Table of Contents:

iOS Games
by Tutorials

By the raywenderlich.com Tutorial Team

Mike Berg, Tom Bradley, Mike Daley, Jacob Gundersen, Kauserali Hafizji,
Matthijs Hollemans, Christopher LaPollo, Rod Strougo, Marin Todorov,
Ray Wenderlich

iOS Games by Tutorials

Mike Berg, Tom Bradley, Mike Daley, Jacob Gundersen, Kauserali Hafizji, Matthijs Hollemans, Christopher LaPollo, Rod Strougo, Marin Todorov, Ray Wenderlich

Copyright ©2013 Razeware LLC.

ISBN: 978-0-9896751-1-6

Dedications

"To my wonderful wife and family, who make it possible to do what I do."
-Mike Berg

"To my wonderful wife Sally and my kids, Jessica, Breanna-Lyn and Rhys."
-Tom Bradley

"To my incredible wife Alison and my fantastic kids Caragh, Alex and Matthew.
Thanks for all your support and patience :o)"
–Mike Daley

"To my folks. Thanks for your unwavering support."
-Jacob Gundersen

"To my beautiful wife Batul and my parents - Thanks for supporting and
believing in me."
-Kauserali Hafizji

"To the crazy ones, the misfits, the rebels and the troublemakers."
–Matthijs Hollemans

"To Darwin and Bram, who amuse, inspire, and encourage me every day, and
to Archana, for everything."
-Chris LaPollo

"To my always supportive and understanding wife Agata, and my family. I love you very much."

-Rod Strougo

"To my parents - ever so supportive and loving. To Mirjam."

—Marin Torodov

"To the editors, authors, and translators at raywenderlich.com – it's an honor working (and playing) with such a talented and hard working group. Let's continue making the coolest stuff fun and easy to learn, and helping others (and ourselves) achieve our dreams."

—Ray Wenderlich

Introduction

By Ray Wenderlich

In this book, you will learn how to make iOS games using Apple's built-in 2D game framework: Sprite Kit. However, this raises a number of questions:

- **Why iOS?** For a game developer, there's no better platform. The development tools are well-designed and easy to learn, and the App Store makes it incredibly simple to distribute your game to a massive audience – and get paid for it!

- **Why 2D?** As impressive as 3D games may be, 2D games are a lot easier to make. The artwork is far less complicated, and programming is faster and doesn't require as much math. All of this allows you as a developer to focus on creating killer gameplay.

  If you're a beginner, making 2D games is definitely the best way to get started.

  If you're an advanced developer, you can still make a 2D game much faster than a 3D game. Since it's not necessarily the case that you earn more money with 3D games, why not go for the easier win? Plus, some people (like myself) prefer 2D games anyway!

- **Why Sprite Kit?** Sprite Kit is a brand new framework for making 2D games in iOS, introduced in iOS 7. It is presently the best option for making 2D games on iOS, hands down – it's user-friendly, powerful and fully-supported by Apple.

So rest easy – with iOS, 2D games and Sprite Kit, you're making great choices!

About this book

If I may say so, this book is something special. Our goal at raywenderlich.com is for this to be the best book on game programming you've ever read.

There are a lot of game programming books out there, and many of them are quite good, so this is a lofty goal! Here's what we've done to try to accomplish it:

- **Learn by making games**: All the books teach the high-level concepts and show code snippets, but many leave you on your own to put together a complete, functioning game. In this book, you will learn by making five games in a variety of genres – games that are actually fun. Our hope is that you can and will reuse techniques or code from these games to make your own games.

- **Learn by challenges**: Every chapter in this book includes some challenges at the end that are designed to help you practice what you've learned. Following a tutorial is one thing, but applying it yourself is quite another. The challenges in this book take off the training wheels and push you to solidify your knowledge by grappling with a problem on your own. (We also provide the answers, of course.) You'll have a blast doing them, too!

- **Focus on polish**: The key to making a hit game is *polish* – adding loads of well-considered details that set your game apart. Because of this, we've put our money where our mouths are and invested in a top-notch artist and sound designer to create resources for the games in this book. We've also included two chapters all about polishing your game with special effects – otherwise known as adding "Juice" – which we think you will love.

- **High-quality tutorials**: Our site is known for its high-quality programming tutorials, and we've put a lot of time and care into the tutorials in this book to make them equally valuable, if not more so. Each chapter has been put through a rigorous multi-stage editing process – resulting in some chapters being rewritten several times! We've strived to ensure that each chapter contains great technical content while also being fun and easy to follow.

After you finish reading this book, please let me know if you think we were successful in meeting these goals. You can email me anytime at ray@raywenderlich.com.

We hope you enjoy the book, and we can't wait to see what games you come up with!

iOS game development: a history

As you will see, it's easy to make games for iOS with SpriteKit – but it wasn't always so. In the early days of iOS, your only option was to make your game with OpenGL ES, which is the lowest-level graphics API available on the platform. OpenGL ES is notoriously difficult to learn, and it was a big barrier to entry for many beginning game developers.

After a while, third-party developers released some game frameworks on top of OpenGL, the most popular of which was called Cocos2D – in fact, several of us wrote a book on the subject! Many of the games at the top of the App Store charts were made with Cocos2D, and many developers can say that Cocos2D was their entry point into the world of game development.

Cocos2D was a great framework, but it wasn't written or supported by Apple. Because of this, there were often problems when new versions of iOS were released, or with integrating other Apple APIs into the system.

To resolve this, with iOS 7 Apple released a brand new framework for making 2D games: Sprite Kit. Its API is very similar to Cocos2D, with similar types for the sprites, actions and scenes that Cocos2D developers know and love, so fans of the older framework will have no trouble getting up to speed. Sprite Kit also has a few extra bells and whistles, like support for playing videos, making shapes and applying special image effects.

The Sprite Kit API is well-designed and easy to use, especially for beginners. Best of all, you can use it knowing that it's fully supported by Apple and heavily optimized to make 2D games on iOS.

From here on out, if you want to make a 2D game on iOS, we definitely recommend you use Sprite Kit rather than other game frameworks. There are only two exceptions to this:

1. **If you need to write custom OpenGL code.** At the time of writing this book, Sprite Kit does not currently support writing your own OpenGL code so if you need that you might want to use a different game framework.

2. **If you want to make a cross platform game.** Sprite Kit is an Apple-only API so it will be more challenging to port your game from Sprite Kit to other platforms than using other options such as Unity or Cocos2D-X.

If neither of these options apply to you, Sprite Kit is the way to go. So let's get you up to speed with Sprite Kit – the future of 2D games on iOS!

What you need

To follow along with the tutorials in this book, you need the following:

- **A Mac running OS X Mountain Lion or later**. This is so you can install the latest version of the required development tool: Xcode.

- **Xcode 5 or later**. Xcode is the main development tool for iOS. You need to use Xcode 5 or later in this book, because Xcode 5 is the first version of Xcode that supports Sprite Kit and iOS 7 development. You can download the latest version of Xcode for free from the Mac App Store here:
  https://itunes.apple.com/app/xcode/id497799835?mt=12

- **An iPhone or iPod Touch running iOS 7 or later, and a paid membership to the iOS development program [optional]**. For most of the chapters in the book, you can run your code on the iOS 7 Simulator that comes with Xcode. However, there are a few chapters later in the book that require a device for testing, like the chapter on using the built-in accelerometer. Also note that Sprite Kit performs better on devices than it does in the Simulator, so your frame rates will appear lower than expected when running your game in the Simulator.

If you don't have the latest version of Xcode installed, be sure to do that before continuing with the book.

Who this book is for

This book is for beginning to advanced iOS developers. Wherever you fall on that spectrum, you will learn a lot from this book, because Sprite Kit is new for everyone!

This book does require some basic knowledge of Objective-C. If you do not know Objective-C, you can still follow along with the book because all of the instructions are in step-by-step format. However, there will likely be parts that are confusing due to gaps in your knowledge. Before beginning this book, you might want to go through our *iOS Apprentice* series, which covers the basics of Objective-C and iOS development:

http://www.raywenderlich.com/store/ios-apprentice

How to use this book

There are two ways to use this book, depending on whether you are a complete beginner to iOS game development or an advanced developer with knowledge of other 2D game frameworks like Cocos2D.

If you are a complete beginner

If you're a complete beginner to iOS game development, the best way to read this book is from cover to cover. We have arranged the chapters to introduce the material in the most logical manner to build up your skills one layer at a time.

However, there are a few exceptions to this. There are several topics (like Core Image filters) that it made sense to include earlier in the book, even though they are on the advanced side.

For every such chapter, we included a note at the beginning suggesting that novice developers might want to skip past the chapter and return to it later, after gaining more experience or upon finding a need for the advanced technique in question.

So, in a nutshell: read through from cover to cover, optionally skipping certain chapters per our suggestions. By the time you're done, you should have a solid basis for making your own 2D iOS games.

If you are an advanced developer

If you're an advanced developer with knowledge of other 2D game frameworks such as Cocos2D, you will have an easier time adapting to Sprite Kit, as the core concepts and syntax will look very familiar.

Our suggestion is to skim through the early chapters and focus more on the later, more advanced chapters, or where you have a particular interest.

We worked hard to make sure there's plenty of interesting material in the book, even if you're a Cocos2D guru. For example, you may find it particularly worthwhile to take a peek at these chapters:

- **Chapter 11, Crop, Video, and Shape Nodes**

- **Chapter 12, Effect Nodes**

- **Chapter 17, Juice Up Your Game, Part 1**

You will build this game across two chapters, in stages:

6. **Chapter 6, Labels**: Create the player and enemy ships, score, health bar and plasma cannon, all with Sprite Kit labels.

7. **Chapter 7, Particle Systems:** Through the power of particle systems, create a star field background, a propulsion engine for the player ship and yes, explosions.

Section III: Physics and nodes

In this section, you will learn how to use the built-in 2D physics engine included with Sprite Kit to create movement as realistic as that in *Angry Birds* or *Cut the Rope*. You will also learn how to use special types of nodes that allow you to play videos, create shapes and apply image filters in your game.

In the process, you will create a physics puzzle game called Cat Nap, where you take the role of a cat who has had a long day and just wants to go to bed.

You will build this game across five chapters, in stages:

8. **Chapter 8, Beginning Physics:** Before starting on the game itself, create a simple test app to get familiar with the core concepts of the physics engine, such as creating physics bodies and setting properties.

9. **Chapter 9, Intermediate Physics:** Create the first level of the game, pictured above, and learn about debug drawing, physics-based collision detection and creating levels from property list files.

10. **Chapter 10, Advanced Physics:** Add two more levels to the game as you learn about interactive bodies, joints between bodies, complex body shapes and more.

11. **Chapter 11, Crop, Video, and Shape Nodes:** Add some special new blocks to Cat Nap while learning about additional types of nodes that allow you to do some amazing things – like play videos, crop images and create dynamic shapes.

12. **Chapter 12, Effect Nodes:** Wrap up Cat Nap by adding image filters to parts of the game, resulting in some very cool special effects.

Section IV: Tile maps and juice

At the time of writing, Sprite Kit doesn't come packaged with tile map support – but in this section, you're going to learn how to create your own tile map engine! You'll also learn how to take a good game and make it great by adding a ton of special effects and excitement – a.k.a. "juice."

In the process, you will create a tile map-based action game called Pest Control, where you take the role of Arnold, a guy so badass he *never* wears a shirt. Giant bugs have invaded Arnold's town, and he's just the guy to dish out a good smashing.

You will build this game across six chapters, in stages:

13. **Chapter 13, Beginning Tile Maps:** Create the bulk of Pest Control. Write code to create a tile map from a simple text format and add the hero and bug-monsters to the game.

14. **Chapter 14, More Tile Maps:** Add the core gameplay and learn about coordinate conversions and collision detection with tile maps.

15. **Chapter 15, Imported Tile Maps:** Import tile maps into your game that are stored in a popular tile-map format called TMX files, and use an open-source map editor to create your maps.

16. **Chapter 16, Saving and Loading Games:** Implement an autosave feature that stores a player's progress in Pest Control. Also add gameplay features like timers, winning and losing and progressing through multiple levels.

17. **Chapter 17, Juice Up Your Game, Part 1:** Demonstrate how adding simple visual effects can make Pest Control, or any game you write, much more entertaining.

18. Chapter 18, Juice Up Your Game, Part 2: Add sounds and even more special effects, because adding fewer effects at this point would be ridiculous.

Section V: Other game APIs

In this section, you'll learn about some APIs other than Sprite Kit that are good to know when making games for iOS. In particular, you will learn how to make user interfaces with UIKit; control movement with the accelerometer; add Game Center leaderboards, achievements, and multiplayer support into your game; and display your game on a TV or external monitor with AirPlay.

In the process, you will create a top-down racing game called Circuit Racer, where you take the role of an elite racecar driver out to set a world record. It would be no problem if it weren't for the debris on the track!

You will build this game across six chapters, in stages:

19. **Chapter 19, UIKit:** Integrate Sprite Kit with UIKit to create view controllers for different screens of your game, as well as use standard iOS controls within your main game scene itself (such as creating an on-screen joypad).

20. **Chapter 20, Accelerometer:** Use the accelerometer to move your sprites around the screen!

21. **Chapter 21, Game Center Achievements**: Enable Game Center for your game and award the user achievements for accomplishing certain feats.

22. **Chapter 22, Game Center Leaderboards**: Set up various leaderboards for your game and track and report the player's scores.

23. **Chapter 23, Game Center Multiplayer**: Add multiplayer support so players can race against each other in real-time across the Internet!

24. **Chapter 24, AirPlay**: Display the game on a TV or external display and use your device as a controller.

Bonus chapters

And that's not all – on top of the above, we have some bonus chapters for you!

These bonus chapters come as an optional PDF download, which you can download for free here:

- http://www.raywenderlich.com/store/ios-games-by-tutorials/bonus-chapters

We hope you enjoy the bonus chapters!

25. **Chapter 25, Performance: Texture Atlases**: Take a deep dive into one of the most important aspects in making your game perform well and use less memory: using texture atlases.

26. **Chapter 26, Performance: Tips and Tricks**: Learn how to get the most performance out of your game and gain an understanding of what's fast and what's slow when it comes to making 2D games on iOS.

27. **Chapter 27, Making Art for Programmers**: If you liked the art in these mini-games and want to learn how to either hire an artist or make some art of your own, look no further than this chapter! This chapter guides you through drawing a cute cat in the style of this book with Illustrator.

Book source code and forums

You can get the source code for the book here: http://www.raywenderlich.com/store/ios-games-by-tutorials/source-code

We've also set up an official forum for the book at raywenderlich.com/forums. This is a great place to ask any questions you have about the book or about Sprite Kit in general, or to submit any errata you may find.

We hope to see you on the forums! ☺

PDF Version

We also have a PDF version of this book available, which can be handy if you ever want to copy/paste code or search for a specific term through the book as you're developing.

And speaking of the PDF version, we have some good news!

Since you purchased the physical copy of this book, you are eligible to buy the PDF version at a significant discount if you would like (if you don't have it already). For more details, see this page:

- http://www.raywenderlich.com/store/ios-games-by-tutorials/upgrade

License

By purchasing *iOS Games by Tutorials*, you acquire the following license:

- You are allowed to use and/or modify the source code provided with *iOS Games by Tutorials* in as many games as you want, with no attribution required.

- You are allowed to use and/or modify all art, music and sound effects that are included with *iOS Games by Tutorials* in as many games as you want, but must include this attribution line somewhere inside your game: "Artwork/sounds: from *iOS Games by Tutorials* book, available at http://www.raywenderlich.com".

- The source code included in *iOS Games by Tutorials* is for your personal use only. You are NOT allowed to distribute or sell the source code in *iOS Games by Tutorials* without prior authorization.

All materials provided with this book are provided on an "as-is" basis, without warranty of any kind, express or implied, including but not limited to the warranties of merchantability, fitness for a particular purpose and non-infringement. In no event shall the authors or copyright holders be liable for any claim, damages or other liability, whether in an action of contract, tort or otherwise, arising from, out of or in connection with the software or the use or other dealings in the software.

All trademarks and registered trademarks appearing in this guide are the property of their respective owners.

Acknowledgements

We would like to thank many people for their assistance in making this book possible:

- **Our families**: For bearing with us during this hectic time as we worked all hours of the night to get this book ready for publication!

- **Everyone at Apple**: For developing an amazing 2D game framework and other helpful APIs for games, for constantly inspiring us to improve our apps and skills, and for making it possible for many developers to have their dream jobs!

- **Ricardo Quesada**: Ricardo is the lead developer of Cocos2D, which got many of us into making games. Sprite Kit seems to draw quite a bit of inspiration from Cocos2D, so Ricardo deserves "mad props" for that as well.

- And most importantly, **the readers of raywenderlich.com and you**! Thank you so much for reading our site and purchasing this book. Your continued readership and support is what makes this all possible!

About the authors

Harken all genders! You may or may not have noticed that all of this book's authors are men. This is unfortunate, and not by design. If you are a woman developing for iOS and are interested in joining the Tutorial Team to write about gaming topics, we'd love to hear from you! ☺

Mike Berg is a full-time game artist who is fortunate enough to work with many indie game developers from all over the world. When he's not manipulating pixel colors, he loves to eat good food, spend time with his family, play games and be happy. You can check out his work at http://www.weheartgames.com.

Tom Bradley has been coding since he was six years old and has over 14 years of industry experience. More recently, he cofounded 71Squared Ltd., known for its Mac-based game development tools, Particle Designer and Glyph Designer. When not in front of the computer or playing with cameras, he can be found spending time with his wife Sally and two children, Jessica and Rhys.

Mike Daley has been developing software for over 25 years. Mike is cofounder of 71Squared Ltd, known for its Mac-based game development tools, Particle Designer and Glyph Designer. When not in front of his computer writing software, he can be with his wife and three children or indulging his other passion, flying light aircraft.

Jake Gundersen is a gamer, maker and programmer. He is cofounder of the educational game company Third Rail Games. He has a particular interest in gaming, image processing and computer graphics. You can find his musings and codings at http://indieambitions.com.

Kauserali Hafizji (a.k.a. Ali) is a developer at heart. He is an avid programmer and loves writing code, even over the weekend. A good read, cool dip in the pool and a hot cheesy meal would be the perfect end to his weekend. You can find Ali on Twitter as @Ali_hafizji.

Vinnie Prabhu created all of the music and sounds for the games in this book. Vinnie is a music composer/software engineer from Northern Virginia who has done music and sound work for concerts, plays and video games. He's also a staff member on OverClocked ReMix, an online community for music and video game fans. You can find Vinnie on Twitter as @palpablevt.

Vicki Wenderlich created many of the illustrations in this book. Vicki discovered a love of digital art three years ago, and has been making app art and digital illustrations ever since. She is passionate about helping people pursue their dreams and makes free app art for developers available on her website, http://www.vickiwenderlich.com.

Section I: Getting Started

This section covers the basics of making 2D games with Sprite Kit. These are the most important techniques, the ones you'll use in almost every game you make. By the time you reach the end of this section, you'll be ready to make your own simple game.

Throughout this section you will create an action game called Zombie Conga, where you take the role of a happy-go-lucky zombie who just wants to party!

Chapter 1: Sprites

By Ray Wenderlich

Now that you know what Sprite Kit is and why you should use it, it's time to try it out for yourself!

The first minigame you will build in this book is called Zombie Conga. Here's what it will look like when you're finished:

In Zombie Conga, you take the role of a happy-go-lucky zombie who just wants to party!

Luckily, the beach town you occupy has an overly abundant cat population. All you need to do is bite them and they'll join your zombie conga line.

But watch out for the crazy cat ladies! They won't take kindly to anyone stealing their beloved cats, and will do their best to make the player rest in peace – permanently.

You will build this game across the next five chapters, in stages:

1. **Chapter 1, Sprites:** You are here! You will get started by adding your first sprites to the game: the background and the zombie.

2. **Chapter 2, Manual Movement:** You will make the zombie move around the screen following your touches, getting a crash-course in basic 2D vector math in the process.

3. **Chapter 3, Actions:** You will add the cats and crazy cat ladies to the game, as well as some basic collision detection and gameplay.

4. **Chapter 4, Scenes:** You will add a main menu to the game, and a win and lose scenes.

5. **Chapter 5, Scrolling:** You will make the game scroll from left to right, and finally add the conga line itself.

Let's get this party started!

Getting started

Start Xcode and select **File\New\Project...** from the main menu. Select the **iOS\Application\SpriteKit Game** template and click **Next**.

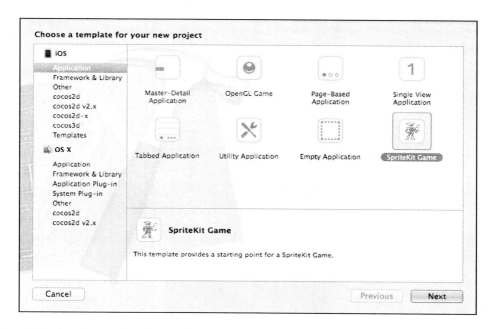

Enter **ZombieConga** for the Product Name, choose **iPhone** for Devices, leave the **Class Prefix** blank and click **Next**.

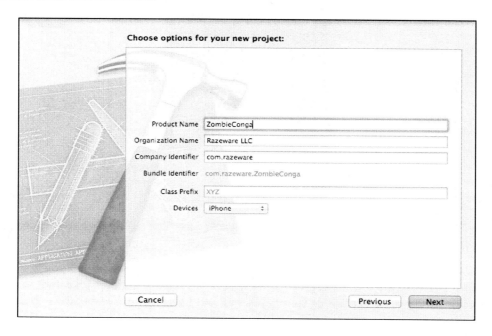

Choose somewhere on your hard drive to save your project and click **Create**. At this point Xcode will generate a simple Sprite Kit starter project for you.

Take a look at what Sprite Kit made. In Xcode's toolbar, select the **iPhone Retina (4-inch) Simulator** and click **Play**.

You'll see a single label that says "Hello, World!" and when you click on the screen, a rotating space ship will appear.

In Sprite Kit, a single object called a `scene` controls each "screen" of your app. A `scene` is a subclass of Sprite Kit's `SKScene` class.

Right now this app just has a single scene, `MyScene`. Open **MyScene.m** and you'll see the code that displays the label and rotating space ship. It's not important to understand this code quite yet – you're going to remove it all and build up your game one step at a time.

For now, delete everything in **MyScene.m** and replace it with the following:

```
#import "MyScene.h"

@implementation MyScene

-(id)initWithSize:(CGSize)size
{
  if (self = [super initWithSize:size]) {
    self.backgroundColor = [SKColor whiteColor];
  }
  return self;
}

@end
```

`initWithSize:` is the method that gets called when the scene is first created. Here, you simply set the background color to white.

Zombie Conga is designed to run in landscape mode, so let's configure the app to launch in landscape. To do this, select the **ZombieConga** project in the Project Navigator and then select the **ZombieConga** target. Go to the **General** tab and uncheck Portrait so that only **Landscape Left** and **Landscape Right** are checked.

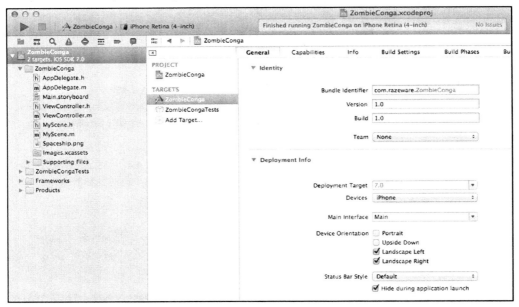

Since you changed the device orientation to landscape, you have to make a change to the code as well. At the time of writing, the Sprite Kit template uses the View Controller's main view's size as the size to create the scene in `viewDidLoad`, but this size is not guaranteed to be correct at `viewDidLoad` time.

There are many ways to fix this, but it's easiest to open **ViewController.m**, rename `viewDidLoad` to `viewWillLayoutSubviews:`, and make a few minor changes as highlighted below:

```
- (void)viewWillLayoutSubviews
{
    [super viewWillLayoutSubviews];

    // Configure the view.
    SKView * skView = (SKView *)self.view;
    if (!skView.scene) {
      skView.showsFPS = YES;
      skView.showsNodeCount = YES;

      // Create and configure the scene.
      SKScene * scene = [MyScene
        sceneWithSize:skView.bounds.size];
      scene.scaleMode = SKSceneScaleModeAspectFill;

      // Present the scene.
      [skView presentScene:scene];
    }
}
```

This works because `self.view.frame.size` is guaranteed to be correct at `viewWillLayoutSubviews` time, so it will properly use the landscape size. The reason you now check to see if `skView.scene` exists before creating it is to avoid creating the scene twice (this method can be called more than once).

There's two last things: to get this game started on the right foot, you should disable the status bar and set up an app icon. To disable the status bar, open **ViewController.m** and add this to the bottom:

```
-(BOOL)prefersStatusBarHidden
{
   return YES;
}
```

And to set up an app icon, open **Images.xcassets** and select the **AppIcon** entry. Then in the resources for this chapter, drag all of the files from the "App Icon" folder into the area on the right (where the icon placeholders are). You should see the following when you're done:

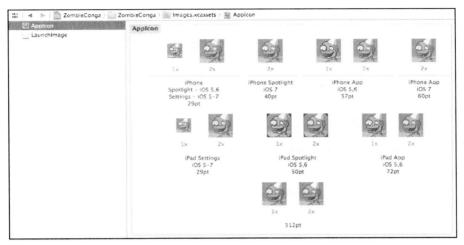

Build and run your app again. This time you should see a (mostly) blank, white screen:

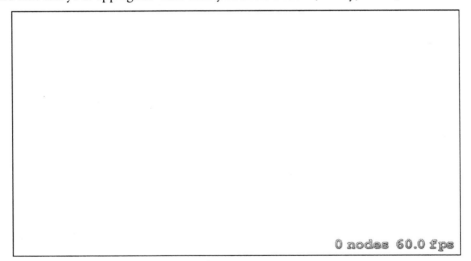

This may not look like much, but you now have a starting point upon which to build your first Sprite Kit game.

Let's move on to the simplest possible task, which also happens to be one of the most important and common tasks when making games – getting an image to appear on the screen.

Displaying a sprite

When making 2D games, you usually put images on the screen representing your game's hero, monsters, bullets, and so on. Each of these images is called a **sprite**.

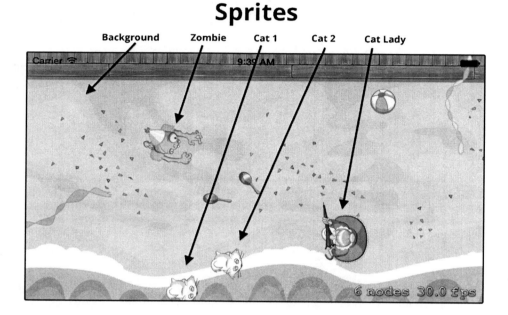

Sprite Kit has a special class that makes it easy to create and work with sprites, called `SKSpriteNode`. This is what you'll use to add all your sprites to the game. Let's give it a try.

Adding the resources

First things first – before you can add sprites to the game, you need some images to work with.

In the resources for this chapter, you will find a folder called **Art** that includes all the images and sounds you need for Zombie Conga. Drag this folder into your project and make sure that **Copy items into destination group's folder (if needed)**, **Create groups for any added folders**, and the **ZombieConga** target are all checked.

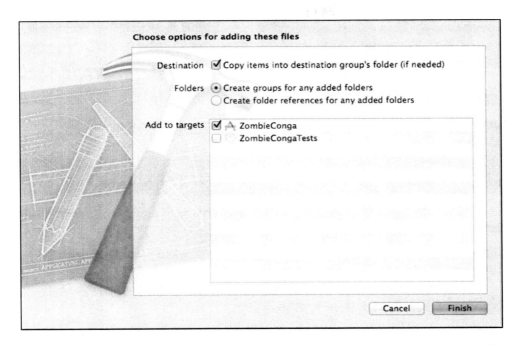

You should now see the list of files in your Xcode project. Feel free to look through the art to get familiar with it.

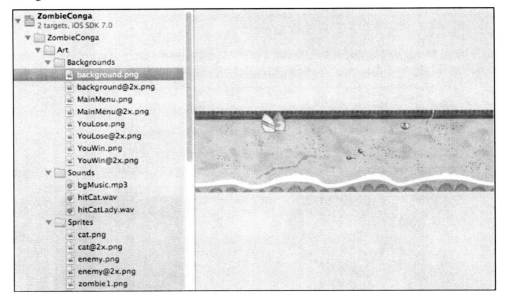

In particular, look for an image called **background.png** as shown above. This represents the beach town the zombie lives in – and this is what you're going to use to create your first sprite!

Creating a sprite

Open **MyScene.m**, and add this line to `initWithSize:`, right after setting the background color:

```
SKSpriteNode *bg =
  [SKSpriteNode spriteNodeWithImageNamed:@"background"];
```

Note that you do not need to pass the image's extension, as Sprite Kit will automatically determine that for you.

Build and run. Ah, you thought it was simple, but at this point you still see a blank white screen – what gives?

Adding a sprite to the scene

It actually is simple. It's just that a sprite will not show up onscreen until you add it as a child of the scene, or one of the scene's descendent **nodes**.

To do this, add this line of code right after the previous line:

```
[self addChild:bg];
```

You'll learn about nodes and scenes later. For now, build and run again, and you'll see part of the background appear in the bottom left of the screen:

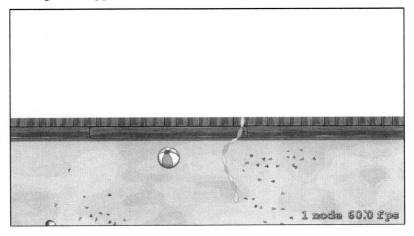

Obviously that's not quite what you want. To get the background in the correct spot, you have to set its position.

Positioning a sprite

By default, a sprite is positioned at (0, 0), which in Sprite Kit represents the bottom left. Note that this is different from the UIKit coordinate system in iOS, where (0, 0) represents the top left.

Try positioning the background somewhere else by setting the `position` property. Add this line of code right before calling `[self addChild:bg]`:

```
bg.position =
    CGPointMake(self.size.width/2, self.size.height/2);
```

Here you are setting the background to the center of the screen. Even though this is just one line of code, there are four important things to understand:

1. The type of the `position` property is `CGPoint`, which is a simple structure that has `x` and `y` components:

```
struct CGPoint {
  CGFloat x;
  CGFloat y;
};
```

2. You can easily create a new `CGPoint` with the macro shown above, `CGPointMake`.

3. Since you are writing this code in an `SKScene` subclass, you can access the size of the scene at any time with the `self.size` property. The `self.size` property's type is `CGSize`, which is a simple structure like `CGPoint` that has `width` and `height` components.

```
struct CGSize {
  CGFloat width;
  CGFloat height;
};
```

4. Note that a sprite's position is within the coordinate space of its parent node, which in this case is the scene itself. You'll learn more about what this means in Chapter 5, "Scrolling".

Build and run, and now your background will be fully visible:

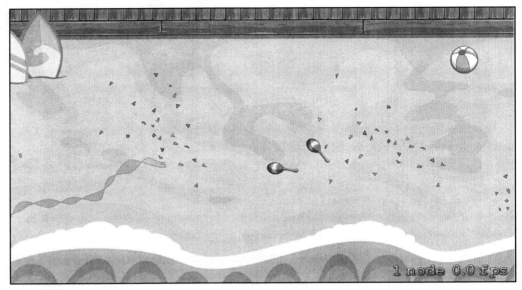

Setting a sprite's anchor point

Note that when you set the position of the background sprite, you're actually setting the *center* of the background sprite to that position. This means two things:

1. Since this background image is bigger than the size of the screen, you are actually looking at the center part of the image right now. Look at the original image to see for yourself.

2. This also explains why you could only see the upper half of the sprite earlier. Before you set the position, the position defaulted to (0, 0). This was placing the center of the sprite at the lower left corner of the screen – so you could only see the top half.

You can change this behavior by setting a sprite's anchor point. Think of the anchor point as "the spot within a sprite that you pin to a particular position." For example, here is an illustration showing a sprite positioned at the center of the screen, but with different anchor points:

Position: center screen

anchor point (0.5, 0.5)   anchor point (0, 0)   anchor point (1, 1)

To see how this works, replace the line that set the background's position to the center of the screen with the following:

```
bg.anchorPoint = CGPointZero;
bg.position = CGPointZero;
```

`CGPointZero` is a handy shortcut for (0, 0). Here you set the anchor point of the sprite to (0, 0) to pin the lower-left corner of the sprite to wherever you set the position – in this case also (0, 0).

Build and run, and this time you'll see a different portion of the background image – the far left half. Notice how the surf boards are now in the middle of the screen?

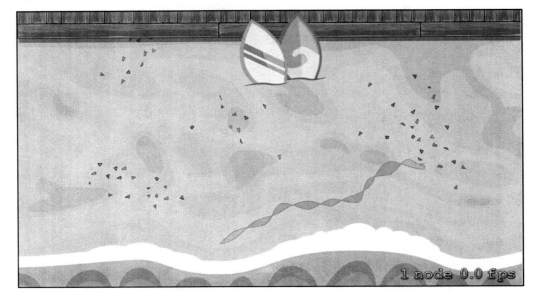

This works because now you are pinning the lower left corner of the background image to the lower left of the screen.

Here you changed the anchor point for the background for learning purposes. However, usually you can leave the anchor point at its default of (0.5, 0.5), unless you have a specific need to rotate the sprite around a particular point – an example of which is described in the next section.

So in short: when you set the position of a sprite, by default it's the center of the sprite that you're positioning.

Rotating a sprite

To rotate a sprite, simply set its `zRotation` property. Try it out on the background sprite by adding this line right before calling `[self addChild:bg]`:

```
bg.zRotation = M_PI / 8;
```

Rotation values are in radians, which are a method of measuring angles. This example rotates the sprite pi / 8 radians, which is equal to 22.5 degrees.

I don't know about you, but I find it easier to think about rotations in degrees, rather than in radians. Later on, you'll create helper routines to convert between degrees and radians.

Build and run, and you'll notice the background sprite has now been rotated:

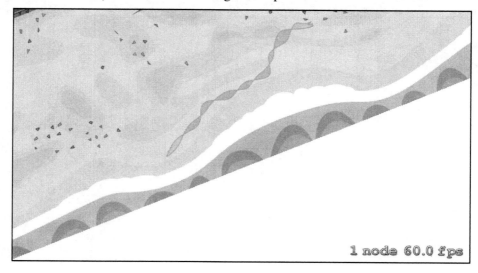

This brings up an interesting point. Sprites are rotated about their anchor points. Since you set the anchor point to (0, 0), this sprite rotates around the bottom-left corner.

Try rotating it around the center instead. Replace the lines that set the position and anchor point with these:

```
bg.position =
   CGPointMake(self.size.width / 2, self.size.height / 2);
bg.anchorPoint = CGPointMake(0.5, 0.5); // same as default
```

Build and run, and this time the background sprite will have rotated around the center instead:

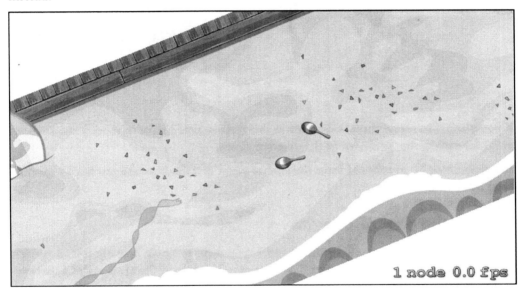

That's good to know! But for this game you don't want a rotated background, so comment out that line:

```
//bg.zRotation = M_PI / 8;
```

If you're wondering when you might want to change the anchor point in a real game, consider the case where you're creating a character's body out of different sprites – one for the head, torso, left arm, right arm, left leg and right leg:

If you wanted to rotate these body parts at their joints, you'd have to modify the anchor point for each sprite, as shown in the diagram above.

But again, usually you should leave the anchor point at default unless you have a specific need like shown here.

Getting the size of a sprite

Sometimes when you're working with a sprite, you want to know how big it is. A sprite's size defaults to the size of the image. The class representing this image is called a **texture** in Sprite Kit.

Add these lines after the call to [self addChild:bg] to get the size of the background and log it out:

```
CGSize mySize = bg.size;
NSLog(@"Size: %@", NSStringFromCGSize(mySize));
```

Build and run, and in your console output you should see something like this:

```
ZombieConga[5316:70b] Size: {1024, 320}
```

Sometimes it's useful to programmatically get the size of sprites like this instead of hard-coding numbers. This makes your code much more robust and adaptable in the future.

Sprites and nodes

Earlier you learned that if you want to make a sprite to appear onscreen, you need to add it as a child of the scene, or as one of its descendent **nodes**. This section will delve more deeply into the concept of nodes.

Everything that appears on the screen in Sprite Kit derives from a class called SKNode. The scene class (SKScene) derives from SKNode, and the sprite class (SKSpriteNode) also derives from SKNode.

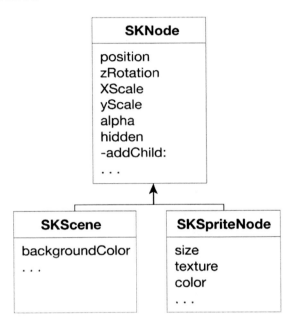

SKSpriteNode inherits a lot of its capabilities from SKNode. It turns out the position and rotation properties are derived from SKNode, not something particular to SKSpriteNode. This means that, just as you can set the position or rotation of a sprite, you can do the same thing with the scene itself, or anything else that derives from SKNode.

You can think of everything that appears on the screen as a graph of nodes, often referred to as a **scene graph**.

Here's an example of what such a graph might look like for Zombie Conga if there was one zombie, two cats and one crazy cat lady in the game:

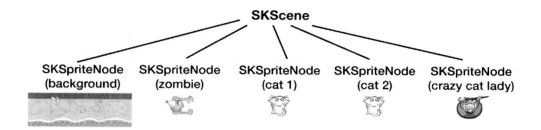

You'll learn more about nodes and the neat things you can do with them in *Chapter 5, Scrolling*. For now, you will be adding your sprites as direct children of the scene itself.

Finishing Touches

And that's it! As you can see, adding a sprite to a scene takes only three lines of code:

1. Create the sprite.

2. Position the sprite.

3. Add it to the scene graph.

Now it's time for you to test your new-found knowledge by adding the zombie to the scene.

Challenges

At this point, it's important for you to practice what you've learned on your own. Each chapter in this book has 1-3 challenges, progressing from easy to hard.

I highly recommend giving all the challenges a try, because while following a step-by-step tutorial is educational, you'll learn a lot more solving a problem by yourself. In addition, each chapter will continue where the previous chapter's challenges left off.

If you get stuck, you can find solutions in the resources for this chapter – but to get the most from this book, try doing these yourself first!

Challenge 1: Adding the zombie

So far your game has a nice background, but it's missing the star of the show. Let's give your zombie a grand entrance.

To start, open **MyScene.m** and, immediately after `@implementation MyScene`, add these three lines:

```
{
    SKSpriteNode *_zombie;
}
```

This creates a section to store private variables for the scene, with a single variable that you'll use to store a reference for the zombie. You're doing this because you'll need to access the zombie a lot in this game, and it'll be nice to have a quick reference to it.

> **Note:** This book will be using modern Objective-C syntax – private interfaces, literal syntax, blocks, and more. If you need a refresher on modern Objective C style, check out Chapter 1 in *iOS 6 by Tutorials*, "Modern Objective-C."

Now it's time for your first challenge – add the zombie to the scene! Here are a few hints:

- You'll need to add three lines of code, which should go inside `initWithSize:` right after the line that logs the size of the background.

- The first line should create an `SKSpriteNode` using **zombie1.png** and store it in `_zombie`.

- The second line should position the zombie sprite at (100, 100).

- The third line should add the zombie to the scene.

If you've got it right, you should see the zombie appear on the screen like this:

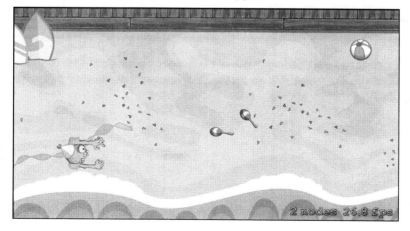

Challenge 2: Further documentation

This chapter covered everything you need to know about sprites and nodes in order to keep working on the game.

However, it's good to know where to find more information in case you ever have questions or get stuck. I highly recommend you check out Apple's *SKNode Class Reference* and *SKSpriteNode Class Reference,* as these are the two classes you'll use most often in Sprite Kit and it's good to have a basic familiarity with the properties and methods they contain.

You can find the references in Xcode by selecting **Help\Documentation and API Reference** from the main menu and searching for SKNode or SKSpriteNode.

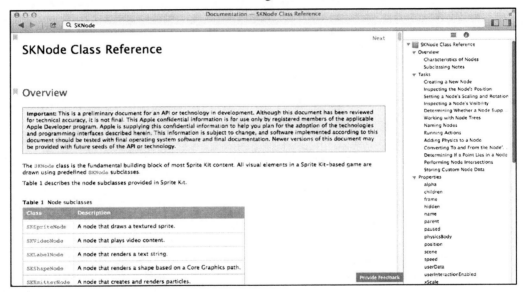

And now for your second challenge: use the information in these docs to double (scale to 2x) the zombie's size. Answer this question: Did you use a method of SKSpriteNode or SKNode to do this?

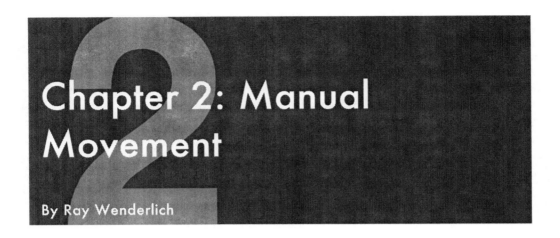

Chapter 2: Manual Movement

By Ray Wenderlich

If you completed the challenges from the previous chapter, you should now have a rather large zombie on the screen:

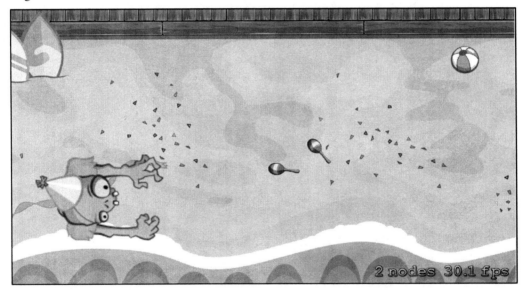

If you were unable to complete the challenges or skipped ahead from a previous chapter, don't worry – you can simply open **ZombieConga-Starter** from the resources for this chapter to pick up where we left off.

Of course, you want this sprite to move around, not just stand there – this zombie's got an itch to boogie!

There are two ways to make a sprite move in Sprite Kit. The first, which you might have noticed in the last chapter if you looked at the template code provided by Apple, is to use a concept called **actions**. You'll learn more about actions in the next chapter.

The second way to make a sprite move is the more "classic" way – and that's to set the position yourself manually over time. It's important to learn this way first, because it gives you the most control and helps you understand what actions do for you.

However, in order to set a sprite's position over time, you need to have a method that is called periodically as the game runs. This introduces a new topic – the Sprite Kit game loop.

The Sprite Kit game loop

A game works like a flipbook animation. You draw a successive sequence of images, and when you flip through them fast enough, it gives the illusion of movement.

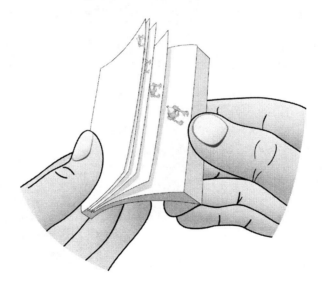

Each individual picture that you draw is called a **frame**. Games typically try to draw frames between 30 to 60 times per second so that the animations feel smooth. This rate of drawing is called the **frame rate**, or specifically **frames per second (FPS)**. By default, Sprite Kit shows you this in the bottom right corner of your game:

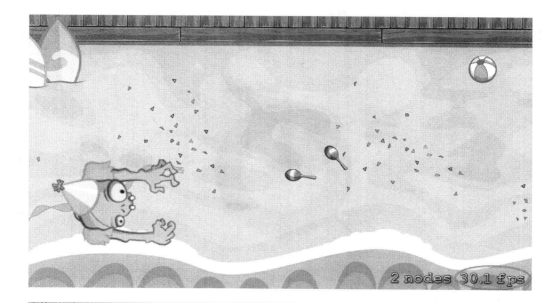

Note: It's handy that Sprite Kit shows your frames per second on the screen by default, because it's good to keep an eye on this as you develop your game to make sure your game is performing smoothly. Ideally you want at least 30 FPS.

Note that you should only pay attention to the FPS display on an actual device, as you'll get very different performance on the Simulator.

In particular, your Mac has a faster CPU, way more memory, but abysmally slow emulated rendering, so you can't count on any accurate performance measurements from your Mac – again always test performance on a device!

In addition to displaying the frames per second, Sprite Kit also displays the count of nodes that it rendered in the last pass.

You can turn off the display of the frames per second and node count by going into **ViewController.m** and setting both `skView.showsFPS` and `skView.showsNodeCount` to `NO`.

Behind the scenes Sprite Kit runs an endless loop, often referred to as the **game loop**, that looks like this:

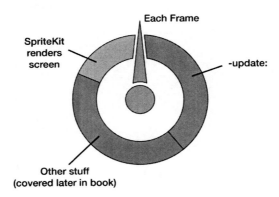

This illustrates that each frame, Sprite Kit does the following:

1. **Calls a method on your scene called** `update:`. This is where you can put code that you want to run every frame. It's a perfect spot for code that updates the position or rotation of your sprites.

2. **Does some other stuff**. You'll revisit the game loop in other chapters, filling in your understanding of the rest of this diagram as you go.

3. **Renders the scene**. Sprite Kit then draws all of the objects that are in your scene graph. Behind the scenes, this is issuing OpenGL draw commands for you.

Sprite Kit tries to draw frames as fast as possible, up to 60 FPS. However, note that if you take too long in your `update:` method, or if Sprite Kit has to draw more sprites at once than the hardware can handle, the frame rate might decrease.

You'll learn more about ways to resolve performance issues like this in Chapters 25 and 26, "Performance: Texture Atlases" and "Performance: Tips and Tricks", but for now you just need to know two things:

1. **Keep your `update:` method fast**. For example, you want to avoid slow algorithms in this method since it's called each frame.

2. **Keep your count of nodes as low as possible**. For example, it's good to remove nodes from the scene graph when they're off screen and you no longer need them.

Now that you know that `update:` is called each frame and is a good spot to update the position of your sprites, let's make this zombie move!

Moving the zombie

You're going to implement the zombie moving code in four iterations. This is so that you can see some common beginner mistakes and solutions, and in the end understand how movement works step-by-step.

To start, you'll implement a simple but not ideal method: moving the zombie a fixed amount per frame.

Before you begin, comment out the line that sets the zombie to double-sized:

```
//[_zombie setScale:2.0]; // SKNode method
```

Zombies scare me enough in normal size! :]

Iteration 1: Fixed movement per frame

Inside **MyScene.m**, add (or update if it's already there) the following method:

```
- (void)update:(CFTimeInterval)currentTime
{
    _zombie.position = CGPointMake(_zombie.position.x + 2,
                                   _zombie.position.y);
}
```

Here you update the position of the zombie to be two more points along the x-axis than last time, and keep the same position along the y-axis. This makes the zombie move from left to right.

Build and run, and you'll see the zombie move across the screen:

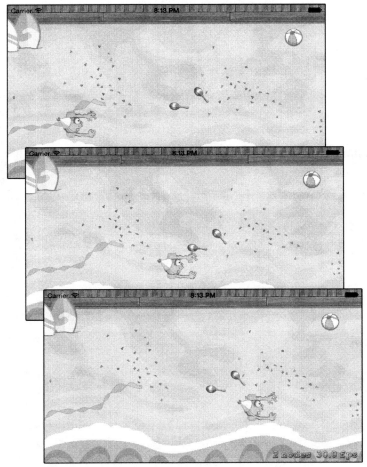

This is great stuff, but you might notice that the movement feels a bit jagged or stuttered. The reason for this goes back to the Sprite Kit game loop.

Remember that Sprite Kit tries to draw frames as quickly as possible. However, there will usually be some variance in the amount of time it takes to draw each frame: sometimes a bit longer, sometimes a bit quicker.

This means that the amount of time between calls to your update: loop can vary. To see this yourself, add some code to print out how much time has elapsed since the last update. Add these variables to MyScene's private variables section, right after the _zombie variable:

```
NSTimeInterval _lastUpdateTime;
NSTimeInterval _dt;
```

Here you create a variable to keep track of the last time update: was called, and the delta time since the last update (often abbreviated as dt).

Then add these lines to the beginning of update:

```
if (_lastUpdateTime) {
    _dt = currentTime - _lastUpdateTime;
} else {
    _dt = 0;
}
_lastUpdateTime = currentTime;
NSLog(@"%0.2f milliseconds since last update", _dt * 1000);
```

Here you calculate the time since the last call to update: and store that in _dt, then log out the time in milliseconds (1 second = 1000 milliseconds).

Build and run, and you'll see something like this in the console:

```
ZombieConga[80642:70b] 0.00 milliseconds since last update
ZombieConga[80642:70b] 23.37 milliseconds since last update
ZombieConga[80642:70b] 16.88 milliseconds since last update
ZombieConga[80642:70b] 16.90 milliseconds since last update
ZombieConga[80642:70b] 16.17 milliseconds since last update
ZombieConga[80642:70b] 17.28 milliseconds since last update
```

As you can see, the amount of time between calls to update: always varies slightly. Since you're updating the position of the zombie a fixed amount each frame rather than taking this time variance into consideration, this can result in movement that looks jagged or stuttered.

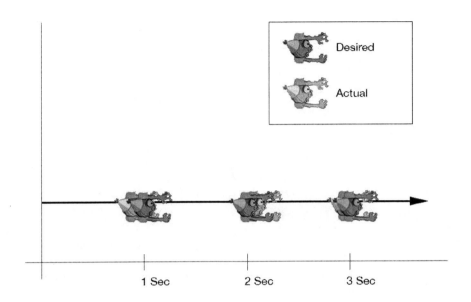

The correct solution is to figure out how fast you want the zombie to move per second, and then multiply this by the fraction of a second since the last update. Let's give this a shot.

Iteration 2: Velocity multiplied by delta time

Start by adding this constant to the top of the file, right after #import "MyScene.h":

```
static const float ZOMBIE_MOVE_POINTS_PER_SEC = 120.0;
```

Here you're saying that in one second, the zombie should move 120 points (about 1/5 of the screen).

Next, add a new private variable where you added _zombie and the others:

```
CGPoint _velocity;
```

So far you have seen CGPoints used to represent positions. However, it's also quite common and handy to use CGPoints to represent **2D vectors** instead.

A 2D vector represents a **direction** and a **length**:

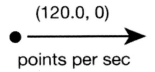

points per sec

The diagram above shows an example of a 2D vector you might use to represent how you want the zombie to move. You can see that the orientation of the arrow shows the **direction** in which the zombie should move, while the arrow's **length** indicates how fast the zombie should move in a second.

However, note that the velocity has no set position. After all, you should be able to make the zombie move in that direction, at that speed, no matter where the zombie starts.

Try this out by adding the following new method:

```
- (void)moveSprite:(SKSpriteNode *)sprite
          velocity:(CGPoint)velocity
{
  // 1
  CGPoint amountToMove = CGPointMake(velocity.x * _dt,
                                     velocity.y * _dt);
  NSLog(@"Amount to move: %@",
        NSStringFromCGPoint(amountToMove));

  // 2
  sprite.position =
    CGPointMake(sprite.position.x + amountToMove.x,
                sprite.position.y + amountToMove.y);
}
```

Here you've refactored the code into a reusable method that takes the sprite to be moved and a velocity vector by which to move it. Let's go over this line-by-line:

1. Velocity is in points per second, and you need to figure out how much to move the zombie this frame. To determine that, this section multiplies the points per second by the fraction of seconds since the last update. You now have a point representing the zombie's position (which you can also think of as a vector from the origin to the zombie's position), and a vector representing the distance and direction to move the zombie this frame:

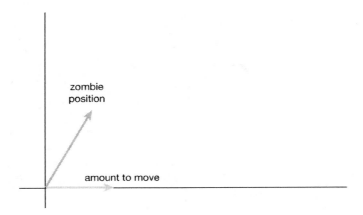

2. To determine the new position for the zombie, just add the vector to the point:

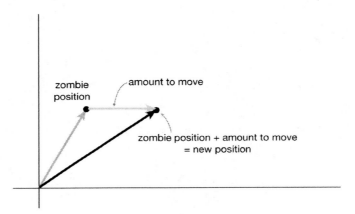

You can visualize this with the diagram above, but in code you simply add the x and y components of the point and the vector together.

> **Note:** To learn more about vectors, check out this great guide:
> http://www.mathsisfun.com/algebra/vectors.html.

Finally, inside update:, replace the line that sets the zombie's position with the following:

```
[self moveSprite:_zombie
        velocity:CGPointMake(ZOMBIE_MOVE_POINTS_PER_SEC, 0)];
```

Build and run, and now the zombie will move much more smoothly across the screen. If you look at the console log, you'll also see that the zombie is now moving a different amount each frame, based on how much time has elapsed.

```
ZombieConga[81339:70b] 0.00 milliseconds since last update
ZombieConga[81339:70b] Amount to move: {0, 0}
ZombieConga[81339:70b] 38.74 milliseconds since last update
ZombieConga[81339:70b] Amount to move: {4.6488085, 0}
ZombieConga[81339:70b] 17.22 milliseconds since last update
ZombieConga[81339:70b] Amount to move: {2.0663457, 0}
ZombieConga[81339:70b] 16.26 milliseconds since last update
ZombieConga[81339:70b] Amount to move: {1.9517885, 0}
```

If this still looks jittery to you, be sure to try it out on an actual device instead of on the Simulator, which has different performance characteristics.

Iteration 3: Moving toward touches

So far, so good, but now you'll make the zombie move toward wherever you touch. After all, everyone knows zombies are attracted to noise!

The goal is for the zombie to move toward where you tap, and keep going even after passing the tap, until you tap another location to draw his attention.

There are four steps to make this work – let's cover them one at a time.

Step 1: Find the offset vector

First you need to figure out the offset between the location of the player's tap and the location of the zombie. You can get this by simply subtracting the zombie's position from the tap position.

Subtracting points and vectors is similar to adding them, but instead of adding the x and y components, you you subtract the x and y components.

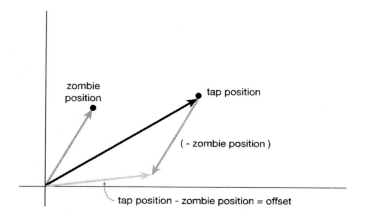

This diagram shows how if you subtract the zombie position from the tap position, you get a vector that shows the offset amount. If you move the offset vector so that it begins from the zombie's position, you can see this even more clearly:

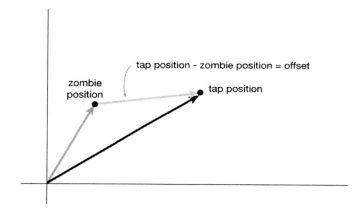

By subtracting these two positions, you get something with a direction and length. Call this the offset vector.

Try this out by adding the following method:

```
- (void)moveZombieToward:(CGPoint)location
{
  CGPoint offset = CGPointMake(location.x - _zombie.position.x,
                               location.y - _zombie.position.y);
}
```

Don't worry about Xcode's warning about the unused variable `offset`; you're not done writing this method yet.

Step 2: Find the length of the offset vector

Now you need to figure out the length of the offset vector, a piece of information you will need in the next step.

Think of the offset vector as the hypotenuse of a right triangle, where the lengths of the other two sides of the triangle are defined by the x and y components of the vector:

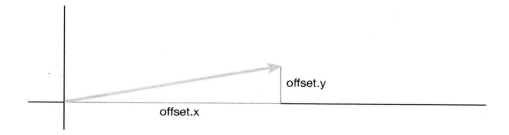

You want to find the length of the hypotenuse. To do this, you can use the Pythagorean theorem. You may remember this simple formula from geometry – it says the length of the hypotenuse is equal to the square root of the sum of the squares of the two sides.

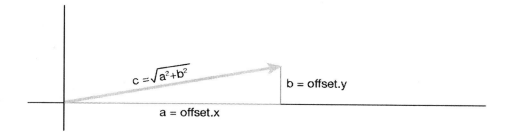

Put this theory into practice. Add the following line to the bottom of `moveZombieToward`:

```
CGFloat length =
    sqrtf(offset.x * offset.x + offset.y * offset.y);
```

Now Xcode isn't complaining about `offset`, but it's warning you that `length` isn't used. You're not done yet!

Step 3: Make the offset vector a set length

Currently, you have an offset vector where:

- The **direction** of the vector points toward where the zombie should go.
- The **length** of the vector is the length of the line between the zombie's current position and where the player taps.

What you want is a velocity vector where:

- The **direction** points toward where the zombie should go.
- The **length** is `ZOMBIE_MOVE_POINTS_PER_SEC` (the constant you defined earlier – 120 points per second).

So you're halfway there – your vector points in the right direction, but isn't the right length. How do you make a vector pointing in the same direction as the offset vector, but a certain length?

The first step is to convert the offset vector into a **unit vector**, which means a vector of length 1. According to geometry, you can do this by simply dividing the offset vector's x and y components by the offset vector's length.

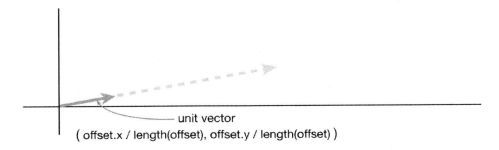

Note that this process of converting a vector into a unit vector is called **normalizing** a vector.

Once you have this unit vector, which you know is length 1, it's easy to multiply it by `ZOMBIE_MOVE_POINTS_PER_SEC` to make it the exact length you want.

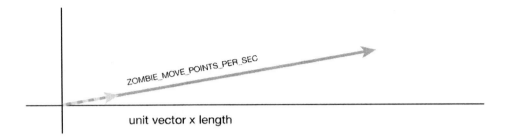

unit vector x length

Give it a try. Add the following lines to the bottom of moveZombieToward:

```
CGPoint direction = CGPointMake(offset.x / length,
                                offset.y / length);
_velocity =
  CGPointMake(direction.x * ZOMBIE_MOVE_POINTS_PER_SEC,
              direction.y * ZOMBIE_MOVE_POINTS_PER_SEC);
```

Now you've got a vector with the correct direction and length, and Xcode is no longer giving you warnings about this method.

Step 4: Hook up to touch events

In Sprite Kit, to get notifications of touch events on a node, you simply need to set that node's userInteractionEnabled property to YES and then override that node's touchesBegan:, touchesMoved: and/or touchesEnded: methods. Unlike other SKNode objects, SKScene's userInteractionEnabled property is set to YES by default.

To see it in action, implement these touch handling methods for MyScene as follows:

```
- (void)touchesBegan:(NSSet *)touches withEvent:(UIEvent *)event
{
  UITouch *touch = [touches anyObject];
  CGPoint touchLocation = [touch locationInNode:self];
  [self moveZombieToward:touchLocation];
}

- (void)touchesMoved:(NSSet *)touches withEvent:(UIEvent *)event
{
  UITouch *touch = [touches anyObject];
  CGPoint touchLocation = [touch locationInNode:self];
  [self moveZombieToward:touchLocation];
}
```

```objc
- (void)touchesEnded:(NSSet *)touches withEvent:(UIEvent *)event
{
  UITouch *touch = [touches anyObject];
  CGPoint touchLocation = [touch locationInNode:self];
  [self moveZombieToward:touchLocation];
}
```

Finally, inside update:, edit the call to moveSprite: so that it passes in _velocity instead of the hardcoded amount:

```objc
[self moveSprite:_zombie velocity:_velocity];
```

That's it! Build and run, and now the zombie will chase toward where you tap. Just don't get too close – he's hungry!

Note: You can also use gesture recognizers with Sprite Kit if you would like. They can be especially handy if you're trying to implement complicated gestures like pinching or rotating.

To do this, you can add the gesture recognizer to self.view – just make sure you do so at some point after init or it won't work. Also, you can use SKScene's convertPointFromView: and SKNode's convertPoint:toNode: methods to get the touch in the coordinate space you need.

For a demonstration of this, see the sample code for this chapter – I've put a commented out demonstration of gesture recognizers in there for you. Since it does the same thing as the touch handlers you implemented, comment out your touch handlers when you run with the gesture recognizers if you want to be sure the gestures are working.

Iteration 4: Bounds checking

As you played the latest version of the game, you might have noticed that the zombie happily runs straight off the screen if you let him. While I admire his enthusiasm, in Zombie Conga you would like him to stay on the screen at all times, bouncing off an edge if he hits one.

The basic idea is this: you need to check if the newly calculated position is beyond any of the screen edges, and make the zombie bounce away if so. To do this, add this new method:

```objc
- (void)boundsCheckPlayer
{
  // 1
  CGPoint newPosition = _zombie.position;
  CGPoint newVelocity = _velocity;

  // 2
  CGPoint bottomLeft = CGPointZero;
  CGPoint topRight = CGPointMake(self.size.width,
                                 self.size.height);

  // 3
  if (newPosition.x <= bottomLeft.x) {
    newPosition.x = bottomLeft.x;
    newVelocity.x = -newVelocity.x;
  }
  if (newPosition.x >= topRight.x) {
    newPosition.x = topRight.x;
    newVelocity.x = -newVelocity.x;
  }
  if (newPosition.y <= bottomLeft.y) {
    newPosition.y = bottomLeft.y;
    newVelocity.y = -newVelocity.y;
  }
  if (newPosition.y >= topRight.y) {
    newPosition.y = topRight.y;
    newVelocity.y = -newVelocity.y;
```

```
    }

    // 4
    _zombie.position = newPosition;
    _velocity = newVelocity;
  }
```

Let's go over this section-by-section:

1. You store the position and velocity in variables. This is required because when you set the position property on a node, you can't just set one component – you have to set the entire position in one shot,.For example, `_zombie.position = CGPointMake(100, 100)` is OK, but `_zombie.position.x = 100` will result in a compiler error. Making a temporary `CGPoint` works around this.

2. This gets the bottom left and top right coordinates of the screen.

3. Here you check the position to see if it's beyond or at any of the screen edges. If it is, you clamp the position and reverse the appropriate velocity component to make the zombie bounce in the opposite direction.

4. You set the zombie to the new position.

Now call your new method at the end of **update**:

```
[self boundsCheckPlayer];
```

Build and run, and now you have a zombie bouncing around the screen. I told you he was ready to party!

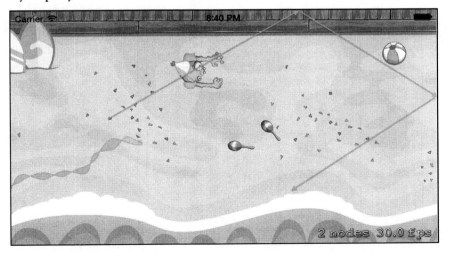

Rotating the zombie

The zombie is moving nicely, but he always faces the same direction. Granted, he is undead, but this zombie is on the curious side and would like to turn to see where he's going!

You already have a vector that includes the direction the zombie is facing: `_velocity`. You just need to get the angle to rotate so that the zombie faces in that direction.

Once again, think of the direction vector as the hypotenuse of a right triangle. You want to find the angle:

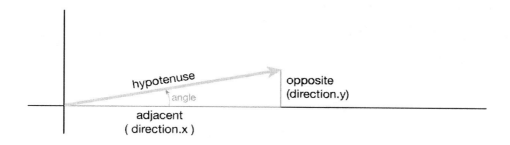

You may remember from trigonometry the mnemonic SOH CAH TOA, where the last part stands for:

```
tan(angle) = opposite / adjacent
```

Since you have the lengths of the opposite and adjacent sides, you can rewrite the above formula as follows to get the angle of rotation:

```
angle = arctan(opposite / adjacent)
```

If none of this trigonometry rings any bells, don't worry. Just think of it as a formula that you type in to get the angle – that's all you need to know.

Try it out by adding the following new method:

```
- (void)rotateSprite:(SKSpriteNode *)sprite
```

```
                 toFace:(CGPoint)direction
{
    sprite.zRotation = atan2f(direction.y, direction.x);
}
```

This just uses the equation from above. Note that this works because the zombie image is set up to be facing to the right. If the zombie were facing up instead, you'd have to add an additional rotation to compensate.

Now call this new method at the end of update:

```
[self rotateSprite:_zombie toFace:_velocity];
```

Build and run, and now the zombie rotates to face the direction in which he's moving:

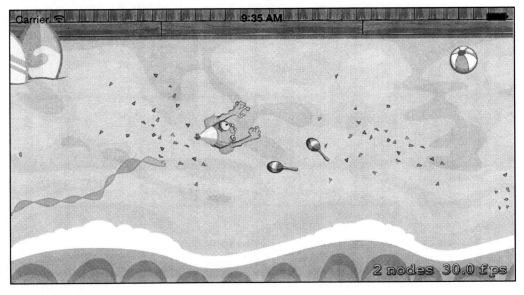

Congratulations, you've given your zombie some life! The sprite moves smoothly, bounces off the edges of the screen and rotates – a great start to a game.

But you're not done yet – it's time for you to try out some of this on your own to make sure you've got this stuff down!

Challenges

This chapter has three challenges, and they're particularly important ones. Performing these challenges will give you useful practice with vector math and introduce some new math utilities you will be using throughout the rest of the book.

As always, if you get stuck, you can find solutions in the resources for this chapter – but give it your best shot first!

Challenge 1: Math utilities

As you may have noticed while working on this game, you frequently have to perform calculations on points and vectors: adding and subtracting points, finding lengths, and so on.

So far in this chapter, you've done this all yourself inline. That's a fine way of doing things, but can get tedious and repetitive in practice. It's also error-prone.

Open **MyScene.m** and add the following functions to your file, right after `#import` "MyScene.h":

```
static inline CGPoint CGPointAdd(const CGPoint a,
                                 const CGPoint b)
{
    return CGPointMake(a.x + b.x, a.y + b.y);
}

static inline CGPoint CGPointSubtract(const CGPoint a,
                                      const CGPoint b)
{
    return CGPointMake(a.x - b.x, a.y - b.y);
}

static inline CGPoint CGPointMultiplyScalar(const CGPoint a,
                                            const CGFloat b)
{
    return CGPointMake(a.x * b, a.y * b);
}

static inline CGFloat CGPointLength(const CGPoint a)
{
    return sqrtf(a.x * a.x + a.y * a.y);
}

static inline CGPoint CGPointNormalize(const CGPoint a)
{
```

```
    CGFloat length = CGPointLength(a);
    return CGPointMake(a.x / length, a.y / length);
}

static inline CGFloat CGPointToAngle(const CGPoint a)
{
    return atan2f(a.y, a.x);
}
```

These are helper functions that implement many of the operations you've been working with already. For example, look at moveSprite:velocity::

```
- (void)moveSprite:(SKSpriteNode *)sprite
          velocity:(CGPoint)velocity
{
    // 1
    CGPoint amountToMove = CGPointMake(velocity.x * _dt,
                                       velocity.y * _dt);
    NSLog(@"Amount to move: %@",
          NSStringFromCGPoint(amountToMove));

    // 2
    sprite.position =
      CGPointMake(_zombie.position.x + amountToMove.x,
                  _zombie.position.y + amountToMove.y);
}
```

You could simplify the first line by calling CGPointMultiplyScalar, and you could simplify the second line by calling CGPointAdd.

Your challenge is to modify the game to use these new routines, and verify that the game still works as expected. When you're done, you should have the following calls (including the two mentioned already):

• CGPointAdd: 1 call

• CGPointSubtract: 1 call

• CGPointMultiplyScalar: 2 calls

• CGPointNormalize: 1 call

• CGPointToAngle: 1 call

You should also notice when you're done that your code is a lot cleaner and easier to understand. In future chapters, you will be using a math library we made very similar to this, but optimized for speed.

Challenge 2: Stop that zombie!

In Zombie Conga, when you tap the screen the zombie moves toward that point – but then continues to move beyond that point.

That is the behavior you want for Zombie Conga, but in some games you might want the zombie to stop where you tap. Your challenge is to modify the game to do this.

Here are a few hints for one possible way to do this:

- Create a new private variable called `_lastTouchLocation`, and update that whenever the user begins, moves or ends their touch.

- Inside `update:`, check the distance between the last touch location and the zombie's position. If that remaining distance is less than or equal to the amount the zombie will move this frame (`ZOMBIE_MOVE_POINTS_PER_SEC * _dt`), then set the zombie's position to the last touch location and the velocity to zero. Otherwise, call `moveSprite:velocity:`, `boundsCheckPlayer`, and `rotateSprite:toFace:` like normal.

- Make one call to `CGPointSubtract` and one call to `CGPointLength` using the helper code from the previous challenge.

Challenge 3: Smooth moves

Currently, the zombie immediately rotates to face where you tap. This can be a bit jarring – it would be nicer if the zombie would smoothly rotate over time to face the new direction.

To do this, you need two new helper routines. Add these to the top of your file:

```
static inline CGFloat ScalarSign(CGFloat a)
{
  return a >= 0 ? 1 : -1;
}

// Returns shortest angle between two angles,
// between -M_PI and M_PI
static inline CGFloat ScalarShortestAngleBetween(
  const CGFloat a, const CGFloat b)
{
  CGFloat difference = b - a;
  CGFloat angle = fmodf(difference, M_PI * 2);
  if (angle >= M_PI) {
    angle -= M_PI * 2;
  }
```

```
    else if (angle <= -M_PI) {
      angle += M_PI * 2;
    }
    return angle;
}
```

ScalarSign returns a 1 if the number is greater than or equal to 0; otherwise it returns -1.

ScalarShortestAngleBetween returns the shortest angle between two angles. It's not as simple as subtracting the two angles, for two reasons:

1. Angles "wrap around" after 360 degrees (2 * M_PI). In other words, 30 degrees and 390 degrees represent the same angle.

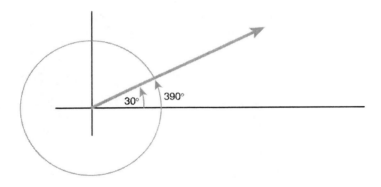

2. Sometimes the shortest way to get between two angles is to go left, and other times to go right. For example, if you start at 0 degrees and want to turn to 270 degrees, it's shorter to turn -90 degrees than 270 degrees. You don't want your zombie turning the long way around – he may be undead, but he's not stupid!

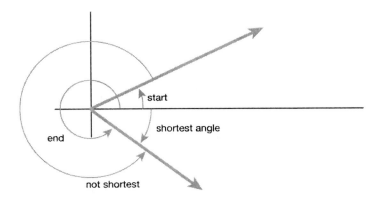

So this routine finds the difference between the two angles, chops off any amount > 360 degrees, then figures out if it's faster to go right or left.

Your challenge is to modify `rotateSprite:toFace:` to take and use a new parameter of how many radians the zombie should rotate per second.

Define the constant as follows:

```
static const float ZOMBIE_ROTATE_RADIANS_PER_SEC = 4 * M_PI;
```

And modify the method signature as follows:

```
- (void)rotateSprite:(SKSpriteNode *)sprite
              toFace:(CGPoint)velocity
  rotateRadiansPerSec:(CGFloat)rotateRadiansPerSec
{
  // Your code here!
}
```

Here are a few hints for implementing this method:

• Use `ScalarShortestAngleBetween` to find the distance between the current angle and the target angle. Call this `shortest`.

• Figure out the amount to rotate this frame based on `rotateRadiansPerSec` and `_dt`. Call this `amtToRotate`.

• If the absolute value of `shortest` is less than the `amtToRotate`, use that instead.

- Use `ScalarSign` on `shortest` to determine whether to add or subtract `amtToRotate` from the current rotation.

- Don't forget to update the call to rotate the sprite in `update:` to use the new parameter.

If you've completed all three of these challenges, great work! You really understand moving and rotating sprites, using the "classic" approach of updating the values yourself over time.

Ah, but the classic, while essential to understand, always gives way to the modern. In the next chapter, you'll learn how Sprite Kit can make some of these common tasks much easier, through the magic of actions!

Chapter 3: Actions

By Ray Wenderlich

So far, you have learned how to move or rotate Sprite Kit nodes – a node being anything that appears onscreen – by manually setting their position and rotation over time.

This do-it-yourself approach works and is quite powerful, but Sprite Kit provides an easier way to move sprites incrementally: **actions**.

Actions are great because they allow you to do things like rotate, scale or change a sprite's position over time with just one line of code! You can also chain actions together to create some neat movement combinations quite easily.

In this chapter, you'll learn all about Sprite Kit actions as you add enemies, collectibles and basic gameplay logic to your game.

You'll see how actions can simplify your game-coding life, and by the time you're done this chapter, Zombie Conga will resemble an actual game!

> **Note:** This chapter begins where Challenge 3 left off in the last chapter. If you were unable to complete the challenges or skipped ahead from a previous chapter, don't worry – you can simply open **ZombieConga-Starter** from the resources for this chapter to pick up where we left off.

Move action

Right now your zombie's life is a bit too carefree, so let's add some action into this game by introducing some enemies to dodge — crazy cat ladies!

Open **MyScene.m** and create the start of a new method to spawn an enemy:

```
- (void)spawnEnemy
{
  SKSpriteNode *enemy = [SKSpriteNode
    spriteNodeWithImageNamed:@"enemy"];
  enemy.position = CGPointMake(
    self.size.width + enemy.size.width/2, self.size.height/2);
  [self addChild:enemy];
}
```

This code should be a review from the previous two chapters — you create a sprite, positioned at the vertical center of the screen, just out of view to the right.

Now, you'd like to move the enemy from the right of the screen to the left. If you were doing this manually, you might update the enemy's position each frame according to a velocity.

No need to trouble yourself with that this time! Simply add these two lines of code to the bottom of spawnEnemy:

```
SKAction *actionMove =
  [SKAction moveTo:CGPointMake(-enemy.size.width/2,
                                enemy.position.y)
          duration:2.0];
  [enemy runAction:actionMove];
```

To create an action in Sprite Kit, you call one of several static constructors on the SKAction class, such as the one you see here, moveTo:duration:. This particular constructor returns an action that moves a sprite to a specified position, over a specified duration (in seconds).

Here you set up the action to move the enemy along the x-axis at whatever speed is necessary to take it from its current position to just off the left side of the screen in two seconds.

Once you've created an action, you need to run it. You can run an action on any SKNode by calling runAction:, as you did in the above code.

Give it a try! For now, just call this method inside `initWithSize:`, right after calling `[self addChild:_zombie]`:

```
[self spawnEnemy];
```

Build and run, and you should see the crazy cat lady race across the screen:

Not bad for just two lines of code, eh? You could have even done it with a single line of code if you didn't need to use the `actionMove` variable for anything else.

Here you saw an example of `moveTo:duration:`, but there are a few other move action variants:

- `moveToX:duration:` and `moveToY:duration:` These allow you to specify a change in only the x or y position – the other is assumed to remain the same. You could have used `moveToX:duration:` in the example above, to save a bit of typing.

- `moveByX:y:duration:` The "move to" actions move the sprite to a particular point, but sometimes it's convenient to move a sprite as an offset from its current position, wherever that may be. You could have used `moveByX:y:duration` for this example, passing `-(self.size.width + enemy.size.width)` for x and 0 for y.

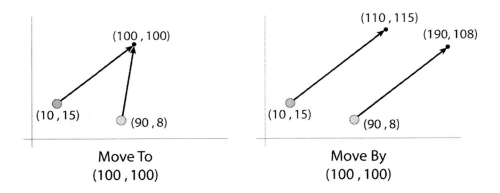

You'll see this pattern of "[action] to" and "[action] by" variants for other action types as well. In general, you can use whichever of these is more convenient for you – but keep in mind that if either works, the "[action] by" actions are preferable because they are reversible. For more on this topic, keep reading.

> **Note:** You may be used to extending classes to implement new functionality. However, there is no way to extend the SKAction class. The *only* way to create an SKAction is via one of its static constructor methods.
>
> In this chapter, you'll learn about specific methods that allow you to create SKActions that run custom code, and you'll learn how to combine SKActions to create complex behaviors. Using these two techniques, you should be able to accomplish your goals without subclasses.

Sequence action

The real power of actions lies in how easily you can chain them together. For example, say you want the cat lady to move in a V – down toward the bottom of the screen, then up to the goal position.

To do this, replace the lines that create and run the move action in spawnEnemy with the following:

```
// 1
SKAction *actionMidMove =
```

```
    [SKAction moveTo:CGPointMake(self.size.width/2,
                                  enemy.size.height/2)
         duration:1.0];
// 2
SKAction *actionMove =
  [SKAction moveTo:CGPointMake(-enemy.size.width/2,
                                enemy.position.y) duration:1.0];
// 3
SKAction *sequence =
  [SKAction
  sequence:@[actionMidMove, actionMove]];
// 4
[enemy runAction:sequence];
```

Let's go over this line-by-line:

1. Here you've created a new move action, just like you did before, except this time it represents the "mid-point" of the action – the bottom middle of the screen.

2. This is the same move action as before, except the duration has been decreased to 1.0, since it will now represent moving only half the distance: from the bottom of the V, off-screen to the left.

3. Here's the new sequence action! As you can see, it's incredibly simple – you use the `sequence:` constructor and pass in an `NSArray` of actions. The sequence action will run one action after another.

> **Note:** As mentioned in Chapter 2, this book uses modern Objective-C syntax, like the literal syntax you see here to declare an `NSArray`, as well as blocks, which you'll see a bit later on. If you need a refresher on modern Objective-C style, check out Chapter 1 in *iOS 6 by Tutorials*, "Modern Objective-C."

4. You call `runAction:` in the same way as before, but pass in the sequence action this time.

That's it – build and run, and you'll see the crazy cat lady "bounce" off the bottom of the screen:

The sequence action is one of the most useful and commonly used actions – chaining actions together is just so powerful! You will be using the sequence action many times in this chapter and throughout the rest of this book.

Wait for duration action

The wait for duration action does exactly what you'd expect: makes the sprite wait for a period of time, during which the sprite does nothing.

"What's the point of that?", you may be wondering. Well, wait for duration actions only truly become interesting when combined with a sequence action.

For example, let's make the cat lady briefly pause when she reaches the bottom of the V-shape. To do this, simply modify your list of actions in **spawnEnemy:**, like so (changes highlighted):

```
SKAction *actionMidMove =
  [SKAction moveTo:CGPointMake(self.size.width/2,
                               enemy.size.height/2)
          duration:1.0];
```

```
SKAction *actionMove =
  [SKAction moveTo:CGPointMake(-enemy.size.width/2,
                               enemy.position.y) duration:1.0];
SKAction *wait = [SKAction waitForDuration:0.25];
SKAction *sequence =
  [SKAction sequence:@[actionMidMove, wait, actionMove]];
[enemy runAction:sequence];
```

To create a wait for duration action, call the `waitForDuration:` constructor with the amount of time to wait in seconds. Then, simply insert it into the sequence of actions where you want the delay to occur.

Build and run, and now the cat lady will briefly pause at the bottom of the V:

Run block and selector actions

At times when you're running a sequence of actions, you'll want to run your own block of code at some point. For example, say you want to log out a message when the cat lady reaches the bottom of the V.

To do this, just modify your list of actions in `spawnEnemy:` like so (changes highlighted):

```
SKAction *actionMidMove =
  [SKAction moveTo:CGPointMake(self.size.width/2,
                               enemy.size.height/2)
          duration:1.0];
SKAction *actionMove =
  [SKAction moveToX:-enemy.size.width/2 duration:1.0];
SKAction *wait = [SKAction waitForDuration:0.25];
SKAction *logMessage = [SKAction runBlock:^{
  NSLog(@"Reached bottom!");
}];
SKAction *sequence = [SKAction sequence:
    @[actionMidMove, logMessage, wait, actionMove]];
[enemy runAction:sequence];
```

To create a block action, simply call the `runBlock:` constructor and pass in a block of code to execute.

Build and run, and when the cat lady reaches the bottom of the V, you should see the following in the console:

```
ZombieConga[9644:70b] Reached bottom!
```

> **Note:** If your project still includes the `NSLog` statements from earlier chapters, now would be a great time to remove them. Otherwise, you'll have to search your console for the above log statement – it's doubtful you'll notice it within the sea of messages scrolling by.

Of course, you can do far more than just log a message here – since it's an arbitrary code block, you can do anything you want!

You should be aware of a few other actions related to running blocks of code:

- `runBlock:queue:` Allows you to run the block of code on an arbitrary dispatch queue instead of in the main Sprite Kit event loop. You can learn more about this in Chapter 26, "Performance: Tips and Tricks."

- `performSelector:onTarget:` Allows you to run any method on a target object, rather than having a block of code inline. Whether you use this or the `runBlock:` action to execute code is a matter of personal preference – mostly. You'll see an example where your choice actually matters in Chapter 16, "Saving and Loading Games."

Reversed actions

Let's say you want to make the cat lady go back the way she came – after she moves in a V to the left, she should move in a V back to the right.

One way to do this is, after she goes off-screen to the left, you could have her run the existing `actionMidMove` action to go back to the middle, and create a new `moveTo:duration:` action to go back to the start position.

But Sprite Kit gives you a better option. You can reverse certain actions in Sprite Kit simply by calling `reversedAction` on them. This results in a new action that is the opposite of the original action.

For example, if you run a `moveByX:y:duration:` action, you can run the reverse of that action to go back the other way:

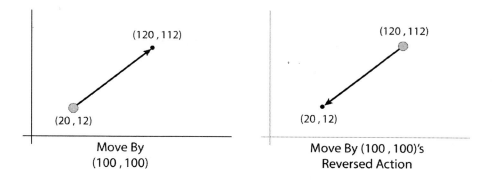

Not all actions are reversible – for example, `moveTo:duration:` is not. To find out if an action is reversible, look it up in the `SKAction` class reference, which indicates it plainly (see image on next page).

moveByX:y:duration:

Creates an action that moves a node relative to its current position.

+ (SKAction *)moveByX:(CGFloat)*deltaX* y:(CGFloat)*deltaY* duration:(NSTimeInterval)*sec*

Parameters
deltaX
   The x-value, in points, to add to the node's position.
deltaY
   The y-value, in points, to add to the node's position.
sec
   The duration of the animation.

Return Value
A new move action.

Discussion
When the action executes, the node's `position` property animates from its current position to its new position.

This action is reversible; the reverse is created as if the following code were executed:

```
[SKAction moveByX: -deltaX y: -deltaY duration: sec];
```

Let's try this out. Modify your list of actions in **spawnEnemy:** like so (changes highlighted):

```
SKAction *actionMidMove =
  [SKAction moveByX:-self.size.width/2-enemy.size.width/2
                 y:-self.size.height/2+enemy.size.height/2
           duration:1.0];
SKAction *actionMove =
  [SKAction moveByX:-self.size.width/2-enemy.size.width/2
                 y:self.size.height/2+enemy.size.height/2
           duration:1.0];
SKAction *wait = [SKAction waitForDuration:1.0];
SKAction *logMessage = [SKAction runBlock:^{
  NSLog(@"Reached bottom!");
}];
SKAction *reverseMid = [actionMidMove reversedAction];
SKAction *reverseMove = [actionMove reversedAction];
  SKAction *sequence =
    [SKAction sequence:@[
      actionMidMove, logMessage, wait, actionMove,
      reverseMove, logMessage, wait, reverseMid]];
[enemy runAction:sequence];
```

First you switch the `moveTo:duration:` actions to the related `moveByX:y:duration:` variant, since that is reversible.

Then you create the reverse of those actions by calling `reversedAction` on each, and insert them into the sequence.

Build and run, and now the cat lady will go one way, then back the other:

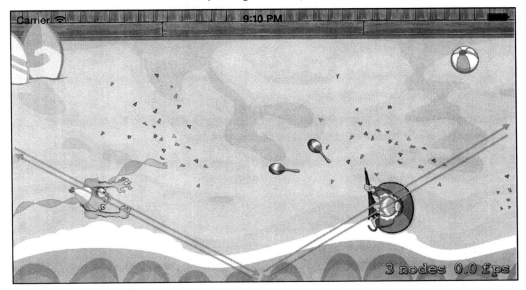

One last thing about reversible actions: if an action is *not* reversible, then it will return the same action. And because sequence actions are also reversible, you can simplify the above code as follows. **Remove** the lines where you create the reversed actions and replace the sequence creation with the following lines:

```
SKAction *sequence =
  [SKAction sequence:
   @[actionMidMove, logMessage, wait, actionMove]];
sequence =
  [SKAction sequence:@[sequence,[sequence reversedAction]]];
```

This simply creates a sequence of actions moving the sprite one way, and then reverses the sequence to go the other way.

Astute observers may have noticed that the first half of this action logs a message as soon as it reaches the bottom of the screen, but on the way back the message is not logged until after the sprite has waited at the bottom for one second.

This is because the reversed sequence is the exact opposite of the original, unlike how you wrote the first version. Later in this chapter you'll read about the group action, which you could use to fix this.

Repeat action

So far, so good, but what if you want the cat lady to repeat this sequence multiple times? Of course, there's an action for that!

You can repeat an action a certain number of times using `repeatAction:count:`, or an endless number of times using `repeatActionForever:`.

Let's go with the endless variant. Replace the line that runs your action in `spawnEnemy` with the following two lines:

```
SKAction *repeat = [SKAction repeatActionForever:sequence];
[enemy runAction:repeat];
```

Here you create an action that repeats the sequence of other actions endlessly, and run that repeat action on the enemy.

Build and run, and now your cat lady will continuously bounce back and forth. I told you she was crazy!

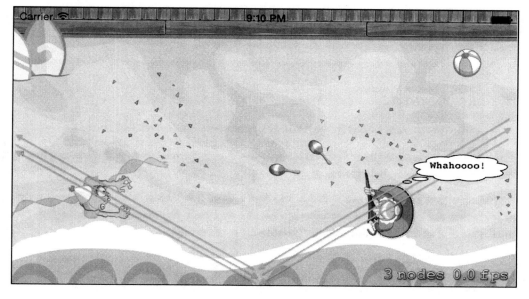

Congratulations, now you understand many useful types of actions:

- Move actions

- Sequence actions

- Wait for duration actions

- Run block and selector actions

- Reversing actions

- Repeat actions

Next, you're going to put these all together in a new and interesting way: you're going to make cat ladies spawn periodically over time, instead of spawning just one cat lady at launch.

Periodic spawning

To prepare for periodic spawning, you'll revert the spawnEnemy code to the original version that simply moves the cat lady from right to left. You'll also introduce some random variance so the cat lady doesn't always spawn at the same y-position.

First things first: you need a helper method to generate a random number within a range of values. Add this new method to the top of your file, along with the other math utilities you added in the first challenge in the previous chapter:

```
#define ARC4RANDOM_MAX      0x100000000
static inline CGFloat ScalarRandomRange(CGFloat min,
                                        CGFloat max)
{
  return floorf(((double)arc4random() / ARC4RANDOM_MAX) *
              (max - min) + min);
}
```

It's not important for you to understand this method, except that you can use it to get a random number between a minimum and maximum value. But if you're really curious, feel free to read the note below.

> **Note:** Here's how the above method works. `arc4random()` gives you a random integer between 0 and ARC4RANDOM_MAX. If you divide that number by ARC4RANDOM_MAX, you get a float between 0 and 1.
>
> If you multiply this value by the range of values (max – min), you'll get a float between 0 and the range. If you add to that the min value, you'll get a float between min and max. Violà, job done!

Next, replace the current version of `spawnEnemy` with the following (important new lines are highlighted):

```objc
- (void)spawnEnemy
{
  SKSpriteNode *enemy =
    [SKSpriteNode spriteNodeWithImageNamed:@"enemy"];
  enemy.position = CGPointMake(
    self.size.width + enemy.size.width/2,
    ScalarRandomRange(enemy.size.height/2,
                      self.size.height-enemy.size.height/2));
  [self addChild:enemy];

  SKAction *actionMove =
    [SKAction moveToX:-enemy.size.width/2 duration:2.0];
  [enemy runAction:actionMove];
}
```

All you did here was modify the fixed y-position to be a random value between the bottom and top of the screen, and revert the movement back to the original implementation. Well, the `moveToX:duration:` variant of the original implementation, anyway.

Now it's time for some action. Inside `initWithSize:`, replace the call to `spawnEnemy:` with the following:

```objc
[self runAction:[SKAction repeatActionForever:
  [SKAction sequence:@[
    [SKAction performSelector:@selector(spawnEnemy)
                     onTarget:self],
    [SKAction waitForDuration:2.0]]]]];
```

This is an example of how you can chain actions together inline if you'd like, instead of creating separate variables for each action.

This example creates a sequence of calling the `spawnEnemy` method and waiting two seconds. It repeats this sequence forever.

Note that you're running the action on `self`, which is the scene itself. This works because the scene is a node, and any node can run actions.

Build and run, and now the crazy cat ladies will spawn endlessly, at varying positions:

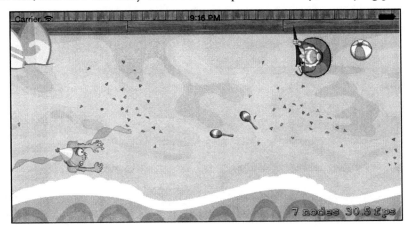

Remove from parent action

If you keep the game running for a while, you'll notice that the node count in the bottom right keeps increasing. Here's a screenshot of the game running after a few minutes:

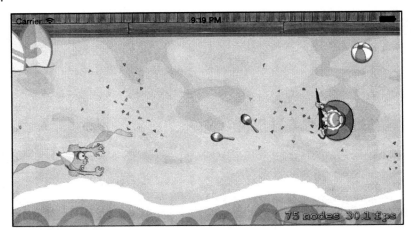

A never-ending list of nodes in a game is not a good thing. This node army will eventually consume all of the memory on the device, and the OS will automatically terminate your app, which from a user's perspective will look like your app crashed.

You'll learn more about best ways to deal with this in Chapter 25, "Performance", but for now a good rule of thumb is, "if you don't need it anymore, remove it."

And as you may have guessed, there's an action for that, too! When you no longer need a node and can remove it from the scene, you can either call removeFromParent directly, or use the remove from parent action.

Let's give this a try. Modify your list of actions in spawnEnemy: like so (changes highlighted):

```
SKAction *actionMove =
  [SKAction moveToX:-enemy.size.width/2 duration:2.0];
SKAction *actionRemove = [SKAction removeFromParent];
[enemy runAction:
  [SKAction sequence:@[actionMove, actionRemove]]];
```

Build and run, and now the node count should always stay about constant, regardless of how long you run the game. Ah – much better!

> **Note:** The removeFromParent action removes the node that's running that action from its parent. But this brings up an interesting point: what happens to actions after you run them? Calling runAction: stores a strong reference to the action you give it, so won't that slowly eat up your memory?
>
> The answer is no. Sprite Kit nodes do you the favor of automatically removing their references to actions when the actions finish running. So you can tell a node to run an action and then forget about it, feeling confident that you haven't leaked any memory.

Animation action

This one is super-useful, because adding animations is a super easy way to add a lot of polish and fun to your game.

To run an animation action, you first need to gather a list of images called **textures** that make up the frames of the animation. A sprite has a texture assigned to it, but you can always swap out the texture with a different one at runtime by setting the `texture` property on the sprite.

In fact, this is what animations do for you – automatically swap out your sprite's textures over time, with a slight delay between each.

Zombie Conga already includes some animation frames for the zombie. As you can see below, you have four textures to use as frames to show the zombie walking:

zombie1.png   zombie2.png   zombie3.png   zombie4.png

You want to play the frames in this order:

1   2   3   4   3   2

You can then repeat this endlessly for a continuous walk animation.

Give it a shot. First create a private instance variable for the zombie action:

```
SKAction *_zombieAnimation;
```

Then add the following code to `initWithSize:`, right after adding the zombie as a child to the scene:

```
// 1
NSMutableArray *textures =
  [NSMutableArray arrayWithCapacity:10];
// 2
for (int i = 1; i < 4; i++) {
  NSString *textureName =
    [NSString stringWithFormat:@"zombie%d", i];
  SKTexture *texture =
    [SKTexture textureWithImageNamed:textureName];
  [textures addObject:texture];
}
// 3
for (int i = 4; i > 1; i--) {
  NSString *textureName =
    [NSString stringWithFormat:@"zombie%d", i];
```

```
    SKTexture *texture =
      [SKTexture textureWithImageNamed:textureName];
    [textures addObject:texture];
  }
  // 4
  _zombieAnimation =
    [SKAction animateWithTextures:textures timePerFrame:0.1];
  // 5
  [_zombie runAction:
    [SKAction repeatActionForever:_zombieAnimation]];
```

Let's go over this one section at a time:

1. You create an array that will store all of the textures to run in the animation.

2. The animation frames are named zombie1.png, zombie2.png, zombie3.png, and zombie4.png. This makes it nice and easy to create a loop that creates a string for each image name, and then makes a texture object from each name using SKTexture's textureWithImageNamed: constructor.

3. The first for loop adds frames 1 to 3, which is most of the "forward walk." This for loop reverses the order and adds frames 4 to 2 to create the "backward walk" animation.

4. Once you have the array of textures, running the animation is easy – just use SKAction's animateWithTextures:timePerFrame: constructor.

5. Finally, run the action wrapped in a repeat forever action. This will seamlessly cycle through the frames 1,2,3,4,3,2,1,2,3,4,3,2,1,2....

Build and run, and now your zombie will strut in style!

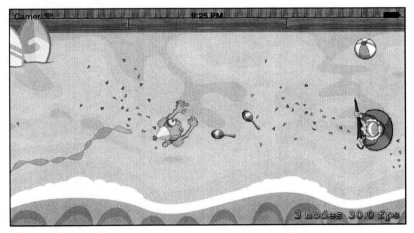

Stopping action

Your zombie's off to a good start, but one annoying thing is that when the zombie stops moving, his animation keeps running. Ideally, you'd like to stop the animation when the zombie stops moving.

In Sprite Kit, whenever you run an action, you can give the action a key simply by using a variant of the `runAction:` method called `runAction:withKey:`. This is handy because then you can stop the action later by calling `removeActionForKey:`.

Give it a shot by adding these two new methods:

```
- (void)startZombieAnimation
{
  if (![_zombie actionForKey:@"animation"]) {
    [_zombie runAction:
     [SKAction repeatActionForever:_zombieAnimation]
           withKey:@"animation"];
  }
}

- (void)stopZombieAnimation
{
  [_zombie removeActionForKey:@"animation"];
}
```

The first method starts the zombie animation. It runs the animation the same as before, except it tags it with a key called "animation".

Also note that the method first uses `actionForKey:` to make sure there is not already an action running with the key "animation"; it doesn't bother running the action if one is already running (i.e. if there's already an action for that key).

The second method stops the zombie animation. It removes the action with the key "animation".

Now, go to `initWithSize:` and comment out the line that ran the action there:

```
//[_zombie runAction:
// [SKAction repeatActionForever:_zombieAnimation]];
```

Call `startZombieAnimation` at the beginning of `moveZombieToward::`

```
[self startZombieAnimation];
```

And call `stopZombieAnimation` inside `update:`, right after the line of code that sets
`_velocity = CGPointZero`:

```
[self stopZombieAnimation];
```

Build and run, and now your zombie will only move when he should!

Scale action

You now have an animated zombie and some crazy cat ladies, but the game is missing
one very important element – cats! Remember that the purpose of the game is for the
player to gather as many cats as he can into the zombie's conga line.

In Zombie Conga, the cats won't move from right to left like the cat ladies do – instead,
they will appear at a random location on the screen and stay stationary. Rather than have
them appear instantly, which would be jarring, you'll have them start at a scale of 0 and
grow to a scale of 1 over time. This will make the cats appear to "pop in" to the game.

To implement this, add the following new method:

```
- (void)spawnCat
{
  // 1
  SKSpriteNode *cat =
    [SKSpriteNode spriteNodeWithImageNamed:@"cat"];
  cat.position = CGPointMake(
    ScalarRandomRange(0, self.size.width),
    ScalarRandomRange(0, self.size.height));
  cat.xScale = 0;
  cat.yScale = 0;
  [self addChild:cat];

  // 2
  SKAction *appear = [SKAction scaleTo:1.0 duration:0.5];
  SKAction *wait = [SKAction waitForDuration:10.0];
  SKAction *disappear = [SKAction scaleTo:0.0 duration:0.5];
  SKAction *removeFromParent = [SKAction removeFromParent];
  [cat runAction:
    [SKAction sequence:@[appear, wait, disappear,
                         removeFromParent]]];
}
```

Let's go over each section:

1. You create a cat at a random spot on the screen. Note that you set the xScale and yScale to 0, which makes the cat 0 size – effectively invisible.

2. You create an action to scale the cat up to normal size by calling the scaleTo:duration: constructor. This action is not reversible, so you also create a similar action to scale the cat back down to 0. The sequence is the cat appears, waits for a bit, disappears, and is then removed from the parent.

You want the cats to spawn continuously from the start of the game, so add the following inside initWithSize:, just after the line that spawns the enemies:

```
[self runAction:[SKAction repeatActionForever:
  [SKAction sequence:@[
    [SKAction performSelector:@selector(spawnCat)
                     onTarget:self],
    [SKAction waitForDuration:1.0]]]]];
```

This is very similar to how you spawned the enemies. You simply run a sequence that calls spawnCat, waits for one second and then repeats.

Build and run, and now you will see cats pop in and out of the game:

You should be aware of a few other variants of the scale action:

- `scaleXTo:duration:`, `scaleYTo:duration:`, and `scaleXTo:y:duration:`: These allow you to scale just the x-axis or y-axis of a node independently, which you can use to stretch or squash a node.

- `scaleBy:duration::` The "by" variant of scaling, which multiples the passed-in scale by the current node's scale. For example, if the current scale of a node is 1.0, and you scale it by 2.0, it is now at 2x. If you scale it by 2.0 again, it is now at 4x. Note that you could not use `scaleBy:duration:` in the previous example, because anything multiplied by 0 is still 0!

- `scaleXBy:y:duration::` Another "by" variant, but this one allows you to scale x and y independently.

Rotate action

The cats in this game should be appealing to the player to try to pick up, but right now they're just sitting motionless.

MEH

Let's give them some charm by making them wiggle back and forth while they sit.

To do that, you'll need the rotate action. To use it, you call the `rotateByAngle:duration:` constructor, passing in the angle (in radians) by which to rotate. Replace the list of actions in **spawnCat** with the following (changes highlighted):

```
cat.zRotation = -M_PI / 16;

SKAction *appear = [SKAction scaleTo:1.0 duration:0.5];

SKAction *leftWiggle = [SKAction rotateByAngle:M_PI / 8
                                      duration:0.5];
```

```
SKAction *rightWiggle = [leftWiggle reversedAction];
SKAction *fullWiggle =[SKAction sequence:
                          @[leftWiggle, rightWiggle]];
SKAction *wiggleWait =
  [SKAction repeatAction:fullWiggle count:10];

//SKAction *wait = [SKAction waitForDuration:10.0];
SKAction *disappear = [SKAction scaleTo:0.0 duration:0.5];
SKAction *removeFromParent = [SKAction removeFromParent];
[cat runAction:
  [SKAction sequence:
    @[appear, wiggleWait, disappear, removeFromParent]]];
```

Rotations go counter-clockwise in Sprite Kit, so negative rotations go clockwise. First you rotate the `cat` clockwise by 1/16 of `PI` (11.25 degrees) by setting its `zRotation` to – `M_PI/16`. The user won't see this because at this point, the cat's scale is still 0.

Then you create `leftWiggle`, which rotates counter-clockwise by 22.5 degrees over a period of 0.5 seconds. And since the cat starts out rotated clockwise by 11.25 degrees, this results in the cat being rotated counter-clockwise by 11.25 degrees.

Since this is a "by" variant, it is reversible, so you use `reversedAction` to create `rightWiggle`, which simply rotates back the other way to where the cat started.

You create a `fullWiggle` by rotating left and then right. Now the cat has wiggled left and right and is back to its start position. This "full wiggle" takes one second total, so in `wiggleWait` you repeat this 10 times to have a 10-second wiggle duration.

Build and run, and now your cats look like they've had some catnip!

Group action

So far you know how to run actions one after another in sequence, but what if you want to run two actions at the exact same time? For example, in Zombie Conga you want to make the cat wiggle and scale up and down slightly as he's wiggling.

For this sort of multitasking, you can use something called the group action. It works in a similar way to the sequence action, where you pass in a list of actions. However, instead of running them one at a time, a group action runs them all at once.

Let's try this out. Replace the list of actions in **spawnCat** with the following (changes highlighted):

```
SKAction *appear = [SKAction scaleTo:1.0 duration:0.5];

SKAction *leftWiggle = [SKAction rotateByAngle:M_PI / 8
                                      duration:0.5];
SKAction *rightWiggle = [leftWiggle reversedAction];
SKAction *fullWiggle =[SKAction sequence:
                     @[leftWiggle, rightWiggle]];
//SKAction *wiggleWait =
//   [SKAction repeatAction:fullWiggle count:10];
//SKAction *wait = [SKAction waitForDuration:10.0];

SKAction *scaleUp = [SKAction scaleBy:1.2 duration:0.25];
SKAction *scaleDown = [scaleUp reversedAction];
SKAction *fullScale = [SKAction sequence:
  @[scaleUp, scaleDown, scaleUp, scaleDown]];

SKAction *group = [SKAction group:@[fullScale, fullWiggle]];
SKAction *groupWait = [SKAction repeatAction:group count:10];

SKAction *disappear = [SKAction scaleTo:0.0 duration:0.5];
SKAction *removeFromParent = [SKAction removeFromParent];
[cat runAction:
  [SKAction sequence:
    @[appear, groupWait, disappear, removeFromParent]]];
```

This code creates a sequence similar to that of the wiggle sequence, except it scales up and down instead of wiggling left and right.

It then sets up a group action to run the wiggling and scaling at the same time. To use a group action, you simply provide it with the list of actions which should run at the same time.

Build and run, and your cats are now bouncing with excitement:

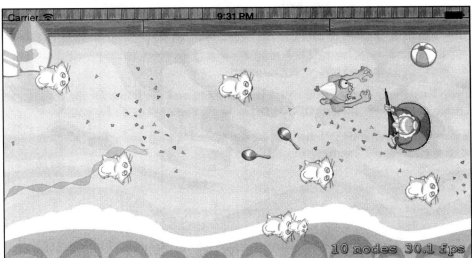

> **Note:** The duration of a group action is equal to the longest duration of any of the actions it contains. So if you add one action that takes one second, and another that takes 10 seconds, both actions will begin to run at the same time, and after one second the first action will be complete. The group action will continue to execute for nine more seconds until the other action is complete.

Collision detection

You've got a zombie, you've got cats, you've even got crazy cat ladies – but what you don't have is a way to detect when they collide.

There are multiple ways to detect collisions in Sprite Kit, including using the built-in physics engine, as you'll learn in Chapter 9, "Intermediate Physics". In this chapter, you'll take the simplest and easiest approach: bounding box collision detection.

There are three basic ideas you'll use to implement this:

1. You need a way of getting all of the cats and crazy cat ladies in a scene into lists so that you can check for collisions one-by-one. An easy way to do this is to give nodes a name when you create them. Then you can use the

enumerateChildNodesWithName:usingBlock: method on the scene to find all of the nodes with a certain name.

2. Once you have the lists of cats and cat ladies, you can loop through them to check for collisions. Each node has a frame property that gives you a rectangle representing where the node is onscreen.

3. If you have the frame for either a cat lady or a cat, and the frame for the zombie, you can use the built-in method CGRectIntersectsRect to see if they collide.

Let's give this a shot. First you need to set the name for each node. Inside spawnEnemy, right after creating the enemy sprite, add this line:

```
enemy.name = @"enemy";
```

Similarly, inside spawnCat, right after creating the cat sprite, add this line:

```
cat.name = @"cat";
```

Then add this new method to the file:

```
- (void)checkCollisions
{
  [self enumerateChildNodesWithName:@"cat"
                         usingBlock:^(SKNode *node, BOOL *stop){
    SKSpriteNode *cat = (SKSpriteNode *)node;
    if (CGRectIntersectsRect(cat.frame, _zombie.frame)) {
      [cat removeFromParent];
    }
  }];

  [self enumerateChildNodesWithName:@"enemy"
                         usingBlock:^(SKNode *node, BOOL *stop){
    SKSpriteNode *enemy = (SKSpriteNode *)node;
    CGRect smallerFrame = CGRectInset(enemy.frame, 20, 20);
    if (CGRectIntersectsRect(smallerFrame, _zombie.frame)) {
      [enemy removeFromParent];
    }
  }];
}
```

Here you enumerate through any child of the scene that has the name "cat" or "enemy" and cast it to an SKSpriteNode, since you know it is a sprite node if it has that name.

You then check if the frame of the cat or enemy intersects with the frame of the zombie. If there is an intersection, you simply remove the cat or enemy from the scene.

Also, notice that you do a little trick for the cat lady. Remember that the frame of a sprite is the entire image of the sprite, including transparent space:

So that means that transparent space at the top of the cat lady image would "count" as a hit if the zombie went into that area. Totally unfair!

To resolve this, you shrink the bounding box a little bit by using the CGRectInset method. It's still not perfect, but it's a start. You'll learn a better way to do this in Chapter 10, "Advanced Physics".

Add the following call to this method at the end of update::

```
[self checkCollisions];
```

Build and run, and now when you collide with the cats or enemies they disappear from the scene. It's your first small step toward the zombie apocalypse!

The Sprite Kit game loop, round 2

There's a slight problem with the way you're doing the collision detection here that I should point out, which is related to how Sprite Kit's game loop and actions interrelate.

The last time you saw the Sprite Kit game loop, you saw that the update: method gets called, then some "other stuff" occurs, and finally Sprite Kit renders the screen:

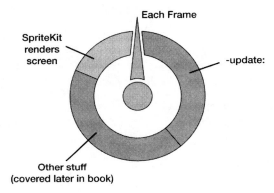

Well, it turns out that one of the things in the "other stuff" section is evaluating the actions that you've been learning about in this chapter:

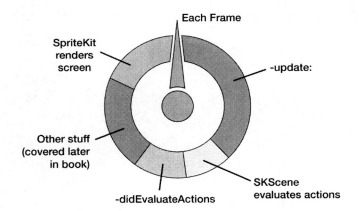

This leads to the problem with the way you're currently doing collision detection. You check for collisions at the end of the update: loop, but Sprite Kit doesn't evaluate the actions until *after* this update: loop. Therefore, your collision detection code is always one frame behind!

As you can see in the updated event loop diagram, a much better place to perform the collision detection would be after Sprite Kit evaluates the actions and all the sprites are in their new spots. So comment out the call at the end of update::

```
//[self checkCollisions];
```

And implement didEvaluateActions as follows:

```
- (void)didEvaluateActions {
  [self checkCollisions];
}
```

You probably won't notice much difference in this case because the frame rate is so fast that it is hard to tell it was behind – but in some games this may be more noticable so it's good to do things properly.

Sound action

The last type of action you'll learn about in this chapter also happens to be one of the most fun – the one that plays sound effects!

Using the playSoundFileNamed:waitForCompletion: action, playing a sound effect with Sprite Kit takes just one line of code. Note that the node on which you run this action doesn't matter, so typically you'll just run it as an action on the scene itself.

You've already added the sounds to your project earlier, so you just need to write the code. Inside checkCollisions, add the following line just after [cat removeFromParent];:

```
[self runAction:[SKAction playSoundFileNamed:@"hitCat.wav"
                      waitForCompletion:NO]];
```

Then add this line just after [enemy removeFromParent];:

```
[self runAction:[SKAction playSoundFileNamed:@"hitCatLady.wav"
                      waitForCompletion:NO]];
```

Here you play the appropriate sound action for each type of collision. Build and run, move the zombie around and enjoy the sounds of the smash-up!

Sharing actions

In the previous section, you may have noticed a slight pause the first time the sound plays. This can occur when the sound system is initialized the first time it is used. The solution to this problem also demonstrates one of the most powerful features of Sprite Kits actions: sharing.

The SKAction object does not actually maintain any state itself, and that allows you to do something cool – reuse actions on any number of nodes simultaneously! For example, the action you create to move the cat ladies across the screen looks something like this:

```
SKAction *actionMove =
  [SKAction moveToX:-enemy.size.width/2 duration:2.0];
```

But you create this action for every cat lady. Instead, you could create a private or static SKAction variable, store this action in it, and then use that variable wherever you are currently using actionMove.

In fact, you could modify Zombie Conga so it reuses most of the actions you've created so far. Doing so would reduce the amount of memory your system uses, but that's a performance improvement you probably don't need to make in such a simple game. You'll learn more about things like this in Chapter 25, "Performance."

But how does this relate to the sound delay?

The application is loading the sound the first time you create an action that uses it. So to prevent the sound delay, you can create the actions in advance and then use them when necessary.

Create the following private variables:

```
SKAction *_catCollisionSound;
SKAction *_enemyCollisionSound;
```

These variables will hold shared instances of the sound actions you want to run.

Now create the sound actions by adding the following lines at the end of initWithSize:, just after the line that runs the action that calls spawnCat:

```
_catCollisionSound = [SKAction playSoundFileNamed:@"hitCat.wav"
                            waitForCompletion:NO];
_enemyCollisionSound =
  [SKAction playSoundFileNamed:@"hitCatLady.wav"
            waitForCompletion:NO];
```

These are the same actions you create in checkCollisions, but now you create them just once for the scene. That means your app will load these sounds as soon as the scene is initialized.

Finally, find this line in checkCollisions:

```
[self runAction:[SKAction playSoundFileNamed:@"hitCat.wav"
                            waitForCompletion:NO]];
```

Replace the above line with this one:

```
[self runAction:_catCollisionSound];
```

Also find this line:

```
[self runAction:[SKAction playSoundFileNamed:@"hitCatLady.wav"
                            waitForCompletion:NO]];
```

And replace it with this one:

```
[self runAction:_enemyCollisionSound];
```

Now you are reusing the same sound actions for all collisions rather than creating a new one for each collision.

Build and run again. You should no longer experience any pauses before the sound effects play.

As for music, stay tuned (no pun intended!) – you'll learn about that in the next chapter, when you'll wrap up the core gameplay by adding a win/lose scene to the game.

But before you move on, be sure to get some practice with actions by trying out the challenges for this chapter!

Challenges

This chapter has three challenges, and as usual they progress from easiest to hardest.

Be sure to do these challenges. As a Sprite Kit developer you will be using actions all the time, so it's important to get some practice with them before moving further.

As always, if you get stuck you can find solutions in the resources for this chapter – but give it your best shot first!

Challenge 1: The ActionsCatalog demo

This chapter covers the most important actions in Sprite Kit, but it doesn't cover all of them. To help you get a good understanding of all the actions that are available to you, I've created a little demo called ActionsCatalog, which you can find in the resources for this chapter.

Open the project in Xcode and build and run. You'll see something like the following:

Each scene in the app demonstrates a particular set of actions, shown as the first part of the label, before the backslash. This first example demonstrates the various move actions.

Each time you tap the screen, you'll see a new set of actions. As the scenes transition, you'll also see different transition effects, shown as the second part of the label, after the backslash.

Your challenge is to flip through each of these demos, then take a look at the code to answer the following questions:

1. What action constructor would you use to make a sprite follow a certain pre-defined path?

2. What action constructor would you use to make a sprite 50% transparent, regardless of what its current transparency settings are?

3. What are "custom actions" and how do they work at a high level?

You can check your answers in a comment at the top of the solution project for this chapter.

Challenge 2: An invincible zombie

Currently, when an enemy hits the zombie, you destroy the enemy. This is a sneaky way of avoiding the problematic scenario of the enemy colliding with the zombie multiple times in a row as it moves through the zombie, resulting in the squish sound effect being played just as many times in rapid succession.

Usually in a video game, you resolve this problem by making the player invincible for a few seconds after getting hit, so the player has time to get his or her bearings.

Your challenge is to modify the game to do just this. When the zombie collides with a cat lady, he should become temporarily invincible instead of destroying the cat lady.

While the zombie is invincible, he should blink. To do this, you can use the custom blink action that is included in ActionsCatalog. Here's the code for your convenience:

```
float blinkTimes = 10;
float blinkDuration = 3.0;
SKAction *blinkAction =
  [SKAction customActionWithDuration:blinkDuration
                         actionBlock:
  ^(SKNode *node, CGFloat elapsedTime) {
    float slice = blinkDuration / blinkTimes;
    float remainder = fmodf(elapsedTime, slice);
    node.hidden = remainder > slice / 2;
  }];
```

If you'd like a detailed explanation of how this method works, see the comment in the solution for the previous challenge.

Here are some hints for solving this challenge:

- You should create an instance variable to keep track of whether or not the zombie is invincible.

- If the zombie is invincible, you shouldn't bother enumerating the scene's cat ladies.

- If the zombie collides with a cat lady, don't remove the cat lady from the scene. Instead, set the zombie as invincible. Then run a sequence of actions where you make the zombie blink 10 times over three seconds, then run the block of code as described below.

- The block of code should set hidden to NO on the zombie (making sure he's visible at the end no matter what), and set the zombie as no longer invincible.

Challenge 3: The conga train

This game is called Zombie Conga, but there's no conga line to be seen just yet!

Your challenge is to fix that. You'll modify the game so that when the zombie collides with a cat, instead of disappearing, the cat joins your conga line!

In the process of doing this, you'll get some more practice with actions, and you'll also review the vector math material you learned in the last chapter. Yes, that stuff still comes in handy when working with actions!

Here are the steps to implement this challenge:

1. Create a constant float variable to keep track of the cat's move points per second at the top of the file. Set it to 120.0.

2. Set the zombie's zPosition to 100. This makes the zombie appear on top of the other sprites. Larger z values are "out of the screen" and smaller values are "into the screen", and the default value is 0.

3. When the zombie collides with a cat, don't remove the cat from the scene. Instead, do the following:

   a. Set the cat's name to "train" (instead of "cat").

   b. Stop all actions currently running on the cat by calling removeAllActions.

   c. Set the scale to 1 and rotation of the cat to 0.

   d. Run an action to make the cat turn green over 0.2 seconds. If you're not sure what action to use for this, check out ActionsCatalog.

4. Make a new method called moveTrain. The basic idea for this method is that every so often, you make each cat move toward where the previous cat currently is. This creates a conga line effect!

Use the following template:

```
- (void)moveTrain
{
    __block CGPoint targetPosition = _zombie.position;
    [self enumerateChildNodesWithName:@"train"
                           usingBlock:^(SKNode *node, BOOL *stop){
        if (!node.hasActions) {
            float actionDuration = 0.3;
            CGPoint offset = // a
            CGPoint direction = // b
            CGPoint amountToMovePerSec = // c
            CGPoint amountToMove = // d
            SKAction *moveAction = // e
            [node runAction:moveAction];
        }
        targetPosition = node.position;
    }];
}
```

You need to fill in **a through d** by using the math utility functions you created last chapter, and **e** by creating the appropriate actions.

Here are some hints:

a. You need to figure out the offset between the cat's current position and the target position.

b. You need to figure out a unit vector pointing in the direction of the offset.

c. You need to get a vector pointing in the direction of the offset, but with a length of the cat's move points per second. This represents where the cat should move in a second.

d. You need to get a fraction of the `amountToMovePerSec` vector, based on the `actionDuration`. This represents the offset the cat should move over the next `actionDuration` seconds.

e. You should move the cat a relative amount based on the `amountToMove`.

5. Call `moveTrain` at the end of `update:`.

And that's it – who said you couldn't herd cats? If you got this working, you've truly made this game live up to its name: Zombie Conga!

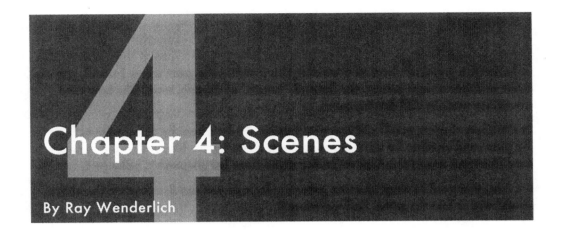

Chapter 4: Scenes

By Ray Wenderlich

Zombie Conga is beginning to look like a real game – it has character movement, enemies, sounds, animation, collision detection – and if you finished the challenges from last chapter, even a conga line!

However, right now all the action takes place in a single **scene** of the game: the default MyScene created for you by the Sprite Kit project template.

In Sprite Kit, you don't have to place everything within the same scene. Instead, you can create multiple unique scenes, one for each "screen" of the app, much like how view controllers work in iOS development.

In this short chapter, you'll add two new scenes: one for when the player wins or loses the game, and another for the main menu. You'll also learn a bit about using the cool transitions you saw in the ActionsCatalog demo from last chapter's Challenge 1.

But first, you need to wrap up some gameplay logic so you can detect when the player should win or lose the game. Let's get started!

> **Note:** This chapter begins where Challenge 3 left off in the last chapter. If you were unable to complete the challenges or skipped ahead from a previous chapter, don't worry – you can simply open **ZombieConga-Starter** from the resources for this chapter to pick up where we left off.

Win and lose conditions

Here's how the player will win or lose Zombie Conga:

- **Win Condition**: If the player creates a conga line of 30 cats or more, the player wins!

- **Lose Condition**: The player will start with five lives. If the player spends all of his or her lives, the player loses.

Right now when the crazy cat ladies collide with the zombie, nothing bad happens – there's only a sound. To make this game challenging, you'll change this so that collisions with a cat lady result in the following effects:

1. The zombie loses a life.

2. The zombie loses two cats from his conga line.

Let's make it so. Inside **MyScene.m**, add a new private instance variable to keep track of the zombie's lives, and another to keep track of whether the game is over:

```
int _lives;
BOOL _gameOver;
```

Inside `initWithSize:`, right after setting the background color, initialize `_lives` to 5 and `_gameOver` to `NO`:

```
_lives = 5;
_gameOver = NO;
```

Next, add this new helper method to make the zombie lose two cats from his conga line:

```
- (void)loseCats
{
  // 1
  __block int loseCount = 0;
  [self enumerateChildNodesWithName:@"train" usingBlock:
    ^(SKNode *node, BOOL *stop) {

    // 2
    CGPoint randomSpot = node.position;
    randomSpot.x += ScalarRandomRange(-100, 100);
    randomSpot.y += ScalarRandomRange(-100, 100);

    // 3
    node.name = @"";
    [node runAction:
      [SKAction sequence:@[
        [SKAction group:@[
          [SKAction rotateByAngle:M_PI * 4 duration:1.0],
          [SKAction moveTo:randomSpot duration:1.0],
          [SKAction scaleTo:0 duration:1.0]
          ]],
        [SKAction removeFromParent]
        ]]];

    // 4
    loseCount++;
    if (loseCount >= 2) {
      *stop = YES;
    }
  }];
}
```

Let's go over this section-by-section:

1. Here you set up a variable to keep track of how many cats have been removed from the conga line so far, then you enumerate through the conga line.

2. You find a random offset from the cat's current position.

3. You run a little animation to make the cat move toward the random spot, spinning around and scaling to 0 along the way. Finally, the animation removes the cat from the scene. You also set the cat's name to an empty string so that it's no longer considered a normal cat or a cat in the conga line.

4. You update the variable that is keeping track of how many cats have been removed from the conga line. Once two or more have been removed, you set the stop Boolean to YES, which causes Sprite Kit to stop enumerating the conga line at that point.

Now that you have this helper method, call it in checkCollisions, right after playing the enemy collision sound:

```
[self loseCats];
_lives--;
```

You are ready to add the code to check if the player should win or lose. Begin by checking for a lose condition. Add this to the end of update:

```
if (_lives <= 0 && !_gameOver) {
  _gameOver = YES;
  NSLog(@"You lose!");
}
```

Here you check if the player's remaining lives number 0 or less, and also make sure it isn't game over already. If both of these conditions are met, you set the game to be over and log out a message.

To check for the win condition, make the following modifications to moveTrain (some of the code is snipped for brevity, and changes are highlighted):

```
- (void)moveTrain
{
  __block int trainCount = 0;
  __block CGPoint targetPosition = _zombie.position;
  [self enumerateChildNodesWithName:@"train" usingBlock:
    ^(SKNode *node, BOOL *stop) {
    trainCount++;
    // Rest of code...
  }];

  if (trainCount >= 30 && !_gameOver) {
    _gameOver = YES;
    NSLog(@"You win!");
  }
}
```

Here you keep track of how many cats are in the train, and if they're greater than 30, and the game isn't over already, you set the game to be over and log out a message.

Build and run, and see if you can collect 30 cats.

If you do, you should see the following message in the console:

`ZombieConga[13307:70b] You win!`

That's great, but when the player wins the game, you want something a bit more dramatic than that. Let's create a proper game over scene.

Creating a new scene

To create a new scene, you simply create a new class that derives from `SKScene`. You can then implement `initWithSize:`, `update:`, `touchesBegan:`, or any of the other methods that you overrode in `MyScene` to implement the behavior you want.

For now, you're going to keep things simple with a bare-bones new scene. In Xcode's main menu, select **File\New\File...**, select the **iOS\Cocoa Touch\Objective-C class** template, and click **Next**.

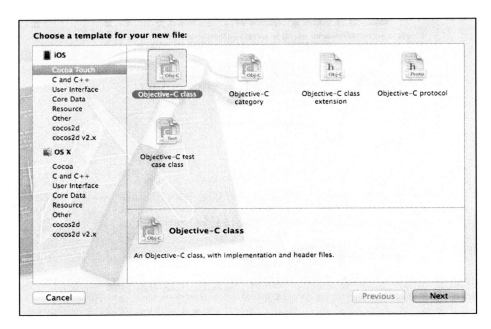

Enter **GameOverScene** for **Class**, enter **SKScene** for **Subclass of**, and click **Next**.

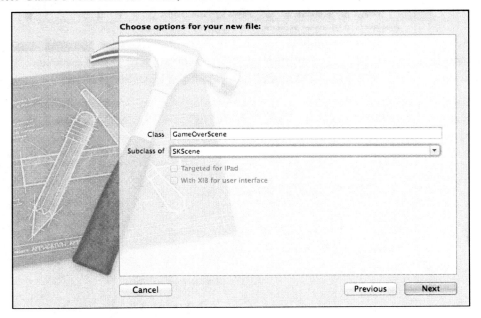

Finally, make sure the **ZombieConga** target is checked and click **Create**.

You'll see that Xcode has created two new files for you – GameOverScene.h and GameOverScene.m. For now they'll stay empty, but later on you'll come back and add some code to make them display the appropriate game over sprite.

Transitioning to a scene

There are three steps to transition from one scene to another:

1. **Create the new scene**. First you create an instance of the new scene itself. Typically you'd use the default `initWithSize:` initializer, although you can always choose to create your own custom initializer if you want to be able to pass in some extra parameters. Later in this chapter, you'll do just that.

2. **Create a transition object**. Next you create a transition object to specify the type of animation you would like to display the new scene. For example, there are cross fade transitions, flip transitions, door-opening transitions, and many more.

3. **Call the** `SKView`'s `presentScene:transition:` **method**. In iOS, `SKView` is the `UIView` that displays Sprite Kit content on the screen. You can get access to this via a property on the scene – `self.view`. You can then call the `presentScene:transition:` method to animate to the passed-in scene (created in step 1) with the passed-in transition (created in step 2).

Let's try this out. Open **MyScene.m** and add the following import to the top of the file:

```
#import "GameOverScene.h"
```

Next add the following lines in `moveTrain`, right after where you log "You Win!" to the console:

```
// 1
SKScene * gameOverScene =
  [[GameOverScene alloc] initWithSize:self.size];
// 2
SKTransition *reveal =
  [SKTransition flipHorizontalWithDuration:0.5];
// 3
[self.view presentScene:gameOverScene transition:reveal];
```

These three lines correspond exactly to the three steps above.

Notice that to create a transition, there are various constructors on `SKTransition`, just as there are various constructors for actions on `SKAction`. Here you choose a flip horizontal animation, which flips up from the bottom of the screen. For a demo of all the transitions, refer to ActionsCatalog, as discussed in the previous chapter's challenges.

Now add those exact same lines to update:, right after where you log "You lose!" to the console.

Build and run, and either win or lose the game. Feel free to cheat and change the number of cats to win to less than 30 – after all, you're the developer! When you do, you should see the scene transition to a new blank scene:

That's really all there is to scene transitions! Now that you have a new scene, you can do whatever you like in it – just as you did in MyScene.

> **Note:** There are two methods you may find it useful to implement in your SKScene subclasses. These are didMoveToView: and willMoveFromView:. As their names imply, these methods are called on your scene just after it's presented by a view and just before it's removed from a view, respectively.
>
> You won't be using them in this chapter, but keep them in mind if you ever need to execute logic at those points in your program.

For Zombie Conga, you'll modify this new scene to show either a "You Win" or "You Lose" background. To make this possible, you'll need to create a custom scene initializer to pass in whether the player won or lost.

Creating a custom scene initializer

Open **GameOverScene.h** and declare your custom initializer right before the @end:

```
- (id)initWithSize:(CGSize)size won:(BOOL)won;
```

This custom initializer takes just one extra parameter: a Boolean that should be YES if the player won and NO if the player lost.

Now open **GameOverScene.m** and start the implementation of the method as follows:

```
- (id)initWithSize:(CGSize)size won:(BOOL)won
{
  if (self = [super initWithSize:size]) {
    SKSpriteNode *bg;
    if (won) {
      bg = [SKSpriteNode
              spriteNodeWithImageNamed:@"YouWin.png"];
      [self runAction:[SKAction sequence:@[
        [SKAction waitForDuration:0.1],
        [SKAction playSoundFileNamed:@"win.wav"
          waitForCompletion:NO]]]
      ];
    } else {
      bg = [SKSpriteNode
              spriteNodeWithImageNamed:@"YouLose.png"];
      [self runAction:[SKAction sequence:@[
        [SKAction waitForDuration:0.1],
        [SKAction playSoundFileNamed:@"lose.wav"
          waitForCompletion:NO]]]
      ];
    }
    bg.position = CGPointMake(
      self.size.width/2, self.size.height/2);
    [self addChild:bg];

    // More here
  }
  return self;
}
```

This first calls the superclass's `initWithSize:` initializer, passing in the size. It then looks at the `won` Boolean to choose the proper background image to set and sound effect to play.

In Zombie Conga, you want the game over scene to display for a few seconds and then automatically transition back to the main scene. To do this, first import the header for your main scene at the top of **GameOverScene.m**:

```
#import "MyScene.h"
```

Then add these lines of code right after the "More here" comment:

```
SKAction * wait = [SKAction waitForDuration:3.0];
SKAction * block =
  [SKAction runBlock:^{
     MyScene * myScene =
       [[MyScene alloc] initWithSize:self.size];

     SKTransition *reveal =
       [SKTransition flipHorizontalWithDuration:0.5];

     [self.view presentScene:myScene transition: reveal];
  }];
[self runAction:[SKAction sequence:@[wait, block]]];
```

By now, this should all be review for you. The code runs a sequence of actions on the scene, first waiting for 3 seconds, and then calling a block of code. The block of code creates a new instance of `MyScene` and transitions to that with a flip animation.

One last step – you need to modify your code in `MyScene` to use this new custom initializer. Open **MyScene.m** and inside `update:`, change the line that creates the `GameOverScene` to indicate that this is the lose condition:

```
SKScene * gameOverScene =
  [[GameOverScene alloc] initWithSize:self.size won:NO];
```

Inside `moveTrain`, change the same line but indicate that this is the win condition:

```
SKScene * gameOverScene =
  [[GameOverScene alloc] initWithSize:self.size won:YES];
```

Build and run, and try to win the game. If you do, you'll see the win scene, which will then flip back to a new game after a few seconds:

Gratuitous music

You almost have a complete game, but you're missing one thing – some awesome background music!

Luckily, we've got you covered. Add the following import to the top of **MyScene.m**:

```
@import AVFoundation;
```

There is no built-in way to play background music in Sprite Kit, so you'll have to fall back on other iOS APIs to do it. One easy way to play music in iOS is by using the `AVAudioPlayer` class inside the AVFoundation framework. The first step is to import the framework using iOS 7's new `@import` keyword.

Next, add the following private instance variable to store the music player:

```
AVAudioPlayer *_backgroundMusicPlayer;
```

Then add a helper routine to play the background music:

```
- (void)playBackgroundMusic:(NSString *)filename
{
  NSError *error;
```

```
    NSURL *backgroundMusicURL =
      [[NSBundle mainBundle] URLForResource:filename
                              withExtension:nil];
    _backgroundMusicPlayer =
      [[AVAudioPlayer alloc]
        initWithContentsOfURL:backgroundMusicURL error:&error];
    _backgroundMusicPlayer.numberOfLoops = -1;
    [_backgroundMusicPlayer prepareToPlay];
    [_backgroundMusicPlayer play];
}
```

This creates an instance of AVAudioPlayer, passes in the URL of the sound to play, sets up a few properties and then calls play to start the music rolling.

Finally, add this line to initWithSize:, right after setting the background color:

```
[self playBackgroundMusic:@"bgMusic.mp3"];
```

Here you set up the game to play the background music when the scene first loads.

Next, you need to stop the background music when the player switches scenes, so they can hear the "you win" or "you lose" sound effects. To do this, add this line right after the "You Win!" log line in moveTrain:

```
[_backgroundMusicPlayer stop];
```

Also add that same line right after the "You Lose!" log line in update:.

Build and run, and enjoy your groovy tunes!

Challenges

This was a short and sweet chapter, and the challenges will be equally so. There's just one challenge this time – adding a main menu scene to the game.

As always, if you get stuck, you can find the solution in the resources for this chapter – but give it your best shot first!

Challenge 1: Main menu scene

Usually it's not good to start a game right in the middle of the action – first you want the player to encounter an opening or main menu scene. Usually it will include options to start a new game, continue a game, access game options, and so on.

For Zombie Conga, the main menu scene will be very simple – it will simply show an image and allow the player to tap to continue straight to a new game.

Your challenge is to implement a main menu scene that shows the MainMenu.png image as a background and transitions upon screen tap to the main action scene using a "doorway" transition over 0.5 seconds.

Here are a few hints for how to accomplish this:

- Create a new class that derives from `SKScene` named `MainMenuScene`.

- Implement the `initWithSize:` method on `MainMenuScene` to display MainMenu.png in the center of the scene.

- Import MainMenuScene.h at the top of ViewController.m.

- Inside ViewController.m, edit `viewWillLayoutSubviews` to make it start with `MainMenuScene` instead of `MyScene`.

- Build and run and make sure the main menu image appears. So far, so good!

- Finally, implement `touchesBegan:withEvent:` in `MainMenuScene` so that when the user taps, it transitions to `MyScene` using a "doorway" transition over 0.5 seconds. Don't forget to import MyScene.h from MainMenuScene.m for this to work.

If you've gotten this working, congratulations – you now have a firm understanding of how to work with multiple scenes and transitions in Sprite Kit!

Chapter 5: Scrolling

By Ray Wenderlich

So far, the background in Zombie Conga is stationary. In contrast, many games have large scrolling worlds, like the original *Super Mario Bros.*:

The red box shows what you can see on the screen, but the level continues beyond to the right. As the player moves to the right, you can think of the background as moving to the left:

Typically in these kinds of games, the player, enemies and power-ups are considered children of the "background layer." To scroll the game, you simply move the background layer from right to left, and its children move with it.

Of course, the children can move within the background layer as well – for example, in the *Super Mario Bros.* level above, the mushroom power-up, Goomba enemies and Mario all move around within the background layer's space.

In this chapter, you're going to modify Zombie Conga so that the level endlessly scrolls from right to left. In the process, you'll learn more about nodes, children and coordinate spaces. Let's get scrolling!

> **Note:** This chapter begins where Challenge 1 left off in the last chapter. If you were unable to complete the challenges or skipped ahead from a previous chapter, don't worry – you can simply open **ZombieConga-Starter** from the resources for this chapter to pick up where we left off.

A scrolling background

As you may remember from Chapter 2, the background you are using in Zombie Conga is actually much longer than the length of a single screen. In fact, it is a repeating background designed so that if you line the right side up with the left side, it appears seamless.

Take a look at the image in **Art\Backgrounds\background.png** to see for yourself:

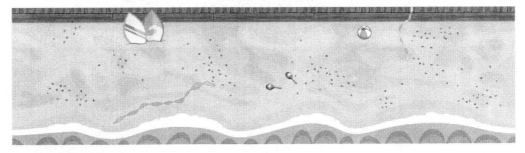

Your first task is simple: make this background scroll from right to left.

Open **MyScene.m** and add a constant for the background's scrolling speed at the top of the file:

```
static const float BG_POINTS_PER_SEC = 50;
```

Then find the code that adds the background in initWithSize:, and replace it with the following:

```
SKSpriteNode * bg =
  [SKSpriteNode spriteNodeWithImageNamed:@"background"];
bg.anchorPoint = CGPointZero;
bg.position = CGPointZero;
bg.name = @"bg";
[self addChild:bg];
```

Previously you had the background centered on the screen. Here you pin the lower left corner to the lower left of the scene instead.

Changing the anchor point to the lower left like this will make it easier to calculate positions when the time comes. You also name the background "bg" so that you can find it readily.

Next add this helper method to move the background:

```
- (void)moveBg
{
  [self enumerateChildNodesWithName:@"bg" usingBlock:
    ^(SKNode *node, BOOL *stop) {
      SKSpriteNode * bg = (SKSpriteNode *) node;
      CGPoint bgVelocity = CGPointMake(-BG_POINTS_PER_SEC, 0);
      CGPoint amtToMove =
        CGPointMultiplyScalar(bgVelocity, _dt);
      bg.position = CGPointAdd(bg.position, amtToMove);
    }];
}
```

This finds any child with the "bg" name and moves it to the left according to the velocity. If you are unsure how the above lines of code work, refer back to Chapter 3, "Manual Movement."

Finally, call this new method inside update:, right after the call to moveTrain:

```
[self moveBg];
```

Build and run, and now you have a scrolling background:

There's one big problem, though. After the background runs out, you're left with empty space:

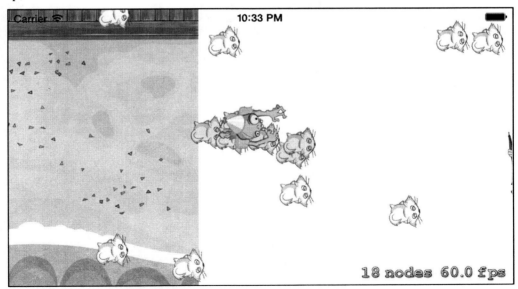

An endlessly scrolling background

The most efficient way to fix this is to simply make two background images instead of one and lay them side-by-side:

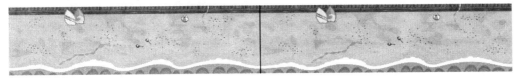

Then, as you scroll both images from right to left, once one of the images goes off-screen, you simply reposition it to the right:

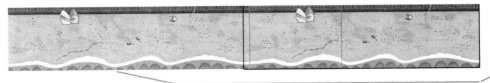

Let's see how this works. Modify the code that creates the background sprite in `initWithSize:` as follows (changes highlighted):

```
for (int i = 0; i < 2; i++) {
  SKSpriteNode * bg =
    [SKSpriteNode spriteNodeWithImageNamed:@"background"];
  bg.anchorPoint = CGPointZero;
  bg.position = CGPointMake(i * bg.size.width, 0);
  bg.name = @"bg";
  [self addChild:bg];
}
```

Also, if you still have the lines that get the background's size and log them, comment them out.

This wraps the code in a `for` loop that creates two copies of the background, then sets the position so the second copy begins after the first ends.

Next add the following code in `moveBg`, inside the `enumerateChildNodesWithName:` block, after setting the bg's `position`:

```
if (bg.position.x <= -bg.size.width) {
    bg.position = CGPointMake(bg.position.x + bg.size.width*2,
                              bg.position.y);
}
```

This checks to see if the background's position is less than 0 by at least the width of the background. In other words, since the sprite's anchor point is the lower left, if the position of that anchor point is the negative width of the sprite, it means the sprite is fully off-screen.

In that case, the code simply moves the background sprite double the width of the background to the right. Since there are two background sprites, this places the first sprite immediately to the right of the second.

Build and run, and now you have an endlessly looping background!

Moving to layers

As you play the game, you might notice that the behavior of the cats now seems a little strange – even for cats!

Since the cats are supposed to remain in the same spots until picked up by the zombie, they should be moving to the left as the background moves to the left.

In other words, the cats should be children of the background so that they move along with it. This raises an issue: there are two different background sprites, but a node can only have a single parent. What should you do?

The solution is to create an empty node that you'll treat as the "background layer." To this you'll add the background sprites, cats and other children – the zombie and crazy cat ladies. Then with each frame you can update the position of the background layer, and all its children will move with it.

> **Note:** You could also, if you wanted, move the position of the scene itself from right to left, since everything is already a child of the scene.
>
> However, it's usually better to create a separate layer, as you're doing here. That way you can easily position sprites at fixed points on the screen, even if the rest of the scene is scrolling – if, for example, you wanted to make a Heads-Up Display to show the zombie's remaining lives.

Give this a try. Create a new private instance variable for the background layer node:

```
SKNode *_bgLayer;
```

Then create the `_bgLayer` at the very beginning of `initWithSize:`, before setting the background color:

```
_bgLayer = [SKNode node];
```

```
[self addChild:_bgLayer];
```

Now every place you add something as a child of the scene, you should add it as a child of the _bgLayer instead. There are four cases:

1. In initWithSize:, when adding the zombie sprite:

```
[_bgLayer addChild:_zombie];
```

2. In initWithSize:, when adding the background sprites:

```
[_bgLayer addChild:bg];
```

3. In spawnEnemy, when adding the enemy sprite:

```
[_bgLayer addChild:enemy];
```

4. In spawnCat, when adding the cat sprite:

```
[_bgLayer addChild:cat];
```

You also have to fix the code that enumerates child nodes of the scene, now that the nodes have been made children of the background layer instead. Modify the line that enumerates the cats in checkCollisions to the following:

```
[_bgLayer enumerateChildNodesWithName:@"cat" usingBlock:
    ^(SKNode *node, BOOL *stop) {
```

And in the same method, modify the line that enumerates the enemies to the following:

```
[_bgLayer enumerateChildNodesWithName:@"enemy" usingBlock:
    ^(SKNode *node, BOOL *stop) {
```

Also modify the line that enumerates the conga line in **both** loseCats and moveTrain to the following:

```
[_bgLayer enumerateChildNodesWithName:@"train" usingBlock:
    ^(SKNode *node, BOOL *stop) {
```

Finally, modify moveBg so that it moves the position of the _bgLayer rather than the individual background sprites themselves:

```
- (void)moveBg
{
  CGPoint bgVelocity = CGPointMake(-BG_POINTS_PER_SEC, 0);
```

```
CGPoint amtToMove = CGPointMultiplyScalar(bgVelocity, _dt);
_bgLayer.position = CGPointAdd(_bgLayer.position, amtToMove);

[_bgLayer enumerateChildNodesWithName:@"bg" usingBlock:
   ^(SKNode *node, BOOL *stop) {
      SKSpriteNode * bg = (SKSpriteNode *) node;
      if (bg.position.x <= -bg.size.width) {
         bg.position =
            CGPointMake(bg.position.x + bg.size.width*2,
                        bg.position.y);
      }
   }];
}
```

Build and run. At first it looks all right, but then… oh no, everything goes flying off the screen!

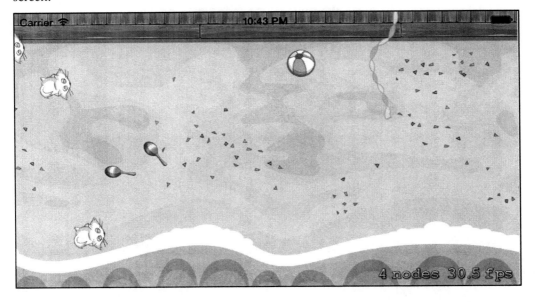

Something is very wrong here! And it's all due to comparing coordinate system apples to oranges.

Coordinate systems

Recall back to Chapter 2, where you learned that a sprite's position is within the coordinate space of its parent node, which up until this chapter was the scene itself.

You've switched the sprites to be children of the background layer, so their positions are now within the coordinate space of that layer.

For example, when the level begins, the zombie is at position (100, 100) in both the screen coordinate system, where (0, 0) represents the bottom left of the screen, and in the background layer coordinate system, where (0, 0) represents the bottom left of the background layer.

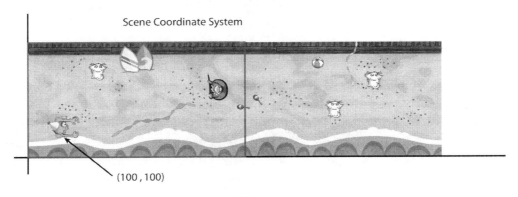

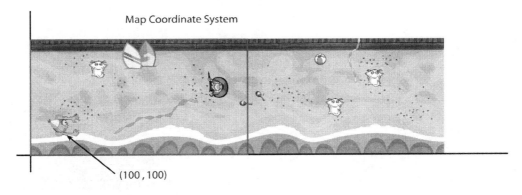

Here the red box indicates what's currently visible on the screen. At first, the positions correspond.

The problem comes when you start moving the background layer to the left. Now the two coordinate systems don't match:

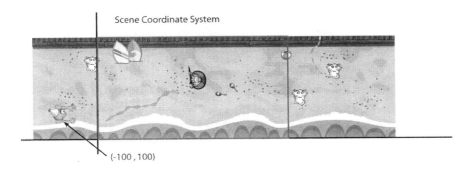

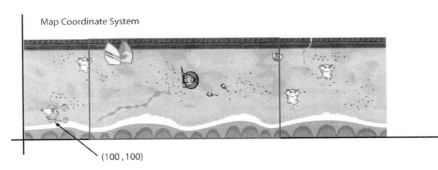

Again, the red box indicates what's visible on the screen.

As you can see, after moving the background layer 200 points to the left, the zombie is at (-100, 100) in scene coordinates, but is still at (100, 100) in map coordinates. The position now depends on which coordinate system you are using!

Currently you have a bunch of code that attempts to compare apples (scene coordinates) to oranges (background layer coordinates). Your goal is to make sure you are comparing apples to apples instead, by converting one set of coordinates to the other.

Let's fix these one at a time, starting with boundary checking for the player.

Fixing the bounds checking

Take a look at this snippet from **boundsCheckPlayer** (below are only the lines that are relevant to this discussion):

```
CGPoint newPosition = _zombie.position;

CGPoint bottomLeft = CGPointZero;
CGPoint topRight =
```

```
    CGPointMake(self.size.width, self.size.height);

if (newPosition.x <= bottomLeft.x) {
  newPosition.x = bottomLeft.x;
}
```

This is trying to compare background layer coordinates (_zombie.position) to scene coordinates (CGPointZero and CGPointMake(self.size.width, self.size.height)), which won't work.

Luckily, this is easy to fix – all you need to do is convert the scene coordinates to background layer coordinates, so that you're comparing the same coordinate types.

To do this, replace the lines that set the bottomLeft and topRight points with the following:

```
CGPoint bottomLeft =
  [_bgLayer convertPoint:CGPointZero fromNode:self];
CGPoint topRight =
  [_bgLayer convertPoint:CGPointMake(self.size.width,
                                     self.size.height)
              fromNode:self];
```

To convert points from one coordinate system to another, you can use the convertPoint:fromNode: method. Here's how it works:

• Pass the node that has the coordinate space you want to convert **from** in the fromNode: parameter. In this case, you're dealing with a scene coordinate, so you pass in the scene here (self).

• Pass the point you want to convert as the convertPoint: parameter.

• The node that has the coordinate space you want to convert **to** should be the object on which you call this method. In this case, you want to convert to the background layer coordinate space.

Build and run, and now you'll see your zombie is correctly prevented from moving off-screen:

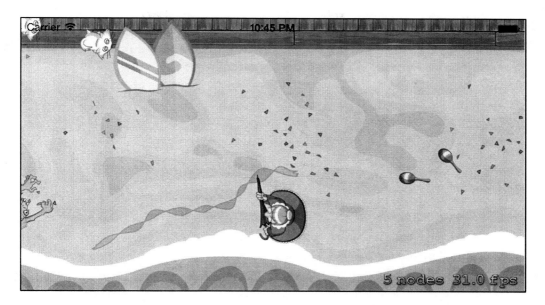

As you play around, though, you'll notice that the touch behavior is no longer working properly – once the background scrolls far enough to the left, the app feels unresponsive. Let's fix this next.

Fixing the touches

Take a look at touchesBegan:withEvent::

```
- (void)touchesBegan:(NSSet *)touches withEvent:(UIEvent *)event
{
  UITouch *touch = [touches anyObject];
  CGPoint touchLocation = [touch locationInNode:self];
  [self moveZombieToward:touchLocation];
}
```

This method gets the touch location by using [touch locationInNode:self], which gives the location of the zombie in scene coordinates. Instead, you want the location of the zombie in background layer coordinates.

To fix this, simply replace self with _bgLayer in the line referenced above, like so:

```
CGPoint touchLocation = [touch locationInNode:_bgLayer];
```

Repeat this for the other touch methods as well (touchesMoved:withEvent: and touchesEnded:withEvent:).

Also, since the background is continuously scrolling, this game now works a lot better if you disable the code that stops the zombie once he reaches the target point. To fix this, just comment the relevant code in **update:**, as shown below:

```
/*if (CGPointLength(offset) <= ZOMBIE_MOVE_POINTS_PER_SEC * _dt)
{
  _zombie.position = _lastTouchLocation;
  _velocity = CGPointZero;
  [self stopZombieAnimation];
} else {*/
  [self moveSprite:_zombie velocity:_velocity];
  [self boundsCheckPlayer];
  [self rotateSprite:_zombie toFace:_velocity
     rotateRadiansPerSec:ZOMBIE_ROTATE_RADIANS_PER_SEC];
//}
```

Build and run, and movement should now work properly.

> **Note:** You'll notice that the zombie moves more slowly to the right. That's because his speed is relative to the background layer, and since the background layer is scrolling to the left, the zombie has to use up some of his velocity just to keep up with the scrolling!
>
> I like this behavior for Zombie Conga because it feels more realistic, so I left it this way. However, if you want a different behavior for your game, you could make the zombie a direct child of the scene to make its movement independent.

As you play around, you might notice another problem: the background no longer scrolls continuously. I bet you can guess why – yep, coordinate systems again!

Fixing the background scrolling

So that the background will once more repeat endlessly, make the following change to moveBg:

```
- (void)moveBg
{
  CGPoint bgVelocity = CGPointMake(-BG_POINTS_PER_SEC, 0);
  CGPoint amtToMove = CGPointMultiplyScalar(bgVelocity, _dt);
  _bgLayer.position = CGPointAdd(_bgLayer.position, amtToMove);

  [_bgLayer enumerateChildNodesWithName:@"bg"
                     usingBlock:^(SKNode *node, BOOL *stop){
    SKSpriteNode * bg = (SKSpriteNode *) node;
    CGPoint bgScreenPos = [_bgLayer convertPoint:bg.position
                                   toNode:self];
    if (bgScreenPos.x <= -bg.size.width) {
      bg.position = CGPointMake(bg.position.x+bg.size.width*2,
                                bg.position.y);
    }
  }];
}
```

The problem was that you were again comparing apples (background layer coordinates) to oranges (scene coordinates). Here you convert the background layer coordinates to scene coordinates so that they are the same.

Notice that this time instead of using convertPoint:fromNode:, you are using convertPoint:toNode:. Here's how this variant works:

- Pass the node that has the coordinate space you want to convert **to** in the toNode: parameter. In this case, you want to convert these coordinates to scene coordinates, so you pass in the scene (self).

- Pass the point you want to convert as the convertPoint: parameter.

- The node that has the coordinate space you want to convert **from** should be the object on which you call this method. In this case, you want to convert it from the background layer coordinate space.

Build and run, and the background should scroll endlessly again.

> **Note:** There's one more thing to keep in mind when scrolling. For most games it won't be a factor, but in some cases, you may encounter rounding errors as your background's position moves farther and farther away from (0,0).
>
> These rounding errors can start to introduce errors in your display when items need to line up perfectly. If you find yourself in such a situation, you'll want to periodically move your background back to (0,0). When doing so, you'll need to adjust the positions of all child nodes to compensate.
>
> For example, if your player node is at (100,50) and your background is at (-100,0), moving the background to the right by 100 would bring it to (0,0) but would require you to compensate by moving your player to the left by 100 to go to (0,50). Of course, to see these rounding errors, you'll need to be working with values much farther away from the origin than the ones shown here.

w00t, you're almost done – the only things left to fix are the cats and the enemies!

And those are your final challenges. Once completed, you will have fulfilled your work with Zombie Conga and will be ready to move on to your next mini-game – where you'll learn all about game physics!

Challenges

This is your final set of challenges for Zombie Conga – you're 99% done with the game, so don't leave it hanging! All you have to do is fix the cats and enemies to work with the new scrolling behavior.

As always, if you get stuck you can find the solutions in the resources for this chapter – but give it your best shot first!

Challenge 1: Fixing the cats

Currently, the cats spawn correctly at the beginning of the level, but seem to no longer appear after the background scrolls. Take a look at spawnCat:

```
- (void)spawnCat
{
  SKSpriteNode *cat =
```

```
    [SKSpriteNode spriteNodeWithImageNamed:@"cat_bw"];
  cat.name = @"cat";
  cat.position =
    CGPointMake(ScalarRandomRange(0, self.size.width),
                ScalarRandomRange(0, self.size.height));
```

Can you think what the apples to oranges are here?

Since this is the easy challenge, I'll tell you: the code above is trying to place the position of the cat, which is in background layer coordinates, based on screen coordinates.

Your challenge is to fix this by converting the scene screen coordinates to background layer coordinates.

Here are some hints:

• Create a new CGPoint called catScenePos, set to the same random value that the current code uses.

• Then use the convertPoint:fromNode: method to convert this point from scene coordinates to background layer coordinates.

Build and run, and now the cats should always spawn!

Challenge 2: Fixing the enemies

Your next challenge is to fix the enemy spawning behavior. There are currently two problems:

1. Enemies appear to stop spawning after a while, due to a coordinate conversion problem.
2. Once you fix the first problem, you'll see enemies appear to spawn faster and faster over time.

Here are some hints to get you started:

• The solution to the first problem is very similar to the solution to Challenge 1, above.

• There are two ways to solve the second problem. You can either do another coordinate conversion, or you can change the action type that you use to move the enemies.

If you've made it this far, a huge congratulations – you have completed your first Sprite Kit mini-game from scratch!

Think of all you've learned how to do:

• Add sprites to a game.

- Move them around manually.

- Move them around with actions.

- Create multiple scenes in a game.

- Make a scrolling game and convert between coordinate systems.

Believe it or not, the information you've learned so far is sufficient to make 90% of Sprite Kit games. The rest is just icing on the cake! ☺

Section II: Labels and Particle Systems

In this section, you'll learn how to add labels to your game to display text and how to create special effects with particle systems, like explosions and star fields.

In the process, you will create a space shooter game called XBlaster, where all of the artwork is ASCII-based!

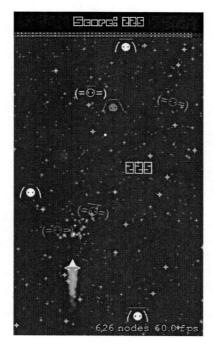

Chapter 6: Labels

Chapter 7: Particle Systems

Chapter 6: Labels

By Mike Daley & Tom Bradley

It's often useful in games to display text to help keep your player informed. There is little point going into battle with an enemy boss if you don't know how much health you have left, or how many bullets are in your weapon of choice!

In this chapter, you'll learn how to display fonts and text within your games. Specifically, you'll create a brand new space shooter game called XBlaster. It will be a space shooter with a twist: *all* of the graphics you use will be made from text – yes, you read that right, text!

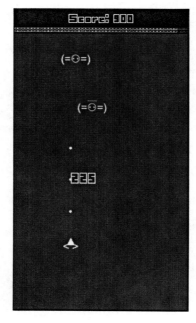

Note that you will not build the full XBlaster game in this chapter – instead, you will focus on the core functionality related to text and fonts.

This is because covering the gameplay logic would repeat too much information covered in the previous chapters. We want to keep this chapter short and focused on the core subject at hand – fonts and text – so you have time and energy to continue with the rest of the book, which contains a lot of awesome information you'll want to know about.

By the time you're done this chapter, you'll have a thorough understanding of fonts and text in Sprite Kit – and you'll have the honor of bringing ASCII art back to the modern era!

Built-In fonts and font families

In iOS, fonts are broken into a set of "families". A font "family" consists of variants of the same font, which may be useful in different situations – for example lighter or heavier versions of the fonts.

For example, the "Thonburi" font family has three fonts inside:

1. **Thonburi-Light**: A thin/light version of the font

2. **Thonburi**: A standard version of the font

3. **Thonburi-Bold**: A bold version of the font

Some font families have even more variants than this – for example, the "Avenir" font family has 12 font variants!

iOS 7 ships with a number of built-in font families and fonts – so before you start using labels, you need to know what's available to you. To find this out, you'll create a simple Sprite Kit project that lets you see these at a glance.

Create a new project in Xcode as you have done in previous chapters by selecting **File\New\Project...** from the main menu. Select the **iOS\Application\SpriteKit Game** template and click **Next**.

Enter **AvailableFonts** for the Product Name, choose **iPhone** for Devices, leave the Class Prefix blank and then click **Next**.

Select a location on your hard drive to store the project and then click **Create**. You now have a simple Sprite Kit project open in Xcode that you will use to list out the font families and fonts you can play with.

You want this app to run in landscape rather than portrait. So just like you did in Chapter 1, "Sprites", select the **AvailableFonts** project in the Project Navigator and then select the **AvailableFonts** target. Go to the **General** tab and uncheck Portrait so that only **Landscape Left** and **Landscape Right** are checked.

Also like you did in Chaper 1, "Sprites", open **ViewController.m**, rename `viewDidLoad` to `viewWillLayoutSubviews:`, and make a few minor changes as highlighted below:

```
- (void)viewWillLayoutSubviews
{
    [super viewWillLayoutSubviews];

    // Configure the view.
    SKView * skView = (SKView *)self.view;
    if (!skView.scene) {
      skView.showsFPS = YES;
      skView.showsNodeCount = YES;

      // Create and configure the scene.
      SKScene * scene = [MyScene
        sceneWithSize:skView.bounds.size];
      scene.scaleMode = SKSceneScaleModeAspectFill;

      // Present the scene.
      [skView presentScene:scene];
    }
}
```

Build and run the project on the iPhone Retina (4-inch) Simulator. You should see the **Hello World** message nicely positioned in the center of the screen in landscape mode.

Next, open **MyScene.m** and replace the contents with the following:

```
#import "MyScene.h"

@implementation MyScene {
  int _familyIdx;
}

-(id)initWithSize:(CGSize)size {
  if (self = [super initWithSize:size]) {
    [self showCurFamily];
  }
  return self;
}
```

```
-(void)showCurFamily
{
  // TODO: Coming soon...
}

-(void)touchesBegan:(NSSet *)touches withEvent:(UIEvent *)event
{
  _familyIdx++;
  if (_familyIdx >= [UIFont familyNames].count) {
    _familyIdx = 0;
  }
  [self showCurFamily];
}

@end
```

The idea is you start displaying the font family with index 0. Every time the user taps, you advance to display the next font family name. Notice you can get a list of the built-in font family names in iOS 7 by calling [UIFont familyNames].

The code to display the fonts in the current font family will be in showCurFamily. So implement that now by placing the following code inside the method:

```
// 1
[self removeAllChildren];

// 2
NSString * familyName = [UIFont familyNames][_familyIdx];
NSLog(@"%@", familyName);

// 3
NSArray * fontNames = [UIFont
fontNamesForFamilyName:familyName];

// 4
[fontNames enumerateObjectsUsingBlock:
^(NSString *fontName, NSUInteger idx, BOOL *stop) {
  SKLabelNode * label =
    [SKLabelNode labelNodeWithFontNamed:fontName];
  label.text = fontName;
  label.position = CGPointMake(self.size.width/2,
    (self.size.height * (idx+1)/(fontNames.count+1)));
  label.fontSize = 20.0;
  label.verticalAlignmentMode =
    SKLabelVerticalAlignmentModeCenter;
  [self addChild:label];
}];
```

Let's go over this section by section:

1. Removes all of the children from the scene so you start with a blank slate.

2. Gets the current family name based on the index that you increment each time you tap. Also logs it out in case you're curious.

3. `UIFont` has another helper method to get the names of the fonts within a family, called `fontNamesForFamilyName:`. You call this here and store the results.

4. You then loop through the block, and create a label using each font, with text showing the name of that font. Since this is the subject of this chapter let's go over it in more detail.

Creating a label

Creating a label is easy – you simply call `labelNodeWithFontName:`, and pass in the name of the font:

```
SKLabelNode * label =
    [SKLabelNode labelNodeWithFontNamed:fontName];
```

The most important property to set is the text – this is what you want the font to display.

```
label.text = @"w00t your text here!";
```

You also usually want to set the font size.

```
label.fontSize = 20.0;
```

Finally, just like any other node, you should position it and add it as a child of another node (the scene itself in this case).

```
label.position = yourPosition;
[self addChild:label];
```

Don't worry too much about the positioning code or the usage of `verticalAlignmentMode` – that's just some magic to get the labels to be spaced evenly up and down the screen. You'll also learn more about alignment later in this chapter.

Build and run, and now every time you tap the screen, you can see a different built-in font family.

Tap through and get an idea of what's available to you. This app can be a handy reference in the future when you're wondering what font would be the perfect match for your game.

Loading custom fonts

While the list of built-in fonts is pretty large, there will be times when you want to use fonts that aren't included by default. The mini-game you will start in this chapter, for instance, is going to be a little retro, so it would be great to use a font that has a retro, pixelated look to it.

None of the fonts included by default are going to meet your needs. Luckily for you, Apple has made it super simple to take a **True Type Font** (TTF) and use it in your project.

First you need to find the font you want to use. One great source of fonts is http://www.dafont.com. Open up your browser of choice and enter the URL. You will see that there is a large selection of categories from which to choose, including one called **Pixel/Bitmap**.

Click on that category and you'll see a huge list of fonts with examples of how they look. Some people could spend hours looking through these fonts just for fun, so take as much time as you'd like to see what's available.

Now that you're back, the font you are going to use is called **Thirteen Pixel Fonts** by 30100flo. Type that name into the search bar on the **dafont.com** website. A preview for that font will appear:

This nice boxy-looking font is a perfect fit for the mini-game you're creating. Click the **Download** button. Once the download is complete, unzip the package and find the file named **thirteen_pixel_font.ttf**. This is the file you need for this project, so place it somewhere safe.

> **Note:** It's important to check the license for any fonts you want to use in your project. Some fonts require permission or a license before they can be used, so checking now could save a lot of heartache and cost later on.
>
> You'll see that the Thirteen Pixels Font you are using is marked as Free, just above the download button, but always check the license information that's included in the downloaded zip file. In this case, you'll see that specifically if uses the Creative Commons Attribution Share Alike license, which you can read about here:
>
> http://creativecommons.org/licenses/by-sa/3.0/

Now that you've got your font, create a new project by selecting **File\New\Project...** from the main menu, just as you did earlier. Select the **iOS\Application\SpriteKit Game** template and click **Next**.

Enter **XBlaster** for the Product Name, choose **iPhone** for Devices, leave the Class Prefix blank and then click **Next**. Select a location on your hard drive to store the project and then click **Create**. This is the project you'll use throughout the rest of this chapter to build the mini-game.

Unlike Zombie Conga and Cat Nap, you want XBlaster to run in portrait mode instead of landscape. So select the **XBlaster** project in the Project Navigator and then select the **XBlaster** target. Go to the **General** tab and uncheck Landscape Left and Landscape Right so that only **Portrait** is checked.

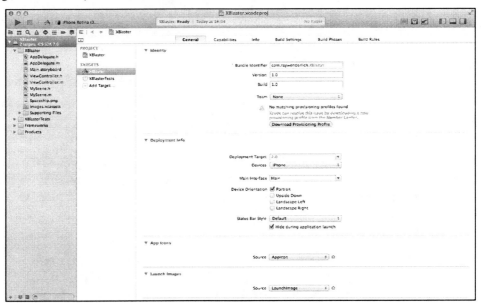

Next you need to add **Thirteen Pixels Fonts** to the project. Click on the **Info** tab at the top of the page and you'll be shown the **Custom iOS Target Properties**. Click on the last entry in the list, called **Bundle versions string, short**, and you'll see a plus and minus button appear next to that title.

Click the plus button and a new entry will appear in the table with a drop-down list of options:

In the drop-down box, type **Fonts**, making sure to use a capital **F**. The first option that comes up will be **Fonts provided by application**. Hit **Return** to select that option and then hit **Return** again to add that entry to the list. This will create an entry with a type of array that allows you to add any number of custom fonts to your project.

Click the triangle to the left of the new entry to expand it and double-click inside the value field. Inside the textbox that appears, type **thirteen_pixel_fonts.ttf**. This is the name of the font file you downloaded and that you're going to use in the game.

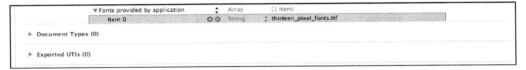

The last step is to copy the actual font file into the project. In the project navigator in Xcode, right-click on the **XBlaster** group and choose **New Group**. Name the newly created group **Resources**. Use the same technique to create a group named **Fonts** inside the **Resources** group.

Drag the **thirteen_pixel_fonts.ttf** file you downloaded earlier into the new **Fonts** group. Make sure to tick **Copy items into destination group's folder (if needed)** and to select **XBlaster** in the Add to Targets panel.

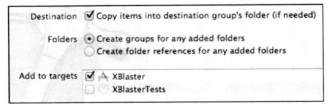

Click **Finish** and you're done.

Now let's try out this font! Open **MyScene.m** and you'll see the code that places the Hello, World! label on the screen along with the rotating space ships. Inside

initWithSize:, you'll see code that already creates a label called myLabel, using the
SKLabelNode class that displays text labels onscreen in Sprite Kit.

Remove touchesBegan:withEvent: and modify initWithSize:, changing the line
that creates myLabel to look like this:

```
SKLabelNode *myLabel =
  [SKLabelNode labelNodeWithFontNamed:@"Thirteen Pixel Fonts"];
```

This change causes the label to use the new font you added to the project. Note you use
the full name of the font itself, not the name of the TTF file.

There's two last things: to get this game started on the right foot, you should disable the
status bar and set up an app icon. To disable the status bar, open **ViewController.m** and
add this to the bottom:

```
-(BOOL)prefersStatusBarHidden
{
    return YES;
}
```

And to set up an app icon, open **Images.xassets** and select the **AppIcon** entry. Then in
the resources for this chapter, drag all of the files from the "App Icon" folder into the
area on the right. You should see the following when you're done:

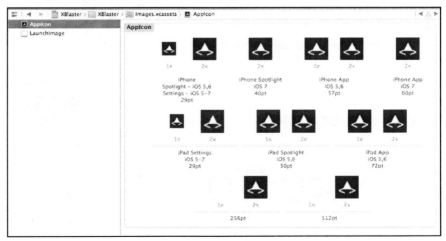

Build and run, and you'll see **Hello, World!** displayed in the center of the screen using
the new font:

Wow, I suddenly feel a lot older! ☺

Alignment modes

So far you know that you can place a label by setting its position – but how can you control where the text is placed in relation to the position?

Unlike `SKSpriteNode`, `SKLabelNode` doesn't have an `anchorPoint` property. In its place, you can use the `verticalAlignmentMode` and `horizontalAlignmentMode` properties.

The `verticalAlignmentMode` controls where the text is placed vertically in relation to the label's position, and the `horizontalAlignmentMode` controls where the text is placed horizontally in relation to the label's position. You can see this visually in the diagram below:

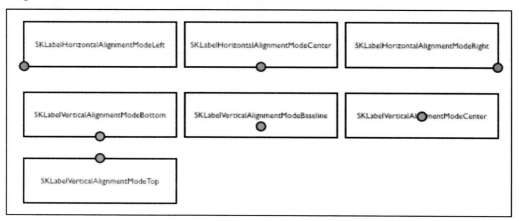

The points in the above diagram show where each label's bounding box will be rendered in relation to its position for the different alignment modes. There are two things to point out here:

- SKLabelNode's default alignment modes are
  SKLabelHorizontalAlignmentModeCenter and
  SKLabelVerticalAlignmentModeBaseline.

- The SKLabelVerticalAlignmentModeBaseline uses the actual font's baseline
  which you can think of as the "line" a font should be drawn on if you were writing on
  ruled paper. For example, the tails of letters such as **g** and **y** will hang below the
  position defined.

Let's try this out. Add the following to initWithSize: after setting
myLabel.position:

```
myLabel.horizontalAlignmentMode =
    SKLabelHorizontalAlignmentModeRight;
```

Build and run the app and you'll see that the label now hangs off the left-hand side of
the screen.

This is because you are now aligning the right side of the text to the position (which is
the center of the screen). Similarly, if you were to change the
horizontalAlignmentNode to SKLabelHorizontalAlignmentModeLeft, the label
would hang off the right-hand side of the screen.

Feel free to play around with different alignment modes for this text to get a feeling for
how they work. In your games, simply choose the alignment that makes it easiest for you
to position your text where you want it.

Layer by layer

Now that you have a good understanding of how to create a label with a custom font
and position it, let's crack on with building up the mini-game. This chapter will give you
plenty of practice using labels, as everything rendered in this game will start life as a
label.

As you've seen in Chapter 5, "Scrolling", it's a good idea to build your scene using a number of different layers, where a layer is usually a plain **SKNode**. This makes it easier to move everything in a layer at once, or to place items in one layer above or below another layer.

For the work you're going to do in this chapter, you're only going to need two layers:

• The heads up display or HUD, which will show the player's score and health

• The player's ship

In one of the challenges, you'll take a peek at the final project with gameplay added, that includes some other layers for the bullets and enemy ships.

For now, you'll just add the two you need right away. Open **MyScene.m** and add the following private instance variables:

```
@implementation MyScene {
  SKNode *_playerLayerNode;
  SKNode *_hudLayerNode;
}
```

You're going to be accessing these layers frequently, so it's handy to have a reference to them.

Now create a new method called `setupSceneLayers`:

```
- (void)setupSceneLayers
{
  _playerLayerNode = [SKNode node];
  [self addChild:_playerLayerNode];

  _hudLayerNode = [SKNode node];
  [self addChild:_hudLayerNode];
}
```

This method simply creates a number of **SKNode** instances, to which you will be adding child nodes later, and adds them to the scene.

The order is important. As you are not setting the nodes' `zPosition`, the nodes are rendered in the order they are added to the scene. For this reason the HUD layer is added to the scene last, as it should be rendered on top of everything else.

Now replace the contents of `initWithSize:` with the following:

```
if (self = [super initWithSize:size]) {
  [self setupSceneLayers];
```

```
  }
  return self;
```

This calls `setupSceneLayers:` when the scene is created so that the layers you're using all get set up. It's handy placing functions like this in their own methods, as it keeps the configuration functions easy to read and extend, should you need to.

You can also delete the `touchesbegan:withEvent:` method – you don't need that right now.

Build and run the app. All you'll see is a dark grey screen, because as yet nothing has been added to the layers for rendering, but don't worry – you'll soon change that.

Creating the HUD

With the layers set up, you can move on to adding the HUD information, which will be comprised of the players' score and health displayed on a black background. You're starting with this because it involves a lot of practice with labels and positioning, and making a HUD is a common need for a game.

Start by creating a new method called `setupUI`:

```
- (void)setupUI
{
  int barHeight = 45;
  CGSize backgroundSize =
    CGSizeMake(self.size.width, barHeight);

  SKColor *backgroundColor =
    [SKColor colorWithRed:0 green:0 blue:0.05 alpha:1.0];
  SKSpriteNode *hudBarBackground =
    [SKSpriteNode spriteNodeWithColor:backgroundColor
                                 size:backgroundSize];
  hudBarBackground.position =
    CGPointMake(0, self.size.height - barHeight);
  hudBarBackground.anchorPoint = CGPointZero;
  [_hudLayerNode addChild:hudBarBackground];
}
```

This code draws a colored background for the HUD using a `SKSpriteNode`.

This is an example of using a `SKSpriteNode` in a different way than you've seen in the past. In addition to creating a `SKSpriteNode` by passing in the name of an image, you can also create a `SKSpriteNode` by passing in a color and a size. This is great if you're trying to quickly prototype a game, or if you're trying to draw a simple colored background like you're doing here.

Next add the following line straight after the call to setupSceneLayers inside initWithSize::

```
[self setupUI];
```

Build and run the app, and you'll see a subtle black box is now drawn at the top of the screen. This forms the basis for the main HUD in the game.

In the next few sections, you will flesh this out by adding the score label, making it "pop", and finally adding a player health label.

Adding a score label

Now you can add the score label that will display the player's score. Add the following to the end of setupUI:

```
// 1
SKLabelNode *scoreLabel =
  [SKLabelNode labelNodeWithFontNamed:@"Thirteen Pixel Fonts"];
// 2
scoreLabel.fontSize = 20.0;
scoreLabel.text = @"Score: 0";
scoreLabel.name = @"scoreLabel";
// 3
scoreLabel.verticalAlignmentMode =
  SKLabelVerticalAlignmentModeCenter;
// 4
scoreLabel.position =
  CGPointMake(self.size.width / 2,
    self.size.height - scoreLabel.frame.size.height + 3);
// 5
[_hudLayerNode addChild:scoreLabel];
```

Let's run through this in detail:

1. First you create a label using the custom font you added to the project.

2. You then set properties on the label to define its size, text and name. The name is useful should you want to access this node later.

3. You set the vertical alignment so that the text will render with its vertical center at the label's position.

4. You then set the position by calculating half the width of the screen for the x-position and then the height of the screen minus the height of the label node, plus 3 to make it look just right.

5. Finally, you add the label as a child of the hud layer.

Run the app now and you'll see the dark background bar for the HUD, along with the score label:

Actions and labels

Since `SKLabelNode` derives from `SKNode`, you can run actions on them just like you can any other node.

Let's try this out by creating an action to run on the score label every time the score changes. Open **MyScene.m** and add the following private instance variable:

```
SKAction *_scoreFlashAction;
```

Then add this code to the end of `setupUI`:

```
_scoreFlashAction = [SKAction sequence:
                     @[[SKAction scaleTo:1.5 duration:0.1],
                       [SKAction scaleTo:1.0 duration:0.1]]];
[scoreLabel runAction:
  [SKAction repeatAction:_scoreFlashAction count:10]];
```

This is a simple action that scales the node it is run against to 1.5 over 0.1 seconds, and then scales it back to 1.0 over 0.1 seconds. Running this action on the score label will give the score a nice little pop when it changes, adding some juice to an otherwise plain label.

The second line is just a quick test to bounce it 10 times on startup so you can make sure it's working.

Build and run, and enjoy your juiced up label!

Displaying the player's health

Now that you're displaying the score, you'll add support to display the player's health. Add the following private variables:

```
SKLabelNode *_playerHealthLabel;
NSString    *_healthBar;
```

Then add the following code to **setupUI** for the player's health meter:

```
// 1
_healthBar =
   @"=================================================";
float testHealth = 75;
NSString * actualHealth = [_healthBar substringToIndex:
   (testHealth / 100 * _healthBar.length)];

// 2
SKLabelNode *playerHealthBackground =
   [SKLabelNode labelNodeWithFontNamed:@"Thirteen Pixel Fonts"];
playerHealthBackground.name = @"playerHealthBackground";
playerHealthBackground.fontColor = [SKColor darkGrayColor];
playerHealthBackground.fontSize = 10.0f;
playerHealthBackground.text = _healthBar;

// 3
playerHealthBackground.horizontalAlignmentMode =
   SKLabelHorizontalAlignmentModeLeft;
playerHealthBackground.verticalAlignmentMode =
   SKLabelVerticalAlignmentModeTop;
playerHealthBackground.position =
   CGPointMake(0,
            self.size.height - barHeight +
               playerHealthBackground.frame.size.height);
[_hudLayerNode addChild:playerHealthBackground];

// 4
```

```
_playerHealthLabel =
  [SKLabelNode labelNodeWithFontNamed:@"Thirteen Pixel Fonts"];
_playerHealthLabel.name = @"playerHealth";
_playerHealthLabel.fontColor = [SKColor whiteColor];
_playerHealthLabel.fontSize = 10.0f;
_playerHealthLabel.text = actualHealth;
_playerHealthLabel.horizontalAlignmentMode =
  SKLabelHorizontalAlignmentModeLeft;
_playerHealthLabel.verticalAlignmentMode =
  SKLabelVerticalAlignmentModeTop;
_playerHealthLabel.position =
  CGPointMake(0,
              self.size.height - barHeight +
              _playerHealthLabel.frame.size.height);
[_hudLayerNode addChild:_playerHealthLabel];
```

This looks like a lot of code, but it's really just setting up a couple of labels.

1. _healthBar holds the string used to render the health bar when the player's health is at 100%. actualHealth holds the substring that represent's the player's current health. For now you hard-code the player's current health to 75/100 so you can test this out.

2. You use the playerHealthBackground label to render a dark version of the player's health meter. This means that as the player's health goes down, you see the background version of the health bar left behind. This simply enhances the appearance of the health meter. You don't define this label as an instance variable or property because, since its not going to be changed, you won't need to access it.

3. You set the label's alignment so that horizontally the position represents the very left-hand edge of the label, while vertically it represents the top of the label. You calculate the x-position to be at the very left of the screen and you calculate the y-position based on the heights of the background bar and the label.

4. You're going to draw _playerHealthLabel over the top of the background label. You set it up as an instance variable, as it will change during game play, and referencing it through a variable makes that easy. Everything else about this label matches the background label. You'll set the color later in the update: method.

Build and run the app. You'll see the score label inside the header background bar and then a line of white = characters representing the player's health:

Now that all of your score label is set up, I'd like to introduce you to someone with whom I hope you become good friends.

Introducing SKTUtils

In the first few chapters of this book while you were working on Zombie Conga, you created some handy helper methods like `CGPointAdd`, `CGPointNormalize`, and `ScalarRandomRange`.

Rather than make you continuously re-add these helper methods in each minigame, we have gathered them all together into a handy little library called SKTUtils.

In addition to pulling the helper methods you know and love into a common spot, we have made a few improvements:

- **Improved performance**. We have modified some of the helper methods to run a little faster on your devices. Sometimes we make use of a library written by Apple called GLKMath that is highly optimized for performance.

- **A few extra methods**. We have added a few additional methods into the library, such as a helper method to easily play background music in your game.

In this section, you are going to add SKTUtils into your project so you can make use of these handy methods in the rest of the chapter. Let's go!

You can find **SKTUtils** in the root folder for this book. Drag the entire **SKTUtils** folder into the project navigator in Xcode. Make sure **Copy items into destination group's folder (if needed)** and the **XBlaster target** are both checked. Click **Finish**.

Feel free to peek around the contents of the library to get a feel of what's inside. It should look quite familiar, with a few additions and tweaks.

```
SKT_INLINE CGPoint CGPointFromGLKVector2(GLKVector2 vector) {
    return CGPointMake(vector.x, vector.y);
}

SKT_INLINE GLKVector2 GLKVector2FromCGPoint(CGPoint point) {
    return GLKVector2Make(point.x, point.y);
}

SKT_INLINE CGPoint CGPointAdd(CGPoint point1, CGPoint point2) {
    return CGPointMake(point1.x + point2.x, point1.y + point2.y);
}

SKT_INLINE CGPoint CGPointSubtract(CGPoint point1, CGPoint point2) {
    return CGPointMake(point1.x - point2.x, point1.y - point2.y);
}

SKT_INLINE CGPoint CGPointMultiply(CGPoint point1, CGPoint point2) {
    return CGPointMake(point1.x * point2.x, point1.y * point2.y);
}
```

Finally, open **Supporting Files\XBlaster-Prefix.pch**, found inside the **Supporting Files** group, and add the following statement with the other imports in the file:

```
#import "SKTUtils.h"
```

This provides every class in your project with access to our handy math functions, useful when performing calculations.

Inheritance-Based Game Architecture

So far in this book, all of the code for your minigames has been inside a single class – the scene's class.

Although this works for extremely simple games like Zombie Conga and Cat Nap, this can rapidly result in a large file with spaghetti code!

So in this chapter, you will create a separate class for the player's ship to keep your code nicely organized. You will also put some common code that will be useful for other objects in the game like bullets and enemy ships into a base class, to avoid code duplication.

> **Note:** The method you are using here is called inheritance-based game architecture. This method works out great for many simple to medium-level complexity games, and is easy and straightforward to develop.

As your games get more complex, you might want to investigate alternative kinds of game architectures, such as component-based game architecture. To learn more about component-based game architecture, check out this post:

http://www.raywenderlich.com/24878/introduction-to-component-based-architecture-in-games

Let's start by creating the base class that will create the common code used by all objects in the game.

Right-click on the **XBlaster** group in Xcode and choose **New Group** to create a new group called **Entities**. Create a new file in this group by right-clicking on the group and choosing **New File…** from the popup menu.

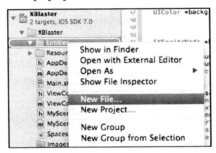

From the template selection panel, select **Objective-C class** and click **Next**. Set Class to `Entity` and Subclass of to `SKSpriteNode` and hit **Next**. Make sure that the **XBlaster** target is selected and then click **Create**.

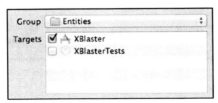

This class will act as an abstract class for all the entities in the game, including the player's ship, bullets and the enemy ships. You will never create an instance of this class, but other entity classes such as `PlayerShip` will inherit from this class.

Open **Entity.h** and add the following properties to the interface:

```
@property (assign,nonatomic) CGPoint direction;
```

```
@property (assign,nonatomic) float   health;
@property (assign,nonatomic) float   maxHealth;
```

All the entities in the game that inherit from this class will now have access to these properties. These are common properties that the majority of entities will need to use.

Next declare the following methods in the same file:

```
+ (SKTexture *)generateTexture;
- (instancetype)initWithPosition:(CGPoint)position;
- (void)update:(CFTimeInterval)delta;
```

Since this chapter is all about labels, you are going to use labels to represent all of the objects in this game – the player's ships, the bullets, and the enemies. However, using labels directly would be inefficient, as behind the scenes Sprite Kit would need to generate a new texture every time you create a new object.

It is much more efficient to generate the texture for a type of ship once, and then re-use that texture multiple times. generateTexture is a class method that will do just that.

You use initWithPosition: to create a new instance of an entity at a specific position. The scene's update: will call the above update: each frame, allowing the entity to perform any logic specific to that entity.

Open **Entity.m** and add the following methods inside the implementation:

```
- (instancetype)initWithPosition:(CGPoint)position
{
  if (self = [super init]) {
    self.texture = [[self class] generateTexture];
    self.size = self.texture.size;
    self.position = position;
    _direction = CGPointZero;
  }
  return self;
}

- (void)update:(CFTimeInterval)delta
{
  // Overridden by subclasses
}

+ (SKTexture *)generateTexture
{
  // Overridden by subclasses
  return nil;
}
```

initWithPosition: uses generateTexture to create the entity's texture. Notice how it calls generateTexture on [self class]. This ensures that it calls the correct version of the generateTexture class method when initializing an instance of a subclass.

Also notice how initWithPosition: sets the object's size to the size of the texture –just setting the texture does not update the size. It goes on to set the position property to the passed-in position and the direction to {0, 0}.

Entity's implementations of update: and generateTexture do nothing, as the subclasses will implement the necessary logic.

Generating a texture from a node

With the abstract entity class in place, you can now do something more exciting and create the player's ship. This will include generating a texture for the ship from some SKLabelNodes.

Create a new file inside the **Entities** group called PlayerShip that subclasses Entity.

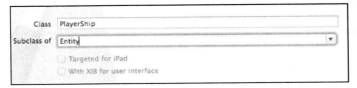

Open **PlayerShip.m** and add the initWithPosition: method:

```
- (instancetype)initWithPosition:(CGPoint)position
{
    if (self = [super initWithPosition:position]) {
        self.name = @"shipSprite";
    }
    return self;
}
```

PlayerShip's initWithPosition: simply calls Entity's version of the method and then sets its name to shipSprite. Setting the name is a good practice because it makes it easy to search for the node in your scene using enumerateChildNodesWithName:usingBlock: or childNodeWithName:.

Remember that `Entity` returns nil from its implementation of `generateTexture.`, so add the following implementation of the method for `PlayerShip`:

```
+ (SKTexture *)generateTexture
{
  // 1
  static SKTexture *texture = nil;
  static dispatch_once_t onceToken;
  dispatch_once(&onceToken, ^{

    // 2
    SKLabelNode *mainShip =
      [SKLabelNode labelNodeWithFontNamed:@"Arial"];
    mainShip.name = @"mainship";
    mainShip.fontSize = 20.0f;
    mainShip.fontColor = [SKColor whiteColor];
    mainShip.text = @"▲";

    // 3
    SKLabelNode *wings =
      [SKLabelNode labelNodeWithFontNamed:@"Arial"];
    wings.name = @"wings";
    wings.fontSize = 20.0f;
    wings.text = @"< >";
    wings.fontColor = [SKColor whiteColor];
    wings.position = CGPointMake(0, 7);

    // 4
    wings.zRotation = DegreesToRadians(180);

    [mainShip addChild:wings];

    // 5
    SKView *textureView = [SKView new];
    texture = [textureView textureFromNode:mainShip];
    texture.filteringMode = SKTextureFilteringNearest;
  });

  return texture;
}
```

This is an important method, so let's go over it section by section.

1. While the game will have only one instance of `PlayerShip`, you're generating the texture in such a way that there is only ever one texture, regardless of how many instances of `PlayerShip` there are. For this reason you create a **static** texture variable

and use the call to **dispatch_once** to guarantee that the code inside its block is only ever run once.

2. You create an SKLabelNode with a size and color and set the text to the shape of the main hull of the player's ship. Note that the text for the hull is using a special "triangle-looking" character. You may wonder how to type this!

The characters you have available to use depend on the font you specify when setting up the label. If you want to access special characters, you can go to **Edit\Special Characters…**, or use the shortcut **CTRL + CMD + SPACE**. This displays a popup from which you can select the special characters you want:

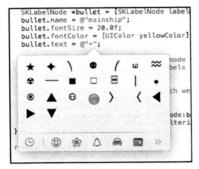

If your window does not look like this, you can click the button in the upper right to switch to the condensed view:

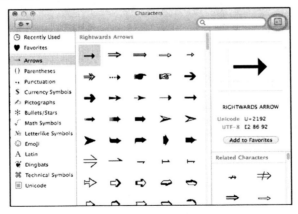

Note that the character you choose will look different based on the font that is being used to render the text. The Arial font is usually a good font to start with, as it contains a large number of different characters in different languages – that's why you use it for this SKLabelNode instead of the custom font.

3. You create another SKLabelNode to represent the wings of the player's ship. You then adjust the position to place the wings correctly on the ship's main hull. This position is in node space.

4. To finish off the wings, you rotate the node 180 degrees using a helper method from SKTUtils.h that converts degrees to radians.

5. This part is the key to this method, in that it creates a new SKView that you use to render to a texture with textureFromNode:. You pass in the mainShip node and end up with a texture that you can use with the PlayerShip.

Again, the above process ensures that you need only a single texture for all instances of this object, which helps with performance. Although there will only be one player ship, you can re-use this same technique for classes where there will be many copies, such as bullets or enemies.

Now that you've created the player's ship, you need to add it to the scene so that it gets rendered.

Open **MyScene.m** and add the following import to the top of the screen:

```
#import "PlayerShip.h"
```

Also add a private variable that you'll use to access the PlayerShip instance inside the scene:

```
PlayerShip *_playerShip;
```

With those additions in place, create a new method called setupEntities::

```
- (void)setupEntities
{
  _playerShip =
    [[PlayerShip alloc]
      initWithPosition:CGPointMake(self.size.width / 2,
                                   100)];
  [_playerLayerNode addChild:_playerShip];
}
```

This creates an instance of PlayerShip and positions the ship in the center of the screen horizontally and 100 points up from the bottom of the screen. It then adds the PlayerShip instance to the _playerLayerNode.

Add a call to this new method inside `initWithSize:`, after your call to `setupUI`:

```
[self setupEntities];
```

Now build and run the app, and you'll see the result of all your hard work – a cool-looking space ship sitting in the middle of the screen.

I bet you never thought of using labels in quite this way! ☺

Moving the player

Once you've calmed down from the excitement of seeing your player's ship rendered onscreen, there's one last thing before you get to try out some of this on your own in the challenges – moving the player.

Although this isn't specifically about fonts or text, you can't just leave the player ship sitting there doing nothing – it's time to get that ship moving! Rather than putting some kind of virtual D-Pad onscreen, you'll allow the player to simply slide their finger around the screen to move the ship.

Add the following private variable in **MyScene.m**, which you'll use to track the amount the player's finger has moved per game update:

```
CGPoint _deltaPoint;
```

Now you need to capture the player's touches, so add the following methods:

```
- (void)touchesMoved:(NSSet *)touches withEvent:(UIEvent *)event
{
  CGPoint currentPoint =
    [[touches anyObject] locationInNode:self];
  CGPoint previousPoint =
    [[touches anyObject] previousLocationInNode:self];
  _deltaPoint = CGPointSubtract(currentPoint, previousPoint);
}

- (void)touchesEnded:(NSSet *)touches withEvent:(UIEvent *)event
```

```
{
  _deltaPoint = CGPointZero;
}

- (void)touchesCancelled:(NSSet *)touches
              withEvent:(UIEvent *)event
{
  _deltaPoint = CGPointZero;
}
```

`touchesMoved:withEvent:` sets the `currentPoint` variable to the current position of the player's finger onscreen and `previousPoint` to the previous position. It then calculates the difference between these two points using the `CGPointSubtract` function from SKTUtils.h and stores it in `_deltaPoint`.

Inside `touchesEnded:withEvent:` and `touchedCancelled:withEvent:`, the code simply sets `_deltaPoint` to a zero point, as the player has now removed their finger from the screen or slid their finger off of a screen edge.

If you run the app now, you're not going to notice much of a difference. Although you are capturing touches and calculating the delta, you aren't using this information anywhere. This is where `update:` comes in.

In previous chapters, you've seen how the scene's `update:` is called once per frame, allowing you to update the logic of your game. This is the perfect place for code that will update the position of the player's ship based on the player's input.

Add the following to `update::`

```
// 1
CGPoint newPoint =
  CGPointAdd(_playerShip.position, _deltaPoint);

// 2
newPoint.x =
  Clamp(newPoint.x,
        _playerShip.size.width / 2,
        self.size.width - _playerShip.size.width / 2);

newPoint.y =
  Clamp(newPoint.y,
        _playerShip.size.height / 2,
        self.size.height - _playerShip.size.height / 2);
// 3
_playerShip.position = newPoint;
_deltaPoint = CGPointZero;
```

1. First you calculate the new position of the ship by adding the `_deltaPoint` updated in the touch methods.

2. You use another function from SKTUtils.h, named `Clamp`, to ensure the ship cannot be moved off the edge of the screen. There is nothing more annoying than losing your player's ship to the depths of space and not being able to retrieve it!

3. You update the position of the player's ship with the new position. You also reset the delta point back to zero since you've already moved the ship this amount.

Build and run the app, and move your finger around the screen. You'll see that the player's ship now moves relative to the movements of your finger – whoohoo!

And with that, it's time for you to take a break to try out some of your new found knowledge. You'll start by adding some shooting to the game, then you'll check out the project with the gameplay added and add a new feature involving moving score labels.

All of this makes for a fun game, but XBlaster doesn't end there. In the next chapter on particle systems, you'll be adding some cool special effects like sparks where the bullet hits the enemy ships, and explosions when the enemy ships die!

Challenges

These are two short challenges to give you practice with labels, and introduce you to the next version of the project which you will continue with in the next chapter. It's important to do these so you can solidify your knowledge and make the most of the next chapter.

As always, if you get stuck you can find the solutions in the resources for this chapter – but give it your best shot first!

Challenge 1: the plasma cannon

Your first challenge is to add something rather important: a plasma cannon. No self-respecting space fighter goes into battle without a big gun!

Here are a few hints on doing this:

• Create a new class that derives from `Entity` named `Bullet`.

• Implement `initWithPosition` similarly to how you did for `PlayerShip`, except set the name to bullet.

• Implement `generateTexture` similarly to how you did for `PlayerShip`, except use a new character for the bullet of your choosing! Also, you probably only need one label unless you're getting fancy.

• Inside **MyScene.m**, import Bullet.h.

• Also add the following new private instance variables:

```
float _bulletInterval;
CFTimeInterval _lastUpdateTime;
NSTimeInterval _dt;
```

• Then add the following code to the bottom of **update**:

```
if (_lastUpdateTime) {
    _dt = currentTime - _lastUpdateTime;
} else {
    _dt = 0;
}
_lastUpdateTime = currentTime;
```

```
_bulletInterval += _dt;
if (_bulletInterval > 0.15) {
  _bulletInterval = 0;

  // 1: Create Bullet
  // 2: Add to scene
  // 3: Sequence: Move up screen, remove from parent
}
```

- Implement comment #1 to create a new instance of your `Bullet` class using your new constructor.

- Implement comment #2 to add the new bullet to the scene.

- Implement comment #3 to run a sequence of actions. The first action in the sequence should move the bullet the height of the screen along the y-axis. The second action in the sequence should remove the bullet from its parent.

Build and run, and if all goes well you should have a ship shooting bullets made from labels!

Challenge 2: A moving score label

Find **Challenge 2 – Starter** in the resources for this chapter and open the project in Xcode. You will see that I have added some basic gameplay to the game (again, so you can keep focused on the subject of this chapter). The biggest change is that the game now has enemies to fight!

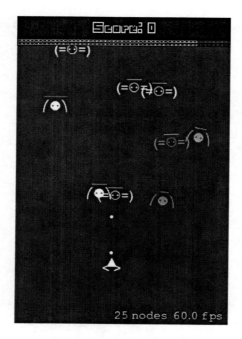

Take a look through the project and get familiar with what's inside – it will be good practice reading other's code, and a good review of the concepts you've learned previously in this book.

Your challenge is to add one more feature to this game involving labels. It's often cool in a game to show informational labels when an event of interest occurs near where the event occurs – for example, showing the HP damage you caused on an enemy right near the enemy.

In this game, you will add a score label that appears when you destroy a ship. This label should be added to the screen at the location the enemy was killed and fade and slide up the screen at the same time and then fade out while still moving up the screen slowly.

Here are some hints:

- Add a new SKLabelNode property to **EnemyA.h** called scoreLabel.

- Inside **EnemyA.m**, create a new static action called scoreLabelAction, along with the other actions right above loadSharedAssets.

- Inside loadSharedAssets, create the scoreLabelAction. It should run a sequence of two groups.

- The first group is the "label appears" effect. It should scale to 1 over 0 seconds (resetting the scale to 1), fade in over 0 seconds (resetting the alpha to 0), fade in over 0.5 seconds (the "real" fade-in), and move 20 points up along the y-axis over 0.5 seconds.

- The second group is the "label disappears" effect. It should move by 40 along the y axis over 1 second, and fade out over 1 second.

- Inside initWithPosition:, create the scoreLabel. Set the font to "Thirteen Pixel Fonts", with 25 font size, R=0.5, G=1.0, B=1.0, Alpha=1.0, and the text displaying the _score field formatted as a string.

- Inside collideWith:contact:, inside the clause where the enemy's health is less than or equal to 0, set the label to the enemy's current position, and add it to the mainScene's hudLayerNode. Finally, remove all actions on the label and run the scoreLabelAction you created earlier.

- (Optional) Repeat these steps for EnemyB.

If you've got it working, build and run and when you destroy an enemy ship, you should see something like the image on the following page.

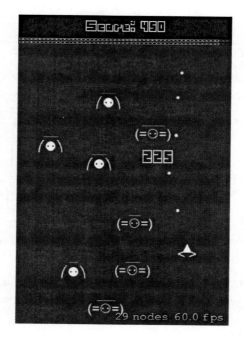

If you have made it this far and completed the challenges, CONGRATULATIONS, you have achieved a great deal in this chapter. Now it's time for some explosions – and remember not to look back!

Chapter 7: Particle Systems

By Mike Daley & Tom Bradley

There's nothing that spices up your game quite like particle systems. Particle systems are an easy way to create special effects in your game, such as this awesome explosion:

You can use them for a wide range of special effects beyond just explosions, cool as they may be. Here are just a few of the things you might simulate with a particle system:

smoke	water	fog
star fields	snow	rain
fire	explosions	magical potions
sparks	blood	bubbles

And this is just the beginning! It's impossible to imagine all that you could do with particle systems, and it pays to be creative. For instance, they would be a great fit for generating subatomic particles emanating from a rip in the space-time continuum.

What else makes particle systems so great? To achieve a special effect like this without particle systems, you'd have to make a traditional frame-by-frame animation, which would require many images taking up significant texture space and memory requirements. With particle systems, the special effects are generated by one small texture and a configuration file, greatly reducing the memory requirements and allowing real-time editing.

In this chapter, you will get hands-on experience with particle systems by adding cool special effects to the XBlaster game you created in the previous chapter. You will learn how to create particle systems both programmatically, as well as by using the built-in Xcode editor.

Here's how your XBlaster project will look after completing this chapter:

Quite an improvement, eh? That's the power of particle systems!

Note: This chapter begins where Challenge 2 left off in the last chapter. If you were unable to complete the challenges or skipped ahead from a previous chapter, don't worry – you can simply open **XBlaster-Starter** from the resources for this chapter to pick up where we left off.

How do particle systems work?

Before you dive into code, let's talk a bit more about how particle systems work – both in theory, and with Sprite Kit specifically.

Particle systems in theory

A particle is two triangles drawn together to create a square or quad. This quad is then textured, colored and rendered to the screen. For example, here's an example of using a rain drop as a particle:

During each frame, the particle system looks at each individual particle it owns and advances it according to the system's configuration. For example, the configuration might say "move each particle between 2-10 pixels toward the bottom of the screen." The effect of this configuration can be seen in the following diagram.

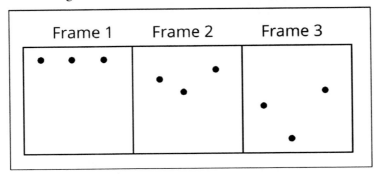

A particle system will typically create a cache of particles when it's initialized, known as the **particle pool**. If a new particle is to be born, the particle system will obtain an available particle from its particle pool. It will set the initial values of the new particle and then add it to the rendering queue. If a particle has reached the end of its life, the system will remove it from the render queue and return it to the particle pool to be used at a later time.

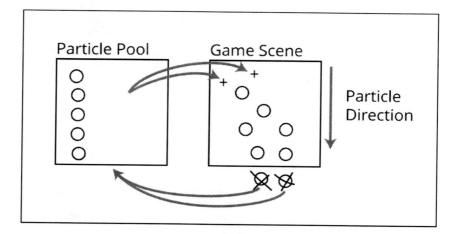

That's the high level of how particle systems work in theory – let's take a look at how they work in practice with Sprite Kit.

Particle systems in practice

One of the great things about Sprite Kit is that it makes it very easy to create and use particle systems in your games. It contains a special node called SKEmitterNode whose sole purpose is to make it easy to create particle systems, and to render them as quickly as possible.

This section will give you a quick overview of how to use particle systems, then you'll try it out for yourself in the rest of the chapter.

To use a SKEmitterNode programatically, you simply declare an instance of the node and set up its properties, like this:

```
SKTexture *_rainTexture = [SKTexture
textureWithImageNamed:@"rainDrop.png"];
SKEmitterNode *_emitterNode = [SKEmitterNode new];
_emitterNode.particleTexture = _rainTexture;
_emitterNode.particleBirthRate = 80.0;
_emitterNode.particleColor = [SKColor whiteColor];
_emitterNode.particleSpeed = -450;
_emitterNode.particleSpeedRange = 150;
_emitterNode.particleLifetime = 2.0;
_emitterNode.particleScale = 0.2;
_emitterNode.particleAlpha = 0.75;
_emitterNode.particleAlphaRange = 0.5;
_emitterNode.particleColorBlendFactor = 1;
_emitterNode.particleScaleRange = 0.5;
```

```
_emitterNode.position =
  CGPointMake(CGRectGetWidth(self.frame) / 2,
              CGRectGetHeight(self.frame) + 10);
_emitterNode.particlePositionRange =
CGVectorMake(CGRectGetMaxX(self.frame), 0);
[self addChild:_emitterNode];
```

Don't worry about what all these properties mean yet – you'll learn about them later in this chapter. To see the effect this code produces open and run the **Rain** project included in the resources for this chapter.

Not only can you create particle systems programmatically, but you can also use Xcode's built-in editor to create and configure particle systems visually:

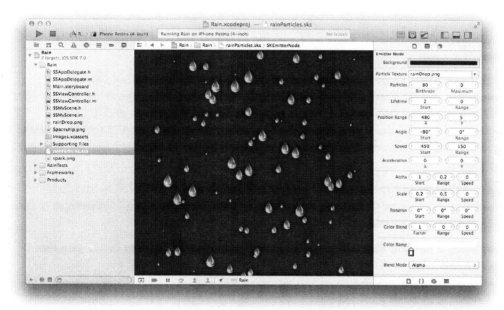

To create a particle system with the visual editor, you simply create a new file with the **iOS\Resource\SpriteKit Particle File** template, which will create a **.sks** file that you can edit with the built-in particle system editor. Then in code you create an **SKEmitterNode** with the file like this:

```
SKEmitterNode *emitter =
  [NSKeyedUnarchiver unarchiveObjectWithFile:
    [[NSBundle mainBundle] pathForResource:@"rain"
                                    ofType:@"sks"]];
```

```
engineEmitter.position = CGPointMake(100, 100);
[self addChild:engineEmitter];
```

This visual editor is super convenient because you can visualize what the particle system looks like in real-time as you tweak its properties. This makes it easy to get the exact effect you're looking for quickly.

In this chapter, you will get practice with both creating SKEmitterNodes programmatically, as well as by using the visual editor. Let's have a play!

Programmatic particle systems

Every space shooter needs a star field moving subtly in the background, and particle systems are perfect for that!

In this section you'll get your first taste of particle systems by creating a star field simulation. You'll create this programmatically rather than using the visual editor. This will help you better understand what's going on behind the scenes, and help you understand how you can programmatically tweak settings on a particle system to make it dynamic (i.e. programmatically make an explosion bigger or smaller based on an event in the game).

Open **XBlaster** and make sure the project still builds and runs OK. The star field simulation is going to sit beneath everything in your scene, so open **MyScene.m** to start setting up your star field.

Add a single method that will create and configure a particle system based on a few parameters:

```
- (SKEmitterNode *)starfieldEmitterNodeWithSpeed:(float)speed
                lifetime:(float)lifetime scale:(float)scale
                birthRate:(float)birthRate color:(SKColor*)color
{
}
```

Sprite Kit renders every particle displayed onscreen using a single texture attached to the particle system. This texture can be anything you wish and allows you to really customize the look of the particle system.

Your star field needs a texture that looks like a star, so let's borrow one of the techniques you learned in the previous chapter and generate a texture from an SKLabelNode.

Add the following in
`starfieldEmitterNodeWithSpeed:lifetime:scale:birthRate:color::`

```
SKLabelNode *star =
  [SKLabelNode labelNodeWithFontNamed:@"Helvetica"];
star.fontSize = 80.0f;
star.text = @"✦";

SKTexture *texture;
SKView *textureView = [SKView new];
texture = [textureView textureFromNode:star];
texture.filteringMode = SKTextureFilteringNearest;
```

The code above will be familiar from the previous chapter. It creates an **SKLabelNode** using the built-in Helvetica font and sets its size and text value. Notice you are using the star symbol from the Helvetica font, which should fit in nicely with your star field.

> **Note**: As a reminder, you can add the star character by going to **Edit\Special Characters...**, or use the shortcut **CTRL + CMD + SPACE**. This displays a popup from which you can select the special characters you want:

```
SKLabelNode *star =
  [SKLabelNode
  labelNodeWithFontNamed:@'
star.fontSize = 80.0f;
star.text = @"✦";

SKTextur
SKView *                                    [Sk
texture                         BLACK FOUR POINTED STAR €
texture.
```

You then turn this **SKLabelNode** into a usable texture using an **SKView**. You set the filtering mode to **SKTextureFilteringNearest** in order to get clean edges on the characters.

Now that you have a texture, you can create the actual particle system. Add the following code below the lines you just added:

```
SKEmitterNode *emitterNode = [SKEmitterNode new];
emitterNode.particleTexture = texture;
emitterNode.particleBirthRate = birthRate;
```

```
emitterNode.particleColor = color;
emitterNode.particleLifetime = lifetime;
emitterNode.particleSpeed = speed;
emitterNode.particleScale = scale;
emitterNode.particleColorBlendFactor = 1;
emitterNode.position = CGPointMake(CGRectGetMidX(self.frame),
                                   CGRectGetMaxY(self.frame));
emitterNode.particlePositionRange =
  CGVectorMake(CGRectGetMaxX(self.frame), 0);
return emitterNode;
```

This method is a convenience method allowing you to easily create particle emitters by simply calling this method and specifying the values you want to use inside the SKEmitterNode.

In the method, you first create a brand new SKEmitterNode. Then you set several properties on the emitter using the values that were passed into the starfieldEmitterNodeWithSpeed:lifetime:scale:birthRate:color:

- **particleTexture**: This is the texture to use for each particle – probably the most important property to set. The default value is nil and if no texture is set then a colored rectangle is used to draw the particle. If a non-nil value is provided then that texture is used to draw the particles and is colorized based on other SKEmitterNode settings.

- **particleBirthRate**: This is the rate at which particles are generated in particles per second. It defaults to 0. If the birth rate is left as 0.0 then NO particles are be generated by the emitter. In the following example this will be set to 1 particle per second.

- **particleColor**: The color that you set for this property is blended with the particles texture using the particleColorBlendColorFactor. The default value for this property is [SKColor clearColor]. In the following example this will be set to [SKColor lightGrayColor].

- **particleLifetime**: This is the duration in seconds for which each particle should be active. The default value is 0.0, and if this is not changed then NO particles are generated by the emitter. In the following example this will be calculated to a value allowing each particle to live long enough to move from the top of the screen to the bottom of the screen.

- **particleSpeed**: This is the initial speed for a new particle generated. It is defined in points per second and it's default value 0.0. In the following example this will be set to -24 causing the particles to move down the screen 24 points per second.

- **particleScale**: This is the scale at which each particle is rendered. The default value is 1 which means that the texture for each particle is rendered at the textures full size. Values greater than 1 will cause the particle texture to scale up and less that 1 will cause them to scale down. In the following example the scale will be set to 0.2 (20%) the original size of the texture being used.

- **particleColorBlendFactor**: This is the amount of color to apply to the texture when rendering each particle. It defaults to 0 , which means that the color of the texture is used and none of the color specified in `particleColor` is blended with the texture. A value greater than 1 causes the texture color to be blended with the `particleColor` using the `particleBlendMode` defined. In the following example the blend factor will be set to 1 causes the `particleColor` to be fully blended with the texture color.

- **position:** This is the starting point of new particles within the parent node's coordinate system. The default is (0.0). As seen already, the x position is set to the center of the screen and the y postion set to the very top of the screen.

- **particlePositionRange**: This is the maximum distance around the starting point that a particle will be generated. It defaults to (0.0, 0.0) meaning all particles will be generated on the starting point. As seen already the x position range is set to the width of the screen causing particles x position to be generated randomly across the width of the screen.

There are many other properties you can set on an **SKEmitterNode** which you'll learn about later in this chapter, but these are all you'll need for the star field.

Now that you've created and configured your particle system, add it to your scene to see what it looks like. Add the following code at the top of **setupSceneLayers**:

```
SKNode *starfieldNode = [SKNode node];
starfieldNode.name = @"starfieldNode";
[starfieldNode addChild:[self starfieldEmitterNodeWithSpeed:-24
              lifetime:(self.frame.size.height / 23)
                 scale:0.2
              birthRate:1
                 color:[SKColor lightGrayColor]]];

[self addChild:starfieldNode];
```

Here you are creating an **SKNode** to hold your star field, adding a particle system to it and adding the **starfieldNode** to your scene. You'll notice that when calculating the lifetime of the particles the window height is divided by 23 not 24, the speed of the particles. This causes the particles to live long enough to move completely off the bottom of the screen before disappearing. If you divided the height by 24 then you would notice particles suddenly vanishing when only half of their height has moved past the bottom of the screen.

Build and run the game. At this stage, you may be wondering why you don't see the particle system. If you play the game for 30 seconds or so, you'll begin to see the particles falling from the top of the screen.

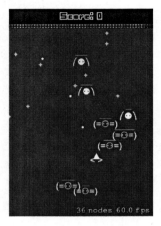

It's a good start, but the delay before the particles start appearing is quite annoying. Let's fix that.

Advancing a particle simulation

The delay is because the particle system is set up to make one particle system appear every second, and they move slowly down the screen. The problem is you want the entire screen to be populated with stars, but as-is it will take some time for enough stars to be generated and move down the screen for this to be the case.

Basically, you want to "fast forward" the particle system a bit before the game starts. Fortunately, `SKEmitterNode` exposes a method called `advanceSimulationTime:` that allows you to advance the emitter to a future point in time.

Go back to your `starfieldEmitterNodeWithSpeed:lifetime:scale:birthRate:color:` method and add the following line after you configure the emitter, just above the `return` statement:

```
[emitterNode advanceSimulationTime:lifetime];
```

Remember that each particle lives for an amount of time (in seconds) represented by the lifetime variable. Therefore, after lifetime seconds, the first star particle will have finished moving to the bottom of the screen and will be destroyed. Other particles generated after the first will be at varying stages throughout their lifetimes, filling the screen from top to bottom.

This is the perfect time to advance the simulation and represent the earliest possible moment where the star field fully fills the screen. Build and run the game again, and it will look much better:

Great! Any time you want to advance a particle system to a point beyond its initial state, you might find this method handy.

More basic particle system properties

As I mentioned earlier, there are a lot more properties on a particle system beyond the ones you've set so far. Let's play around with a few, then I'll mention all the others for a handy reference.

One of the most useful properties is the **emissionAngle**. This controls the direction in which angles are emitted (clockwise from the 6 o'clock position). This defaults to 0 (going straight down).

Let's see what this looks like. Add the following line to the bottom of starfieldEmitterNodeWithSpeed:lifetime:scale:birthRate:color:, before the call to advance the simulation time:

```
emitterNode.emissionAngle = M_PI_4;
```

This sets the emission angle to 45 degrees. Build and run, and you'll see the stars now emit at an angle of 45 degrees toward the left hand edge of the screen:

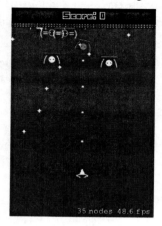

Being able to define the direction in which particles are emitted can be used when creating effects such as fountains where you want the water to move up the screen before slowing down and then moving back down the screen, as if affected by gravity. In combination with the **emissionAngleRange** property, it's also super handy when creating explosions.

For XBlaster you want the stars to just move down the screen, so remove that line from your project.

Another neat property you should know about is **particleAction**. This is a normal SKAction that will run on every particle in the system. Give it a shot by adding the following line to the bottom of starfieldEmitterNodeWithSpeed:lifetime:scale:birthRate:color:, before the call to advance the simulation time:

```
emitterNode.particleAction = [SKAction repeatActionForever:
  [SKAction sequence:@[
    [SKAction rotateToAngle:-M_PI_4 duration:1],
    [SKAction rotateToAngle:M_PI_4 duration:1],
  ]]];
```

This makes the stars rotate back and forth as they move down the screen. You might find setting a **particleAction** useful to add additional effects to your particle systems that the built in engine doesn't allow you to do. The example shown above could be used to simulate leaves falling from a tree and rotating back and forth as they fall to the ground.

Note: You must be careful when using particle actions in conjunction with the `advanceSimulationTime:` method. This method does not run any attached actions while advancing the particle system so you could end up with unexpected results. Performance should also be considered as running actions on a large number of particles can adversely affect performance.

There are a number of other core particle system properties beyond these. Here's a handy reference of what's available:

- **particleZPosition**: This is the starting Z position for each particle and defaults to 0.

- **particleBlendMode**: This is the blend mode used when rendering particles. Possible values are:

  a. `SKBlendModeAlpha`: Multiply the alpha component of the source texture with red, green and blue components then add them to the pixel values in the destination buffer.

  b. `SKBlendModeAdd`: Add the pixel values of the source texture to the pixel values in the destination buffer.

  c. `SKBlendModeMultiply`: Multiply the pixel values of the source texture with the pixel values in the destination buffer.

  d. `SKBlendModeMultiplyX2`: Multiply the pixel values of the source texture with the pixel values in the destination buffer, and double the result.

  e. `SKBlendModeReplace`: Simply copy the values of the source texture into the destination buffer.

  f. `SKBlendModeScreen`: Divide the pixel values of the source texture with the pixel values in the destination buffer.

  g. `SKBlendModeSubtract`: Subtract the pixel values of the source texture from the pixel values in the destination buffer.

- **particleColorRed/Green/Blue/AlphaSpeed**: The rate at which each color component changes per second, per particle. This defaults to 0.

- **particleColorBlendFactorSpeed**: The rate at which the blend factor changes per second. Defaults to 0.

- **xAcceleration**: The amount of x acceleration to apply to the velocity of each particle. Defaults to 0.

- **yAcceleration**: The amount of y acceleration to apply to the velocity of each particle. Defaults to 0.

- **numParticlesToEmit**: The number of particles the emitter should emit before stopping. Defaults to 0 meaning there is no limit. This is a useful property when creating an explosions as you can set a high birth rate that will initially generate a large number of particles, but as soon as the `numParticlesToEmit` value is reached particle emission will stop, while the particles that have already been created continue to move as defined

- **particleRotation**: The starting rotation to apply to each particle. Defaults to 0.

- **particleRotationSpeed**: The rate at which the amount of rotation should change in 1 second. Defaults to 0.

- **particleSize**: The initial size of each particle. Defaults to `CGSizeZero` causing the particle to use the assigned texture size as its initial size.

- **particleScaleSpeed**: The rate at which to modify the particles scale in 1 second. Defaults to 0.

- **particleAlpha**: The initial alpha value of each pixel. Defaults to 1.

- **particleAlphaSpeed**: The rate at which to modify the particles alpha in 1 second. Defaults to 0.

- **targetNode**: This allows particles to be rendered as if they belong to another node. This is an important property that allows you to create some unique effects and will be covered in more detail later in this chapter.

Range properties

There is another set of properties on `SKEmitterNode` designed to allow you to add random variance to a related property. You have actually seen an example of this already, when you used `particlePositionRange` to set some random variance for the `position` property so stars would spawn randomly across the screen.

Let's take a look at some other range properties, by adding some variation to the speed of the stars. Right now the stars are the same size and moving together, as though they are all on the same plane. That's not very convincing as it looks a little flat!

Add this line to `starfieldEmitterNodeWithSpeed:lifetime:scale:birthRate:color:`, before the call to advance the simulation time:

```
emitterNode.particleSpeedRange = 16.0;
```

The `particleSpeedRange` represents a random variance about the starting speed for each particle. It defaults to 0, so usually there is no variance. Here you set it to 16 so now the speed will vary randomly by plus or minus half the range value.

Run the game again and you'll observe each particle moving at a different pace:

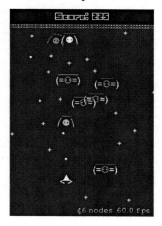

Just as you can modify the speed of a particle by a random value, you can also add random variance to other properties as well:

- **particleZPositionRange**: This will set the initial z position of each particle will be randomly determined and may vary by plus or minus half the range value. Defaults to 0.

- **particleColorRed/Green/Blue/AlphaRange**: Each particle will be created with random red/green/blue/alpha component values according to the range. Defaults to 0.

- **particleColorBlendFactorRange**: Randomize the initial blend factor of each particle. Defaults to 0.

- **particlePositionRange**: Every particle will start in a random position. Defaults to (0.0, 0.0) meaning all particles would originate from the same location.

- **emissionAngleRange**: Use this to randomize the angle at which new particles are emitted. Defaults to 0.

- **particleLifetimeRange**: Randomize the lifetime of each particle. Setting this will mean some particles will live longer than other particles.

- **particleRotationRange**: Randomize the initial rotation of each particle. Defaults to 0.

- **particleScaleRange**: Randomize the initial scale according to this range. Defaults to 0.

- **particleAlphaRange**: Randomize the amount of alpha applied to each particle. Defaults to 1.

Keyframe properties

There are four properties on SKEmitterNode left to discuss, and they all use a very cool technique: key framing.

The idea is, instead of just varying the property between a single value and a random range, with key frames you can change a property to several specific values over time.

For example, there is a property on SKEmitterNode called particleColorSequence that is a keyframe property (i.e. its type is SKKeyframeSequence *):

```
@property (SK_NONATOMIC_IOSONLY, retain)
  SKKeyframeSequence *particleColorSequence;
```

To use a keyframe property, you first initialize it, then you add one or more keyframes. Each keyframe has two properties:

- **time**: The time when the keyframe occurs within the lifetime of the particle. This is a value in the range of 0 (the particle is created) to 1 (the particle is destroyed). For example, if the lifetime of a particle is 10 seconds and you put 0.25 for the time for a keyframe, it would occur at 2.5 seconds.

- **value**: The value that the property will be set to when this keyframe occurs. For the particleColorSequence, it expects an SKColor instance for the value, such as [SKColor yellowColor]. For other properties, it may expect a different type of value based on the property (more on that later).

- Let's give this a shot and use the particleColorSequence to make the stars "twinkle" between white and yellow periodically over time. Add this code to starfieldEmitterNodeWithSpeed:lifetime:scale:birthRate:color:, right before the call to advance the simulation time:

```
// 1
float twinkles = 20;
SKKeyframeSequence *colorSequence =
  [[SKKeyframeSequence alloc] initWithCapacity:twinkles*2];
// 2
```

```
float twinkleTime = 1.0/twinkles;
for (int i = 0; i < twinkles; i++) {

  // 3
  [colorSequence addKeyframeValue:[SKColor whiteColor]
time:((i*2)*twinkleTime/2)];
  [colorSequence addKeyframeValue:[SKColor yellowColor]
time:((i*2+1)*(twinkleTime/2))];
}

// 4
emitterNode.particleColorSequence = colorSequence;
```

Let's go over this section in detail:

1. You will make the stars twinkle 20 times. Each twinkle is two keyframes: one where the star is white, and one where the star is yellow. So you create a keyframe sequence with a capacity of 40 keyframes.

2. Since there will be 20 twinkles, each twinkle will take 1/20th of the particle's lifetime. You then start a loop to create the keyframes for each twinkle.

3. As I mentioned in step 1, each twinkle consists of two keyframes: one where the star is white, and one where the star is yellow. You just specify the time to begin and end each keyframe, based on where it is in the loop. Each keyframe takes 1/40th of the particle's lifetime.

4. Finally, set the `particleColorSequence` to the keyframe sequence you just created. Note that by setting a keyframe property, it overrides the non-keyframe variants (`particleColor`, `particleColorAlphaRange`, `particleColorRedRange`, `particleColorGreenRange`, `particleColorBlueRange`, `particleColorAlphaSpeed`, `particleColorRedSpeed`, `particleColorGreenSpeed`, and `particleColorBlueSpeed` in this case).

Build and run, and enjoy your twinkling stars:

Keyframe sequences are very powerful. In this example you only alternated between two colors, but you could have used multiple colors at different times to create some very cool effects!

There are three other properties that support keyframe sequences:

- **particleColorBlendFactorSequence**: This allows you to accurately control the blend factor applied to each particle during its lifetime.

- **particleScaleSequence**: Using this sequence allows you to scale each particle up and down multiple times during its lifetime.

- **particleAlphaSequence**: This sequence gives you full control over each particles alpha channel during its lifetime.

- **particleRotationSequence:** This sequence gives you full control over each particles rotation value during its lifetime.

There are two important properties on SKKeyframeSequence. These are the interpolationMode and repeatMode.

The interpolationMode property determines how the values for times between keyframes are calculated.

The available values are:

- `SKInterpolationModeLinear`: The interpolation values are calculated linearly.

- `SKInterterpolationModeSpline`: The interpolation values are calculated using a spline. What this means is that the values calculated give the effect of easing at the start and end of a keyframe sequence. If you were scaling with this mode then the scale change would start off slowly, pick up speed and then slow down until it comes to the end of the sequence. This provides a nice smooth transition.

- `SKInterpolationModeStep`: The interpolation values between keyframes are not interpolated when using this mode. The value is simply calculated as that of the most recent keyframe.

The `repeatMode` property is used to control how values are calculated if they are outside the keyframes defined in the sequence. It's possible to define keyframes from 0.0 all the way to 1.0, but you don't have to. You could have a keyframe that runs from 0.25 to 0.75. The `repeatMode` property defines what values should be used from 0.0 to 0.25 and from 0.75 to 1.0. The available values are:

- `SKRepeatModeClamp`: This clamps the value to the range of time values found in the sequence. If for example the last keyframe in a sequence had a time of 0.5. Any time from 0.5 to 1.0 would return the last keyframes value.

- `SKRepeatModeLoop`: This causes the sequence to loop. If the time value of the last keyframe in the sequence was 0.5, then the sample at any time from 0.5 to 1.0 returns the same value as the sequence did from 0.0 to 0.5.

Parallax scrolling with particle systems

To improve your star field even more, you're going to add a second layer of stars that are smaller in size and slower moving. This will create a 3D-like effect and is commonly known as **parallax scrolling**.

Go back to `setupSceneLayers` and add a second particle system to the `starfieldNode`. Add this line before the line that adds the existing particle system child node:

```
[starfieldNode addChild:
  [self starfieldEmitterNodeWithSpeed:-16
                          lifetime:(self.frame.size.height/10)
                             scale:0.14
                         birthRate:2
                             color:[SKColor grayColor]]];
```

In this emitter node, the particles will be slower and smaller but there will be more of them.

Build and run to partake of the nifty illusion you've just created:

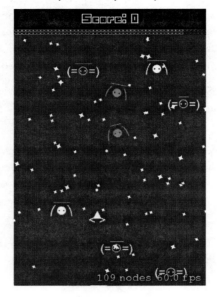

> **Note:** Remember that the order in which nodes are added determine the order in which they appear on the screen. If you had added this star field after the first star field, the smaller stars would render on top the larger stars.

Why stop there? Now let's create a third layer, adjusting the properties further to simulate even more distant stars. Add this line *before* the one you just added:

```
[starfieldNode addChild:
 [self starfieldEmitterNodeWithSpeed:-10
                          lifetime:(self.frame.size.height/5)
                             scale:0.10
                         birthRate:5
                             color:[SKColor darkGrayColor]]];
```

Build and run once more and peer into the depths of space:

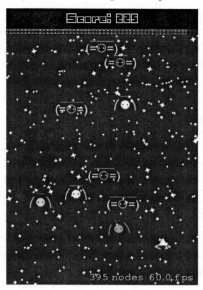

And there you have it – you built an impressive star field using particle systems and the parallax scrolling technique. You also applied what you learned in the previous chapter by using an SKLabelNode as a texture.

Visual particle systems

Your ship looks a little boring floating through space, especially with those fancy stars in the background. Let's improve its look by upgrading its engine to a state-of-the-art plasma propulsion system. First off, this requires an introduction to Apple's SKS file.

Creating an SKS file

Adding particle systems programmatically is not your only option. For iOS 7, Apple has added a new Xcode file type called an SKS file. This file allows you to store all the necessary settings for a particle system in a single file as part of your project, so you can take advantage of the built-in Xcode editor as well as easy loading and saving via NSCoding.

Let's create a new group in Resources to hold all of your particle systems. Highlight the **XBlaster** group in the project tree and select **File\New\Group** to add a new group. Call this group **Particles** and press enter to confirm.

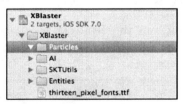

With the **Particles** group highlighted, select **File\New\File...** from the main menu. Select **iOS\Resource\SpriteKit Particle File**.

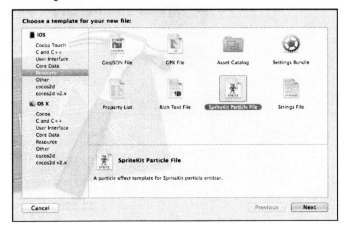

Click **Next** and on the next screen you will see a drop down that contains a number of different particle templates.

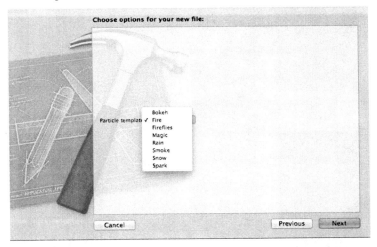

These templates give you a starting point from which to create your own particles. The items in the list are common particle configurations that you can adapt to your own needs. The following images show you what each of these templates looks like.

Bokeh   Fire

FireFlies   Magic

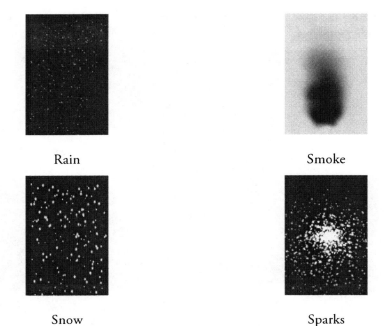

Rain   Smoke

Snow   Sparks

You could use any of these templates to get started on the engine effect, but fire is the closest to an engine flame so select the fire template from the list.

Click **Next** once more, enter **engine** for the file name (Xcode will automatically add the file extension), ensure the **XBlaster** target is selected, and click **Create**.

> **Note:** You'll notice that when you add your first particle system file to a project, Xcode automatically adds a second file, **spark.png**, alongside it. This image file is the default texture used when using particle templates built into Xcode apart from one, the Bokeh template has it's own image that is added to the project called **bokeh.png**.
>
> You do not have to use this texture for your particle system. If you would like to use your own texture simply add it to the project, then select the SKS file. In the utilities bar on the right, select the third tab (the **SKNode** inspector), and you can then choose your alternative texture file:

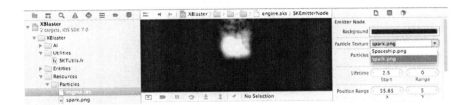

Loading an SKS file

The SKEmitterNode is fully NSCoding-compliant, making the loading process simple. NSCoding is an Apple technology that makes it easy to save and load objects from an archive. To find out more about NSCoding, take a look at the "Saving and Loading" chapter.

When you edit and save a particle system using Xcode, your SKS file will be updated and included in the application bundle, ready to be deployed to a device. To load a particle system in code, simply look for the particle system file in the application bundle and unarchive it. The result is a fully-configured SKEmitterNode, ready to add to your scene or another node.

Before you start tweaking any of the values of the particle system, let's just get the default particle system you made with the template loaded and rendering in the game.

Open **PlayerShip.m** and locate initWithPosition:. Since XBlaster calls this method when it creates your ship, it's a good place to add your particle emitter. After setting the name, add the following code:

```
SKEmitterNode *engineEmitter =
  [NSKeyedUnarchiver unarchiveObjectWithFile:
   [[NSBundle mainBundle] pathForResource:@"engine"
```

```
                                            ofType:@"sks"]];
engineEmitter.position = CGPointMake(1, -4);
engineEmitter.name = @"engineEmitter";
[self addChild:engineEmitter];
```

First you load the SKS file from your bundle and unarchive it to obtain an
SKEmitterNode. Next you position the particle emitter just below your ship, give it a
name and add it to the ship node.

That's it for loading a particle emitter and adding it to a node. Build, run and give it a
whirl.

Mayday – Mayday – Mayday – Fire detected!

That's not quite the look you were after, so this is a good opportunity to learn how to
edit your particle system using the built-in Xcode editor.

The Xcode particle editor

Not all properties of an SKEmitterNode are configurable through Xcode's built-in
particle editor such as the sequence properties for scale, blend factor and alpha, but the
most important ones are. To access the editor, highlight the **engine.sks** file in the
project navigator and ensure the inspector is visible on the right and set to the third tab
(the SKNode inspector):

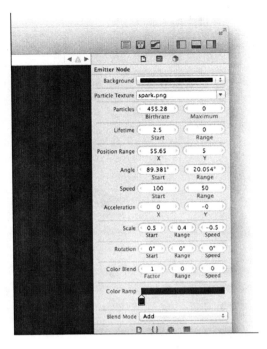

Play around with the settings in the inspector to change how the particle system behaves. Notice the `Particle Texture` property? It's set to use the default texture file, **spark.png**.

The first property for you to change is the color. The engine is supposed to be a state-of-the-art plasma propulsion drive and the flame effect doesn't cut it, not to mention there is no air in space so you wouldn't get a flame anyway.

Locate the Color Ramp property in the editor and click on the color stop at the left of the color selection panel. This will display a standard OS X color picker. Change the color in the picker and you will see how the color of the particles changes.

For the plasma engine you will need to set the color to a dark pink/purple. Select the **Color Sliders** tab and make sure that the drop down shows **RGB Sliders**.

Now enter **188** for the red value, **26** for green and **107** for blue making sure the Opacity slider is at **100%:**

The Color Ramp in the editor is actually creating a **particleColorSequence**. Double click towards the end if the color well and a new color stop will be added. The color will match the color of the nearest color stop to its left.

With the new color stop selected, change the opacity of the color to **0%**. You will now have a pink flame in the emitter editor.

You could continue to add colors to the color ramp and the particles would transition smoothly from one color to the next over their lifetime.

With the color set you can now start to edit the shape, speed and position of the emitter using the following steps.

Change the **Particles Birthrate** to **1000** with a **Maximum** of 0. This causes the emitter to generate 1000 particles per second. You want to keep the number of particles as low as possible to get the effect you want to help performance. Even though 1000 seems high, 1000 particles per second * 0.1 seconds lifetime per particle means only about 100 particles will be on the screen at a time.	
Change the **Lifetime Start** to **0.1** with a **Range** of **0.4**. This reduces the amount of time particles are alive which causes the length of the plasma trail to be reduced	
Change the **Position Range X** to **8** and **Y** to **0**. This causes the position of the particles on the x axis to range from **-4** to **4**.	
Change **Angle** to **-90** with a **Range** of **0**. This causes the particles to be emitted down the screen rather than up.	
Change **Speed Start** to **300** with a **Range** of 10. This causes the default speed of the particles to be 300 with a range of 10, so the speed would be in the range **295** to **305.**	
Change **Scale Start** to **0.25** with a **Range** of **0** and a **Speed** of **-0.3**. This scales the texture being used to 25% of its original size and reduces that scale by **0.3** per second.	

> **Note:** At the time of writing, Xcode's particle editor is still a work in progress. Selecting fields to edit is often difficult because the fields don't appear to respond. Pressing tab from any field brings the keyboard focus back to the texture field, so you will sometimes edit that without realizing it. And the editor crashes. A lot.
>
> This crash may be related to archiving the particle file, so once it crashes, it may keep crashing until you delete the particle file and start fresh. Hopefully Apple will resolve these issues soon.

After all that hard work you should now see a plasma trail in the editor fit for any state-of-the-art propulsion system.

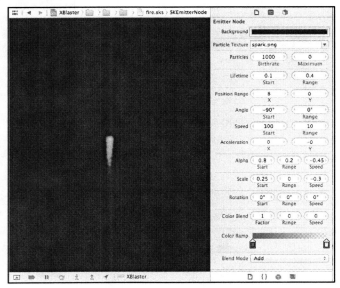

Give it another run to see how it's looking. Woo-hoo! You've upgraded the ship's propulsion and it looks like it's ready for a fight!

Play once particle systems

So far, you have made particle systems that run continuously (like the starfield effet and the ship's engine). This time, let's make a particle system designed to make an explosion effect once, rather than playing continuously like the others.

Specifically, let's have a little fun and ignite an enemy ship's plasma core when it dies instead of just making the ship disappear from the screen.

Highlight the Particles group and select **File\New\File...** from the main menu.

Select **iOS\Resource\SpriteKit Particle File**. Select Spark from the list of templates and press Next.

In the save dialogue call the file **enemyDeath** and press Create.

You'll now have a new particle file which you can start to edit. Select the **enemyDeath.sks** file to bring up the editor and change the configuration of the emitter based on the following steps.

Change **Particles Birthrate** to **10000** particles per second with a **Maximum** of 1000. Setting the maximum will cause the emitter to spit out 1000 particles at a time (last time you had 0 for unlimited). This particle system will only run once as the emitter will stop emitting particles once it has emitted the **Maximum** number of particles. You want this particular explosion to look substantial. Given the particles are very small, rendering 1000 particles, even on a mobile device, should not cause any problems. If performance is an issue then you can reduce the number of particles being generated.	
Change **Lifetime Start** to **0.5** and **Range** to 3. This reduces the overall lifetime of the particles getting you closer to the explosion effect you're creating. Things will look pretty similar to the previous step.	
Change **Position Range X** to **0** and **Y** to **0**. You want all the particles to originate from the same point in this example.	You will not see any noticable difference at this point.
Change **Angle Start** to **0** and **Range** to **360**. For an explosion in space you want particles to be ejected in all directions.	Things will still look pretty similar

Change **Speed Start** to **100** and **Range** to **20**. By having a small range on the speed you will end up with a ring of particles getting larger. That's more like the kind of impressive explosions you see in space films.	
Change **Acceleration X** to **0** and **Y** to **0**. This will stop the particles being pulled to the bottom of the screen and you will start to see a much more convincing explosion effect starting to appear.	
Change **Scale Start** to **0.1** and **Range** to **0.0** and **Speed** to **0.0**. This causes the texture being used to be scaled to 10% of its original size and for that size to not change over the lifetime of the particle.	
Change the **Color Ramp** color stop to white with 100% opacity.	Color Ramp
Add a new color stop to the **Color Ramp** and set **Red** to **255**, **Green** to **128** and **Blue** to **0.** Position this color stop very close to the first color stop so the color changes very quickly from bright white to orange.	Color Ramp
Add a third color stop to **Color Ramp** and set the color to **white** with **0%** opacity. This causes the explosion to fade out while getting brighter over time for a cool effect.	Color Ramp

Nice! You now have a cool looking explosion you can use when an enemy ship dies.

To add the explosion to the game you need to create a new layer in **MyScene.m** for the explosion emitters. This will allow you to add particle emitters into their own layer that is not attached to the enemy ships.

If you attached an emitter to an enemy ship it will move with the ship, which is not what you want. Adding the emitter to another node means you can move the ship around and the explosion stays where it is, just as it should be. You will see another method for detaching an emitters particles from the emitter node in the next section on the **targetNode** property.

Open **MyScene.h** and add the following property:.

```
@property (strong,nonatomic) SKNode *particleLayerNode;
```

Next create the layer and add it to the scene. Open **MyScene.m** and find the `setupSceneLayers` method. Just before you create the bullet layer and add the following code:.

```
_particleLayerNode = [SKNode node];
[self addChild:_particleLayerNode];
```

With the new layer in place you can now add the explosion emitter. As you are using this emitter when an enemy dies, **EnemyA.m** is the perfect place to load up the emitter file ready for use, allowing each enemy to run its own particle emitter when it bites the dust.

First add a private instance variable to store the particle emitter:

```
@implementation EnemyA {
    SKEmitterNode *_deathEmitter;
}
```

Next you need to load the SKS file from your application bundle. The game calls `initWithPosition:` every time it creates an enemy, so add this code to load the particle emitter just after the call to `configureCollisionBody`:

```
_deathEmitter =
    [NSKeyedUnarchiver unarchiveObjectWithFile:
      [[NSBundle mainBundle] pathForResource:@"enemyDeath"
                                      ofType:@"sks"]];
```

All that's left to do now is run the emitter when the enemy dies. Every time a bullet collides with an enemy the update method in the scene calls `collidedWith:contact:` In this method you reduce the enemy's health until it has none left and then spawn it at the top of the screen to start over again.

With this in mind, add the following code *after* displaying the score label, but *before* changing the object's position:

```
_deathEmitter.position = self.position;
if (!_deathEmitter.parent)
  [mainScene.particleLayerNode addChild:_deathEmitter];
[_deathEmitter resetSimulation];
```

You set the position of the death emitter in the same way that you set the position of the score label in the last chapter. Next you add your emitter to `mainScene`'s `particleLayerNode` if it hasn't already been added.

Finally, you call `resetSimulation` on the death emitter. This handy method completely resets the running state of the emitter and starts it off again. This is good to use for effects like this that you want to start from the beginning each time, play once, and then be done with it.

Build and run the game, and when an enemy dies you'll see your cool explosion as their plasma coils overload and their ship is blown into tiny little pieces.

Targeted particle systems

In the last section you added the particle emitter node to a layer in the main scene called **particleLayerNode**. This then allows you to set off a particle emitter explosion that would not follow the enemy ship when you reset its position to the top of the screen.

Another way of achieving this is to use the **targetNode** property of SKEmitterNode. The **targetNode** property allows you to define a node, other than the SKEmitterNode that should influence the emitter particles while they are alive.

By default this property is set to nil which means that all particles generated by an emitter are treated as children of that emitter. Therefore while particles are alive their properties are affected by the emitter nodes properties such as position and scale.

When particles are first created the calculations about their position and scale etc. are performed based on the emitter node, but from that point onwards and throughout their lifetime, the particles are affected by the properties of the node which has been defined as the **targetNode**.

Currently the plasma trail from the back of the players ship is static i.e. as you move the ship around the trail continues to flow straight out from the ship which doesn't look very good. To fix this you will use the **targetNode** property.

Open **PlayerShip.m** and add this import to the top of the file:

```
#import "MyScene.h"
```

Then add the following new method:

```
- (void)update:(CFTimeInterval)delta
{
  SKEmitterNode *emitter = (SKEmitterNode *)
    [self childNodeWithName:@"engineEmitter"];
  MyScene * scene = (MyScene *)self.scene;
  if (!emitter.targetNode) {
    emitter.targetNode = [scene particleLayerNode];
  }
}
```

This checks to see if the engine emitters **targetNode** has already been set and if not sets it to the **particleLayerNode** in the main scene.

Now run and build and as you move the player around you will see that the engine trail acts much more naturally.

You're almost done – just one more thing before you go.

Gratuitous Music and Sound Effects

We can't just let you leave before adding some fun music and sound effects to wrap up the game!

In the resources for this chapter, you will find a folder named **Sounds**. Drag it into your project, make sure **Copy items into destination group's folder** is selected, the **XBlaster** target is checked, and click **Finish**.

First go to **MyScene.h** and declare these two methods:

```
- (void)playExplodeSound;
- (void)playLaserSound;
```

Open **MyScene.m** and add this import to the top of the file:

```
#import "SKTAudio.h"
```

And add these private instance variables:

```
SKAction *_laserSound;
SKAction *_explodeSound;
```

Then add these lines to initWithSize, right after the call to setupEntities:

```
[[SKTAudio sharedInstance] playBackgroundMusic:@"bgMusic.mp3"];
_laserSound = [SKAction playSoundFileNamed:@"laser.wav"
  waitForCompletion:NO];
_explodeSound = [SKAction playSoundFileNamed:@"explode.wav"
  waitForCompletion:NO];
```

Then implement the methods you defined earlier:

```
- (void)playExplodeSound {
  [self runAction:_explodeSound];
}

- (void)playLaserSound {
  [self runAction:_laserSound];
}
```

Call playLaserSound in update:, right before running the action on the bullet:

```
[self playLaserSound];
```

And to play the explosion sound, open **EnemyA.m** and **EnemyB.m** and add this line in the collideWith:contact:, right after resetting the death emitter:

```
[mainScene playExplodeSound];
```

Also call this in PlayerShip.m at the top of collideWith:contact::

```
MyScene * scene = (MyScene *)self.scene;
[scene playExplodeSound];
```

Build and run, and enjoy your new game!

And that's it – believe it or not, you've learned almost everything there is to know about particle systems in Sprite Kit!

Throughout this chapter you have learned how to add some awesome visual effects to your game. You've also learned one of the coolest things about particle systems: the ease with which you can create so many different effects by changing just a few properties.

Now it's time to try out your newfound knowledge with a few fun challenges!

Challenges

Particle systems can be a lot of fun – with the built in particle editor, it's a lot of fun to mess around and see what you can create.

This chapter contains two challenges – one to get practice creating your own particle system in the built-in editor, and a second to add it into the game.

If you get stuck, you can find the solutions in the resources for this chapter – but give yourself a chance to succeed first!

Challenge 1: Create a venting plasma effect

For the first challenge you are going to create a new particle effect to represent plasma being vented from the players ship. Now, while I've never actually seen venting plasma for real, I've watched way too much Sci-Fi channel so the effect you are looking for is:

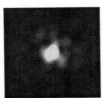

To kick things off you should create a new Particle file resource using the **Spark** template. That template already has particles moving in all directions so is a good place to start.

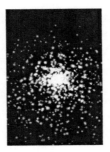

The following properties should be reviewed to turn the Spark template into the effect you are looking for:

- Particle birthrate

- Position range

- Speed

- Scale

- Color Ramp

By using what you have learnt in this chapter you should be able to adjust the properties above to achieve the venting plasma effect. If you get stuck you can check out the finished particle system inside the **XBlaster – Challenge 1** inside the resources for this chapter

Challenge 2: Add your new effect to the game

For the second challenge you are going to take the venting plasma particle effect you created in challenge 1 and add it to the game. To make this a little more interesting the venting plasma should only appear on the players ship when their health is 30% of less.

Here are some hints:

1. Add a new `SKEmitterNode` instance variable to **PlayerShip.m** called `_ventingPlasma`

2. Load the particle file called **ventingPlasma.sks** inside `initWithPosition:` making sure that it is set to hidden using its `hidden` property.

3. Add a check inside the update: method on the value of `self.health`. If this is equal to or below 30 and `_ventingPlasma` is not already visible then set its hidden property to NO

4. Don't forget to also check if `self.health` is greater than 30 so that you can hide `_ventingPlasma`.

Once you have made the necessary changes, build and run the project and once the players health gets equal or less than 30% the players ship should start venting plasma:

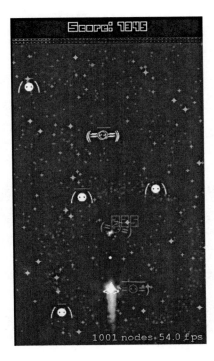

I'm sure you will agree that adding particle effects to XBlaster has really made a difference to the game. It feels more dynamic with the explosions, engine and leaking plasma. Having made it this far you really have earned the right to sit in the Captain's chair commanding all the particle effects at your disposal.

Just one thing left to say really…..”Make it so number one!”

Section III: Physics and Nodes

In this section, you will learn how to use the built-in 2D physics engine included with Sprite Kit to create movement as realistic as that in *Angry Birds* or *Cut the Rope*. You will also learn how to use special types of nodes that allow you to play videos, create shapes and apply image filters in your game.

In the process, you will create a physics puzzle game called Cat Nap, where you take the role of a cat who has had a long day and just wants to go to bed.

Chapter 8: Beginning Physics

Chapter 9: Intermediate Physics

Chapter 10: Advanced Physics

Chapter 11: Crop, Video, and Shape Nodes

Chapter 12: Effect Nodes

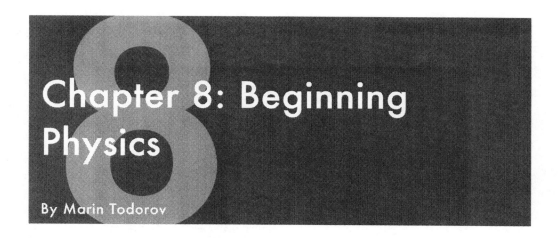

Chapter 8: Beginning Physics

By Marin Todorov

So far, you have learned how to move sprites around by manual positioning, or by running actions. But what if you want to simulate real-life behavior, like bouncing a ball against a wobbly pillar, making a chain of dominos fall down, or making a house of cards collapse?

You could accomplish the above with a bunch of math, but there's an easier way. Sprite Kit contains a powerful and easy to use physics engine that you can use to easily make objects move in a realistic way.

By using a physics engine, you can accomplish effects like you see in many popular iOS games:

- **Angry Birds**: Uses a physics engine to simulate what happens when the bird collides with the tower of bricks.

- **Tiny Wings**: Uses a physics engine to simulate the bird riding the hills and flying into the air.

- **Cut the Rope**: Uses a physics engine to simulate the movement of the ropes and the gravity affecting the candy.

Physics engines are great when combined with touch controls, because they make your game seem realistic, dynamic – and like you see in Angry Birds, sometimes destructive!

If you like this kind of reckless behavior and you want to know how to build your own physics-based game, you're in for a treat.

In this chapter, you'll get started with Sprite Kit physics by making a little test project. You'll add a few physics shapes with different properties, and add tiny sand particles that flow around them in a cool and dynamic manner.

In the next two chapters, you'll then build upon this foundational knowledge to create your own physics-enabled game with touch controls, realistic movement, and yes – being reckless (with cats)!

Sprite Kit physics

Under the hood, Sprite Kit uses a library called Box2D. This library performs all the physics calculations. Box2D is a great open source physics library – it's full featured, fast and powerful. In fact, it's already used in a lot of popular games on the iPhone, Android, BlackBerry, Nintendo DS, Wii, OSX and Windows – so it's nice to see it as part of Sprite Kit.

However, Box2D has two main drawbacks for iOS developers: it is written in C++ rather than Objective-C, and it could stand to be more user-friendly, especially to beginning developers.

Apple doesn't expose Box2D directly – instead, it abstracts it behind its own Objective-C API calls in Sprite Kit. In fact, Box2D is walled so well that Apple could choose to change the physics engine in a later version of iOS and you wouldn't know a thing.

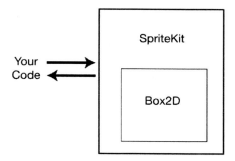

Long story short – in Sprite Kit, you get access to all the power of a super-popular engine, but through a friendly, polished Apple-style API.

Physics bodies

In order for the physics engine to control the movement of one of your sprites, you have to create a **physics body** for your sprite. You can think of a physics body as a rough boundary for your sprite that is used for collision detection.

The illustration below shows what a physics body for a sprite might look like. Note that the shape of the physics body does not need to match the boundaries of the sprite exactly. Usually, you choose a simpler shape so the collision detection algorithms can run faster.

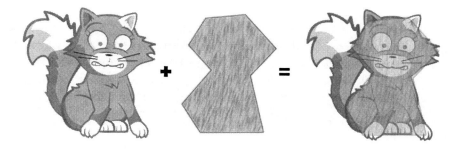

Once you set a physics body for your sprite, it will move similarly to how it would in real life – it will fall with gravity, be affected by impulses and forces, and move in response to collisions with other objects.

You can adjust the nature of your physics bodies, such as how heavy or bouncy they are. You can also alter the laws of the whole simulated world – for example, you can decrease the gravity so a ball would bounce back off the ground higher and will go further. On the image below two balls are thrown and bounce for a while –the red one in normal Earth gravity, the blue one in low gravity (for example on the Moon):

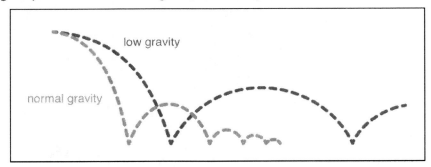

There are few things you should know about physics bodies:

- **Physics bodies are rigid**. In other words, physics bodies can't get squished or deformed under pressure, and do not change shape as a consequence of the physics simulation. For example, you cannot simulate a squishy ball that deforms as it rolls along the floor.

- **Physics bodies must be convex**. A body can be one of the following shapes: a rectangle, a circle, a chain, or a convex polygon. A convex polygon is a fancy way of saying "all of the inner angles of the shape must be less than 180 degrees." You'll learn more about why this is and ways to get around it in Chapter 10, "Advanced Physics."

- **Physics bodies are moved by forces or impulses**. Physics bodies are moved by applying forces or impulses. Impulses adjust the object's momentum immediately (such as the transfer of energy when two physics bodies collide), while forces affect the object gradually over time (such as gravity moving a physics body). You can apply your own forces or impulses to physics bodies as well – for example, you might use an impulse to simulate firing a bullet from a gun, but a force to simulate launching a rocket. You'll learn more about forces and impulses later in this chapter.

The great thing about Sprite Kit is that it makes all of these features, and many more, incredibly easy to use. In Apple's typical manner, most of the configuration is fully pre-defined. This means a blank Sprite Kit project already includes life-like physics with absolutely no setup.

Getting started

Let's try this out. Start Xcode and select **File\New\Project...** from the main menu. Select the **iOS\Application\SpriteKit Game** template and click **Next**.

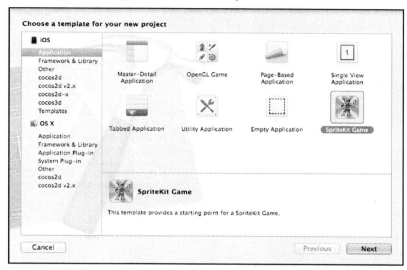

Enter **SpriteKitPhysicsTest** for the Product Name, choose **iPhone** for Devices, leave the **Class Prefix** blank and click **Next**.

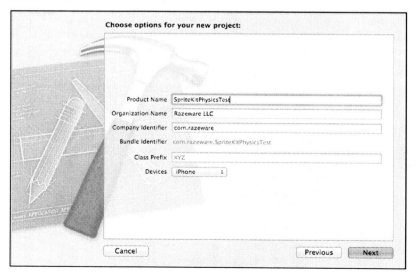

Choose somewhere on your hard drive to save your project and click Create. At this point Xcode will generate a simple Sprite Kit starter project for you.

You want this app to run in landscape rather than portrait. So just like you did in Chapter 1, "Sprites", select the **SpriteKitPhysicsTest** project in the Project Navigator and then select the **SpriteKitPhysicsTest** target. Go to the **General** tab and uncheck Portrait so that only **Landscape Left** and **Landscape Right** are checked.

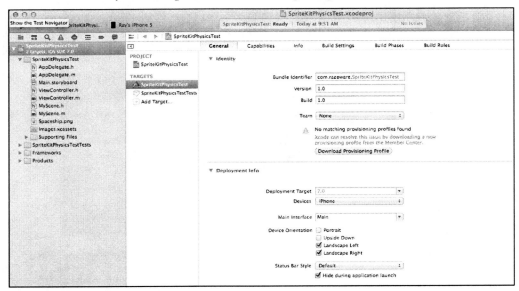

Also like you did in Chapter 1, "Sprites", open **ViewController.m**, rename `viewDidLoad` to `viewWillLayoutSubviews:`, and make a few minor changes as highlighted below:

```
- (void)viewWillLayoutSubviews
{
    [super viewWillLayoutSubviews];

    // Configure the view.
    SKView * skView = (SKView *)self.view;
    if (!skView.scene) {
        skView.showsFPS = YES;
        skView.showsNodeCount = YES;

        // Create and configure the scene.
        SKScene * scene = [MyScene
            sceneWithSize:skView.bounds.size];
```

```
        scene.scaleMode = SKSceneScaleModeAspectFill;

        // Present the scene.
        [skView presentScene:scene];
    }
}
```

To start with a blank slate, open **MyScene.m** and replace the contents with the following:

```
#import "MyScene.h"

@implementation MyScene

-(instancetype)initWithSize:(CGSize)size
{
  if(self = [super initWithSize:size])
  {
    // Your code goes here
  }
  return self;
}

@end
```

Here you create a scene with just an empty `initWithSize:` stub. In the rest of this chapter, any code you add to `initWithSize:` will go inside the `if` statement where the comment reads, "Your code goes here".

In the resources for this chapter, you will find a folder called **Shapes** that includes all the artwork you need for this physics test. Drag this folder into your project and make sure that **Copy items into destination group's folder (if needed)**, **Create groups for any added folders**, and the **SpriteKitPhysicsTest** target are all checked.

Destination	☑ Copy items into destination group's folder (if needed)
Folders	⦿ Create groups for any added folders
	◯ Create folder references for any added folders
Add to targets	☑ SpriteKitPhysicsTest
	☐ SpriteKitPhysicsTestTests

Build and run your project in the **iPhone Retina (4-inch) Simulator**, and make sure you have a blank black screen in landscape mode.

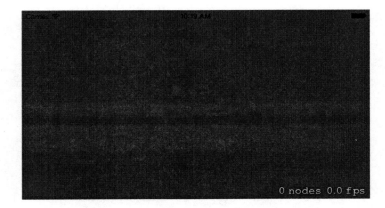

Now that you have a nice blank slate, let's add some sprites into the scene to work with. First add some private variables:

```
@implementation MyScene
{
  SKSpriteNode *_square;
  SKSpriteNode *_circle;
  SKSpriteNode *_triangle;
}
```

Here you define three SKSpriteNode instance variables that will store some test sprites you will add to the scene. Next initialize these sprites in initWithSize:

```
_square = [SKSpriteNode spriteNodeWithImageNamed:@"square"];
_square.position = CGPointMake(self.size.width * 0.25,
                               self.size.height * 0.50);
[self addChild:_square];

_circle = [SKSpriteNode spriteNodeWithImageNamed:@"circle"];
_circle.position = CGPointMake(self.size.width * 0.50,
                               self.size.height * 0.50);
[self addChild:_circle];

_triangle = [SKSpriteNode spriteNodeWithImageNamed:@"triangle"];
_triangle.position = CGPointMake(self.size.width * 0.75,
                                 self.size.height * 0.5);
[self addChild:_triangle];
```

This creates three sprites in the center of the screen — a square, a circle and a triangle. Build and run the project to check them out:

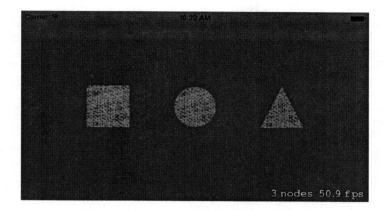

So far, this is review from what you learned in the previous chapters. It's time to introduce something new – let's make these objects physics-controlled!

Circle bodies

Remember two things from earlier in this chapter:

1. In order for the physics engine to control the movement of one of your sprites, you have to create a **physics body** for your sprite.

2. You can think of a physics body as a rough boundary for your sprite that is used for collision detection.

Let's try this out by attaching a physics body the circle. After the other code you added to `initWithSize:`, add:

```
_circle.physicsBody =
   [SKPhysicsBody bodyWithCircleOfRadius:_circle.size.width/2];
```

Since the `_circle` sprite uses an image shaped like a circle, you want to create a physics body of roughly the same shape. `SKPhysicsBody` has a simple factory method called `bodyWithCircleRadius:` that creates a circle-shaped body.

Believe it or not, thanks to Sprite Kit's pre-configured physics simulation, you are all done!

Build and run the project and you will see the circle drop with gravity:

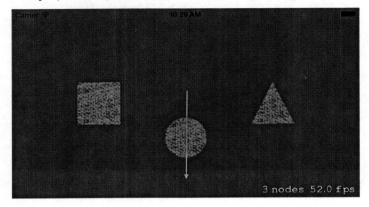

But wait a minute – the circle keeps going off-screen and disappears! For this app, you want the circle to stop when it hits the bottom of the screen.

Luckily, Sprite Kit provides an easy way to do this by using something called an edge loop body.

Edge loop bodies

To add a boundary for the scene, add this line to `initWithSize`:

```
self.physicsBody =
  [SKPhysicsBody bodyWithEdgeLoopFromRect:self.frame];
```

First, notice you are setting the physics body for the scene itself. Any Sprite Kit node can have a physics body, and a scene is a node too!

Next, notice you are creating a different type of body this time – an edge loop body, rather than a circle body. These two types of bodies have a major difference:

- The circle body is a **dynamic** physics body (i.e. it moves). It is solid, has mass and can collide with any other type of physics body. The physics simulation can apply various forces to move volume-based bodies.

- The edge loop body is a **static** physics body (i.e. it does not move). As the name implies, an edge loop only defines the edges of a shape. It does not have mass, cannot collide with other edge loop bodies and it is never moved by the physics simulation. Other objects can be inside or outside of the edges.

The most common use for an edge loop is to define collision areas to describe your game's boundaries, ground, walls, trigger areas or any other type of unmoving collision space.

Since you want to restrict bodies so that they can only move within the screen boundaries, you create the scene's physics body to be an edge loop with the scene's `frame CGRect`:

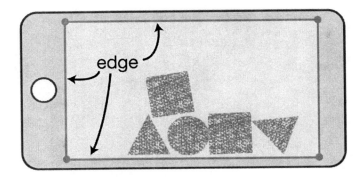

Build and run to see how this works. Now the ball stops when it hits the bottom of the screen, and even bounces a bit:

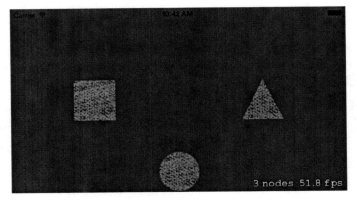

Rectangle bodies

Next let's add the physics body for the square sprite. Add the following line to the end of `initWithSize`:

```
_square.physicsBody =
    [SKPhysicsBody bodyWithRectangleOfSize:_square.size];
```

You can see that creating a rectangle-based physics body is very similar to creating a circle body. The only difference is that instead of passing in the radius of the circle, you pass in a CGSize representing the width and height of the rectangle.

Build and run, and now the square will fall down to the bottom of the scene too:

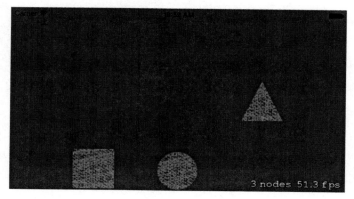

Custom shaped bodies

So far you've some very simple shapes – a circle and a square. This is great if your sprite is similar to these basic forms, but what if your shape is more complicated? For example, there is no built-in triangle shape.

Luckily, Sprite Kit provides a way for you to create arbitrarily shaped bodies, by giving Sprite Kit a **Core Graphics path** that defines the boundary of the body. The easiest way to understand how this works is by looking at an example – so let's try this out with the triangle shape.

Add the following code to the end of initWithSize:

```
//1
CGMutablePathRef trianglePath = CGPathCreateMutable();

//2
CGPathMoveToPoint(
    trianglePath, nil, -_triangle.size.width/2, -
_triangle.size.height/2);
```

```
//3
CGPathAddLineToPoint(
  trianglePath, nil, _triangle.size.width/2, -
_triangle.size.height/2);
CGPathAddLineToPoint(trianglePath, nil, 0,
_triangle.size.height/2);
CGPathAddLineToPoint(
  trianglePath, nil, -_triangle.size.width/2, -
_triangle.size.height/2);

//4
_triangle.physicsBody =
  [SKPhysicsBody bodyWithPolygonFromPath:trianglePath];

//5
CGPathRelease(trianglePath);
```

Let's go through this step-by-step:

1. First you create a new **CGMutablePathRef**, which you will use to draw the triangle.

2. You move your virtual "pen" to the starting point where you want to draw by using **CGPathMoveToPoint()**. Note that the coordinates are relative to the sprite's anchor point, which is by default its center.

3. You then draw three lines to the three corners of the triangle by calling **CGPathAddLineToPoint()**.

4. You create the body by passing the **trianglePath** to **bodyWithPolygonFromPath:**.

5. Finally, do not forget to call **CGPathRelease()**, because **CGPathCreateMutable()** gave you a retained copy of the path through the ARC bridge. To learn more about this, check out Chapter 2 and 3 of *iOS 5 by Tutorials*, "Beginning and Intermediate ARC".

Build and run the project, and now all of the objects will fall down:

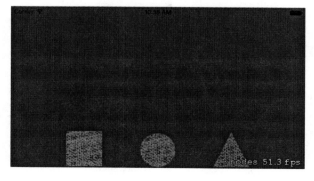

Visualizing the bodies

Each of the three objects now has a physics body that matches its shape, but right now you can't prove that the physics bodies are different for each sprite.

Let's pour some particles over the objects to observe their true physical shapes. Add this new method:

```
- (void)spawnSand
{
  //create a small ball body
  SKSpriteNode *sand =
    [SKSpriteNode spriteNodeWithImageNamed:@"sand"];
  sand.position = CGPointMake(
      (float)(arc4random()%(int)self.size.width),
      self.size.height - sand.size.height);
  sand.physicsBody =
    [SKPhysicsBody bodyWithCircleOfRadius:sand.size.width/2];
  sand.name = @"sand";
  [self addChild:sand];
}
```

In this method, you make a small circular body (just like you did before) out of the texture called **sand.png** and you position the sprite in a random location at the top of the screen.

Let's add 100 of these sand particles and see what happens! Add this code at the end of your other code in `initWithSize::`:

```
[self runAction:
 [SKAction repeatAction:
  [SKAction sequence:
   @[[SKAction performSelector:@selector(spawnSand)
                      onTarget:self],
     [SKAction waitForDuration:0.02]
     ]]
                  count:100]
 ];
```

You create a sequence of actions that calls `spawnSand` and then waits for 0.02 seconds. Then you execute the sequence 100 times on the scene instance.

Build and run the project. You should see small particles – the "sand" – rain down and fill in the spaces between the three bodies on the ground. Doesn't that look great?

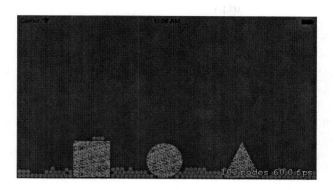

Physics body properties

There's more to physics bodies than just collision detection. A physics body also has several properties you can set, such as how slippery, bouncy, or heavy the object is.

To see how a body's properties affect the game physics, let's adjust the properties for the sand. Right now the sand falls down as if it is very heavy – much like granular rock. What about if the pieces were made out of soft, elastic rubber?

Add the following line to spawnSand:

```
sand.physicsBody.restitution = 1.0;
```

The restitution property describes how much energy the body retains when it bounces off of another body. Basically it's a fancy way of saying "bounciness".

Values can range from 0.0 (the body does not bounce at all) to 1.0 (the body bounces with the same force with which it started the collision). The default value is 0.2.

Build and run the project again. Oh my! The balls go crazy.

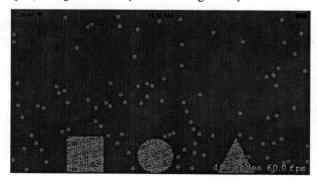

Note: Sprite Kit sets all properties of physics bodies to *reasonable* values by default. An object's default weight is based on how big it looks on screen; restitution and friction are set to values matching the material of most everyday objects, and so forth.

One more thing: while valid values for `restitution` must be from 0 to 1, the compiler won't complain if you supply values outside of that range. However, think about what it means to have a value greater than 1, for example. The body would actually end a collision with *more* energy than it had initially. That's not realistic behavior and it would quickly break your physics simulation, as the values grow too large for the physics engine to calculate accurately. It's not something I'd recommend in a real app, but give it a try if you want for fun.

Next, let's make the particles much more dense, so they are effectively heavier than the other shapes. Provided how bouncy they are, it should be an interesting sight!

Add this line to the end of spawnSand:

```
sand.physicsBody.density = 20.0;
```

Density is defines as mass per unit volume – in other words, the higher the density of an object is and the bigger it is, the heavier it will be. Density defaults to 1.0, so here you are setting the sand as being 20x as dense as usual.

This results in the sand being heavier than the other shapes – the other shapes behave as if they are styrofoam. Build and run and you should end up with something like this on the screen after the simulation settles down:

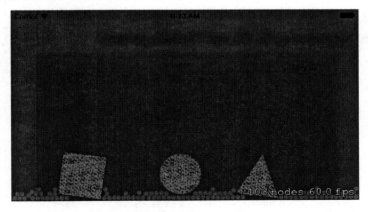

The red particles now literally throw their considerable weight around and push the bigger (but lighter) blue shapes aside. When you control the physics, size doesn't necessarily have to matter!

Here's a quick tour of the rest of the properties on a physics body:

- **friction**: This sets how "slippery" an object is. Values can range from 0.0 (the body slides smoothly along surfaces like an ice cube) to 1.0 (the body is quickly stopped while sliding along surfaces). The default value is 0.2.

- **dynamic**: Sometimes you want to use physics bodies for collision detection, but move the node yourself with manual movement or actions. If this is what you want, simply set dynamic to NO, and the physics engine will ignore all forces and impulses on the physics body and let you move the node yourself.

- **usesPreciseCollisionDetection**: By default, Sprite Kit does not perform precise collision detection, because it's faster to avoid doing this unless absolutely necessary. However, this has a side effect in that if an object is moving very quickly (like a bullet), it might pass through another object. If this ever occurs, you should try turning this flag on to enable more accurate collision detection.

- **allowsRotation**: Sometimes you might have a sprite that you want the physics engine to simulate, but never rotate. If this is the case, simply set this flag to NO.

- **linearDamping** and **angularDamping**: These values affect how much the linear velocity (translation) or angular velocity (rotation) decreases over time. Values can range from 0.0 (the speed never decreases) to 1.0 (the speed decreases immediately). The default value is 0.1.

- **affectedByGravity**: All objects default as affected by gravity, but you can set this off for a body simply by setting this to NO.

- **resting**: The physics engine has an optimization where objects that haven't moved in a while are flagged as 'resting' so the physics engine does not have to perform calculations on them any more. If you ever need to "wake up" a resting object manually, simply set this flag to NO.

- **mass and area**: These are automatically calculated for you based on the shape and density of the physics body. However, if you ever need to manually override these values, they are here for you.

- **node**: The physics body has a handy pointer back to the **SKNode** it belongs to.

- **categoryBitMask**, **collisionBitMask**, **contactBitMask**, and **joints**: You will learn all about these in Chapter 9, "Intermediate Physics" and Chapter 10, "Advanced Physics."

Applying an impulse

To wrap up with this introduction to physics in Sprite Kit, you're going to add some interactivity to your test app. When the user taps the screen, you'll apply an impulse to the particles – making them jump up like so:

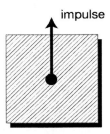

Remember that impulses adjust an object's momentum immediately, like a bullet firing from a gun.

To test this out, add this new method to **MyScene.m**:

```
- (void)touchesBegan:(NSSet *)touches withEvent:(UIEvent *)event
{
  for (SKSpriteNode *node in self.children) {
    if ([node.name isEqualToString:@"sand"])
      [node.physicsBody applyImpulse:
        CGVectorMake(0, arc4random()%50)];
  }
}
```

In this method you loop over all sprites in the scene and apply an impulse to the ones named "sand".

You create the impulse as a `CGVector`, which is just like a CGPoint, but named so that it's more clear it's used as a vector instead of a point. You then apply the impulse to the anchor point of each particle. Since the strengths of the impulses are random, the shake effect will look pretty natural.

Build and run, and give it a try. Note it's best to wait until the particles settle down before tapping the screen.

That impressive! But you can do even more than make the particles jump – why not shake the screen as well for an even cool effect?

Also add these few lines to the end of touchesBegan:withEvent:

```
SKAction *shake = [SKAction moveByX:0 y:10 duration:0.05];
[self runAction:
  [SKAction repeatAction:
    [SKAction sequence:@[shake, [shake reversedAction]]]
                     count:5]];
```

You create a new action that moves the whole scene up by 10 pixels, and then animates it back to its original position – and repeats this process 5 times.

Build and run the project again – you'll feel the difference!

> **Note:** The animation you just added had nothing to do with physics. That is, moving the scene isn't affecting the physics simulation; it's just making it *look* more spectacular, providing the illusion that the ground shook and caused the objects to move.
>
> If you enjoyed this shake effect and want to learn even more kinds of cool special effects like this you can add to your games, check out Chapters 17 and 18, "Juice Up Your Game."

You have now covered the basics of the physics engine in Sprite Kit, and you are almost ready to put these concepts to use in a real game. But first, it's time to push yourself to prove all that you've learned so far!

Challenges

This chapter has two challenges that will get you ready to create your first physics game. You'll create a custom shape, learn about forces, and create a dynamic sprite with collision detection.

As always, if you get stuck you can find the solutions in the resources for this chapter — but give it your best shot first!

Challenge 1: Octagon shape

Think back to how you created the custom path for the triangle shape earlier in this chapter:

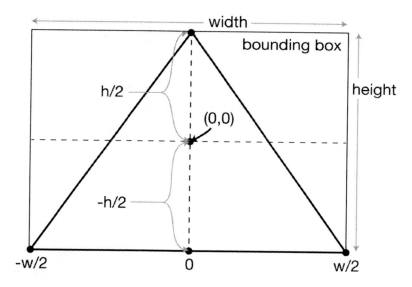

Remember you used `CGPath` methods to start at the bottom left corner of the triangle, and then move to each point around the edge.

Following a similar approach, replace the square shape in your game's scene with an octagon. Use the **octagon.png** image you already imported into your Xcode project within the Shapes folder.

When looking at the octagon, remember that point (0,0) is in the center. Each of its corner points, called a vertex, can be calculated by moving either ¼ or ½ of the width or height. Move x-coordinate in the negative direction for points to the left of the center point, and move y-coordinates in the negative direction for points below the center point.

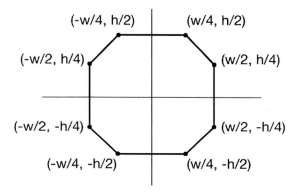

This is an important technique to understand, because if you know how to do this, you'll understand how to create physics bodies for any shape you may have in the future.

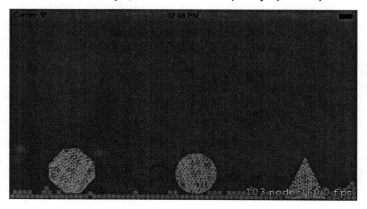

Challenge 2: Forces

So far you've learned how to make the sand move immediately when you tap by applying an impulse. But what if you wanted to make objects move more gradually over time?

In this challenge, your goal is to simulate a very windy day that will blow your objects back and forth across the screen. Here are some guidelines on how to accomplish this:

First add the helper function to generate a number within a random range from Zombie Conga:

```
#define ARC4RANDOM_MAX      0x100000000
static inline CGFloat ScalarRandomRange(CGFloat min, CGFloat
max)
{
   return floorf(((double)arc4random() / ARC4RANDOM_MAX) *
     (max - min) + min);
}
```

Then add these private instance variables:

```
NSTimeInterval _dt;
NSTimeInterval _lastUpdateTime;
CGVector _windForce;
BOOL _blowing;
NSTimeInterval _timeUntilSwitchWindDirection;
```

Finally add this stub implementation of **update**:

```
- (void)update:(NSTimeInterval)currentTime
{
  // 1
  if (_lastUpdateTime) {
    _dt = currentTime - _lastUpdateTime;
  } else {
    _dt = 0;
  }
  _lastUpdateTime = currentTime;

  // 2
  _timeUntilSwitchWindDirection -= _dt;
  if (_timeUntilSwitchWindDirection <= 0) {
    _timeUntilSwitchWindDirection = ScalarRandomRange(1, 5);
    _windForce = CGVectorMake(0, 0); // 3 - Replace me!
    NSLog(@"Wind force: %0.2f, %0.2f",
      _windForce.dx, _windForce.dy);
```

```
    }

    // 4 - Do something here!
  }
```

Let's go over this section-by-section:

1. This is the same code from Zombie Conga that determines how much time has elapsed since the last frame.

2. This keeps track of how much time until the wind direction should switch (a random time between 1-5 seconds). Once the time elapses, it resets the time and sets the wind force.

3. Right now the wind forces is set to be 0. Modify this to be between -50 and 50 along the x-axis, and 0 along the y-axis.

4. In section 4, apply this force to all nodes in the scene (both the sand and the objects).

Note that the difference between applying forces and impulses is that forces are something you apply every frame while the force is active, but impulses are something you fire once and only once.

If you get this working, you should see the objects slide back and forth across the screen as the wind direction changes:

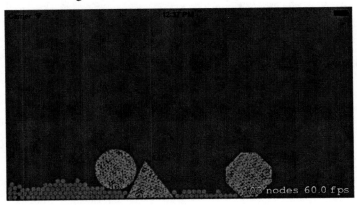

Challenge 3: Kinematic Bodies

In your games you might have some sprites you want to move with manual movement or custom actions, and others you want the physics engine to move. However, you still want collision detection to work even with sprites you move yourself.

As you learned earlier in this chapter, you can accomplish this by setting the `dynamic` flag on a physics body to `NO`. Bodies that you move yourself (but that still have collision detection) are sometimes called **kinematic bodies**.

Here your challenge is to try this out for yourself, by making the circle sprite move wherever you tap. Here are a few hints:

- Set the `dynamic` property of the circle's physics body to `NO` (after creating it).

- Inside `touchesBegan:withEvent:`, choose a single touch from the set and get the touch's location in the scene. You can use the same method you did in Zombie Conga to do this.

- Remove all actions from the circle, and then run a move to action to move the circle to the touch location.

If you get this working, you should see that everything is affected by the gravity, wind, and impulses except for the circle. However, the objects still collide with the circle as usual:

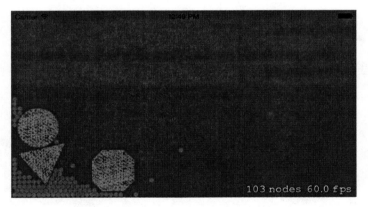

If you made it through all three of these challenges, congratulations! You now have a firm grasp of the most important concepts of the Sprite Kit physics engine, and you are now 100% ready to put these concepts to use in a physics-enabled game.

Over the next few chapters, you'll create a puzzle game that features a lazy cat, trampolines and, of course, out-of-this-world physics. Meow!

In the last chapter, you got started with Sprite Kit physics by making a little test project. You learned how to create shapes, customize physics properties, and even apply forces and impulses.

In this chapter, you will start building the second minigame in this book: a game called Cat Nap. Here's what it will look like when you're finished:

In Cat Nap, you take the role of a cat who's had a long day and just wants to go to bed.

However, some thoughtless human has placed a bunch of junk on top of the cat bed, preventing the cat from falling asleep!

Your job is to destroy the blocks by tapping them, so the cat can comfortably fall into place. However, if you cause the cat to fall out onto the floor or on his side, he'll wake up and get really cranky.

The puzzle is that you must destroy the blocks in the correct order so that the cat falls straight down. One wrong choice and – face the Wrath of Kitteh!

You will build this game across the next three chapters, in stages:

1. **Chapter 9, Intermediate Physics**: You are here! You will get started by creating the first level of the game, which is pictured above. You'll learn about debug drawing, physics-based collision detection, and creating levels from property list files.

2. **Chapter 10, Advanced Physics**: You will add two more levels to the game as you learn about interactive bodies, joints between bodies, complex body shapes, and more.

3. **Chapter 11, Crop, Video, and Shape Nodes**: You will add some special new blocks to Cat Nap while learning about additional types of nodes that allow you to do some amazing things – like play videos, crop images, and create dynamic shapes.

4. **Chapter 12, Effect Nodes and Core Image**: You will wrap up Cat Nap by adding image filters to parts of the game, resulting in some very cool special effects.

Let's get started – there's nothing worse (or perhaps funnier[1]) than an impatient cat!

---

[1] http://www.youtube.com/watch?v=70wuAWxOEZA

Getting Started

Start Xcode and select **File\New\Project...** from the main menu. Select the **iOS\Application\SpriteKit Game** template and click **Next**.

Enter **CatNap** for the Product Name, choose **iPhone** for Devices, leave the Class Prefix blank and click **Next**. Choose somewhere on your hard drive to save your project and click **Create**.

You want this app to run in landscape rather than portrait. So just like you did in Chapter 1, "Sprites", select the **CatNap** project in the Project Navigator and then select the **CatNap** target. Go to the **General** tab and uncheck Portrait so that only **Landscape Left** and **Landscape Right** are checked.

Also like you did in Chapter 1 "Sprites", open **ViewController.m**, rename `viewDidLoad` to `viewWillLayoutSubviews:`, and make a few minor changes as highlighted below:

```
- (void)viewWillLayoutSubviews
{
    [super viewWillLayoutSubviews];

    // Configure the view.
    SKView * skView = (SKView *)self.view;
    if (!skView.scene) {
      skView.showsFPS = YES;
      skView.showsNodeCount = YES;

      // Create and configure the scene.
      SKScene * scene = [MyScene
        sceneWithSize:skView.bounds.size];
      scene.scaleMode = SKSceneScaleModeAspectFill;

      // Present the scene.
      [skView presentScene:scene];
    }
}
```

There's two last things: to get this game started on the right foot (or should we say paw), you should disable the status bar and set up an app icon. To disable the status bar, open **ViewController.m** and add this to the bottom:

```
-(BOOL)prefersStatusBarHidden
{
```

```
    return YES;
}
```

And to set up an app icon, open **Images.xassets** and select the **AppIcon** entry. Then in the resources for this chapter, drag all of the files from the "App Icon" folder into the area on the right. You should see the following when you're done:

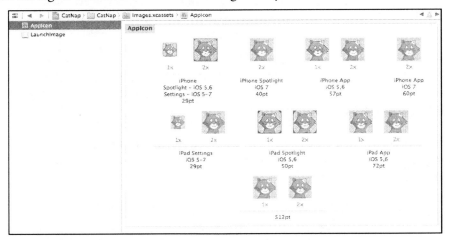

Build and run the project on the iPhone Retina (4-inch) Simulator. You should see the **Hello World** message nicely positioned in the center of the screen in landscape mode.

Before you can add sprites to the scene, you need some sprite images, right? In the resources for this chapter, you will find a folder called **Art** that includes all the images, sounds, and other files you need for Cat Nap. Drag this folder into your project and make sure that **Copy items into destination group's folder (if needed)**, **Create groups for any added folders**, and the **CatNap** target are all checked.

At this point, you should see folders for the backgrounds, sounds, and sprites in your Project Navigator:

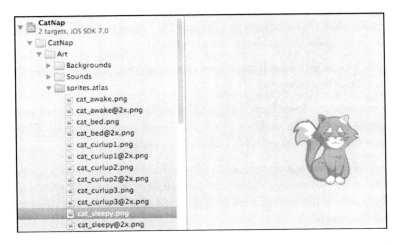

You might also notice something new about the way these files were imported. The folder containing the sprites (**sprites.atlas**) is colored blue – what's that all about?

In Sprite Kit, if you import a folder that ends with the extension **.atlas**, Sprite Kit will automatically pack all of the sprites in that folder into a special image called a texture atlas (also known as a sprite sheet). The texture atlas for Cat Nap looks something like this:

You'll learn more about sprite sheets in Chapter 25, "Performance". For now, you just need to know three main things about texture atlases:

1. It's good practice to put your images into texture atlases. This will make your game run faster and use less memory.

2. Generally you want to keep large images (like backgrounds) outside of texture atlases. Texture atlases are best for packing a bunch of small images together. This is why Cat Nap has one folder for backgrounds and another for sprites.

3. To put a set of images in a texture atlas, all you have to do is put the sprites in a folder that ends in **.atlas** and import them into your project. You create sprites the same way you usually would if the sprites were in individual files - Sprite Kit takes care of the rest behind the scenes!

> **Note:** Want to see how Xcode generates texture atlases for your app? Open Terminal, switch to Cat Nap's art directory, and run this command:
>
> ```
> /Applications/Xcode.app/Contents/Developer/Tools/../
> usr/bin/TextureAtlas sprites.atlas ~/Desktop/
> ```
>
> Xcode will then generate a directory called **sprites.atlasc** on your desktop that contains image files (one with normal art, and one with retina art) as well as a property list that describes where each sprite is in the images. Cool!

The project setup is done – back to physics!

Adding the cat bed

Now that you have some art ready to go, let's add the cat bed into the scene. Open **MyScene.m** and replace the contents of the file with the following:

```
#import "MyScene.h"

@implementation MyScene
{
    SKNode *_gameNode;
    SKSpriteNode *_catNode;
```

```
    SKSpriteNode *_bedNode;

    int _currentLevel;
}

@end
```

_gameNode will contain all objects in the current level, while **_catNode** and **_bedNode** are the cat and cat bed sprite nodes, respectively. You also declare a helper instance variable to keep track which level is the player solving right now.

Next add this initial version of your new `initWithSize:` method and a custom `initializeScene` method:

```
- (instancetype)initWithSize:(CGSize)size
{
  if (self = [super initWithSize:size]) {
    [self initializeScene];
  }
  return self;
}

- (void)initializeScene
{
  self.physicsBody =
    [SKPhysicsBody bodyWithEdgeLoopFromRect:self.frame];

  SKSpriteNode* bg =
    [SKSpriteNode spriteNodeWithImageNamed:@"background"];
  bg.position =
    CGPointMake(self.size.width/2, self.size.height/2);
  [self addChild: bg];

}
```

`initWithSize:` simply calls `initializeScene:`. There you create an edge loop around the screen, just as you did in the last chapter. You also add the background image to the center of the screen.

Next add this helper method to add the cat bed and initialize its physics body:

```
- (void)addCatBed
{
  _bedNode =
    [SKSpriteNode spriteNodeWithImageNamed:@"cat_bed"];
  _bedNode.position = CGPointMake(270, 15);
  [self addChild:_bedNode];
```

```
}
```

As you've done many times before, you create a new SKSpriteNode instance, load up an image (automatically fetched from your sprite sheet), and position it toward the bottom of the screen.

> **Note:** In Cat Nap, you're using fixed values for the sprite position in order to have shorter and cleaner code. Usually you would like those values in a configuration file or relative to the screen size.

Let's add a physics body to the cat bed. Append to the end of addCatBed:

```
CGSize contactSize = CGSizeMake(40, 30);
_bedNode.physicsBody =
  [SKPhysicsBody bodyWithRectangleOfSize:contactSize];
_bedNode.physicsBody.dynamic = NO;
```

The physics body doesn't necessarily have to match the sprite's size or shape exactly. For the cat bed you want the size of the physics shape to be much smaller than the size of the sprite itself. This is because you want the cat only to happily fall asleep when he hits the exact center of the bed. Cats are known to be picky, after all!

For this purpose, you first create a CGSize that is 40 by 30 points, and then you initialize a rectangular body for the bed with that size.

Since you never want the cat bed to move, you set its dynamic property to NO. This makes the body static, which allows the physics engine to optimize its calculations because it can ignore any forces applied to this object.

As a final step, add this code to initializeScene:

```
[self addCatBed];
```

Build and run, and you will see the background and cat bed:

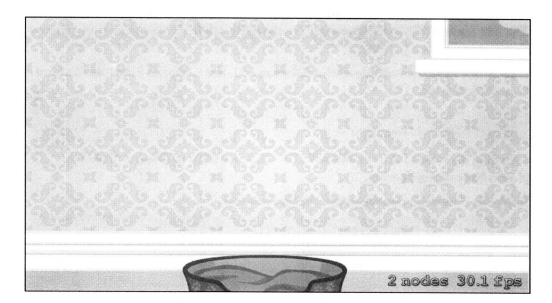

But right now there's no way to see that the physics body for the cat bed is actually smaller than the cat bed itself. Visualizing the shapes of physics bodies are incredibly handy for debugging purposes, so let's see how you can do that next.

Physics debug drawing

To visualize the physics bodies, you will write a method that can create a visual shape for a physics body. You will add to a category on SKSpriteNode so it's easy to use for any sprite.

In Xcode's main menu, select **File\New\File...**, select the **iOS\Cocoa Touch\Objective-C category** template, and click **Next**. Enter **DebugDraw** for Category, enter **SKSpriteNode** for Category on, and click **Next**. Finally, make sure the **CatNap** target is checked and click **Create**.

Open **SKSpriteNode+DebugDraw.h** and add these two method declarations inside the class interface:

```
- (void)attachDebugRectWithSize:(CGSize)s;
- (void)attachDebugFrameFromPath:(CGPathRef)bodyPath;
```

The first method adds a debug rectangle to the sprite, while the second adds an arbitrary shape created from a `CGPath`.

Now switch to **SKSpriteNode+DebugDraw.m** and, just above the `@implementation` line, add a variable:

```
//disable debug drawing by setting this to NO
static BOOL kDebugDraw = YES;
```

Changing the value of this variable will allow you to quickly enable and disable the physics body debug drawing.

Inside the class implementation, add the first method:

```
- (void)attachDebugFrameFromPath:(CGPathRef)bodyPath
{
  //1
  if (kDebugDraw==NO) return;

  //2
  SKShapeNode *shape = [SKShapeNode node];

  //3
  shape.path = bodyPath;
  shape.strokeColor = [SKColor colorWithRed:1.0 green:0 blue:0
                                      alpha:0.5];
  shape.lineWidth = 1.0;

  //4
  [self addChild:shape];
}
```

This is quick and dirty method to show the physics body:

1. If `kDebugDraw` is `NO`, you exit the method.

2. You create a blank `SKShapeNode` instance. A shape node is similar to a sprite, but instead of an image it can display a rectangle, a circle or an arbitrary path shape. You will learn more about shape nodes in Chapter 11, "Crop, Video, and Shape Nodes".

3. You then set the `path` property to define the node's shape. You also set the `strokeColor` and `lineWidth` to define how the shape should render.

4. Finally, you add the node as a child of the sprite itself.

If you change the body later, this debug shape will no longer represent it, but for the simple purposes of this chapter, it will suffice. Now also add the rectangle shape helper:

```
- (void)attachDebugRectWithSize:(CGSize)s
{
  CGPathRef bodyPath = CGPathCreateWithRect(
    CGRectMake(-s.width/2, -s.height/2, s.width, s.height),nil);

  [self attachDebugFrameFromPath:bodyPath];
  CGPathRelease(bodyPath);
}
```

This method gets a `CGSize` as its sole parameter and creates a `CGPath` rectangle by using `CGPathCreateWithRect`. In the end you simply use the method you already have – `attachDebugFrameFromPath:` – to attach the rectangular shape to the sprite.

Let's try this out. Open up **MyScene.m** again and, under the existing `#import` at the top of the file, add:

```
#import "SKSpriteNode+DebugDraw.h"
```

Now append to `addCatBed`:

```
[_bedNode attachDebugRectWithSize:contactSize];
```

All done. Run the project and now you can see both the bed image and its physics body:

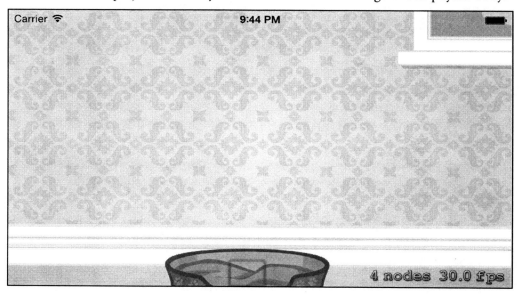

This visual feedback will help you better understand what's going on from a physics perspective. If you ever want to turn this off, you can disable it by setting kDebugDraw to NO in **SKSpriteNode+DebugDraw.m**.

Loading a level dynamically

You could continue to place down the rest of the sprites for this level by hard-coding values like you did for the cat bed, but there's a better way.

Open **Art\Levels\level1.plist**, and you'll see that I've created a file for you that specifies where the rest of the sprites should be placed in the level:

Key		Type	Value
▼ Root		Dictionary	(3 items)
▼ blocks		Array	(4 items)
▼ Item 0		Dictionary	(1 item)
rect		String	{{270, 30}, {30, 60}}
▼ Item 1		Dictionary	(1 item)
rect		String	{{330, 30}, {30, 60}}
▼ Item 2		Dictionary	(1 item)
rect	◎ ◎	String	{{270, 70}, {120, 40}}
▼ Item 3		Dictionary	(1 item)
rect		String	{{270, 100}, {120, 40}}
catPosition		String	{270,175}
bedPosition		String	{270,15}

This file is a **property list**. A property list is a type of file created by Apple that makes it extremely easy to store common types of data used in Objective-C programming, like strings, numbers, dictionaries, and arrays. Xcode contains a built in editor for property lists (which you can see above), and iOS contains built in methods to read and write property lists.

You can expand the entries in the property list by clicking the arrows next to them. Peek through the file and you'll see the root object is a dictionary, containing the following entries:

- blocks is an array of objects, each containing a rectangle that represents the bounds of the wooden block to place. You will be using these to add the obstacles "block"-ing the cat from his bed. Horrible pun intended! ☺

- catPosition is a string containing the initial coordinates of the cat.

- bedPosition is a string containing the initial coordinates of the bed.

The advantage of putting these coordinates in a property list is that you can change the level layout without having to change any code. In fact, someone who doesn't even know programming could edit one of these files to create a level, or you could create your own level editor that generates these files.

Your task is to read the data from this .plist file and create the objects at the appropriate positions.

Adding the cat

Let's start with the cat – we've made her wait long enough! Add the following method to **MyScene.m**:

```
- (void)addCatAtPosition:(CGPoint)pos
{
  //add the cat in the level on its starting position
  _catNode = [
    SKSpriteNode spriteNodeWithImageNamed:@"cat_sleepy"];
  _catNode.position = pos;

  [_gameNode addChild:_catNode];
}
```

By now you should be a champion at adding sprites to the scene. In this code, you simply create a new sprite out of cat_sleepy.png, set her size and position and add her as a child of _gameNode (you'll create this later).

And now, to get the simulation running, add the body of the cat to the end of addCatAtPosition::

```
CGSize contactSize = CGSizeMake(_catNode.size.width-40,
    _catNode.size.height-10);

_catNode.physicsBody =
  [SKPhysicsBody bodyWithRectangleOfSize: contactSize];
[_catNode attachDebugRectWithSize: contactSize];
```

This creates a physics body for the cat by using a size a bit smaller than the actual texture size – this way the physics body matches the outline of the cat in the sprite texture.

Next add this new method:

```
- (void)setupLevel:(int)levelNum
{
  //load the plist file
  NSString *fileName =
```

```
    [NSString stringWithFormat:@"level%i",levelNum];
  NSString *filePath =
    [[NSBundle mainBundle] pathForResource:fileName
                                    ofType:@"plist"];
  NSDictionary *level =
    [NSDictionary dictionaryWithContentsOfFile:filePath];

  [self addCatAtPosition:
    CGPointFromString(level[@"catPosition"])];
}
```

The method takes in a level number, reads the property list for that level, and sets up the scene appropriately. The first three lines simply build the file name and then load the property list into an **NSDictionary** called **level**.

Right now you're interested in the entry in the property list's dictionary called "catPosition". This is a string, so you need to convert it to a point using the **CGPointFromString()** method. You then pass it to the **addCatAtPosition:** method you wrote earlier.

Last but not least, you need to call **setupLevel:**. Add these lines to the end of **initializeScene**:

```
  _gameNode = [SKNode node];
  [self addChild:_gameNode];

  _currentLevel = 1;
  [self setupLevel: _currentLevel];
```

Here you create a new node, stored in **_gameNode**, where all the action will be happening and you add it to your scene.

Then you set the value of **_currentLevel** to 1 and pass it to **setupLevel:** so that it loads level1.plist and builds your level on the scene.

Build and run, and your cat will drop into the screen:

The cat has reached her bed, but she doesn't get to sleep quite yet – there's a pesky human causing trouble!

Adding the blocks

You might have guessed it already, that pesky human is you. ☺ In this section, you will add the blocks that are preventing the cat from her well-deserved rest. Poor kitty!

To do this, add the following new methods:

```
-(void)addBlocksFromArray:(NSArray*)blocks
{
  // 1
  for (NSDictionary *block in blocks) {

    //2
    SKSpriteNode *blockSprite =
      [self addBlockWithRect:CGRectFromString(block[@"rect"])];
    [_gameNode addChild:blockSprite];
  }
}

-(SKSpriteNode*)addBlockWithRect:(CGRect)blockRect
{
  // 3
  NSString *textureName = [NSString stringWithFormat:
    @"%.fx%.f.png",blockRect.size.width, blockRect.size.height];

  // 4
  SKSpriteNode *blockSprite =
  [SKSpriteNode spriteNodeWithImageNamed:textureName];
  blockSprite.position = blockRect.origin;
```

```
// 5
CGRect bodyRect = CGRectInset(blockRect, 2, 2);
blockSprite.physicsBody =
  [SKPhysicsBody bodyWithRectangleOfSize:bodyRect.size];

//6
[blockSprite attachDebugRectWithSize:blockSprite.size];

return blockSprite;
}
```

Let's go over this bit-by-bit:

1. In the first method `addBlocksFromArray:` you take in a list of blocks (as defined in the .plist file) and you loop over that list.

2. For each block you use `CGRectFromString` to create a `CGRect` from the **rect** key of each block object, then call another helper method which creates a block sprite for you. Finally, you add that sprite to the scene by using `addChild:`.

3. In the second method `addBlockWithRect:`, depending on the block size, you need an image in the format [width]x[height].png. For example, the first block in the property list is 30 by 60 pixels, so it looks for **30x60.png**.

4. As next step you create the sprite with the texture name you already have and place it at the proper position.

5. You use the handy `CGRectInset` function to shrink the bounding box a bit and you create a physics body from the result. You shrink the box so that the block sprites will rest against each other tightly.

6. Finally, you add a debug shape for the block's body.

Now back in `setupLevel:` call your new method:

```
[self addBlocksFromArray:level[@"blocks"]];
```

Build and run, and oh my - the level already looks impressive!

Note how the blocks are resting on top of the bed's body somewhat in the air, rather than resting on the ground or in the bed. Don't worry about it for now – you will make a short detour in the next section and then you will come back to fixing this.

Now that all of your level is set up, let's get the player in the right mood for puzzles by starting up some soothing but cute background music.

Gratuitous background music

Just like you did in Chapter 6, "Labels", you'll integrate our handy SKTUtils library so you can easily play some background music. In the next chapter some of the other methods will come in handy as well.

You can find **SKTUtils** in the root folder for this book. Drag the entire **SKTUtils** folder into the project navigator in Xcode. Make sure **Copy items into destination group's folder (if needed)** and the **CatNap target** are both checked. Click **Finish**.

Then jump to the top of **MyScene.m** and import `SKTAudio`:

```
#import "SKTAudio.h"
```

Finally, add this code to `setupLevel:` to start the music:

```
[[SKTAudio sharedInstance] playBackgroundMusic:@"bgMusic.mp3"];
```

Build and run, and enjoy the happy tune!

Controlling your bodies

So far you know how to create physics bodies for sprites and let the physics engine do its thing.

But in Cat Nap, you want a bit more control than that:

- **Categorizing bodies.** You want to make the cat bed and blocks not collide. To do this, you'll need a way to categorize bodies and set up collision flags.

- **Finding bodies.** You want to be able to tap a block to destroy it. To do this, you'll need a way to find a body at a given point.

- **Detecting collisions between bodies.** You want to detect when the cat hits the cat bed, so she can get her beauty sleep. To do this, you'll need a way to detect collisions.

In the next three sections, you will investigate these areas. By the time you're done, you'll have implemented the most important parts of the minigame!

Categorizing bodies

In Sprite Kit, the default behavior is for all physics bodies to collide with all other physics bodies. If two objects are placed at the same point (like the bottom left brick and the cat bed), one of them will be automatically moved aside by the physics engine. This is why the bottom left block is horizontal (it should be vertical like the lower right block):

The good news is you can override this default behavior and specify whether two physics bodies collide with each other.

There are two steps to do this:

1. **Define the categories.** The first step is to define categories of physics bodies – for example, block bodies, cat bodies, cat bed bodies, etc.

   In Sprite Kit, you define those categories using a bit mask. A bit mask is a way to use a 32-bit integer as a set of 32 individual flags you can turn on or off.

   Note this means at most you can have 32 unique object categories in your app – so choose your categories wisely!

2. **Set the category bit mask.** Once you have your set of categories, you specify what categories each physics body belongs to by setting its category bit mask.

3. **Set the collision bit mask.** You should also specify the collision bit mask for each physics body. This controls what categories of bodies it should collide with.

Let's start with step 1 and define the categories for Cat Nap. Open **MyScene.m** and under the last **#import**, add this enumeration:

```
typedef NS_OPTIONS(uint32_t, CNPhysicsCategory)
{
  CNPhysicsCategoryCat   = 1 << 0,  // 0001 = 1
  CNPhysicsCategoryBlock = 1 << 1,  // 0010 = 2
  CNPhysicsCategoryBed   = 1 << 2,  // 0100 = 4
};
```

This defines three categories: cats, blocks, and cat beds. If you're unfamiliar with the bitwise shift operator shown here ("<<"), you can think of "1 << 0" as "category #0", "1 << 1" as "category 2", and so on – up to 32 categories max.

> **Note:** You can read more about bitwise operations here:
> http://en.wikipedia.org/wiki/Bitwise_operation

Let's move to step 2 and 3 and set the category and collision bit masks for each object, starting with the blocks. Inside **addBlocksFromArray:**, add the following lines just *above* the line where you add **blockSprite** to **_gameNode**:

```
blockSprite.physicsBody.categoryBitMask =
  CNPhysicsCategoryBlock;
blockSprite.physicsBody.collisionBitMask =
  CNPhysicsCategoryBlock | CNPhysicsCategoryCat;
```

Here you assign each block's physics body to the block category, and set them to collide with both the cat and block categories (blocks should collide with other blocks).

Notice that to set `collisionBitMask` with a value referring to more than one body category, you use the bitwise OR operator (denoted by a single pipe symbol).

Next move to the cat. Add the following line to `addCatAtPosition:` to assign the cat's category:

```
_catNode.physicsBody.categoryBitMask = CNPhysicsCategoryCat;
```

For the cat, you'll leave the `collisionBitMask` at its default value, which is all bits set. That means it will collide with any category of physics object.

Finally, head to `addCatBed` and add at the end:

```
_bedNode.physicsBody.categoryBitMask = CNPhysicsCategoryBed;
```

This sets the bed physics body's category to the bed category. You don't need to set the `collisionBitMask` in this case either, for reasons explained in the note below.

Note: A physics body's `collisionBitMask` value specifies which categories of objects should affect the movement of *that* body when those two bodies collide. But remember, you set the bed's **dynamic** property to **NO**, which already ensures that no forces will ever affect the bed. So there is no need to set the bed's `collisionBitMask`.

Generally, there is never a reason to set the `collisionBitMask` for an object whose **dynamic** property is set to **NO**. Likewise, edge loop physics are always treated as if their **dynamic** property is **NO**, even if it isn't. So there is never a reason to set the `collisionBitMask` for an edge loop, either.

Because of the way you set up the various collision bit masks, blocks will now fall through the cat bed and rest on the floor, but the cat will stop and sit on the bed – if it falls right onto it, that is.

Build and run the project, and you'll see the bottom left block is now vertical like it should be, and no longer collides with the cat bed:

Now you know now how to make a group of bodies pass through some bodies and collide with others.

This technique can come in handy for many types of games. For example, in some games you want players on the same team not to collide with each other, but to collide with enemies from the other team.

Finding bodies

Often in games, you want to be able to find out what physics bodies are at a given point. Sprite Kit provides a method on the physics world called `enumerateBodiesAtPoint:usingBlock:` that does exactly that:

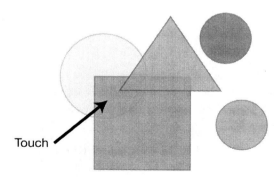

Touch

In Cat Nap you'll use this method to find any physics body where the user taps. If there's a block at the location, you'll destroy it.

To try this method out, implement `touchesBegan:` like so:

```
- (void)touchesBegan:(NSSet *)touches withEvent:(UIEvent *)event
{
  [super touchesBegan:touches withEvent:event];

  // 1
  UITouch *touch = [touches anyObject];
  CGPoint location = [touch locationInNode:self];

  // 2
  [self.physicsWorld enumerateBodiesAtPoint:location
                                 usingBlock:
    ^(SKPhysicsBody *body, BOOL *stop) {
      // 3
      if (body.categoryBitMask == CNPhysicsCategoryBlock) {
        [body.node removeFromParent];
        *stop = YES; // 4

        // 5
        [self runAction:[SKAction playSoundFileNamed:@"pop.mp3"
                                  waitForCompletion:NO]];
      }
    }];
}
```

Let's go over this section by section:

1. You get the position of the touch in the scene, same as you did for Zombie Conga.

2. You enumerate over all the bodies in the physics world of the current scene by passing the touch location and a block. The block takes in two parameters, a body and a boolean parameter called `stop`.

3. Since all destructible bodies are of the category `CNPhysicsCategoryBlock`, it's easy to determine whether to destroy the current body. If so, you use the body's `node` property to access the `SKNode` represented by this physics body and call `removeFromParent` on it.

4. Finally you set `stop` to `YES`, so that the enumerator won't loop over the rest of the world's bodies. You want only one body destroyed at a time.

5. As a final touch (yet another horrible pun intended!): make the blocks *pop*.

Build and run the project, and now you should be able to tap blocks to destroy them:

Try destroying the blocks in different orders – the following illustration shows the way to correctly land the cat in the cat bed, or send her tumbling! Note you haven't added any win/lose capability yet, so you'll have to restart the game each try.

Detecting collisions between bodies

Very often in games, you'd like to know if certain bodies are in contact. Two or more bodies can "touch" or pass through each other, depending upon whether or not they're set to collide. In both cases they are in contact:

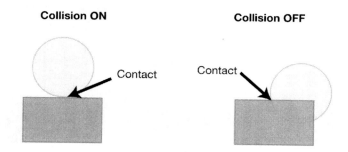

In Cat Nap, you want to know whether certain pairs of bodies touch:

1. If the **cat touches the floor**, it means that it's on the ground, but out of its bed, and the player fails the level.

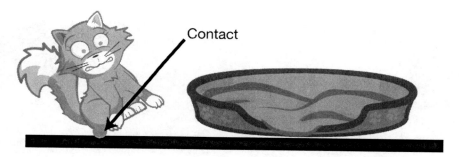

2. If the **cat touches the bed**, it means it landed successfully on the bed, and the player solved the level.

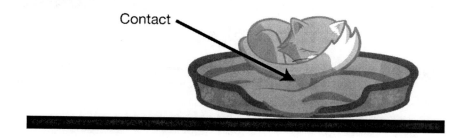

Sprite Kit makes it easy for you to receive a callback when two physics bodies collide. The first step to do this is to implement the SKPhysicsContactDelegate method. In Cat Nap, you will implement these methods in MyScene.

Scroll to the top of **MyScene.m** and, just above the @implementation line, add:

```
@interface MyScene ()<SKPhysicsContactDelegate>
@end
```

The SKPhysicsContactDelegate protocol defines two methods you can implement in MyScene:

- didBeginContact: will tell you when two bodies have first made contact.

- didEndContact: will tell you when two bodies end their contact.

The diagram below shows how these methods will be called for the case where two bodies pass through each other:

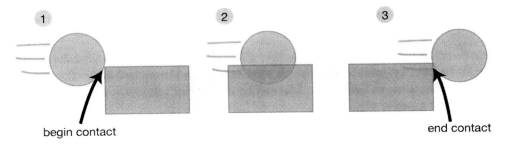

begin contact   end contact

You'll most often be interested in didBeginContact:, because much of your game logic will occur when two objects touch.

However, there are times when you'll want to know when objects stop touching. For example, you may want to use the physics engine to test when a player is within a trigger area. Perhaps entering the area sounds an alarm, while leaving the area silences it. In a case such as this, you'll need to implement didEndContact: as well.

Let's try this out. The first thing is you need to add a new category constant for the edges of the screen, since you want to be able to detect when the cat collides with the floor. To do this, scroll to the top of **MyScene.m** and add this value to the CNPhysicsCategory enumeration:

```
CNPhysicsCategoryEdge   = 1 << 3,  // 1000 = 8
```

Then find this line inside `initializeScene`:

```
self.physicsBody =
  [SKPhysicsBody bodyWithEdgeLoopFromRect:self.frame];
```

And just below, add:

```
self.physicsWorld.contactDelegate = self;
self.physicsBody.categoryBitMask = CNPhysicsCategoryEdge;
```

First you set `MyScene` as the contact delegate of the scene's physics world. Then you assign `CNPhysicsCategoryEdge` as the body's category.

Build and run to see the result of your actions so far.

Hmm… that's not right. All the blocks fall through the edge! And just seconds ago the project worked fine.

Let me pinpoint the problem for you right away: the world edge now has a category (`CNPhysicsCategoryEdge`) but the blocks are not set to collide with it. Therefore, they fall through the floor.

The cat, on the other hand, is set to collide with anything. Because you kept the default value for its `collisionBitMask`, the cat rests happily on the cat bed or the floor, whichever it happens to land upon. Meanwhile the cat bed's `dynamic` property is set to `NO`, so it can't move at all.

Fix that now. Inside the `addBlocksFromArray:` method, find:

```
blockSprite.physicsBody.collisionBitMask =
  CNPhysicsCategoryBlock | CNPhysicsCategoryCat;
```

And add to it the edge bit mask, like so:

```
blockSprite.physicsBody.collisionBitMask =
  CNPhysicsCategoryBlock | CNPhysicsCategoryCat |
    CNPhysicsCategoryEdge;
```

It's all good now – build and run the project again and everything will appear as normal.

Now for the new part. Just like you've learned about `categoryBitMask` (to set what categories a physics body belongs to), and `collisionBitMask` (to set what categories a physics bodies collides with), there's another bit mask: `contactTestBitMask`.

`contactTestBitMask` is used to set the categories a physics body should detect contacts with. Once you set this up, your physics contact delegate methods will be called.

You want to receive callbacks when the cat collides with either the edge or bed bodies, so add this line to the end of `addCatAtPosition`:

```
_catNode.physicsBody.contactTestBitMask =
  CNPhysicsCategoryBed | CNPhysicsCategoryEdge;
```

That's all the configuring you need. Now to handle those contact messages, add this contact delegate protocol method to your class:

```
- (void)didBeginContact:(SKPhysicsContact *)contact
{
  uint32_t collision = (contact.bodyA.categoryBitMask |
                        contact.bodyB.categoryBitMask);
  if (collision == (CNPhysicsCategoryCat|CNPhysicsCategoryBed))
  {
    NSLog(@"SUCCESS");
  }

  if (collision == (CNPhysicsCategoryCat|CNPhysicsCategoryEdge))
  {
    NSLog(@"FAIL");
  }
}
```

Have a look at the parameter this method receives. It is of class `SKPhysicsContact` and tells you a lot about the contacting bodies:

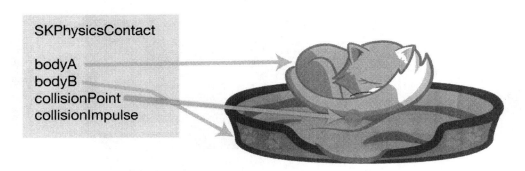

There is no way to guarantee a particular object will be in bodyA or bodyB. There are various ways you can find out, such as by checking the body's category or for some property of the body's node.

But this simple game contains only four categories, which correspond to the int values 1, 2, 4, 8. That makes it simple to check for contact combinations – you can use addition for easy-to-read and accurate checks.

Categories	2-Category Combinations
Cat: 1	Cat (1) | Block (2) = 3
Block: 2	Block (2) | Block (2) = 2
Bed: 4	Cat (1) | Bed (4) = 5
Edge: 8	... other combinations

Note: If you feel the ground loosening under your feet when you hear about comparing bitmasks and such, feel free to read this short but informative article: http://en.wikipedia.org/wiki/Mask_(computing).

Inside your implementation of `didBeginContact:`, you first add the categories of the two bodies that collided and store the result in `collision`. The two `if` statements check `collision` for the combinations of bodies in which you are interested:

• If the two contacting bodies are the cat and the bed, print out *SUCCESS*.

• If the two contacting bodies are the cat and the edge, print out *FAIL*.

> **Note**: When the cat falls on the ground, you see several FAIL messages. That's because the cat bounces off the ground just a tiny bit by default, so it ends up making contact with the ground more than once. You'll fix this a bit later.

Finishing touches

You're almost there – you already know when the player should win or lose, you just need to do something about it!

There are three steps and you'll be done: adding an in-game message, handling losing, and handling winning.

Adding an in-game message

First, add this new category value to the `CNPhysicsCategory` enum:

```
CNPhysicsCategoryLabel  = 1 << 4,  // 10000 = 16
```

Then add a new method to show messages on the screen – with the help of the physics engine.

```
- (void)inGameMessage:(NSString*)text
{
  // 1
  SKLabelNode *label =
    [SKLabelNode labelNodeWithFontNamed:@"AvenirNext-Regular"];
  label.text = text;
  label.fontSize = 64.0;
  label.color = [SKColor whiteColor];

  // 2
  label.position = CGPointMake(self.frame.size.width/2,
                               self.frame.size.height - 10);
```

```
    label.physicsBody =
      [SKPhysicsBody bodyWithCircleOfRadius:10];
    label.physicsBody.collisionBitMask = CNPhysicsCategoryEdge;
    label.physicsBody.categoryBitMask = CNPhysicsCategoryLabel;
    label.physicsBody.restitution = 0.7;

    // 3
    [_gameNode addChild:label];

    // 4
    [label runAction:
      [SKAction sequence:@[
        [SKAction waitForDuration:3.0],
        [SKAction removeFromParent]]]];
  }
```

Let's go over this step by step.

1. In step one, you create a Sprite Kit label node just like you learned in Chapter 6, "Labels."

2. You then set physics body for the label and set it to collide with the edge of the screen. You also make it pretty bouncy. Note that you can add a physics body to any kind of node, not just sprite nodes!

3. You add the label to the scene.

4. Finally you run a sequence action, which waits for a bit and then removes the label from the screen.

The effect of invoking this method is that you get a label on the screen that falls down and bounces a bit before it disappears.

Now you are going to add a method to help you restart the current level. Add the newGame method to your scene:

```
- (void)newGame
{
  [_gameNode removeAllChildren];
  [self setupLevel: _currentLevel];
  [self inGameMessage:[NSString stringWithFormat:
    @"Level %i", _currentLevel]];
}
```

In just three lines of code, you:

1. Remove all sprites from _gameNode and sweep the level clean.

2. Load up the level configuration and build everything anew.

3. With one more code line to spare, you show a message to the player.

With all the helper methods in place, you can continue implementing *lose* and *win* sequences.

Handling losing

Begin with losing. Add the initial version of the `lose` method:

```
- (void)lose
{
  // 1
  _catNode.physicsBody.contactTestBitMask = 0;
  [_catNode setTexture:
    [SKTexture textureWithImageNamed:@"cat_awake"]];

  // 2
  [[SKTAudio sharedInstance] pauseBackgroundMusic];
  [self runAction:[SKAction playSoundFileNamed:@"lose.mp3"
                              waitForCompletion:NO]];

  [self inGameMessage:@"Try again ..."];

  // 3
  [self runAction:
    [SKAction sequence:
      @[[SKAction waitForDuration:5.0],
        [SKAction performSelector:@selector(newGame)
                         onTarget:self]]]];
}
```

Let's go over this section-by-section:

1. You disable further contact detection by setting `_catNode`'s `contactTestBitMask` to `0`. This fixes the problem you saw earlier where you received multiple contact messages. Then you change `_catNode`'s texture to the awakened kitty.

2. You play a fun sound effect when the player loses. To make the effect more prominent, you pause the in-game music by calling `pauseBackgroundMusic` on `SKTAudio`. Then you run an action to play the effect on the scene.

3. Finally, tell the user that they lost and restart the level.

That's it for now – head to `didBeginContact:` and replace `NSLog(@"FAIL");` with:

```
[self lose];
```

Now you have a working fail sequence. Give it a try:

The five-second delay after the player fails is just enough time for the player to witness the raging cat animation and the onscreen message.

Oh, but now the label hits the cat on its head when it falls down. It's because the cat collides with everything on the scene. Go to `addCatAtPosition:` and add a proper collision bitmask for the cat:

```
_catNode.physicsBody.collisionBitMask =
    CNPhysicsCategoryBlock | CNPhysicsCategoryEdge;
```

That should keep the message from banging the poor cat on the head. :]

Handling winning

Now it would only be fair to add a success sequence, right? Add this new method to your scene class:

```
- (void)win
{
    // 1
    _catNode.physicsBody=nil;

    // 2
    CGFloat curlY = _bedNode.position.y+_catNode.size.height/2;
    CGPoint curlPoint = CGPointMake(_bedNode.position.x, curlY);
```

```
// 3
[_catNode runAction:
 [SKAction group:
  @[[SKAction moveTo:curlPoint duration:0.66],
    [SKAction rotateToAngle:0 duration:0.5]]]];

    [self inGameMessage:@"Good job!"];

// 4
[self runAction:
  [SKAction sequence:
   @[[SKAction waitForDuration:5.0],
     [SKAction performSelector:@selector(newGame)
                      onTarget:self]]]];

// 5
[_catNode runAction:
 [SKAction animateWithTextures:
  @[[SKTexture textureWithImageNamed:@"cat_curlup1"],
    [SKTexture textureWithImageNamed:@"cat_curlup2"],
    [SKTexture textureWithImageNamed:@"cat_curlup3"]]
                  timePerFrame:0.25]];

// 6
[[SKTAudio sharedInstance] pauseBackgroundMusic];
[self runAction:[SKAction playSoundFileNamed:@"win.mp3"
                           waitForCompletion:NO]];
}
```

There's a lot of code here, but luckily it's mostly review. Let's go over it step by step:

1. First you set the `physicsBody` of the cat to `nil`, so that the physics simulation no longer affects _catNode.

2. You want to animate the cat *onto* the bed, so you calculate the proper y-coordinate for the cat to settle down upon, and use that with _bedNode's x-coordinate as the target.

3. You run an action on _catNode to move the cat to the target position, while rotating it to zero degrees to ensure it is nice and straight.

4. You show a success message and restart the level. This part is identical to the lose method.

5. You animate the cat so she curls up in happiness, using the same technique you learned in Zombie Conga.

> **Note:** At the time of writing this chapter there is a bug where the animation frames of the cat appear stretched when this occurs. This appears to be a bug in Sprite Kit, and hopefully it will be fixed soon.

6. Plays a happy musical ditty to congratulate the player.

As a last step, in `didBeginContact:`, find the line `NSLog(@"SUCCESS");` and replace it with:

```
[self win];
```

Build and run the project now, and you have a winning sequence in place – in both senses of the word:

Believe it or not, you just developed another mini-game! And this time, your game also has a complete physics simulation in it. Congratulations!

Don't be sad that your game has only one level – you'll continue to work on Cat Nap in the next chapter, adding two more levels and some crazy features before you're done.

Make sure you aren't rushing too fast through these chapters. You are learning a lot of new concepts and APIs, so iterating over what you learn is the key to retaining it.

That's one reason why the challenges at the end of each chapter are your best friends. If you feel confident about everything you've covered so far in Cat Nap, why not take on the one below?

Challenge

This chapter only has one challenge – so be sure to give it your best shot. If you get stuck, the solutions are in the resources for this chapter.

Challenge 1: Count the bounces

Think about that in-game message that you show when the player wins or loses the level. Your challenge is to implement a more fine-tuned control when it disappears from the scene.

Your challenge is to count how many times the label bounces off the bottom margin of the screen, and kill the message on exactly the fourth bounce. This challenge will teach you more about **SKNode** and custom actions during contact detection. Base your solution on the fact that you can attach an arbitrary object to any node in the scene.

You can attach an object to a node by storing it in **SKNode**'s **userData** property, which is a **NSMutableDictionary**. Count the bounces and store the count in an **NSNumber**, then attach the **NSNumber** to the label sprite.

Your solution should follow this guide:

- Delete the code that removes the label after a timeout.

- Implement a new condition in **didBeginContact:** that checks for a contact between the edge and the label.

- Add the proper contact bitmasks to the contacting bodies.

- Remember there is no way to guarantee whether the label's body will be in **bodyA** or **bodyB**. So check the category bit mask to figure out which body is the label's body, and get the a reference to that physics body's node (i.e. the label).

- Check to see if the label's **userData** dictionary is nil. If it is, create a new mutable dictionary with a single entry with the key "bounceCount", and the value an **NSNumber** of 1. If it isn't nil, look up the "bounceCount" entry and increment the number.

- If the number of bounces equals 4, kill the label. (e.g. remove it from its parent node.)

This exercise should get you on the right path to implementing more complicated contact handlers. Imagine the possibilities – all the custom actions that could happen in a game depending on how many times two bodies touch, or how many bodies of one category touch the edge, and so forth.

Chapter 10: Advanced Physics

By Marin Todorov

In the last chapter, you saw how easy it is to create responsive game worlds with Sprite Kit. By now you are champion of creating sprites and physics bodies and configuring them to interact under simulated physics.

But perhaps you're already thinking in bigger terms than what you built in the last chapter. So far you only can move shapes by having them be affected by gravity and forces. What if you want to pin a sprite to a particular position, weld two sprites together, or enforce other constraints on their behavior?

In this chapter, you will learn all of that and more by adding two new levels to Cat Nap - three if you successfully complete the chapter challenge! By the time you're done, you'll bring up your knowledge of Sprite Kit physics to an advanced level and will be able to apply this newfound force in your own apps.

The Sprite Kit game loop, round 3

To get you back on track with Cat Nap, you are going to add one last touch to Level 1. You are going to implement a smarter detection system for when the player fails the level.

Specifically, you're going to detect whether the cat is leaning to either side by more than 25 degrees and if yes, you'll wake up the cat, at which point the player should fail the level.

To achieve this, you'll check the position of the cat every frame after the physics engine does its job. But in order to do this, you have to understand a bit more about the Sprite Kit game loop.

Back in Chapter 3, "Actions", you learned that the Sprite Kit game loop looks something like the following:

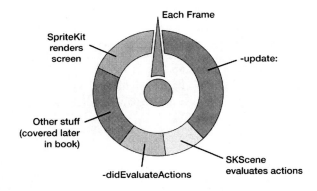

Now it's time to introduce the final piece of the puzzle:

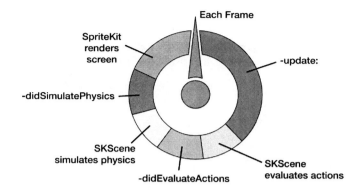

After executing `update:` and evaluating the sprite actions, and just before rendering the sprites onscreen, Sprite Kit performs the physics simulation and moves the sprites and bodies accordingly. After this occurs, you have a chance to perform any code you might like by implementing `didSimulatePhysics` – this is a perfect spot to check to see if the cat is tilting too much.

Inside **MyScene.m**, add this import to the top of the file:

```
#import "SKTUtils.h"
```

This imports the library of helper methods you added in the last chapter. Specifically, you'll be using a handy helper method to convert degrees to radians.

Next implement `didSimulatePhysics` as follows:

```
- (void)didSimulatePhysics
{
    if (_catNode.physicsBody.contactTestBitMask &&
        fabs(_catNode.zRotation) > DegreesToRadians(25)) {
      [self lose];
    }
}
```

Here you perform two tests:

1. **Is the cat still active?** To determine this you check whether its `contactTestBitMask` is set. Remember that you disable the cat's contact bitmask when the player completes the level.

2. **Is the cat tilted too much?** Specifically, is the absolute value of the `zRotation` property more than the radian equivalent of 25 degrees?

When **both** of these conditions are true, then you can call `[self lose]` right away, because obviously the cat is falling over and should wake up immediately.

Build and run, then fail the level on purpose. The cat wakes up while it's still in the air, before it even touches the ground.

This is a bit more realistic behavior, as it's kinda hard to sleep when you're 45 degrees vertical! Although I admit, I probably could have done that in my college days.

Level 2: springs and joints

Open **level2.plist** and have a look inside:

Key	Type	Value
▼ Root	Dictionary	(5 items)
▼ blocks	Array	(2 items)
▶ Item 0	Dictionary	(1 item)
▶ Item 1	Dictionary	(1 item)
▼ springs	Array	(1 item)
▼ Item 0	Dictionary	(1 item)
position	String	{270,110}
catPosition	String	{270,190}
bedPosition	String	{270,15}
hook	String	

You can see that this level introduces some new elements. There's a curious top-level object called `springs`, which is a list of positions where you will display springs on the scene – except we'll call them catapults for this game!

Fortunately for the cat, in this level, there's just one.

Then there is an element called `hook`. This is a flag to instruct the game to show a certain element. You'll learn more about `hook` in a moment.

The finished level will look like this:

Notice that catapult just underneath the cat and the hook on the ceiling. This looks rather nefarious, but I promise no animals will be harmed in the making of this game.

To win the level, the player needs to tap the catapult first. This will launch the cat up, the hook will catch her, and the player can then destroy the blocks and then release the cat. If the player destroys the blocks and then taps the catapult, the cat will be too low for the hook to catch her, causing the player to lose the level.

Let's dive straight into coding. Head to `initializeScene` in **MyScene.m** and replace this line:

```
_currentLevel = 1;
```

With this one:

```
_currentLevel = 2;
```

This should start the game from Level 2. Give it a run right now to see the result.

You start with two ordinary blocks and the cat. You are already halfway to a complete level!

Springs

Since catapults are a whole new category of objects in your game, you also need a new method to set them up on the scene. The code is almost identical to the method that adds the blocks onscreen, so I won't spell out all the details, and you can move through this part quickly.

First add a new category bitmask to the **CNPhysicsCategory** enumeration for the new body types:

```
CNPhysicsCategorySpring = 1 << 5,  // 100000 = 32
```

Then add a new method to **MyScene** that will take in the list of catapult locations and create the sprites:

```
- (void)addSpringsFromArray:(NSArray *)springs
```

```
{
  for (NSDictionary *spring in springs) {

    SKSpriteNode *springSprite =
      [SKSpriteNode spriteNodeWithImageNamed: @"spring"];
    springSprite.position =
      CGPointFromString(spring[@"position"]);

    springSprite.physicsBody =
      [SKPhysicsBody bodyWithRectangleOfSize:springSprite.size];
    springSprite.physicsBody.categoryBitMask =
      CNPhysicsCategorySpring;
    springSprite.physicsBody.collisionBitMask =
      CNPhysicsCategoryEdge | CNPhysicsCategoryBlock |
        CNPhysicsCategoryCat;

    [springSprite attachDebugRectWithSize: springSprite.size];

    [_gameNode addChild: springSprite];
  }
}
```

Just as with the blocks, you loop over the list coming in from the .plist file and for each object, you create a new sprite, along with a physics body, and add them to the scene. This way you can have more than one catapult in another level.

For the catapult bodies, you use the new body category constant, `CNPhysicsCategorySpring`.

Now head to `addCatAtPosition:` to set the `_catNode` so that it collides with catapults. Change the last line to include `CNPhysicsCategorySpring` in the collision bitmask, like so:

```
_catNode.physicsBody.collisionBitMask =
  CNPhysicsCategoryBlock | CNPhysicsCategoryEdge |
    CNPhysicsCategorySpring;
```

All that is left is to call `addSpringsFromArray:` to add the springs to the scene. Add to the end of `setupLevel`:

```
[self addSpringsFromArray: level[@"springs"]];
```

Now your catapult should be visible. Build and run the game, and check it out.

Next, let's make the catapult hurl that kitty. It's actually quite easy – if the player taps on the catapult, you apply an impulse to its body. Scroll to `touchesBegan:withEvent:` and add the following code where indicated (new code is highlighted):

```
    // 5
    [self runAction:[SKAction playSoundFileNamed:@"pop.mp3"
                      waitForCompletion:NO]];
}

if (body.categoryBitMask == CNPhysicsCategorySpring) {
    SKSpriteNode *spring = (SKSpriteNode*)body.node;

    [body applyImpulse:CGVectorMake(0, 12)
              atPoint:CGPointMake(spring.size.width/2,
                                  spring.size.height)];

    [body.node runAction:
      [SKAction sequence:@[[SKAction waitForDuration:1],
                           [SKAction removeFromParent]]]];

    *stop = YES;
}
}];
```

Let's have a look at what happens in the code above.

In the case when the tapped body is a catapult, you first fetch the `SKSpriteNode` instance and store it in the `spring` variable. Then you apply an impulse to its body by using `applyImpulse:atPoint:`, similar to what you used in Chapter 7, "Beginning Physics" on the sand particles. Finally you remove the catapult after a delay of one second and play a sound effect.

Run the game again and tap on the catapult:

You have liftoff!

Joints: an overview

Joints are a way in Sprite Kit to constrain the positions of two bodies relative to each other. Let's have a look at what kind of practicle use you might find in a game for the 5 different types of joints that Sprite Kit offers.

Fixed joint

A fixed joint gives you the ability to fix two physics bodies together. Imagine you have two objects and you nail them to each other with a number of big rusty nails. The two objects are fixed so if you take one of them and throw it also the other one will fly with it. Fixed!

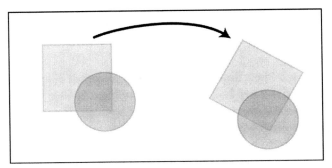

Often times you want an object to be immoveable – just fix it to the scene edge loop and you are ready to go. Other times you will need to have a complex object that the player can destroy into pieces – just fix the parts together and remove the joints when the body has to fall apart.

Limit joint

A limit joint sets the maximum distance two objects can be from each other. That means the two bodies can be closer than that distance, but not further apart. You can imagine the limit joint as a soft but strong rope that connects two objects. On the diagram below the ball is connected to the square via a limit join – it can bounce around, but can never go farther than the length of the limit joint:

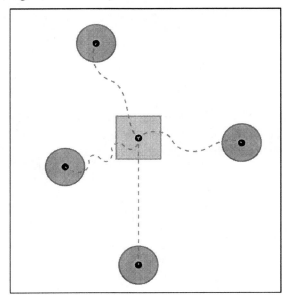

Spring joint

A spring joint acts much like a limit joint, but the connection between the two bodies is also elastic, much like if the two bodies are connected by a spring. This joint is useful to simulated real world rope connections, elastics, and so forth. If you have a game about bungee jumping, the spring joint will be of great help!

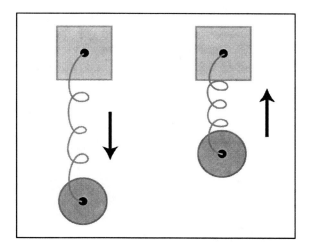

Pin joint

A pin joint fixes two objects around a certain point – the anchor of the joint. This allows both to rotate freely around this point (if they do not collide of course). You can imagine the pin joint as a big screw that keeps two objects tightly together, but still allows them to rotate around it:

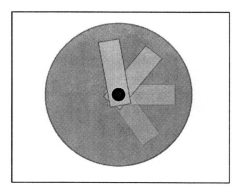

If you were to build a clock you would use a pin joint to fix the hands to the dial. Or in case you were building a physics body of an airplane you will use pin joint to attach the propeller to the plane nose.

Sliding Joint

A sliding joint fixes two bodies on an axis that they can slide along; you can further also define the smallest and biggest distance the two bodies can be from each other while sliding on the axis.

The two connected bodies act as if they go on a rail and there's a soft connection between them controlling their distance:

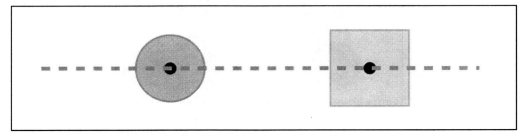

You can use the sliding joint for more complex interactive bodies – like a crane with a control cabin on top and a robotic arm both hanging on the crane's jib (the cabin and the robotic arm being the two bodies that slide along the crane's jib axis; they also can be connected by a cable definining the max distance between them).

Using joints for good

Consider this production plan for the hook object that you are going to create and attach to the ceiling:

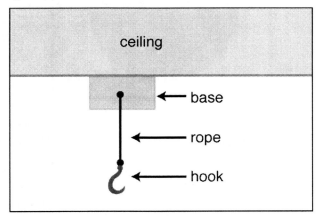

You will have one body (the base) fixed to the ceiling, another body that will be the hook itself, and finally you will have the rope (or string) that "connects" them together.

To make this structure work, you will use joints. Specifically, you will use two types of joints:

1. **A fixed joint** to fix the base to the ceiling.

2. **A spring joint** to connect the hook to the base.

> **Note**: Usually for such a setup you would use a limit joint to connect the hook to the base, but at the time of this writing this chapter the limit joint still has some bugs so should be avoided. The good news is the spring joint behaves just like a limit joint with its default settings.

The easiest way to understand how to use joints is to try them out – so let's get started by attaching the base to the ceiling.

Fixed joint

Add the following private instance variables to **MyScene.m** – you'll need them to access all the parts of the hook construction:

```
BOOL _isHooked;

SKSpriteNode *_hookBaseNode;
SKSpriteNode *_hookNode;
SKSpriteNode *_ropeNode;
```

Besides the three nodes, you need to build a hook structure matching the three objects in the construction plan above. You also need a flag to determine whether or not the cat is currently hanging on the hook.

Create this new method stub to initialize the hook structure:

```
- (void)addHookAtPosition:(CGPoint)hookPosition
{
  _hookBaseNode = nil;
  _hookNode = nil;
  _ropeNode = nil;

  _isHooked = NO;
}
```

You will pass to this method the hook key from the .plist file. The code you just added cleans up the instance variables and makes sure there is a hook object found in the .plist data.

> **Note:** It is particularly important to not leave garbage between levels, because as with the case of the hook – some levels will have hook, some won't therefore you need to reset the hook construction each time you load up a new level. Just be a good iOS citizen ☺

Append the following to addHookAtPosition: to create the sprite and its body on the scene:

```
_hookBaseNode =
  [SKSpriteNode spriteNodeWithImageNamed:@"hook_base"];
_hookBaseNode.position = CGPointMake(hookPosition.x,
  hookPosition.y-_hookBaseNode.size.height/2);
_hookBaseNode.physicsBody =
  [SKPhysicsBody bodyWithRectangleOfSize:_hookBaseNode.size];

[_gameNode addChild:_hookBaseNode];
```

This code creates the piece attached to the ceiling, along with its physics body, and positions them at the top of the screen.

You're probably curious to see what you have so far, so add this line to setupLevel:

```
if (level[@"hookPosition"]) {
  [self addHookAtPosition:
    CGPointFromString(level[@"hookPosition"])];
}
```

With this code you check if there's a hookPosition key defined in the level .plist file and if so convert it to a CGPoint and pass it to addHookAtPosition:. Run the game again to see the hook base:

Ack, the hook falls down onto the cat's head! Let's add a joint to fix that.

Imagine the fixed joint as a very big nail that'll keep the piece attached to the ceiling. Add this code to the end of addHookAtPosition: to create the joint:

```
SKPhysicsJointFixed *ceilingFix =
  [SKPhysicsJointFixed
    jointWithBodyA:_hookBaseNode.physicsBody
           bodyB:self.physicsBody
          anchor:CGPointZero];
[self.physicsWorld addJoint:ceilingFix];
```

You use SKPhysicsJointFixed's factory method to get an instance of a joint between the _hookBaseNode's body and the scene's own body, which is the edge loop. You also provide a CGPoint to tell the scene where to create the connection between the two bodies.

You always specify the anchor point in scene coordinates, and the sprites must already be added as children of the scene before creating the joint. When you attach a body to the scene's body, you can safely pass any value as the anchor point, so you used ({0, 0}).

> **Note:** When creating a fixed joint, the two bodies do not actually need to be touching – each body simply maintains its relative position from the anchor point.
>
> Also, not that you could get this same behavior by setting the physicsBody's dynamic property to NO, and avoid using the joint completely. This would

> actually be more efficient, but you're using a fixed joint here for learning purposes.

Finally, you add the joint to the scene's physics world. Now these two bodies are connected until death does them apart – or until you remove that joint.

Build and run the game, and you should see the holder piece soundly fixed to the top of the screen now, instead of just falling down due to the gravitational pull:

So far, so good. Let's see how to create some other types of joints, as this is a heavily used concept in physics-based games.

Spring joint

You need one more body category for the hook, so add this new value to the PCPhysicsCategory enum:

```
CNPhysicsCategoryHook   = 1 << 6,  // 1000000 = 64
```

Now add the following lines to the end of addHookAtPosition: to add the hook sprite:

```
_hookNode = [SKSpriteNode spriteNodeWithImageNamed:@"hook"];
_hookNode.position = CGPointMake(hookPosition.x,
  hookPosition.y-63);
_hookNode.physicsBody =
  [SKPhysicsBody bodyWithCircleOfRadius:
    _hookNode.size.width/2];
_hookNode.physicsBody.categoryBitMask = CNPhysicsCategoryHook;
_hookNode.physicsBody.contactTestBitMask = CNPhysicsCategoryCat;
_hookNode.physicsBody.collisionBitMask = kNilOptions;
```

```
  [_gameNode addChild: _hookNode];
```

You create a sprite as usual, set its position and create a physics body. Then you set the category bitmask to `CNPhysicsCategoryHook` and instruct the physics world to detect contacts between the hook and the cat.

You position the hook sprite just under the ceiling base, as the distance between the base and the hook is precisely the length of the rope that'll hold them together.

Now create a spring joint to connect the hook and its ceiling holder together by adding this:

```
  SKPhysicsJointSpring *ropeJoint = [SKPhysicsJointSpring
    jointWithBodyA:_hookBaseNode.physicsBody
    bodyB:_hookNode.physicsBody
    anchorA:_hookBaseNode.position
    anchorB: CGPointMake(_hookNode.position.x,
      _hookNode.position.y+_hookNode.size.height/2)];

  [self.physicsWorld addJoint:ropeJoint];
```

Using a factory method similar to the one you just used for the ceiling joint, you connect **_hookNode**'s body and **_hookBaseNode**'s body. You also specify the precise points (in the scene's coordinate system) where the rope connects to the two bodies.

Run the game now and you will see the hook hanging in the air just under the ceiling. However, there's one little problem:

The rope joint works fine, but there is no rope sprite for the player to see. It's almost as if the poor cat's house is haunted – now she'll never get any sleep!

Updating sprites by using physics

So far, you've modeled your physics bodies after the sprites you see onscreen. However, sometimes you'll need to remodel your sprites according to what's happening in your physics world.

In this section, you will position the rope on the screen yourself, based on the coordinates that the physics simulation calculates for the hook and the holder piece.

Scroll to the middle of the body of addHookAtPosition: and find this line:

```
_hookNode = [SKSpriteNode spriteNodeWithImageNamed:@"hook"];
```

Just above it add the rope sprite node (this way the rope appears under the hook sprite):

```
_ropeNode = [SKSpriteNode spriteNodeWithImageNamed:@"rope"];
_ropeNode.anchorPoint = CGPointMake(0, 0.5);
_ropeNode.position = _hookBaseNode.position;
[_gameNode addChild: _ropeNode];
```

As usual, you add a new sprite from an atlas texture and you set its position on the scene. This time, let's highlight few details:

- You create the rope oriented horizontally towards the scene – it's easier this way when the initial rotation of this sprite is 0 degrees with respect to the scene's x-axis.

- You don't create a physics body for the rope because you don't want it to collide or contact with other bodies.

- Finally, to make the sprite swing like a pendulum, you set its anchor point to one of its ends (you kind of *pin* it to the scene on that end).

The best place to update your rope is the game loop. Find the didSimulatePhysics method and add this **before** the existing code:

```
CGFloat angle =
  CGPointToAngle(CGPointSubtract(_hookBaseNode.position,
                                 _hookNode.position));

_ropeNode.zRotation = M_PI + angle;
```

Using helper methods from SKTUtils, you calculate the angle between the ceiling fixture and the hook, and then you rotate the rope sprite so that it has the correct direction onscreen.

Run the game again and check out your moving customized level-object!

Nice! It looks like the whole construction does exactly what you wanted.

There's just one thing I really should mention to keep my conscience clear: the rope right now is represented by just one physics body and as you know in Sprite Kit physics bodies are stiff. So right now the rope is more like a rod. If you would like to create an object resembling a rope better, create many shorter segments connected to each other like shown below:

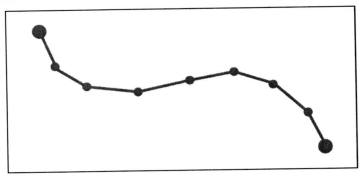

Creating and removing joints dynamically

There are some final touches to make for the whole hooking-up process to work: you need to check for hook-to-cat contact and create and remove a joint to fix the cat to the rope dynamically.

Add this to the end of your `didBeginContact:` method:

```
if (collision == (CNPhysicsCategoryHook|CNPhysicsCategoryCat)) {
  //1
  _catNode.physicsBody.velocity = CGVectorMake(0, 0);
```

```
_catNode.physicsBody.angularVelocity = 0;

//2
SKPhysicsJointFixed *hookJoint =
  [SKPhysicsJointFixed
    jointWithBodyA: _hookNode.physicsBody
    bodyB: _catNode.physicsBody
    anchor: CGPointMake(_hookNode.position.x,

    _hookNode.position.y+_hookNode.size.height/2) ];

[self.physicsWorld addJoint:hookJoint];

//3
_isHooked = YES;
}
```

First you alter the physics simulation manually a bit. You intervene in Sprite Kit's business and force a zero velocity and angular velocity on the cat's body. You do this to calm him down mid-air when it's about to get hooked, because otherwise the cat might swing for a long time on the hook. (And you don't want to make the player wait too much for their next move.)

So, the important point here is that you just learned that you can also manually alter the physics simulation, how great is that? Don't be afraid to do this – making the game fun is your top priority.

Next you get all the data for the new dynamic joint instance from your SKPhysicsContact object – the two bodies and the point where they touched. Using this data, you simply create a new SKPhysicsJointFixed and add it to the world.

Finally you set _isHooked to YES, so the cat does not wake up while it hangs around. You can try commenting out this line, and you'll find that the cat wakes up every time because of all the swinging.

Now you also have to make didSimulatePhysics respect the _isHooked flag. Scroll to that method and change the line [self lose] to:

```
if (_isHooked==NO) [self lose];
```

This way when the cat swings on the hook he won't wake up. Run the game again and play around!

> **Note:** Notice how the hook is getting fixed to just left of the cat's ear. Leave that for now, and in the next section you will learn how to create much more precise physics bodies and you will have the skills to fix that if you want.

Now when the cat hangs from the ceiling, you can safely destroy the blocks over the cat bed. But you're still missing one thing – the cat needs to jump off the hook and into the bed. To do that, you need to remove the joint you just added.

Add the following method to `MyScene`:

```
- (void)releaseHook
{
    _catNode.zRotation = 0;

    [self.physicsWorld removeJoint:
    _hookNode.physicsBody.joints.lastObject];
    _isHooked = NO;
}
```

First you set the `zRotation` of the cat to zero, so it won't accidentally wake up when unhooked.

Next - meet the `joints` property of `SKPhysicsBody` – it's an array of all the joints that are connected to a given physics body at the moment. You are more specifically interested in the last joint added to `_hookNode.physicsBody.joints`, because it is the one that connects the rope to the cat.

Removing the joint is as easy as calling `removeJoint` on your physics world object. Finally, you also set `_isHooked` to `NO`.

Now call this method when the player taps the cat. Inside `touchesBegan:withEvent:`, add this at the end of the `enumerateBodiesAtPoint:usingBlock:`'s block parameter:

```
if (body.categoryBitMask == CNPhysicsCategoryCat && _isHooked) {
    [self releaseHook];
}
```

If the player taps the cat while it's hooked, you invoke your `releaseHook` method.

Start the game again and try to land the cat on the bed. You probably don't need this advice, but: tap on the catapult; tap on all the blocks, and then tap the cat to solve the level:

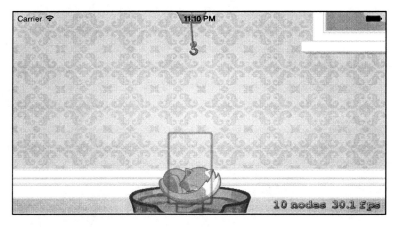

Creating joints dynamically like this is a really fun and powerful technique – I hope to see you use it a lot in your own games!

Level 3: compound shapes

In Level 3 you will tackle a whole new concept in game physics, related to physics body shapes. With this in mind, have a look at the completed Level 3 and try to guess what's new compared to the previous levels:

You guessed it if you said that in Level 3 one of the blocks has a more complicated L-shape to it. You might even notice that the shape is broken into two sub shapes, and wonder why it was done that way instead of just making a polygon shape like you did in Challenge 1 in Chapter 8, "Beginning Physics".

The reason is because Sprite Kit does not allow you to make shapes that are concave – you can only make convex shapes.

What are concave and convex shapes? Well, consider these two shapes:

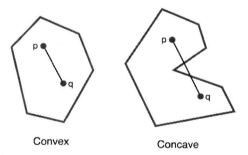

Convex   Concave

The convex polygon does not have any angles of more than 180 degrees. Therefore, if you draw a line between any two points inside the polygon, the line never crosses the outline of the body. However, doing the same thing with a concave polygon can produce intersections between the body's outline and your imaginary line (like on the diagram above).

Box2D only works with convex polygons because calculating collisions, contacts, mass, and so forth for concave polygonss is too expensive. Believe it or not, calculating collisions for one concave shape requires many more calculations than for two or three convex shapes.

But in games, sometimes you want to use concave shapes, like the new block in Level 3. It is made of stone and has a distinctive rotated "L" shape, which is clearly concave. You can see for yourself by drawing a line, like on the image below:

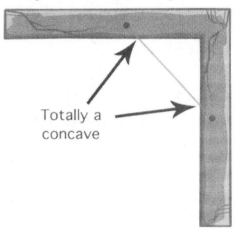

Totally a
concave

While you can't use concave polygons directly as physics bodies, there's a workaround: create multiple shapes, and use joints to weld them together!

Let's give this a shot. Just as before, replace the starting level in `initializeScene`:

```
_currentLevel = 3;
```

If you build and run the game right now you will see a level, which fails right away — you'll have to hold your horses buddy! You first need to implement some code to handle the new type of block.

Making concave shapes out of convex bodies

In order to create a body for the new "L" block you will use two normal rectangle bodies and you will fix them together to create a concave physics body.

Note: You can actually create a body out of a concave `CGPath`, but Sprite Kit will automatically convert it to convex by cutting out pieces of it, so you really have to make sure on your own that your bodies are convexes. Otherwise, you'll have strange physics collisions and might not realize the bodies you create have been automatically modified.

Let's get started!

Open up Art/Levels/level3.plist in your Xcode project navigator and have a look at the data definition of your new block:

Key	Type	Value
▼ Root	Dictionary	(3 items)
▼ blocks	Array	(5 items)
▶ Item 0	Dictionary	(1 item)
▶ Item 1	Dictionary	(1 item)
▶ Item 2	Dictionary	(1 item)
▶ Item 3	Dictionary	(1 item)
▼ Item 4	Dictionary	(1 item)
▼ tuple	Array	(2 items)
Item 0	String	{{270,130},{140,20}}
Item 1	String	{{330,60},{20,120}}
catPosition	String	{270,202}
bedPosition	String	{270,310}

Your new block contains (instead of a **rect** key) a key called **tuple** which contains two rectangle definitions. As you see since the "L" is made out of two rectangles – you just define its body shape by bundling two rectangles together. Easy, peasy!

Now alter the code to handle this new **tuple** construct. Navigate within **MyScene.m** and find the `addBlocksFromArray:` method, and make the following highlighted changes:

```objc
-(void)addBlocksFromArray:(NSArray*)blocks
{
  for (NSDictionary *block in blocks) {

    if (block[@"tuple"]) {
      //handle tuples here
    } else {
      SKSpriteNode *blockSprite = [self
addBlockWithRect:CGRectFromString(block[@"rect"])];
      blockSprite.physicsBody.categoryBitMask =
        CNPhysicsCategoryBlock;
      blockSprite.physicsBody.collisionBitMask =
        CNPhysicsCategoryBlock | CNPhysicsCategoryCat |
      CNPhysicsCategoryEdge;
      [_gameNode addChild:blockSprite];
    }
  }
}
```

Here you added an `if` inside the for loop that checks if the block contains a tuple key. Now add the actual code to handle tuples where the `//handle tuples here` comment is:

```
//1
CGRect rect1 = CGRectFromString([block[@"tuple"] firstObject]);
SKSpriteNode* block1 = [self addBlockWithRect: rect1];
block1.physicsBody.friction = 0.8;
block1.physicsBody.categoryBitMask =
  CNPhysicsCategoryBlock;
block1.physicsBody.collisionBitMask =
  CNPhysicsCategoryBlock | CNPhysicsCategoryCat |
CNPhysicsCategoryEdge;
[_gameNode addChild: block1];

//2
CGRect rect2 = CGRectFromString([block[@"tuple"] lastObject]);
SKSpriteNode* block2 = [self addBlockWithRect: rect2];
block2.physicsBody.friction = 0.8;
block2.physicsBody.categoryBitMask =
  CNPhysicsCategoryBlock;
block2.physicsBody.collisionBitMask =
  CNPhysicsCategoryBlock | CNPhysicsCategoryCat |
CNPhysicsCategoryEdge;
[_gameNode addChild: block2];
```

You start by fetching the first element of the tuple array and you turn it into a `CGRect`. By using the fetched rectangle you call **addBlockWithRect:** in order to create a new sprite. You alter the block's friction so that the cat won't slide too much on it and finally you add it to the scene.

The code handles the second block of the tuple in precisely the same way, except that it takes the second element from the **tuple** array.

You are almost there! Now just fix the two bodies together and that was it! Just add below this code to create a fixed joint:

```
[self.physicsWorld addJoint: [SKPhysicsJointFixed
  jointWithBodyA: block1.physicsBody
  bodyB: block2.physicsBody
  anchor:CGPointZero]
];
```

That was easy, wasn't it? Just run the game and behold the stone "L"!

Victory! You have a concave body in your scene and it's even dynamically created from the level configuration file! Nice.

However if you play around you will probably notice a little annoyance – if you tap the stone shape you destroy its two parts separately and that does not feel very "concavy".

Luckily you already posses all necessary skills to make the two parts of the block disappear when any of them is tapped! Scroll to `touchesBegan:withEvent:` and find the code which destroys blocks and specifically this line:

```
[body.node removeFromParent];
```

Immediately before this line add the code to destroy all adjacent bodies to the tapped body:

```
for (SKPhysicsJoint* joint in body.joints) {
    [self.physicsWorld removeJoint: joint];
    [joint.bodyA.node removeFromParent];
    [joint.bodyB.node removeFromParent];
}
```

This code goes over all joints applied to the current body and destroys first the joints themselves and then all bodies that were connected by these joints. At the end of the loop run you will have all blocks, both the tapped one and its adjacent ones, removed from the scene.

That's that! Now you can try to solve the level! Build and run and good luck with getting the cat to fall asleep in his bed:

Level progression

So far you have worked on one level at a time, so you have been setting `_currentLevel` manually. However, that won't work for players – they expect to proceed to the next level after winning!

Luckily this is quite easy to do, so let's add this in. Start by setting the `_currentLevel` in `initializeGame` to 1:

```
_currentLevel = 1;
```

Then at the beginning of the method called `win` add:

```
if (_currentLevel<3) {
  _currentLevel++;
}
```

Now every time the player completes a level they will move on to the next one. And to make the game more challenging and interesting add also this to the beginning of `lose`:

```
if (_currentLevel>1) {
  _currentLevel--;
}
```

That'll certainly make the player think twice before tapping a block!

Challenges

I hope that by now you already feel like you have mastered physics in Sprite Kit.

And you better have because I prepared for you a challenge, which will require solid understanding of everything you did in the last three chapters and will also ask of you some more!

In this chapter's challenge you will develop a whole new level by yourself, if you do everything just right the finished level will look like this:

As you can see this time besides blocks there's also a seesaw on the way of poor cat to her bed. This cat's life isn't easy, is it?

And yes – it's a real seesaw; it rotates around its base and is fully interactive. And you developed all this yourself! Ehm, sorry – you will develop all this yourself. ☺

I'll just lay down the main points and you take it from there.

Your project already includes the level file for this challenge – you can find it under **Art\Levels\level4.plist**. The interesting part is the position for the seesaw element:

Key	Type	Value
▼ Root	Dictionary ⏷	(4 items)
▼ blocks	Array	(2 items)
▶ Item 0	Dictionary	(1 item)
▶ Item 1	Dictionary	(1 item)
seesawPosition	String	{140,65}
catPosition	String	{265,185}
bedPosition	String	{270,15}

As with other level elements you will have to check for **seesawPosition** in setupLevel and if present call a separate method (let's say `addSeesawAtPosition:`) to add it to the scene.

Inside `addSeesawAtPosition:` first create a base to pin the seesaw board to. Create a sprite node out of the 45x45.png image texture position it at the seesaw position and fix it on the scene by using a fix joint. (Also set its collision bit mask and category to 0, since it won't interact with any other objects.)

At this point the game should look pretty much like this (notice the seesaw base on the left):

Not so much left to do from here (I'll go ahead and assume that you did everything perfect so far).

Create a new sprite node out of the 430x30.png texture image and position it at the point coming from the .plist file. Set it to collide with the cat and the blocks (otherwise you'll witness funny defects in your level.)

You'll then only need to fix the seesaw board to its base on the wall. You'll do that by creating a pin joint – it'll anchor the center of the board to the center of the base and allow the board to rotate around that anchor.

Use [SKPhysicsJointPin jointWithBodyA:bodyB:anchor:] to pin the board like so:

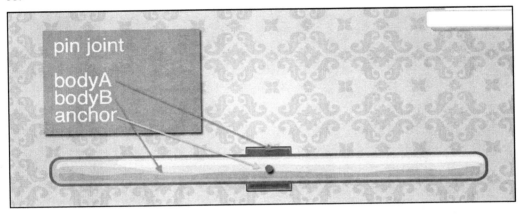

That should get you all done! Try solving the level yourself – I'm not going to give away any other tip besides the fact the order that you destroy the blocks matter!

Although you are now done with physics, you are not done with Cat Nap yet! Stay tuned for the next two chapters, where you'll learn about the four remaining types of nodes in Sprite Kit that you haven't seen yet. In the process, you'll make this poor cat's life even more difficult! ☺

Chapter 11: Crop, Video, and Shape Nodes

By Jacob Gundersen

As you learned in the first chapter of this book, everything that appears on the screen in Sprite Kit derives from a class called SKNode. So far, you have used four types of SKNodes in this book:

1. **SKSpriteNode**: This node displays images. You learned about this in Chapter 1, "Sprites", and have used this in every chapter since then.

2. **SKScene**: This node represents a "screen" in your app and usually contains a bunch of other nodes. You learned about this in Chapter 4, "Scenes".

3. **SKLabelNode**: This node displays text. You learned about this in Chapter 6, "Labels".

4. **SKEmitterNode**: This node displays particle systems. You learned about this in Chapter 7, "Particle Systems".

There are four more advanced types of nodes that you haven't learned about yet, and in this chapter you'll learn about three of them:

5. **SKCropNode**: This node allows you to apply a mask to a node or node tree, effectively "cropping" its children to only display a certain region.

6. **SKVideoNode**: This node allows you to easily play video files right from within your games.

7. **SKShapeNode**: This node draws a shape (with a stroke, fill, and glow color) from a CGPath path. You have briefly touched on this when implementing debug drawing drawing in Chapter 9, "Intermediate Physics", but we'll go into more detail here.

You'll learn about the final node type in the next chapter:

8. **SKEffectNode:** This node applies a Core Image filter (a filter that applies a post-processing special effect to an image) to its children.

These four nodes allow you to create some cool and unique effects in your games that would be quite difficult to do in other game frameworks, so they're well worth learning about.

Make no mistake! These nodes are powerful weapons in your game development arsenal. But, with great power comes . . . Well, you know the rest. These nodes all require greater resources. When using these nodes, it's important to keep an eye on performance, because you may find that your brilliant game only runs on the latest hardware.

Over the next two chapters, you'll get hands-on experience with these nodes by adding them into Cat Nap. By the time you're done, you'll be able to create effects like these:

Cropping   **Videos**   **Shapes**

> **Note:** This chapter begins where Challenge 1 left off in the last chapter. If you were unable to complete the challenges or skipped ahead from a previous chapter, don't worry – you can simply open **CatNap-Starter** from the resources for this chapter to pick up where we left off.

Crop nodes

Let's say you want to put this picture:

Inside this picture frame:

Should be easy, right? Just draw the picture, then draw the photo frame on top. To do this, add the following method to the bottom of **MyScene.m**:

```
- (void)createPhotoFrameWithPosition:(CGPoint)position
{
  SKSpriteNode *photoFrame =
    [SKSpriteNode spriteNodeWithImageNamed:@"picture-frame"];
  photoFrame.name = @"PhotoFrameNode";
  photoFrame.position = position;

  SKSpriteNode *pictureNode =
    [SKSpriteNode spriteNodeWithImageNamed:@"picture"];
  pictureNode.name = @"PictureNode";
  pictureNode.position = position;

  [_gameNode addChild:pictureNode];
  [_gameNode addChild:photoFrame];
}
```

This should be review – you simply create a `SKSpriteNode` for each and add them to the scene. You give the node names so you can easily look these nodes later in the chapter.

Now call this new method at the end of `initializeScene`:

```
[self createPhotoFrameWithPosition:CGPointMake(120, 220)];
```

Build and run, and you will see the following:

You can see that the zombie bleeds outside the photo frame — and everybody knows zombies shouldn't bleed!

Wouldn't it be cool if you could dynamically crop this picture so only the parts inside the photo frame showed up? Enter the power of SKCropNode.

Using crop nodes

To use a crop node, you need to do three things:

1. **Create the crop node.** This is as simple as calling [SKCropNode node].

2. **Add children nodes** to display. The children should be the things you want to be cropped. In this example, you would want to add the zombie picture sprite node.

3. **Set a mask node.** This is an node that represents the portion of the children nodes that should be drawn to the screen. Any part where the mask is transparent will not show up to the screen.

   For this example, let's say you have an image of a white circle that matches up to the "open area" of the picture frame. All you'd need to do is create a SKSpriteNode using this image, and set it as the crop node's mask node.

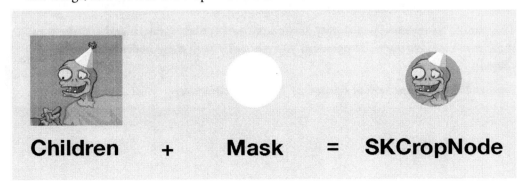

Children   +   Mask   =   SKCropNode

4. **Add it to the scene.** As usual, the last step is to add the crop node to the scene.

And that's it! Once you add the crop node to the scene, it will apply the mask to its children, so only the part that is not transparent shows through.

Let's try this out. Replace `createPhotoFrameWithPosition:` with the following:

```
- (void)createPhotoFrameWithPosition:(CGPoint)position
{
  // 1
  SKSpriteNode *photoFrame =
  [SKSpriteNode spriteNodeWithImageNamed:@"picture-frame"];
  photoFrame.name = @"PhotoFrameNode";
  photoFrame.position = position;

  SKSpriteNode *pictureNode =
  [SKSpriteNode spriteNodeWithImageNamed:@"picture"];
  pictureNode.name = @"PictureNode";

  // 2
  SKSpriteNode *maskNode =
  [SKSpriteNode spriteNodeWithImageNamed:@"picture-frame-mask"];
  maskNode.name = @"Mask";

  // 3
  SKCropNode *cropNode = [SKCropNode node];
  [cropNode addChild:pictureNode];
  [cropNode setMaskNode:maskNode];
  [photoFrame addChild:cropNode];

  [_gameNode addChild:photoFrame];
}
```

There are just three steps here:

1. This part is the same as what you had earlier. There's one difference – you no longer set the position of the picture node. This is because you'll be adding it as a child of the `cropNode`, and you want it centered at the crop node's position.

2. You load an image I have prepared for you that indicates the region of the zombie picture that you want to show through. This image is white where the center of the photo frame is, and transparent otherwise. Note it doesn't matter what color you use – all that matter is if it is transparent or not.

3. Finally you create the crop node following the three steps you learned about above. Note that you add the crop node as a child of the photo frame. This is so that all parts of the picture frame (border, crop node, mask, and children) can all be positioned or

moved by a single node – the photoFrame. This will make some code later in this chapter easier.

Build and run, and check out your picture now:

Ahh, much better – this house is looking more homey already!

Dynamic cropping

You might be thinking to yourself that you could have saved several lines of code if you had just cropped the source image in Photoshop:

That would work in this case, but there are a lot of times where this would not work:

- **Different shapes**. What if you want to put this zombie picture in different picture frames with different shapes? You'd have to save another version of the zombie image for each picture frame, which would waste memory and storage, plus be an all-around pain.

- **Dynamic images**. What if the image you want to put in the frame comes from a dynamic source, like from a web server or the user's photo library? You can't pre-crop that in Photoshop.

So to show you the real power of crop nodes, you'll try out the second of these cases – you'll modify this app to allow the user to choose their own picture to display in the picture frame.

Detect tap on node

You want to let the user select a photo when they tap on the picture frame, so the first thing you need to do is write some code to do that.

You already have code in `touchesBegan:withEvent:` that looks through all of the bodies in the physics world and detects if any of them are at the current touch point. It makes sense to leverage that same code – but to do that you'll need to create a physics body for the picture frame.

To do that, the following code to the end of `createPhotoFrameWithPosition::`

```
photoFrame.physicsBody =
[SKPhysicsBody bodyWithCircleOfRadius:
  photoFrame.size.width / 2.0 - photoFrame.size.width * 0.025];
photoFrame.physicsBody.categoryBitMask = CNPhysicsCategoryBlock;
photoFrame.physicsBody.collisionBitMask =
  CNPhysicsCategoryBlock | CNPhysicsCategoryCat |
    CNPhysicsCategoryEdge;
```

This code should look familiar. It's the same code you used to create a body for the blocks already in the game, with one small change: you use `bodyWithCircleOfRadius` instead of a rectangular physics body.

Note you use a radius that's slightly smaller than the radius of the sprite itself. This is a little trick to make the game look better – this way the borders of the sprite will seem to slightly overlap other sprites as if it's "sinking in". Just a personal preference of mine.

Now that you have a physics body for the picture frame, add the following code to `touchesBegan:withEvent:` at the beginning of the `enumerateBodiesAtPoint:usingBlock:` block parameter:

```
if ([body.node.name isEqualToString:@"PhotoFrameNode"]) {
  NSLog(@"Picture tapped!");
  *stop = YES;
  return;
}
```

Build and run, and you'll notice the picture frame drops to the ground now. That's because it has a physics body so it's under control of the physics simulation. Tap the photo, and you should see a message in the console log like the following:

```
CatNap[34882:70b] Picture tapped!
```

Displaying the image picker

Next you want to display the image picker when the user taps the photo. iOS comes with a built in view controller to do this: `UIImagePickerController`.

However, usually you display view controllers from inside another view controller, and your game code is running inside a scene class. You could pass a reference to the `ViewController` to the `MyScene` class, but there's a more elegant way to do this that won't tie the classes so tightly together.

Instead, you'll create a delegate protocol on the `MyScene` class that has a method to request a `UIImagePickerController`. The `ViewController` class will implement this delegate protocol. When the user chooses an image, the `ViewController` will call then a method on `MyScene`.

Start with the delegate protocol. Add this code to **MyScene.h** (before the `@interface` block):

```
@protocol ImageCaptureDelegate
- (void)requestImagePicker;
@end
```

Then add this property to `MyScene` to set the delegate, and declare the method that will set the texture after the user has chosen a photo:

```
@property (nonatomic, assign)
  id <ImageCaptureDelegate> delegate;
-(void)setPhotoTexture:(SKTexture *)texture;
```

`setPhotoTexture` will replace the texture for the existing `SKSpriteNode` that contains the image in the photo frame node. You're replacing the texture instead of replacing the entire node so that you can keep the same rectangle and positioning in place.

In **ViewController.m**, add an `@interface` block that includes the following delegate protocols:

```
@interface ViewController() <
  ImageCaptureDelegate,
  UINavigationControllerDelegate,
  UIImagePickerControllerDelegate>
@end
```

First implement the `ImageCaptureDelegate` method `requestImagePicker`:

```
#pragma mark ImageCaptureDelegate methods
```

```
- (void)requestImagePicker
{
  UIImagePickerController *imagePicker =
    [[UIImagePickerController alloc] init];
  imagePicker.delegate = self;
  [self presentViewController:imagePicker animated:YES
                  completion:nil];
}
```

This code is simple. You just create the `UIImagePickerController` object, set the `ViewController` class as the delegate and call `presentViewController`. Setting the delegate allows you to handle the callback when the user has chosen an image from their album. Add that method next:

```
#pragma mark UIImagePickerControllerDelegate methods
- (void)imagePickerController:(UIImagePickerController *)picker
didFinishPickingMediaWithInfo:(NSDictionary *)info
{
  //1
  UIImage *image =
    [info objectForKey:@"UIImagePickerControllerOriginalImage"];
  //2
  [picker dismissViewControllerAnimated:YES completion:^{
    //3
    SKTexture *imageTexture =[SKTexture textureWithImage:image];
    //4
    SKView *view = (SKView *)self.view;
    MyScene *currentScene = (MyScene *)[view scene];
    //Place core image code here
    [currentScene setPhotoTexture:imageTexture];
  }];
}
```

Let's go over this one part at a time:

1. This delegate method receives an `NSDictionary` in which one of the keys is `UIImagePickerControllerOriginalImage`. The value for this key is a `UIImage` object containing the chosen photo.

2. The `UIImagePickerController` has to be told to dismiss itself and takes a block callback.

3. Here you create a texture from a `UIImage`. `textureWithImage:` works with `UIImage` objects in iOS and `NSImage` objects in OS X. You can also initialize an `SKTexture` using its `textureWithCGImage:` method, passing a `CGImageRef` from a `UIImage`'s `CGImage` property.

4. The next three lines get a reference to the `MyScene` object and then call `setPhotoTexture`, passing the texture created from the chosen photo.

There's one last thing you need to do in **ViewController.m**: set the delegate for the `MyScene` class in `viewWillLayoutSubviews`. Change the following line:

```
SKScene * scene = [MyScene sceneWithSize:skView.bounds.size];
```

To this:

```
MyScene * scene = [MyScene sceneWithSize:skView.bounds.size];
scene.delegate = self;
```

Now that you have all the pieces in place, open **MyScene.m** and find the "Picture tapped!" log line in `touchesBegan:withEvent:`. Replace that with the following:

```
[self.delegate requestImagePicker];
```

This calls the delegate method to request the image picker when the user taps the photo frame.

Also implement the callback method at the bottom of the file:

```
- (void)setPhotoTexture:(SKTexture *)texture
{
  SKSpriteNode *picture =
    (SKSpriteNode *)[self childNodeWithName:@"//PictureNode"];
  [picture setTexture:texture];
}
```

You need to add one more thing to get the `UIImagePickerController` to work, The controller only works in portrait orientation. Right now this game only runs in landscape. You have to add support for portrait orientation somewhere in the app in order for it to show the `UIImagePickerController`.

Open **AppDelegate.m** and add this method:

```
- (NSUInteger)application:(UIApplication *)application
    supportedInterfaceOrientationsForWindow:(UIWindow *)window
{
  return UIInterfaceOrientationMaskAllButUpsideDown;
}
```

Build and run now. Tap on the photo frame and it will launch the picker:

Tap OK. If you pick a photo from your album, you should see it appear in the picture frame.

However, you may notice a problem here. When you rotate the game to portrait, it will resize and adjust. You don't want it doing that, but you still need to support portrait mode in the appDelegate for the UIImagePickerController.

Fortunately, there's a simple fix for this, too. Replace the contents of supportedInterfaceOrientations in **ViewController.m** with the following:

```
return UIInterfaceOrientationMaskLandscape;
```

Now the picker is presented in portrait, but the game view won't rotate to portrait.

At this point, you now have a custom image cropped to fit inside the photo frame – pretty cool, eh? Now that you've got this cool new feature working, let's integrate it properly into the game itself.

Interlude: level integration

Up to this point, you have added your new photo node directly to the scene no matter what. This means it will show up in every level of the game, often messing up the puzzles and making some impossible!

Let's fix this by treating the photo node just the same as the other types of blocks – loadable from level property list files.

I've provided several new CatNap levels to use the new nodes that you'll be creating in this chapter and the next. You need to make some modifications to the code that loads the level plist files in order to create these new kinds of nodes.

You'll be building levels five through seven in this tutorial. Inside **MyScene.m**, find the line in initializeScene that sets the current level and change it to 5:

```
_currentLevel = 5;
```

You will eventually modify addBlocksFromArray: to support several new types. To help with that, you'll refactor it a bit. First add the following two new lines to the top of the for loop (new lines are highlighted):

```
for (NSDictionary *block in blocks) {
  NSString * blockType = block[@"type"];
  if(!blockType) {
    if (block[@"tuple"]) {
```

These lines look for a new "type" field in the block definition from the plist files. The original block definitions do not include this field, so they will return `nil` and then the old logic will execute.

Now add the following code to the bottom of the `for` loop to close the new `if` clause and add an `else` clause:

```
} else {
  if ([blockType isEqualToString:@"PhotoFrameBlock"]) {
    [self createPhotoFrameWithPosition:
            CGPointFromString(block[@"point"])];
  }
}
```

In cases where the "type" field is present, this checks the type to see if it equals "PhotoFrameBlock." If it does, you call `createPhotoFrameWithPosition:` and pass in the position of where to place it from the plist.

Key	Type	Value
▼ Root	Dictionary	(3 items)
▼ blocks	Array	(7 items)
▼ Item 0	Dictionary	(2 items)
type	String	PhotoFrameBlock
point	String	{300, 130}
▼ Item 1	Dictionary	(1 item)
rect	String	{{150, 100}, {30, 85}}
▼ Item 2	Dictionary	(1 item)
rect	String	{{350, 100}, {30, 85}}
▼ Item 3	Dictionary	(1 item)
rect	String	{{100, 30}, {45, 45}}
▼ Item 4	Dictionary	(1 item)
rect	String	{{400, 30}, {45, 45}}
▼ Item 5	Dictionary	(2 items)
material	String	ice
rect	String	{{250, 50}, {430, 30}}
▶ Item 6	Dictionary	(2 items)
catPosition	String	{270,225}
bedPosition	String	{270,15}

You can see here that special node types have a new "type" string that tells the method which type to create. You can see that regular blocks have no "type" key, which means they will have a nil value for that string.

This should allow you to load Level 5 from the plist, but there are a couple of other things to do. Comment out this line from `initializeScene`:

```
//[self createPhotoFrameWithPosition:CGPointMake(120, 220)];
```

Now that the plist is loading the blocks, you don't want to add that extra photo frame block to every level.

Then change the first line of `win` to this:

```
if (_currentLevel<5) {
```

This just makes sure you can get back to this level if you fail to clear it while playing.

Build and run. You should see Level 5 and have a round photo frame block in your scene:

This level actually makes for a nice challenge – you have to time the sliding and destruction of the blocks right so the cat gets into the bed. Changing the picture to your own image is just for fun. ☺

But this is just the beginning of what you can do with crop nodes – lemme show you one last thing.

Different types of mask nodes

One of the coolest things about `SKCropNode` is that the `maskNode` can be any kind of node – not just a `SKSpriteNode`!

To see what I mean, open **MyScene.m** and find the lines that create the background in `initializeScene`. Add these lines right afterwards:

```
SKSpriteNode* bg2 =
```

```
[SKSpriteNode spriteNodeWithImageNamed:@"background-desat"];

SKLabelNode *label = [SKLabelNode
labelNodeWithFontNamed:@"Zapfino"];
label.text = @"Cat Nap";
label.fontSize = 96;

SKCropNode *cropNode = [SKCropNode node];
[cropNode addChild:bg2];
[cropNode setMaskNode:label];
cropNode.position = CGPointMake(self.size.width/2,
self.size.height/2);
[self addChild:cropNode];
```

This project includes a second version of the background named background-desat.png that is "desaturated" to be slightly grayer. Here you create a label that says "Cat Nap", and use a crop node to crop the desaturated background with the label as its mask.

Build and run, and you'll see the following:

Pretty cool, eh? I am sure you can come up with all kinds of creative ways to use SKCropNode in your own games.

Video nodes

Video nodes allow you to easily play video content right within your game. They work just like any other node, so you can move them, scale them, rotate them, have them be affected by physics, and much more!

SKVideoNode supports the following types of video files (from AVFoundation Constants Reference):

- Quicktime Movies (.mov, .qt)
- MPEG4 (.mp4)
- Apple MPEG4 (.m4v)
- 3GP Formate (.3gp, .3gpp)

In this section, you'll create a TV that plays the trailer for this book. If you've ever had cats, you know how they can be pretty vain! ☺

Using video nodes

To use a video node, you need to do 3 things:

1. **Create a SKVideoNode.** The first step is to create an instance of SKVideoNode. You can either simply pass in the URL of the video to play or initialize it with an AVPlayer (more on that later).

2. **Call play.** When you're ready to play the video, just call the play method.

3. **Add it to the scene.** As usual, the last step is to add the crop node to the scene.

That's all that is absolutely required – it's pretty simple stuff. Here are a few optional steps you might sometimes want to do:

- **Create an AVPlayer (optional).** When you create a SKVideoNode you can optionally pass in an AVPlayer, which is a class in AVFoundation introduced in iOS 5 that makes it nice and easy to play video.

  This is great if you want more control over the video. It allows you to control the playback rate so you can play a video at half speed or double speed, create a seamless video loop, jump to specific locations in the video, and much more.

- **Mask the video (optional).** Sometimes you might want the video to play within a certain boundary – like the inside of the TV sprite in Cat Nap. Yes, you can use SKCropNode to crop videos too!

Let's try this out by adding the TV to Cat Nap. Since implementing the TV will be slightly more complicated than creating the photo frame, you are going to create a separate class to contain all its code.

In Xcode's main menu, select **File\New\File...,** select the **iOS\Cocoa Touch\Objective-C class** template and click **Next**. Enter **OldTVNode** for **Class**, enter **SKSpriteNode** for **Subclass of** and click **Next**. Finally, make sure the **CatNap** target is checked and click **Create**.

Declare the following initializer in **OldTVNode.h**:

```
- (id)initWithRect:(CGRect)frame;
```

You use an initWithRect: initializer so that you can pass the position and size of the block in from the levels plist, just as you did with the photo frame block.

Inside **OldTVNode.m**, add the following import to get access to AVPlayer:

```
#import <AVFoundation/AVFoundation.h>
```

Now add the following private instance variables:

```
AVPlayer *_player;
SKVideoNode *_videoNode;
```

Like you did for the picture frame, the root object of the TV hierarchy will be a sprite node with the TV image. It will have a crop node as a child, which in turn has the video node as a child.

Therefore, you create a property here for the inner video node, and a reference to the AVPlayer you are creating so you have a high amount of control over the video playback.

Next implement the initializer as follows:

```
- (id)initWithRect:(CGRect)frame
{
  // 1
  if (self = [super initWithImageNamed:@"tv"]) {
    self.name = @"TVNode";
    // 2
    SKSpriteNode *tvMaskNode =
      [SKSpriteNode spriteNodeWithImageNamed:@"tv-mask"];
    tvMaskNode.size = frame.size;
    SKCropNode *cropNode = [SKCropNode node];
    cropNode.maskNode = tvMaskNode;
    // 3
    NSURL *fileURL =
    [NSURL fileURLWithPath:
     [[NSBundle mainBundle] pathForResource:@"BookTrailer"
                                     ofType:@"m4v"]];
    _player = [AVPlayer playerWithURL: fileURL];
    // 4
    _videoNode = [[SKVideoNode alloc] initWithAVPlayer:_player];
    _videoNode.size =
      CGRectInset(frame,
                  frame.size.width * .15,
                  frame.size.height * .27).size;
    _videoNode.position = CGPointMake(-frame.size.width * .1,
                                      -frame.size.height * .06);
    // 5
    [cropNode addChild:_videoNode];
    [self addChild:cropNode];
    // 6
    self.position = frame.origin;
    self.size = frame.size;
    // 7
    _player.volume = 0.0;
    [_videoNode play];
  }
  return self;
}
```

Let's go over this section-by-section:

1. You initialize the **SKSpriteNode** superclass with the **initWithImageNamed:** method, passing in a string @"tv", to load the file tv.png. As this is the parent node, all the child nodes that you add will be drawn on top of this node.

   You set the name of the node in order to look it up later.

2. As you did with the picture frame, you set up an **SKCropNode** to crop another node so that it fit nicely inside the bounds of the TV screen image. tvmask.png is a white, screen-shaped image surrounded by transparent space. It's the same shape and size as the screen in tv.png, so the masked section of the **SKCropNode**'s child node will line up exactly where you want it. You set the mask's size and position with the **frame** parameter.

3. Here you set up the **AVPlayer** to play a local movie file. This video is the trailer for this very book!

4. In this section, you create an **SKVideoNode** passing in the **AVPlayer** you just created. You also set the size and position of the video node. By default, an **SKVideoNode** has a **size** property that's the same as the input video. In your case you want to scale and position the video to be about the size of the TV screen, which you do by setting the **size** and **position** properties.

   You're using the **CGRectInset** function to easily shrink the video's height and width by some percentage of the width and height of the input rectangle.

5. In this step, you're adding the **SKVideoNode** as a child of the **SKCropNode**. Now it will be cropped to the inside of the TV screen. After that you add the crop node as a child of main node.

6. Now it's time to set the position and size of **self** based on the input frame.

7. These last two lines start the video playing and set the volume to mute so the movie's music doesn't play over the game music. There's a corresponding method to pause the video as well.

It's time to test your new node type. First add the following to **MyScene.m**:

```
#import "OldTVNode.h"
```

Now you need to add that node to you scene. Add this code to the end of **initializeScene**:

```
OldTVNode *tvNode =
  [[OldTVNode alloc] initWithRect:CGRectMake(100,250,100,100)];
[self addChild:tvNode];
```

This code simply creates an instance of the TV node and adds it to the scene. Build and run, and you should see a TV node up on the wall with the trailer for the book playing:

Just like SKCropNode, the ability to play videos so easily like this is pretty cool. There's a ton of creative ways you could apply this in your own games, from special effects to intro videos to tutorials and more – your imagination is the only limit!

Interlude: level integration

Just like last time, now that you've got the basics working you need to integrate the logic that creates levels from the property lists.

First add this code to **OldTVNode.m**, inside initWithRect: before the call to [_videoNode play]:

```
CGRect bodyRect = CGRectInset(frame, 2, 2);
self.physicsBody = [SKPhysicsBody bodyWithRectangleOfSize:
bodyRect.size];

self.physicsBody.categoryBitMask = CNPhysicsCategoryBlock;
self.physicsBody.collisionBitMask = CNPhysicsCategoryBlock |
CNPhysicsCategoryCat | CNPhysicsCategoryEdge;
```

This code should look familiar. However, it won't compile like this because back in Chapter 9, "Intermediate Physics", you declared the CNPhysicsCategory type in

MyScene.m. You need to move this to a location where both `MyScene` and `OldTVNode` can access them.

To do this, from Xcode's main menu select **File\New\File...**, select the **iOS\C and C++\Header File class** template and click **Next**. Enter **Physics.h** for the filename, make sure the **CatNap** target is checked and click **Create**.

Remove the following lines from **MyScene.m** and use them to replace the contents of **Physics.h**:

```
typedef NS_OPTIONS(uint32_t, CNPhysicsCategory)
{
  CNPhysicsCategoryCat    = 1 << 0,  // 0001 = 1
  CNPhysicsCategoryBlock  = 1 << 1,  // 0010 = 2
  CNPhysicsCategoryBed    = 1 << 2,  // 0100 = 4
  CNPhysicsCategoryEdge   = 1 << 3,  // 1000 = 8
  CNPhysicsCategoryLabel  = 1 << 4,  // 10000 = 16
  CNPhysicsCategorySpring = 1 << 5,  // 100000 = 32
  CNPhysicsCategoryHook   = 1 << 6,  // 1000000 = 64
};
```

Now import Physics.h in **OldTVNode.m** and **MyScene.m**:

```
#import "Physics.h"
```

Still in **MyScene.m**, add a condition to the last `if` statement in `addBlocksFromArray:` to create a TV node if the type string is "TVBlock". The complete `if` statement at the bottom of the `for` loop should look like this (new lines are highlighted):

```
if ([blockType isEqualToString:@"PhotoFrameBlock"]) {
  [self createPhotoFrameWithPosition:
              CGPointFromString(block[@"point"])];
}
else if ([blockType isEqualToString:@"TVBlock"]) {
  [_gameNode addChild:
    [[OldTVNode alloc]
     initWithRect:CGRectFromString(block[@"rect"])]];
}
```

I've set up level6.plist to contain the TV block in the level, so let's switch the game to starrt on that level. Find the line in `initializeScene` in **MyScene.m** that sets the `_currentLevel` and change it to 6:

```
_currentLevel = 6;
```

Likewise, change the first line of `win` to the following:

```
if (_currentLevel<6) {
```

One final thing: you can now remove the lines that add the TV node at the end of `initializeScene`:

```
//OldTVNode *tvNode =
//   [[OldTVNode alloc]
//     initWithRect:CGRectMake(100,250,100,100)];
//[self addChild:tvNode];
```

Build and run, and you should now have a new level using your TV node!

Controlling video playback

That's all you're going to do with video nodes in this chapter, but before you move on I wanted to mention a few other things you can do with video nodes.

If you want to play or pause your video, you can simply call the `play` and `pause` methods on the video node. Unfortunately that's all the control you have from `SKVideoNode` directly – to do more, you have to go one level deeper and and use the methods on `AVPlayer`.

The good news is `AVPlayer` has just about everything you might need. It contains methods to increase the play rate, seek to a spot in the video, perform a callback when the video ends, and much more. For a more details, see Apple's official AVPlayer Class Reference.

That's it for video playback – let's move on to the last type of node in this chapter!

Shape nodes

Shape nodes allow you to generate a visual element from an arbitrary Core Graphics path. They are great for when you need to visualize something quickly, or for when you need to create dynamic shapes in your game based on user input or randomness (rather than prerendered graphics).

You've actually been using shape nodes all throughout Cat Nap, for the debug drawing of your physics shapes:

But in this section you'll go a little bit deeper, and learn about some more things you can do with shape nodes. In particular, you're going to add a new type "Wonky Blocks" into your game that vary slightly each time you run the level. These blocks will use random numbers to create shapes that are somewhat, but not completely, rectangular.

This means the blocks (and the levels) will be slightly different each time you play the game. Some might not even be solvable – but hey, cats have nine lives for a reason!

Using shape nodes

To use shape nodes, you need to do 4 things:

1. **Create a SKShapeNode.** This is as simple as calling [SKShapeNode node].

2. **Create a path.** The most important part of creating a SKShapeNode is to set the path that defines the shape. There are a number of ways to create a path. For example, you can use Core Graphics, which is a C API, or you can use the higher-level

UIBezierPath (or NSBezierPath on OS X). In this chapter, you'll use
UIBezierPath because it's simpler.

3. **Set properties (optional).** An SKShapeNode has properties to control the stroke color
and width, the fill color and the glow around the stroke.

4. **Add it to the scene.** As usual, the last step is to add the crop node to the scene.

Let's try this out by implementing the new "wonky blocks" feature into Cat Nap.

First, you're going to create a couple of helper methods to make the code more usable.
You'll pass each point in the rectangle through a random number generator that will
return a number that can vary up to 15% of the block size from the provided location.

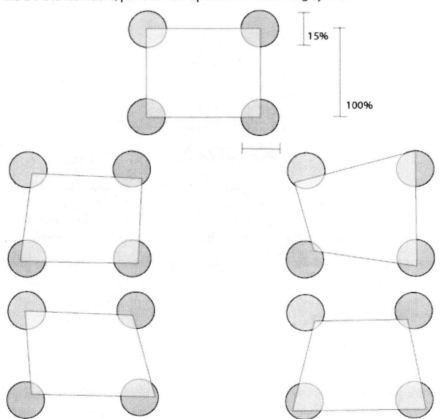

First add a method to **MyScene.m** that takes in a CGPoint and CGSize and returns a randomized point:

```
CGPoint adjustedPoint(CGPoint inputPoint, CGSize inputSize)
{
  //1
  float width = inputSize.width * .15;
  float height = inputSize.height * .15;
  //2
  float xMove = width * RandomFloat() - width / 2.0;
  float yMove = height * RandomFloat() - height / 2.0;
  //3
  return CGPointMake(inputPoint.x + xMove,
                     inputPoint.y + yMove);
}
```

Let's quickly go through these sections:

1. This section finds the maximum height and width of the deviation (15% of width or height) and stores them in the variables width and height.

2. This section multiplies a random number between 0.0 and 1.0 by the width or height and then subtracts half the input width or height. You do the subtraction to create a movement range that's centered between positive and negative movement. The ultimate range of the point's movement is between -0.075 * and 0.075 *, width or height.

3. Finally, you add that random movement amount to the input point. You now have a random output point.

Now that you've got some helper methods, you're ready to add the method that creates a Wonky Block. Add this to **MyScene.m**:

```
- (SKShapeNode *)createWonkyBlockFromRect:(CGRect)inputRect
{
  //1
  CGPoint origin =
    CGPointMake(inputRect.origin.x - inputRect.size.width / 2.0,
                inputRect.origin.y - inputRect.size.height/2.0);
  CGPoint pointlb = origin;
  CGPoint pointlt =
    CGPointMake(origin.x,
                inputRect.origin.y + inputRect.size.height);
  CGPoint pointrb =
    CGPointMake(origin.x + inputRect.size.width, origin.y);
  CGPoint pointrt =
    CGPointMake(origin.x + inputRect.size.width,
```

```
                    origin.y + inputRect.size.height);

//2
pointlb = adjustedPoint(pointlb, inputRect.size);
pointlt = adjustedPoint(pointlt, inputRect.size);
pointrb = adjustedPoint(pointrb, inputRect.size);
pointrt = adjustedPoint(pointrt, inputRect.size);

//3
UIBezierPath *shapeNodePath = [UIBezierPath bezierPath];
[shapeNodePath moveToPoint:pointlb];
[shapeNodePath addLineToPoint:pointlt];
[shapeNodePath addLineToPoint:pointrt];
[shapeNodePath addLineToPoint:pointrb];

//4
[shapeNodePath closePath];

//5
SKShapeNode *wonkyBlock = [SKShapeNode node];
wonkyBlock.path = shapeNodePath.CGPath;

//6
UIBezierPath *physicsBodyPath = [UIBezierPath bezierPath];
[physicsBodyPath moveToPoint:
 CGPointSubtract(pointlb, CGPointMake(-2, -2))];
[physicsBodyPath addLineToPoint:
 CGPointSubtract(pointlt, CGPointMake(-2, 2))];
[physicsBodyPath addLineToPoint:
 CGPointSubtract(pointrt, CGPointMake(2, 2))];
[physicsBodyPath addLineToPoint:
 CGPointSubtract(pointrb, CGPointMake(2, -2))];
[physicsBodyPath closePath];

//7
wonkyBlock.physicsBody =
  [SKPhysicsBody
   bodyWithPolygonFromPath:physicsBodyPath.CGPath];
wonkyBlock.physicsBody.categoryBitMask =
  CNPhysicsCategoryBlock;
wonkyBlock.physicsBody.collisionBitMask =
  CNPhysicsCategoryBlock | CNPhysicsCategoryCat |
    CNPhysicsCategoryEdge;

//8
wonkyBlock.lineWidth = 1.0;
wonkyBlock.fillColor =
  [SKColor colorWithRed:0.75 green:0.75 blue:1.0 alpha:1.0];
```

```
    wonkyBlock.strokeColor =
        [SKColor colorWithRed:0.15 green:0.15 blue:0.0 alpha:1.0];
    wonkyBlock.glowWidth = 1.0;
    return wonkyBlock;
}
```

There's a lot to go through here, so let's take it one step at a time:

1. In order to modify each of the four corners of a rectangle individually, you first need the location of each corner. This section of code creates a variable for the points at the left-bottom, left-top, right-bottom, and right-top.

   First you have to create an origin point that's half the width and height to the bottom-left of the provided point, because a CGRect is positioned from the bottom-left, but an SKNode is positioned by default from the center point. You use the information about the origin and size of the CGRect to find those points.

2. Here you pass each of the points into the helper method you created to randomly modify them. You also pass in the size so that the magnitude of the change is appropriate for the size of the rectangle you have.

3. To create a UIBezierPath, you use the bezierPath convenience method. There are number of ways to use a UIBezierPath.

   Some of the ways you create a path is to provide a CGRect, draw straight lines by calling addLineToPoint, create Bezier curves with a call to addCurveToPoint:controlPoint1:controlPoint2:, or a number of other shape drawing methods. For a comprehensive list of the API methods, see the UIBezierPath Class Reference on Apple's developer documentation. The first line moves the "pencil" to the starting point, then each call after that draws a line to the next point in the list. Order matters here.

4. Calling closePath draws a line between the very first point and the last point, guaranteeing that you have a closed shape.

5. Now it's time to create the SKShapeNode and set its shape. SKShapeNode has a CGPath property that takes a CGPathRef. Luckily, UIBezierPath has a CGPath property that returns a CGPath. CGPathRef is a lower-level, C representation of the path.

6. This time, you add the physics body now, instead of doing so in a later step. If you wanted a physics body that was exactly the same size as your shape, you could just pass the same CGPath to the physics body. Usually, though, you want a physics body that's just a little smaller than the visual representation, so this block creates a new path and

shrinks the corner points by 2 pixels at each point, for a total of 4 pixels narrower and shorter. You use the convenience method `CGPointSubtract` that's provided in the code that comes with this book.

7. Next, you create the physics body by using `bodyWithPolygonFromPath`. This method takes a `CGPath` and, as long as it meets the requirements, creates a physics body. You then assign it the same physics properties for all the other block types.

Note: The requirements for a polygon physics body are that it must be a convex polygon, non of its corners can point inward. It must have a counterclockwise winding. And, it must not intersect itself, or none of its lines can cross.

8. Finally, you set the width of the stroke line, the fill color of the shape, the color of the stroke and the `glowWidth`, which is the size of the glow effect on the stroke line.

Now that you have a new block type, you should add it to the process that loads blocks from the plist. To do this, add another `else if` block to the series of `if` statements that handles different block types in `addBlocksFromArray:`. The following is the entire `if` statement block (new lines are highlighted):

```
if ([blockType isEqualToString:@"PhotoFrameBlock"]) {
  [self createPhotoFrameWithPosition:
              CGPointFromString(block[@"point"])];
}
else if ([blockType isEqualToString:@"TVBlock"]) {
  [_gameNode addChild:
    [[OldTVNode alloc]
      initWithRect:CGRectFromString(block[@"rect"])]];
}
else if ([blockType isEqualToString:@"WonkyBlock"]) {
  [_gameNode addChild:
    [self createWonkyBlockFromRect:
      CGRectFromString(block[@"rect"])]];
}
```

To test this, change the `_currentLevel` variable in `initializeScene` to 7:

```
_currentLevel = 7;
```

And change the first line of `win` to this:

```
if (_currentLevel<7) {
```

Build and run now.

Level 7 is full of Wonky Blocks! Each time you replay this level, you'll get a slightly different puzzle — and maybe some that aren't solvable — but that's what you get with Wonky!

Note: In my testing at the time of writing, unfortunately you cannot use an SKShapeNode as a maskNode for an SKCropNode. Instead of using the shape in the path, the crop node appears to crop to some bounding box that approximately contains the shape.

There's one work around that I've found and tested that will help in a limited capacity. You can make an SKShapeNode a child of an SKEffectNode (which you'll learn about in the next chapter) and set the SKEffectNode's shouldRasterize property to YES. This will draw the shape into the SKEffectNode's buffer (without any filter, because you don't have to set the filter property or the shouldEnableEffects property). Then, setting the SKEffectNode as the maskNode property on the SKClipNode will clip to the shape drawn by the path.

This solution is limited. In order to update the shape, you must repeat the entire process, which is even more expensive (SKShapeNodes are already expensive) than using the SKShapeNode on its own.

Another quick note about using SKEffectNodes, if you don't need to change the shape of your SKShapeNodes often, this is actually a good way to save on performance. Using an SKEffectNode (with a shape node) without a filter, is going to perform much better than using an SKShapeNode directly. Once the shape node is rendered into the effect node, it's much more like an SKSpriteNode, the image data is cached and can be drawn very quickly. Of course, it's static in this state.

And that's it for the new block types! At this point, you've learned about 7 of the 8 types of SKNodes available in Sprite Kit. Before you move on to the final type of SKNode, take a break to play around a bit more with video nodes!

Challenge

There's just one challenge for you in this chapter – making a video loop endlessly.

As always, if you get stuck you can find the solution in the resources for this chapter – but give it your best shot first!

Challenge 1: Endless looping

Because video files are quite large, you might want to take a small video file in your game and loop it endlessly. You can do this by setting up a key-value observer on the AVPlayer's AVPlayerItemDidPlayToEndTimeNotification key. When the observer receives that notification, you set the video to start over.

I've provided another video in the starter project called **loop.mov**. This is a 16-second video whose end frame matches seamlessly with its beginning frame, allowing you to play that video for as long as you want.

Your challenge is to modify **OldTVNode.m** to play this video file endlessly. The rest of this challenge gives you a few hints on how to do this.

AVPlayer has a property called actionAtItemEnd. This is an enum that tells the AVPlayer what it should do when the currently playing item has ended. The default behavior is that AVPlayer stops the video. You want to change actionAtItemEnd to AVPlayerActionATItemEndNone so that it won't stop the video.

Instead, you want to call [AVPlayer seekToTime:kCMTimeZero] to reset the playback to the very beginning of the video. This should happen without any noticeable jitter in playback.

Here's what that code should look like:

```
_player.actionAtItemEnd = AVPlayerActionAtItemEndNone;
[[NSNotificationCenter defaultCenter]
  addObserverForName:AVPlayerItemDidPlayToEndTimeNotification
           object:nil queue:[NSOperationQueue mainQueue]
       usingBlock:^(NSNotification *note) {
  [_player seekToTime:kCMTimeZero];
}];
```

Don't forget that you need to remove the observer in `dealloc`.

```
- (void)dealloc
{
  [[NSNotificationCenter defaultCenter] removeObserver:self
   name:AVPlayerItemDidPlayToEndTimeNotification object:nil];
}
```

All of this code can be efficiently placed in the `OldTVNode` class. You'll need to load Level 6 or add a `TVNode` to another level to see it in action.

Once you've got it working, you should see something like this:

That's just a taste of what you can do with `AVPlayer` — there's a lot more handy methods in there if you find you ever need them.

And with that, you've made it to the end of the chapter! Stay tuned for the last chapter on Cat Nap, where you'll learn how to add special effects to your game using Core Image filters.

Chapter 12: Effect Nodes

By Jacob Gundersen

So far, you have learned about 7/8 of the types of nodes in Sprite Kit.

In this chapter you will learn about the last type of node: `SKEffectNode`.

An `SKEffectNode` allows you to apply special effects to its children nodes. For example, you could use it to modify a sprite's vibrance, hue, or exposure, blur the sprite, or convert it to black and white.

These special effects are created with a technology introduced in iOS 5 called Core Image. Core Image allows you to perform many of the functions that writing custom shaders would perform in other game engines. However, the benefit of using effect nodes is that they are much easier to use than writing OpenGL and GLSL code!

Sprite Kit provides three ways to use Core Image to process an image, of which `SKEffectNode` is just one of the options:

1. **SKTexture**. This class has a method called `textureByApplyingCIFilter:`, which takes the texture object and creates a new texture by processing it with the provided filter.

2. **SKEffectNode**. All the children of this node will be rendered and post-processed by the provided Core Image filter chain. This could be the entire scene or some child node tree.

3. **SKTransition**. This class has a method called `transitionWithCIFilter:duration:`. You can write a custom `CIFilter` subclass that takes in two input images (the previous scene and the one to which you want to transition) and use whatever combination of filters you wish to create a transition effect. This could be as simple as a fade, but you can do more complex things.

In this chapter, you will first get hands-on experience using Core Image in all three of these ways. To do this, you'll add a lot of special effects to Cat Nap, such as this "old projector" effect:

Effect nodes and Core Image is a great way to make your game stand out and look unique. So let's dive in and make this game look funky!

More about Core Image

Core Image is an image processing framework available on OS X and iOS. It provides a number of predefined filters that you can use to do anything from altering the brightness or contrast of an image, to combining multiple images, to applying a 3D transformation to an image.

Core Image has a number of classes available in its API. However, in the context of Sprite Kit, you'll only use one main filter class, `CIFilter`. `CIFilter` has a class method that creates a `CIFilter` subclass called `filterWithName:`. This method returns a subclass for a given filter name, such as "CISepiaTone", "CIBloom", "CIGaussianBlur", and many more.

Each filter has a different set of parameters that you can alter from their default values in order to customize the filter's effects. This can range from changing the center point of the effect, to changing the intensity, to changing the color of a `CIFilter`.

This chapter will explain the basics of using Core Image as you go along, but to learn more, check out our four chapters on Core Image in our books *iOS 5 and 6 by Tutorials*, which delve much deeper into the subject.

Performance notes

Using Core Image to process a node may require a lot of processing power. The resources required to process an image depends on the pixel size of the tree. As a rule of thumb, the bigger the element you're trying to filter, the more processing power it will take.

It also depends on the complexity of the filter or filter chain. A Gaussian blur, for example, is a particularly expensive filter because it has to calculate each pixel using inputs from the pixels that surround it.

Throughout this chapter, I'll mention the performance issues and limitations of using Core Image filters. In most cases, you won't be able to process the entire scene each frame on older hardware – iPhone 4 is particularly slow, as it has an older GPU.

Long story short – using Core Image and effect nodes can be expensive, so use them with care and keep performance in mind.

Filtering a texture

To get started, you're going to try out the first of the three ways to use Core Image in Sprite Kit listed at the beginning of this chapter: filtering a texture.

Specifically, you're going to apply a sepia filter to the image that you chose to place in your photo frame in the last chapter. A sepia filter makes an image look yellowed and old.

Go to **ViewController.m** and replace the line "//Place core image code here" in
`imagePickerController:didFinishPickingMediaWithInfo:` with this code:

```
//1
CIFilter *sepia = [CIFilter filterWithName:@"CISepiaTone"];
//2
[sepia setValue:@(0.8) forKey:@"inputIntensity"];
//3
imageTexture = [imageTexture textureByApplyingCIFilter:sepia];
```

Let's review this line-by-line:

1. In order to create a `CIFilter`, you call `filterWithName:` and supply a string that is
   the name of the filter. In this case, "CISepiaTone" is the name of the filter.

   You always call the class method `filterWithName:` to create a Core Image filter from
   the built-in set of filters.

2. In order to set a parameter on a `CIFilter`, you call `setValue:forKey:` and supply a
   valid value (it can be an `NSNumber`, `CIVector`, `CIImage`, `CIColor`, etc.) and key
   name.

3. Finally, you apply the filter to the image texture by calling
   `textureByApplyingCIFilter:` and passing in the filter you just created. This
   returns to you a new (modified) texture.

To test this, you need to switch back to Level 5, because that's the level that has the
photo frame node. Change `_currentLevel` back to 5 in `initializeScene` in
MyScene.m:

```
_currentLevel = 5;
```

Build and run now. If you tap on the photo frame, it will present the photo picker as
before, but now when you choose a photo, it will insert it into the frame with a sepia
filter applied.

Performance Note: The `CISepiaTone` filter is a fairly lightweight filter. Even if it weren't, this operation would work just fine on any device that supports Sprite Kit.

This is because in this example you only apply the filter once, so even if it takes a while to process it's a one-time performance hit (rather than continuously each frame).

The app then saves the result as the texture for the photo node. In fact, it replaces the previous texture – the node no longer has a reference to the image the way it was before the filter was applied. Only the sepia version remains.

Applying a filter to a texture when a node is first created is a great way to reuse one image. For example, you could use the `CIHueAdjust` filter to create differently colored enemies from the same original image.

There's a challenge at the end of this chapter where you'll do exactly that.

Listing available filters

You may be wondering how I knew to put "CISepiaFilter" for the filter name, and that it took "inputIntensity" as a parameter. You might also be wondering what other filter types are available on iOS.

Core Image provides over 100 filters for iOS and even more for OS X. Fortunately, there are built-in methods you can use to determine which filters are available on the current platform and the parameters they accept.

To try this out, open **ViewController.m** and add the following code to `viewWillLayoutSubviews::`

```
NSArray *ciFilters =
  [CIFilter filterNamesInCategory:kCICategoryBuiltIn];
for (NSString *filter in ciFilters) {
  NSLog(@"filter name %@", filter);
  NSLog(@"filter %@",
        [[CIFilter filterWithName:filter] attributes]);
}
```

`filterNamesInCategory:` returns an array of all the names (`NSStrings`) of the filters in that category. The constant `kCICategoryBuiltIn` will return a list of all the filters available on the platform that you are running, in this case iOS.

In the above code, you use the `NSString` name of the filter to create an instance of that filter. You can then call the `attributes` method, which returns an `NSDictionary` containing the attributes of that filter. These include the name of the filter, the input parameters the filter accepts, and information about each input parameter: acceptable range, data type, `UISlider` values, and so on.

Build and run and you'll see a list of filters in the console, that looks something like this:

```
2013-08-16 16:46:35.197 CatNap[8877:a0b] filter name CIAdditionCompositing
2013-08-16 16:46:35.199 CatNap[8877:a0b] filter {
    CIAttributeFilterCategories =     (
        CICategoryCompositeOperation,
        CICategoryVideo,
        CICategoryStillImage,
        CICategoryInterlaced,
        CICategoryNonSquarePixels,
        CICategoryHighDynamicRange,
        CICategoryBuiltIn
    );
    CIAttributeFilterDisplayName = Addition;
    CIAttributeFilterName = CIAdditionCompositing;
    inputBackgroundImage =     {
        CIAttributeClass = CIImage;
        CIAttributeType = CIAttributeTypeImage;
    };
    inputImage =     {
        CIAttributeClass = CIImage;
        CIAttributeType = CIAttributeTypeImage;
    };
}
2013-08-16 16:46:35.199 CatNap[8877:a0b] filter name CIAffineClamp
2013-08-16 16:46:35.200 CatNap[8877:a0b] filter {
    CIAttributeFilterCategories =     (
        CICategoryTileEffect,
        CICategoryVideo,
        CICategoryStillImage,
        CICategoryBuiltIn
    );
    CIAttributeFilterDisplayName = "Affine Clamp";
    CIAttributeFilterName = CIAffineClamp;
    inputImage =     {
        CIAttributeClass = CIImage;
        CIAttributeType = CIAttributeTypeImage;
    };
    inputTransform =     {
        CIAttributeClass = NSValue;
        CIAttributeDefault = "CGAffineTransform: {{1, 0, 0, 1}, {0, 0}}";
        CIAttributeIdentity = "CGAffineTransform: {{1, 0, 0, 1}, {0, 0}}";
    };
}
2013-08-16 16:46:35.200 CatNap[8877:a0b] filter name CIAffineTile
2013-08-16 16:46:35.200 CatNap[8877:a0b] filter {
    CIAttributeFilterCategories =     (
        CICategoryTileEffect,
        CICategoryVideo,
```

For example, if you search through the console log you'll find a filter named "CIBloom" that has three attributes:

1. **inputImage**: The input image – almost all filters have this. Sprite Kit will set this property for you, and you will only need to set it yourself if you create a filter chain.

2. **inputIntensity**: A number ranging between 0-1, that represents how strong the bloom effect should be.

3. **inputRadius**: A number ranging between 0-100, that represents the radius of the bloom effect.

Apple has a Core Image Filter Reference in the developer docs that has a pretty comprehensive list of filters and better explanations on their usage and function. However, this API is a more up to date reference. A few of the available filters aren't up on the developer sight yet, and a few filters have different names in the API than the developer portal.

Even the API is not always accurate. I've found that some of the listed default, minimum, and maximum values returned by the API aren't actually the defaults, or I've been able to use values outside the returned minimum and maximum values.

Filtering a SKEffectNode

Next you're going to try out the second of the three ways to use Core Image in Sprite Kit listed at the beginning of this chapter: filtering a SKEffectNode.

Remember that a SKEffectNode will apply its Core Image effect to all of its children node. So you could create a SKEffectNode, add the cat sprite as a child, and it would apply the Core Image effect to just the cat.

But what if you want to apply an effect to the entire scene? It turns out that SKScene is a subclass of SKEffectNode, so you can simply set a Core Image filter on the scene itself to filter the entire scene!

In this section, you are going to try this out by adding an "Old Timey" effect to the entire scene. But to accomplish this effect, you're going to need more than just one simple filter – you're going to need to chain multiple filters together, one after another.

And to do this, you're going to need to understand how to use filter chains.

Filter chains

Filter chains are just what it sounds like – they are a way to tell Core Image to efficiently run a sequnce of filters on an input image.

There are a number of ways to construct a filter chain when using Core Image. However, if you're using Sprite Kit, you need to contain your filter chain in a CIFilter subclass. This is because every method in Sprite Kit takes only a single CIFilter object as a parameter.

So to create a filter chain in Sprite Kit, you need to perform these steps:

1. Create a subclass of CIFilter for your filter chain.

2. Make sure your CIFilter has an inputImage property.

3. Override setDefaults to initialize any parameters you may need.

4. Override outputImage to create the chain of filters. You basically chain the input image from the user to the input of filter A, then the output of filter A to the input of filter B, and so on – returning the final result.

Let's try this out by creating the "Old Timey" filter chain!

The Old Timey filter chain

The "Old Timey" filter chain will make your game look like it's being run on an old projector. It will work by applying the following effects in order:

1. **Color controls effect**: It will first use a color controls effect to turn the scene black and white, and make it randomly flicker from bright to dark.

2. **Vignette effect**: It will then use a vignette effect to darken the edges of the scene like worn photo.

3. **Affine Transform Effect**: Finally, it will use an affine transform effect to move the image around a bit randomly to make it seem like a shaky camera.

Remember, the first step is to create a subclass of `CIFilter` for the filter chain, so let's do this now.

In Xcode's main menu, select **File\New\File...**, select the **iOS\Cocoa Touch\Objective-C class** template and click **Next**. Enter **OldTimeyFilter** for **Class**, enter **CIFilter** for **Subclass of** and click **Next**. Finally, make sure the **CatNap** target is checked and click **Create**.

The second step is to create a property for the `inputImage`. Add this line to **OldTimeyFilter.h**:

```
@property (strong, nonatomic) CIImage *inputImage;
```

Now switch to **OldTimeyFilter.m** and add the following import:

```
#import "perlin.h"
```

You import a file called **perlin.h**, which you have already included this file in your project under **Art\Code**. This contains a C implementation of the Perlin noise algorithm, which you can think of as "smooth noise". It's a common algorithm used to generate 2D textures like clouds or dirt, and when you visualize it it makes something that looks like this:

> **Note:** For more information than you may want to know about Perlin noise, see here: http://webstaff.itn.liu.se/~stegu/TNM022-2005/perlinnoiselinks/perlin-noise-math-faq.html

In the case of your `CIFilter` subclass, you're going to set all your parameters in `outputImage`, so you don't need to do the third step (implementing `setDefaults`).

So you're onto the fourth and last step – implementing `outputImage`. All the important stuff goes here, so let's build this up one step at a time. Start by adding the following:

```
- (CIImage *)outputImage
{
  CFAbsoluteTime time = CFAbsoluteTimeGetCurrent();
  float v1[] = {sin(time / 15.0) * 100, 1.5};
  float v2[] = {sin(time / 2.0) * 25, 1.5};
  double randVal1 = noise2(v1);
  double randVal2 = noise2(v2);
}
```

The perlin noise function `noise2` takes two floats as an input that represent the X and Y coordinates, and returns to you the value of the noise at those coordinates. Here you are always passing 1.5 for the Y coordinate, and changing the X coordinate each frame.

Remember that perlin noise generates random (but smoothly changing) values over time, so you'll get a natural feeling random value that you can then pass to your core image filters as input (like brightness and intensity of the vignette).

You may wonder how I came up with the values for the X coordinates to the perlin noise function: v1 and v2. Here are a few notes on that:

- `CFAbsoluteTimeGetCurrent()` returns a value that is the system clock in seconds. This becomes an input value you use to drive the random noise values. You could have set up your own variable to keep track of the time since program execution, but this built-in method works just fine.

- Putting this time value into the `sin` function will return a value between 1.0 and -1.0 that will cycle smoothly over time. By dividing time by 15 in the v1 float, you are making the cycle take 15 times as long. Multiplying by 100 scales up the resulting value.

- I found the exact values "15" and "100" through trial and error.

Next, add some code to create the first filter to the bottom of `outputImage`:

```
CIFilter *colorControls =
   [CIFilter filterWithName:@"CIColorControls"];
[colorControls setValue:@(0.0) forKey:@"inputSaturation"];
[colorControls setValue:@(randVal2 * .2)
             forKey:@"inputBrightness"];
```

This creates the first filter in the chain: "CIColorControls". This filter has three parameters you can use to adjust the image: brightness, contrast and saturation. You set the saturation to 0.0 first. This takes a color image and turns it to black and white.

Next you use the `randVal2`, along with some scaling of that value, as the inputBrightness. You can set the brightness value between -1.0 and 1.0, with 0.0 meaning no change,

`randVal2` will return a random value between 0.0 and 1.0, so by multiplying it by .2 you will set the brightness to a random value between 0.0 and 0.2.

It's time for the second filter. Add this code to the bottom of `outputImage`:

```
CIFilter *vignette = [CIFilter filterWithName:@"CIVignette"];
[vignette setValue:@(0.2 + randVal2) forKey:@"inputRadius"];
[vignette setValue:@(randVal2 * .2 + 0.8)
          forKey:@"inputIntensity"];
```

The vignette filter adds a vignette effect to the image, which causes the edges of the image to be darkened. You set both the size and intensity of the vignette based on the randVal2. This will cause the vignette to change size and darken based on the changes in randVal2.

There's still one more filter left to add. Add this code to the bottom of outputImage:

```
CIFilter *transformFilter =
  [CIFilter filterWithName:@"CIAffineTransform"];
CGAffineTransform t =
  CGAffineTransformMakeTranslation(0.0, randVal1 * 45.0);
NSValue *transform = [NSValue valueWithCGAffineTransform:t];
[transformFilter setValue:transform forKey:@"inputTransform"];
```

The next filter in the chain is a "CIAffineTransform". You can do many kinds of things to an image with this filter: scale, move (translate), rotate or skew. In this case, you simply want it to make the image jump up and down.

In this step, you are creating a CGAffineTransform with a call to CGAffineTransformMakeTranslation. A translation is a transform that moves the position of an element. There are also constructor methods for rotation and scale transformations. All these transformations can be combined, as well.

Here you are passing in the randVal1 noise result and multiplying by 45.0 (chosen again through trial and error) in the y-dimension.

You can't pass a CGAffineTransform into the CIFilter directly, as it is C struct. You need to wrap it in an NSValue.

Now that you have created the three filters, it's time to chain them together. Add this code to the bottom of outputImage:

```
[colorControls setValue:self.inputImage
               forKey:kCIInputImageKey];
[vignette setValue:colorControls.outputImage
          forKey:kCIInputImageKey];
[transformFilter setValue:vignette.outputImage
                  forKey:kCIInputImageKey];
return transformFilter.outputImage;
```

First you set the inputImage property to the input of the color controls filter. You're using Core Image constant kCIInputImageKey instead of the @"inputImage" string for convenience, but they are identical.

Next you set the `outputImage` value of the color controls filter to the input image property of the vignette filter. Finally, you connect the output image from the vignette filter to the input image of the transform filter.

This is how you construct CIFilter chains – by connecting the outputImage from one filter to the inputImage of the next filter.

Finally, the outputImage method needs to return a CIImage, so it returns the outputImage from the transform filter.

Now that you've set up your subclass, put it to some use.

Filtering an entire scene

Switch to **MyScene.m** and import your new class:

```
#import "OldTimeyFilter.h"
```

You'll set the filter to operate on the entire scene. Add the following code to the end of `initializeScene`:

```
self.filter = [[OldTimeyFilter alloc] init];
self.shouldEnableEffects = YES;
```

The `SKEffectNode` has a `filter` property that contains a reference to the `CIFilter` or `CIFilter` subclass. You need to set the `shouldEnableEffects` property to YES to apply the filter.

There's another property on `SKEffectNode` called `shouldRasterize`. That property is set to NO by default. When set to YES, it will apply the filter and save the contents to a buffer, rather than re-applying the filter each frame.

If you're filtering a large node or using a complex filter chain, this can be very helpful. Applying a complex image filter 30 or 60 times a second is sometimes too much for good performance. If the node doesn't change every frame, you can avoid the overhead by setting `shouldRasterize` to YES until the node needs updating.

> **Note:** This filter chain has three different filters in it and you're applying it to the entire screen. On an iPhone 4, this filter will reduce the frames per second to about 10, which is pretty slow.
>
> If you need to support these devices, you probably want to find a way to run this filter periodically (rather than every frame) in your game. In order to save on

processing resources, you can set the `shouldRasterize` property to YES. This will keep a rendered version of the filters output and display that instead of re-rendering the scene.

By switching that flag on and off every other frame, you only have to apply the expensive filter half of the time. If the game runs at 30 fps, the screen refreshes 15 times per second (which is about the rate a 8mm projector runs at). However, input still is accepted at 30fps.

Alternatively, if you are applying a filter to a subtree of the scene, and those elements don't change every frame, you can set the filter to only run after a change has been registered, further saving resources.

Build and run now. You should have a game that looks like an old projector:

That was a lot of work, but the result is worth it!

Note: At this point, if you are running on the simulator, or an older device, your FPS has dropped a bit. This is no surprise, as full-screen Core Image effects with multiple filters can be very expensive!

This also creates an interesting problem: when the cat collides with the bed, the win method is sent. Similarly, when the cat collides with the floor, the `lose` method is sent. It's possible with a low frame rate for both collisions to be called at once, meaning you both lose and win the game simultaneously!

If you'd like to resolve this, simply add a boolean to the class, called `gameOver`. It will initialize to NO and then set it to YES whenever the player wins or loses. Finally, check to make sure `gameOver` is NO before letting the player win or lose in the future.

Filtering transitions

You already learned about the `SKTransition` class in Chapter 5, "Scenes". Remember, this is the class that you can use to run special effects between scenes, like a door opening effect or a flip effect. The ActionsCatalog demo that comes with this book gives you a way to preview all of these built in transitions.

But what if the built in transitions aren't enough, and you want to create one of your own? Well you can do this with the third and final way to use Core Image in Sprite Kit: filtering transitions.

`SKTransition` has a method named `transitionWithCIFilter:duration:`. You can pass a specially constructed `CIFilter` object to this method, along with a duration, and the method will use the filter to create the transition effect.

To use a `CIFilter` subclass in a `SKTransition`, it needs to have two parameters for `CIImage` input images: `intputImage` and `inputTargetImage`. It also needs to have an `inputTime` property.

The `inputTime` property will be passed in at render time, and ranges from 0.0 to 1.0 for the duration time passed in to the method. For example, if the duration of the transition is 0.8 seconds, after .4 seconds in the transition, the `inputTime` property will have a value of 0.5.

You can use the value of `inputTime` to determine where you are in the transition. Then you can create an `outputImage` based on this time location.

To illustrate this point, you're going to create a very simple fade transition.

Interlude: Refactoring CatNap for transitions

Before you begin, you need to alter the **CatNap** project to use a transition between each scene, instead of cleaning up all the child nodes and reloading them as it does now.

It's necessary to do some refactoring of the current code to accomplish this. You'll first change the initializer in MyScene that takes a level number parameter.

Go to **MyScene.h** and declare the following method:

```
- (instancetype)initWithSize:(CGSize)size
  andLevelNumber:(int)currentLevel;
```

Inside **MyScene.m**, delete initWithSize: and add the implementation of your new initializer method:

```
- (instancetype)initWithSize:(CGSize)size
  andLevelNumber:(int)currentLevel {
  if (self = [super initWithSize:size]) {
    [self initializeSceneWithLevelNumber:currentLevel];
  }
  return self;
}
```

This should be clear – you're only changing the initializeScene call to include the level parameter as well. Next, alter initializeScene's method signature to look like this:

```
- (void)initializeSceneWithLevelNumber:(int)levelNumber
```

Now find the line where you set the _currentLevel variable and change it to use the passed-in argument:

```
_currentLevel = levelNumber;
```

Instead of hard-coding a level number, you are passing it in from the initializer.

Now replace the contents of newGame with the following:

```
SKScene *nextLevel =
  [[MyScene alloc] initWithSize:self.size
                 andLevelNumber:_currentLevel];
SKTransition *levelTransition =
  [SKTransition flipVerticalWithDuration:0.5];
[self.view presentScene:nextLevel transition:levelTransition];
```

Here you are simply using the new initializer with the _currentLevel variable, which the program will have incremented if you successfully completed the level. For now, you're using a simple flipVerticalWithDuration transition. You'll change that to a custom transition in a minute.

Finally, because you've replaced the old newGame, you need to add the inGameMessage call again. Add it to the end of initializeSceneWithLevelNumber::

```
[self inGameMessage:
  [NSString stringWithFormat: @"Level %i", _currentLevel]];
```

One last thing: add code to **ViewController.m** to use the new initializer method. Change the line that creates the scene in viewWillLayoutSubviews to look like the following:

```
MyScene * scene =
  [[MyScene alloc] initWithSize:skView.bounds.size
                  andLevelNumber:1];
```

Build and run. Play through Level 1 and witness your new transition in action!

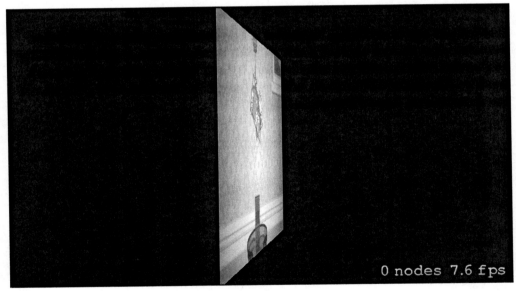

0 nodes 7.6 fps

Creating a custom transition

It's time to create a custom CIFilter to make a custom transition.

This custom transition will perform a simple fade from one scene's image to the next, but it will also rotate the scene as it does so.

In Xcode's main menu, select **File\New\File…**, select the **iOS\Cocoa Touch\Objective-C class** template and click **Next**. Enter **CustomTransitionFilter** for Class, enter **CIFilter** for **Subclass of** and click **Next**. Finally, make sure the **CatNap** target is checked and click **Create**.

Add the following properties to **CustomTransitionFilter.h**:

```
@property (strong,nonatomic) CIImage *inputImage;
@property (strong,nonatomic) CIImage *inputTargetImage;
@property (assign,nonatomic) NSTimeInterval inputTime;
```

These properties will automatically be set by Sprite Kit when you run set this filter on a SKTransition. inputImage will be the source scene, inputTargetImage will be the destinationScene, and inputTime will always range from 0.0 to 1.0.

That last part may be confusing. Regardless of how much time you pass the duration parameter when you call transitionWithCIFilter:duration:, inside the CIFilter subclass that value is scaled to a value between 0.0 and 1.0. For example, if you pass a transition duration of 0.75 seconds, half way through the transition, or at .375 seconds into the transition, inputTime will be 0.5;

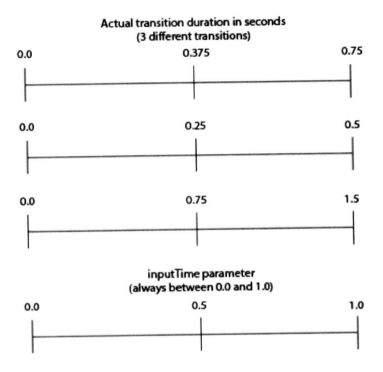

Now add the following method to **CustomTransitionFilter.m**:

```objc
- (CIImage *)outputImage
{
  //1
  CIFilter *color =
    [CIFilter filterWithName:@"CIConstantColorGenerator"];
  [color setValue:[CIColor colorWithRed:1.0 green:1.0 blue:1.0
                                  alpha:self.inputTime]
          forKey:@"inputColor"];
  //2
  CIFilter *blendWithMask =
    [CIFilter filterWithName:@"CIBlendWithAlphaMask"];
  [blendWithMask setValue:color.outputImage
                   forKey:@"inputMaskImage"];
  [blendWithMask setValue:self.inputImage
                   forKey:@"inputBackgroundImage"];
  [blendWithMask setValue:self.inputTargetImage
                   forKey:@"inputImage"];
  //3
  CIFilter *spinFilter =
```

```
    [CIFilter filterWithName:@"CIAffineTransform"];
  [spinFilter setValue:blendWithMask.outputImage
            forKey:kCIInputImageKey];
  //4
  CGAffineTransform t =
    CGAffineTransformMakeRotation(self.inputTime * 3.14 * 4.0);
  NSValue *transformValue =
    [NSValue valueWithCGAffineTransform:t];
  [spinFilter setValue:transformValue forKey:@"inputTransform"];
  //7
  return spinFilter.outputImage;
}
```

This filter is not so complicated when you break it down into steps:

1. The first filter you create in the chain is called CIConstantColorGenerator. There is a class of CIFilters called generators that don't require an input image. Other generators include linear and radial gradients, noise and checkerboards.

   The constant color generator outputs a single color. In this case, you need to create an alpha mask that ranges from 0.0 to 1.0. The color doesn't matter as much as the last parameter for the alpha argument. Here you pass in self.inputTime.

   The second filter blends the source and destination scenes according to the alpha mask.

   The way the filter works is for any given pixel, it interpolates between the 'inputImage' and the 'inputBackgroundImage' based on the alpha value of the pixel in the mask image 'inputMaskImage'. When the alpha value is 0.0, the 'inputBackgroundImage' is fully displayed, in this case, that's set to the inputImage property of your CIFilter subclass, or the source scene. When the alpha pixel value is 1.0, the image displayed is the 'inputImage', in this case the inputTargetImage or destination scene image.

2. The final filter is another CIAffineTransform. As you saw before, it takes a transformation matrix that can rotate, scale, and translate the scene's image. The first thing to do with the new filter is set its inputImage.

3. Here you create an affine transformation matrix using CGAffineTransformMakeRotation. There are corresponding methods for scaling and translation (moving). You need to wrap the transform in an NSValue object for the CIFilter to take it as a parameter. Then you set the NSValue object as the inputTransform key for the filter.

4. Finally, you return the result of the filter.

That's it for this filter. As the value in `self.inputTime` moves from 0.0 to 1.0, it masks more and more of the image from the original scene and you see more and more the target scene. The scene will also spin as the time increments, making two rotations, as 3.14 is half a rotation.

To see your custom transition `CIFilter` class in action, import it into **MyScene.m**:

```
#import "CustomTransitionFilter.h"
```

Replace the current scene transition in `newGame` with your new custom transition filter:

```
SKTransition *levelTransition =
  [SKTransition transitionWithCIFilter:
   [[CustomTransitionFilter alloc] init] duration:0.5];
```

Build and run now, and enjoy your simple fade transition.

> **Note:** If you have trouble seeing the transition, make sure you run the code on an actual device (and that the device is relatively new, like an iPhone 5 for example). Remember Core Image filters are expensive so might not perform well on older hardware (or the simulator).

At this point, you now have experience using Core Image in all three of the ways you can in Sprite Kit: filtering textures, filtering an `SKEffectNode`, and filtering transitions.

But before you bid farewell to Cat Nap for good, why not practice what you just learned by adding a special effect to the game on your own? The cat will love you for it! ☺

Challenges

There are two challenges for you in this chapter. Both help you get more practice using SKEffectNode – but this time to apply an effect to just part of the scene instead of the entire scene.

As always, if you get stuck you can find the solution in the resources for this chapter – but give it your best shot first!

Challenge 1: A crazy dream

Since you're pretty much done with Cat Nap at this point, you'll just apply a gratuitous special effect to the game just for fun and practice. It will represent the state of mind of the cat as she begins to fall asleep – the world will begin to distort like a fun house mirror!

Instead of applying your new filter to the entire game, it would be nice to restrict it to just a part of the node tree. Your challenge is to apply a filter called `CIBumpDistortion` to only the blocks. You also want to change the magnitude of the effect each frame, for a pulsating effect.

Here are some hints:

1. Create an **SKEffectNode.**

2. Make the **SKEffectNode** a child of the main **SKScene** (probably a child of **_gameNode**).

3. Instead of putting the block nodes into **_gameNode**, put them into the **SKEffectNode.**

4. Create the filter and set your parameters according to hints 5-8 below.

5. Set the **SKEffectNode.filter** property to the "CIBumpDistortion" filter.

6. Set the "inputScale" attribute on the filter to an **NSNumber** equal to 1.0.

7. Set the "inputCenter" attribute on the filter to a **CIVector** (270, 180).

8. Set the **SKEffectNode.shouldEnableEffects** to YES.

9. Create an update loop.

10. Within the update loop, alter the input parameter on the bump distortion filter based on the current time, so that it ranges from -1.0 to 1.0.

Give that a shot on your own, but if you get stuck some additional hints follow.

You'll need a new instance variable in **MyScene.m** for the effect node and the filter – remember that you need to keep a reference to the filter to alter its properties:

```
SKEffectNode *_blockNode;
CIFilter *_bumpFilter;
```

You'll need to set up that node in the initialization of the layer, after you create the _gameNode:

```
_blockNode = [SKEffectNode node];
_blockNode.shouldEnableEffects = YES;
_bumpFilter = [CIFilter filterWithName:@"CIBumpDistortion"];
[_bumpFilter setValue:@(1.0) forKey:@"inputScale"];
[_bumpFilter setValue:
  [CIVector vectorWithCGPoint:CGPointMake(270, 180)]
                    forKey:@"inputCenter"];
_blockNode.filter = _bumpFilter;
[_gameNode addChild:_blockNode];
```

Anywhere you normally would have added a block to the **_gameNode**, you want to add it to **_blockNode** instead, as in the following example:

```
[_blockNode addChild:blockNode];
```

Now for the fun part: add an **update:** method in which you change the **inputIntensity** of the _bumpFilter:

```
- (void)update:(NSTimeInterval)currentTime
{
    float distortionAmount = (float)sin(currentTime);
    [_bumpFilter setValue:@(distortionAmount)
                forKey:@"inputScale"];
}
```

I think it's best at this point to remove the **OldTimeyFilter** effect, because its jitter combined with the distortion created by the new blocks filter will be too much. Comment out the lines in **initializeSceneWithLevelNumber:** that set **self.filter** and **self.shouldEnableEffects**.

Keep in mind that these filters are only affecting the visual representation of the blocks –
the touches are still interpreted where they would be without any filter applied.

Good job! Now you have an effect that only applies to a subtree of your scene – and
your cat is looking more tired than ever.

And with that, you're done with Cat Nap! May she rest in peace. ☺

Challenge 2: A Colorful Ressurection

Remember the zombie from Zombie Conga? Well, he's about to be arisen from the
grave!

In the resources for this chapter, you will find a starter projet called **HueAdjust-Starter**.
Open it in Xcode and build and run, and you will see that your favorite zombie has
returned!

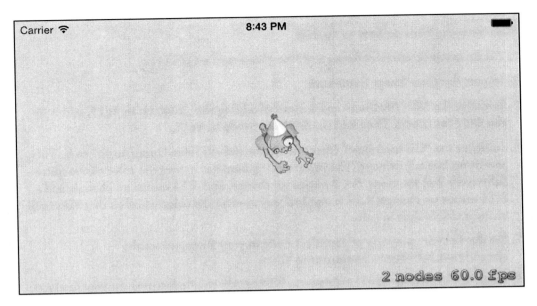

Take a look through the code – you'll see it's very similar to the Zombie Conga project, but there are two main differences:

1. The zombie just automatically moves around, bouncing off walls. Maybe the crazy cat ladies have worn off on him!

2. This time the zombie is made of two images: one sprite for the zombie itself, and a child sprite for the zombie's hat. I'll explain why I did this later on.

   However, note that both the zombie and the hat are added as children of the main scene, and their position and rotation are updated so they always stay in sync.

Your challenge is to adjust the hue of the zombie to be a random color. This is a very handy technique if you want to have lots of different types of enemies in your game, but not have them all look exactly the same.

This gets to the reason why I split out his hat into a different sprite. Often, you want to adjust some parts of a sprite's color, but keep other parts unchanged. By making the hat a different sprite, you can apply a filter to the zombie sprite but the hat can rest on top, unchanged.

To adjust the zombie's color, you need to apply a `CIHueAdjust` filter to the zombie. The goal is that ever you tap the screen, you update the `CIFilter` to make the zombie switch to a new color.

Here are some hints on how to do this:

1. Create instance variables for an `SKEffectNode` and a `CIFilter`.

2. Import the Core Image framework

3. Initialize the `SKEffectNode` and instead of adding the `_zombie` to `self`, add it to the `SKEffectNode`. Then add the `SKEffectNode` to `self`.

4. Initialize the "CIHueAdjust" filter and set the default value "inputAngle" to 0. This means no hue adjustment. The input angle parameter rotates the color of the sprite fully every 2 pi rotations. So, 0 means no change, and 6.14 means no change, and -6.14 means no change. 3.14 is one half way around the color wheel so that value will create a visible shift in color.

5. Set the `filter` property of the effect node to your filter and set the `shouldEnableEffects` parameter to YES;

6. Now, in the existing `touchesBegan:withEvent:` method, inside the touches loop, add a method that creates a random number between 0.0 and 6.14 (there's already a method included to create a random number inside a given range). Then set that random value to the "inputAngle" property of the filter instance variable.

Each time you tap the screen, the zombie will change color, but his hat will remain the same:

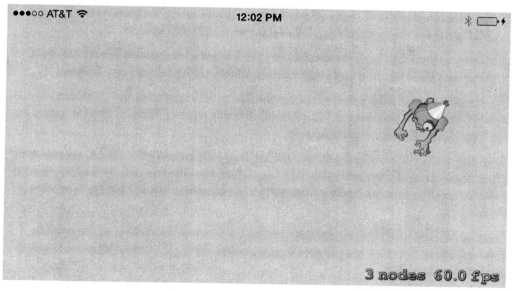

You may wonder why you bothered doing this, when you could have simply set the `color` property on the zombie. Try this for yourself by commenting out the lines in `touchesBegan:withEvent:` that update the filter's "inputAngle" value, and replace them with the following:

```
_zombie.color = [SKColor colorWithRed:RandomRange(0, 1)
                                green:RandomRange(0, 1)
                                 blue:RandomRange(0, 1)
                                alpha:1];
_zombie.colorBlendFactor = 1.0;
```

Build and run, and notice how the zombie looks when you tap:

Notice setting the color sets the entire zombie to be that color, while varying the hue gives you some nice variance between different parts of the zombie and generally looks better. So this is definitely a neat technique to have in your toolbelt!

Now bring out your shotgun and put this zombie to rest – permanently. It's time to move onto a new game about a bad-ass with an attitude, and a whole lotta bugs.

Section IV: Tile Maps and Juice

At the time of writing, Sprite Kit doesn't come packaged with tile map support – but in this section, you're going to learn how to create your own tile map engine! You'll also learn how to take a good game and make it great by adding a ton of special effects and excitement – a.k.a. "juice."

In the process, you will create a tile map-based action game called Pest Control, where you take the role of Arnold, a guy so badass he *never* wears a shirt. Giant bugs have invaded Arnold's town, and he's just the guy to dish out a good smashing.

Chapter 13: Beginning Tile Maps

Chapter 14: More Tile Maps

Chapter 15: Imported Tile Maps

Chapter 16: Saving and Loading Games

Chapter 17: Juice Up Your Game, Part 1

Chapter 18: Juice Up Your Game, Part 2

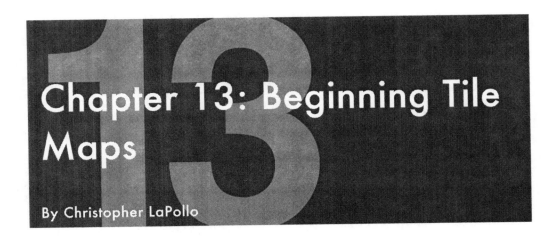

Chapter 13: Beginning Tile Maps

By Christopher LaPollo

Since the early days of computers, developers have had to find ways to get more performance out of limited CPU cycles, RAM and disk space. Video game makers discovered one trick early on: building up level backgrounds by combining and repeating smaller images, referred to as **tiles**. You've seen tiles in countless games, like Mega Man, Contra, Super Mario Brothers, and The Legend of Zelda.

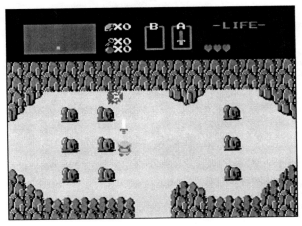

Using tile maps in games is a great choice for indie iOS developers for a number of reasons:

- **Improved performance**. Tile maps require less memory and processing time than many alternative methods. They're a particularly good choice for iOS, since processing power is quite limited compared to PCs or consoles.

- **Reduced art costs**. Tile maps allow you to reuse a small set of tiles to make large levels, allowing you to make the most of an often limited art budget.

- **Reduced time to market**. Tile maps are quite simple to create and to work with, allowing you to create and iterate on levels quickly.

Over the next few chapters, you'll create a new minigame: Pest Control. Here's what it will look like when you're finished:

In Pest Control, you take the role of Arnold, a guy so bad-ass he *never* wears a shirt. Arnold's town has been invaded by giant bugs in need of a good smashing.

Pest Control uses very simple pixel art. Each of its animations consists of only two frames, and its backgrounds are plain. This is by design, to show you what you can accomplish with some relatively simple art.

You'll start by building a solid foundation for the game, and then see how you can add a bit of polish or "juice" to really bring your game to life.

You will build this game across the next six chapters, in stages:

1. Chapter 13, Beginning Tile Maps: You are here! In this chapter, you'll create the bulk of Pest Control. You'll write some code to create a tile map from a simple text format, and add the hero to the game.

2. **Chapter 14, More Tile Maps:** You'll add the core gameplay in this chapter and learn about coordinate conversions and collision detection with tile maps.

3. **Chapter 15, Imported Tile Maps:** You'll learn how to import tile maps into your game that are stored in a popular tile-map format called TMX files, and use an open-source map editor to create your maps.

4. **Chapter 16, Saving and Loading Games:** You'll learn how to implement an autosave feature that stores a player's progress in Pest Control. You'll also add gameplay features like timers, winning and losing, and progressing through multiple levels.

5. **Chapter 17, Juice Up Your Game, Part 1:** You'll learn how adding simple visual effects can make Pest Control, or any game you write, more entertaining.

6. **Chapter 18, Juice Up Your Game, Part 2:** You'll add sounds and even more effects, because adding fewer effects at this point would be ridiculous.

Controlling pests takes a lot of work, so let's get started.

Getting started

Start Xcode and select **File\New\Project...** from the main menu. Select the **iOS\Application\SpriteKit Game** template and click **Next**.

Enter **PestControl** for the Product Name, choose **iPhone** for Devices, leave the **Class Prefix** blank and click **Next**. Choose somewhere on your hard drive to save your project and click **Create**.

Inside your new project, modify the **PestControl** target to support only **Landscape Left** and **Landscape Right**.

You'll want access to the math functions in your old friend SKTUtils, so drag the **SKTUtils** folder from the book's resources into your project. Make sure **Copy items into destination group's folder (if needed)**, **Create groups for any added folders**, and the **PestControl** target are all checked.

Open **PestControl-Prefix.pch** in the **Supporting Files** group and add the following import with the other imports:

```
#import "SKTUtils.h"
```

This gives all of your files access to **SKTUtils.h**, so you won't need to import it anywhere else to use it.

You don't want players distracted by the time, so you'll hide the iPhone's status bar while your app runs. To do so, add the following method to **ViewController.m**:

```
- (BOOL)prefersStatusBarHidden
{
    return YES;
}
```

Finally, to get this game off on the right foot open **Images.xassets** and select the **AppIcon** entry. Then in the resources for this chapter, drag all of the files from the "App Icon" folder into the area on the right. You should see the following when you're done:

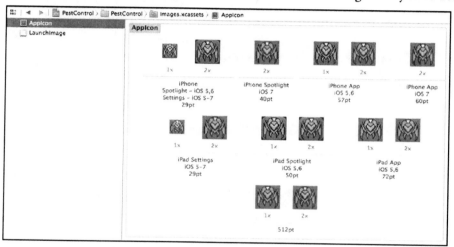

Import resources

The next step is to import the resources you need for this project. To do this, drag the **Resources** folder from this chapter's resources into your project. Make sure **Copy items into destination group's folder (if needed)**, **Create groups for any added folders**, and the **PestControl** target are all checked.

The **Resources** folder you just added includes three subfolders: **Levels**, **Art**, and **Extra Source Code**:

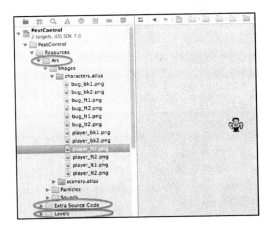

Levels contains configuration data that you can ignore for now, and **Extra Source Code** contains files you'll use in later chapters. Inside **Art** are three more folders, **Sounds**, **Particles**, and **Images**. You'll use **Sounds** and **Particles** in Chapter 18, "Juice Up Your Game, Part 2."

Images contains folders named **scenery.atlas** and **characters.atlas**. As you learned in Chapter 9, "Intermediate Physics", Xcode automatically creates a texture atlas from the images in a folder whose name ends with **.atlas**. It might create more than one atlas image if there are too many images to fit within its size constraints.

There aren't many images in Pest Control, so they could all easily fit into a single texture atlas. But in order to demonstrate some additional Sprite Kit features in this chapter, I've divided the images into two groups:

- Those you'll use to create the map, stored in **scenery.atlas**. For this folder, Xcode will create a texture atlas named **scenary**.

- Those that make up the player and bug animations, stored in **characters.atlas**. For this folder, Xcode will create a texture atlas named **characters**.

With the project created and its resources in place, let's make a map.

Map-building with tiles

In most games, the background art takes up the most screen space. That means it threatens to take up most of your art budget and the most space in your app's bundle, too.

In this section, you'll see how you can create a background using only a few different images, repeated and laid out in a grid. You'll create your scene using multiple layers: one for the bugs, a second for background objects like the grass and water, and a third for some special decorations, the trees. Finally, Arnold will run around on top of those layers.

Note: Separating your scene into multiple layers has a number of benefits.

First, it keeps your code cleaner and easier to understand. For example, if you know the background tiles are in the background layer, and the bugs are in the bug layer, you can code accordingly.

Second, multiple layers in your scene make it easy to put tiles in front of or behind other layers. For example, in Pest Control the tree tiles will be partially transparent so you can see the grass behind them. You can also do even fancier things like have another layer on top of the bug layer, so bugs could hide behind a bush, or use multiple background layers to implement parallax scrolling.

Third, it can result in better performance. Sprite Kit attempts to speed up its rendering by drawing as much as it can with a single texture atlas before loading a different texture atlas into the GPU. It's actually more complicated than that, but one way you can drastically improve rendering performance is to organize your sprite nodes by texture atlas.

Put another way, your game might run really slowly if you mix texture atlases within a single node and its children. In fact, even if all the sprites in a node use the same texture atlas, you may still need to put them on different layers if they are treated differently in some other way, like if they all don't use the same blend mode. For more information see Chapter 25, "Performance".

Ok, before Arnold can rid his town of its bug infestation, you need to build him a town filled with bugs. Start things off with the background layer.

Tile layers

Go to **File\New\File...**, choose the **iOS\Cocoa Touch\Objective-C class** template, and click **Next**. Name your class **TileMapLayer**, make it a subclass of **SKNode** and click **Next** again. Be sure the **PestControl** target is checked and click **Create**.

Open **TileMapLayer.h** and add the following property and method declarations:

```
@property (readonly,nonatomic) CGSize tileSize;

- (instancetype)initWithAtlasNamed:(NSString *)atlasName
                          tileSize:(CGSize)tileSize
                              grid:(NSArray *)grid;
```

The `tileSize` property simply provides access to the `tileSize` passed into `initWithAtlasNamed:tileSize:grid:`.

As for `initWithAtlasNamed:tileSize:grid:`, it initializes a `TileMapLayer` object with the following parameters:

- `atlasName` is the name of a texture atlas created by Xcode, in which it will find images for this layer's tiles. As previously mentioned, Pest Control will have two atlases: **scenery** and **characters**. The way you'll implement the game, each `TileMapLayer` will only use images from a single atlas. In the next chapter, you'll create layers without this limitation.

- `tileSize` is the width and height of this layer's tiles, measured in points. You'll use this value to position tiles in the map, and the math you'll use to do so only works if every tile in the grid is the same size. If your app needs to support multiple tile sizes, group them into different `TileMapLayer` objects.

- `tileCodes` is an `NSArray` of `NSStrings`. This array defines the layout of the map itself. You'll learn more about this soon.

Open **TileMapLayer.m** and add the following private variable to the `TileMapLayer` implementation:

```
SKTextureAtlas *_atlas;
```

The previous games haven't covered the `SKTextureAtlas` class. `SKTextureAtlas` provides direct access to the texture atlases Xcode generates for you. It only has a few methods, but as you'll soon see, there are some benefits in using it to create your sprites.

Creating tiles

In this chapter, you're going to create tile maps using simple text files. For now, you'll only support two different tile types: grass and walls. You'll put the 'o' character wherever you want grass to appear, and the 'x' character wherever you want a wall. I chose these two characters just because I liked the way they looked.

For example, the following line:

```
@"xooooooooooooooooox"
```

Will be converted into 1 wall tile, 16 grass tiles, and 1 wall tile, like this:

You need a method that takes a character and returns the right kind of tile for that character. For the wall and grass tiles, you will simply create an SKSpriteNode with the appropriate image set.

To do this, add the following new method:

```
- (SKSpriteNode*)nodeForCode:(unichar)tileCode
{
  SKSpriteNode *tile;

  // 1
  switch (tileCode) {
    case 'o':
      tile = [SKSpriteNode spriteNodeWithTexture:
              [_atlas textureNamed:@"grass1"]];
      break;
    case 'x':
      tile = [SKSpriteNode spriteNodeWithTexture:
              [_atlas textureNamed:@"wall"]];
      break;
    default:
      NSLog(@"Unknown tile code: %d",tileCode);
      break;
  }
  // 2
  tile.blendMode = SKBlendModeReplace;
  return tile;
}
```

This is the heart of your operation. Or the brains. Maybe the guts? It's definitely something important. This method takes a character and returns an appropriate SKSpriteNode for it. There are two things to note here:

1. You use a switch statement to create the correct sprite based on the value of tileCode. For now, it only supports two characters, o and x, used to create grass and wall tiles, respectively. But you'll be adding more tile types to this statement throughout this chapter.

Note that you're creating your `SKSpriteNode` in a different way here than you have in previous chapters. Instead of using `SKSpriteNode`'s `spriteNodeWithImageNamed:` method, you call `spriteNodeWithTexture:`, passing in textures retrieved by name from `_atlas`. I'll cover this in more detail below.

2. You set the tile's `blendMode` property to `SKBlendModeReplace`. By default, Sprite Kit uses a blend mode of `SKBlendModeAlpha`, which supports combining a sprite's pixels with whatever pixels are below it. This is necessary when layering sprites that contain transparent pixels. But most of your images are background tiles that you know don't have transparent pixels, so setting the blend mode this way allows Sprite Kit to speed up its rendering by ignoring the pixels below this sprite. Later, when you add sprites that include transparency, you'll make sure their blend modes remain set to the default mode.

Now – back to why you're using the new `spriteNodeWithTexture:` API in this method. There are two potential benefits to creating `SKSpriteNode`s this way, instead of the image-name-based method you've been using.

1. **You control the source texture.** When you call `textureNamed:` on an `SKTextureAtlas`, Sprite Kit knows exactly where to find the texture. If you use `SKSpriteNode`'s `spriteWithImageNamed:` or `SKTexture`'s `textureWithImageNamed:`, Sprite Kit first searches your app's bundle for an image file with that name; if it can't find one, it searches your app's texture atlases.

   If your app contains multiple files with the same name, each in a different atlas, then Sprite Kit will just pick one. For example, maybe you have multiple atlases arranged by map area, but each contains a different image named "tree.png".

   `textureNamed:` is called on a specific atlas, so Sprite Kit bypasses that search and returns the correct texture immediately. This means you can have image files with the same name in different atlases, allowing you to name your images descriptively without worrying about file names in other atlases.

2. **Increased performance.** Because you specify the texture the image comes from directly, Sprite Kit doesn't have to search for it. This makes finding images this way a tiny bit faster,. To be clear, I'm not touting this as a performance optimization tip because it's doubtful your app's overall performance will be noticeably different either way. However, I thought it's worth mentioning so you can get a better idea of what's going on behind the scenes. The *real* performance increase comes from `SKTextureAtlas`'s ability to share objects efficiently, but I'll come back to that later.

Still inside **TileMapLayer.m**, add the following method that initializes a `TileMapLayer` from some strings:

```
- (instancetype)initWithAtlasNamed:(NSString *)atlasName
                          tileSize:(CGSize)tileSize
                              grid:(NSArray *)grid
{
  if (self = [super init])
  {
    _atlas = [SKTextureAtlas atlasNamed:atlasName];

    _tileSize = tileSize;

    for (int row = 0; row < grid.count; row++) {
      NSString *line = grid[row];
      for(int col = 0; col < line.length; col++) {
        SKSpriteNode *tile =
          [self nodeForCode:[line characterAtIndex:col]];
        if (tile != nil) {
          // add tiles here
        }
      }
    }
  }
  return self;
}
```

The code above initializes a `TileMapLayer` object. It assigns `_atlas` an `SKTextureAtlas` to access the texture atlas named in `atlasName`. It stores `tileSize` in the `tileSize` property you added. Finally, it loops through `grid` to build sprites for the tiles.

`grid` contains `NSStrings`, where each string represents a row of tiles in the map, and each of the string's characters represents a single tile in that row. You create a sprite for each character using the `nodeForCode:` method you just added.

Notice you check to see if `nodeForCode:` returns `nil`. That's because it returns `nil` if it doesn't know what sprite to create, or if a character represents empty space. Objective-C is usually great about safely handling `nil` objects, but if you pass `nil` to an `SKNode`'s `addChild:` method, your app *will* crash. If you aren't already certain, a best practice is to check that nodes are not `nil` before you try to add them.

Positioning tiles

Once you create a sprite, you need to position it correctly in the map. Add the following method to calculate a tile's x- and y-positions, based on its row and column in the tile grid:

```
- (CGPoint)positionForRow:(NSInteger)row col:(NSInteger)col
{
  return CGPointMake(col * self.tileSize.width +
                          self.tileSize.width / 2,
                  row * self.tileSize.height +
                          self.tileSize.height / 2);
}
```

This isn't complicated. (It's also not completely correct, but you'll fix it soon.) Take a look at this diagram and the explanation that follows to see how you find the position for a tile:

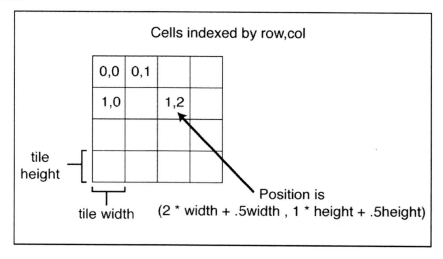

Rows count from top to bottom, and columns count from left to right. So you multiply col by the tile width to find its x-position, and multiply row by the tile height to find its y-position. You add half the tile's width and height to those x- and y-values, because you are calculating the tile's center point.

Inside initWithAtlasNamed:tileSize:grid:, replace the comment that reads, "add tiles here" with the following:

```
tile.position = [self positionForRow:row col:col];
[self addChild:tile];
```

The code above sets the tile's position and adds it to the layer.

Almost done! You just need to create your new `TileMapLayer` object to see it in action.

Your first map

Open **MyScene.m** and import your new class, like this:

```
#import "TileMapLayer.h"
```

Remove the methods this file currently contains – those were provided by the SpriteKit Game template, but you'll implement each one as you need it.

In order to keep things neat, you'll organize your scene initialization code into several methods. Add the first one to `MyScene` now, named `createScenery`:

```
- (TileMapLayer *)createScenery
{
  return [[TileMapLayer alloc]
         initWithAtlasNamed:@"scenery"
                   tileSize:CGSizeMake(32, 32)
                       grid:@[@"xxxxxxxxxxxxxxxxxx",
                              @"xoooooooooooooooox",
                              @"xoooooooooooooooox",
                              @"xoooooooooooooooox",
                              @"xoooooooooooooooox",
                              @"xooooooooooxoooooox",
                              @"xooooooooooxoooooox",
                              @"xooooooxxxxoooooox",
                              @"xoooooxoooooooooox",
                              @"xxxxxxxxxxxxxxxxxx",]];
}
```

This is really only one line of code. It returns a new `TileMapLayer` that creates tiles from the texture atlas named **scenery**, all of which are **32** points wide and tall. It defines a grid made of `x`s and `o`s that's 18 tiles wide and 10 tiles high.

Because you already know that `x` translates to a `wall` tile and `o` translates to `grass`, you can imagine what the map will look like just by glancing at this grid of characters. But using your imagination is no fun, right? So add the following method to actually create your map and add it to the scene:

```
- (id)initWithSize:(CGSize)size
{
  if (self = [super initWithSize:size]) {
    [self addChild:[self createScenery]];
```

```
    NSLog(@"Size: %@", NSStringFromCGSize(self.size));
  }
  return self;
}
```

Build and run in the **iPhone Retina (4-inch) Simulator**. You should see the following:

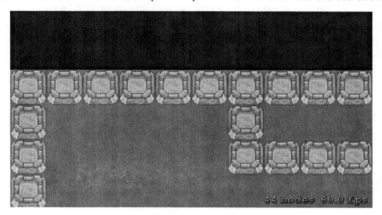

Hmm. That doesn't seem right. You made a tile map that was 18 tiles wide by 10 tiles high, and since each tile should be 32x32 points, your map should fill the entire view. However, the tiles don't seem to be the right size, and what's with that dark bar across the top?

The problem is that the Sprite Kit template kindly – and incorrectly – scaled your scene's content when your device entered landscape mode. This is because of two things:

1. **Scene initialized with portrait size**. By default, the template initializes the Sprite Kit scene in `viewDidLoad`, passing in the size of the view's frame as the scene size. At this time the view's frame has portrait, not landscape dimensions. Later on, iOS changes the orientation of the view to landscape, and updates the size of your scene.

2. **Scene streches content on size change**. Also by default in the Sprite Kit template, when your scene changes size, it stretches its contents to match the new scene size. In some games, this behavior might be fine, but it causes the tile map (made in portrait mode) to be incorrectly positioned and sized in landscape mode, like you see here.

In previous chapters, you solved this by initializing your scene at a later time, when the view's frame was already oriented in landscape mode. In this way, the scene's size never changes and there's no problem.

However, I want to show you another way to handle this problem: telling Sprite Kit not to stretch your scene's content.

Open **ViewController.m** and find `viewDidLoad`. Change the line that sets `scene`'s `scaleMode` property to the following:

```
scene.scaleMode = SKSceneScaleModeResizeFill;
```

That tells Sprite Kit to resize the scene's dimensions to match those of its view, but to leave the scene's contents unscaled.

Also add this method in **MyScene.m** so you can see what's going on:

```
- (void)didChangeSize:(CGSize)oldSize
{
  NSLog(@"Changed size: %@", NSStringFromCGSize(self.size));
}
```

Run the app, and now you should see this:

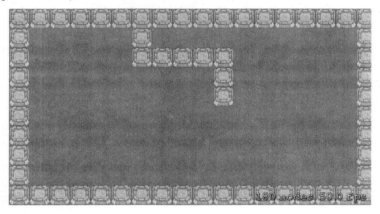

And in the log you'll see the following:

```
PestControl[1336:60b] Changed size: {320, 568}
PestControl[1336:60b] Size: {320, 568}
PestControl[1336:60b] Changed size: {568, 320}
PestControl[1336:60b] Changed size: {568, 320}
```

Here you see that the size of the scene started out in portrait, but then iOS switched the app to landscape orientation and it updated the scene's size to match, without stretching the tiles.

> **Note:** Sprite Kit calls `didChangeSize:` on your scene whenever its size changes, and even sometimes when it doesn't. If you write a game that supports both portrait and landscape modes, implement this method to update anything in your scene that depends on the screen size, such as the placement of UI elements.

Before moving on, delete the `NSLog` statement in `initWithSize:` and delete `didChangeSize:` completely. You don't want to be bugged by all those log statements every time you run. See what I did there, with the bugged?

Filtering modes

The tiles are sized correctly now, but they still don't look the way they should. If you look very closely, you'll see they're blurry, when they should appear with a sharp pixel-art style.

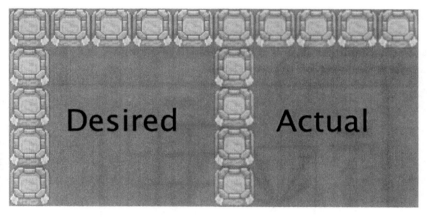

You are displaying the tiles as 32x32 points so that Pest Control shows the same number of tiles on both retina and non-retina displays. However, the image you are using for the tile is actually 32x32 pixels, so on retina devices it gets scaled by 2 to account for its double pixel density. But why's it blurry?

By default, Sprite Kit produces scaled images that are antialiased, or smooth. To achieve this result, it blends pixel colors in such a way that sharp lines are often lost. That looks great for a lot of art, but Pest Control uses pixel art, which is meant to show the stark outline of individual pixels.

Fortunately, there's a simple way to fix this. Open **TileMapLayer.m** and add the following line to nodeWithCode:, immediately after the line that sets tile's blendMode property:

```
tile.texture.filteringMode = SKTextureFilteringNearest;
```

Run again, and now you'll see your map in all its pixelated glory!

Upside-down maps

Looks good now, right? Not quite.

You may not have noticed it, but if you compare the image with the grid you defined in createScenery, you'll find that the map is upside down!

The problem lies in your implementation of positionForRow:col: in **TileMapLayer.m**.

You built the tile map using standard array syntax, counting left to right, top to bottom. But remember that in Sprite Kit's coordinate system, y values move *up* the screen as they increase. So tile coordinate (0,0) is at the upper-left of your grid, but your math will place that tile at the lower-left of your screen.

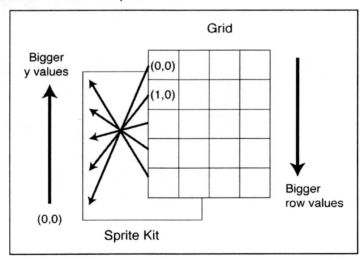

To fix this, you need to adjust the y-positions of all your tiles. Instead of counting up from (0,0), you want to count down from the top of the map.

To do so, you'll need access to a couple more pieces of information about your tile map. Open **TileMapLayer.h** and add the following properties:

```
@property (readonly,nonatomic) CGSize gridSize;
@property (readonly,nonatomic) CGSize layerSize;
```

You're adding these properties to `TileMapLayer`'s public interface because they return information that other classes may find useful, too.

- `gridSize` returns the width and height of the grid, measured in tiles. For example, this map will be 18x10.

- `layerSize` returns the layer's width and height, measured in points. Conceptually, it's `gridSize * tileSize`. For example, this map will be 576x320.

Inside **TileMapLayer.m**, add the following code to `initWithAtlasNamed:tileSize:grid:`, just *before* the `for` loop that creates the tiles:

```
_gridSize = CGSizeMake([grid.firstObject length], grid.count);
_layerSize = CGSizeMake(_tileSize.width * _gridSize.width,
                        _tileSize.height * _gridSize.height);
```

Notice how it assigns `gridSize`'s `width` using the length of the first string in `grid`. `TileMapLayer` assumes every item in `grid` is the same size, but to keep things short, it doesn't include any error-checking. So make sure your grids are sized properly, or you may experience errors.

Now replace the contents of `positionForRow:col:` with this:

```
return
  CGPointMake(
    col * self.tileSize.width + self.tileSize.width / 2,
    self.layerSize.height -
      (row * self.tileSize.height + self.tileSize.height / 2));
```

This starts by calculating the same y-value as the original version, but it subtracts that from the layer's height. This effectively flips the map's x,y coordinates, making it return higher y-values for higher row values.

Build and run. Here's what you'll get:

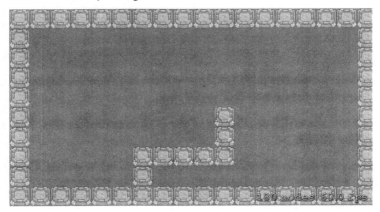

OK, the map is displayed correctly. Notice, though, some of the tiles on the right hand side are cut off, while they're not on the left. Wouldn't you feel better if the map were centered?

Centering the scene

It's not hard to center your scene. However, as you add more and more nodes, moving things around becomes problematic, so you'll refactor the scene a bit while you're at it.

Instead of adding nodes directly to the scene, you'll add them all to a single node like you did in Chapter 5, "Scrolling." This will allow you to move everything in your scene by moving just that node. Later, you'll add UI elements like labels directly to the scene, so you can move the map while the labels remain in place.

Open **MyScene.m** and add the following private variables:

```
SKNode *_worldNode;
TileMapLayer *_bgLayer;
```

_worldNode is the single node that will contain all the scene's elements. _bgLayer will store the TileMapLayer returned from createScenery. You'll be accessing it a lot, so this variable will come in handy.

Now add the following method:

```
- (void)createWorld
{
  _bgLayer = [self createScenery];
```

```
_worldNode = [SKNode node];
[_worldNode addChild:_bgLayer];
[self addChild:_worldNode];

self.anchorPoint = CGPointMake(0.5, 0.5);
_worldNode.position =
    CGPointMake(-_bgLayer.layerSize.width / 2,
              -_bgLayer.layerSize.height / 2);
}
```

Much like `createScenery`, this method organizes some of your scene's setup. It assigns the `TileMapLayer` returned from `createScenery` to `_bgLayer`. It creates `_worldNode`, adds `_bgLayer` as a child of `_worldNode` and adds `_worldNode` to the scene.

Finally, it changes the scene's `anchorPoint` to (0.5,0.5) and sets `_worldNode`'s position. These two lines are what actually center the scene:

1. The new `anchorPoint` value moves the scene's origin – point (0,0) – to the center of the screen.

2. Then you move the `_worldNode` down and to the left. Remember, though: the way you positioned your tiles, (0,0) in the layer is the lower-left corner of the map. By moving the map in a negative direction by half its width and half its height, the map's center is now at the scene's origin.

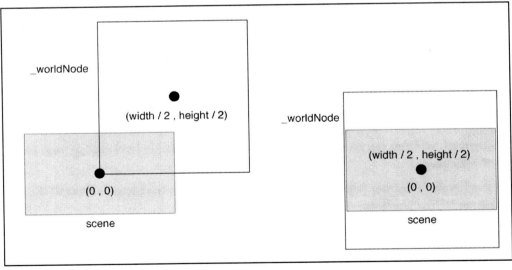

Inside `initWithSize:`, replace this line:

```
[self addChild:[self createScenery]];
```

With this one:

```
[self createWorld];
```

Build. Run. Centered. Yay!

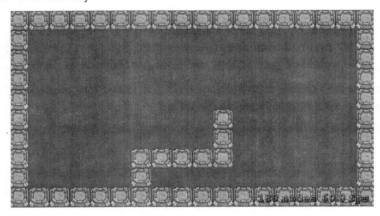

You finally have your map onscreen exactly as intended. But your hero in Pest Control is a cardio nut – he's going to need a bit more running space.

Loading layers from text files

Hard-coding your levels, like you're doing now in `createScenery`, isn't a very good idea. In Chapter 15, "Imported Tile Maps," you'll see how to load TMX files, which are a nice way to define tile maps. For now, you'll implement a simple mechanism for loading levels defined with text files. This is a good way to start because it's easy to understand, and you can reuse this concept for other bare-bones level editing tools in your own games.

In the **Levels** folder you imported (inside **Resources**), there is a file called **level-1-bg.txt**. Here are its first few lines:

```
scenery
32x32
xxxxxxxxxxxxxxxxxxxxxxxxxxxxxxxx
xooooooooooooooooooooowwwwwwwwx
xooooooooooooooooooooowwwwwwwwx
```

It simply contains the same type of information that you've been providing to
`TileMapLayer`'s `initWithAtlasNamed:tileSize:grid:` method: an atlas name, tile
size and rows of characters representing tiles.

The **Levels** folder also includes a helper class I wrote for you called
`TileMapLayerLoader`. This class contains a single method named
`tileMapLayerFromFileNamed:` that uses the contents of a text file formatted like the
one shown above to initialize and return a new `TileMapLayer`.

This helper class is straightforward and well commented, so its contents are not included
here. However, please feel free to take a peek to make sure you understand it.

> **Note:** There is one thing you do need to know about `TileMapLayerLoader` if
> you use it to load layer data files you've edited yourself. It's written in the same
> style as the rest of Pest Control, in that it lacks production-level error checking. If
> it loads a file that includes any empty lines where the rows of tile characters
> should appear—including any blank lines at the end of the file—it will produce
> gaps in the tile map.
>
> If you ever run and see an extra row's worth of space at the bottom of the map,
> you probably hit return/enter at the end of the last row of characters in your layer
> data file.

Inside **MyScene.m**, import the `TileMapLayerLoader` class:

```
#import "TileMapLayerLoader.h"
```

Then replace the contents of `createScenery` with the following call to load the level
defined in **level-1-bg.txt**:

```
return [TileMapLayerLoader tileMapLayerFromFileNamed:
        @"level-1-bg.txt"];
```

Run the app and you should see this:

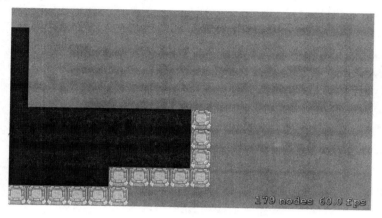

What is that dark area? Look in your console and you should see a bunch of log messages similar to this one:

```
PestControl[44048:70b] Unknown tile code: 61
```

That's just because level-1-bg.txt contains a couple of characters your project doesn't yet support. I wanted you to see what happens when your level contains an unsupported character, in case you try to extend this app and run into this situation.

Open **TileMapLayer.m** and add support for these new characters by adding the following `case` statements to the `switch` statement in `nodeForCode::`

```
case '=':
  tile = [SKSpriteNode spriteNodeWithTexture:
          [_atlas textureNamed:@"stone"]];
  break;
case 'w':
  tile = [SKSpriteNode spriteNodeWithTexture:
          [_atlas textureNamed:@"water1"]];
  break;
```

Run again and you should no longer have that dark area.

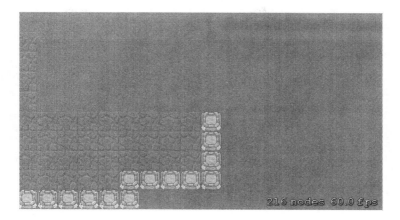

But wouldn't you like to move around and see the whole map?

Moving the camera

In Pest Control, you'll keep the camera focused on your pest-smashing hero as he runs around the map. As you learned in Chapter 5, "Scrolling," you can simulate a moving camera in Sprite Kit by moving the scene's nodes.

Your scene's nodes are all children of _worldNode, so you'll find the player's position in _worldNode and place the center of the screen on top of it. Astute readers will note there is no player yet – all in due time.

You won't be able to simply center the view on the player's position, however, because if he's too close to the edge of the map, the camera will appear to move over too far and expose the blank nothingness that lies beyond. This means you'll have to do some math to enforce limits on the camera.

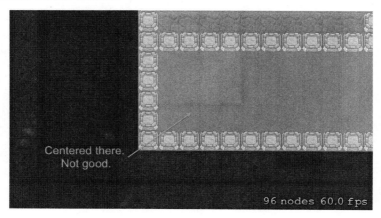

Open **MyScene.m** and add this method:

```
- (void)centerViewOn:(CGPoint)centerOn
{
  CGSize size = self.size;

  CGFloat x = Clamp(centerOn.x, size.width / 2,
                    _bgLayer.layerSize.width - size.width / 2);

  CGFloat y = Clamp(centerOn.y, size.height / 2,
                    _bgLayer.layerSize.height - size.height/2);

  _worldNode.position = CGPointMake(-x, -y);
}
```

There's a bit of math to explain here, so let's review this in detail.

First, it gets the size of the scene. The scene's size defines the limits for how close to the map's edge the center can be. For example, if the scene is 320 points tall, the scene's origin is 160 points from the top and bottom of it. That means you don't want to center on any point less than 160, or more than the map's height minus 160.

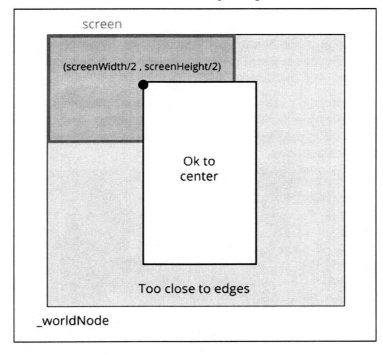

The next lines determine the best x- and y-values that satisfy the above constraints. It uses the `Clamp` function from `SKUtils` to choose either the coordinate from `centerOn` or the minimum/maximum allowed value if `centerOn`'s value is outside the allowable range. The allowable sizes are based on `_bgLayer`'s dimensions because it's assumed the background layer defines the largest area that you want visible in the level.

You then negate the values and use those to position `_worldNode`. Remember how you originally centered the map by negating half its width and height? Here you're doing the same thing, except you aren't centering over the center of the map, but rather over the position you just calculated.

To see it in action, add this method to center the view on a touch location (or replace the existing `touchesBegan:withEvent:` method if you still have it from the template):

```
- (void)touchesBegan:(NSSet *)touches withEvent:(UIEvent *)event
{
  UITouch *touch = [touches anyObject];
  [self centerViewOn:[touch locationInNode:_worldNode]];
}
```

Build and run. Tap the screen and notice how the map moves so that the point you touched is as close to the screen's center as possible, without ever revealing anything beyond the map's edges.

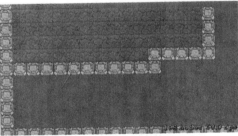

Take a look around the map. You'll see some walls, some water and a lot of grass. Maybe too much grass. You're about to learn a tip for making your maps look less repetitive.

Randomizing the tiles

There are several ways to improve a tile map. For example, if you look at the boundaries between the water and grass tiles, it's pretty blocky. You could use special tiles along these transition points to show a more gradual, pleasing border between the two tile types.

However, placing such tiles manually can be time consuming, and implementing logic so your app can choose appropriate boundary tiles automatically is a bit too complicated for this chapter. The open-source tool you use in Chapter 15, "Imported Tile Maps", does support this sort of behavior, but even using the tool to do it is complicated to explain in this book.

But keeping it simple doesn't mean you can't mix it up a little. One simple trick is to return one of several different images for a type, rather than always returning the same image.

Open **TileMapLayer.m** and replace the `case` statements that create the grass and water tiles with these:

```
case 'o':
  tile = [SKSpriteNode spriteNodeWithTexture:
          [_atlas textureNamed:
            RandomFloat() < 0.1 ? @"grass2" : @"grass1"]];
  break;
case 'w':
  tile = [SKSpriteNode spriteNodeWithTexture:
          [_atlas textureNamed:
            RandomFloat() < 0.1 ? @"water2" : @"water1"]];
  break;
```

These simply choose a different grass or water tile about 10 percent of the time.

Build and run, and now the large areas of grass or water have a bit more visual interest. And as an added bonus, your map will look slightly different every time you play.

You've defined a nice, peaceful map. But it's a bit desolate. Hey, who's that I hear banging on the door?

Adding and moving the player

In Pest Control, your hero is a bad-ass named Arnold who can't stand idly by while giant bugs roam free across his land. In fact, he can't stand still at all, and he's more than willing to destroy everything he sees in pursuit of a giant-bug-free world.

When you tap the screen, Arnold will start running and either bounce off or run straight through anything he comes across. There's no stopping this guy once he gets going. Speaking of which, let's get going with some code.

Go to **File\New\File...**, choose the **iOS\Cocoa Touch\Objective-C class** template and click **Next**. Name your class **Player**, make it a subclass of **SKSpriteNode** and click **Next** again. Be sure the **PestControl** target is checked and click **Create**.

Inside **Player.m**, add the following initializer method:

```
- (instancetype)init
{
  SKTextureAtlas *atlas =
    [SKTextureAtlas atlasNamed: @"characters"];
  SKTexture *texture = [atlas textureNamed:@"player_ft1"];
  texture.filteringMode = SKTextureFilteringNearest;

  if (self = [super initWithTexture:texture]) {
    self.name = @"player";
    // more setup later
  }
  return self;
}
```

Once again, you access textures using an `SKTextureAtlas`. You're hard-coding the atlas name because you know all of Pest Control's player images are in the atlas named `characters`.

If you wanted to use more than one atlas, you could easily add an initializer that includes an atlas name parameter. You might want to do something like that if your player character wears different costumes in different levels, for example.

You also name the sprite `player` so it will be easy to find using Sprite Kit's node-searching features. That will come in handy a bit later.

Now go back to **MyScene.m** to add your player to the scene.

First, import your new **Player** class:

```
#import "Player.h"
```

Then add this private variable to provide convenient access to the **Player** object:

```
Player *_player;
```

Once again, you'll keep the scene's configuration code organized by adding a new method to create your characters. Add this method:

```
- (void)createCharacters
{
  _player = [Player node];
  _player.position = CGPointMake(300, 300);
  [_worldNode addChild:_player];
}
```

This creates a player at a set position in the map. Later on, you'll learn how to define a custom spawn point and will add more types of characters (like the bugs) to the map.

Finally, add the following lines to **initWithSize:**, just after your call to **createWorld**:

```
[self createCharacters];
[self centerViewOn:_player.position];
```

This simply calls your new method to create the player, and then uses the **centerViewOn:** method you created earlier to make sure you can see your hero.

Build and run. Tough guy? Check.

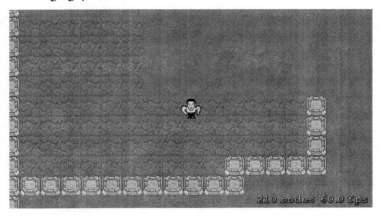

Stoic heroes are great and all, but it sure would be cool if this guy could move.

Physics-based motion

In Pest Control, your hero is obsessed with one thing: crushing bugs. Tapping the screen will send the hero running determinedly in the tap's direction. Nothing will deter him. If he hits something, he'll either smash right through it or bounce off and keep running in a new direction.

To create this behavior, you'll use Sprite Kit's physics engine. You've already read a lot about physics in earlier chapters, so I won't explain every detail here.

Open **Player.m** and replace the comment inside `init` that reads, "more setup later" with the following code:

```
// 1
CGFloat minDiam = MIN(self.size.width, self.size.height);
minDiam = MAX(minDiam-16, 4);
self.physicsBody =
  [SKPhysicsBody bodyWithCircleOfRadius:minDiam/2.0];
// 2
self.physicsBody.usesPreciseCollisionDetection = YES;
// 3
self.physicsBody.allowsRotation = NO;
self.physicsBody.restitution = 1;
self.physicsBody.friction = 0;
self.physicsBody.linearDamping = 0;
```

The above code adds a physics body to the player sprite, configured as follows:

1. It uses a circle that's a bit smaller than the sprite to provide more visually satisfying collision behavior.

2. It enables precise collision detection. Your hero moves fast, and you want the physics engine to keep up.

3. Finally, you want your hero to run forever, and you don't want him to tip over while he's doing it. These lines create that behavior by disabling the body's rotation, friction and linear damping, and setting restitution to 1. For a refresher on what these properties mean, check out Chapter 8, "Beginning Physics."

Users will always want to see Arnold as he runs around, so open **MyScene.m** and add this method:

```
- (void)didSimulatePhysics
{
  [self centerViewOn:_player.position];
}
```

Remember from Chapter 10, "Advanced Physics" that this is the method that gets called after the physics engine has updated the positions of each node based on the physics simulation. Therefore, it is the perfect spot to center the view to the (newly updated) position of Arnold.

Build, run, and watch as Arnold makes a mad dash to the bottom of the map and then runs right off the screen. Hmm. Got somewhere to be, Arnold?

Come on, Arnold. If you run away now, what will you to do when the giant bugs show up?

Help your hero look more heroic by turning off gravity. To do so, add this line to **MyScene.m** at the end of `createWorld`:

```
self.physicsWorld.gravity = CGVectorMake(0, 0);
```

Run again, and you'll see that Arnold stands still. Actually, he won't budge, as if he's frozen with fear. Let's make him move again, but this time, where *you* want him to go.

Much like you did when building Zombie Conga, you're going to provide a target position, which the player's sprite will then run toward and beyond.

Open **Player.h** and declare the following method:

```
- (void)moveToward:(CGPoint)targetPosition;
```

Then add its implementation in **Player.m**:

```
- (void)moveToward:(CGPoint)targetPosition
{
  CGPoint targetVector =
```

```
    CGPointNormalize(CGPointSubtract(targetPosition,
                                     self.position));

    targetVector = CGPointMultiplyScalar(targetVector, 300);
    self.physicsBody.velocity = CGVectorMake(targetVector.x,
                                             targetVector.y);
}
```

This math should look familiar if you've completed the minigames up to this point. It simply sets the sprite's velocity to a vector pointing at `targetPosition` with a length of 300. Remember, the length is interpreted as a speed, so the larger this number, the faster he goes!

Open **MyScene.m** and replace the contents of `touchesBegan:withEvent:` with the following:

```
UITouch *touch = [touches anyObject];
[_player moveToward:[touch locationInNode:_worldNode]];
```

This just tells the player sprite to move toward the location of the user's tap.

Build and run. Now Arnold goes back to running right off screen, but at least he does it in the direction you tell him to go. Tap the screen again, and you'll eventually see him run back into view, only to run away once more. I suppose that's progress.

It looks like Arnold needs a little encouragement to stick around. Much as you've done in some of this book's other minigames, you'll define a world boundary into which he'll collide. Basically, you're going to trap Arnold in a box. But *trapping* sounds so ugly. Let's say you're going to *convince* him to stay.

First, you need to define a physics category. Open **MyScene.h** and define the following type:

```
typedef NS_OPTIONS(uint32_t, PCPhysicsCategory)
{
  PCBoundaryCategory = 1 << 0,
};
```

This defines a category for the edge of the world. You'll add more types later, but this will do for now.

Inside **MyScene.m**, define a world boundary at the end of createWorld:

```
SKNode *bounds = [SKNode node];
bounds.physicsBody =
  [SKPhysicsBody bodyWithEdgeLoopFromRect:
    CGRectMake(0, 0,
               _bgLayer.layerSize.width,
               _bgLayer.layerSize.height)];
bounds.physicsBody.categoryBitMask = PCBoundaryCategory;
bounds.physicsBody.friction = 0;
[_worldNode addChild:bounds];
```

Notice how this adds the physics boundary to a new node that is then added to _worldNode. That's because you're moving _worldNode and you need the physics boundary to move with it.

The player sprite is already set to collide with everything, so build and run. Tap the screen and watch that guy bounce around the map.

Moving the camera, revisited

Currently, the game centers its view on Arnold, keeping perfect pace with him as he runs around the map, stopping only when necessary to ensure the player never sees anything beyond your tile grid's boundaries. That works fine, and for some games that's exactly what you'll want.

However, consider the poor camera operator who has to keep up with Arnold, lugging around all that heavy equipment while desparately trying to keep Arnold perfectly centered in the frame. That's hard work, and it may be a little much to expect anyone to keep up with someone as fit as Arnold. More importantly, it's harder for your players to appreciate the scenery if the whole world moves so quickly; sometimes, it's downright unpleasant.

It would be more realistic, and more pleasing to the eye, if the view lagged behind Arnold ever so slightly, giving your players the feeling that Arnold moves so quickly that it's difficult for the game to keep up with him.

It's really quite easy to implement this effect. First, you'll refactor the code slightly. Create this new method in **MyScene.m**, which contains the exact same code that's currently in `centerViewOn:`, except instead of setting `_worldNode`'s position, it simply returns the new position:

```objc
- (CGPoint)pointToCenterViewOn:(CGPoint)centerOn
{
  CGSize size = self.size;

  CGFloat x = Clamp(centerOn.x, size.width / 2,
              _bgLayer.layerSize.width - size.width / 2);

  CGFloat y = Clamp(centerOn.y, size.height / 2,
              _bgLayer.layerSize.height - size.height/2);

  return CGPointMake(-x, -y);
}
```

And change `centerViewOn:`'s contents, replacing everything in it with the following single line:

```objc
_worldNode.position = [self pointToCenterViewOn:centerOn];
```

This simply sets `_worldNode.position` using `pointToCenterViewOn:`, which should result in exactly the same behavior you had before. After all, you're still executing the same code; you just moved it to a different method.

The scene currently keeps itself centered over Arnold in `didSumulatePhysics`, so that's the method you need to change. Replace its code with the following:

```
CGPoint target = [self pointToCenterViewOn:_player.position];

CGPoint newPosition = _worldNode.position;
newPosition.x += (target.x - _worldNode.position.x) * 0.1f;
newPosition.y += (target.y - _worldNode.position.y) * 0.1f;

_worldNode.position = newPosition;
```

This method calculates the target position using the `pointToCenterViewOn:` method you just added, but rather than setting `_worldNode`'s position to this value, it does some math to calculate a different position to use. This math moves the camera from its current position *toward* the target position, but only 10% of the way there. This 10% is what makes the camera lag behind Arnold, because it's always trying to catch up to where he is but never quite gets there. (Actually, if he stays put, the camera *will* catch up to him due to the limited precision with which you can position sprites on a display.)

> **Note:** If you're curious about the math in `didSimulatePhysics`, then consider this: if the distance between the positions of Arnold and the `_worldNode` is 100 points, then it moves `_worldNode` by 10% of that, so 10 points.
>
> The next time `didSimulatePhysics` runs, assuming Arnold hasn't moved, the distance is now only 90 points and the camera moves 9 points closer to him. The distance shrinks to 81 points the next time, moving the camera 8.1 points. The camera keeps getting closer, but it gradually slows down, which makes the movement look smooth.

Run the app and notice how much more natural the motion appears. It's now easier for your players to discern details in your levels, which is good when so much of your app development time will be spent designing those levels.

You can also see a side effect of this code when the level first loads. Instead of being centered on Arnold, the camera starts someplace else and pans over to him. It's a cool effect, but may not look good depending on where you position Arnold's spawn point (you'll be doing that as one of this chapter's challenges).

If it doesn't look good, you may need to adjust the code a bit. For example, you'll be adding game states in Chapter 16, "Saving and Loading Games," after which point it would be easy to change `didSimulatePhysics` to only move `_worldNode` when the game is in an appropriate state.

This simple trick can make your apps appear much more polished. You'll learn more of these sorts of techniques in Chapters 17 and 18, "Juice Up Your Game, Parts 1 & 2."

In the next chapter, you'll add collisions with other things, like the walls and water. But for now, you've got a guy trapped in a box. Wouldn't it be fun to fill it with giant bugs? Whoa, this chapter just got creepy.

Challenges

Here are two short challenges to get you more familiar with the process of editing your level files to create different types of objects and behavior. First, you'll add some bugs, and then you'll add the ability to specify Arnold's spawn point in the level file.

As always, if you get stuck, you can find solutions in the resources for this chapter – but give it your best shot first!

Challenge 1: Bring on the bugs

A giant-bug invasion without giant bugs is not the kind of giant-bug invasion you're going for, am I right? Here's your chance to fix that.

Look inside the **Levels** folder you imported, and you'll find a file called **level-1-bugs.txt**. Here are its first few lines:

```
characters
32x32
.............................
........b....................
...b............b...........
```

This file is formatted exactly like level-1-bg.txt, so it can be turned into a `TileMapLayer` using `TileMapLayerLoader`. It includes an atlas name and tile size at the beginning, followed by a grid of characters. In the grid, each **b** represents a bug, and each period (**.**) represents empty space. The periods make it possible to see the area covered by the grid.

Your challenge is to create a new `Bug` class, similar to your `Player` class, and then populate the world with bugs based on this file.

Here are some detailed hints on how to do this:

1. Create a new `Bug` class that derives from `SKSpriteNode`. It should have just one method – init. This method should be very similar to `Player`'s init method, except a) use the sprite named **bug_ft1**, and b) set the `name` property to "bug", and c) don't add in any of the code related to the `physicsBody` yet (you'll make the bug move in the next chapter).

2. Open **TileMapLayer.m** and edit `nodeForCode:` to return nil for a ".". character, and `[Bug node]` for a "b" character. Be sure to return the new `Bug` object directly from the `case` statement rather than setting the `tile` variable, because you want the bugs to use Sprite Kit's default blend mode that supports transparency.

3. Open **MyScene.m** and add a new private instance variable called _bugLayer of type `TileMapLayer *`. Then add this code to the *beginning* of `createCharacters`:

```
_bugLayer = [TileMapLayerLoader tileMapLayerFromFileNamed:
            @"level-1-bugs.txt"];
[_worldNode addChild:_bugLayer];
```

Build and run. Now your app is filled with bugs – but hopefully not the coding kind! ☺

Note: I know I snuck it into a challenge, but the code you just wrote demonstrates a major benefit of using textures from `SKTextureAtlas`. Every time you request a texture using the same name, you receive the exact same Objective-C object.

In fact, if you implemented `Bug` like you did `Player`, then each `Bug` instance creates an `SKTextureAtlas` inside its init. It turns out that multiple

SKTextureAtlas objects created with the same atlas name all return references to the same texture objects! That means no matter how many wall tiles, grass tiles or bugs you create, you'll never create more than one SKTexture object to reference each of their textures.

Now you may be asking yourself, "Don't SKSpriteNodes that reference the same image share their texture data, too?"

Yes, it's true that Sprite Kit stores the actual *texture* data only once, which is a significant performance feature of Sprite Kit. But each time they're called, SKSpriteNode spriteWithImageNamed: and SKTexture textureWithImageNamed: create unique Objective-C objects to access their texture data.

If you're creating many copies of the same sprite, as is common in a tile-based game (reusing image assets is one of the biggest benefits of tile-based games, right?), the memory savings you get by creating fewer Objective-C objects is measurable. And that can improve performance.

Challenge 2: Player spawn, revisited

Even though hard-coding the player's spawn point is easier than doing it for a bunch of bugs, it's still not a very good idea. For one thing, you probably want to place the player in relation to where you put the bugs. You don't want Arnold spawning on top of a bug, do you?

Open **level-1-bugs.txt** and change any *single* character you like to be a p (and don't forget to change the existing p character to a period). That will be where you'll spawn the player. From a gameplay standpoint, it's probably best to choose a spot away from any bugs.

Your challenge is to add support for this new character to TileMapLayer, just like you did for the others. Here are some detailed hints on how to do this:

1. Open **TileMapLayer.m** and edit nodeForCode: to return [Player node] for a "p" character. Just as you did with the Bug objects in the last challenge, be sure to return the new Player object directly rather than setting the tile variable, because you want the player to use Sprite Kit's default blend mode.

2. Open **MyScene.m** and delete the last three lines of createCharacters – the ones that create and position _player. Then add three lines: a) find the child of

_bugLayer named "player" and assign it to _player, b) remove this node from its parent (you want it as a child of _worldNode, not _bugLayer), and c) add it as a child of _worldNode instead.

Build and run. Now the player will appear in whatever position you put the p at in the file.

Pop quiz, hotshot. You're surrounded by giant bugs. They aren't moving, but you don't like that look in their eyes. What do you do? What do you do?

Actually, just head to the next chapter to find out!

Chapter 14: Intermediate Tile Maps

By Christopher LaPollo

So far, you have a world filled with bugs and a hero rampaging around wondering why he can't do anything about it. You're missing one critical element: collisions!

In this chapter, you'll continue investigating tile maps in Sprite Kit by adding some physics based collisions between Arnold and the bugs, as well as between Arnold and certain tiles in the map.

In addition, you'll add some code to make the bugs move around randomly while avoiding certain types of tiles, and you'll animate your characters based on which direction they're facing. By the time you're done this chapter, you will have developed Pest Control's core logic.

> **Note:** This chapter begins where Challenge 2 left off in the last chapter. If you were unable to complete the challenges or skipped ahead from a previous chapter, don't worry – you can simply open **PestControl-Starter** from the resources for this chapter to pick up where we left off.

Killing bugs

After finishing the challenges from the last chapter, you're probably itching to kill something. Well so is Arnold. Wait. We *are* talking about bugs, here, right?

Arnold already uses physics to move around, so you'll use physics to detect collisions with the bugs as well.

First you need to define new physics categories for the player and the bugs, so add these to the `PCPhysicsCategory` type in **MyScene.h**:

```
PCPlayerCategory     = 1 << 1,
PCBugCategory        = 1 << 2,
```

Open **Player.m** and add the following import to get access to `PCPhysicsCategory`:

```
#import "MyScene.h"
```

Add the following lines with the other `physicsBody` setup in `init`:

```
self.physicsBody.categoryBitMask = PCPlayerCategory;
self.physicsBody.contactTestBitMask = 0xFFFFFFFF;
```

You assign the player's physics category to `PCPlayerCategory` so that it will be easy to identify this object during collisions. You set the player's `contactTestBitMask` such that it generates contact notifications if the player touches anything. There won't be any physics bodies in Pest Control that can escape his wrath.

Now you need to set up the `Bug`'s physics properties.

In **Bug.m**, add the following import:

```
#import "MyScene.h"
```

Inside `init`, add the following lines after setting the name of the bug:

```
CGFloat minDiam = MIN(self.size.width, self.size.height);
minDiam = MAX(minDiam-8, 8);
self.physicsBody =
  [SKPhysicsBody bodyWithCircleOfRadius:minDiam/2.0];
self.physicsBody.categoryBitMask = PCBugCategory;
self.physicsBody.collisionBitMask = 0;
```

This code is simpler than the player's setup, because the bug won't use the physics engine for movement. You just create a circular physics body, assign the bug's physics category, and set its collision bit mask so that the bug is not affected by collisions.

Finally, whenever Arnold collides with a bug, you need to remove the bug from the scene. Open **MyScene.m** and add the following private interface category above the line that reads `@implementation MyScene`:

```
@interface MyScene () <SKPhysicsContactDelegate>
@end
```

As you learned earlier in the book, this states that MyScene conforms to the SKPhysicsContactDelegate protocol, and as such can register to receive callbacks when physics bodies contact each other.

Register for contact notifications by adding this line at the end of createWorld:

```
self.physicsWorld.contactDelegate = self;
```

Finally, add the following method to process contacts when they occur:

```
- (void)didBeginContact:(SKPhysicsContact *)contact
{
  SKPhysicsBody *other =
  (contact.bodyA.categoryBitMask == PCPlayerCategory ?
   contact.bodyB : contact.bodyA);

  if (other.categoryBitMask == PCBugCategory) {
    [other.node removeFromParent];
  }
}
```

The way you've configured the physics bodies in Pest Control, your program will only call this method when the player contacts another body. That is, two bugs touching will not generate an event. This method finds which of the two bodies is *not* the player (the other body) and checks its physics category. If it's a bug, the method removes it from the scene.

Build and run. Tap the screen and watch as Arnold gets his first taste of dead bug. Crunchy!

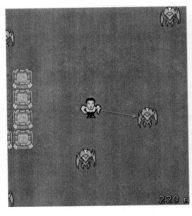
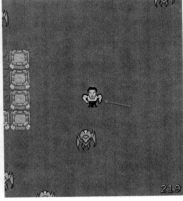

Unfortunately, Arnold doesn't smash right through the bugs as you had planned. Instead, he bounces off them. That's because the `Player` object's `physicsBody` still uses the default `collisionBitMask`, which allows collisions with any type of object to affect the player's motion.

For now, you only want Arnold's motion affected by the world's boundary. Open **Player.m** and add the following line with the other `physicsBody` setup in `init`:

```
self.physicsBody.collisionBitMask = PCBoundaryCategory;
```

Run the app again and now Arnold plows right through bugs like a hot knife through… bugs! But for their part, the bugs just sit there; it almost seems mean to squash them. Let's make them move around a bit so they at least have a fighting chance.

Moving bugs on the map

The player sprite uses the physics engine to run around the map, but to move the bugs from one tile to another, you'll use actions instead of physics. That will give the bugs more purpose, plus it will let you explore some other tile-related issues.

When it's time for a bug to leave its current tile, it needs to answer a few questions. Where is it now? Where does it want to go? Is the desired position even a valid location? You'll add a few more methods to `TileMapLayer` to help it answer these questions.

Open **TileMapLayer.h** and add the following methods to the interface:

```
- (BOOL)isValidTileCoord:(CGPoint)coord;
- (CGPoint)pointForCoord:(CGPoint)coord;
- (CGPoint)coordForPoint:(CGPoint)point;
```

These methods will help you convert between grid coordinates and (x,y) positions in your map.

Open **TileMapLayer.m** and add the following implementations for these methods:

```
- (BOOL)isValidTileCoord:(CGPoint)coord
{
  return (coord.x >= 0 &&
          coord.y >= 0 &&
          coord.x < self.gridSize.width &&
          coord.y < self.gridSize.height);
}

- (CGPoint)coordForPoint:(CGPoint)point
{
```

```
    return CGPointMake((int)(point.x / self.tileSize.width),
                       (int)((point.y - self.layerSize.height) /
                             -self.tileSize.height));
}

- (CGPoint)pointForCoord:(CGPoint)coord
{
    return [self positionForRow:coord.y col:coord.x];
}
```

These methods are straightforward helper methods that you'll use to convert between grid coordinates and points.

- isValidTileCoord: checks tile coordinates against the layer's grid size to ensure they are within the range of possible grid coordinates.

- coordForPoint: returns the grid coordinates (row,column) for the given (x,y) position in the layer. It's basically the reverse of the positionForRow:col: that you wrote in the previous chapter.

- pointForCoord: returns the (x,y) position at the center of the given grid coordinates. This uses positionForRow:col: to find the position. Notice how the coord parameter is in (column,row) order. This keeps it in line with the other ways you interact with the layer, such as (x,y) positions and (width,height) measurements.

With those methods in place, you can add some brains to your bugs to make them walk.

Open **Bug.m** and import the TileMapLayer class:

```
#import "TileMapLayer.h"
```

Put the logic for picking tiles and moving between them inside walk, like so:

```
- (void)walk
{
    // 1
    TileMapLayer *tileLayer = (TileMapLayer*)self.parent;

    // 2
    CGPoint tileCoord = [tileLayer coordForPoint:self.position];
    int randomX = arc4random() % 3 - 1;
    int randomY = arc4random() % 3 - 1;
    CGPoint randomCoord = CGPointMake(tileCoord.x+randomX,
                                      tileCoord.y+randomY);
    // 3
    BOOL didMove = NO;
    if ([tileLayer isValidTileCoord:randomCoord]) {
```

```
  // 4
  didMove = YES;
  CGPoint randomPos = [tileLayer pointForCoord:randomCoord];
  SKAction *moveToPos =
  [SKAction sequence:
   @[[SKAction moveTo:randomPos duration:1],
     [SKAction runBlock:^(void){
     [self walk];
  }]]];
  [self runAction:moveToPos];
}
// 5
if (!didMove) {
  [self runAction:
   [SKAction sequence:
    @[[SKAction waitForDuration:0.25 withRange:0.15],
      [SKAction performSelector:@selector(walk)
                       onTarget:self]]]];
  }
}
```

There's a fair bit of code here, so let's go over it carefully section by section.

1. This line casts the bug's parent to type `TileMapLayer`. It's important that you only add `Bug` objects directly to `TileMapLayer`s. Otherwise, your app will crash when this method tries to call missing `TileMapLayer` methods on `tileLayer`.

2. You then use one of `TileMapLayer`'s new helper methods, `coordForPoint:`, to find the bug's current location within the tile grid. Using that cell as a starting point, you choose random coordinates from one of the eight tiles surrounding this tile.

3. Next you call `isValidTileCoord:` on the layer to make sure the random tile you chose is valid. That is, you make sure it's actually on the map. If the bug was already on the edge of the map when you asked, you may have chosen a position off the map.

4. If the random tile location you chose is valid, you find the new tile's (x,y) position using `pointForCoord:` and create a sequence action to move the bug to the new location and then call `walk` when it gets there. That creates a cycle that looks like this: call `walk`, choose a tile, move to the tile and repeat. It keeps the bug walking continuously from tile to tile.

5. Finally, if you didn't move the bug (because the randomly chosen tile was invalid), you run an action that waits 0.25 seconds and then calls `walk` again. In these cases, the bug will remain in its current tile a bit longer before it continues on its way.

Now that you have `walk` implemented, you need to start each bug walking. At first you might think to call `walk` from within `init`, but there's a problem with that: in order to move around, the bug needs access to the tile map, which may not be fully initialized yet. For example, if the bug decides where to walk based on the types of tiles around it, it can't start walking until those tiles are set up.

The solution is to add a new method – call it `start` – that your scene calls after all the nodes have been added.

Open **Bug.h** and declare this method:

```
- (void)start;
```

And add this implementation in **Bug.m**:

```
- (void)start
{
  [self walk];
}
```

`start` simply calls `walk` to start the bug walking. The reason you define a `start` method instead of having the scene access `walk` directly is so subclasses can perform additional setup before walking. (You'll be extending `Bug` in one of this chapter's challenges.)

Open **MyScene.m** and import the **Bug** class:

```
#import "Bug.h"
```

Add the following at the end of `createCharacters` to get your bugs moving:

```
[_bugLayer enumerateChildNodesWithName:@"bug"
                            usingBlock:
 ^(SKNode *node, BOOL *stop){
   [(Bug*)node start];
 }];
```

> **Note:** Since you know `_bugLayer` only contains `Bug` objects, you could have used a `for` loop instead of `enumerateChildNodesWithName:usingBlock:`, such as the following:
>
> ```
> for (Bug *bug in _bugLayer.children)
> ```

> However, the solution you're actually using lets you put non-**Bug** objects in this
> layer as well, as long as you don't name them @"bug".

Build and run, and watch your bugs, well, run.

Now the bugs are moving, but they're doing it right over the walls! Between the bugs climbing over everything and Arnold bouncing around wherever he wants, it seems no one respects your boundaries. Or at least, the boundaries you've set up in the map. Time to take care of that.

Collisions with tiles, two ways

When you have tiles that represent solid or otherwise impassible objects, you want the characters in your game to behave accordingly. In this section, you'll see two different methods to keep characters from moving through solid tiles. The player will use physics-based collision detection, while the bugs will query tile properties to decide where to walk.

Physics-based tile collisions

You want the player to bounce off walls (for now – in Chapter 18, "Juice Up Your Game, Part 2," you'll give him the ability to smash right through them!), and you probably don't want him to walk on water. (Maybe you'll want to add that as a power up after you've finished going through the book?)

To accomplish this, you need some additional physics settings. Open **MyScene.h** and add the following categories for walls and water to the `PCPhysicsCategory` type:

```
PCWallCategory        = 1 << 3,
PCWaterCategory       = 1 << 4,
```

Then go to **Player.m** and add the new categories to the player's `collisionBitMask`, so that it looks like this:

```
self.physicsBody.collisionBitMask =
    PCBoundaryCategory | PCWallCategory | PCWaterCategory;
```

Now the player wants to bounce off not only the world's boundary, but wall and water tiles as well. However, the wall and water tiles need physics bodies in order for this to work.

Open **TileMapLayer.m**, where you'll modify the nodes returned for walls and water. First, give `TileMapLayer` access to the `PCPhysicsCategory` type by adding the following import:

```
#import "MyScene.h"
```

Replace the 'x' `case` of the `switch` statement in `nodeForCode:` with the following code:

```
case 'x':
  tile = [SKSpriteNode spriteNodeWithTexture:
            [_atlas textureNamed:@"wall"]];
  tile.physicsBody =
    [SKPhysicsBody bodyWithRectangleOfSize:tile.size];
  tile.physicsBody.categoryBitMask = PCWallCategory;
  tile.physicsBody.dynamic = NO;
  tile.physicsBody.friction = 0;
  break;
```

This creates a physics body the same size as the tile. It sets its dynamic property to NO because the wall won't move, and sets its friction to 0 so the player doesn't slow down when he hits it.

Now do the same for water tiles by replacing the 'w' `case` with the following:

```
case 'w':
  tile = [SKSpriteNode spriteNodeWithTexture:
            [_atlas textureNamed:
              RandomFloat() < 0.1 ? @"water2" : @"water1"]];
```

```
tile.physicsBody =
    [SKPhysicsBody bodyWithRectangleOfSize:tile.size];
tile.physicsBody.categoryBitMask = PCWaterCategory;
tile.physicsBody.dynamic = NO;
tile.physicsBody.friction = 0;
break;
```

Build and run. Tap the screen and watch Arnold run around bouncing off walls and water just like he should.

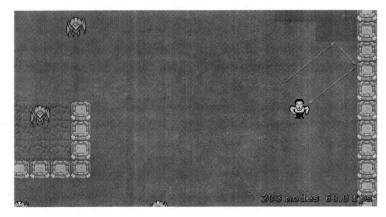

Now that Arnold obeys the rules, it doesn't seem fair that the bugs are walking through walls like your stones are made of nothing more than flat pixels! Let's fix that.

Property-based tile avoidance

Instead of moving the bugs using physics, you're using Sprite Kit actions to move the bugs between tiles, so you'll use the tiles' properties to determine where a bug can walk. Basically, they'll check to see if the way is clear before trying to move.

To do that, `TileMapLayer` needs to provide access to its tiles by position. It would be convenient to access tiles using either their grid coordinates (row,column) or their x,y positions. Open **TileMapLayer.h** and declare the following new methods:

```
- (SKNode*)tileAtCoord:(CGPoint)coord;
- (SKNode*)tileAtPoint:(CGPoint)point;
```

Inside **TileMapLayer.m**, implement these new methods like so:

```
- (SKNode*)tileAtCoord:(CGPoint)coord
{
```

```
    return [self tileAtPoint:[self pointForCoord:coord]];
}

- (SKNode*)tileAtPoint:(CGPoint)point
{
    SKNode *n = [self nodeAtPoint:point];
    while (n && n != self && n.parent != self)
        n = n.parent;
    return n.parent == self ? n : nil;
}
```

`tileAtCoord:`'s implementation is straightforward. It simply uses the `pointForCoord:` method you added earlier to find the x,y position of the given grid location, and then uses `tileAtPoint:` to find the tile.

`tileAtPoint:`'s implementation may look needlessly complicated, but it's not so bad. It uses `SKNode`'s `nodeAtPoint:` method to find the node at the given position, and then checks to make sure this `TileMapLayer` is the discovered node's parent. If it isn't, the code walks up the parent chain until it finds a node whose parent *is* this object.

Why do all that? At this point, `nodeForCode:` only returns nodes with no children – a single wall tile, for example. Later, though, you may have nodes that contain child nodes, like a tree on top of some grass. To be clear, you'll be adding breakable trees as a challenge at the end of this chapter, but you won't be adding them like this. The tree-on-grass example here is only for the purposes of this discussion.

When multiple sprites overlap, as shown in the following image, `nodeAtPoint:` returns the one on top. That's usually what you want when handling touches, for example, but in this case, you want to find the *bottom* sprite – the one you returned from `nodeForCode:` – not one of its children.

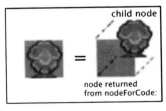

Now that `TileMapLayer` provides access to its tiles, your bugs need to check for tiles they cannot traverse, but the bugs don't even know about the layer that contains the walls. As far as they're concerned, the world contains nothing but themselves. Is there anything worse than a narcissistic bug?

The scene itself is a good place to provide this access. You'll add a method that returns whether or not a map location has certain properties, such as PCWallCategory. Open **MyScene.h** and declare the following two methods to query tile properties:

```
- (BOOL)tileAtPoint:(CGPoint)point hasAnyProps:(uint32_t)props;
- (BOOL)tileAtCoord:(CGPoint)coord hasAnyProps:(uint32_t)props;
```

These are two variations of the same method: each will find a tile *in the scene's background layer*, either by point or grid location, and return YES if the tile has a physicsBody with any of the given props bits set in its categoryBitMask.

> **Note:** To reduce the size of this chapter, the only properties you'll test for are the categories assigned to the physics body. In your own app, you could use the node's userData dictionary or some other mechanism to store other types of properties.

Inside **MyScene.m**, implement these two methods like this:

```
- (BOOL)tileAtCoord:(CGPoint)coord hasAnyProps:(uint32_t)props
{
  return [self tileAtPoint:[_bgLayer pointForCoord:coord]
            hasAnyProps:props];
}

- (BOOL)tileAtPoint:(CGPoint)point hasAnyProps:(uint32_t)props
{
  SKNode *tile = [_bgLayer tileAtPoint:point];
  return tile.physicsBody.categoryBitMask & props;
}
```

Here's what these methods are doing:

Since you know the map tiles are in _bgLayer, you find the tile at that location in _bgLayer using the tileAtPoint: method you just added. You then compare the tile's physics category to the bits in props. The methods return YES if any bit is set in both props and tile.physicsBody.categoryBitMask, or NO otherwise. Tile might be nil if you provided an invalid location, and the physics body won't be present on some tiles, such as grass, but it won't matter, because Objective-C returns NO in those cases.

One last thing to do, and these bugs will finally know their places. In **Bug.m**, replace the following line in walk:

```
if ([tileLayer isValidTileCoord:randomCoord]) {
```

With these lines:

```
MyScene *scene = (MyScene*)self.scene;
if ([tileLayer isValidTileCoord:randomCoord] &&
    ![scene tileAtCoord:randomCoord
            hasAnyProps:(PCWallCategory | PCWaterCategory)]) {
```

This changes the bug logic, so that now they will only walk into valid tiles that are not currently occupied by a wall or water.

Build and run. Finally, your walls are doing their jobs.

OK, you've got a level made of tiles and filled with bugs. You've got a hero with an almost disturbing need to crush those bugs. Life is good. But wouldn't things be better if they were a bit more... animated?

> **Note:** This next section is for polish, fun, and practicing the material you've learned so far in this book – it has little to do with tile maps. If you'd like to stay focused on tile map material, feel free to skip ahead to the challenges section. You can pick up the finished project there, and we have some fun challenges in store for you!
>
> But if you'd like some extra practice with animating sprites in a semi-tricky use case – making objects animate differently based on the direction they're facing – read on!

Animating sprites

In Pest Control, both Arnold and the bugs will animate. There will be some similarity in how you implement these animations, so you'll create a class that contains stuff both the bugs and Arnold can use. Then you'll refactor Player and Bug so they subclass this new class.

Go to **File\New\File…**, choose the **iOS\Cocoa Touch\Objective-C class** template and click **Next**. Name your class **AnimatingSprite**, make it a subclass of **SKSpriteNode** and click **Next** again. Be sure the **PestControl** target is checked and click **Create**.

Inside **AnimatingSprite.h**, add the following declarations:

```
@property (strong,nonatomic) SKAction *facingForwardAnim;
@property (strong,nonatomic) SKAction *facingBackAnim;
@property (strong,nonatomic) SKAction *facingSideAnim;

+ (SKAction*)createAnimWithPrefix:(NSString *)prefix
                           suffix:(NSString *)suffix;
```

These properties each hold an SKAction for animating the sprite while facing in one of four directions: forward, back or to the left or right sides. Player and Bug will use createAnimWithPrefix:suffix: to create the animations, which they'll use to set these properties.

This method expects the image names to follow a specific convention, as follows: **prefix_direction#**, where **direction** is one of **ft**, **bk**, or **lt**, for front, back, and left, and **#** is the animation frame number, starting at 1. Notice there is no option for the direction right. You'll see later how you use the same image for both directions.

Open **AnimatingSprite.m** and add the following implementation of createAnimWithPrefix:suffix::

```
+ (SKAction*)createAnimWithPrefix:(NSString *)prefix
                           suffix:(NSString *)suffix
{
  SKTextureAtlas *atlas =
    [SKTextureAtlas atlasNamed:@"characters"];

  NSArray *textures =
  @[[atlas textureNamed:[NSString stringWithFormat:@"%@_%@1",
                         prefix, suffix]],
    [atlas textureNamed:[NSString stringWithFormat:@"%@_%@2",
                         prefix, suffix]]];
```

```
[textures[0] setFilteringMode:SKTextureFilteringNearest];
[textures[1] setFilteringMode:SKTextureFilteringNearest];

return [SKAction repeatActionForever:
        [SKAction animateWithTextures:textures
                        timePerFrame:0.20]];
}
```

The above code creates an animation action using textures from the atlas named `characters`. It generates the texture names using `stringWithFormat:` with the file name format described earlier. It then sets the `filteringMode` on those textures to account for the app's pixel art.

As you can see, each animation in Pest Control consists of just two frames, but for more fluid animations, you'd want to include more. If anything related to the `SKAction` code above seems unfamiliar to you, revisit Chapter 3, "Actions."

With that helper method in place, it's time to refactor `Player` and `Bug` to use it.

Player animations, part 1

In this section, you'll modify `Player` to support animation. Later, you'll implement logic to control those animations.

Inside **Player.h**, import `AnimatingSprite`, like this:

```
#import "AnimatingSprite.h"
```

And change the interface to subclass `AnimatingSprite`, like this:

```
@interface Player : AnimatingSprite
```

Finally, you need to initialize the animation properties declared in `AnimatingSprite`. Inside **Player.m**, add the following code inside `init`, just after you set up the `physicsBody`:

```
self.facingForwardAnim =
  [Player createAnimWithPrefix:@"player" suffix:@"ft"];
self.facingBackAnim =
  [Player createAnimWithPrefix:@"player" suffix:@"bk"];
self.facingSideAnim =
  [Player createAnimWithPrefix:@"player" suffix:@"lt"];
```

This simply uses the `createAnimWithPrefix:suffix:` method you defined in `AnimatingSprite` to create the three animations. It will create animations from frames named `player_ft1` and `player_ft2`, `player_bk1` and `player_bk2`, and `player_lt1` and `player_lt2`.

To test the animations, temporarily add the following line in `init`, after the ones you just added:

```
[self runAction:self.facingForwardAnim];
```

Build and run. Your hero starts running in place. So that's how he stays so fit!

If you'd like to see the other two animations, modify the line you just added and run again, using `facingBackAnim` and then `facingSideAnim`. When you're done, remove that line completely.

Bug animations, part 1

Just as you did with `Player`, you'll first modify `Bug` to support animating. Later, you'll implement logic to control those animations.

Inside **Bug.h**, import `AnimatingSprite`, like this:

```
#import "AnimatingSprite.h"
```

And change the interface to subclass `AnimatingSprite`, like this:

```
@interface Bug : AnimatingSprite
```

You need to implement the animation properties declared in `AnimatingSprite`, but you'll do it a bit differently from what you did in `Player`.

Open **Bug.m** and add the following static variables, along with the property getter methods that access them:

```
static SKAction *sharedFacingBackAnim = nil;
- (SKAction*)facingBackAnim {
  return sharedFacingBackAnim;
}

static SKAction *sharedFacingForwardAnim = nil;
- (SKAction*)facingForwardAnim {
  return sharedFacingForwardAnim;
}

static SKAction *sharedFacingSideAnim = nil;
- (SKAction*)facingSideAnim {
  return sharedFacingSideAnim;
}
```

These property getters may look strange to you. Instead of using the methods that Xcode creates for you automatically when it synthesizes the properties, you provide your own implementations that access static variables. Why do that?

There are a lot of bugs running around your scenes. If the bugs created their animations the same way the player does, each one would have an identical set of three actions. But as you learned in Chapter 3, "Actions," actions can be shared amongst any number of nodes. So in an effort to conserve memory at runtime, your bugs store their actions in these static variables shared by all the bugs. Awfully considerate bugs, aren't they?

Notice how you did not include property setter methods to access the static variables. That's because you only want to set these static animation variables once. Still inside **Bug.m**, add the following method:

```
+ (void)initialize
{
  static dispatch_once_t onceToken;
  dispatch_once(&onceToken, ^{
    sharedFacingForwardAnim =
      [Bug createAnimWithPrefix:@"bug" suffix:@"ft"];
    sharedFacingBackAnim =
      [Bug createAnimWithPrefix:@"bug" suffix:@"bk"];
    sharedFacingSideAnim =
      [Bug createAnimWithPrefix:@"bug" suffix:@"lt"];
  });
}
```

This defines `initialize`, a special class method your app calls the first time it accesses a class. The code here creates animations the same way `Player` does, but it assigns them to the static variables you added, and it does so within a `dispatch_once` block to ensure it only ever occurs once during a run of the app.

> **Note:** While the app calls `initialize` the *first* time you access a class, that doesn't mean it only calls it once. When accessing a *subclass* of that class, and that subclass either does not provide its own implementation of `initialize` or it includes a call to `super initialize`, your app will call this method again. So you still need to ensure this method only contains code that is safe to run multiple times, or implement it as you've done here to ensure the code only runs once no matter how many times you call the method.

To test the animations, temporarily add the following line in `init`, after the ones you just added:

```
[self runAction:self.facingForwardAnim];
```

Build and run. Your bugs are on the march!

As with the player, if you'd like to see the other two animations, modify the line you just added and run again, using `facingBackAnim` and then `facingSideAnim`. When you're done, remove that line completely.

Changing directions

You need the ability to get and set the direction the sprite faces. For example, when a sprite is moving toward the bottom of the screen, you want to make sure it's animating with the `facingForwardAnim` action. Let's add one last property to access the direction the sprite is currently facing.

Open **AnimatingSprite.h** and add the following enumeration above the `AnimatingSprite` interface:

```
typedef NS_ENUM(int32_t, PCFacingDirection)
{
  PCFacingForward,
  PCFacingBack,
  PCFacingRight,
  PCFacingLeft
};
```

This type defines the four different directions the sprite can face.

Add the following property and helper method to the `AnimatingSprite` interface. Subclasses will use these to keep their animations pointing in the right direction.

```
@property (assign,nonatomic) PCFacingDirection facingDirection;
```

You'll rely on Xcode to autosynthesize the `facingDirection` getter method, but add the following custom setter inside **AnimatingSprite.m**:

```
- (void)setFacingDirection:(PCFacingDirection)facingDirection
{
  // 1
  _facingDirection = facingDirection;
  // 2
  switch (facingDirection) {
    case PCFacingForward:
      [self runAction:self.facingForwardAnim];
      break;
    case PCFacingBack:
      [self runAction:self.facingBackAnim];
      break;
    case PCFacingLeft:
      [self runAction:self.facingSideAnim];
      break;
    case PCFacingRight:
      [self runAction:self.facingSideAnim];
      // 3
      if (self.xScale > 0.0f) {
        self.xScale = -self.xScale;
      }
      break;
  }
  // 4
```

```
    if(facingDirection != PCFacingRight && self.xScale < 0.0f) {
      self.xScale = -self.xScale;
    }
  }
```

This method does quite a bit for a property setter, so let's go through it step-by-step:

1. It sets the property's value.

2. This `switch` statement choses and runs the animation action that matches the direction the sprite currently faces.

3. Remember how you only provided left-facing images? If you set the sprite's `xScale` to a negative value, it renders flipped around the y-axis. The check here ensures it only flips the image if it isn't already facing that direction. Flipping images like this is a great trick to get more use out of image assets.

4. This bit of code flips the sprite back to its native orientation when the sprite is not facing to the right.

> **Note:** Developers often debate whether or not it's OK to use a setter in this manner, where it does more than just set the variable it claims to set. This is referred to as a side effect. In this case, `facingDirection` is meant to indicate the state of the animation, so setting it separately from the animation felt wrong to me. However, it would be simple to separate this logic into two methods, if that was something you wanted to do.

Now that you can manipulate the direction the sprites face, it's time to complete this portion of Pest Control.

Player animations, part 2

You already added animation support to Player. In this section, you'll make sure Arnold always looks where he is going.

In **Player.m**, add this method:

```
- (void)faceCurrentDirection
{
  // 1
  PCFacingDirection facingDir = self.facingDirection;

  // 2
```

```
    CGVector dir = self.physicsBody.velocity;
    if (abs(dir.dy) >  abs(dir.dx)) {
      if (dir.dy < 0) {
        facingDir = PCFacingForward;
      } else {
        facingDir = PCFacingBack;
      }
    } else {
      facingDir = (dir.dx > 0) ? PCFacingRight : PCFacingLeft;
    }

    // 3
    self.facingDirection = facingDir;
}
```

Here's what's going on:

1. You save the current value of `facingDirection`. You do this because the series of checks that follows is not guaranteed to find a new direction, but you need a valid value to set at the end.

2. This bit of code checks the player's velocity to see if it's moving vertically more than horizontally. If so, it chooses to face either forward or backward, based on which direction it's headed. If it's movement is primarily horizontal, it chooses to face either to the right or to the left.

3. Finally, you set the player's `facingDirection` property. Remember, setting that property also runs the correct animation for the given direction.

Set the player sprite's direction by calling this new method at the end of `moveToward:`, like so:

```
[self faceCurrentDirection];
```

Now every time you tell the hero to start running, he should face the appropriate direction.

Build and run. Things should look good each time you tap the screen, but Arnold's animation doesn't change direction when he bounces off of things. What now?

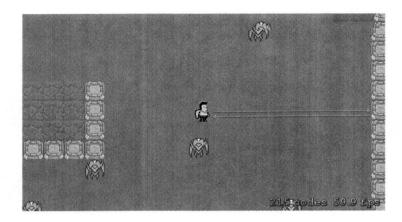

You're adjusting the player's direction inside moveToward:, which you call only when the user touches the screen. But you should also adjust the direction the sprite faces when it bounces off of something. Fortunately, the scene already registered to receive contact notifications, so you can handle it there.

First, add a public declaration of faceCurrentDirection to the Player interface. Inside **Player.h**, add the following:

```
- (void)faceCurrentDirection;
```

Now you can call faceCurrentDirection from outside Player.

Open **MyScene.m** and add this method:

```
- (void)didEndContact:(SKPhysicsContact *)contact
{
  // 1
  SKPhysicsBody *other =
  (contact.bodyA.categoryBitMask == PCPlayerCategory ?
   contact.bodyB : contact.bodyA);

  // 2
  if (other.categoryBitMask &
      _player.physicsBody.collisionBitMask) {
    // 3
    [_player faceCurrentDirection];
  }
}
```

The physics engine will call `didEndContact:` when the player ceases to touch a physics object it had been touching. Here's what your implementation of `didEndContact:` does:

1. You know that the player is one of the objects involved in the callback, so here you find the other one.

2. This compares the object's physics category with the player's `collisionBitMask` – if it gets a non-zero value, it means this collision was with something solid enough to cause the player to change directions.

3. You call `faceCurrentDirection`. That method will use the player's current velocity to ensure the player is facing in the correct direction.

> **Note:** Instead of making `faceCurrentDirection` public, you could have called `moveToward:` here, passing in the sum of the player's current position and its velocity. However, that would perform extra processing, first to do that sum, and then for `moveToward:` to calculate the player's new velocity, which would end up being the same as its current velocity anyway. It's more efficient to call `faceCurrentDirection` directly.

Build and run. Arnold should be running around *and* looking where he's going.

With `Player` complete (for this chapter, anyway), let's finish up the bugs.

Bug animations, part 2

Now that Arnold looks where he's going, it's only fair that the bugs do the same. `Bug` already has access to `setFacingDirection:` from its super class, `AnimatingSprite`, and it chooses a direction to move in `walk`. Now it needs a method that chooses which direction to face based on which direction the bug is moving. However, because `bug` isn't using the physics engine like `Player` does, the logic here will be a little different.

Open **Bug.m** and add the following method for choosing a direction to face:

```objc
- (void)faceDirection:(CGPoint)dir
{
  // 1
  PCFacingDirection facingDir = self.facingDirection;
  // 2
  if (dir.y != 0 && dir.x != 0) {
    // 3
    facingDir = dir.y < 0 ? PCFacingBack : PCFacingForward;
    self.zRotation = dir.y < 0 ? M_PI_4 : -M_PI_4;
    if (dir.x > 0) {
      self.zRotation *= -1;
    }
  } else {
    // 4
    self.zRotation = 0;

    // 5
    if (dir.y == 0) {
      if (dir.x > 0) {
        facingDir = PCFacingRight;
      } else if (dir.x < 0) {
        facingDir = PCFacingLeft;
      }
    } else if (dir.y < 0) {
      facingDir = PCFacingBack;
    } else {
      facingDir = PCFacingForward;
    }
  }
  // 6
  self.facingDirection = facingDir;
}
```

There's a lot going on here, so let's go over it one section at a time:

1. Store the direction the sprite currently faces. Depending on the value of `dir`, you may not end up finding a new direction to face, but you need a valid value to set at the end.

2. `dir` will represent the relative direction from the bug's current tile, in grid coordinates. That is, its x- and y-components will each be one of 0, 1 or -1. This first `if` statement determines whether or not the new tile is located diagonally from the current tile.

3. For diagonal motion, you choose the appropriate facing direction, but then you rotate the sprite to add a bit more visual interest. The rotation values used here are based on the direction the image faces in the original image files.

4. If the movement direction is *not* diagonal, you set the rotation to zero. Without that line, bugs that had been rotated for diagonal movement would remain rotated if they began moving horizontally or vertically.

5. This series of checks figures out if the movement is horizontal (`y == 0`) or vertical, and chooses the correct direction to face based on what it finds.

6. Finally, you set the bug's `facingDirection` property. Remember, setting that property also runs the correct animation for the given direction.

Now you need to call this method. Add the following line to `walk`, just after the line that runs the `moveToPos` action:

```
[self faceDirection:CGPointMake(randomX,randomY)];
```

It uses the `randomX` and `randomY` offset values you calculated earlier in the method. Unlike how `Player` uses its velocity, this method calculates the bug's facing direction using tile grid offsets from the current position.

Build and run. Take a moment. You just got a lot done.

These two chapters laid the groundwork for what will turn into a fun game, but it also showed you a lot of what you'll need to build any number of your own games in the future.

The next few chapters describe easier ways to make your maps, and add gameplay features like timers, support for multiple levels, winning and losing, and autosaving progress. Then, in the Chapters 17 and 18, "Juice Up Your Game, Parts 1 & 2," you'll learn how you take this or any other game to an amazing new level.

Before you move on, try the following challenges to add some cool new features on your own.

Challenges

If you've made it this far into the book, I'm convinced you can tackle some more advanced challenges – so this time, we've ramped up the difficulty level a notch. Do you think you have what it takes to make Arnold proud?

CHALLENGE ACCEPTED

Of course, if you have any trouble, you can find solutions to these challenges in the resources for this chapter.

Challenge 1: Breakables

The background tiles you've created so far have been single images, sometimes with a physics body attached, but tiles don't have to be so simple. For example, what if you planted a few trees in your level?

Sure, you could add support for a new character that returned a sprite that looked like a tree, just as you made the other tiles. But this is supposed to be a challenge, so let's take this opportunity to explore the notion of interactive tiles.

For example, instead of just plain trees, you could have trees that your player can smash and potentially reveal hidden objects in your game, like you may have seen in games from the Super Mario or Zelda series.

For this challenge, you won't go as far as creating hidden pickups, but you *will* create trees that Arnold can smash, leaving behind nothing but a stump. Later, in Chapter 17, "Juice Up Your Game, Part 1," you'll see how to make this destruction even more satisfying.

Take a look at the following hints and then give it a try.

You'll need a new `PCPhysicsCategory` value: call it `PCBreakableCategory`. Be sure to modify `Bug`'s `walk` method so it avoids breakables – no one wants bugs crawling all over their trees.

By the way, you're using the term "breakable" instead of "tree" because the class you're about to write will be generic. The only thing that makes these objects trees instead of rocks or crates will be the images you use to render them.

Create a new class named `Breakable` that extends `SKSpriteNode` and includes the following initializer method:

```
- (instancetype)initWithWhole:(SKTexture *)whole
                       broken:(SKTexture *)broken;
```

Here are some tips to help you implement `initWithWhole:broken::`

1. Initialize the sprite using the `whole` texture. The sprite appears with this image before Arnold smashes it.

2. Create an instance variable named `_broken` and use it to store the `broken` texture. You'll use this image to display debris left behind after a collision.

3. Add a physics body of type `PCBreakableCategory`. Make it a static (not dynamic) rectangle that is 80% of the size of the tile.

When Arnold collides with a `Breakable`, he should break it. Add the following method to the `Breakable` interface:

```
- (void)smashBreakable;
```

Implement `smashBreakable` to do the following:

1. Remove the sprite's physics body. Doing this means once the breakable has been smashed, the player will no longer collide with it, and the bugs will consider that space empty.

2. Replace the sprite's texture with `_broken`. This gets rid of the pre-smashed image, which in this case is the full tree, and displays the post-smash wreckage, which in this case is the tree stump. Be sure to set `self.size` equal to `_broken.size` after setting the texture, because at the time of this writing, Sprite Kit sometimes warps your textures if you don't do that.

Back in **MyScene.m**, check for collisions with `PCBreakableCategory` objects in `didBeginContact:`. When the player hits one, call `smashBreakable` on it (be sure to call smash breakable on the physics body's node – not the physics body itself).

You'll need to modify `TileMapLayer` to return `Breakables` when appropriate. Add a `case` statement for '`t`' that returns a `Breakable` using the images **tree.png** and **tree-stump.png**. Look at the `case` statements for the bugs or player if you need help.

Finally, the trees should sit on a layer above the background layer, like how you put the bugs on their own layer. This will require several changes in **MyScene.m**:

1. Add a new private instance variable called `_breakableLayer` of type `TileMapLayer *`.

2. Then add a new method called `createBreakables` that returns a new `TileMapLayer` created from the file **level-2-breakables.txt**. This file looks just like the other level data files you've used, except with "t" characters to indicate tree positions.

3. Initialize `_breakableLayer` at the *end* of `createWorld` by assigning it the result returned from `createBreakables`, and then add `_breakableLayer` as a child of `_worldNode`. Before adding it to `_worldNode`, make sure `_breakableLayer` is not `nil`.

4. Finally, you need to make sure the scene checks these objects in addition to the background tiles when checking for properties, otherwise your bugs will walk all over them. Replace the first line of `tileAtPoint:hasAnyProps:` with the following code, which finds the tile by looking for breakables first, only retrieving a background tile if no tile can be found in the breakable layer:

```
SKNode *tile = [_breakableLayer tileAtPoint:point];
if (!tile)
```

```
tile = [_bgLayer tileAtPoint:point];
```

If you got it working, congratulations! Now you can plant some trees to improve Arnold's environment, and then revel in their destruction. You've got issues.

Challenge 2: Other enemies

Most games have more than one type of enemy. This challenge will show how you can add another type of bug with just a few tweaks to existing code.

Instead of bugs that just disappear when the player hits them, your task is to create a bug that is impervious to collisions. Rather than disappear when hit, it will simply bounce a short distance away, sending the player off in a new direction as well.

Of course, it wouldn't be fair if there were *no* way to kill these new bugs. Instead of smashing them, you'll make it so they drown when bounced into water. That big, strong exoskeleton isn't helping you now, is it, Mr. Sinky?

Completing this challenge will require quite a bit of what you've learned in this book. Here are a few tips to help you with it:

This new bug will be red and die in water, so create a new class named `FireBug` that extends `Bug`.

You'll need a new `PCPhysicsCategory` value: call it `PCFireBugCategory`. This will let you perform different logic when colliding with these versus regular bugs. Remember, you want the player to bounce off these bugs, so be sure to modify `Player`'s collision bit mask to include `PCFireBugCategory`.

Put `FireBug`'s initialization code in a method named `init`. Inside `init`, do the following:

1. Call `[super init]`.

2. Set the physics category to `PCFireBugCategory`.

3. Set the collision bit mask so the fire bugs collide with the player, walls, breakables and the world boundary.

4. Set the linear and angular damping values to `1`. That will keep the bugs from sliding too far when they get bumped.

5. Set the sprite's `color` to red. Remember, in Sprite Kit, you should use `SKColor` values.

6. Adjust the sprite's `colorBlendFactor` to `0.45`.

Add the following method to the `FireBug` interface:

```
- (void)kickBug;
```

Implement `kickBug` to do the following:

1. Remove all running actions. (You could remove just the action that walks the bug between tiles. However, there are a few more steps involved in doing that.)

2. Run an action that waits for one second before calling a new method called `resumeAfterKick`.

Next, implement `resumeAfterKick` to do the following:

1. Set the sprite's physics body's velocity to (0, 0). That will bring the bug to a complete stop just in case it's still sliding a bit.

2. Then query the scene to see if the fire bug currently sits on top of a water tile. If it does, run the following code:

```
SKAction *drown =
  [SKAction group:@[[SKAction rotateByAngle:4*M_PI duration:1],
                    [SKAction scaleTo:0 duration:1]]];
[self runAction:
  [SKAction sequence:@[drown,[SKAction removeFromParent]]]];
```

This creates a simple action that makes the bug look like it's getting sucked into a whirlpool and then removes the bug from the scene.

If the bug is not on a water tile, you should resume walking by calling `walk`.

At this point, walk is a private method in **Bug.m**. For the above code to compile, you'll need to declare `walk` in **Bug.h**.

Once you have all of that complete (it's a lot, I know), inside **MyScene.m** add a check for collisions with `PCFireBugCategory` objects in `didBeginContact:`. When the player hits a fire bug, call `kickBug` on it.

Finally, you'll need to modify `TileMapLayer` to return `FireBugs` when appropriate. Add a `case` statement for 'f' that returns a `FireBug`. Look at the other `case` statements if you need help.

You can test your code by adding some fs to your bug layer file. Or, change `createCharacters` in **MyScene.m** to use **level-2-bugs.txt**. Build and run, and you should have fire bugs!

That one was tough. If you got it working without looking at the completed project, nice job! If not, don't be discouraged; we both know those guys who said they got it without looking are liars. ☺

Just look through the completed project and try to make sure you know what's going on, because you'll work with both `Breakable` and `FireBug` again in Chapters 17 and 18, "Juice Up Your Game, Parts 1 & 2."

Chapter 15: Imported Tile Maps

By Christopher LaPollo

The previous two chapters showed you how to build the foundation of Pest Control, a game about a man, some giant bugs and the smashing of said bugs. To those of you who worked through those chapters, welcome back! We had some good times, didn't we? Yeah, we did.

For those of you who didn't follow the earlier chapters, don't worry – so long as you understand the basics of tile maps, you can complete this chapter on its own. You just might not laugh at our inside jokes.

In the last two chapters, you created tile maps using rows of characters in text files. While that's a good technique to know, it does have a few drawbacks, such as:

- **It's error prone.** A single misplaced newline or incorrect letter and your map breaks, and sometimes these errors are difficult to find. For instance, if your bug layer doesn't have the same dimensions as your background layer, your bugs will check the wrong tiles when choosing a destination, potentially causing them to walk where they're not wanted. That's what bugs normally do, but these are *your* bugs.

- **You can't *really* see what the level looks like without loading it into the game**, or creating a tool for your designers so they can load levels without the game. For example, consider this line from a map:

```
@"xoooooooooooooooooox"
```

Although you can kinda imagine the end-result (and don't get excited, Sprite Kit doesn't have a crush on you), seeing something nice and visual like this is a big improvement:

- **It's difficult to see the relationships between items when editing different layers.** Are you placing a bug right on top of a wall? You can either spend time squinting at character grids trying to compare positions of letters in different files, or you can build levels through trial and error, repeatedly loading levels to test how they look.

  For example, try to line up this line from the background layer:

  ```
  ooooooooooooooowwwwww
  ```

  With this line from the bug layer:

  ```
  ....b.p.............
  ```

  While trying to line up characters is fun, for sure, is this the most efficient use of your time?

- **If you want an artist or designer to create your levels, it's easier to let them use a GUI.** Those people just don't appreciate numbers and letters as much as we programmer-types do.

In this chapter, you'll see how to alleviate these problems using Tiled, an open source application that lets you build tile maps using a GUI. Tiled saves its maps in a file format known as Tile Map XML, or TMX. You'll learn how to load TMX files into Pest Control, which will make it much easier for you to create new levels.

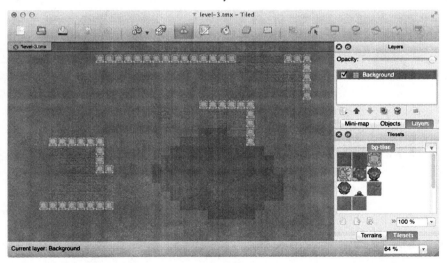

Oh, and to those of you who already know about Tiled and are joining us just because you want to learn how to get your precious TMX files into Sprite Kit, welcome! The rest of us will try not to judge you too harshly for skipping ahead. (Spoiler alert: We try, but we fail. Consider yourself judged.)

> **Note:** This chapter begins where Challenge 2 left off in the last chapter. If you were unable to complete the challenges or skipped ahead from a previous chapter, don't worry – you can simply open **PestControl-Starter** from the resources for this chapter to pick up where we left off.

> **Note:** If you already know how to use Tiled, you can skip various sections throughout this chapter that cover using that software to create a level, as the project already includes a sample TMX file you can use to complete the tutorial.
>
> However, you *need to read the section* titled "Tilesets" because in it you will import some required assets, as well as learn the best way to create your own texture atlases for use with both Sprite Kit and Tiled. From there you'll be directed to the next required section.
>
> Now go forth and choose your own adventure!

Introduction to Tiled

Tiled is a popular open source tile map editor that you can download for free at http://www.mapeditor.org.

The core functionality of Tiled is to paint tiles visually onto a map. It supports multiple layers, and different tile sets. Tiled also includes some other cool features that you'll learn about in this chapter such as tile properties, object layers, and more.

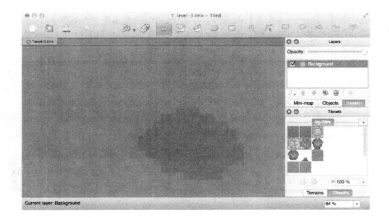

Tiled has an easy to use interface, and saves out map data in an XML format that you can read in your game. In this chapter, you will use Tiled to create your maps, and then add a third party library to read the files that it exports.

In order to create a map for Pest Control in Tiled, you first need to set up your tile images in a particular manner that Tiled supports. So let's get started with this first.

Tilesets

Tiled allows you to access tiles from what it calls **tilesets**. I don't know why they spell it "tileset" instead of "tile set," but they do, so I'll do the same. Tiled also lets you place images in your maps that do not come from such a tileset, but you won't be using that feature here.

A tileset is simply a single image file, such as a PNG file, made up of a grid of smaller images and, optionally, some fixed amount of space between them. It's basically the image portion of a texture atlas, but one whose images must all be the same size, arranged in a grid, and not rotated.

> **Note:** Texture atlases also include a plist file that describes the contents of the image, but Tiled doesn't need it. This is because Tiled makes some assumptions about how things are laid out as described earlier (i.e. that all tiles are the same size, they are arranged in a grid, and they are not rotated).

The following image shows the tileset you'll use in Pest Control:

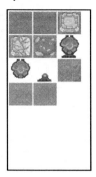

In the next section, you'll create a texture atlas that includes the above image. If you already know how to do this or just want to skim through, you can skip ahead to the section titled "Importing texture atlases into Xcode" where you'll find instructions for using a prebuilt texture atlas.

Using TexturePacker to create tilesets

Unfortunately the Texture Atlas tool that comes built-in with Xcode doesn't have enough configuration options to generate a texture atlas in this grid-based format that Tiled expects. So unless you really enjoy doing a ton of copying and pasting in Photoshop, you'll have to turn to a third party tool to help you out.

The good news is there's a great tool for this called TexturePacker. TexturePacker is a well-known tool for creating sprite sheets (a.k.a. packed texture files or texture atlases) for use with many different platforms, including cocos2d, Unity and even HTML. And now TexturePacker supports creating Sprite Kit texture atlases, too!

What's great about this is that you'll be able to access this TexturePacker-generated texture atlas exactly like you've been accessing the atlases created for you by Xcode. You can create SKSpriteNodes using image names, get SKTextures from an SKTextureAtlas object... the works. This will come in handy a bit later.

This section is not meant to be a thorough tutorial on TexturePacker – there are many of those available on the Internet and I encourage you to explore the software on your own. The point of this section is simply to show you an easy way to create a texture atlas suitable for use in both Tiled and Sprite Kit.

If you don't already have the latest version of TexturePacker, download it here: http://www.codeandweb.com/texturepacker. There is a free version you can use or you can purchase a license for the pro version.

Open TexturePacker and take a look at the interface. If it does not have the three sections shown in the following image, you should open the **View** menu and enable the display of both **TextureSettings** and **Sprites**:

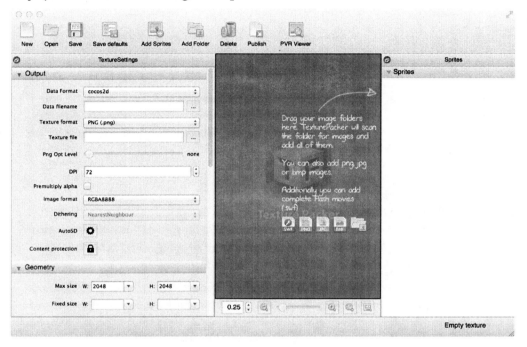

If you've run TexturePacker before, click **New** in the toolbar at the top of the interface to make sure you are starting with all default settings.

Inside the **Output** section of the **TextureSettings** on the left, choose **SpriteKit** for **Data Format** and choose **RGBA5551** for **Image format**, as follows:

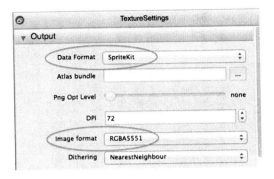

Choosing **SpriteKit** for the data format instructs TexturePacker to create a texture atlas suitable for use with Sprite Kit.

> **Note:** Setting the image format is actually optional – the default settings will work just fine. However, when creating texture atlases, you often want to tailor your settings to get the best image quality using the least amount of disk space. Since Pest Control's tiles have very few colors, and pixels that are either fully opaque or fully transparent, you can choose this image format to produce a smaller file, as well as reduce memory usage by 50%!
>
> Just remember, this setting won't work for all of your art – check the TexturePacker documentation for more information on the available formats. You can also learn more about this in Chapter 26, "Sprite Kit Performance: Texture Atlases".

Next, click the **...** button to the right of the **Atlas bundle** field (still in the **Output** section) and choose a location to save the texture atlas. **Do not** pick anywhere within your project folders, because that will cause errors when you follow the import instructions in the next section. Name your atlas **tmx-bg-tiles** and click **Save**.

Now click **Add Sprites** in the toolbar at the top of the interface. In the dialog that appears, navigate to the **scenery.atlas** directory within your project hierarchy. Select all of the image files and click **Open**.

The center of TexturePacker's interface shows you what the packed texture would look like if you published it with the current settings. The right side of the interface shows the sprites that are part of the atlas, and the lower right displays the size of the image that TexturePacker will produce, as shown on the next page:

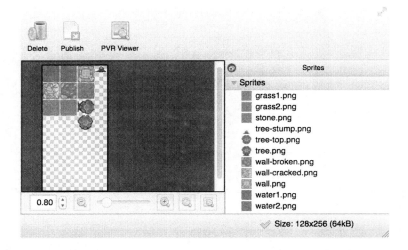

If you were *not* planning to use the texture atlas with Tiled, then you could publish at this point, as TexturePacker has produced an efficiently packed texture. There does appear to be quite a bit of empty space in the image, but that's because by default TexturePacker extends images to be a power of two, which is optimal for some types of hardware. (Currently, it's unclear if Sprite Kit in general performs better with images sized like this, but it certainly doesn't perform worse.) In this case, the smallest power of two image that can fit all of these tiles is 128x256 pixels.

However, because you *are* going to use Tiled, you have to change a couple more settings. Tiled requires that all tile images within the grid are the same size. If they aren't, you'll get strange drawing behavior. Also, as mentioned earlier Tiled expects tiles not to be rotated, but by default TexturePacker rotates tiles when appropriate to pack images as tightly as possible (as you can see with the tree image).

To fix these issues, inside the **Layout** section of the **TextureSettings** on the left, **uncheck Allow rotation**. Also choose **None** for **Trim mode**. This keeps TexturePacker from trimming transparent space around the edges of tiles, which is important to make sure each tile remains its native size in the atlas. Again, all of the tile images must have the exact same size for use in Tiled.

You should now see the following:

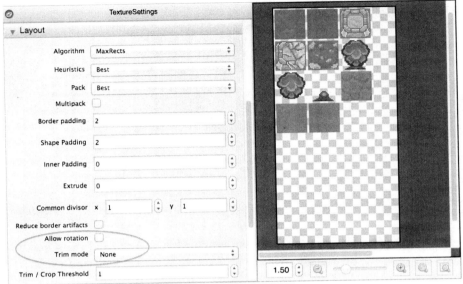

Notice that the tree images are no longer rotated, and the tree stump image has more transparent space around it.

This is one price you pay for using Tiled – if you have many tiles containing lots of transparent pixels, your texture atlases may be larger than they would be if you were using a non-TMX solution, such as what you implemented in the previous two chapters. However, for a small tileset like this it makes very little difference.

One more thing: you *might* be able to get away with the settings you have right now, but using these settings, I've sometimes seen tiles render with gaps between them. You can avoid this problem by extruding the edges of your tiles.

That is, you'll copy extra rows and columns of the pixels along the outer edges of each sprite in the texture atlas, effectively making them larger than their 32x32 pixel size, but you'll still try to use only the central 32x32 pixels. This gives Sprite Kit some extra appropriately-colored pixels in case it accidentally renders a little more than 32x32 pixels due to rounding errors and the like.

Still inside the **Layout** section of the **TextureSettings** on the left, set the **Extrude** value to **2**, as shown on the next page.

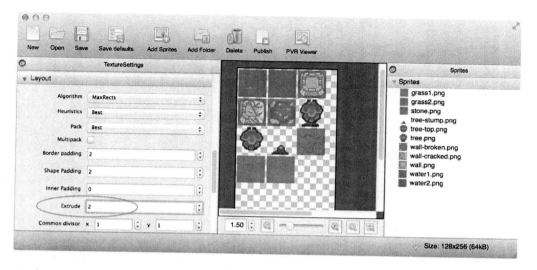

As shown in the above image, your tiles have grown a bit, and some of them look a little strange. For example, the tree tile seems to have grown some extra pixels on top.

In general, tiles that include transparent pixels run the risk of looking the worst when extruded, because it tends to look strange when the extra pixels aren't added evenly around the entire image. They'll look fine when you see them in Pest Control, but keep in mind that for sprites with lots of transparency, especially those that make up character animations, it's advisable to include a margin of at least one transparent pixel to avoid such display anomalies.

Click **Publish** in the toolbar at the top of the interface and TexturePacker will write your texture atlas to the location you specified in the **Atlas bundle** field.

You should now have a directory named **tmx-bg-tiles.atlasc** that contains two files, named **tmx-bg-tiles.1.png** and **tmx-bg-tiles.plist**. In the next section, you'll add these to your project in Xcode.

Importing texture atlases into Xcode

Note: If you skipped ahead to this section, you can find the texture atlas we generated in the **tmx-bg-tiles.atlasc** folder in the resources for this chapter.

At this point, you've either built or found the premade directory named **tmx-bg-tiles.atlasc**, which contains two files, named **tmx-bg-tiles.1.png** and **tmx-bg-tiles.plist**.

The image file **tmx-bg-tiles.1.png** contains every tile used to create Pest Control's maps (some of which aren't used until Chapters 17 and 18, "Juice Up Your Game, Parts 1 & 2."); Sprite Kit uses **tmx-bg-tiles.plist** to find specific images within **tmx-bg-tiles.1.png**. Together, these two files form the texture atlas named **tmx-bg-tiles**.

The one tricky thing about adding this texture atlas to your project is that you need a *folder reference* in Xcode, not a standard group.

If you haven't done so already, open the PestControl project in Xcode. Highlight the **PestControl/Resources/Levels** group in the Project Navigator on the left and then either right-click or go to the **File** menu and choose **Add Files to "PestControl"**....

Select the **tmx-bg-tiles.atlasc** folder, either the one you made or the one from the project resources, and make sure **Copy items into destination group's folder (if needed)** and the **PestControl** target are both selected. Finally, choose **Create folder references for any added folders** and click **Add**. This is different from what you usually choose when importing, as shown below:

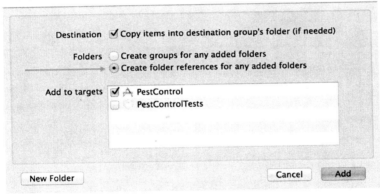

If everything went correctly, your **tmx-bg-tiles.atlasc** folder should look like this in the Project Navigator:

If the icon next to **tmx-bg-tiles.atlasc** is not blue like in the image above (and is yellow instead), this means you selected **Create groups** instead of **Create folder references**. To fix this, you should delete it and try again. Be sure to choose **Move to Trash** when prompted during the delete operation.

My apologies to the readers of this printed book viewing a black and white image, but just use your imagination — pretend that one shade of gray is yellow, and that other shade of gray is blue. No, you've got them backwards. Come on, you're not even trying!

> **Note:** You imported this folder into the **Levels** group for an important reason. At the time of this writing, the class you'll be using to load TMX files requires those TMX files to only reference images from their same directory or from a subdirectory of that directory. The **Levels** group seemed like the best place for the TMX file, so the image had to be in this folder or in a descendent of this folder.

So you have your tiles all lined up neatly in a grid and you've imported your texture atlas into Xcode. Next stop: Tiled town.

Creating maps in Tiled

> **Note:** If you're already familiar with making maps in Tiled and just want to know how to load TMX files into Sprite Kit, you can skip ahead to "Importing your maps." The starter project contains a TMX file named **level-3-sample.tmx** that you can use so that you can focus on the code.

Now that you've created your tileset, you can finally start to create your map in Tiled.

Creating maps in Tiled is a straightforward affair. You define the size of the map and its tiles, load in your tilesets and start painting. In this chapter you won't cover much more than the basics — just what's necessary to create a level for Pest Control — but you should explore Tiled on your own afterwards to see what you can do with some of its other features.

To install Tiled, go to http://www.mapeditor.org, click the **Download** button and then choose your preferred OS from the **Latest Release** area at the top of the page. After your download completes, double-click the disk image and follow any instructions provided.

Configuring your map

Create a new map by choosing **File\New...**. Set its **Orientation** to **Orthogonal**, its **Map size** to **30 tiles** wide by **20 tiles** tall, and its **Tile size** to **32 x 32 pixels**, as shown below:

Before you continue, go to **File\Save As...**, name your file **level-3.tmx** and save it inside your project's **Resources/Levels** folder.

> **Note:** For your app to work properly throughout this tutorial, you must configure your map exactly as described above. Certain steps in this tutorial mix TMX-based tiles with non-TMX tiles, and if you use different values here, those steps will not work correctly.
>
> After you've completed the chapter and the full TMX solution is in place, you can freely create maps with different sizes, but if you want to change the tile size, you'll need to supply your own graphics. You've been warned.

Maps in Tiled are comprised of layers similar to those used in Photoshop and most other image-editing programs. This means you don't need to try to cram all of your data into a grid that's only a single tile deep. You can instead, for example, create a background layer for your grass and water, with a layer above it for decorations like trees. In fact, that is exactly what you're about to do.

New maps in Tiled always start with a single layer named **Tile Layer 1**. You can see it, along with any other layers you make, in the **Layers** pane. Double-click **Tile Layer 1** in the **Layers** pane and rename it **Background**, as shown on the next page:

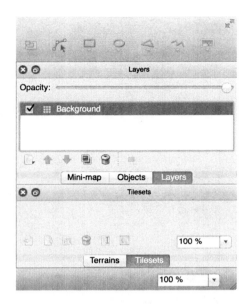

> **Note:** if you don't see the panes as shown above, toggle them on in the **View** menu. Be sure to show at least **Tilesets**, **Layers** and **Objects**, as you'll need each of those in this chapter.

You've completed your initial map setup. The next step is to add your tilesets.

Adding tilesets

As mentioned earlier, a tileset is an image that contains multiple smaller images, each of which you can place into your map any number of times. Think of it as a palette you use to paint your map.

Pest Control has only a single tileset, but Tiled allows you to use multiple tilesets in a map. In fact, you can use multiple tilesets within the same layer of a map. But it's best to group your tiles into sets based on their expected uses together in a scene, because Sprite Kit's performance decreases as the number of tilesets it simultaneously needs to access increases.

Create a new tileset by choosing **Map\New Tileset...**. Name it **bg-tiles**, click **Browse...**, and locate **tmx-bg-tiles.1.png** in your project's **Resources/Levels/tmx-bg-tiles.atlasc** directory. Be sure **Tile width** and **height** are both **32 px**, and **Drawing Offset X** and **Y** are both **0 px**. Finally, set **Margin** to **4px** and **Spacing** to **6px**.

Your dialog should look like the one below. Click **OK**.

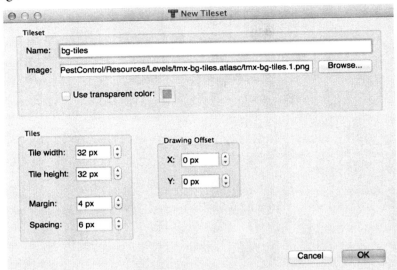

The margin and spacing settings above may seem odd, but they are necessary to account for the extruded tiles you added to your images. Here is what each of these settings mean:

- **Margin** indicates how many pixels Tiled should skip (for both width and height) before reading the first tile. The margin setting of 4 accounts for the actual 2-pixel margin added around the entire atlas image by TexturePacker, as well as the two extruded pixels along the top edge of the tiles in the top row and the two extruded pixels along the left edge of the tiles in the left column.

- **Spacing** indicates how many pixels Tiled should skip (for both width and height) to get from one tile to the next. The 6-pixel spacing accounts for the two pixels TexturePacker added between each tile, plus two extruded pixels in each of the two tiles on either side of that gap.

Phew. That's more accounting than I generally like to do.

bg-tiles is now available for you to use, visible in the **Tilesets** tab.

Your tiles are loaded, so it's time to start putting them into place.

Placing tiles

Tiled's shining attribute is the ease with which it lets you create maps using controls similar to any standard paint program. In this chapter, you'll use a few different techniques to make your level. To begin, you'll create a randomized field of grass with just five clicks.

Random fills

1. Click the **Random Mode** button in the toolbar, which looks like a pair of dice. Using this mode, you select multiple tiles and let Tiled randomly choose which one to use to paint.

2. Click the **Bucket Fill Tool** button in the toolbar, which looks like a paint bucket. (You can also press the letter F shortcut key.) This lets you modify any contiguous group of identical tiles with a single click.

3. **Shift+click** the **two grass tiles** in the **bg-tiles** tileset. This counts as two of those five clicks I mentioned. Since you're in Random Mode, Tiled will randomly choose between these two tiles for any paint actions you perform.

4. Move your mouse cursor over the large map area. As soon as the cursor enters this area, you'll see a preview the map if you were to click. Notice that the background continues to change as you move your mouse cursor. That's because Tiled is constantly re-evaluating its random tile placement. When you like the general look of the background, **click** in the map. Don't worry if it's not perfect – you'll learn how to fix it next.

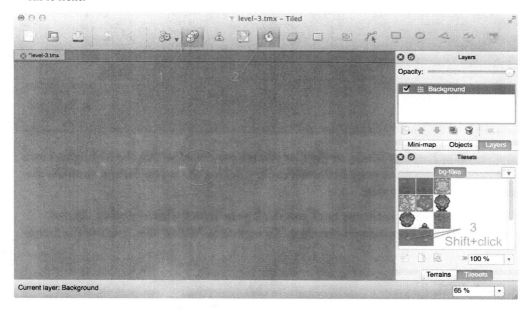

You may not like certain things about the way Tiled distributed the grass tiles. Perhaps there is too much tall grass, or maybe you just don't like a few specific clumps. There are a couple of easy ways to fix that.

Hover your mouse cursor over any part of the map and you'll see a preview of what it would look like if you clicked on that spot. Because you're still using the Bucket Fill Tool, Tiled highlights not only the tile you hover over, but also every identical tile that touches that tile, as shown below:

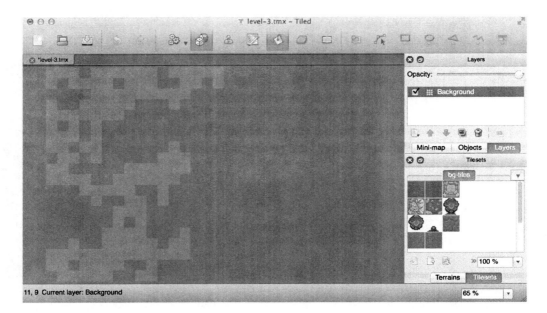

You're still in Random Mode, so the tiles you see previewed within the highlighted area will change as you move your cursor within it. Clicking the mouse button commits the changes you see to the area.

Continue to make adjustments until you think your lawn is almost perfect. At that point, it's time to do some spot weeding. To replace individual tiles, you use the Stamp Brush.

Single Tiles

Click the **Random Mode** button again to toggle it **off**, and then click the **Stamp Brush** in the toolbar, which looks like a rubber stamp. You can also enable the Stamp Brush by pressing the letter **B** shortcut key.

Now click one or the other grass tile in your tileset so that only one is selected, and then click in the map to place the selected tile in that spot on the grid. You can also click and drag if you'd like to paint a larger area with the chosen tile, and you can continue to paint with that tile until you choose a different one in this or another tileset.

Once you're tired of watching grass grow, move on to the next section to get your feet wet with... oh, forget it. Next, you'll paint some water tiles.

Random painting

Your lawn looks great, but it could use a little water. **Shift+click** the two water tiles in the **bg-tiles** tileset, choose **Random Mode** and the **Stamp Brush** (if it isn't already selected).

Use your mouse cursor to click and/or click and drag in the map to create a small pond. Notice how the Random Mode option works with the Stamp Brush as well as the Bucket Fill Tool, so you can repeatedly paint over the same area and see it change slightly each time.

Tweak the appearance of the water using the same techniques you used with the grass, until you've created an inviting pond, similar to the one shown below:

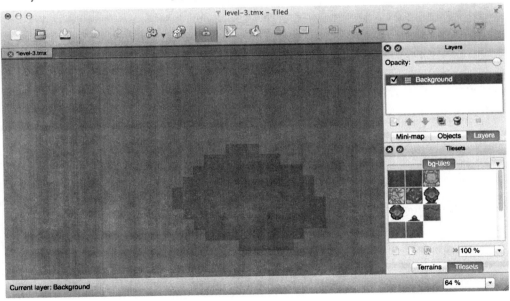

Wow, computer graphics have come a long way, don't you think? But I assure you that if you try to jump in for a swim, it will likely end in damage to your monitor, embarrassment, and potentially, bodily harm. You've been warned.

Finishing touches

Use the **Stamp Brush** to finish up the background layer, adding some solid walls and stone floor tiles wherever you see fit. Don't use the other tiles at this point, as you'll use those later for specific things. Here's what I made:

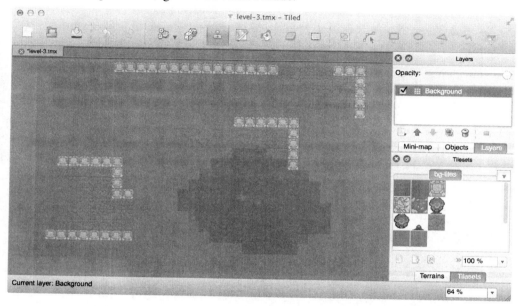

You've got a lovely field of grass, a cool, refreshing pond, and some oddly placed walls that look a bit like old ruins. Now you need to add some trees for shade.

Adding layers

One of the benefits of using Tiled over the text files you used in the previous chapters is that you can see all of your layers simultaneously. In this section, you'll add a separate layer for your trees.

Choose **Layer\Add Tile Layer,** which creates a new layer named **Tile Layer 2**. By default, the name field will have keyboard focus so you should be able to simply start typing to change its name, but if not, double-click **Tile Layer 2** in the **Layers** pane and rename it to **Breakables**, as shown in the following image.

With the **Breakables** layer selected, choose the tree tile that shows an entire tree, not just the top or the stump. Using the **Stamp Brush** (with Random Mode turned off), add several trees to the **Breakables** layer.

You may find it useful to turn on **View\Highlight Current Layer**. This makes the **Background** layer dimmed to indicate that it is not the active layer, as shown below:

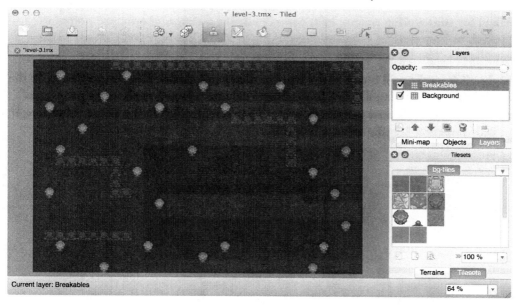

This is useful because it's very easy to forget what layer you're working within Tiled and accidentally draw to the wrong layer. With the dimming option, it's more clear at a glance what layer you're in.

If you don't like where you planted a tree, use the **Eraser** tool to remove it.

Once you've made a level you think Arnold would be happy to call home, move on to the next section to learn how you can pass data to your app by attaching it to your tiles.

Adding tile properties

One of Tiled's coolest features is that it lets you assign properties to your tiles. You can also assign properties to other things, such as layers and tilesets, but for our purposes, tile properties will suffice.

You'll use properties to indicate tile types to your app, so that you'll be able to query your tiles to find out whether or not they are walls, for example. But properties are just arbitrary key-value pairs that you can use to store any metadata you like.

You could use properties to store specific physics settings to make ice tiles more slippery than stone tiles; a class name to tell your app what type of object to instantiate; point values for your scoring system; item names to define pickups; or even just notes for yourself to keep track of things while working in Tiled, like how you planned to use a specific tile. The list is endless.

Right-click on the wall image in the **bg-tiles** tileset and choose **Tile Properties…**. In the dialog that appears, double-click in the **Name** column where it reads **<new property>** and enter **wall** as the new property's name. Then double-click in the **Value** column next to **wall** and enter **1** as the value. Click **OK**.

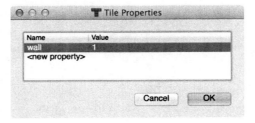

As I just mentioned, you can use properties for all sorts of things and the values you set will depend on your intended use. In this case, the code you write is simply going to check if a property named wall is present on a tile, so the actual value you set here doesn't matter.

Now follow those steps again to add a property named **tree** to the tree tile containing the entire tree (not just the tree top or tree stump).

OK, you've seeded grass, planted trees, erected walls, paved floors and even dug a pond. You must be tired. It's time to take a break and see how it all looks in Sprite Kit.

Importing your maps

First you need to add your TMX file to the Xcode project. If you skipped the previous section and didn't build **level-3.tmx** yourself, then ignore the next paragraph because your project already includes the TMX file you'll be using.

Select the **PestControl/Resources/Levels** group in the Project Navigator and either right-click or open the **File** menu, then choose **Add Files to "PestControl"…**. Choose the TMX file that you just made, which should be named **level-3.tmx** and should be right there in the Levels folder. Be sure that **PestControl** is checked in the **Add to targets** section of the dialog and click **Add**.

Now you've got a TMX file in your app's bundle, but what can you do with it? At the time of writing, Sprite Kit does not have built-in support for TMX files. However, the open source community has been working hard on various solutions of its own. You'll probably have plenty of options to choose from by the time you're reading this, but the one you'll use in Pest Control is called JSTileMap.

JSTileMap: an open source TMX solution for Sprite Kit

JSTileMap is a custom subclass of SKNode that renders TMX files in Sprite Kit. It parses a TMX file and instantiates various objects to model the contents of the file, such as TMXLayers for each tile layer, TMXTilesetInfo objects for each tileset and SKSpriteNodes for each tile. It's a work in progress, so these things may change in the future.

Jeremy Stone started the JSTileMap project. JS – get it? He based his original implementation on the TMX parsing code from the open source cocos2d-iPhone project. He continues to work on it, with contributions from myself and other members of the community, making it more Sprite Kit-centric, improving performance and adding support for features not included in the cocos2d version. For more information on JSTileMap, to download the latest version or to contribute code, go to https://github.com/slycrel/JSTileMap.

> **Note:** Because an open source project like JSTileMap can change quickly and often, you're not going to download the latest code to follow along with this chapter. Instead, we've included a folder in this chapter's resources named **JSTileMap** that includes a version of the code that we know works at the time of this writing. We'll update that file periodically with newer versions of JSTileMap as we test them and know they still work with the chapter. Of course, after going through the chapter, you are encouraged to download the latest version of JSTileMap to use in your own apps.
>
> Also note, this chapter won't be covering the inner workings of JSTileMap and its supporting classes, so you should take a look at the source code if you want a detailed understanding of how it works.

Find the **JSTileMap** folder in this chapter's resources. Inside Xcode, choose **File\Add Files to "PestControl"...** and select the **JSTileMap** folder. Be sure **Copy items into destination group's folder (if needed)**, **Create groups for any added folders**, and the **PestControl** target are all checked, and then click **Add**.

Your app would fail to build if you tried right now, because part of what you just imported was a compression utility named LFCGzipUtility, which requires you to link your app with an additional library. This compression utility is required because Tiled compresses the map data in order to make TMX files smaller.

Choose the **PestControl** project in the Project Navigator and then choose the **PestControl** target. Inside the **General** tab, click the + button in the section labeled **Linked Frameworks and Libraries**, as shown below:

Select the library named **libz.dylib** and click **Add**.

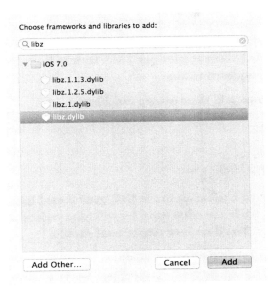

Build your project to make sure everything compiles OK. With `JSTileMap` and `libz` added to your app, you're now ready to write some code.

Rendering TMX maps in Sprite Kit

In order to support TMX files along with the text files you used in the previous two chapters, you'll create a subclass of `TileMapLayer`. This lets you leverage all the code you've already written, so you won't have to write much new code to add TMX support. However, if you were only supporting TMX files, it might make more sense to replace `TileMapLayer` instead.

Go to **File\New\File...**, choose the **iOS\Cocoa Touch\Objective-C class** template and click **Next**. Name your class **TmxTileMapLayer**, make it a subclass of **TileMapLayer** and click **Next** again. Be sure the **PestControl** target is checked and click **Create**.

Open **TmxTileMapLayer.h** and import `JSTileMap`:

```
#import "JSTileMap.h"
```

Declare the following initializer:

```
- (instancetype)initWithTmxLayer:(TMXLayer*)layer;
```

`TMXLayer` is a class declared in JSTileMap.h. You created multiple layers in Tiled when you made your map, and instances of this class give you access to those layers individually. For some games, you won't need this access, because a single JSTileMap object can display all of its layers simultaneously. In the case of Pest Control, however, you'll create a single TmxTileMapLayer per TMX layer to fit the current TileMapLayer-based implementation.

In **TmxTileMapLayer.m**, add these private variables:

```
TMXLayer *_layer;
CGSize _tmxTileSize;
CGSize _tmxGridSize;
CGSize _tmxLayerSize;
```

You'll use _layer to hold a reference to the TMXLayer passed into initWithTmxLayer:, while the other variables will store various pieces of size-related data regarding the layer. You'll see how they're used shortly.

Now implement initWithTmxLayer: as follows:

```
- (instancetype)initWithTmxLayer:(TMXLayer *)layer
{
  if (self = [super init]) {
    _layer = layer;
    _tmxTileSize = layer.mapTileSize;
    _tmxGridSize = layer.layerInfo.layerGridSize;
    _tmxLayerSize = CGSizeMake(layer.layerWidth,
                               layer.layerHeight);
  }
  return self;
}
```

Notice how this method calls super init rather than initWithAtlasNamed:tileSize:grid:. This is because you don't want any of TileMapLayer's default grid processing to occur for TmxTileMapLayer objects. However, you still want this class to be a kind of TileMapLayer so that you can use it wherever you've used those objects, such as in MyScene.

The rest of the method simply stores some of the layer's data, which you'll use in the next methods you add.

You need to override the getters for some of TileMapLayer's properties because they currently return values that were initialized in initWithAtlasNamed:tileSize:grid:, but as you just saw, TmxTileMapLayer doesn't call that method.

Add the following new getter implementations:

```
- (CGSize)gridSize {
```

```
    return _tmxGridSize;
}

- (CGSize)tileSize {
  return _tmxTileSize;
}

- (CGSize)layerSize {
  return _tmxLayerSize;
}
```

It doesn't get much more straightforward than that. You may be wondering, though, why you don't return this data directly from the _layer object you're holding. Why make a copy of the data and return that instead?

Because I can see into the future, that's why. Specifically, I know that you'll add another initializer method later that doesn't take a TMXLayer, which means _layer will sometimes be nil. Rather than make these getters more complicated by having them check which objects are available and doing different things for different cases, you simply store the data into a separate variable and use that. You'll do something similar in the other initializer you're going to write. This way, no matter the source of the data, you know you can find it in the same variable. Doesn't that sound convenient?

Most of TileMapLayer's methods use other TileMapLayer methods. For example, isValidTileCoord: calls both self.tileSize and self.layerSize to perform its range checks. That means by overriding those three getter methods, you've given TmxTileMapLayer access to most of the functionality of TileMapLayer.

You'll override one more method later in this chapter. Can you guess which one? No, not that one! Actually, maybe that one. I don't really know because I can't hear you. You *do* know how books work, don't you?

Now you're ready to load your TMX file into your scene. Inside **MyScene.m**, import your new class:

```
#import "TmxTileMapLayer.h"
```

And add this private instance variable:

```
JSTileMap *_tileMap;
```

This variable holds a reference to your JSTileMap, which is an SKNode that you'll create from a TMX file.

In order to create your `JSTileMap`, you need to actually load a level from a TMX file. In the next chapter, you'll refactor your level-loading code to support multiple levels, but for now, you'll continue to hard-code things.

Comment out the contents of `createScenery` and add the following lines in their place. Readers who did not work through the sections to create **level-3.tmx** should load the map named **level-3-sample.tmx** instead:

```
_tileMap = [JSTileMap mapNamed:@"level-3.tmx"];
return [[TmxTileMapLayer alloc]
        initWithTmxLayer:[_tileMap layerNamed:@"Background"]];
```

You first initialize `_tileMap` with a TMX file. Because `JSTileMap` extends `SKNode`, you could (and will, soon) add it to your scene and it would render the map it contains. That really couldn't be any easier. But you also return a new `TmxTileMapLayer` backed by the TMX file's `Background` layer.

Remember, your app initializes `_bgLayer` with the return value from `createScenery`, so the `TmxTileMapLayer` you return here is what you'll access when you interact with `_bgLayer`. For example, when your scene checks for valid tile positions or queries tile properties, it will be using this object – and hence, data from your TMX file – to do so.

Inside `createWorld`, add the following highlighted lines where shown:

```
_worldNode = [SKNode node];
if (_tileMap) {
  [_worldNode addChild:_tileMap];
}
[_worldNode addChild:_bgLayer];
```

This just adds `_tileMap` to `_worldNode`, which will display the TMX file's contents in the scene. You first check to make sure `_tileMap` exists so that you can still support the text file approach from the previous chapters. Now you've got options!

Build and run. Remember when you were creating Pest Control and you had to keep iterating over it to get exactly the behavior you wanted? Well, all that work seems to have gone out the window: you've got trees all over the place, only some of which get smashed when Arnold runs through them, and Arnold and the bugs are once again running around wherever they want. It's a sprite mutiny!

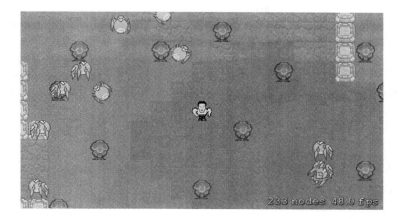

While this behavior is undesirable, it's perfectly reasonable based on the code you've written so far. First of all, you are rendering two sets of trees. Remember, your TMX file now contains a layer with tree sprites, but your app is also still loading trees from the text file like it did before. You'll fix that problem a bit later.

The other problem is that your background tiles are no longer rendered from `_bgLayer` like they had been when loading from text files. Instead, you created `_tileMap` and added *it* in `createWorld`. Yes, you initialized `_bgLayer` from the layer named `Background` inside your TMX file, and you added it as a child of `_worldNode`, but remember—you created a new initializer that bypassed all the initialization code in `TileMapLayer`. That means your `TmxTileMapLayer` *never creates any tiles*. No walls, no water, no nothing. Instead, `_bgLayer` only acts as a pass-through object that lets you ask things like how big are its tiles, or what are the dimensions of the background layer's grid?

It looks like there are a few more things to do to get TMX files working properly in Pest Control. First, you'll reinforce those flimsy walls with some sturdy physics bodies.

Adding physics bodies

When you created **level-3.tmx**, you added a property named **wall** to the wall tile. (If you're running with **level-3-sample.tmx**, the `wall` property was defined for you.) Now you're going to use that property to determine where in your scene to add physics bodies of type `PCWallCategory`.

Inside **TmxTileMapLayer.m**, add this import to get access to `PCPhysicsCategory`:

```
#import "MyScene.h"
```

Add the following method to process the layer's tiles. You could add any custom tile-based setup here, but for now, you'll just process wall tiles:

```
- (void)createNodesFromLayer:(TMXLayer *)layer
{
  JSTileMap *map = layer.map;
  //1
  for (int w = 0 ; w < self.gridSize.width; ++w) {
    for(int h = 0; h < self.gridSize.height; ++h) {

      CGPoint coord = CGPointMake(w, h);
      //2
      NSInteger tileGid =
        [layer.layerInfo tileGidAtCoord:coord];
      if(!tileGid)
        continue;
      //3
      if([map propertiesForGid:tileGid][@"wall"]) {
        //4
        SKSpriteNode *tile = [layer tileAtCoord:coord];

        tile.physicsBody =
        [SKPhysicsBody bodyWithRectangleOfSize:tile.size];
        tile.physicsBody.categoryBitMask = PCWallCategory;
        tile.physicsBody.dynamic = NO;
        tile.physicsBody.friction = 0;
      }
    }
  }
}
```

The above code does the following:

1. It loops through all the cell locations in the layer.

2. At each location, it finds the global identifier for that cell's tile. TMX files reference specific tile types by unique global identifiers, or GIDs, with a value of zero meaning there is no tile at that location. If there is no tile, the code skips to the next cell location. This isn't absolutely necessary, but it's more efficient than running through the remaining logic for a tile that isn't even there. For more information about the TMX format, consult its documentation here:
https://github.com/bjorn/tiled/wiki/TMX-Map-Format

3. For each tile, the code checks for the existence of the **wall** property. As was mentioned when you added the property in Tiled, this code doesn't check the value, just whether or not the key exists.

4. Whenever this method finds a tile with the **wall** property, it attaches a physics body to that tile, just like the ones you made in `TileMapLayer`. The important thing to notice is that the code adds the physics body to a sprite that is in the `JSTileMap`, not the `TmxTileMapLayer` — the `TmxTileMapLayer` still contains no sprites of its own.

Don't worry about the water tiles for now: you'll handle those later using a different technique.

Now call this method from within `initWithTmxLayer:`, just after the line that initializes `_tmxLayerSize`:

```
[self createNodesFromLayer:layer];
```

Build and run. Arnold's back to banging his head into walls, just the way he likes it, but those bugs still don't seem to care about the walls.

You may recall from the previous chapter, the bugs don't use physics for collisions. Instead, they query the scene to find out if it's safe to travel on a tile. And how does the scene determine that? It checks the properties of tiles in `_breakableLayer` and `_bgLayer`. However, you just saw that `_bgLayer` no longer *has* any tiles.

And that brings us to that other method you need to implement in `TmxTileMapLayer`. The one you guessed earlier, remember? Or was that someone else? Speak up, please. Ha! Just kidding — still a book.

Add this method to **TmxTileMapLayer.m**:

```
- (SKNode*)tileAtPoint:(CGPoint)point
{
    SKNode *tile = [super tileAtPoint:point];
    return tile ? tile : [_layer tileAt:point];
}
```

This does two things. First, it checks for a tile using the method's `super` implementation from `TileMapLayer`, which looks for tiles that are children of this object. If there happens to be a tile there — and there sometimes will be before you're done with this chapter — the method returns it. But if there isn't a tile in this layer node, then this method asks the `TMXLayer` object `_layer` for a tile at this position. This bridges the gap between the `TileMapLayer` logic and the `JSTileMap`. Now your layer object can access your walls and their physics bodies, even though they actually exist inside the `JSTileMap`.

Build and run, and now your bugs are back to avoiding walls. However, they still walk on water and half the trees — the half defined in the TMX layer.

Adding breakables

It's time to get rid of the old trees and add proper support for the trees from the TMX file.

Open **MyScene.m** and add the following to the beginning of `createBreakables`, which will put the method's current contents into an `else` clause:

```
if (_tileMap) {
  TMXLayer *breakables = [_tileMap layerNamed:@"Breakables"];
  return
    (breakables ?
    [[TmxTileMapLayer alloc] initWithTmxLayer:breakables] :
    nil);
}
else
```

If `_tileMap` is present, the above code checks for a layer named `Breakables`. If such a layer exists, the method returns a `TmxTileMapLayer` created from it, or `nil` otherwise. However, if `_tileMap` is `nil`, the code falls into the `else` clause and executes your old logic.

Run now and you'll see that all the old trees have disappeared.

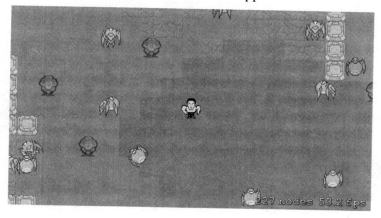

Unfortunately, the old trees were the ones that worked! Arnold and the bugs both happily pass right over the remaining trees as if there's nothing there.

You'll handle trees a bit differently than you did the walls. Instead of modifying the tiles directly in the `JSTileMap`, you'll remove those tiles and add `Breakable` objects to the `TmxTileMapLayer` in their place.

Modifying tile maps at runtime

Sometimes, you'll want to modify your map at runtime. For example, you might have player pickups, destructible elements or scenery changes that occur based on in-game events. In this section, you'll get a taste of how to accomplish this sort of thing by removing tiles from the `JSTileMap` and adding `Breakables` to your `TmxTileMapLayer`. In the process, you'll learn how to create sprites using the same tileset images referenced by the TMX file.

Inside **TmxTileMapLayer.m**, import `Breakable`:

```
#import "Breakable.h"
```

At the top of `createNodeFromLayer:`, add the following line:

```
SKTextureAtlas *atlas =
  [SKTextureAtlas atlasNamed:@"tmx-bg-tiles"];
```

This gives you access to a texture atlas backed by exactly the same image this layer uses in the TMX file. Now you can create sprites knowing you're using the same images you saw when you were working in Tiled. Yes, this is a bit of hard-coding trickery that won't work if your TMX file uses multiple atlases. But don't worry – you'll see how you could correct for that in a moment.

To handle tree tiles, add this `else` clause after the `if` block inside `createNodesFromLayer::`

```
else if([map propertiesForGid:tileGid][@"tree"]) {
  SKNode *tile =
    [[Breakable alloc]
     initWithWhole:[atlas textureNamed:@"tree"]
            broken:[atlas textureNamed:@"tree-stump"]];
  tile.position = [self pointForCoord:coord];
  [self addChild:tile];
```

```
    [layer removeTileAtCoord:coord];
}
```

The code above checks for any tile that has the **tree** property – remember, it's in a loop inside `createNodesFromLayer:`. When it finds one, it creates a `Breakable` object and places it inside this `TmxTileMapLayer` object. Finally, it removes the tile it found from the `TMXLayer` object. The important thing to note is that, unlike with the walls, the tree sprite the game displays to the user is now in the `TmxTileMapLayer`, not the `JSTileMap`.

If you didn't want to hard-code the texture atlas name used in this method, then you could use the code below to find the name of the texture atlas containing a specific tile GID:

```
TMXTilesetInfo* info = [map tilesetInfoForGid:tileGid];
NSString *atlasName =
  [[[info.sourceImage lastPathComponent]
    stringByDeletingPathExtension]
  stringByDeletingPathExtension];
```

Note that this code will only work if you didn't use any periods in your texture atlas names. It first finds the tileset used by the current tile (as a `TMXTilesetInfo` reference), and then strips the path and unnecessary text from the file name, resulting in the atlas name.

You would then get the atlas using `atlasName` and proceed as before, but you'd have to do that once for each tile. Technically, you could cache references to the atlases by tile type. However, for the purposes of Pest Control, none of this is necessary.

Run again and help Arnold prune some branches. Not too much, mind you – just take a little off the top.

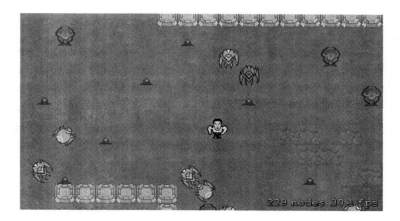

Also notice that once again, the bugs avoid your trees. How'd that happen? While it may look like Arnold invested in some bug repellent, this is the result of code you wrote just a few steps ago.

Remember when you implemented `tileAtPoint:` in `TmxTileMapLayer` to check for tiles in the `TmxTileMapLayer` node before checking the `TMXLayer` object? The `Breakables` are now stored in the `TmxTileMapLayer`, and as such `tileAtPoint:` returns them when appropriate. Since Pest Control calls this method when the bugs are planning their movements, they now correctly identify the trees as impassable tiles.

With your background and trees both coming from the TMX file, it's time to turn your attention to Arnold and the bugs.

Defining spawn points

Right now you've got parts of the level loading from a TMX file and parts of it loading from the text files you were using in the previous chapters, but you really want to store all the level data in a single TMX file. In this section, you'll add to the file the starting positions, or spawn points, for the player and all the bugs. To do that, you'll use a different type of layer called an **Object Layer**.

> **Note:** If you aren't following along in Tiled, you can skip ahead to "Accessing TMX data layers in Sprite Kit," where you'll see how to use data in an object layer to spawn the player and the bugs.

Adding data layers in Tiled

In much the same way you made the Breakables tile layer, you'll make a new layer to store character spawn points. However, instead of adding tiles to this layer, you'll just store metadata used by your app to create the appropriate objects. To accomplish this, you'll create what is called an Object Layer.

Open **level-3.tmx** in Tiled and choose **Layer\Add Object Layer**, which creates a new layer named **Object Layer 1**. Rename **Object Layer 1** to **Bugs**, as shown below:

Select the **Insert Rectangle** tool (shortcut **R**) from the toolbar and with the Bugs layer selected, click someplace on the map where you'd like a bug to spawn. That will create a small square at that position, as shown below:

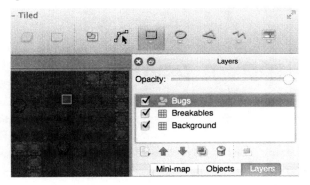

Now do more of that until you have a nice field of squares, making sure each square is positioned where it makes sense to spawn a bug.

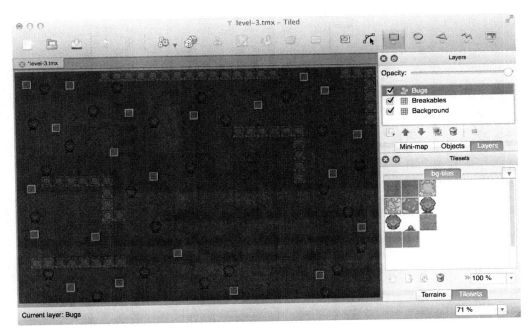

Each of these squares defines a bug's spawn point that you'll need to process in your code. To make that easier, you'll name each square. Click the **Objects** tab and then expand the **Bugs** layer, which will show you the name and type for every object it currently contains. Because you haven't assigned any names or types, your list will look like the one below:

Double-click in the **Name** column to the right of one of the checkmarks and then enter the name **bug**. Do that for every object in the **Bugs** layer, which should result in something similar to the image on the next page:

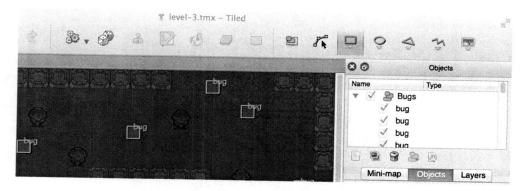

Notice how each object in the map view also displays its name.

In your original implementation, you also defined Arnold's spawn point in the bug data file, and you'll do the same thing here. To make Arnold's point easier to see, you'll define it using a different shape.

Select the **Insert Ellipse** tool (shortcut **C**) from the toolbar and with the **Bugs** layer selected, click someplace on the map where you'd like Arnold to appear. That will create a small circle at that position. Inside the **Objects** list, name that object **player**, as shown below:

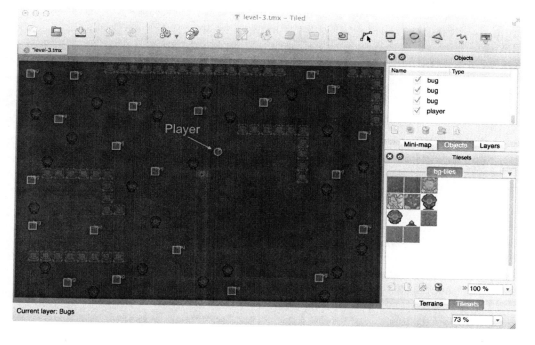

It's hard to see it, but the circle is displaying the object's name on the map just like the squares do. It's truncated though, because the object is so small. If you had created a larger object, you'd see the name.

You're done for now, so save your map in Tiled.

You've defined all your spawn points and you can see at a glance exactly how your level is arranged. Now you need to use this spawn data in your app.

Accessing TMX data layers in Sprite Kit

JSTileMap creates TMXLayers for each tile layer in a TMX file and you've already added support for those inside TmxTileMapLayer. But object layers are accessed via TMXObjectGroup objects, not TMXLayers, so you'll need to support those differently.

Declare the following new method in **TmxTileMapLayer.h**:

```
- (instancetype)initWithTmxObjectGroup:(TMXObjectGroup *)group
                              tileSize:(CGSize)tileize
                              gridSize:(CGSize)gridSize;
```

Unlike TMXLayer, TMXObjectGroup has no concept of tile or grid sizes. But for your purposes, you still want to interact with the TmxTileMapLayer object in terms of tiles and cells. For these reasons, this initializer requires you to pass in the tile and grid sizes along with the group reference.

Open **TmxTileMapLayer.m** and import both the Player and Bug classes:

```
#import "Player.h"
#import "Bug.h"
```

Much like how you handled tiles with different properties in createNodesFromLayer:, you'll add support for objects with different names in a new method called createNodesFromGroup:. For now, add this implementation to handle spawning the player character:

```
- (void)createNodesFromGroup:(TMXObjectGroup *)group
{
  NSDictionary *playerObj = [group objectNamed:@"player"];
  if (playerObj) {
    Player *player = [Player node];
    player.position = CGPointMake([playerObj[@"x"] floatValue],
                                  [playerObj[@"y"] floatValue]);
```

```
        [self addChild:player];
    }
}
```

This simply asks the group for the object named **player**. In the current version of the library, TMXObjectGroup returns objects as dictionaries of data. If one is found named **player**, then this method creates a new Player object, sets its position using the x- and y-values stored in the playerObj dictionary and adds it to the layer. But where did those position values come from?

Tiled defined those keys and values for you when you placed the object in the Bugs layer. This dictionary contains other data, too, which will vary depending on the object type, and it would contain any user-defined properties added to the object in Tiled.

Now implement the new initializer method that handles TMXObjectGroups instead of TMXLayers:

```
- (instancetype)initWithTmxObjectGroup:(TMXObjectGroup *)group
                              tileSize:(CGSize)tileSize
                              gridSize:(CGSize)gridSize
{
  if (self = [super init]) {
    _tmxTileSize = tileSize;
    _tmxGridSize = gridSize;
    _tmxLayerSize = CGSizeMake(tileSize.width * gridSize.width,
                               tileSize.height*gridSize.height);

    [self createNodesFromGroup:group];
  }
  return self;
}
```

This implementation is similar to initWithTmxLayer:, except it doesn't store a layer — there isn't one — and it calls createNodesFromGroup: instead of createNodesFromLayer:.

Next you need to replace the current bug layer with a TmxTileMapLayer. To do so, you need to modify createCharacters inside **MyScene.m**. Comment out its first line (the one that creates _bugLayer) and put the following in its place:

```
_bugLayer = [[TmxTileMapLayer alloc]
            initWithTmxObjectGroup:[_tileMap
                  groupNamed:@"Bugs"]
                    tileSize:_tileMap.tileSize
                    gridSize:_bgLayer.gridSize];
```

Run the app. Arnold appears right where you put him and the bugs are nowhere to be seen. Just how Arnold likes it.

The bugs are gone because you're now loading the bugs from the TMX file's Bugs group, but you only added support in createNodesFromGroup: for the object named player.

To remedy this, open **TmxTileMapLayer.m** and add this inside createNodesFromGroup::

```
NSArray *bugs = [group objectsNamed:@"bug"];
for (NSDictionary *bugPos in bugs) {
  Bug *bug = [Bug node];
  bug.position = CGPointMake([bugPos[@"x"] floatValue],
                             [bugPos[@"y"] floatValue]);

  [self addChild:bug];
}
```

Run again and the bugs are back in town!

Your app is rendering a map from a TMX file. Your player and bugs are spawning where they should and colliding properly with the walls and trees. There's just one thing left to fix: water tiles. You could handle water tiles the same way you did the walls, but instead you'll use a more efficient approach: another object layer.

Object layers for collisions areas

Previously, you created separate physics bodies for each wall tile. This works and in such small levels, it performs fine. But as the number of physics bodies in a scene increases, performance eventually suffers. To improve performance, you'll use object layers to define larger, more efficient physics bodies.

> **Note:** If you aren't following along in Tiled, you can skip ahead to "Using TMX object layers for collision areas in Sprite Kit," where you'll see how to use object layers to define physics objects.

Defining collision areas in Tiled

Open **level-3.tmx** in Tiled. Choose **Layer\Add Object Layer** and name the new layer **CollisionAreas**. With the **CollisionAreas** layer selected, choose **Insert Rectangle** (shortcut **R**) in the toolbar and find some water on your map.

Click and hold down the mouse button over the upper-left corner of a water tile and then drag the mouse cursor down and to the right to draw the largest rectangle you can that contains only water tiles. Don't worry if the rectangle doesn't line up perfectly with your tiles – you'll see an easy way to fix that next.

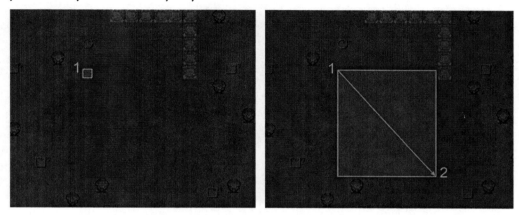

You now have a single large rectangle covering several water tiles, but it probably isn't covering them perfectly. To fix this, choose the **Objects** tab and expand **CollisionAreas** to see all the objects it contains. Select the single unnamed object in **CollisionAreas** and then click the **Object Properties** button, as shown below:

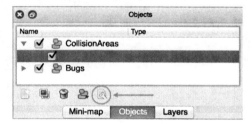

This brings up a dialog in which you can name your object and set its properties. You're most interested in the **X, Y, Width** and **Height** properties. You want to change each value to a whole number. In general, if you kept the rectangle smaller than the area of water tiles its meant to cover, you'll adjust the **X-** and **Y-**values **down** to the next whole number and then adjust the **Width** and **Height** values **up** to the next whole number. See the example below:

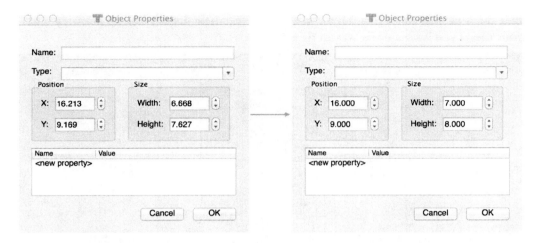

Of course, if any of your rectangle's edges are beyond the boundary of the area of water you meant to cover, you'll have to adjust these properties differently. But in general it's pretty easy to line them up. After making the above adjustments, here is what this rectangle looks like:

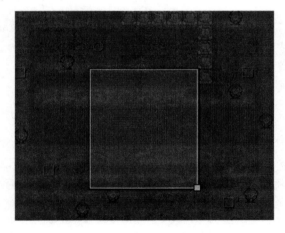

Now repeat that process and continue to make rectangles, covering as much as you can with as few rectangles as possible. Don't bother running algorithms trying to come up with the most efficient coverage that uses the fewest possible rectangles – the idea is simply to use fewer rectangles than you would if you created a separate one for each tile, which is essentially the path you took when creating the physics bodies for the walls.

Name each of these rectangles **water**.

Here is one possible set of rectangles that covers the water tiles in this map:

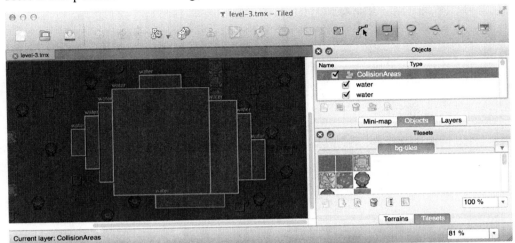

Tiled also lets you create polygons with arbitrary vertices, so you could create a single polygon that encompasses all of the water tiles in the above image. However, Sprite Kit currently imposes a vertex limit on physics bodies, so you'd have to do extra work in code to break the large polygon into multiple smaller ones anyway. The technique shown here is much simpler to understand and implement and still provides a large savings over using a separate physics body per tile.

Using TMX object layers for collision areas in Sprite Kit

You *could* create a new TmxTileMapLayer for the group named CollisionAreas, much like you did for the Bugs group, but recall that your app logic already checks _bgLayer when testing for water tiles. In order to reuse as much code as possible between the TMX and non-TMX versions, and because _bgLayer is already created from the Background tile layer, you'll simply add your collision areas to _bgLayer.

This time open **MyScene.m** and add the following new method:

```
- (void)createCollisionAreas
{
  TMXObjectGroup *group =
    [_tileMap groupNamed:@"CollisionAreas"];

  NSArray *waterObjects = [group objectsNamed:@"water"];
  for (NSDictionary *waterObj in waterObjects) {
    CGFloat x = [waterObj[@"x"] floatValue];
```

```
    CGFloat y = [waterObj[@"y"] floatValue];
    CGFloat w = [waterObj[@"width"] floatValue];
    CGFloat h = [waterObj[@"height"] floatValue];

    SKSpriteNode* water =
      [SKSpriteNode spriteNodeWithColor:[SKColor redColor]
                                   size:CGSizeMake(w, h)];
    water.name = @"water";
    water.position = CGPointMake(x + w/2, y + h/2);

    water.physicsBody =
      [SKPhysicsBody bodyWithRectangleOfSize:CGSizeMake(w, h)];

    water.physicsBody.categoryBitMask =  PCWaterCategory;
    water.physicsBody.dynamic = NO;
    water.physicsBody.friction = 0;

    [_bgLayer addChild:water];
  }
}
```

The method above handles objects named "water" in the group named CollisionAreas much like `createNodesFromGroup:` in `TmxTileMapLayer` handles objects named "people."

It uses the object's dictionary to create a rectangle of the appropriate size and then creates a red sprite with that size. You'll use the red color for debugging. Finally it creates a physics body with the same properties as the water tiles you've made in the past and adds it to `_bgLayer`.

Add the following code at the end of `createWorld`:

```
if (_tileMap) {
  [self createCollisionAreas];
}
```

Once again, in order to support the older data files you have from the previous chapters, you ensure `_tileMap` exists before proceeding. If it does exist, you call your new method to create collision areas.

Build and run the app. Now that the water looks like hot lava, no one wants to touch it!

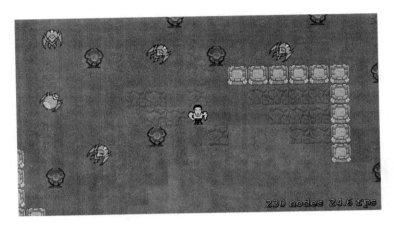

The red color helps you see that your objects were indeed created in the proper locations. Now that you've verified it's working correctly, modify `createCollisionAreas` as shown below (new line highlighted):

```
water.physicsBody.friction = 0;
water.hidden = YES;
[_bgLayer addChild:water];
```

Run once more and your water looks like water again, but now Arnold bounces off of it and the bugs avoid it. I guess no one in this game can swim.

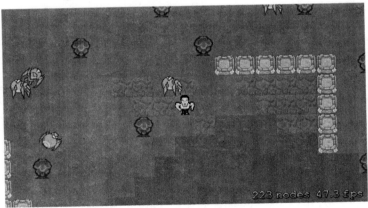

In this chapter, you added TMX support for almost every aspect of a Pest Control level. You'll take care of the one remaining item – fire bugs – as this chapter's single challenge. Afterwards spend some time with Tiled, create your own tilesets and see what you can make. `JSTileMap` already supports more features of the TMX file format than you used in this chapter and the plan is to support them all. However, there are other options available, so look into them and let us know on the forums which solution you end up preferring!

In the next chapter you'll add various gameplay elements to Pest Control, like UI elements, progressing through multiple levels and win/lose states. Plus you'll use Sprite Kit's NSCoding support to implement autosaving.

Challenge: spawning fire bugs

The last chapter had larger-than-average challenges, so let's keep it simple this time around.

You already support spawn points for the player and the regular bugs – now you'll add them for the fire bugs. To do so, add objects named **firebug** to the **Bugs** layer in **level-3.tmx**. Then modify createNodesFromGroup: in **TmxTileMapLayer.m** to get all the objects named **firebug** and create a FireBug for each of them. Take another look at how you create the regular bugs if you need any help.

If you still need help, you can find the solution in the resources for this chapter, but Arnold will know if you didn't try your best!

Chapter 16: Saving and Loading Games

By Christopher LaPollo

Players come and players go. That's never been truer than it is with mobile, where play sessions for even the most successful games can be on the order of just a few seconds or minutes. If you don't want everyone who ever tries your game to walk away angry, chances are you need to save their game state between sessions.

There are various ways you can save game data: using plain text files, property files or binary files; storing data locally, in iCloud, on your own server or maybe even using one of various other services, like Dropbox. Due to the existence of all these possibilities, it doesn't make much sense to try to show *the* way for you to save game state.

However, one of the most exciting features of Sprite Kit, at least from a tool developer's standpoint, is that users can archive any of its nodes and later make new objects from those archives. That means you can do a lot of fun things, such as create a level editor that uses Sprite Kit to let you see, modify and even test game levels, and then save those levels as SKNodes to use directly in your game.

Making something like a level editor would be a great application of Sprite Kit's archiving feature, but we don't have enough room in the book to show something like that to you. Rather than ignore archiving entirely, this chapter shows you how to implement a nice little autosave feature for Pest Control by saving the actual Sprite Kit scene to disk!

This chapter's first section, "Making a game out of pest control," covers implementing Pest Control's remaining gameplay features, like winning and losing and transitioning between multiple levels. As such, it doesn't actually deal with the chapter's topic, saving and loading games. However, without this logic, there isn't much to save or load. After all, it's hard to save a player's progress in a game if there's no way to make progress in the game, right?

> **Note:** If you're not interested in the details of creating Pest Control's remaining gameplay features, you can skip ahead to "Saving and loading Sprite Kit data." There you'll find a starter project that picks up from that point so that you can focus on saving and loading.

Making a game out of pest control

> **Note:** This chapter begins where the Challenge from the last chapter left off. If you were unable to complete the challenge or skipped ahead from a previous chapter, don't worry – you can simply open **PestControl-Starter** from the resources for this chapter to pick up from there.

Running and using muscles for smashing bugs. That strange sentence fragment came out of nowhere and feels incomplete, right?

Well, Pest Control is currently just like that. The user loads the app and suddenly there are bugs moving around and a guy in the middle of the screen. You haven't indicated what's expected of your player, and once they figure out how to move Arnold and then begin killing bugs, the "game" never ends. Eventually all the bugs are gone and Arnold is left roaming around the screen, forced to live out a solitary, empty existence for the rest of his days, pining for the very things he once sought to destroy.

Doesn't that make you want to cry? No? You, sir or madam, are a monster. Yes? Well then stop it, crybaby. Arnold doesn't want your tears; he wants some direction in life. He wants to win.

You've got sprites that respond to player taps and to collisions with each other, but that doesn't mean you've got a game. Your players will want to decide when to start a level, will want ways to succeed or fail and will want to progress through multiple different levels. Let's begin at the beginning.

Starting the game

Right now, Pest Control just starts. The game appears and the bugs are wandering around and there's no indication of what your user should do. That's not very helpful. In this section you'll add some instructions for your users and you'll modify the scene so that nothing starts moving until the player starts playing.

You'll create a new type to define the possible game states, which will allow you to perform different logic based on simple `if` checks at key points in your game. Inside **MyScene.m**, define the following type just after the imports at the top of the file:

```
typedef NS_ENUM(int32_t, PCGameState)
{
  PCGameStateStartingLevel,
  PCGameStatePlaying,
};
```

You'll add more types later, but for now, these two let you differentiate between starting a level, when the app is still waiting for the player's first input, and playing the game, when Arnold is busy with his smashing spree.

Add this private variable to store the game's current state:

```
PCGameState _gameState;
```

Now add this helper method, which will set up the initial user interface:

```
- (void)createUserInterface
{
  SKLabelNode* startMsg =
    [SKLabelNode labelNodeWithFontNamed:@"Chalkduster"];
  startMsg.name = @"msgLabel";
  startMsg.text = @"Tap Screen to run!";
```

```
    startMsg.fontSize = 32;
    startMsg.position = CGPointMake(0, 20);
    [self addChild: startMsg];
}
```

This simply adds a label to the scene instructing the user to tap the screen to begin running. You named the label `msgLabel` because you'll want to find it later to use for some other messages.

Call this method just after the call to `centerViewOn:` inside `initWithSize:` and then initialize `_gameState`:

```
[self createUserInterface];
_gameState = PCGameStateStartingLevel;
```

Build and run. You'll see the app runs just as it did before, but now it's got a high-tech user interface obscuring your view. So... helpful, right?

With instructions on the screen, the user knows what to do. That's good. But the instructions never go away – that's less good. Since you already handle touches in `touchesBegan:withEvent:`, that's a good place to get rid of the label. It's also where you'll update the game state when the user starts playing.

Replace `touchesBegan:withEvent:` with the following:

```
- (void)touchesBegan:(NSSet *)touches withEvent:(UIEvent *)event
{
  switch (_gameState) {
    case PCGameStateStartingLevel:
    {
      [self childNodeWithName:@"msgLabel"].hidden = YES;
```

```
        _gameState = PCGameStatePlaying;

        // Intentionally omitted break
    }
    case PCGameStatePlaying:
    {
        UITouch* touch = [touches anyObject];
        [_player moveToward:[touch locationInNode:_worldNode]];
        break;
    }
    }
  }
}
```

This method handles touches based on the current value of _gameState. If the state is PCGameStateStartingLevel, the method hides msgLabel, updates the game state to PCGameStatePlaying and then moves _player. If the state is PCGameStatePlaying, the method simply moves _player.

> **Note:** The first case in touchesBegan:withEvent: does not include a break statement but instead has a comment reading Intentionally omitted break. It's a habit of mine to always put such a comment at the end of any case without a break statement, just so there's never any doubt regarding the code's intentions, to others or to my future self.
>
> Here, you don't use a break statement because you want the user's first tap to start Arnold running. (Well, that's what *I* wanted. If that's *not* what you want, add a break there.)

If you run now, the message disappears as soon as you tap the screen. But there's still one issue: the bugs are already moving around even before the player has a chance to start playing. If you waited long enough, there's a chance that all the bugs would walk right into Arnold! Not very sporting.

To keep your sprites from running their SKActions – and hence, keep your bugs from moving – you need to pause the scene. Add the following method:

```
- (void)didMoveToView:(SKView *)view
{
    if (_gameState == PCGameStateStartingLevel)
        self.paused = YES;
}
```

Sprite Kit calls `didMoveToView:` when it presents your scene in an `SKView`. At this point, your scene has been initialized and should be ready to go, so you simply check the state and pause if necessary.

Build and run again, and now no one is moving. At all. Ever.

The problem is that you paused the scene at start up, but you never un-paused it when the user started playing. To do so, add the following line to `touchesBegan:withEvent:`, inside the case that handles `PCGameStateStartingLevel`:

```
self.paused = NO;
```

Now when you run, things stay put until the player taps the screen, at which point the bugs start walking and Arnold darts off in the direction of the tap. Your player is in control and it's time to give them a goal.

Winning the game

The win condition for Pest Control is pretty simple: kill all the bugs and you win. You already have a separate node – `_bugLayer` – which contains all the bugs, so all you have to do is check it to find out when all the bugs are gone.

You *could* maintain a separate counter to keep track of the bugs, updating it every time Arnold collides with a bug, and that may even be the most efficient way to do it. However, if you went that route, you'd also have to add logic in multiple places to update the counter for each type of enemy in the game.

More importantly, you're here to get more practice with Sprite Kit, so you'll query `_bugLayer` directly rather than maintain a separate counter.

Implement `update:` as shown below:

```
- (void)update:(CFTimeInterval)currentTime
{
  if (![_bugLayer childNodeWithName:@"bug"]) {
    NSLog(@"Who's the big winner? You are!");
  }
}
```

This simply searches `_bugLayer` for the first object named `bug` that it can find. Every bug (including the fire bugs) is named `bug`, so if `childNodeWithName:` returns `nil`, the bugs are gone and the player has cleared the level.

Build and run and kill all those bugs! As soon as Arnold runs through the last one, you should see this statement appear repeatedly in the console:

```
PestControl[17638:70b] Who's the big winner? You are!
```

Now that you know the game properly recognizes its win state, you need to replace that console log with a notification to the player.

Add this new method that will handle notifying the player of both wins and losses:

```
- (void)endLevelWithSuccess:(BOOL)won
{
  //1
  SKLabelNode* label =
    (SKLabelNode*)[self childNodeWithName:@"msgLabel"];
  label.text = (won ? @"You Win!!!" : @"Too Slow!!!");
  label.hidden = NO;
  //2
  SKLabelNode* nextLevel =
    [SKLabelNode labelNodeWithFontNamed:@"Chalkduster"];
  nextLevel.text = @"Next Level?";
  nextLevel.name = @"nextLevelLabel";
  nextLevel.fontSize = 28;
  nextLevel.horizontalAlignmentMode =
    (won ? SKLabelHorizontalAlignmentModeCenter :
    SKLabelHorizontalAlignmentModeLeft);
  nextLevel.position =
    (won ? CGPointMake(0, -40) : CGPointMake(0+20, -40));
  [self addChild:nextLevel];
  //3
  _player.physicsBody.linearDamping = 1;
}
```

The above code does the following:

1. It displays msgLabel with an appropriate win/loss message based on the value you pass in for won.

2. It displays a new label named nextLevelLabel that gives the player the option of moving to the next level. Later you'll find this object by name and process touch events that occur over it, effectively making it a button. Note that it positions this label differently based on whether this was a win or a loss, because later you'll add an item next to it in the case of a loss.

3. This line is simply a nicety. Setting the player's linearDamping to 1 will cause Arnold to skid to a halt. It looks better than having him continue to bounce around in the background while you have UI elements for your user to read.

With that method in place, replace the NSLog statement in update: with the following call:

```
[self endLevelWithSuccess:YES];
```

Build and run. Kill all the bugs, and this time Arnold slows to a stop – of course, he continues to run in place, to stay fit – and you see your messages:

Unfortunately, even after squashing all those giant bugs, there is still one bug lurking in your code and it's wreaking havoc on your frame rate.

As you probably know by now, Sprite Kit calls update: once per frame, ideally 60 times per second. However, your scene's update: checks the bug count and calls endLevelWithSuccess: if the count is zero. That makes sense the first time you call it, but what about the next 59 times that second? And so on.

Calling endLevelWithSuccess: over and over is bad for multiple reasons. First it's inefficient – once the app knows you've cleared the level, it shouldn't keep checking. But more importantly, endLevelWithSuccess: adds a new label to the scene. Even though you only see "Next Level?" on the screen once, your app is actually adding a new label in the exact same place every time you call that method, ideally 60 times per second.

Of course, as the node count goes up, Sprite Kit cannot maintain that ideal of 60 fps, so you see the frame rate drop. In the screenshot above, there are 508 nodes (way up from the 220+ nodes that are usually in the scene while playing) and Sprite Kit is rendering at a sluggish 7.5 frames per second. As time passes, that frame rate just keeps getting lower.

The best way to fix this problem is to consider the time when the app is displaying these messages to the user as a new game state and then perform different processing in update: based on the game's current state.

Add the following new value to PCGameState at the top of **MyScene.m**. You will use it to indicate when the game is showing a menu between levels:

```
PCGameStateInLevelMenu,
```

Note that, even though you are showing a sort of menu in the state PCGameStateStartingLevel, these are still unique states because you want to handle touches differently in each case.

Also, you may be confused by all this talk of levels, because Pest Control only has one level at the moment. Don't worry – you'll remedy that in the next section. And one more thing: now that you've added the PCGameStateInLevelMenu value to PCGameState, Xcode warns you that you're not handling PCGameStateInLevelMenu in the switch statement in touchesBegan:withEvent:. You'll fix that in the next section, too.

At the end of endLevelWithSuccess:, add the following line to update the game state:

```
_gameState = PCGameStateInLevelMenu;
```

This updates the game state to indicate the menus are onscreen, but it inadvertently fixes another bug you had as well. Before adding this code, if you tapped the screen after you won, Arnold would try to move again. His linearDamping value was still 1 and your frame rate was dropping to ridiculously low values, so he never got very far. But now when you tap the screen while the menus are visible, Arnold completely ignores the touch event.

Finally add these lines at the beginning of update::

```
if (_gameState != PCGameStatePlaying) {
    return;
}
```

This simply ensures the bulk of update: only executes when the player is actually playing. Run again and the app's performance is back to normal.

When the player has killed all the bugs, you present a hearty message of congratulations and an inviting Next Level button. Unfortunately, you don't have multiple levels. You'll fix that in the next section.

Multiple levels

In Pest Control, you currently hard-code the level to load. That's great for testing, but is not a good long-term solution. In this section, you'll give your players the ability to progress through multiple levels, while giving Arnold a world that he can never truly rid of all its pests.

The first thing you'll add is the notion of a current level. For that, you'll need a custom initializer method that specifies the level to load. Declare this new initializer in **MyScene.h**:

```
- (instancetype)initWithSize:(CGSize)size level:(int)level;
```

And inside **MyScene.m**, add this private variable:

```
int _level;
```

Now modify the top of your implementation of initWithSize: to look like this (changes are highlighted):

```
- (instancetype)initWithSize:(CGSize)size level:(int)level
{
  if (self = [super initWithSize:size]) {
    _level = level;

    // Remainder of the method unchanged...
```

```
    }
```

All you did was add a new parameter to your original initializer method and store its value in a private variable.

Open **ViewController.m** and change the line that creates `scene` to look like this:

```
SKScene * scene =
    [[MyScene alloc] initWithSize:skView.bounds.size level:0];
```

This instructs your scene to load level zero. Of course, running now won't produce any new results, because `MyScene` still hard-codes its level data. Before you can load a specific level, you need a list of levels.

The **Resources\Levels** group project includes a file named **Levels.plist** that defines the app's levels and looks like this:

Key	Type	Value
▼ Root	Dictionary	(1 item)
▼ levels	Array	(3 items)
▼ Item 0	Dictionary	(2 items)
timeLimit	Number	10
▼ layers	Dictionary	(2 items)
background	String	level-1-bg.txt
bugs	String	level-1-bugs.txt
▼ Item 1	Dictionary	(2 items)
timeLimit	Number	200
▼ layers	Dictionary	(3 items)
background	String	level-2-bg.txt
bugs	String	level-2-bugs.txt
breakables	String	level-2-breakables.txt
▼ Item 2	Dictionary	(2 items)
timeLimit	String	200
tmxFile	String	level-3-sample.tmx

The `Root` dictionary contains a single array stored with the key `levels`. Each item in the `levels` array is a dictionary defining a single level. The game will progress through them in order (i.e. `Item 0`, `Item 1`, `Item 2`, and so on) and loop back to the beginning after the final level.

Each level dictionary contains two keys:

1. `timeLimit` specifies the number of seconds the player has to complete a level. You'll use this when you implement a loss state in the next section.

2. One of the following:

a. `layers` is a dictionary containing the file names that define the layers in your tile map. It is only present for levels defined using the non-TMX file approach from Chapters 13 and 14.

b. **tmxFile**, on the other hand, is only present for levels defined using TMX files. It contains the name of the TMX file that defines the level.

You'll change `MyScene` to load the current level's configuration from **Levels.plist**. Open **MyScene.m** and add the following code to `initWithSize:level:`, just *before* the line that sets the value of `_level`:

```
NSDictionary *config =
  [NSDictionary dictionaryWithContentsOfFile:
   [[NSBundle mainBundle] pathForResource:@"Levels"
                                   ofType:@"plist"]];

if (level < 0 || level >= [config[@"levels"] count])
  level = 0;
```

This loads the contents of **Level.plist** into `config` and then performs a bounds check on the `level` value passed into the method. Because `levels` is an array, its indices count from `0` to `[levels count]–1`. If `level` is not within these bounds, you set it to `0`. This will make the game loop back to the first level when a user completes the last level, but you could change it to do something else in this case, such as tell your player that they've completed the game and encourage them to go back to beat their high scores or to make an In-App Purchase.

At this point, you know the current level is in bounds, so it's safe to load its data from **Levels.plist**. Add the following line just *after* the line that sets `_level`:

```
NSDictionary *levelData = config[@"levels"][level];
```

As you can see in **Levels.plist**, and as you learned in the previous chapter, your scene needs to load levels stored in TMX files differently from those stored using plain text files.

Start out by adding this code immediately following the line you just added:

```
if (levelData[@"tmxFile"]) {
  _tileMap = [JSTileMap mapNamed:levelData[@"tmxFile"]];
}
```

This simply creates `_tileMap` if `levelData` contains the key `tmxFile`. Throughout the rest of `MyScene`, wherever there are places that require different logic for TMX vs. non-

TMX levels, you'll add a check for _tileMap – if it's present, you'll perform TMX logic; otherwise, you'll execute non-TMX logic.

Now you'll refactor createScenery, createWorld, createCharacters and createBreakables to each take an NSDictionary parameter and you'll pass the levelData dictionary to each of these methods.

> **Note:** Once you make the next change, the project will no longer compile successfully until you reach the next build and run step.

Start by replacing createScenery with the following:

```
- (TileMapLayer *)createScenery:(NSDictionary *)levelData
{
  if (_tileMap) {
    return [[TmxTileMapLayer alloc] initWithTmxLayer:
            [_tileMap layerNamed:@"Background"]];
  } else {
    NSDictionary *layerFiles = levelData[@"layers"];
    return [TileMapLayerLoader tileMapLayerFromFileNamed:
            layerFiles[@"background"]];
  }
}
```

With these changes, createScenery now uses the data supplied in levelData to create _bgLayer. Notice that levelData goes unused if _tileMap exists – that's because you know you named the background layer "Background" when you created the TMX file. However, you could have stored the TMX layer names in levelData if you didn't want to hard-code their names in this class.

Now change the top of createWorld, including its signature and the creation of _bgLayer, so that it uses the level data dictionary:

```
- (void)createWorld:(NSDictionary *)levelData
{
  _bgLayer = [self createScenery:levelData];

  // Remainder of the method unchanged...
}
```

Modify the signature for createBreakables to take a level data dictionary, like this:

```
- (TileMapLayer *)createBreakables:(NSDictionary *)levelData
```

And replace its current `else` statement with the following:

```
else {
  NSDictionary *layerFiles = levelData[@"layers"];
  return [TileMapLayerLoader tileMapLayerFromFileNamed:
      layerFiles[@"breakables"]];
}
```

This simply replaces the logic for loading breakables from a hard-coded file name with logic to find the file name in the level data dictionary. Remember, if `layerFiles` does not include a value for the key `breakables`, `tileMapLayerFromFileNamed:` will return `nil`.

Change the call to `createBreakables` in `createWorld` to pass it the level data dictionary, like this:

```
_breakableLayer = [self createBreakables:levelData];
```

Inside `createCharacters`, remove the line that creates `_bugLayer`. Then change the signature and top of the method to look like this:

```
- (void)createCharacters:(NSDictionary *)levelData
{
  if (_tileMap) {
    _bugLayer = [[TmxTileMapLayer alloc]
                  initWithTmxObjectGroup:[_tileMap
                                           groupNamed:@"Bugs"]
                  tileSize:_tileMap.tileSize
                  gridSize:_bgLayer.gridSize];
  } else {
    NSDictionary *layerFiles = levelData[@"layers"];
    _bugLayer = [TileMapLayerLoader tileMapLayerFromFileNamed:
                  layerFiles[@"bugs"]];
  }

  // Remainder of the method unchanged...
}
```

This code initializes `_bugLayer` with code similar to what you wrote in `createScenery`, except it creates the TMX-version using a different initializer. That's because, as you learned in Chapter 15, "Imported Tile Maps," `Bugs` is an object layer and not a tile layer.

Finally, change the calls to `createWorld` and `createCharacters` in `initWithSize:level:`, passing in `levelData` to look like the following:

```
[self createWorld:levelData];
[self createCharacters:levelData];
```

Build and run. The app launches showing the level defined in `Item 0` of **Levels.plist**.

Now that you can clear a screen and have multiple levels defined, you can go back and make that **Next Level** button do something.

Add the following to the `switch` statement in `touchesBegan:withEvent::`

```
case PCGameStateInLevelMenu:
{
  UITouch* touch = [touches anyObject];
  CGPoint loc = [touch locationInNode:self];

  SKNode *node = [self childNodeWithName:@"nextLevelLabel"];
  if ([node containsPoint:loc]) {
    MyScene *newScene = [[MyScene alloc] initWithSize:self.size
                                                level:_level+1];

    [self.view presentScene:newScene
              transition:[SKTransition
                           flipVerticalWithDuration:0.5]];

  }
  break;
}
```

The above code simply checks to see if the user touched the **Next Level?** label by finding the touch's location in the scene's coordinate space and then asking the label if it contains that point. If so, it creates a new `MyScene` object initialized to the level after the current one and asks this scene's view to transition to the new scene. Essentially, it replaces the current scene with a new one.

In addition, this `case` statement took care of the warning Xcode has been giving you ever since you added the `PCGameStateInLevelMenu` value.

Build and run. Kill all the bugs in the first level, tap **Next Level?** and watch as the next level transitions into view.

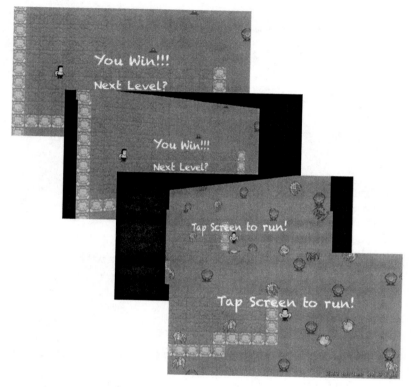

Neat! Except there's a problem. (Why are you always causing problems?) Remember earlier in this chapter when you implemented `didMoveToView:` to pause the game when it wasn't playing? Well, when the new level appears, the bugs are already moving, which means the scene isn't paused.

Here's what's happening. First you create the new scene and ask the view to present it using a transition. Sprite Kit then calls `didMoveToView:`, in which you pause the scene. After that, Sprite Kit performs the visual transition to the new scene. At this point, what you see from the first scene is just an image, *not* a running scene. However, in order to perform the transition, Sprite Kit un-pauses the scene!

In order to fix this, you have to do something that may seem a bit strange. Add the following at the beginning of `update::`

```
if(_gameState == PCGameStateStartingLevel && !self.isPaused){
  self.paused = YES;
}
```

Surprisingly enough, Sprite Kit continues to call `update:` in your scene even while it's paused. The only effect that pausing has on a scene is to stop its nodes from executing `SKActions`. Unfortunately, there's no way to know when the view transition animation completes, so you can't just pause the scene after that, either.

Instead, what you do is pause the scene every time `update:` executes while the game state is `PCGameStateStartingLevel`. You added an additional check so it only attempts to pause the scene if the scene isn't already paused. This probably isn't necessary, because the `paused` property setter most likely performs such a check internally, but I think checking here makes it clearer what the code is trying to accomplish.

Now that you have this code in place, **delete `didMoveToView:`** in its entirety, because here you are overriding the work it's doing anyway.

With multiple levels and a way to clear them, things are starting to shape up. However, there's still nothing at stake for Arnold or the user. "Failure is not an option" may sound cool when you're setting off on a mission to save the world, but it doesn't always make for a challenging game.

Time limits and losing

As you saw in the previous section, each level defined in **Levels.plist** includes a key named `timeLimit`, which specifies the maximum number of seconds the user is allowed to spend attempting to clear that level.

> **Note:** I chose the time limit values in the file to point out specific things in parts of this chapter but in your own games, be careful when choosing values for things like time limits. You want them short enough to be challenging but not so short as to make beating them impossible.

You'll display the remaining time onscreen and make it count down to zero to give Arnold a sense of urgency. To start, add the following private variables:

```
double _levelTimeLimit;
SKLabelNode* _timerLabel;
```

You'll store the current level's time limit in `_levelTimeLimit` and compare the amount of time spent playing a level against this value to determine when the player has lost. You'll display `_timerLabel` onscreen as the user plays the game, counting down from `_levelTimeLimit` to zero. This gives your players useful information and also adds a bit of tension as they watch their time running out.

Store the current level's time limit in `initWithSize:level:` right *before* the call to `createUserInterface`:

```
_levelTimeLimit = [levelData[@"timeLimit"] doubleValue];
```

At the end of `createUserInterface`, use the following familiar-looking code to create `_timerLabel` and add it in the upper-right of the display:

```
_timerLabel =
  [SKLabelNode labelNodeWithFontNamed:@"Chalkduster"];
_timerLabel.text =
  [NSString stringWithFormat:@"Time Remaining: %2.2f",
    _levelTimeLimit];
_timerLabel.fontSize = 18;
_timerLabel.horizontalAlignmentMode =
  SKLabelHorizontalAlignmentModeLeft;
_timerLabel.position = CGPointMake(0, 130);
[self addChild:_timerLabel];
```

Run the app and you'll see you have 10 seconds to kill those bugs. I hope you're better at this game than I am.

Now that you know what the label looks like, hide it until the player taps to start the level. Add the following line to the end of `createUserInterface`:

```
_timerLabel.hidden = YES;
```

Then show the timer when the user taps to start. Add this line to the PCGameStateStartingLevel case in touchesBegan:withEvent:, just *above* the comment that reads Intentionally omitted break:

```
_timerLabel.hidden = NO;
```

Run again. The timer readout will not appear until Arnold starts running.

A timer that never changes isn't very useful, so you need to make it count down to zero. Add the following new private variables:

```
double _currentTime;
double _startTime;
double _elapsedTime;
```

You will use these three variables in conjunction with _levelTimeLimit to handle Pest Control's time keeping, as follows:

1. _currentTime stores the currentTime value passed into update:, so that you can access it from outside of that method.

2. _startTime is the value of _currentTime at the point when the player tapped the screen to start a level.

3. _elapsedTime is calculated from _currentTime and _startTime and you will use it to determine when the player has exceeded the time limit specified in _levelTimeLimit.

Don't worry if you don't fully understand how you will use each of these fields – it will become clear over the next few steps.

When the user taps the screen to start playing the level, you'll store the current time in _startTime. Add this line to the PCGameStateStartingLevel case in touchesBegan:withEvent:, just *above* the comment that reads Intentionally omitted break:

```
_startTime = _currentTime;
```

That was easy. But you may have noticed that you haven't yet set a value for _currentTime. When Sprite Kit calls update:, it passes in a currentTime value. Because Sprite Kit calls update: once every frame, currentTime is constantly changing.

Add the following line at the top of `update:` to store the most recent time:

```
_currentTime = currentTime;
```

It's important that this is the first line in `update:` because there is a conditional `return` statement later in the method that will execute prior to the user tapping the screen. If you put this line anywhere in the method after that `return` statement, the code you added in `touchesBegan:withEvent:` will initialize `_startTime` with an incorrect time.

Each time `update:` executes, you can calculate the amount of time the user has spent on this level by subtracting the start time from the current time. Add the following line to `update:` just *before* the `if` statement that checks `_bugLayer` for a node named `bug`:

```
_elapsedTime = currentTime - _startTime;
```

You store the time spent playing this level in `_elapsedTime`. For now, you'll only use this value in the current method, but you store it in an instance variable because later you'll need it outside of this method, too.

At the end of `update:`, you currently have an `if` statement that checks for a win condition. Add some additional conditions to handle the timer, as shown below (new code highlighted):

```
if (_elapsedTime >= _levelTimeLimit) {
  [self endLevelWithSuccess:NO];
} else if (![_bugLayer childNodeWithName:@"bug"]) {
  [self endLevelWithSuccess:YES];
} else {
  _timerLabel.text =
    [NSString stringWithFormat:@"Time Remaining: %2.2f",
      (_levelTimeLimit - _elapsedTime)];
}
```

The first `if` statement you added checks to see if Arnold's time has run out by comparing the elapsed time to the level's time limit. If so, you call `endLevelWithSuccess:`, passing in `NO`. You changed the existing `if` statement into an `else if` to handle the win condition and you added an `else` statement that updates the onscreen timer display. The timer display should count down to show the player how much time is left, rather than count up to show how much time has elapsed, so you display the time limit minus the elapsed time.

Build and run. Because the time limit for this level is only 10 seconds, you've got an excellent chance of failing.

In the screenshot above, you can see two issues. The first is that the **Next Level?** button is not centered, but that's by design and you'll handle it later.

The second issue is that the readout claims there are still two hundredths of a second left, even while it claims you were too slow. A bit presumptuous, don't you think? What if you were just toying with the bugs, lulling them into feeling safe by waiting until the last possible moment before making a heroic push to win right at the end?

The problem here is that you update the label only *after* you check for wins and losses, which means the final value displayed in the readout is incorrect. The easiest solution is to move the label update logic to earlier in the method, but then you have to worry about showing a negative value for time remaining, because there's no guarantee that the frame won't continue to update after time has expired.

First, remove the final `else` statement in `update:`. Then add the following code just after the line that updates `_elapsedTime`:

```
CFTimeInterval timeRemaining = _levelTimeLimit - _elapsedTime;
if (timeRemaining < 0) {
  timeRemaining = 0;
}
_timerLabel.text =
  [NSString stringWithFormat:@"Time Remaining: %2.2f",
  timeRemaining];
```

Run again, and this time, lose like you mean it!

Now that you've got the countdown timer working and players can win and lose, it would be nice if players who failed to clear a level could try again. Remember when you added the **Next Level?** button earlier and you moved it to the right to make room for another UI element? Today is the day you've been planning for! That is to say, now would be a good time to add a **Try Again?** button.

Add the following code inside `endLevelWithSuccess:`:

```
if (!won) {
  SKLabelNode* tryAgain =
    [SKLabelNode labelNodeWithFontNamed:@"Chalkduster"];
  tryAgain.text = @"Try Again?";
  tryAgain.name = @"retryLabel";
  tryAgain.fontSize = 28;
  tryAgain.horizontalAlignmentMode =
    SKLabelHorizontalAlignmentModeRight;
  tryAgain.position = CGPointMake(0-20, -40);
  [self addChild:tryAgain];
}
```

When the player fails to clear a level, this code adds a label named `retryLabel` that reads **Try Again?**. Just as with the **Next Level?** label, you want to handle touch events over the label so that it functions as a button.

Inside `touchesBegan:withEvent:`, add this `else` statement inside the `PCGameStateInLevelMenu` case, just above the `break` statement:

```
else {
  node = [self childNodeWithName:@"retryLabel"];
  if ([node containsPoint:loc]) {
    MyScene *newScene = [[MyScene alloc] initWithSize:self.size
```

```
                                                        level:_level];
    [self.view presentScene:newScene
             transition:[SKTransition
                         flipVerticalWithDuration:0.5]];
    }
}
```

The above code simply checks to see if the user touched the **Try Again?** label. If so, it creates a new `MyScene` object initialized to the current level and asks this scene's view to transition to the new scene. Essentially, it replaces the current scene with an identical one, but one that's initialized to its start state.

Build and run and lose all over again. You'll get the options to try again or to move on to the next level. Try each button to see how they work:

At this point, you've implemented all of Pest Control's gameplay features. Arnold and the bugs wait patiently for your player to start a level; Arnold runs around smashing bugs; the bugs run around wondering why this guy is smashing them; a timer counts down to make your players anxious; players can beat, retry or skip a level; and you congratulate or chastise them as appropriate.

Now that players can progress through the game, you're ready to start saving and loading that progress.

Saving and loading state

> **Note:** If you skipped ahead to this part of the chapter and did not go through the steps to add the remaining gameplay features to Pest Control, start here from the **PestControl-WithGameLogic** project in this chapter's resources.

The previous part of the chapter focused on getting Pest Control's final gameplay elements in place. In this part, you'll implement autosave using Sprite Kit's archiving support.

To implement autosave, you'll simply write the entire scene to disk and then later present the saved scene to the user. That is, you'll archive a single object – the scene currently in the view – and that will in turn archive all of the scene's child nodes and their actions. Then, when loading from the autosave file, you'll initialize a new scene from the archived one and present it to the user. Well, it's almost as easy as that, anyway.

> **Note:** As mentioned earlier in this chapter, this is only one of many ways to save your game's data. For example, you could take a far simpler approach and simply record the level number the player is in, and make them restart at the beginning of the level upon loading a saved game.
>
> The reason you are learning about archiving the entire scene in this chapter is that it's one of the most unique and generally helpful features of Sprite Kit, and is useful to know even if you choose to use an alternate method of saving and loading data in your game.

In order to save the scene and all of its child nodes, the first thing you need to do is make sure everything *can* be saved....

NSCoding

To archive an object, it must conform to the `NSCoding` protocol. `NSCoding` includes the two methods required to support encoding and decoding an object – `encodeWithCoder:` and `initWithCoder:` – and you use encoding and decoding to archive objects to disk. Your class's implementation of these methods can also encode and decode primitive data types and some `structs`, such as `int`, `double` and `CGSize`, but other class objects to be archived must be `NSCoding`-compliant.

Fortunately, `SKNode` and all of its subclasses, such as `SKScene` and `SKSpriteNode`, along with `SKAction` conform to the `NSCoding` protocol. If you create a subclass of an `SKNode` (or one of its subclasses), you *may* need to add custom `NSCoding` support as well.

Basic encoding/decoding

As a general rule, any class that has its own instance variables and/or properties needs to implement the methods from the `NSCoding` protocol, because those instance variables will receive default values when restored from an archive, and those default values probably won't match the values at the time the object was encoded.

For many classes, encoding is a straightforward matter of passing each of its instance variables to one of the various encoding methods on an `NSCoder`, which encapsulates the encoding and decoding logic into simple method calls. Decoding is simply the reverse of encoding, where you initialize each variable with a call to one of an `NSCoder`'s various decoding methods.

Sometimes, though, you need to do more work. You'll start by adding `NSCoding` support to `AnimatingSprite`, a class that requires the least effort, and eventually handle `MyScene`, which will entail dealing with a few complications.

Open **AnimatingSprite.m** and add the following method:

```
- (void)encodeWithCoder:(NSCoder *)aCoder
{
  //1
  [super encodeWithCoder:aCoder];
  //2
  [aCoder encodeObject:_facingForwardAnim
            forKey:@"AS-ForwardAnim"];
  [aCoder encodeObject:_facingBackAnim
            forKey:@"AS-BackAnim"];
  [aCoder encodeObject:_facingSideAnim
            forKey:@"AS-SideAnim"];
  [aCoder encodeInt32:_facingDirection
            forKey:@"AS-FacingDirection"];
}
```

As you can see, implementing `encodeWithCoder:` is a straightforward affair.

1. When extending Sprite Kit classes, you always need to call `super` `encodeWithEncoder:` to ensure super classes encode their data. It doesn't necessarily

need to be the method's first line – indeed, you'll see an example later where it must not be – but you do need to call it.

2. All of `AnimatingSprite`'s data resides in auto-synthesized properties, so you encode the private variables that Xcode created for them. For example, because you declared the property `facingForwardAnim`, Xcode implements it using a private variable named `_facingForwardAnim`, which is an instance of `SKAction`. Because `SKAction` is `NSCoding`-compliant, you encode it using `encodeObject:forKey:`. The key you use here – `AS-ForwardAnim` – I chose arbitrarily but with the intent that its name would clearly indicate the value it references. I added the `AS-` prefix to make it obvious which class added the key – `AnimatingSprite` – and to reduce the likelihood of reusing a key used by one of `AnimatingSprite`'s ancestor classes.

> **Note:** While `NSCoding` isn't very complicated, it's worth reading up on it to understand it fully. For more information, take a look at this tutorial, http://www.raywenderlich.com/1914/nscoding-tutorial-for-ios-how-to-save-your-app-data, this one, http://nshipster.com/nscoding/, or at this excellent write up, http://www.mikeash.com/pyblog/friday-qa-2010-08-12-implementing-nscoding.html.

`AnimatingSprite`'s encoding logic is about as basic as it comes, as will be its decoding logic. Add the following method to support initializing an `AnimatingSprite` from an `NSCoder`:

```
- (instancetype)initWithCoder:(NSCoder *)aDecoder
{
  //1
  if (self = [super initWithCoder:aDecoder]) {
    //2
    _facingForwardAnim =
      [aDecoder decodeObjectForKey:@"AS-ForwardAnim"];
    _facingBackAnim =
      [aDecoder decodeObjectForKey:@"AS-BackAnim"];
    _facingSideAnim =
      [aDecoder decodeObjectForKey:@"AS-SideAnim"];
    _facingDirection =
      [aDecoder decodeInt32ForKey:@"AS-FacingDirection"];
  }
  return self;
}
```

As you can see, `initWithCoder:` is a special initializer method that reverses the work you did in `encodeWithCoder:`.

1. `initWithCoder:` functions much like any other initializer method and as such you need to assign `self` to the return value of an initializer from the class's super class. When dealing with super classes defined by Sprite Kit, you must always call `super initWithCoder:`.

2. For each key-value pair you encoded in `encodeWithCoder:`, you decode it here using the same key and assign the decoded value directly to the instance variable. You can perform any additional initialization you'd like in `initWithCoder:`, but `AnimatingSprite` requires none.

With those two methods added, you can now safely archive `AnimatingSprite` objects. In fact, since neither `Player` nor `Bug` adds any data of its own and since they each subclass `AnimatingSprite`, you *should* be able to archive those now as well. (I write "should" because there is actually a subtle issue you'll fix later in order to archive `Bug` objects.) But you still have a few other classes to handle before you can archive an entire scene.

Surprise exercise!

In Pest Control, there are five classes that require `encodeWithCoder:` and `initWithCoder:` implementations. You already took care of one – `AnimatingSprite`. The others are `TileMapLayer`, `TmxTileMapLayer`, `Breakable` and `MyScene`. `MyScene` will be more complicated than the others, so you'll cover it in detail in the next section. For now, as an exercise, try adding `encodeWithCoder:` and `initWithCoder:` to `TileMapLayer`, `TmxTileMapLayer` and `Breakable` yourself.

Remember to encode every private variable and every auto-synthesized property in each of these classes. When you're done, check your implementation against what follows below, but don't worry if you used different keys than the ones you see here – all that matters with key names is that they match between the encode and decode operations.

In **TileMapLayer.m**:

```
- (void)encodeWithCoder:(NSCoder *)aCoder
{
  [super encodeWithCoder:aCoder];

  [aCoder encodeObject:_atlas forKey:@"TML-Atlas"];
  [aCoder encodeCGSize:_gridSize forKey:@"TML-GridSize"];
  [aCoder encodeCGSize:_tileSize forKey:@"TML-TileSize"];
  [aCoder encodeCGSize:_layerSize forKey:@"TML-LayerSize"];
```

```
}
- (instancetype)initWithCoder:(NSCoder *)aDecoder
{
  if (self = [super initWithCoder:aDecoder]) {
    _atlas = [aDecoder decodeObjectForKey:@"TML-Atlas"];
    _gridSize = [aDecoder decodeCGSizeForKey:@"TML-GridSize"];
    _tileSize = [aDecoder decodeCGSizeForKey:@"TML-TileSize"];
    _layerSize = [aDecoder decodeCGSizeForKey:@"TML-LayerSize"];
  }
  return self;
}
```

In **TmxTileMapLayer.m**:

```
- (void)encodeWithCoder:(NSCoder *)aCoder
{
  [super encodeWithCoder:aCoder];
  [aCoder encodeObject:_layer forKey:@"TmxTML-Layer"];
  [aCoder encodeCGSize:_tmxTileSize forKey:@"TmxTML-TileSize"];
  [aCoder encodeCGSize:_tmxGridSize forKey:@"TmxTML-GridSize"];
  [aCoder encodeCGSize:_tmxLayerSize
                forKey:@"TmxTML-LayerSize"];
}

- (instancetype)initWithCoder:(NSCoder *)aDecoder
{
  if (self = [super initWithCoder:aDecoder]) {
    _layer = [aDecoder decodeObjectForKey:@"TmxTML-Layer"];
    _tmxTileSize =
      [aDecoder decodeCGSizeForKey:@"TmxTML-TileSize"];
    _tmxGridSize =
      [aDecoder decodeCGSizeForKey:@"TmxTML-GridSize"];
    _tmxLayerSize =
      [aDecoder decodeCGSizeForKey:@"TmxTML-LayerSize"];
  }
  return self;
}
```

In **Breakable.m**:

```
- (void)encodeWithCoder:(NSCoder *)aCoder
{
  [super encodeWithCoder:aCoder];
  [aCoder encodeObject:_broken forKey:@"Breakable-broken"];
}

- (instancetype)initWithCoder:(NSCoder *)aDecoder
```

```
{
  if (self = [super initWithCoder:aDecoder]) {
    _broken = [aDecoder decodeObjectForKey:@"Breakable-broken"];
  }
  return self;
}
```

Hopefully you were able to come up with similar implementations on your own. If not, that's OK – you'll get some more practice now as you tackle encoding and decoding MyScene, a class that requires more complex encoding/decoding logic than what you've seen so far.

Encoding/decoding complex objects

Each of the classes for which you've added NSCoding support so far has required nothing more than the most basic encoding or decoding of data. Unfortunately, that won't always be the case.

For MyScene, you'll have to do a bit more work. To get started, open **MyScene.m** and add the following method:

```
- (void)encodeWithCoder:(NSCoder *)aCoder
{
  //1
  [super encodeWithCoder:aCoder];

  [aCoder encodeObject:_worldNode forKey:@"MyScene-WorldNode"];
  [aCoder encodeObject:_player forKey:@"MyScene-Player"];
  [aCoder encodeObject:_bgLayer forKey:@"MyScene-BgLayer"];
  [aCoder encodeObject:_bugLayer forKey:@"MyScene-BugLayer"];
  [aCoder encodeObject:_breakableLayer
            forKey:@"MyScene-BreakableLayer"];
  [aCoder encodeObject:_tileMap forKey:@"MyScene-TmxTileMap"];

  [aCoder encodeInt32:_gameState forKey:@"MyScene-GameState"];
  [aCoder encodeInt:_level forKey:@"MyScene-Level"];
  [aCoder encodeDouble:_levelTimeLimit
            forKey:@"MyScene-LevelTimeLimit"];
  [aCoder encodeObject:_timerLabel
            forKey:@"MyScene-TimerLabel"];
  //2
  [aCoder encodeDouble:_elapsedTime
            forKey:@"MyScene-ElapsedTime"];
}
```

This method is not yet complete, but here's what you have so far:

1. It starts off with a familiar call to super encodeWithCoder:, followed by encoding *most* of MyScene's instance variables. Here you're using an important aspect of the NSCoder class: when you archive the same object multiple times, NSCoder is smart enough to include the object in the archive only once so the size of your archive won't get out of hand. Later, during the decoding process, NSCoder will ensure all requests for that object reference the same item. In this case, calling super encodeWithCoder: encodes all of the scene's child nodes as well, but then you archive specific child nodes again, like _worldNode, _player and _bgLayer – not to mention that _player is a child of _worldNode, so it's actually archived three times.

2. Notice that you archive _elapsedTime but not _currentTime or _startTime. That's because the current and start times are absolute values that only make sense during a specific run of the game. Instead you'll rely on the code you already have in update: to continuously update _currentTime, and you'll add code later to initialize _startTime.

With most of the encoding completed, add the following method to support decoding a MyScene object:

```
- (instancetype)initWithCoder:(NSCoder *)aDecoder
{
  if (self = [super initWithCoder:aDecoder]) {
    _worldNode =
      [aDecoder decodeObjectForKey:@"MyScene-WorldNode"];
    _player = [aDecoder decodeObjectForKey:@"MyScene-Player"];
    _bgLayer = [aDecoder decodeObjectForKey:@"MyScene-BgLayer"];
    _bugLayer =
      [aDecoder decodeObjectForKey:@"MyScene-BugLayer"];
    _breakableLayer =
      [aDecoder decodeObjectForKey:@"MyScene-BreakableLayer"];
    _tileMap =
      [aDecoder decodeObjectForKey:@"MyScene-TmxTileMap"];

    _gameState =
      [aDecoder decodeInt32ForKey:@"MyScene-GameState"];
    _level = [aDecoder decodeIntForKey:@"MyScene-Level"];
    _levelTimeLimit =
      [aDecoder decodeDoubleForKey:@"MyScene-LevelTimeLimit"];
    _timerLabel =
    [aDecoder decodeObjectForKey:@"MyScene-TimerLabel"];

    _elapsedTime =
      [aDecoder decodeDoubleForKey:@"MyScene-ElapsedTime"];
  }
```

```
    return self;
}
```

The above code simply decodes each item you encoded in `encodeWithCoder:` and sets the appropriate variables, just as you did before. This won't be good enough to make the game work, but it is enough to begin testing – at which point, you'll find the problems.

Archiving and restoring scenes

In order to implement Pest Control's autosave feature, you'll automatically save the state of the scene whenever the user switches away from the game to another app. Then, whenever the player returns to the game, if there is a save game available, you'll ask the user if they'd like to continue playing from that point or restart on the same level.

To begin, open **AppDelegate.m** and import the Sprite Kit framework at the top of the file:

```
#import <SpriteKit/SpriteKit.h>
```

iOS calls `applicationWillResignActive:` when the app is about to become inactive. The first thing you should do, if nothing else, is pause the scene. Otherwise, your app may continue to execute actions even when the user thinks it's not running.

Add the following inside `applicationWillResignActive:`:

```
SKView *view = (SKView*)self.window.rootViewController.view;
view.scene.paused = YES;
```

The way you've written Pest Control, you know that its window contains a view controller whose view is an `SKView`. The above code simply gets that `SKView` and pauses the scene it is currently presenting.

Now un-pause the scene in `applicationDidBecomeActive:`:

```
SKView *view = (SKView*)self.window.rootViewController.view;
view.scene.paused = NO;
```

This code simply gets the current scene and un-pauses it.

Before you can create a save game file, you need to pick a folder in which to store it. Apple recommends putting data like this – things you want backed up but that you don't want accessible to the user via iTunes – inside the **Private Documents** folder in the app's **Library** folder. Add this helper method, which returns a path to that folder:

```
+ (NSString *)getPrivateDocsDir
{
  NSArray *paths =
    NSSearchPathForDirectoriesInDomains(NSLibraryDirectory,
                                        NSUserDomainMask, YES);
  NSString *documentsDirectory = [paths objectAtIndex:0];
  documentsDirectory = [documentsDirectory
    stringByAppendingPathComponent:@"Private Documents"];

  NSError *error;
  [[NSFileManager defaultManager]
   createDirectoryAtPath:documentsDirectory
   withIntermediateDirectories:YES attributes:nil error:&error];

  return documentsDirectory;
}
```

The above code returns the path to the **Private Documents** folder in the app's **Library** folder, creating it if it cannot be found.

With that helper logic in place, you can finally archive your scene. Replace the contents of `applicationDidEnterBackground:` with the following code:

```
//1
SKView *view = (SKView*)self.window.rootViewController.view;
SKScene *scene = view.scene;
//2
NSString *documentsDirectory = [AppDelegate getPrivateDocsDir];
NSString *filePath =
  [documentsDirectory
   stringByAppendingPathComponent:@"autosaved-scene"];
//3
NSMutableData *data = [[NSMutableData alloc] init];
NSKeyedArchiver *archiver =
  [[NSKeyedArchiver alloc]
   initForWritingWithMutableData:data];
//4
[archiver encodeObject:scene forKey:@"AppDelegateSceneKey"];
[archiver finishEncoding];
[data writeToFile:filePath atomically:YES];
```

This logic archives the scene whenever the app moves into the background on the device. Specifically:

1. It gets the scene from the app's current view.

2. It finds the path to a file named **autosaved-scene**, which is where you'll store the archive.

3. Here it creates an `NSKeyedArchiver` backed by an `NSMutableData` object. You'll use these two objects to actually encode the data and write it to disk.

4. Using the archiver, the logic encodes the scene and writes it to disk. Calling `encodeObject:forKey:` runs the scene's `encodeWithCoder:` method on itself as well as on any of its children.

That's all it takes to archive your scene to disk. Now you need to load an archived scene and display it in the view. Replace the contents of `applicationDidBecomeActive:` with the following:

```
SKView *view = (SKView*)self.window.rootViewController.view;
NSString *dataPath =
  [[AppDelegate getPrivateDocsDir]
    stringByAppendingPathComponent:@"autosaved-scene"];
NSData *codedData =
  [[NSData alloc] initWithContentsOfFile:dataPath];
if (codedData != nil) {
  NSKeyedUnarchiver *unarchiver =
    [[NSKeyedUnarchiver alloc]
      initForReadingWithData:codedData];
  SKScene *scene =
    [unarchiver decodeObjectForKey:@"AppDelegateSceneKey"];
  [unarchiver finishDecoding];
  [view presentScene:scene];
}
view.scene.paused = NO;
```

This is mostly the same as what you did in `applicationDidEnterBackground:`, except here you use an `NSKeyedUnarchiver` to unarchive a scene instead of archiving it. The last line of the method ensures the scene is not paused.

It's been a while since you've run the app. To test the autosave feature, start Pest Control and then press the **Home** button on the device or Simulator, and then... crash?

```
436    - (void)encodeWithCoder:(NSCoder *)aCoder
437    {
438        [super encodeWithCoder:aCoder];    Thread 1: EXC_BAD_ACCESS (code=1, address=0xc78914fb)
439
440        [aCoder encodeObject:_worldNode forKey:@"MyScene-WorldNode"];
441        [aCoder encodeObject:_player forKey:@"MyScene-Player"];
442        [aCoder encodeObject:_bgLayer forKey:@"MyScene-BgLayer"];
```

At the time of this writing, this app crashes here due to a bug in Sprite Kit. If it doesn't crash for you, it means you're living in the future, some time after Apple has fixed this bug, but before a new version of this chapter has been released. If that's the case, do we have hover boards yet?

If your app doesn't crash here, skip the "Edge loops cannot be encoded" section and move straight to the section titled "Block actions cannot be encoded."

Issues with archiving in Sprite Kit

This autosave stuff all seemed a bit too easy, didn't it? While Arnold takes a break from squashing bugs, you're going to deal with some bugs in Sprite Kit.

> **Note:** Each of the following subsections provides a workaround for a specific issue caused by Sprite Kit. Each was present at the time of this writing, but that does not mean they are still occurring when you are reading this. If you do not witness an error as described, that means Apple has corrected it in the version of Sprite Kit you are using and you can skip that specific workaround.

Edge loops cannot be encoded

At the time of this writing, apps crash when they attempt to encode physics bodies created with `SKPhysicsBody bodyWithEdgeLoopFromRect:`. While annoying, it's not an insurmountable issue because Pest Control only creates one such object – the world boundary. To work around the problem, you'll make a few small additions to **MyScene.m**.

First add the following line to `createWorld:` to name the world boundary object:

```
bounds.name = @"worldBounds";
```

Then add these lines at the top of `encodeWithCoder:`, *before* the call to `super encodeWithCoder::`

```
SKNode *worldBounds =
  [_worldNode childNodeWithName:@"worldBounds"];
[worldBounds removeFromParent];
```

This finds the boundary object in `_worldNode` and removes it, but stores a reference to it for later. Because the next line after this is the call to `super encodeWithCoder:`, you are actually encoding the scene without the physics world boundary, so the app won't crash.

However, now your world has no physics boundary, which is not good. Add this at the end of `encodeWithCoder::`

```
[_worldNode addChild:worldBounds];
```

This replaces the physics boundary after you're done encoding the scene, but that only fixes part of the problem. The app won't crash when you *encode* it, but later when you *decode* it, the scene won't include a physics boundary! Still not good.

Inside `initWithCoder:`, add the following code to correct this issue:

```
SKNode *bounds = [SKNode node];
bounds.name = @"worldBounds";
bounds.physicsBody =
  [SKPhysicsBody bodyWithEdgeLoopFromRect:
    CGRectMake(0, 0,
               _bgLayer.layerSize.width,
               _bgLayer.layerSize.height)];
bounds.physicsBody.categoryBitMask = PCWallCategory;
bounds.physicsBody.collisionBitMask = 0;
bounds.physicsBody.friction = 0;
[_worldNode addChild:bounds];
```

The above code simply adds a physics boundary to `_worldNode` just like the one added in `initWithSize:level:`. This workaround wouldn't be so easy if you had multiple nodes with these broken physics bodies, but fixing it for just one wasn't too difficult.

Block actions cannot be encoded

Now when you run Pest Control and press the **Home** button, the app doesn't crash. However, you do see a bunch of messages like the following in the console:

```
PestControl[5738:70b] SKAction: Run block actions can not be
properly encoded, Objective-C blocks do not support NSCoding.
```

With Pest Control in the background on your device or the Simulator, tap the app's icon to bring it back into the foreground. At that point you'll see a bunch more messages in the console like this one:

```
PestControl[5738:70b] SKAction: Run block actions can not be
properly decoded, Objective-C blocks do not support NSCoding.
```

The messages are pretty clear – you cannot encode or decode `SKActions` created with `runBlock:` because Objective-C blocks do not support `NSCoding`. You're seeing these messages because `Bug` runs an action created in just this way. No wonder Arnold likes to smash these things.

So you can't use blocks – what now? In some cases, you would be in a tough spot. For example, if you were using custom actions, which are created using blocks via `SKAction customActionWithDuration:actionBlock:`, you'd have to refactor your code in potentially complicated ways. But in other cases, such as now, you can avoid using blocks by calling a selector instead.

Open **Bug.m** and replace the line in `walk` that creates the `moveToPos` action with the following:

```
SKAction* moveToPos =
  [SKAction sequence:
   @[[SKAction moveTo:randomPos duration:1],
     [SKAction performSelector:@selector(walk)
                      onTarget:self]]];
```

This new action moves to the new position and then simply calls `walk` instead of using a block to call it. You may be asking, "Why didn't you write the action this way back in Chapter 14, 'More Tile Maps?'" Well, I could ask you the same question, couldn't I? Also, this has served to point out an issue you need to be aware of when writing apps that support archiving.

Hidden nodes don't stay hidden

If you happened to save the game while playing a level defined by a TMX file, you may have noticed some unhealthy-looking water when you loaded up the saved game, as shown in the following screenshot:

You may remember those red tiles from the previous chapter. They are only there to define physics boundaries and are supposed to be hidden, but Sprite Kit doesn't seem to have gotten the message.

To fix this, add the following code to the end of `initWithCoder:` in **MyScene.m**:

```
if (_tileMap) {
```

```
    [_bgLayer enumerateChildNodesWithName:@"water"
                              usingBlock:
      ^(SKNode *node, BOOL *stop){
        node.hidden = YES;
      }];
  }
```

This code checks to see if there is a **_tileMap** present, which indicates that the level was loaded from a TMX file. If so, it finds every node named **water** in **_bgLayer** and hides it. It's important to only do this for TMX files, because you do *not* want to hide water tiles in any other case. Now when you run, water looks like water again, see?

While testing and fixing these various issues, you may have noticed something else that's very wrong. You can see it in the screenshot above – no matter how much time is remaining when you save the game, when you start playing again, the app claims you've run out of time. That one isn't Sprite Kit's fault, and you'll fix it in the next section, called "Continuing play from a restored archive."

SKActions do not retain state when archived

As the section header states, **SKActions** do not retain their state when archived. That is, if you archive a node that is currently running an action and you later create a new node from that archive, it will have a copy of that **SKAction** on it that will immediately start executing *from the beginning* rather than where it left off.

According to Apple, this behavior is as expected, but this certainly does mess things up if you don't account for it, so let's cover it briefly.

For example, consider a node running an action to move from its current position to (200,200) over two seconds. If you archived such a node after it had been running its action for one second and later created a new node from that archive, the new node would appear at the position it occupied when archived – let's say (100,100) – and then immediately begin running an action to move from its current position to (200,200) *over two seconds*. But since the position of the node is now where you would have expected it to be after one second, it only needs to cover half the expected distance over those two seconds, meaning it will move at half the speed.

This means that any running actions with durations, which are most of them, will have different speeds/rates of change when unarchived.

In addition, any action defined by a relative change, such as `moveByX:y:duration:`, will cause problems, sometimes completely breaking your game. For example, consider a node running an action to move by 100 points along the x-axis over two seconds. If you archive that action after one second, a new node created from that archive will appear at the position it occupied when it was archived and immediately begin to move *100 points along the x-axis* over two seconds. But since it was already about 50 points away from where you started the original action, it will end up moving 50 points too far.

As you can see, you can't archive nodes that are running just any action and assume Sprite Kit will decode your scene in the same state it was in when you encoded it. Maybe Apple assumed developers would only archive actions to be added to nodes later, after unarchiving, rather than archive nodes that include running actions. Or maybe it is too difficult to maintain the necessary state information in the archive, so instead of admitting it as a bug, they decided to say it is working as intended.

Whatever the reason, you will need to do some complicated pre- and post-processing during the encoding/decoding process if you want to support archiving nodes with running actions. And in some cases, because `SKAction` doesn't expose any of the information you would need to make this easy, it may be impossible.

Again, archiving Sprite Kit nodes is probably best suited for level editors and such that can most likely get away with not archiving in-progress actions, because a level editor usually doesn't have running actions but is instead concerned with layout and game data issues, but it's good to understand this limitation.

On the other hand, Pest Control is archiving nodes with running actions – the player and each of the bugs are constantly running actions – but the actions have such short durations and there are so many of them that the problem isn't very noticeable. In the upcoming chapters on adding juice to your game, you'll add more actions, and some of them do sometimes cause anomalies when restored from the save game file.

Continuing play from a restored archive

When the app finds an autosave file, it should ask the user whether to continue playing from the point of the save or to restart the current level. To do so, you'll add a new game state that displays the options and you'll load games into this state if they were saved in-progress.

First add the following PCGameState value in **MyScene.m**:

```
PCGameStateInReloadMenu,
```

Then add this method to display the options to the user:

```
- (void)showReloadMenu
{
  SKLabelNode* label =
    (SKLabelNode*)[self childNodeWithName:@"msgLabel"];
  label.text = @"Found a Save File";
  label.hidden = NO;

  SKLabelNode* continueLabel = (SKLabelNode*)
    [self childNodeWithName:@"continueLabel"];
  if (!continueLabel)
  {
    continueLabel =
      [SKLabelNode labelNodeWithFontNamed:@"Chalkduster"];
    continueLabel.text = @"Continue?";
    continueLabel.name = @"continueLabel";
    continueLabel.fontSize = 28;
    continueLabel.horizontalAlignmentMode =
      SKLabelHorizontalAlignmentModeRight;
    continueLabel.position = CGPointMake(0-20, -40);
    [self addChild:continueLabel];

    SKLabelNode* restartLabel =
      [SKLabelNode labelNodeWithFontNamed:@"Chalkduster"];
    restartLabel.text = @"Restart Level?";
    restartLabel.name = @"restartLabel";
    restartLabel.fontSize = 28;
    restartLabel.horizontalAlignmentMode =
      SKLabelHorizontalAlignmentModeLeft;
    restartLabel.position = CGPointMake(0+20, -40);
    [self addChild:restartLabel];
  }
}
```

This looks like a lot of code, but it just adds labels to the screen the same way you did for winning and losing. There is one important thing to note, though: instead of automatically creating the labels, the code first checks the scene for a node named continueLabel and only creates the labels if it isn't there.

The reason for this check relates to how you're going to use this method. In the next step, you'll call this method when restoring from a saved game. But what if the player had paused the game – and hence created a save file – while they were looking at this menu? If that were to happen, you would restore the labels as part of the decoding process. If this method were to then add new ones, it would cause problems for you later. (By the way, you only check for one of the two labels because if one is there, the other one is, too.)

Now call this method at the appropriate times by adding this switch statement to the end of initWithCoder::

```
switch (_gameState) {
  case PCGameStateInReloadMenu:
  case PCGameStatePlaying:
  {
    _gameState = PCGameStateInReloadMenu;
    [self showReloadMenu];
    break;
  }
  default: break;
}
```

This switch statement calls showReloadMenu if the game had been saved in either the playing state or the reload menu state itself. For all other states, the app restores itself into that state directly. If you think about it, there are only two other states, which occur at the beginning and end of a level, respectively. There is no reason to show the reload menu in those cases because they already have their own interface elements onscreen.

Build and run to see the new menu.

Besides the new labels, there are two other things you should notice. The first is that the **Time Remaining** value is correct. We like it when things work. The other is that Arnold and the bugs are running around even though the player is staring at a menu screen! That one needs to be fixed.

Replace the first `if` statement in **update:** with the following:

```
if((_gameState == PCGameStateStartingLevel ||
    _gameState == PCGameStateInReloadMenu) && !self.isPaused){
  self.paused = YES;
}
```

You were already pausing the game when it loads a new level, but now you pause it while you're displaying this new menu, too.

Build and run again and you'll see the game is properly paused when displaying the reload options screen. Of course, the player can't do anything, because the labels still don't handle touch events. To rectify the situation, add this **case** statement to **touchesBegan:withEvent::**

```
case PCGameStateInReloadMenu:
{
  UITouch* touch = [touches anyObject];
  CGPoint loc = [touch locationInNode:self];
  SKNode* node = [self nodeAtPoint:loc];
  if ([node.name isEqualToString:@"restartLabel"]) {
    MyScene *newScene = [[MyScene alloc] initWithSize:self.size
                                                level:_level];
    [self.view presentScene:newScene
               transition:[SKTransition
                             flipVerticalWithDuration:.5]];
```

```
    } else if ([node.name isEqualToString:@"continueLabel"]) {
        [node removeFromParent];
        node = [self childNodeWithName:@"restartLabel"];
        [node removeFromParent];
        [self childNodeWithName:@"msgLabel"].hidden = YES;

        _gameState = PCGameStatePlaying;
        self.paused = NO;
    }
    break;
}
```

Just as you handle touches while in the PCGameStateInLevelMenu state, you check to see if one of the labels contains the touch event. If the user touched **Restart Level?**, you transition to a newly initialized scene for the same level – the same thing you do when the user taps **Try Again?** after failing to clear a level. But if the user touched **Continue?**, then you remove the two buttons from the scene, hide the msgLabel node, update the game state and un-pause the scene.

Build, run and click **Continue?**. Aw, too slow.

The previous section mentioned this problem, with a promise that this section would fix it.

First, an explanation of the cause: the app archives and restores _elapsedTime and _levelTimeLimit, but not _startTime and _currentTime. As mentioned earlier, that's because those two values only make sense in relation to the current run. That is, if you start a level, play for 10 seconds, pause the game and then resume playing 30 minutes later, _startTime would be 30 minutes and 10 seconds ago. In update:, you use _startTime to calculate the amount of time spent playing this level, which means the app will think the player has been playing for an awfully long time. (If players are having *that* much trouble finding the last bug, you may want to consider adding some sort of radar-type feature to your app.)

To solve this problem, you didn't archive the start or current times. However, whenever a value is not set in `initWithCoder:`, it automatically receives a default value, which for variables of type `double` is zero. As far as your app is concerned, Arnold has been looking for those bugs since the beginning of time!

The fix is simple – you need to initialize `_startTime` to a time that makes sense for the current play session. To do so, add the following line to the `PCGameStateInReloadMenu` case in `touchesBegan:withEvent:`, inside the `else if` block that handles touches for the node named `continueLabel`:

```
_startTime = _currentTime - _elapsedTime;
```

This simply calculates what time the player *would* have started, had they started `_elapsedTime` seconds before right now.

Build and run, and you're really, really done! The game's countdown timer, Arnold and the bugs all pick up where they left off when they were archived and you're right back in the action. After all that, a few minutes of senseless bug destruction may be just what you need.

As this chapter's challenge, you'll implement high score tracking. After that, Pest Control's gameplay features are complete. In the next two chapters, you'll learn how to trick out your game with audio and visual effects that can turn the basic gameplay of Pest Control – or any other game you make – into something even more fun than a field full of bugs!

Challenges

Ready to see if you've mastered saving and loading your games? Try out this challenge!

As always, you can find a solution in this chapter's resources, but first aim to do it yourself.

Challege 1: High Scores

As its name implies, Chapter 22, "Game Center Leaderboards," shows you how to set up leaderboards in Game Center. That's a cool way to track high scores, but for some additional practice with archiving, try tracking a player's high score locally in the save game file.

Every **SKNode** includes a `userData` property, which is a dictionary that lets you add any data you'd like to a node. Since you're already archiving the entire scene anyway, **MyScene**'s `userData` is a convenient place to store the high scores.

> **Note:** In a real app, you'll probably want to store things like high scores in a separate file or using something like Game Center. The solution described here is simply to show how user data can be archived along with the scene.

Start by initializing the `userData` property of the first scene you create (inside **ViewController.m**) with an empty `NSMutableDictionary` (`userData` is `nil` by default). Then add an entry into the dictionary with the key "bestTimes", and the value another empty mutable dictionary.

Next modify `endLevelWithSuccess:` in **MyScene.m** so that each time the user *successfully* clears a level, it does the following:

1. It gets the dictionary stored with the key **bestTimes** in the scene's `userData`.

2. It then checks for a saved high score, using the current level as a key into the dictionary. In a real app you'd probably want something more robust, like a unique

level ID, so that you could reorder levels without breaking your users' high scores, but that's overkill for Pest Control.

3. If there isn't a high saved score or if `_elapsedTime` is less than the saved value, update the saved score.

4. Update the `msgLabel` node to tell the player about the new high score.

There are three places in **MyScene.m** where you create a new scene and present it in the view. In each of these places, you need to pass the current scene's `userData` to the new scene. To do so, add a line like the following before presenting the scene in the view:

```
newScene.userData = self.userData;
```

That's it! Play a level and beat it. The first time you do, you should see the message you added for new high scores.

Again, the high score will be persisted across game loads since **SKNode** automatically persists its `userData` property.

When you get tired of trying to beat your best time, move on to the next chapter to start juicing up Pest Control.

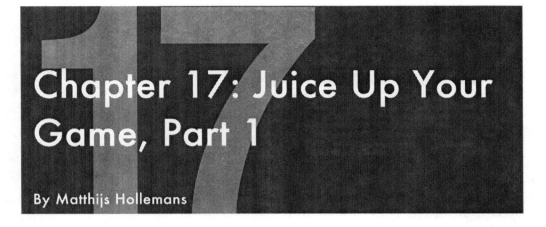

Chapter 17: Juice Up Your Game, Part 1

By Matthijs Hollemans

Pop quiz: what's the difference between a good game and a *great* game? Why does one game delight its players while another is greeted with indifference? Why do some games have raving fans? And what is this magical potion named "polish" that you're supposed to sprinkle on your games to make them awesome?

The answer is all in the details.

Great games are filled to the brim with droves of little details that are often so subtle that you might not even consciously notice them while you're playing. And it gives you great pleasure when you finally *do* notice them. Polishing a game means paying attention to these details. Don't stop developing once your game reaches a playable state and rush it to the App Store. Push your game further. Add some salt and pepper to spice it up!

"Juice", the topic of this chapter and the next, is a special type of polish that is easy to add and serves to bring joy to the game. When a game is *juicy*, it feels alive – every interaction between the player and the game world results in a visually stimulating response.

For example, when two objects collide, you shouldn't just see it happen on the screen – that collision should look so convincing that you can almost *feel* it in your body. Playing a juicy game is a truly visceral experience.

No Juice

With Juice

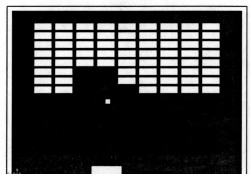
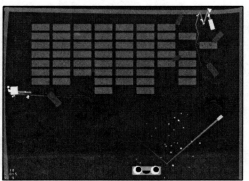

The great thing about juice is that you don't need to invest in a doubly large art budget or hire expensive consultants who used to work for Pixar. Instead, you can use simple animation effects – such as scaling, rotation and movement – to manipulate your sprites. This is great news for programmers like you and me!

On their own, each of these effects isn't that exciting, but put together, every interaction with the game world results in a cascade of visual feedback that keeps players coming back for more. That is what we mean by making your games *juicy*.

In this chapter, you will take the game from the previous chapter, **Pest Control**, and juice it up by adding a myriad of details to it. It's already a good game as it is, but now you will make it totally awesome.

Don't misunderstand: you're not going to change the rules of the game. All you will do in these chapters is add special effects to make the game more appealing to see and experience. And you can apply these same effects to your own games!

Note: This chapter begins where the challenge left off in the last chapter. If you were unable to complete the challenge or skipped ahead from a previous chapter, don't worry – you can simply open **PestControl-Starter** from the resources for this chapter to pick up where we left off.

Getting started

Open the latest Pest Control project. First, you are going to modify the game to load a level that was especially designed to show off the special effects from this chapter. To keep things simple, this chapter only works with the text-based levels, not TMX levels.

Go to **MyScene.m** and in `initWithSize:level:`, change the following line to load the level data from **JuicyLevels.plist** instead of Levels.plist:

```
NSDictionary *config =
  [NSDictionary dictionaryWithContentsOfFile:
    [[NSBundle mainBundle] pathForResource:@"JuicyLevels"
                                    ofType:@"plist"]];
```

Delete your old build from the simulator or device, so that any save file you may currently have is not loaded on the next run. Great, now you're ready to rock!

If you run the game in its current state, you'll find that it works well enough – all the gameplay rules are functioning as they should – but it lacks excitement.

For example, when you catch a bug it simply disappears from the screen. One moment it's there, the next it's gone. As players, we want to see something more gratifying as a reward for catching that bug. Big explosions always work well!

Note that the project already includes a special effect: when you push a red firebug into the water, it appears to drown. This is thanks to a combination of two `SKActions`: a rotation action to make the bug spin and a scaling action to shrink it at the same time. (See the `resumeAfterKick` method in **FireBug.m**.)

These two actions together make it look like the firebug gets sucked into a deadly vortex! Give it a try. Run the game and try to push a firebug into the water.

That is exactly the sort of enhancement you'll be making throughout this chapter and the next, until the entire game feels more alive – and is double the fun to play!

3 steps to juice your game

Juicing up your game is like performing a magic trick. The results may look impressive to an unsuspecting audience, but it is really just sleight of hand. Fortunately, you don't need to go to Hogwarts and study for years to become a special effects wizard.

The rest of this chapter and next will show you some special effects you can use in your game. But before you begin adding effects willy-nilly, you need to know where to apply them. It doesn't make sense to add them randomly – otherwise your game runs the risk of feeling confusing and distracting for players.

The good news is all you have to do is follow a simple algorithm. Without further ado, here are our "3 Steps to Juice Your Game":

1. **List the actors**. First, make a list of all the objects that play a role in your game – often called the *actors*. For example, two of your actors are Arnold and a tree.

2. **List the interactions**. Second, make a list of the interactions that exist between them. For example, one interaction is Arnold colliding with a tree to chop it down. An object can also perform interactions with itself, like moving or changing state.

3. **Add effects to interactions**. Finally, you add as many effects to these interactions as you can. This is what makes the player feel like they're really making something cool happen.

> For example, what if instead of simply making the tree immediately switch from normal to chopped like it does now, you applied a series of actions to make the tree top appear to bounce off as if the hero is chopping it down?

Simple enough, right? Let's give the steps 1 and 2 a try with Pest Control – then in this chapter and the next, you will repeatedly apply step 3.

First, what actors are there in Pest Control? Here is my list:

- **The hero**, making his living as an exterminator. You call him Arnold.

- **Normal bugs**. The antagonists of this story. The hero has to squash them all to win the game.

- **Fire bugs**. These cannot be squashed, but must be shoved into water.

- **Trees**. Just for decoration. They break when the hero runs over them.

- **Walls**. These tiles block the hero's movement, as is usually the case with walls, but he can bounce off them to his advantage.

- **Water**. Like walls, but with a different look.

- **Background**. This includes the grass and stone floor tiles. These serve no real purpose in the game other than to make it look more interesting.

- **The screen itself**. The game world is the container of all the other actors. The player can also bounce off the edges of the screen.

- **Gameplay rules**. Certain gameplay rules might cause interesting things to happen. For example, in Pest Control if the player destroys all the bugs, they win the game.

- **The player**. Yes, the player is an actor in the game, too – and with the most important role, one might argue!

Second, now that you've identified the gameplay actors, what interactions exist between them? Here is a partial list:

- Hero interacts with tree (i.e. hero chops down tree)

- Hero interacts with normal bug (i.e. hero destroys bug)

- Hero interacts with fire bug (i.e. hero kicks bug)

- Fire bug interacts with water (i.e. fire bug is destroyed)

- Hero interacts into wall or water (i.e. hero bounces off wall or water)

- Player interacts with screen (i.e. player taps screen)

- Hero interacts with game world (i.e. the hero performs an action like moving or changing direction)

- Bugs interacts with game world (i.e. the bug performs an action like moving or spawning)

- Game rule interacts with game rule (i.e. win or lose conditions are satisfied)

And much more!

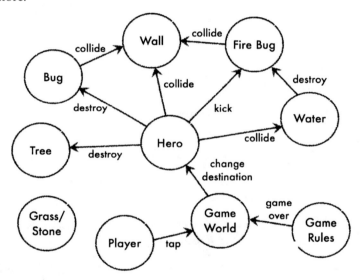

All of these interactions are great places to add effects that will juice up the game. But what effects should you use?

5 basic special effects

In this chapter, you'll start out with five basic special effects. The good news is to use these you just need to know SKActions, and you've had plenty of practice with those already in this book.

There are five basic effects that you can apply to sprite nodes:

1. **Movement** changes a node's position.

2. **Scaling** changes a node's size.

3. **Rotation** changes a node's angle.

4. **Alpha** changes a node's translucency.

5. **Texture** changes to a sprite node's image.

All of these effects can be temporary or permanent, immediate or animated, performed by themselves or – and this is where the magic happens – in combination with others. When you add a bunch of these effects together, they can make the entire screen jump and bounce. That's when things get juicy!

You've already seen in previous chapters how easy it is to make an object move or rotate using an SKAction. That's the great thing about these effects: they are incredibly easy to program, so adding them to your games is a quick win. Although I have to warn you: once you start adding special effects, it's hard to stop!

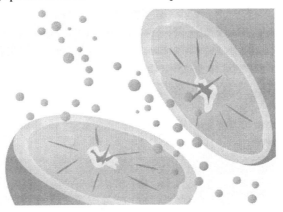

Four effects to fell a tree

You're going to start by applying four of the five basic special effects to the "hero collides with tree" interaction.

This is because smashing things is a lot of fun. You usually get into trouble for it in the real world, but luckily in games you can get away with it. Pest Control already lets you run over trees, after which they get reduced to poor little tree stumps. This is an excellent opportunity to add some cool animations.

Currently, the tree-smashing code looks like this, in **Breakable.m**:

```
- (void)smashBreakable {
  self.physicsBody = nil;
  self.texture = _broken;
  self.size = _broken.size;
}
```

The tree tiles are instances of the Breakable class, which is really an SKSpriteNode with some extra stuff. The Breakable tile starts out displaying one texture, which is the normal, unbroken tree, but it also has a variable named _broken that references a different texture, which is the tree stump.

In smashBreakable, you simply replace the sprite's current texture, the solid tree, with the _broken texture, the tree stump. This is satisfyingly simple to code, but not to watch. Your players want to see something more spectacular!

In this section, you will add a new "treetop" sprite and make it tumble down the screen, so that it looks like the hero is chopping down trees!

Pest Control's **scenery.atlas** folder already contains an image named **tree-top.png**. To use this new image in the Breakable class, you have to rewrite it slightly. First, add a new private instance variable to the top in **Breakable.m**:

```
SKTexture *_flyAwayTexture;
```

Then change the name of the initWithWhole:broken: method to include a new parameter, flyAway:

```
- (instancetype)initWithWhole:(SKTexture *)whole
                       broken:(SKTexture *)broken
                      flyAway:(SKTexture *)flyAway
```

Add the following line inside initWithWhole:broken:flyAway:, just after setting up self.physicsBody:

```
_flyAwayTexture = flyAway;
```

This simply stores the value from the new flyAway parameter into the _flyAwayTexture instance variable.

Of course, you also need to change this method name in the **Breakable.h** file:

```
- (instancetype)initWithWhole:(SKTexture *)whole
                       broken:(SKTexture *)broken
```

```
flyAway:(SKTexture *)flyAway;
```

And finally, change where these methods are called. First in **TileMapLayer.m**'s
nodeForCode: method, modify the case 't' statement so it calls the new initializer:

```
case 't':
  return [[Breakable alloc]
            initWithWhole:[_atlas textureNamed:@"tree"]
                   broken:[_atlas textureNamed:@"tree-stump"]
                  flyAway:[_atlas textureNamed:@"tree-top"]];
```

And in **TmxTileMapLayer.m**, find the following line that allocates the Breakable in
createNodesFromLayer: and replace it with the following (changes are highlighted):

```
SKNode *tile =
  [[Breakable alloc]
    initWithWhole:[atlas textureNamed:@"tree"]
           broken:[atlas textureNamed:@"tree-stump"]
          flyAway:[atlas textureNamed:@"tree-top"]];
```

> **Note:** Remember, this chapter focuses on modifying the non-TMX-related parts
> of Pest Control. You're making the changes in TmxTileMapLayer.m so that the
> project continues to compile, but you'll need to change other areas of the project
> if you want to support the effects shown in this chapter and the next chapter
> when using TMX files.

Finally, since you added a new instance variable, you need to update Breakable's
NSCoding support. Otherwise, these effects won't work properly after continuing from a
saved level.

Add this line to encodeWithCoder: to encode _flyAwayTexture:

```
[aCoder encodeObject:_flyAwayTexture forKey:@"Breakable-
flyAway"];
```

And add this line to initWithCoder: to decode it:

```
_flyAwayTexture =
  [aDecoder decodeObjectForKey:@"Breakable-flyAway"];
```

Build the app to see if everything compiles again without errors. Phew! That was a lot of
work, but now you have everything set up to add some toppling trees to the game.

This diagram illustrates what you're going to implement:

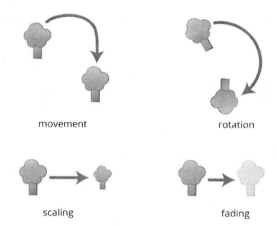

You can see you will be combining four different effects (that's juicy!):

1. **Movement**. You will push the tree upwards slightly and then make it fall down the screen.

2. **Rotation**. You'll rotate the tree by a random amount so that it appears to topple over.

3. **Scaling**. To make the tree "pop", you'll first scale it up so that it appears bigger for a moment, and then scale it down with an animation.

4. **Alpha**. As the scaling animation makes the tree smaller, you will also lower the tree's alpha component so that it becomes more and more transparent, until finally the sprite is no longer visible.

Alone, each of these effects isn't too spectacular, but together they make for a very cool animation.

Instead of adding these effects all at once, you'll do them one-by-one so you can see how to build up a complex effect. You'll begin with the movement.

Effect 1: movement

First, add the following import at the top of **Breakable.m**:

```
#import "SKNode+SKTExtras.h"
```

This file contains handy functions that you will use in a moment. You'll also be using some functions from **SKTUtils.h** again, but since that's already included in **PestControl-Prefix.pch**, there's no need to import that here.

Replace smashBreakable with the following:

```
- (void)smashBreakable
{
  self.physicsBody = nil;
  self.texture = _broken;
  self.size = _broken.size;
  // 1
  SKSpriteNode *topNode = [SKSpriteNode
                           spriteNodeWithTexture:_flyAwayTexture];
  [self addChild:topNode];

  // 2
  SKAction *upAction = [SKAction moveByX:0.0f y:30.0f
                                duration:0.2];
  upAction.timingMode = SKActionTimingEaseOut;

  SKAction *downAction = [SKAction moveByX:0.0f y:-300.0f
                                  duration:0.8];
  downAction.timingMode = SKActionTimingEaseIn;

  // 3
  [topNode runAction:[SKAction sequence:
                      @[upAction, downAction,
                        [SKAction removeFromParent]]]];
}
```

The first part of this method is still largely the same as before, except now:

1. You add a new child node for the treetop image. This is the node that you're going to make fly off the screen.

2. You create two actions, the first one to move the sprite 30 points up in 0.2 seconds and the second to move the sprite 300 points down in 0.8 seconds.

3. This runs the above actions in sequence: first the treetop sprite flies slightly upward, so that it looks like it was pushed up by the hero, then it falls down the screen, and finally – after about one second – the code removes the sprite from the scene altogether. If you're no longer using a node, you can improve performance and save memory by removing it.

Run the game and smash through a tree to see what this looks like:

That already looks great, but you can take this even further by adding some horizontal movement to the treetop. Add the following lines to the bottom of smashBreakable:

```
CGFloat direction = RandomSign();
SKAction *horzAction = [SKAction moveByX:100.0f * direction
                                       y:0.0f duration:1.0];
[topNode runAction:horzAction];
```

The RandomSign() function randomly returns either 1 or -1. That's very handy for situations like this: a value of 1 means the treetop flies to the right (the positive x-direction) while -1 means it flies to the left (negative direction). As a result, this SKAction makes the treetop fly 100 points in a random horizontal direction.

Notice that you're running this as a separate action, so it's independent of the vertical movement that you added earlier. Sprite Kit combines the effects of these two different actions behind the scenes, making it look like the treetop flies in a neat curve.

Run the game to see it in action:

   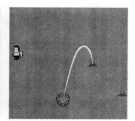

It's all about the timing:

If you look carefully at the `SKActions` in `smashBreakable`, you'll notice the following two lines:

```
upAction.timingMode = SKActionTimingEaseOut;

downAction.timingMode = SKActionTimingEaseIn;
```

Timing is arguably one of the most important aspects of the special effects that you're adding in this chapter. `SKAction` lets you choose one of four possible timing modes for your actions.

The default is `Linear` movement, which looks totally unrealistic. If you comment out the above two lines, then the treetop will appear to fly like this:

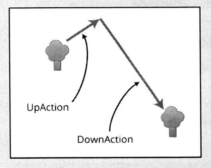

But by using `EaseOut` for the upward push and `EaseIn` for the downward phase, the flight path of the treetop becomes a lot more realistic:

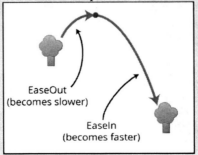

> Unfortunately, SKAction only lets you choose between these two timing modes. Later on in this chapter you will learn to do much crazier things with timing and unlock its full potential.

This concludes the first effect, movement. It looks pretty sweet by itself, but you've only used one trick from a full bag. When it comes to special effects, it's good to always ask yourself, "How far can I take this? What other fun stuff can I add?"

Effect 2: rotation

The movement effect was by far the most complicated because it combined two vertical stages – up and down – with a horizontal movement. Rotation is much simpler. Add the following lines to the bottom of smashBreakable:

```
SKAction *rotateAction = [SKAction rotateByAngle:
            -M_PI + RandomFloat()*M_PI*2.0f duration:1.0];
[topNode runAction:rotateAction];
```

This tells the treetop sprite to rotate by a random angle between -π and +π (-180 and +180 degrees) over the span of one second. You use the RandomFloat() function from **SKTUtils.h** to get a random number between 0.0 and 1.0.

That's all you have to do to make the treetop tumble as it falls. Run the app to try it out:

Effect 3: scaling

Messing with the scale of objects is equally simple but very effective. In fact, if you only add one of the five basic special effects to your game, add scaling – it goes a long way toward making your game super juicy!

Obviously in the real world, most objects don't become larger or smaller when you interact with them, but this is the virtual world and you can do as you please.

Add these lines to the bottom of `smashBreakable`:

```
topNode.xScale = topNode.yScale = 1.5f;

SKAction *scaleAction = [SKAction scaleTo:0.4f duration:1.0];
scaleAction.timingMode = SKActionTimingEaseOut;
[topNode runAction:scaleAction];
```

This first sets the scale of the treetop sprite to 150% so that it immediately becomes a lot bigger, then it slowly scales it down to only 40% of its original size as the treetop tumbles down the screen.

Run the app and smash some trees:

Feels nice, doesn't it?

Notice the use of the `timingMode` property here. `EaseOut` will make the sprite shrink quickly at first, but then it slows down the degree of scaling. This looked better to me than linear animation. Feel free to experiment with the other timing modes, `SKActionTimingLinear`, `SKActionTimingEaseIn`, and the combination of ease-in and ease-out, `SKActionTimingEaseInEaseOut`. The differences are subtle but noticeable.

Effect 4: alpha

The final effect you'll apply to the treetop is a simple fade out by modifying the alpha. For objects that need to disappear from the screen, it's always a good idea to apply a fade out to make the effect less jarring. Put these lines at the bottom of `smashBreakable`:

```
[topNode runAction:[SKAction sequence:@[
  [SKAction waitForDuration:0.6],
  [SKAction fadeOutWithDuration:0.4]]]];
```

This performs a fade out action after 0.6 seconds. Notice that all the effects you've added so far each last for 1.0 second. That's no coincidence! They all need to work together as a well-orchestrated whole, or the whole thing won't look as polished.

Run the app and watch those trees fade into oblivion:

How cool is that? Simply by adding a few of the five basic special effects to `smashBreakable`, you now have trees that are irresistible to smash! When I'm playing this game, I can't keep myself from running into those trees just to see them get chopped up.

Five effects to smash a wall

One of the most important interactions in the game is the "hero collides with wall" interaction. Currently, the player just bounces off the wall, but there is a ton of potential here for special effects.

Before you continue reading, I'd like you to make a list of the things you could do to the wall sprite, as well as to the player sprite, when they collide. Go ahead – give it a shot. Remember the five basic animations that you can apply to any node.

Ready? Good. Compare your list to the one I made below. I'm sure we have some effects in common. This is what I came up with:

1. **Scaling (the wall).** Scale the wall up and then down again. You can apply this trick to any of your nodes in any interaction and it will look good, so this is a no-brainer.

2. **Movement.** Move the wall in the direction of the collision with a bouncing animation. This is totally unrealistic, of course (unless the hero is Arnold), but it does reinforce the idea of the collision.

3. **Scaling (the player).** The wall isn't the only thing that should change. It takes two to tango, so the collision should also have some effect on the player. Squashing is scaling with different horizontal and vertical amounts, so that the player sprite will look flattened – which is exactly what happens to a cartoon character when it bumps into something.

4. **Scaling (other objects).** By putting a tiny scale effect on the actors that weren't directly involved in the collision, for example the bugs, you can strengthen the illusion that the player smacked into the wall.

5. **Texture.** When the player hits the wall, it would be cool to replace the wall's texture with an image of a cracked wall. Letting players deform the terrain of your games in fun and unexpected ways is an excellent opportunity to generate delight.

You will add the first three of these effects now, and then add the final two as challenges. By the time you're done, you will have experience using all five of the basic effects in Pest Control – many of them in several different ways. Let's get cracking!

Effect 1: scaling (the wall)

No, I'm not talking about climbing here! Instead, you will scale the size of the wall up and back down again.

Start by adding the following imports to **MyScene.m**. These files contain handy helper methods that make it a little easier to use nodes and actions:

```
#import "SKNode+SKTExtras.h"
#import "SKAction+SKTExtras.h"
```

To keep the code clean, you will put each special effect into its own method. Add this new method to MyScene:

```
- (void)scaleWall:(SKNode *)node
{
  node.xScale = node.yScale = 1.2f;

  SKAction *action = [SKAction scaleTo:1.0f duration:1.2];
```

```
    action.timingMode = SKActionTimingEaseOut;
    [node runAction:action withKey:@"scaling"];
}
```

You've seen this before. It sets the scale of the wall's sprite node to 120% and then scales it back down to 100% with an animation. You use ease-out to make the effect more natural.

You'll call `scaleWall:` from a new method named `wallHitEffects:`. Implement it as shown below:

```
- (void)wallHitEffects:(SKNode *)node
{
    // 1
    if (node.physicsBody.categoryBitMask & PCBoundaryCategory) {

        // TODO: you will add code here later

    } else {

        // 2
        [node skt_bringToFront];

        // 3
        [self scaleWall:node];
    }
}
```

Some notes on how this works:

1. There is a special situation that you need to deal with here. There is a special node that surrounds the game world with the physics category `PCBoundaryCategory`. This node is not represented by any sprite on the screen, so you only want to perform some of the animations on that node. Scaling it won't make any sense, for example.

2. You need to bring the wall sprite in front of any other nodes, so any animations do not (partially) hide it behind any of the other tiles on the background layer. **SKNode** does not have a "bring to front" method that lets you put a node in front of other nodes, so here you use a small helper method, `skt_bringToFront`, from the **SKNode+SKTExtras** category that you imported earlier.

3. You call `scaleWall:`. You'll be adding more effects here later.

Collisions are detected inside **MyScene.m** by the `didBeginContact:` method. Add this snippet to the bottom of that method:

```
else if (other.categoryBitMask &
        (PCBoundaryCategory | PCWallCategory |
         PCWaterCategory)) {
  [self wallHitEffects:other.node];
}
```

This simply adds another else-if clause that checks whether the collision was with the world boundary or a wall tile (or a water tile, which you'll treat the same for many of the effects) and then calls `wallHitEffects:`.

Run the app to see how it works.

Note that you can make the effect more pronounced by increasing the scale factor from 1.2 to some higher number. But be careful, too much scaling will destroy the illusion.

Interlude: tweening for pros

Before you add the rest of the effects to the wall, let's take a moment to improve what you already have through the power of something called **tweening**.

This scaling effect works, but to be honest it doesn't really give me shivers down my spine. The wall scales up and then neatly shrinks down again. Yawn... I want it to shake and crumble, like it's been hit by a bulldozer or an earthquake!

This is Arnold we're talking about here – have you seen his muscles? That wall needs to take some real damage!

 Arnold
SMASH
wall!!!

If you've used other gaming toolkits before, such as Cocos2d or Unity, then you may have come across so-called **tweening** or **easing** actions. These are special functions that alter the way time is perceived by the animation. The SKAction's timingMode is an example of that, but unfortunately it only supports the most basic of these timing functions.

Why limit yourself to plain ease-in and ease-out when you can choose from among so much more timing goodness? Here is a little preview:

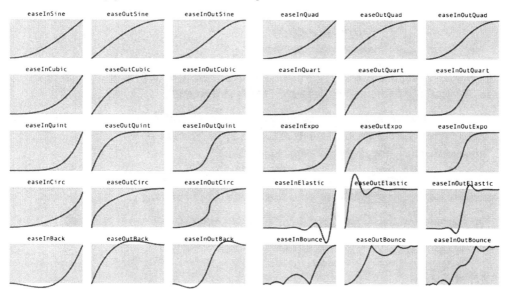

This is an overview of what are known as the Robert Penner easing equations. These are common in many other gaming and animation toolkits but alas, not in Sprite Kit.
(Image by Zeh Fernando from his open source project Tweener.)

Since Sprite Kit does not support anything but the most basic timing functions, you will have to use some tricks to get this working. The **Resources\Extra Source Code** folder you added in Chapter 13 contains some helper code to make this possible: **SKTEffects.h** and **.m**, and **SKTTimingFunctions.h** and **.m**. These source files contain a way for you to do complex tweening using Sprite Kit, even though Sprite Kit does not support this out-of-the-box.

Here's how these helper classes and methods work:

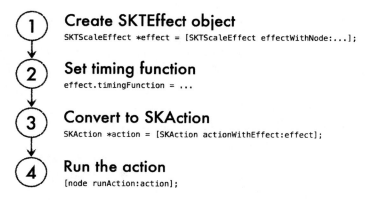

1. **Create an SKTEffect.** An SKTEffect is kind of like an action – for example, there is an SKTScaleEffect, an SKTRotateEffect, and so on.

2. **Set timing function.** SKTEffects allows you to set your own timing function (unlike SKAction). I have created a bunch of handy timing functions you can use, such as "bounce ease in", "smoothstep", and many more.

3. **Convert to action.** After you create an SKTEffect, you convert it into an action with a handy category on SKAction called actionWithEffect:.

4. **Run the action.** Once you have the SKAction, you can just run it as usual.

To use SKTEffects, first import it at the top of **MyScene.m**:

```
#import "SKTEffects.h"
```

Now replace scaleWall: with the following:

```
- (void)scaleWall:(SKNode *)node
{
    if ([node actionForKey:@"scaling"] == nil) {
```

```
// 1
CGPoint oldScale = CGPointMake(node.xScale, node.yScale);
CGPoint newScale = CGPointMultiplyScalar(oldScale, 1.2f);

// 2
SKTScaleEffect *scaleEffect =
  [SKTScaleEffect effectWithNode:node duration:1.2
                       startScale:newScale
                         endScale:oldScale];

// 3
scaleEffect.timingFunction = SKTCreateShakeFunction(4);

// 4
SKAction *action = [SKAction actionWithEffect:scaleEffect];

// 5
[node runAction:action withKey:@"scaling"];
  }
}
```

Let's take this step-by-step:

1. Calculate a new scale but also remember the old scale. The SKTEffects code uses a `CGPoint` object to describe the scale, unlike Sprite Kit itself, which uses two separate float variables, `xScale` and `yScale`. The new scale is 120% larger than the old scale, thanks to the `CGPointMultiplyScalar()` function that simply multiplies the x and y fields of the `CGPoint` with 1.2.

2. Create a new `SKTScaleEffect` that describes the scaling operation. You need to pass in a reference to the affected node, a duration in seconds, and the starting and ending values for the scale size, respectively.

3. This is where the magic happens. `SKTCreateShakeFunction()` creates a fancy timing function that simulates a shaking effect. More about this in a minute.

4. You cannot apply an `SKTScaleEffect` object directly to a node, so you need to wrap it in an `SKAction`. The `actionWithEffect:` method comes from a category that is provided by SKTEffects; it is not a standard `SKAction` method.

5. You give the action the key name "scaling" when you add it to the node. If there is already one of these effects active on the node – which might happen if the player bumps into the wall twice in a row – then you don't want to start another animation.

Run the app to see how this works.

Wow, that's pretty sweet. The wall not only scales up but now as it scales down, its size bounces a few times.

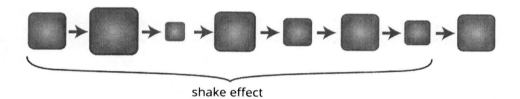

shake effect

To see this better, change the scale factor from 1.2 to 3.0:

```
CGPoint newScale = CGPointMultiplyScalar(oldScale, 3.0f);
```

You may notice a strange black effect – don't worry about that now, we'll discuss it in a bit.

Also feel free to play with the parameter to SKTCreateShakeFunction(). That value represents the number of oscillations in the animation. If you set it to 1, then the animation is very similar to the basic ease-out that you've seen before. But if you set it larger, for example to 10, then wowza! The wall will bounce up and down 10 times.

```
scaleEffect.timingFunction = SKTCreateShakeFunction(10);
```

Run the game to try it out. Also, you may want to increase the duration of the animation to something like 3 seconds or more so you can see the shake motion a bit better.

This is not your grandmother's ease-out; this is mayhem!

Welcome to the power of timing functions. SKTScaleEffect does the same thing as a regular SKAction for scaling – it simply animates the node's xScale and yScale properties – except that it lets you change the timing of the animation using one of these timing functions. While the start and end values of the animation are the same as before, what happens in the meantime is totally determined by the timing function – and this can be as wild as you can imagine it.

Note that SKTEffects contains many other types of timing functions beyond just the shake function. You'll be using some of the others in this chapter and the next, but you're encouraged to look through SKTTimingFunctions.h and experiment on your own as well.

There's one ugly thing here: you can see a black gap behind the wall tile when it's scaled down because there is now nothing drawn in the background.

The black background color of the scene is showing through. This is easily fixed. Add the following line to initWithSize:level:, just after the line that sets the _gameState:

```
self.backgroundColor = SKColorWithRGB(89, 133, 39);
```

This makes the background color of the scene green instead of black, so the gap won't be so noticeable.

Now set the scale factor, duration and number of oscillations back to their old values in scaleWall:. Those are: 1.2f for scale, 1.2 seconds for duration, and 4 for the shakiness.

Try it out:

Effect 2: movement

There is still more you can do to the wall. Don't worry, it can take the abuse. In addition to tinting and scaling the wall, you can also temporarily move it out of the way, as if Arnold actually managed to push it aside during the collision. The combination of these three effects will make for a very convincing collision animation!

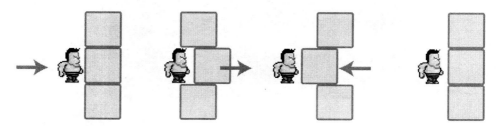

This brings up an interesting question, though: the wall needs to move in the direction of the player's movement against the wall. In other words, if the player hits the wall from above, the wall needs to move downward. Conversely, a collision with the bottom of the wall needs to send the wall moving up. So you need a way to determine: which side of the wall did the player hit?

First, add an enum type that can describe these sides to the top of **MyScene.m** near the other `typedef`:

```
typedef NS_ENUM(NSInteger, Side)
```

```
{
  SideRight = 0,
  SideLeft = 2,
  SideTop = 1,
  SideBottom = 3,
};
```

This is seen from the perspective of the player, so `SideRight` describes a collision on the player's right side.

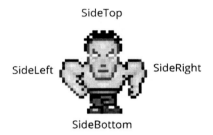

Add the following method:

```
- (Side)sideForCollisionWithNode:(SKNode *)node
{
  CGPoint diff = CGPointSubtract(node.position,
                                         _player.position);
  CGFloat angle = CGPointToAngle(diff);

  if (angle > -M_PI_4 && angle <= M_PI_4) {
    return SideRight;
  } else if (angle > M_PI_4 && angle <= 3.0f * M_PI_4) {
    return SideTop;
  } else if (angle <= -M_PI_4 && angle > -3.0f * M_PI_4) {
    return SideBottom;
  } else {
    return SideLeft;
  }
}
```

This determines the angle between the player sprite and another node (in this case the one it collided with) and then uses that angle to determine which side the collision was on. Remember that angles in Sprite Kit are always in radians, so you'll have to do some mental math to make the conversion. `M_PI_4` is a built-in constant that contains the value of $\pi/4$, which is the same as 45 degrees.

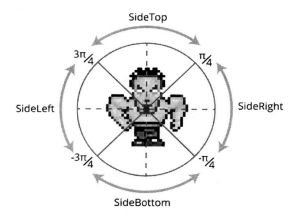

Now add this new method that will move a node appropriately based on a **Side** value:

```objc
- (void)moveWall:(SKNode *)node onSide:(Side)side
{
  if ([node actionForKey:@"moving"] == nil) {

    // 1
    static CGPoint offsets[] = {
      {  4.0f,  0.0f },
      {  0.0f,  4.0f },
      { -4.0f,  0.0f },
      {  0.0f, -4.0f },
    };

    // 2
    CGPoint oldPosition = node.position;
    CGPoint offset = offsets[side];
    CGPoint newPosition = CGPointAdd(node.position, offset);

    // 3
    SKTMoveEffect *moveEffect = [SKTMoveEffect
            effectWithNode:node duration:0.6
            startPosition:newPosition endPosition:oldPosition];

    // 4
    moveEffect.timingFunction = SKTTimingFunctionBackEaseOut;

    // 5
    SKAction *action = [SKAction actionWithEffect:moveEffect];
    [node runAction:action withKey:@"moving"];
  }
}
```

This is similar to the `scaleWall:` method you've just seen, except that now you're using an `SKTMoveEffect` instead of an `SKTScaleEffect`.

1. The `offsets` array is a so-called **look-up table**. It describes how much you will add to the wall's current position. There is one entry in the array for each possible side. So if `side` is `SideRight`, which has value 0, then the first offset from the look-up table is used (4.0, 0.0). In other words, it shifts the wall 4 points to the right. Likewise for the other sides.

2. You find the offset for the current side and add it to the wall node's current position to obtain the new position.

3. You create an `SKTMoveEffect` for the wall node. It will immediately place the wall on its new position, 4 points shifted towards the direction of the collision's impact, and then move it back to its original position over the span of 0.6 seconds.

4. You set the timing function for the animation. Unlike the scaling effect, this does not use the shake timing but something called **back ease-out**. It's a subtle effect that makes the node overshoot its target a little bit.

5. You create an `SKAction` for this effect and add it under the name "moving". You do this so that only one movement action at a time can be active on the wall node.

Now all that's left to do is find the direction of collision and call `moveWall:onSide:`. Add the following line at the top of `wallHitEffects:`.

```
Side side = [self sideForCollisionWithNode:node];
```

This determines which side of the player had the collision.

Then add the following line in `wallHitEffects:`, just after the call to `scaleWall::`

```
[self moveWall:node onSide:side];
```

This tells the wall node to move out of the way.

That should do the trick. Run the game and watch those walls bounce:

Now running into a wall is most definitely fun. Notice that these same effects also apply to the water tiles. It's a totally different sprite, but the animations don't care what the sprite looks like. Give them an SKNode and they will happily twist and pull it out of shape.

> **Note:** There are now two effects on the wall that by themselves are pretty simple – just scale and movement. These effects work together, though, to make bumping into the wall look very cool. To study each effect in detail, comment out the others and play with the various parameters. Maybe you like the scaling effect better if it's longer or shorter, or maybe the wall should move a bit further when it gets pushed. Experimentation is the name of the game!

Effect 3: scaling (the player)

There's one more effect for you to try before we set you loose on your own – and it has to do with cartoons.

I'm sure you watched cartoons when you were a kid (maybe you still do!). Remember how cartoons tend to exaggerate movement? This is actually a scale effect – but one where the x-scale is more or less than the y-scale.

The technical term for this is **squash and stretch**, and it's considered one of the basic principles of animation. Without it, moving objects seem stiff and lifeless.

This is what Arnold would look like if he jumped from a tall building, with squash and stretch applied:

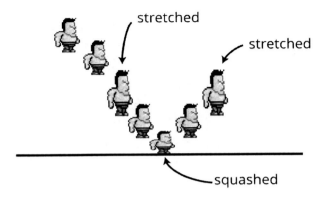

Squash happens when an object collides with something; *stretch* happens when an object accelerates. In this section, you will add both to the most important actor in this game: Arnold.

First the stretch

Right now, when you tap in the game world, the hero simply changes direction and runs towards where you tapped. This is a prime place for adding some juice.

Add the following methods to the bottom of **MyScene.m**:

```
- (void)tapEffectsForTouch:(UITouch *)touch
{
  [self stretchPlayerWhenMoved];
}

- (void)stretchPlayerWhenMoved
{
  CGPoint oldScale = CGPointMake(_player.xScale,
                                 _player.yScale);
  CGPoint newScale = CGPointMultiplyScalar(oldScale, 1.4f);

  SKTScaleEffect *scaleEffect =
    [SKTScaleEffect effectWithNode:_player duration:0.2
                        startScale:newScale endScale:oldScale];

  scaleEffect.timingFunction = SKTTimingFunctionSmoothstep;

  [_player runAction:[SKAction actionWithEffect:scaleEffect]];
}
```

`tapEffectsForTouch:` is where you will add all the effects that happen when the player taps the screen. Right now there is only one effect but in the next chapter you'll add several others – juicy games are about adding as many effects as you can get away with!

The real work happens in `stretchPlayerWhenMoved`. There shouldn't be any surprises for you here. The `SKTScaleEffect` scales the player up and then down again. The only new thing is `SKTTimingFunctionSmoothStep`, which is a special version of ease-in/ease-out. I liked the way that looked for this effect.

You need to call `tapEffectsForTouch:` when a tap happens, which is in `touchesBegan:withEvent:`. Add the following line to the `PCGameStatePlaying` case statement, just before you call `moveToward:` on `_player`:

```
[self tapEffectsForTouch:touch];
```

Run the app and now Arnold should briefly scale up whenever you tap the screen:

Simply scaling up the player sprite for a bit makes Arnold seem more alive.

Note: Granted, this isn't really a stretch. The player sprite simply expands by the same amount in all directions. If this were a true stretch, the sprite would only scale up along its axis of acceleration. However, in this game the player doesn't ever accelerate – the dude is already running all the time! For this particular game, it's easier to uniformly scale up the sprite for a fraction of a second. You have to admit that it still looks good even though it's only a basic scaling effect. What just a few lines of code can do to polish your game!

Then the squash

Exaggeration is the secret to convincing cartoon animation, but it also works well in video games. When the player collides with a wall, you're going to squash his sprite to drive home the idea that there was a collision:

Add the following method to **MyScene.m**:

```
- (void)squashPlayerForSide:(Side)side
{
  if ([_player actionForKey:@"squash"] != nil) {
    return;
  }

  CGPoint oldScale = CGPointMake(_player.xScale,
                                 _player.yScale);
  CGPoint newScale = oldScale;

  const float ScaleFactor = 1.6f;

  if (side == SideTop || side == SideBottom) {
    newScale.x *= ScaleFactor;
    newScale.y /= ScaleFactor;
  } else {
    newScale.x /= ScaleFactor;
    newScale.y *= ScaleFactor;
  }

  SKTScaleEffect *scaleEffect = [SKTScaleEffect
                    effectWithNode:_player duration:0.2
                    startScale:newScale endScale:oldScale];

  scaleEffect.timingFunction =
                      SKTTimingFunctionQuadraticEaseOut;

  [_player runAction:[SKAction actionWithEffect:scaleEffect]
          withKey:@"squash"];
}
```

By now, you should be getting familiar with this sort of thing. First you calculate the starting and ending values, then you create the SKTScaleEffect, set a timing function, and finally run the action. The only new thing here is the method of calculating the amount of squash, which depends upon which side of the player sprite hit the wall.

It's important with these squashing and stretching effects that, no matter how much you scale the object, the total volume of the object appears to remain the same. That means if you're scaling the sprite up in the vertical direction, then you need to scale it down in the horizontal direction to compensate:

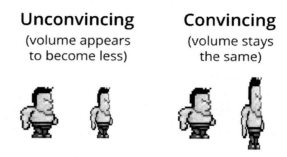

Unconvincing
(volume appears
to become less)

Convincing
(volume stays
the same)

Call this new method at the top of wallHitEffects:, just after you set the side value:

```
[self squashPlayerForSide:side];
```

This applies the squashing effect not only for the wall and water tiles, but also for the edges of the screen.

Try it out!

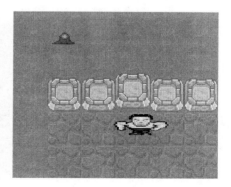

You may have noticed something odd at the edges of the screen. When you bump into a screen edge, the player sprite seems to squash the wrong way around. That's because `sideForCollisionWithNode:` calculates the angle between the player sprite and the node it collided with, by first subtracting their positions and then some trigonometry.

But the screen edge is represented by a special node, named "worldBounds", that is as big as the entire world. The position of this special node is in the center of the world layer because this node is really big. The calculations in `sideForCollisionWithNode:` don't make any sense for this world-bounds node, so you'll have to fix this method to make an exception. Modify the method as follows:

```
- (Side)sideForCollisionWithNode:(SKNode *)node
{
  // Did the player hit the screen bounds?
  if (node.physicsBody.categoryBitMask & PCBoundaryCategory) {

    if (_player.position.x < 20.0f) {
      return SideLeft;
    } else if (_player.position.y < 20.0f) {
      return SideBottom;
    } else if (_player.position.x > self.size.width - 20.0f) {
      return SideRight;
    } else {
      return SideTop;
    }
  } else {  // The player hit a regular node

    // put original contents of this method here
  }
}
```

Run the game again and verify that bumping into the screen edges now gives you the right kind of squash. And not butternut squash, either. I told you the scaling effect was good for a lot of stuff!

At this point you've used 3 out of the 5 special effects to juice up smashing a wall. The remaining two will be challenges for you!

Challenges

There are three challenges in this chapter. The first two challenges are about adding the remaining two basic special effects to the "hero interacts with wall" interaction. Don't worry – you'll get step-by-step hints along the way as usual.

The final challenge is a bit more difficult, so it's optional. Your goal will be to juice up the "hero interacts with bug" interaction using your own creativity, and using what you've learned in this chapter. I won't provide you detailed hints for this one, since your ideas and solution may be different than mine!

As always, if you get stuck you can find the solutions in the resources for this chapter – but give it your best shot first!

Challenge 1: Scaling (other objects)

The next special effect to add to your "hero interacts with wall" interaction is movement for objects other than the wall itself.

Imagine if you were to slam yourself into the wall of your room right now – don't actually do this though! If you were to hit it hard enough, then I'm sure other items in your room would shake from the impact. If you were Arnold, the whole house would tremble!

Your challenge is to make all of the bugs on the screen shake like jelly when the hero collides with the wall. You'll be using the scale effect, since it will give the illusion of them bouncing up and then down. Here are some hints on how to accomplish this:

- Add a new method to **MyScene.m** called `bugJelly` that takes no parameters. It should enumerate through all of the child nodes in `_bugLayer` that have the name "bug". For each of these, it should scale the bug from 1.2 to 1.0.

- You should use the helper class `SKTScaleEffect` and `SKAction` category method `actionWithEffect` to accomplish this, since that will allow you to use a custom timing function. I suggest using the "elastic ease out" timing function.

- Call this method from the bottom of `wallHitEffects:` (outside of the if/else statement so that it applies when the Arnold hits the edges of the screen, not just when he hits a wall).

When you're done, run the game and slam into some walls. You should see the bugs quiver whenever there's a collision:

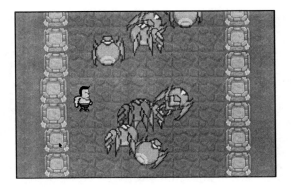

The effect is subtle – as it should be – but if you want to make it more extreme, then feel free to try the following:

- Set the start scale to 1.5
- Set the duration to 3.0
- Set the timing function for a slightly bouncier result:

```
scaleEffect.timingFunction = SKTTimingFunctionBounceEaseOut;
```

Challenge 2: Texture

One very effective way to make your games more delightful is to let the player deform the terrain. That's already what happens with the trees and you've seen how much fun it is to kick them over even though it has no real bearing on the gameplay mechanics. Such effects make it even more obvious to the player that they are really interacting with the game world.

Your challenge is to add the last of the five basic types of effects that you can apply to a Sprite Kit node: changing the texture of a sprite. When the player bumps into a wall, you will temporarily replace the wall image with a cracked version. After a couple of seconds, you'll put the original image back.

Here are some hints on how to accomplish this:

- Add a new method to **MyScene.m** called crackWall: that takes a SKSpriteNode as a parameter.

- Check if the physics body for the node has PCWallCategory in its bitmask.

- If it does, run an action to switch the node's texture to "wall-cracked", then back to "wall" after 2.0 seconds. These textures come from the _bgLayer's atlas.

- You may find it useful to use an `animateWithTexture:timePerFrame:` action to do this.

- You may find it useful to add this method to **TileMapLayer.m** (and expose it in **TileMapLayer.h**):

```
- (SKTexture *)textureNamed:(NSString *)name
{
  return [_atlas textureNamed:name];
}
```

- Call the new `crackWall:` method from `wallHitEffects:`, just after the call to `moveWall::`

```
[self crackWall:(SKSpriteNode *)node];
```

OK, now run the app and crack some walls with your thick skull, Arnold:

I bet now that you see those cracks, you're starting to wish you can bust straight through the walls! Don't worry, you'll get a "crack" at that in the challenges for the next chapter! ☺

Challenge 3: Crush those bugs! [Optional]

So far, you have added special effects to the "hero interacts with wall" interaction, and the "hero interacts with tree" interaction. However, there is still one major interaction that has escaped your attention so far: "hero interacts with bug!"

When you collide with a bug it simply disappears (or gets kicked, in the case of a fire bug), which is a bit of a letdown. You want to feel good about getting rid of this pest!

This is an optional challenge for the most hardcore developers. Your goal is to use the knowledge you have learned so far in this book to add some "juice" to the "hero interacts with bug" and "hero interacts with fire bug" interactions.

To get started, add a method to **MyScene.m** that looks like this:

```
- (void)bugHitEffects:(SKSpriteNode *)bug
{
  // 1
  bug.physicsBody = nil;
  [bug removeAllActions];

  // 2
  SKNode *newNode = [SKNode node];
  [_bugLayer addChild:newNode];
  newNode.position = bug.position;
  bug.position = CGPointZero;
  [bug removeFromParent];
  [newNode addChild:bug];

  // 3
  const NSTimeInterval Duration = 1.3;
  [newNode runAction:
          [SKAction skt_removeFromParentAfterDelay:Duration]];

    // 4: Create and run special effects here!
}
```

This method is intended to be called after a collision between the player sprite and a normal orange bug. Step-by-step, this is what it does:

1. Since the bug sprite is now dead, it should no longer take part in any of the collision detection. To that end, you set its physicsBody property to nil. You also remove all the actions so the bug stops moving.

2. This is a workaround for a problem that I noticed with Sprite Kit. Sometimes when you have multiple actions running on a sprite that combine rotating with scaling, the sprite becomes distorted. This is fixed by creating a new **SKNode** and putting it at the position of the bug sprite. You add the original bug sprite back, but as a child node of this new node. Then you perform all the animations on the new node instead.

3. It is useful to declare a constant for the duration of the animation. Often you want to tweak these times and by having just a single constant to modify you can save yourself some work. All the animation effects that follow will use this same Duration value.

You also start a new action here that removes the bug sprite from the scene after 1.3 seconds.

4. You will add some more code here to perform special effects on the bug. You might want to pull each special effect into a helper method to keep your code nice and clean.

You need to call bugHitEffects: from somewhere. The obvious place is from the method didBeginContact:, also in **MyScene.m**, which handles all the collisions. The following line is currently inside that method's first if statement:

```
[other.node removeFromParent];
```

Replace that line with:

```
[self bugHitEffects:(SKSpriteNode *)other.node];
```

Now it's time for you to fill up bugHitEffects: with special effects - this is where your creativity comes into play!

Remember the five basic special effects you have learned about in this chapter:

1. **Movement** changes a node's position.

2. **Scaling** changes a node's size.

3. **Rotation** changes a node's angle.

4. **Alpha** changes a node's translucency.

5. **Texture** changes to a sprite node's image.

How could these be useful when the hero interacts with the bugs?

Come up with your own ideas and try them out – make it as cool as you can, and don't forget the fire bugs! After you're done, you can check out the solutions to this chapter to see what I came up with.

One final hint for inspiration, in the form of a picture:

 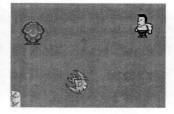 

Have fun, and make it juicy!

Chapter 18: Juice Up Your Game, Part 2

By Matthijs Hollemans

In the previous chapter, you learned that the secret to making a game juicy is to add as many special effects as you can get away with on each interaction. You then learned about 5 basic special effects and applied them to your game to make chopping trees, smashing walls, and squashing bugs super juicy.

In this chapter, you will add a whole set of new tricks to your repertoire. Specifically, you will learn 8 new types of special effects:

1. Tinting: Color nodes differently to indicate status effects.

2. Flashing: Make nodes flash quickly to draw the player's attention.

3. Screen Shake: Make the entire screen shake to (literally) make an impact!

4. Screen Zoom: Or to really wow your audience, give your players a double take.

5. Color Glitch: Make the screen flash to indicate something really shocking.

6. Particle Effects: A game can never have enough particles – learn why!

7. Shape Effects: Use shapes for quick but effective indicators and effects.

8. Sound Effects: Last but not least, sound can make a huge difference – especially when applied with fun in mind!

By the time you are done with this chapter, you will have a huge set of tools in your arsenal, and you will be ready to apply these in your own games to take them to the next level. Let's get started!

> **Note:** This chapter begins where Challenge 3 left off in the last chapter. If you were unable to complete the challenges or skipped ahead from a previous chapter, don't worry – you can simply open **PestControl-Starter** from the resources for this chapter to pick up where we left off.

Custom timing functions

Before you begin learning the new special effects, I wanted to show you a little more about the cool things you can do with timing functions.

As an example, let's take the "hero interacts with bug" case that you were working with in Challenge 3 in the previous chapter. It would be fun to make the dead bug bounce up and down a few times in addition to the other animations. Something like this:

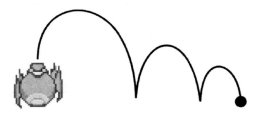

Given what you've seen in this chapter and the last, how would you go ahead and program this sort of effect? The naïve way would be to make a sequence of SKActions that move the bug up and down several times, using ease-out and ease-in to make it look like smooth curves. That is certainly possible but it's also a lot of work. Adding special effects is fun but you're looking for quick gains with little effort here. If it takes you days to program a special effect, it may not be worth the trouble.

So instead of a sequence of movement animations, you're just going to have a single movement action. The bouncing will be achieved through using a timing function.

As you learned in the previous chapter, Sprite Kit only comes with some basic timing functions by default, and has no built-in way to create your own timing functions. However, I created some helper classes for you that make it possible to do this: SKEffects and SKTimingFunctions.

In the last chapter, you used these helper classes to apply a "shake" timing function when Arnold crashes into a wall, and an "elastic ease in/out" when making the bugs shake like jelly. This time, rather than using these pre-created timing functions, you will learn how to create a custom timing function of your own.

Here is all the code you need. Add it to the bottom of **MyScene.m**:

```objc
- (void)bounceBug:(SKNode *)node
        duration:(NSTimeInterval)duration
{
  CGPoint oldPosition = node.position;
  CGPoint upPosition = CGPointAdd(oldPosition,
                              CGPointMake(0.0f, 80.0f));

  SKTMoveEffect *upEffect =
    [SKTMoveEffect effectWithNode:node duration:1.2
                   startPosition:oldPosition
                     endPosition:upPosition];

  upEffect.timingFunction = ^(float t) {
    return powf(2.0f, -3.0f * t) * fabsf(sinf(t * M_PI * 3.0f));
  };

  SKAction *upAction = [SKAction actionWithEffect:upEffect];
  [node runAction:upAction];
}
```

As you can see, defining a timing function to create a bounce effect only takes one line of code.

But how does it work? The timing functions used by SKTEffects are in the form of an Objective-C block that takes a float parameter *t* that represents the normal animation time (a value from 0 to 1). The block returns a new float with the modified time value.

First, you use an SKTMoveEffect to move the bug between its current position and 80 points higher. The exact shape of that movement is determined by the timing function. With a linear timing function, the sprite would simply slide from the start position to the end position, but here it's a little more involved.

The formula for the bouncing timing function is:

$$t_{new} = 2^{-3t} \cdot abs(sin(t \cdot 3\pi))$$

If your math is a little rusty it will help to plot this using the Grapher app. In Finder, go to **Applications/Utilities** and launch **Grapher**. Choose **2D Graph**, **Default** as the template.

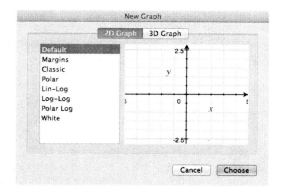

Type the following formula and then press return to plot it:

$$y = sin(x * pi * 3)$$

This gives you a basic sine wave. Because this is a timing function, the only region that is important is between $x = 0$ and $x = 1$, so zoom in on that:

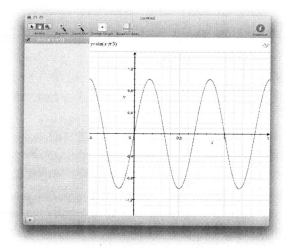

Click the + button in the bottom of the window and choose **New Equation** from the popup menu. This lets you enter a second equation that gets plotted on top of the first, so you can easily see the difference.

Enter:

$$y = abs(sin(x * pi * 3))$$

This takes the absolute value of the sine wave, flipping the negative part to make it positive. This already looks like a basic bouncing motion:

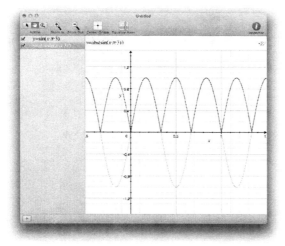

However, the amount of bouncing should diminish over time, just like it would for a bouncing ball. You can make that happen by multiplying the sine wave by something else. In this case, that something else will be an exponent. Add a new equation and enter:

$$y = 2\wedge\text{-}3x$$

Typing the caret symbol creates the exponent. The plot now looks like this:

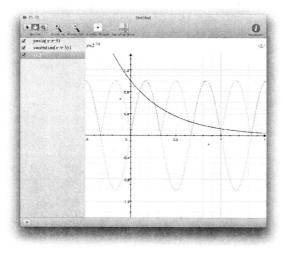

You can see that this creates a curve that grows smaller over time. To apply that to the sine wave, you just multiply the two formulas. Add a new equation and type:

$$y = 2\hat{}\,\text{-}3x * abs(sin(x * pi * 3))$$

(Make sure you press the down arrow key after **−3x** to move out of the exponent part.)

And there you go, a bouncing motion that slowly gets smaller:

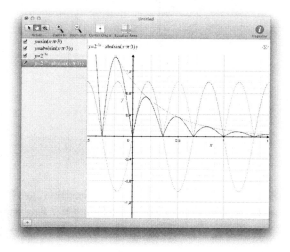

All that is left is calling the new **bounceBug:duration:** method from the bottom of **bugHitEffects:**. This method comes from Challenge 3 in the last chapter, so if you skipped please use the starter project for this chapter.

Add this line to the bottom of **bugHitEffects:**:

```
[self bounceBug:newNode duration:Duration];
```

And you're ready to bounce. Run the game to try it out!

Feel free to experiment with the timing function. For example, to add more bounces, change the 3 inside the *sin()* to a larger number.

Tinting

It's time for a new type of effect – tinting!

As you learned in the challenge for Chapter 4, "Actions", you can set the color of a sprite to something other than the default value (white). This is called tinting, and the way it works is that Sprite Kit multiplies the color value of each of the sprite's pixels with a tint color.

This one is so simple it doesn't even require a method of its own. Just add these two lines to the bottom of `bugHitEffects`:

```
bug.color = SKColorWithRGB(128, 128, 128);
bug.colorBlendFactor = 1.0f;
```

This blends the texture of the bug sprite with a medium gray color to make it darker. There's no need to make this an animation, just set the new color and you're done.

It's useful to change the color of the dead bugs because that makes it clearer that these sprites are no longer participating in the game. Besides, it looks cool.

See for yourself:

It's pretty obvious which of these bugs just got whacked.

> **Note:** Because the tint color is *multiplied* by the original color to get the final result, if you set the color of a sprite to blue the end result won't necessarily be blue — it depends on what the original color is.
>
> Because of this, if you want to dynamically set a sprite's color to a specific color, it is convenient to make the source color of the sprite white (like the cat in Zombie Conga). If you want parts of your sprite to be different colors, you can also split your sprite into different parts, each of which you tint to a different color.
>
> For more information, see the Beat 'Em Up Game Starter Kit available at raywenderlich.com.

Flashing

Sprite Kit has a cool type of node called the `SKCropNode` that is very useful for making special effects. A crop node can have child nodes like any other node, but it doesn't just draw them on the screen. It first applies a mask to it. Only pixels that are also set in the mask get drawn.

That is an excellent way to make a flashing effect. When Arnold runs over them, you will turn the bugs completely white for a fraction of a second. Without a crop node you would have to make white versions of all the animation frames for all the bugs sprites, which adds a lot to the size of your texture atlas and is a bit of a pain. But with a crop node the flash effect is easy peasy.

This is the complete flashing code. Add it to **MyScene.m**:

```
- (void)flashBug:(SKNode *)node mask:(SKNode *)mask
{
  // 1
  SKCropNode *cropNode = [SKCropNode node];
  cropNode.maskNode = mask;

  // 2
  SKSpriteNode *whiteNode =
  [SKSpriteNode spriteNodeWithColor:SKColorWithRGB(255,255,255)
                               size:CGSizeMake(50, 50)];
  [cropNode addChild:whiteNode];

  // 3
  [cropNode runAction:
   [SKAction sequence:@[[SKAction fadeInWithDuration:0.05],
                        [SKAction fadeOutWithDuration:0.3]]]];

  [node addChild:cropNode];
}
```

This is what it does:

1. Create the **SKCropNode** and set its mask. The mask will be a copy of the bug sprite, as you will see momentarily.

2. Create a new sprite node that is completely white. In Sprite Kit, if you create an **SKSpriteNode** without a texture, it will become a rectangle with a solid color. That is handy for debugging, but it's also useful here. The white node is added as a child node to the crop node.

3. Quickly fade in the crop node and then fade it out again. This creates the flashing effect.

Call this new method from bugHitEffects:

```
SKNode *maskNode = [SKSpriteNode
                      spriteNodeWithTexture:bug.texture];
[self flashBug:newNode mask:maskNode];
```

Remember that newNode here refers to the SKNode that you are performing all the effects on and that bug is the original SKSpriteNode with the bug image. You create a copy of that bug image to use as the mask for the crop node.

Here is how it works: the white sprite gets masked by the bug image, leaving you with a bug that looks completely white.

Run the game and crush some bugs:

Any bugs you stomp will flash white, bounce up and down, and then fade to their darker tint color before they disappear completely.

Screen shake effects

It's time to introduce an eighth effect to your collection, one that is probably my favorite: the *screen shake*.

So far all the effects you have applied were to individual gameplay objects: the player sprite, the bugs, the wall sprites, and so on. But you can also consider the game world as a whole as an object that you can apply effects on. And the screen shake is an excellent example of that. As its name implies, the screen shake effect makes the whole screen shake up and down!

Given the nature of this game, where Arnold is running the whole time, the beauty of the screen shake is hard to appreciate. It works best with a screen that doesn't already move so much. So first you'll tweak the code a little just to see what the screen shake does, and after that you will add it into the game for real.

Just for testing out this screen shake effect, comment out the current `PCGameStatePlaying` case in `touchesBegan:withEvent:`, and temporarily replace it with the following:

```
case PCGameStatePlaying:
{
  CGPoint amount = CGPointMake(RandomFloat() * 20.0f,
                               RandomFloat() * 20.0f);

  SKAction *action =
    [SKAction skt_screenShakeWithNode:_worldNode amount:amount
                        oscillations:10 duration:3.0];

  [_worldNode runAction:action];
  return;
}
```

Any time you now tap the screen, it no longer makes Arnold move, but it performs a screen shake.

Try it out. How cool is that! Imagine the impact of this when you combine it with a wall collision. Not only does the wall sprite bounce up and down, the entire game world shakes at its foundations!

I encourage you to play with the parameters of this screen shake effect for a moment. See what happens when you increase or decrease the number of oscillations, or the duration of the animation. For example, try 20 oscillations and 2.0 seconds duration. Boinggg!

OK, if you're done playing then remove the above lines of code and uncomment out the original `PCGameStatePlaying` case so that Arnold is free to run once more.

> **Note:** If you're curious, the screen shake effect is implemented in **SKTEffects.m** in a category on `SKAction` that adds the method
> `skt_screenShakeWithNode:amount:oscillations:duration:`.
>
> Performing a screen shake is as easy as calling this method to create the action object and then running the action on the `_worldNode`. The actual code that performs the screen shake is surprisingly simple. You can see this for yourself in **SKTEffects.m** in the `SKAction (SKTEffects)` category:
>
> ```
> + (instancetype)skt_screenShakeWithNode:(SKNode *)node
>                                  amount:(CGPoint)amount
>                            oscillations:(int)oscillations
>                                duration:(NSTimeInterval)duration
> {
>   CGPoint oldPosition = node.position;
>   CGPoint newPosition = CGPointAdd(oldPosition, amount);
>
>   SKTMoveEffect *effect = [[SKTMoveEffect alloc]
>             initWithNode:node duration:duration
>           startPosition:newPosition endPosition:oldPosition];
>
>   effect.timingFunction = SKTCreateShakeFunction(oscillations);
>
>   return [SKAction actionWithEffect:effect];
> }
> ```
>
> This is all stuff you've seen before. It creates an `SKTMoveEffect` and then gives it a shake function for the timing. The main trick is that you apply this effect to the `_worldNode`, which contains all the other nodes in the game world, so all the game objects move up and down by the same amount, which makes it appear that the whole screen is shaking.

Player + wall

You will now run a screen shake when the player bumps into a wall. Add the following method to **MyScene.m**:

```
- (void)screenShakeForSide:(Side)side power:(CGFloat)power
```

```
{
  static CGPoint offsets[] = {
    {  1.0f,  0.0f },
    {  0.0f,  1.0f },
    { -1.0f,  0.0f },
    {  0.0f, -1.0f },
  };

  CGPoint amount = offsets[side];
  amount.x *= power;
  amount.y *= power;

  SKAction *action =
    [SKAction skt_screenShakeWithNode:_worldNode amount:amount
                      oscillations:3 duration:1.0];

  [_worldNode runAction:action];
}
```

Remember that when a player collides with a wall it is always on one side, which is represented by a value from the Side enum. This side determines the direction of the screen shake. If Arnold slams into a wall on his left, then the screen also shakes to the left. That will really make the force of the impact seem a lot bigger.

The power parameter determines how far you want the screen to shake. The number of oscillations is 3 (how many times the screen shakes up and down) and the duration is one second. You want this effect to be subtle. In this game the player is running all the time already so the screen is constantly in motion. You don't want to add a huge screen shake on top of that or you'll end up with players feeling seasick!

Change wallHitEffects: to make it shake. Replace the comment that reads, "TODO: you will add code here" with the following line:

```
[self screenShakeForSide:side power:20.0f];
```

Then add the following line to the else statement, just after the call to crackWall::

```
[self screenShakeForSide:side power:8.0f];
```

Note that this calls the screen shake method in two spots with different values for power, once for when Arnold hits a wall sprite and once for when he hits the edge of the screen. When the player bumps into the screen edge it's OK to make the shake more pronounced (the camera stops moving at the screen edges, so there is no motion in that direction anyway).

Give it a try! It's a bit hard to tell from a static screenshot but on the left you can see there is a gap between the background tiles and the edge of the screen. That's the screen shake in action (but trust me, it's much better when you run the app).

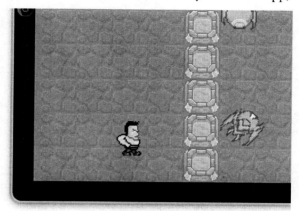

Notice how this screen shake effect, even though it's quite subtle, changes the whole feel of the game. It really does make it seem that Arnold is now slamming into these walls. You can almost feel it in your own body as you're playing. Ouch! Powerful stuff, this screen shake.

Player + bug

The screen shake feels so cool that I'm a little bummed out whenever my guy steps on a bug now. There is no visceral feedback from that. Whereas the wall collision offers real resistance, stepping on a bug doesn't. There's only one remedy: also add a screen shake on the bugs!

Add the following code to the bottom of `bugHitEffects`:

```
[_worldNode runAction:
    [SKAction skt_screenShakeWithNode:_worldNode
                              amount:CGPointMake(0.0f, -12.0f)
                        oscillations:3 duration:1.0]];
```

This creates a screen shake action that moves the screen up by the slightest amount, 12 points. That makes it feel like Arnold really has to stomp down hard on those bugs to squash them. I love this effect! As a player I'm no longer controlling pixels on a screen; I feel like I'm interacting with real objects in a real world. The game has come alive! It's just a delight to run over these bugs. If only pest control was this much fun in the real world. ☺

Screen zoom effects

So what about the firebugs, shall you add a screen shake there too? Nah, I've got something special in mind for that: *screen zoom*!

The screen shake effect applies the shaky timing to an SKTMoveEffect, but there is no reason you cannot do the same thing with a scale effect. That will really make it seem like running into firebugs is a bad idea!

Add the following line to fireBugHitEffects:

```
[_worldNode runAction:
  [SKAction skt_screenZoomWithNode:_worldNode
                        amount:CGPointMake(1.05f, 1.05f)
                    oscillations:6 duration:2.0]];
```

This applies only a little bit of scaling (105%) to the world node but you don't want to go too extreme with this effect anyway.

I dare you to run into a firebug now! Again, the screenshots don't do it justice. You have to see this to believe it.

With Screen Zoom   **Normal Size**

As a rule of thumb, any time you have a large impact in your games, consider using a screen shake effect, and if it's a *really* dramatic impact consider using a screen zoom effect.

> **Note:** The screen zoom code also lives in **SKTEffects.m** and is very similar to the screen shake, except that it uses an SKTScaleEffect instead of a move effect.

Color glitch effects

There is one more thing I'd like to add to firebug collisions and that is an effect known as the *color glitch*. It rapidly displays flashing colors for a fraction of a second, emulating color glitches that sometimes occurred in old arcade games.

This effect is a bit extreme so you should apply it with caution. You don't want to use it all the time or risk your players collapsing from seizures. Firebug collisions don't happen very often – or shouldn't! – so that's a reasonable place to add the color glitch.

The SKTEffects code comes with a handy method that runs a color glitch on an
SKScene. You run it on the scene because that has a backgroundColor property
(regular nodes don't). However, there is a small problem: the scene isn't visible in this
game because of the tile map. There are tiles everywhere. So in order to perform the
color glitch effect, you need to remove these background tiles in order to let the scene's
color show through.

Add the following method to **MyScene.m**:

```
- (void)colorGlitch
{
  // 1
  [_bgLayer enumerateChildNodesWithName:@"background"
                             usingBlock:
    ^(SKNode *node, BOOL *stop) {
      node.hidden = YES;
    }];

  [self runAction:[SKAction sequence:@[

    // 2
    [SKAction skt_colorGlitchWithScene:self
              originalColor:SKColorWithRGB(89, 133, 39)
              duration:0.1],

    // 3
    [SKAction runBlock:^{
      [_bgLayer enumerateChildNodesWithName:@"background"
            usingBlock:^(SKNode *node, BOOL *stop) {
                          node.hidden = NO;
                        }];
    }]]]];
}
```

This looks a little scary, but it's actually quite simple:

1. Look at all child nodes of the background layer with the name "background" and hide
   them. For this game, you will only remove unimportant tiles such as the grass and the
   trees, while the walls and water will remain visible.

2. Run the color glitch action. It only lasts for 0.1 seconds. When the action is done, it
   restores the scene's original background color.

3. After the color glitch action completes, look at the background nodes again and un-
   hide them. So the trees and grass only disappear for a moment while the color glitch is
   happening and then come back when it is over.

Call this new `colorGlitch` method from within `fireBugHitEffects`:

```
[self colorGlitch];
```

There is one more thing you need to do and that is telling the game which nodes are considered background nodes. Open **TileMapLayer.m** and go to the `nodeForCode:` method. Add the following line to both the `case '='` and `case 'o'` clauses, just after the lines creating the stone or grass tiles:

```
tile.name = @"background";
```

Also open **Breakable.m** and make sure that the `initWithWhole:broken:flyAway:` method contains the following line:

```
self.name = @"background";
```

Great, that should do the trick. Now whenever you bump into a firebug, the screen will flash with random colors:

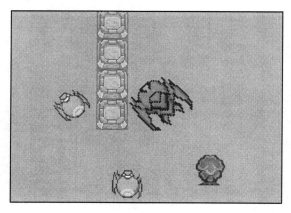

Particle effects

It's now time to introduce special effect number 11, and arguably one of the most powerful: particle effects!

There exists an unspoken rule among game developers everywhere that no game is considered complete unless it has particle effects. You can use particles to create effects such as explosions, fire, smoke, and flying debris, and they are great for juicing up your game. You simply can't have too many of them.

> **Note:** This chapter assumes you already have some experience with particle systems. If you're unsure exactly what particle systems are or how they work, then check out Chapter 7, "Particle Systems", which goes into great detail.

I have created some particle effects fro you for this chapter, and you already added them to your project.

As you have learned in Chapter 7, "Particle Systems", a particle effect consists of a texture image and a number of configuration parameters that determine how the individual particles propagate. The texture image is a PNG file and the parameters are stored in a **.sks** file (which stands for "Sprite Kit Something-or-other").

To put such a particle effect inside your game you use a special type of node, SKEmitterNode. This node reads the configuration from the SKS file and then starts emitting particles onto your scene.

Tree leaves

The sparks are a pretty decent effect already but you can do much more with particles. How about making the tree drop its leaves when you smash it? The effect for this is in **TreeSmash.sks** and it uses a leaf image (**Leaf.png**) as its texture. To see the particle effect, click on the SKS file in the project navigator:

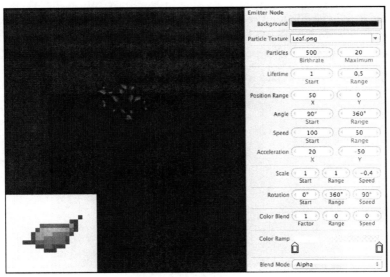

Open **Breakable.m**, which is the class that represents the trees, and add these new imports at the top:

```
#import "SKAction+SKTExtras.h"
#import "SKEmitterNode+SKTExtras.h"
```

You will recall from the previous chapter that the Breakable class has a method smashBreakable that gets called when the player fells a tree. Add the following lines to the bottom of that method:

```
SKEmitterNode *emitter =
  [SKEmitterNode skt_emitterNamed:@"TreeSmash"];

emitter.targetNode = self.parent;

[emitter runAction:
  [SKAction skt_removeFromParentAfterDelay:1.0]];

[self addChild:emitter];
```

The skt_emitterNamed: method comes from the **SKEmitterNode+SKTExtras** category and makes it a little easier to load particle systems from the app's bundle. This is a bit shorter than writing out all the NSKeyedUnarchiver stuff. Here it loads the **TreeSmash.sks** effect.

The emitter node runs for 1.0 seconds and then it is removed from the scene, so the particle effect is only visible for a second. It's a good idea to remove emitter nodes from the scene when you no longer need them, or eventually they will slow your game to crawl. (That advice goes for all types of nodes, by the way, not just particle emitters.)

Try it out. Now when you smack a tree, it sheds its leaves:

Sweet!

> **Note:** To keep the code shorter, this effect was hard-coded into **Breakable**. But **Breakable** is really meant to be a generic class that you could extend for multiple types of breakable objects. In a real app, you should either add an emitter parameter to the initializer, or subclass **Breakable** to put this logic in something like a **Tree** class.

Wall stones

If the trees can drop leaves, then there must also be something you can do about a collision with a wall... How about showing a short particle burst at the point of impact? The effect is **PlayerHitWall.sks** and it uses the **Rock.png** particle.

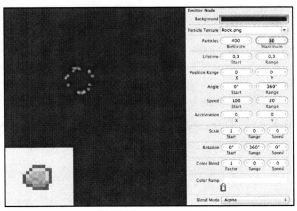

First import the emitter node helper into **MyScene.m**:

```
#import "SKEmitterNode+SKTExtras.h"
```

Then add the following method:

```
- (void)showParticlesForWall:(SKNode *)node onSide:(Side)side
{
  CGPoint position = _player.position;
  if (side == SideRight) {
    position.x = node.position.x - _bgLayer.tileSize.width/2.0f;
  } else if (side == SideLeft) {
    position.x = node.position.x + _bgLayer.tileSize.width/2.0f;
  } else if (side == SideTop) {
```

```
    position.y =
      node.position.y - _bgLayer.tileSize.height/2.0f;
  } else {
    position.y =
      node.position.y + _bgLayer.tileSize.height/2.0f;
  }

  SKEmitterNode *emitter =
    [SKEmitterNode skt_emitterNamed:@"PlayerHitWall"];
  emitter.position = position;

  [emitter runAction:
    [SKAction skt_removeFromParentAfterDelay:1.0]];
  [_bgLayer addChild:emitter];
}
```

Creating and running the emitter node is the same as before, but this method also needs to calculate exactly where to place the emitter. It should go on the side of the wall where the collision took place.

Please notice the `skt_removeFromParentAfterDelay:` near the end of the method. Due to the way this particle system is configured, the emitter's particles will appear on screen for less than a second but the emitter will continue to run for as long as it is parented to a node. So it's smart to remove the emitter when the effect is done.

Finally, call this new method from **wallHitEffects:**. Add it inside the else-clause, just below the call for the screen shake:

```
[self showParticlesForWall:node onSide:side];
```

Try it out. You should now see stones flying away from the wall at the point of impact:

Water drops

There is one odd thing, though. If you bump into a water tile, then you also get flying stones. It would make more sense if these were water drops instead.

The resources for this project don't have a new particle system for water collisions. Instead, they contain an alternative texture image. You can simply load the particle effect for the wall collision and replace its texture image to look like a water drop.

Add the following lines to the bottom of `showParticlesForWall:onSide:`

```
if (node.physicsBody.categoryBitMask & PCWaterCategory) {
  emitter.particleTexture =
  [SKTexture textureWithImageNamed:@"WaterDrop"];
}
```

After you have created the `SKEmitterNode` you can still change its properties. These lines simply assign a different texture image to the emitter.

And that should do it. Run the app and bump into a water tile. Instead of stone particles you should now see water drops:

It's the same particle effect but with a different image.

Motion trail

The game is shaping up nicely – it already feels a lot more polished than the bare game you started out with – but I do think Arnold could still be more awesome. After all, he is the hero of the game and heroes always have that little bit extra.

An easy trick is to give the player a motion trail, which shows you the path Arnold has been running along but it also gives the player the impression of going extra fast. You will use particles to make the motion trail. The project already includes a particle system named **PlayerTrail.sks** that draws stars.

Go to **Player.m** and import the helper category for particle emitters:

```
#import "SKEmitterNode+SKTExtras.h"
```

Also add a new instance variable for the emitter node:

```
SKEmitterNode *_emitter;
```

Because you're adding a new instance variable, you also need to update your archiving methods. Add the following two methods to **Player.m**:

```
- (instancetype)initWithCoder:(NSCoder *)aDecoder
{
  if (self = [super initWithCoder:aDecoder]) {
    _emitter = [aDecoder decodeObjectForKey:@"Player-Emitter"];
  }
  return self;
}

- (void)encodeWithCoder:(NSCoder *)aCoder
{
  [super encodeWithCoder:aCoder];
  [aCoder encodeObject:_emitter forKey:@"Player-Emitter"];
}
```

Also add the following method:

```
- (void)start
{
  _emitter = [SKEmitterNode skt_emitterNamed:@"PlayerTrail"];
  _emitter.targetNode = self.parent;
  [self addChild:_emitter];

  self.zPosition = 100.0f;
}
```

This creates the emitter and sets its `targetNode` to the player's parent, which is the world node. That way the emitter will follow the player wherever it goes, but the actual star particles stay put once they have been emitted, causing the trail effect.

It looks better if the player node is always drawn on top of the particles, which can be achieved by setting the node's `zPosition` property to 100. This makes sure the player is always drawn above everything else (all other nodes have the default `zPosition` of 0).

Go to **Player.h** and add the prototype for this new function so other classes can call it:

```
- (void)start;
```

Finally, go to **MyScene.m** and call this new method from `touchesBegan:withEvent:`, inside the `PCGameStateStartingLevel` case:

```
[_player start];
```

Run the game and you should see a big trail of stars following Arnold wherever he travels:

You may notice times when the particles do not seem to appear, but if you look closely, they are appearing right at Arnold's position and moving with him. This is a bug in Sprite Kit that occurs when the player sprite is flipped.

Particles are pretty easy to use and they add a lot of polish to your game, provided you use them properly. Feel free to tweak the configuration parameters for these effects in Xcode's particle editor. They can be a lot of fun to play with!

Public Safety Warning: There is a high risk that you may get carried away and waste of lot time playing with these particles. ☺

Shape effects

The 12th special effect that you can use in your games is shape effects.

Sometimes you might want to draw a simple shape to indicate an event in your game. As you learned in Chapter 11, "Crop, Video, and Shape Nodes", SKShapeNode is perfect for that!

There is one interaction that you have mostly ignored so far: the user tapping on the screen. Right now that just scales up Arnold for a brief moment, but he usually isn't anywhere near where the user tapped. So let's add a cool little animation to highlight the actual tap location.

Add the following method to **MyScene.m**:

```
- (void)showTapAtLocation:(CGPoint)point
{
  // 1
  UIBezierPath *path =
    [UIBezierPath bezierPathWithOvalInRect:
      CGRectMake(-3.0f, -3.0f, 6.0f, 6.0f)];

  // 2
  SKShapeNode *shapeNode = [SKShapeNode node];
  shapeNode.path = path.CGPath;
  shapeNode.position = point;
  shapeNode.strokeColor = SKColorWithRGBA(255, 255, 255, 196);
  shapeNode.lineWidth = 1;
  shapeNode.antialiased = NO;
  [_worldNode addChild:shapeNode];

  // 3
  const NSTimeInterval Duration = 0.6;

  SKAction *scaleAction = [SKAction scaleTo:6.0f
                                   duration:Duration];
  scaleAction.timingMode = SKActionTimingEaseOut;

  [shapeNode runAction:
    [SKAction sequence:@[scaleAction,
                [SKAction removeFromParent]]]];

  // 4
  SKAction *fadeAction =
    [SKAction fadeOutWithDuration:Duration];
  fadeAction.timingMode = SKActionTimingEaseOut;
```

```
    [shapeNode runAction:fadeAction];
}
```

Let's go through this step-by-step:

1. Create a `UIBezierPath` object that describes a circle with a 6-point diameter. The center of this circle will be placed at the tap position.

2. Create a new `SKShapeNode` with the Bézier path as its shape. Position this shape node at the tap location and add it to the `_worldNode`.

3. Define an action that scales up the shape node to 6 times its size, and then removes it from the scene again.

4. While the shape node is scaling up, also fade it out at the same time.

Call this new method at the end of `tapEffectsForTouch::`

```
[self showTapAtLocation:[touch locationInNode:_worldNode]];
```

Run the app and there should now be a small, animated circle anywhere you tap:

Sound effects

There's one final type of special effect to add to your bag of tricks: sound effects.

So far all the special effects you have dealt with have been visual effects, but sound is just as important. In fact, the quality of the sound effects can make or break your game. If your sound effects are annoying, then people will simply stop playing your game. But if they are amazing, then you've created an experience that people won't easily forget.

Creating compelling sound effects is a job for a good sound designer and is outside the scope of this chapter. Fortunately, playing those sound effects in the game is pretty easy, and in this section you will find out how.

The resources for your project already include a folder named **Sounds** with pre-made sound effects. Feel free to take a listen through to check them out.

It's important to preload your sound effects. Because they can take a while to load you don't want the game to freeze up in the heat of the action. To do this, add the following variable declarations to the top of **MyScene.m**, somewhere between the #import statements and the @implementation line:

```
static SKAction *HitWallSound;
static SKAction *HitWaterSound;
static SKAction *HitTreeSound;
static SKAction *HitFireBugSound;
static SKAction *PlayerMoveSound;
static SKAction *TickTockSound;
static SKAction *WinSound;
static SKAction *LoseSound;
static SKAction *KillBugSounds[12];
```

You will create these objects inside a special method called +initialize. Add this after the @implementation:

```
+ (void)initialize
{
  if ([self class] == [MyScene class]) {

    HitWallSound = [SKAction playSoundFileNamed:@"HitWall.mp3"
                               waitForCompletion:NO];
    HitWaterSound = [SKAction playSoundFileNamed:@"HitWater.mp3"
                               waitForCompletion:NO];
    HitTreeSound = [SKAction playSoundFileNamed:@"HitTree.mp3"
                               waitForCompletion:NO];
    HitFireBugSound =
      [SKAction playSoundFileNamed:@"HitFireBug.mp3"
                  waitForCompletion:NO];
    PlayerMoveSound =
      [SKAction playSoundFileNamed:@"PlayerMove.mp3"
                  waitForCompletion:NO];
    TickTockSound =
      [SKAction playSoundFileNamed:@"TickTock.mp3"
                  waitForCompletion:YES];
    WinSound = [SKAction playSoundFileNamed:@"Win.mp3"
                          waitForCompletion:NO];
    LoseSound = [SKAction playSoundFileNamed:@"Lose.mp3"
```

```
                         waitForCompletion:NO];
    for (int t = 0; t < 12; ++t) {
      KillBugSounds[t] =
        [SKAction playSoundFileNamed:
         [NSString stringWithFormat:@"KillBug-%d.mp3", t+1]
                 waitForCompletion:NO];
    }
  }
}
```

The initialize method is a so-called *class method* (because it has a + in front of its name instead of a –). It gets called just once, automatically, the very first time the app tries to use MyScene (even before any instances get allocated). Here you create the actions to play each sound effect so they're loaded in advance.

Unlike the other sounds, TickTockSound passes YES for its waitForCompletion argument. You'll learn why a bit later.

Now it's simply a matter of running these actions from the right places. Let's take them one-by-one.

Add the following lines to the bottom of wallHitEffects:

```
if (node.physicsBody.categoryBitMask & PCWaterCategory) {
  [self runAction:HitWaterSound];
} else {
  [self runAction:HitWallSound];
}
```

This plays the "wall hit" sound when the collision was with a wall tile or the "water hit" sound when it was a water tile.

Inside didBeginContact:, directly under the line that calls smashBreakable, add this:

```
[self runAction:HitTreeSound];
```

Add this line to the bottom of fireBugHitEffects:

```
[self runAction:HitFireBugSound];
```

And to the bottom of tapEffectsForTouch:

```
[_player runAction:PlayerMoveSound];
```

That takes care of the basic sound effects. Let's also add some funky music.

First import the `SKTAudio` class, which makes it easy to play background music:

```
#import "SKTAudio.h"
```

Add this line to the end of `initWithSize:level:` to start the music:

```
[[SKTAudio sharedInstance] playBackgroundMusic:@"Music.mp3"];
```

And finally, add these lines to the bottom of `endLevelWithSuccess:` to stop the music and play a sound effect based on whether you won or lost:

```
[[SKTAudio sharedInstance] pauseBackgroundMusic];
[self runAction:won ? WinSound : LoseSound];
```

Great, give that a try! When you run the app, you should hear a variety of sound effects.

> **Note:** If the app jumps into the debugger when you run it, then make sure you disable the Exception Breakpoint if you have it enabled. For some reason, loading the sound effects triggers an exception deep inside Sprite Kit.

Making combos

Almost every interaction has a sound effect now, except for crushing orange bugs. You are going to do something special here. Often games become more fun if you can score *combos*. For example, if you kill one bug and then another one really quickly after that, you score extra points. This game doesn't have a score counter, but you can still make use of combos for the special effects.

If you look at the sound files in the project you will see there is not just one "kill bug" sound but there are twelve, each one slightly higher in pitch than the one before. That will be the player's reward for making a combo: they get to hear a cool sound effect. The more bugs you kill in a short time, the higher the pitch rises.

To program this logic you need to add a couple new private instance variables to **MyScene.m**:

```
CFTimeInterval _lastComboTime;
int _comboCounter;
```

Add this bit of logic to the top of `bugHitEffects:`

```
CFTimeInterval now = CACurrentMediaTime();
```

```
if (now - _lastComboTime < 0.5f) {
  _comboCounter++;
} else {
  _comboCounter = 0;
}
_lastComboTime = now;
```

The `_lastComboTime` instance variable keeps track of the last time that the player crushed an orange bug. If the player crushes a new bug and it has been less than half a second since the last time, then this counts as a combo and the value of `_comboCounter` goes up. But if it has been longer than half a second, `_comboCounter` is reset to 0 again, which means no combo was made.

Add the following line to the bottom of `bugHitEffects`:

```
[newNode runAction:KillBugSounds[MIN(11, _comboCounter)]];
```

This plays the corresponding sound effect from the `KillBugSounds` array. If no combo was made, it picks the first sound effect (the lowest tone), but if `_comboCounter` is greater than 0 it picks one of the higher-pitched sounds. The `MIN()` macro makes sure the counter does not go over 11, which is the index of the highest sound. It won't happen often that a player kills 12 bugs in the span of half a second but a little defensive programming never hurt anyone.

> **Note:** You aren't archiving `_lastComboTime` and `_comboCounter`. Each time the app loads a save file, the combo count will reset. It's not so bad if combos reset when you pause the game.

Run the app and try to make some combos!

You're not limited to using the combo counter for just sound effects. You can also use it for other things, for example to increase the size of the bugs as they explode. The larger your combo, the bigger the sprites become.

In the `scaleBug:duration:` method, replace the line that sets the `ScaleFactor` with:

```
const CGFloat ScaleFactor = 1.5f + _comboCounter * 0.25f;
```

Now the scale factor is no longer fixed at 150% but it adds another 25% for every combo that you make.

Try it out:

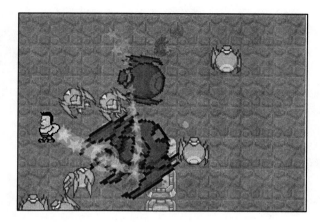

Scaling things up even more than usual is a great way to visualize combos.

Running out of time

This is a time-based game – you need to catch all the bugs before the clock reaches zero – but there currently is no feedback when your time is actually running out, other than the count on the clock. You can make things more exciting by adding a sound effect when the player gets dangerously low on time. You want to get the player's adrenaline pumping!

The project includes a sound effect that sounds like a ticking clock. You will play this sound effect when the user only has a few seconds left.

Add a new private instance variable to **MyScene.m**:

```
BOOL _tickTockPlaying;
```

In `update:` add the following code at the end of the last else-clause:

```
if (timeRemaining < 10 && timeRemaining > 0 &&
    !_tickTockPlaying) {
  _tickTockPlaying = YES;
  [self runAction:TickTockSound withKey:@"tickTock"];
}
```

This starts the tick-tock sound playing when there are only 10 seconds left in the game.

To test this, open the **JuicyLevels.plist** file and change the **timeLimit** field to something like 15 seconds, so you don't have to wait for several minutes before you hear this sound:

Key	Type	Value
▼ Root	Dictionary	(1 item)
▼ levels	Array	(1 item)
▼ Item 0	Dictionary	(2 items)
timeLimit	Number	15
▼ layers	Dictionary	(3 items)
background	String	juicy-level-bg.txt
breakables	String	juicy-level-breakables.txt
bugs	String	juicy-level-bugs.txt

PestControl › PestControl › Resources › Levels › JuicyLevels.plist › No Selection

Run the game. Now tell me that hearing this clock tick down doesn't make you anxious to hurry up!

Note: There is one problem with this effect, and it relates to archiving.

`_tickTockPlaying` doesn't need to be archived the same way you've done for other variables, because you want the game to always load with `_tickTockPlaying` equal to `NO`. If the player chooses to continue with their current level, `update:` will reset `_tickTockPlaying` appropriately based on the remaining time.

However, when you archive `MyScene`, any running actions are also archived. That means the `TickTockSound` action may be playing as soon as the user opens the app, which messes up everything. To fix this, you need to remove the action when you initialize from an archive. Add the following line to `initWithCoder:`, just after that method's `switch` statement:

```
[self removeActionForKey:@"tickTock"];
```

This is why you initialized `TickTockSound` by passing `YES` as its `waitForCompletion` argument. Sound actions that do not wait for completion are considered instantaneous, which means they are not considered to be running at all! If you had passed `NO` when creating `TickTockSound`, and then tried calling `actionForKey:` here instead of `removeActionForKey:`, you would find there is no action running with that key, even though you might hear the sound playing.

The above line should fix most of the problem, but there's one more issue: the sound file plays for ten seconds, but when you continue a level that was already in the final seconds, that sound would continue to play past when the actual time ran out. To fix this, you need to stop the sound when the time runs out. Simply add the same line again, this time at the top of `endLevelWithSuccess::`

```
[self removeActionForKey:@"tickTock"];
```

Unfortunately, there is currently a bug in Sprite Kit where sounds don't always stop playing when their actions are removed, even if they were created like TickTockSound. But some day, when that bug is fixed, this solution should keep your players from going crazy wondering what is that mysterious ticking noise they hear.

Guess what... you're done!

If you've been counting then you know you added about 30 special effects to this project. And it shows! Just for fun, play the original starter project again to see the difference. That game looks very static and stiff in comparison, doesn't it?

Remember that you didn't change any of the gameplay rules. You only added a ton of special effects. And most of these effects didn't take a lot of programming at all.

When you're ready to juice up your game, remember to apply the 3 steps from the previous chapter:

1. List the actors.

2. List the interactions.

3. Add effects to interactions.

And here is the full list of effects you tried out in these chapters:

1. Movement

2. Scaling

3. Rotation

4. Alpha

5. Texture

6. Tinting

7. Flashing

8. Screen Shake

9. Screen Zoom

10. Color Glitch

11. Particle Effects

12. Shape Effects

13. Sound Effects

Feel free to experiment with your own types of effects – this is only the beginning! Remember the goal is to provide feedback to the player that their actions matter. Your players will love you for it!

A lot of the techniques used in this chapter are based on fun talk by Martin Jonasson and Petri Purho. They show how to take a very bland breakout game and turn it into a spectacular display of mayhem by applying the exact same sort of animations that you've seen here. I strongly recommend that you check out the video of their presentation on YouTube for some inspiration: http://bit.ly/juice-it

And with that, you've reached the end of this chapter – but the juice isn't over yet! We have two final challenges for you to add the finishing touches to this game.

Challenges

This time you have two challenges. In the first, you'll add a gratuitous bug squish effect to the game, and for the grand finale you'll let Arnold bust straight through the walls, just like he's been dreaming of.

As always, if you get stuck you can find the solutions in the resources for this chapter – but give it your best shot first!

Challenge 1: Bug guts for breakfast

In this chapter, you added several types of particle systems to the game, including tree leaves, wall stones, water drops, and a motion trail.

Is there anywhere else you can put particles to good use? But of course! What about when you crush a bug? I don't mind seeing some bug goo fly across the screen, do you?

Your challenge is to add a particle effect when the player collides with a bug, using the particle effect **BugSplatter.sks** and the texture image is **Splat.png**.

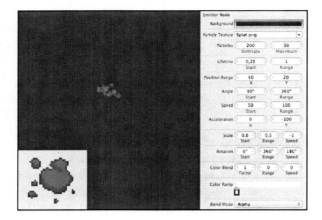

This works in exactly the same way as the other particle effects. If you've done it once, you can do it again. Here are a few hints on how to accomplish this:

• Create a new method in **MyScene.m** called `showParticlesForBug:` that takes an `SKNode` as an argument. It should create a `SKEmitterNode` using "BugSplatter", position it at the node's position, add it as a child of the background layer, and remove it from its parent after 0.4 seconds.

• Then call this method at the bottom of `bugHitEffects:`.

```
[self showParticlesForBug:newNode];
```

Run the game and get ready to get dirty:

Now that's some juice!

Challenge 2: Smashing through walls

This is a fun one! When the player bangs into a wall you currently show a cracked version of the wall texture on that tile, and after a second or two the wall magically heals itself by putting back the original texture.

What if the player were to hit the wall again in that two-second interval? Your challenge is to make the wall bust down and disappear in this event, making Arnold bust straight through the wall!

Here are some hints on how to accomplish this:

- Define a new collision detection category for the wall when it is in its temporary cracked state. Add this to the PCPhysicsCategory type in **MyScene.h**:

```
PCCrackedWallCategory = 1 << 7,
```

- In **MyScene.m** inside crackWall:, inside the case where the wall has the PCWallCategory, set the category mask to PCCrackedWallCategory instead. Also, run an action that sets the category back to regular PCWallCategory after 2 seconds. Finally, set the animate action (created earlier) to have a key of "crackAnim".

- Still inside crackWall:, add an else case that checks if the wall has the PCCrackedWallCategory. In this case, remove the "crackAnim" action, set the wall texture to "wall-broken" from the background layer's atlas, and set the wall's physics body to nil.

- Edit didBeginContact: to add the PCCrackedWallCategory case to the clause that calls wallHitEffects:.

Build and run, and you should be able to smash straight through the walls:

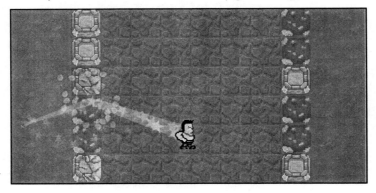

If you've made it this far, you've accomplished a lot – you have made Arnold the master of bugs, and yourself the master of juice! We hope to see many juicy games from you in the future.

Section V: Other Game APIs

In this section, you will learn about some other APIs you need to know to make a game for iOS other than Sprite Kit itself. In particular, you will learn how to make user interfaces with UIKit, control movement with the accelerometer, add Game Center leaderboards, achievements, and multiplayer support into your game, and display your game on your TV or extrernal monitor with AirPlay.

In the process, you will create a top-down racing game called Circuit Racer, where you take the role of an elite race car driver out to set a world record. It would be no problem if it wasn't for the debris on the track!

Chapter 19: UIKit

Chapter 20: Accelerometer

Chapter 21: Game Center Achievements

Chapter 22: Game Center Leaderboards

Chapter 23: Game Center Multiplayer

Chapter 24: AirPlay

Chapter 19: UIKit

By Marin Todorov

If you've made your way through the entire book up to this point, you have created four games: Zombie Conga, XBlaster, Cat Nap, and Pest Control. You have learned a ton about making Sprite Kit games in the process – from sprites to actions to nodes to tile maps and more.

But there's more to making games than just the Sprite Kit APIs themselves. One of the great things about Sprite Kit is that it's easy to integrate the rest of the frameworks in the iOS ecosystem that you may have learned about in our *iOS Apprentice* and *iOS by Tutorials* series. For example, you can use other iOS APIs in your game to make remote calls to web services, save data to iCloud, or make in-app purchases.

In this chapter, you are going to learn how to integrate one of these frameworks into your Sprite Kit games – a user interface library called UIKit.

The games you have created so far all used Xcode's built-in Sprite Kit template, which provides you with a simple starter project. The template provides you with a Storyboard with just one view controller, which is set up to display a Sprite Kit view on the screen. This way, your Sprite Kit scene is displayed as soon as the application launches so that players can immediately begin enjoying your game.

That's indeed a great starting point, but for most games you usually want to provide some sort of menu system first so the player can do things like load saved games (as you can see in the screenshot to the lower left), select game difficulty, select the level they'd like to play (as you can see in the screenshot to the lower right), and more.

You'll also need a GUI *inside* your game for in-game controls (as you can see in the screenshot to the lower left), the head-up display (HUD), in-game menus (as you can see in the screenshot to the lower right), and more.

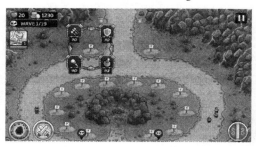 

You could make user interfaces like this in Sprite Kit using sprites and a ton of custom code, but this would be "reinventing the wheel". Apple already has a library called UIKit that's chock full of tons of controls you can use in your apps, such as buttons, table views, scroll views, and more.

If you've ever made any iPhone apps in the past, then you've probably already used UIKit. The goal of this chapter isn't to teach you UIKit, as there are a ton of tutorials and books that cover UIKit already. Rather, the goal of this chapter is to show you how you can integrate UIKit into your Sprite Kit games.

> **Note:** If you're completely new to UIKit, don't worry – you can still follow along with this chapter as the instructions are step by step. However, you might want to go through our *iOS Apprentice* or *iOS by Tutorials* series if you'd like to learn more about what you can do with UIKit.

Throughout this and the next few chapters, you will create the fifth and final game in this book: **Circuit Racer**.

Here's what it will look like when you're finished:

In Circuit Racer, you take the role of an elite racecar driver out to set a world record. It would be no problem if it weren't for the debris on the track!

You will build this game across the next six chapters, in stages:

1. **Chapter 19, UIKit**: You are here! You will get started by learning how to integrate Sprite Kit with UIKit to create view controllers for different screens of your game, as well as use standard iOS controls within your main game scene itself (such as creating an on-screen joypad).

2. **Chapter 20, Accelerometer**: You will learn how to use the accelerometer to move your sprites around the screen.

3. **Chapter 21, Game Center Achievements**: You will learn how to enable Game Center for your game and award the user achievements for accomplishing certain feats.

4. **Chapter 22, Game Center Leaderboards**: You will learn how to set up various leaderboards for your game and track and report the player's scores.

5. **Chapter 23, Game Center Multiplayer**: You will learn how to add multiplayer support so players can race against each other in real-time across the Internet!

6. **Chapter 24, AirPlay**: You will learn how to display the game on a TV or external display and use your device as a controller.

> **Note:** The gameplay idea of Circuit Racer game originates from one of the examples included with the AndEngine game engine. The code you will develop will be completely different than the game from AndEngine but we still thought it was good karma to give them credit for the game.

There's a lot to cover, so let's get started!

Getting started

> **Note:** The first part of this chapter covers building the initial implementation of Circuit Racer, which is a review of material already covered in this book.
>
> If you feel like you have a strong handle on the material so far and just want to jump straight to the UIKit integration, you can skip ahead to the section called **UIKit game controls**. We will have a starter project waiting for you there!

Start Xcode and select **File\New\Project...** from the main menu. Select the **iOS\Application\SpriteKit Game** template and click **Next**.

Enter **CircuitRacer** for the Product Name, choose **iPhone** for Devices, leave the **Class Prefix** blank and click **Next**. Choose somewhere on your hard drive to save your project and click **Create**. At this point Xcode will generate the standard Sprite Kit starter project for you.

On the **General Project properties** screen (open by default when you create a new project) make sure that only **Landscape Left** is selected so that your game will start in landscape mode instead of portrait. You're only supporting Landscape Left instead of both landscape orientations because you'll be adding accelerometer support in the next chapter, and supporting just one device orientation will be easier.

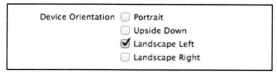

You don't need the boilerplate code that Xcode generated for you, so open **MyScene.m** and delete all methods found between @implementation and @end.

Open the assets folder for this chapter and drag and drop the folder called **Art** onto Xcode's project file list, make sure the checkbox Copy to destination folder is checked. These are all the assets you are going to need throughout the Circuit Racer chapters:

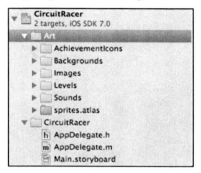

As with previous games in this book, you have your sprite images inside the folder sprite.atlas (so that Xcode will automatically create a texture atlas for you), screen backgrounds are in Backgrounds and level configuration files are in Levels. Feel free to peek inside to see all the coolness coming your way!

One last step, for polish. Open **Images.xassets** and select the **AppIcon** entry. Then in the resources for this chapter, drag all of the files from the "App Icon" folder into the area on the right. You should see the following when you're done:

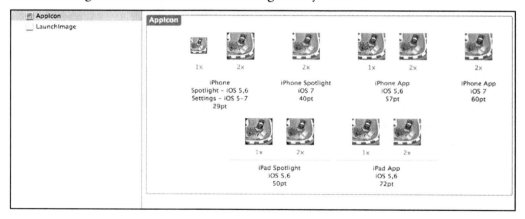

Initializing the scene

It's time to start coding. The completed mini-game will feature several different tracks and cars, so you need to define few constants. Add at the end of **CircuitRacer/Supporting Files/CircuitRacer-Prefix.pch**:

```
typedef NS_ENUM(int, CRCarType)
{
  CRYellowCar = 1,
  CRBlueCar,
  CRRedCar
};

typedef NS_ENUM(int, CRLevelType)
{
  CRLevelEasy = 1,
  CRLevelMedium,
  CRLevelHard
};
```

This uses the **NS_ENUM** helper to declare two enumeration: one for types of cars (yellow, blue, or red), and one for types of levels (easy, medium, and hard).

> **Note**: To learn more about Foundation helpers like **NS_ENUM** and **NS_OPTIONS**, check out Chapter 1 in *Effective Objective-C 2.0*, "Accustomizing Yourself to Objective-C."

Next open **MyScene.h** and add a new init inside the class interface:

```
- (id)initWithSize:(CGSize)size carType:(CRCarType)carType
            level:(CRLevelType)levelType;
```

This method will initialize your scene for the given size and store the level and car types for later use. Inside **MyScene.m**, add the following private variables to store your scene settings:

```
@implementation MyScene
{
    CRCarType _carType;
    CRLevelType _levelType;
}
```

And add these methods:

```
- (id)initWithSize:(CGSize)size carType:(CRCarType)carType
          level:(CRLevelType)levelType
{
  if (self = [super initWithSize:size]) {
    _carType = carType;
    _levelType = levelType;
    [self initializeGame];
  }
  return self;
}

- (void)initializeGame
{
}
```

In your new `initWithSize:carType:level` method, you take the incoming car and level type and store them in your class, and then you call `initializeGame`, which is empty for now. You'll fill it out soon.

Configuring the levels

Now that your scene is in shape, it's time to clean up your view controller. Open **ViewController.m** and just as you did for `MyScene` delete all methods from the implementation body and add this one instead:

```
- (void)viewWillLayoutSubviews
{
  [super viewWillLayoutSubviews];

  SKView *skView = (SKView *)self.view;
  if (!skView.scene) {
    MyScene *scene =
      [[MyScene alloc] initWithSize:skView.bounds.size
                        carType:CRYellowCar
                          level:CRLevelEasy];
    scene.scaleMode = SKSceneScaleModeAspectFill;
    [skView presentScene:scene];
  }
}
```

As you certainly remember from past chapters, an easy way to handle landscape mode is to move your scene initialization code to `viewWillLayoutSubviews:`.

In `viewWillLayoutSubviews:`, as usual, you grab a reference to your `SKView`, create an instance of your scene and present it onscreen. You have the car and level types hard-coded for the moment.

Here are the level details you will load from **LevelDetails.plist**:

Key	Type	Value
▼ Root	Array	(3 items)
▼ Item 0	Dictionary	(2 items)
time	Number	15
laps	Number	2
▼ Item 1	Dictionary	(2 items)
time	Number	25
laps	Number	5
▼ Item 2	Dictionary	(2 items)
time	Number	35
laps	Number	10

As you can see, for each increase in track difficulty, the player has less time to do the required number of laps. To load the level configuration, open **MyScene.m** and add the following private instance variables :

```
NSTimeInterval _timeInSeconds;
int _noOfLaps;
```

You'll use these to store the level settings. Now add this new method:

```
- (void)loadLevel
{
  NSString *filePath =
    [NSBundle.mainBundle pathForResource:@"LevelDetails"
                                  ofType:@"plist"];
  NSArray *level = [NSArray arrayWithContentsOfFile:filePath];

  NSNumber *timeInSeconds = level[_levelType-1][@"time"];
  _timeInSeconds = [timeInSeconds doubleValue];

  NSNumber *laps = level[_levelType-1][@"laps"];
  _noOfLaps = [laps intValue];
}
```

This method loads LevelDetails.plist. Then it fetches the **time** and **laps** keys from the first, second or third elements in the plist file, depending on _levelType's value. It subtracts one from _levelType because the CRLevelType values start at one, but array indices start at zero.

With your level now configured, add this code to initializeGame in order to load the level details and show the level background, depending on the level configuration:

```
[self loadLevel];
```

```
SKSpriteNode *track = [SKSpriteNode spriteNodeWithImageNamed:
  [NSString stringWithFormat:@"track_%i", _levelType]];

track.position = CGPointMake(CGRectGetMidX(self.frame),
                             CGRectGetMidY(self.frame));
[self addChild:track];
```

You create a new sprite with a track image and position it in the center of the screen.

Game on! Build and run. If you are testing in the iPhone Simulator, don't forget to select the **iPhone Retina 4-inch** simulation. Woot!

You see the easiest track in your future game onscreen.

A little physics review

Next let's add your car to the scenery. Nothing too fancy is going to happen – you'll simply create a sprite and display it. Add this new private instance variable to `MyScene`:

```
SKSpriteNode *_car;
```

You'll use that to store a car sprite. Add the following method:

```
- (void)addCarAtPosition:(CGPoint)startPosition
{
  _car =
    [SKSpriteNode spriteNodeWithImageNamed:
      [NSString stringWithFormat:@"car_%i",_carType]];
  _car.position = startPosition;
  [self addChild:_car];
}
```

You initialize _car in addCarAtPosition:, depending on the car type you'll see onscreen: car_1.png, car_2.png or car_3.png. Right now you are hard-coding the car type to CRYellowCar (defined as 1), so this will always be car_1.png for the time being.

Speaking of racing cars... you're going to use physics bodies to detect collisions and contacts with the track fence and some track obstacles. Of course, having completed the **Cat Nap** project from earlier, you are already a master of contacts and collisions.

Scroll up to the beginning of **MyScene.m** and just under the #import statement add the body categories for Circuit Racer:

```
typedef NS_OPTIONS(uint32_t, CRPhysicsCategory)
{
  CRBodyCar = 1 << 0,
  CRBodyBox = 1 << 1,
};
```

You define two categories of bodies – CRBodyCar for the car and another one called CRBodyBox that you will use for a couple of obstacles you're going to add to the racing track in few moments time.

Speaking of bodies, you are going to need one for your car sprite! Add this code to addCarAtPosition:

```
_car.physicsBody =
  [SKPhysicsBody bodyWithRectangleOfSize:_car.frame.size];
_car.physicsBody.categoryBitMask = CRBodyCar;
_car.physicsBody.collisionBitMask = CRBodyBox;
_car.physicsBody.contactTestBitMask = CRBodyBox;
_car.physicsBody.allowsRotation = NO;
```

You should be very familiar with what this code does, since you created many bodies in Chapter 9, "Intermediate Physics" and Chapter 10, "Advanced Physics".

In the code above, you create a rectangular physics body and attach it to the car sprite. Then you set the car body's category to `CRBodyCar` and make it collide with and contact `CRBodyBox` bodies, which you'll add to the scene momentarily.

Finally, you set a property on the car's body that you haven't yet seen in this book. `allowsRotation` instructs the physics simulation whether the physics laws and collisions with other objects should rotate the body (and the sprite image) around its z-axis. Here you set it to `NO` because you are going to change the car's orientation on the track yourself from within your code.

As the last step in setting up your car, add this code to `initializeGame`:

```
[self addCarAtPosition:
  CGPointMake(CGRectGetMidX(track.frame), 50)];

self.physicsWorld.gravity = CGVectorMake(0, 0);
CGRect trackFrame = CGRectInset(track.frame, 40, 0);
self.physicsBody =
  [SKPhysicsBody bodyWithEdgeLoopFromRect:trackFrame];
```

First you position the car on the track's finish line. Then you turn off the world's gravity by setting it to the zero vector – you don't want that car to fall down the screen, do you?

In the last couple of lines, you set the edge loop for your scene by taking the size of the track image and decreasing the width a bit, because the area where the car can go does not span the entire width of the screen. Have a look at the screenshot below to see what I mean.

Run the project and make sure you see the car at the start position:

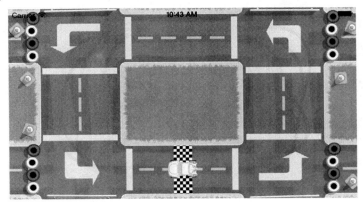

Now you're going to recklessly throw two boxes in the way of the car to make the race a bit more challenging. Add this new method to MyScene:

```
- (void)addBoxAt:(CGPoint)point
{
  SKSpriteNode *box =
    [SKSpriteNode spriteNodeWithImageNamed:@"box"];
  box.position = point;
  box.physicsBody =
    [SKPhysicsBody bodyWithRectangleOfSize:box.size];
  box.physicsBody.categoryBitMask = CRBodyBox;
  box.physicsBody.linearDamping = 1;
  box.physicsBody.angularDamping = 1;
  [self addChild:box];
}
```

The method addBoxAt: takes in a CGPoint and at this position creates a sprite out of box.png. It then adds a square physics body to the box and sets its category to CRBodyBox. Physics bodies collide with everything by default, and the car body is already set up to indicate contacts between it and the boxes, so you do not need to set anything else on the box body.

This also sets some linear and angular damping on the physics body, which reduces the linear and angular velocity of the physics body each frame. This is useful to simulate friction and prevent the boxes from continuously sliding around.

Now add this new method that uses addBoxAt: to create boxes on the track:

```
- (void)addObjectsForTrack:(SKSpriteNode*)track
{
  // 1
  SKNode *innerBoundary = [SKNode node];
  innerBoundary.position = track.position;
  [self addChild:innerBoundary];

  CGSize size = CGSizeMake(180, 120);
  innerBoundary.physicsBody =
    [SKPhysicsBody bodyWithRectangleOfSize:size];
  innerBoundary.physicsBody.dynamic = NO;

  // 2
  [self addBoxAt:
    CGPointMake(track.position.x + 130, track.position.y)];
  [self addBoxAt:
    CGPointMake(track.position.x - 200, track.position.y)];
}
```

Let's briefly go over the code:

1. You first create an empty **SKNode** for the inner track boundary and a physics body based on the size of the inner boundary. You set the inner boundary body to be static, as it shouldn't move, no matter how hard the car hits it.

2. Second you create two obstacles on the track by calling **addBoxAt:**. You can see the two boxes in the screenshot below.

Finally, call this new method at the end of `initializeGame`:

```
[self addObjectsForTrack:track];
```

Run the project again to see the results:

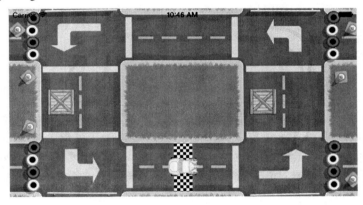

What an outrage! Somebody could crash into those boxes! Well, if your car could move at all, that is.

Your first taste of the user interface

Before you get to the driving, there's one step left.

Although you'll be creating much of the user interface for this game using UIKit controls, there's one part of user interfaces that Sprite Kit can do well, as you may remember from your old friend XBlaster – drawing labels.

So as the last step of the game setup, you will add two labels in the center of the screen to show the player how much time they have left and how many laps left to go. Add these two private instance variables for quick access to the onscreen UI:

```
SKLabelNode *_laps, *_time;
```

And add this new method:

```
- (void)addGameUIForTrack:(SKSpriteNode*)track
{
  _laps = [SKLabelNode labelNodeWithFontNamed:@"Chalkduster"];
  _laps.text =
    [NSString stringWithFormat:@"Laps: %i", _noOfLaps];
  _laps.fontSize = 28;
  _laps.fontColor = [UIColor whiteColor];
  _laps.position = CGPointMake(track.position.x,
                               track.position.y + 20);
  [self addChild:_laps];

  _time = [SKLabelNode labelNodeWithFontNamed:@"Chalkduster"];
  _time.text =
    [NSString stringWithFormat:@"Time: %.lf", _timeInSeconds];
  _time.fontSize = 28;
  _time.fontColor = [UIColor whiteColor];
  _time.position = CGPointMake(track.position.x,
                               track.position.y - 10);
  [self addChild:_time];
}
```

Inside addGameUIForTrack:, you create two label nodes and set up their font size, color and position. The _laps label node displays the laps to go as set from LevelDetails.plist according to the track difficulty, and _time shows the time left to finish the laps remaining. You position both in the center of the track, within the inner boundary area.

Call this new method at the end of initializeGame:

```
[self addGameUIForTrack:track];
```

All done! That was a long stretch, no doubt… but for your trouble, build and run one last time and you'll see the labels on the screen:

That's it for the basic game setup — now let's turn your attention to UIKit, starting with making the car move!

UIKit game controls

> **Note**: If you skipped the last section of the chapter, open the project **CircuitRacer-SkippedSetup** from the chapter's assets folder so that you can continue this tutorial from here.

In this section, you're going to implement a classic joypad control in Circuit Racer that the player will use to control the car. You'll create the joypad as a normal `UIView` and add it on top of the game scene. Then you'll make your scene read the knob position to change the car's velocity.

Here's how the joypad will look when you're finished:

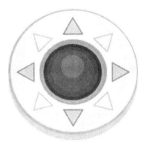

You probably already know how to use one of these from playing games on your iPhone or iPod touch. You touch the knob in the center of the control and then drag it around to control a hero, a car or a gun inside the game. It's actually quite easy to make a joypad, so let's get to it!

Adding the joypad

As you've done for many other games in this book, you'll integrate our handy SKTUtils library into this game. You can find **SKTUtils** in the root folder for this book. Drag the entire **SKTUtils** folder into the project navigator in Xcode. Make sure **Copy items into destination group's folder (if needed)** and the **CircuitRacer** target are both checked. Click **Finish**.

Then from Xcode's menu, select **File/New/File...** and as a template select the **Objective-C class**. Enter **AnalogControl** as the class name and make it a subclass of **UIView**. Finally, make sure the new class is included in your **CircuitRacer** target and create the file.

Switch to **AnalogControl.m** and replace the existing contents with this:

```objective-c
#import "AnalogControl.h"
#import "SKTUtils.h"

@implementation AnalogControl
{
  UIImageView *_knobImageView;
  CGPoint _baseCenter;
}

- (id)initWithFrame:(CGRect)frame
{
  self = [super initWithFrame:frame];
  if (self) {
    //initialize here
  }
  return self;
}

@end
```

In this chunk of code, you add two instance variables – the building parts of the completed joypad:

• _knobImageView is for the joypad knob image on screen.

- **_baseCenter** will store the position that is the "neutral" position of the control (i.e. the center of the control's frame).

As you might know, to customize a **UIView** subclass you usually override its **initWithFrame:** method, as this is the most common way to make view instances. Now let's add some substance to **initWithFrame:** to get something more than an empty transparent view onscreen. Add this code where you see the **//initialize here** placeholder:

```
// 1
[self setUserInteractionEnabled:YES];

// 2
UIImageView *baseImageView =
    [[UIImageView alloc] initWithFrame:self.bounds];
baseImageView.contentMode = UIViewContentModeScaleAspectFit;
baseImageView.image =
    [UIImage imageNamed:@"base.png"];
[self addSubview:baseImageView];

// 3
_baseCenter = CGPointMake(frame.size.width/2,
                          frame.size.height/2);

// 4
_knobImageView =
    [[UIImageView alloc] initWithImage:
        [UIImage imageNamed:@"knob.png"]];
_knobImageView.center = _baseCenter;
[self addSubview:_knobImageView];

// 5
NSAssert(CGRectContainsRect(self.bounds, _knobImageView.bounds),
    @"Analog control size should be greater than the knob size");
```

Let's go over this section by section:

1. You instruct the view to handle touches by setting **userInteractionEnabled** to YES.

2. Then you create an image view out of base.png and make it fit the control's frame.

3. You calculate the center of the control's frame – this will be the "neutral" position for the knob.

4. You create an image view out of knob.png and position it neutrally.

5. Finally you check if the control's bounding box contains the whole knob, just to make sure the knob fits the base image. This check will always pass for the assets you've gotten for Circuit Racer, but if you reuse this class for your own games, the check might save you some debugging time.

This should be enough to already display a nice joypad control onscreen.

Displaying the joypad

Now it's time to step back for a moment and think about where and how to display the joypad on the screen. This is a UIKit view control and therefore you can't add it to `MyScene` – you'll have to add it to your `ViewController`'s view instead.

Here you encounter your first serious problem for this chapter. Your controller's view is an `SKView` and you cannot, at the time of this writing, add `UIView` instances as subviews of an `SKView`.

You can fix that in few easy steps. First open **Main.storyboard** and select the controller's view:

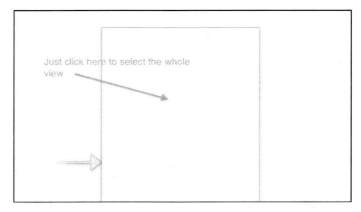

Then, in the **Identity Inspector** (the third tab on the sidebar), delete the contents of the field **Class**.

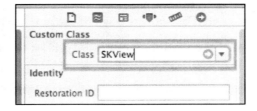

When you delete all the characters in the text field, the default value **UIView** will appear, which is exactly what you want. Now go back to **ViewController.m** to handle that change. Make the highlighted changes to the file:

```
#import "ViewController.h"
#import "MyScene.h"

@implementation ViewController {
  SKView *_skView;
}

- (void)viewWillLayoutSubviews
{
  [super viewWillLayoutSubviews];

  if (!_skView) {
    _skView =
      [[SKView alloc] initWithFrame:self.view.bounds];
    MyScene *scene =
      [[MyScene alloc] initWithSize:_skView.bounds.size
                            carType:CRYellowCar
                              level:CRLevelEasy];
    scene.scaleMode = SKSceneScaleModeAspectFill;
    [_skView presentScene:scene];
    [self.view addSubview:_skView];
  }
}

@end
```

In the new setup, instead of fetching your game's **SKView** from the storyboard, you create it with code. This doesn't make any difference to Sprite Kit, but you win big time because now you can add **UIView** subviews to the controller's view. (And that was your evil plan all along!)

Now it's time to show the joypad on the scene. Import **AnalogControl** to give your **ViewController** access to your new class:

```
#import "AnalogControl.h"
```

Then add this private instance variable:

```
AnalogControl *_analogControl;
```

OK – this code imports your new class and creates an `_analogControl` instance variable in `ViewController`. Now you only need to display the view on the screen, so add this to `viewWillLayoutSubviews`, right after adding the `_skView` subview:

```
const float padSide = 128;
const float padPadding = 10;

_analogControl =
  [[AnalogControl alloc] initWithFrame:
    CGRectMake(
      padPadding, _skView.frame.size.height-padPadding-padSide,
      padSide, padSide)];

[self.view addSubview:_analogControl];
```

You set the bottom-left corner of the screen, where joypads usually reside, as the origin of the control. You give it a size of (128,128).

The following diagram shows you how you use the `padPading` and `padSide` variables to create the frame. Remember in UIKit (0, 0) represents the top left of the screen (rather than the bottom left one in Sprite Kit), so to get the y coordinate you have to subtract `padPadding` from the height of the screen.

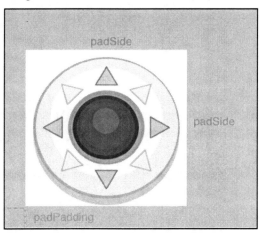

Build and run the project to see your first UIKit game control onscreen:

Wiring up the joypad

It looks good, but it doesn't do much. In fact, to be completely honest, it does not do *anything*! Let's fix that.

The main task of the analog control is to expose the position of the knob to other classes in the game. Therefore you need a new property on the `AnalogControl` class to do that. Open **AnalogControl.h** and, inside the `@interface` declaration, add:

```
@property (nonatomic, assign) CGPoint relativePosition;
```

Now switch to **AnalogControl.m** and add the following method, which will move the knob:

```
- (void)updateKnobWithPosition:(CGPoint)position
{
  // 1
  CGPoint positionToCenter =
    CGPointSubtract(position, _baseCenter);
  CGPoint direction;
  if (CGPointEqualToPoint(positionToCenter, CGPointZero)) {
    direction = CGPointZero;
  } else {
    direction = CGPointNormalize(positionToCenter);
  }

  // 2
  float radius = self.frame.size.width/2;
  float length = CGPointLength(positionToCenter);

  // 3
```

```
  if (length > radius) {
    length = radius;
    positionToCenter = CGPointMultiplyScalar(direction, radius);
  }
}
```

Let's go over this section by section:

1. You subtract the position of the touch from the center of the joystick image. This gives you a relative offset for where the touch is. Also gets the direction of the offset by normalizing the vector as you learned in Chapter 2, "Manual Movement".

2. This joystick is circular, so you don't want the knob to move further outside of the radius of the joystick image. So here you calculate the radius and the length of the relative offset.

3. If the length is greater than the radius, then you make a vector that points in the same direction but has the length of the radius instead. You do this by multiplying the normalizing vector (which has a length of 1) by the radius, as you also learned in Chapter 2.

Continue by adding this code to `updateKnobWithPosition:`:

```
CGPoint relativePosition =
  CGPointMake(direction.x * length/radius,
              direction.y * length/radius);
```

This converts the direction into vector of length (length/radius) – in other words, the closer the knob is toward the edge of the circle, the closer the length will be to 1. This will be helpful when moving the car later.

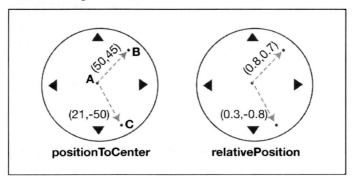

You need to update the control with the calculated position, so add at the end of the method:

```
_knobImageView.center =
  CGPointAdd(_baseCenter, positionToCenter);
self.relativePosition = relativePosition;
```

All right, the last step is to implement the standard `UIView` touch-handling callbacks so that the player will be able to drag the knob around. Add these new methods to `AnalogControl`:

```
- (void)touchesBegan:(NSSet*)touches withEvent:(UIEvent*)event {
  CGPoint touchLocation =
    [[touches anyObject] locationInView:self];
  [self updateKnobWithPosition:touchLocation];
}

- (void)touchesMoved:(NSSet*)touches withEvent:(UIEvent*)event {
  CGPoint touchLocation =
    [[touches anyObject] locationInView:self];
  [self updateKnobWithPosition:touchLocation];
}

- (void)touchesEnded:(NSSet*)touches withEvent:(UIEvent*)event {
  [self updateKnobWithPosition:_baseCenter];
}

- (void)touchesCancelled:(NSSet*)touches
            withEvent:(UIEvent*)event {
  [self updateKnobWithPosition:_baseCenter];
}
```

When the player puts a finger down on the screen and when they drag it around, you call `updateKnobWithPosition:` with the position of the touch. When the touch ends, you call `updateKnobWithPosition:` with `_baseCenter`, which sets the knob back to its neutral position.

Believe it or not – that's all. Run the game again and fool around a bit with the joypad.

Using physics for positioning

Now that you have the car direction vector, you want to be able to move that beast around the track. Luckily that's going to be very easy to implement. A physics body's velocity is also a vector, so all you need to do is take the `relativePosition` of `AnalogControl` and set the current velocity of your car's body.

Using key-value-observing

To connect your UIKit control to your Sprite Kit scene, you're going to use **key-value-observing**. This is a method built into iOS that allows you to get notified on any changes to a property that you are listening to.

This is helpful because it allows more than one class can observe the knob's current position property. If you implemented a delegate pattern to the joypad instead, only one object could be the delegate.

Open **ViewController.m** and add the following private instance variable:

```
MyScene *_scene;
```

And add the following at the end of `viewWillLayoutSubviews:`, right after adding the `_analogControl` subview:

```
[_analogControl addObserver:scene forKeyPath:@"relativePosition"
                    options:NSKeyValueObservingOptionNew
                    context:nil];
_scene = scene;
```

Key-value-observing is a very powerful technique. If you don't use it very often, you should.

Here you add a new instance variable to access your scene and then you set `scene` as an observer of `_analogControl.relativePosition`. Every time the value of this property changes, a certain method will automatically get invoked on the `scene` class. Neat!

To make sure you don't leak memory, you also need to remove the observer when you don't need the updates anymore. You can do this in `dealloc`. Add the method anywhere in the class body:

```
- (void)dealloc {
    [_analogControl removeObserver:_scene
```

```
                        forKeyPath:@"relativePosition"];
    }
```

The method is quite straightforward – `removeObserver:forKeyPath:` simply stops the key-value-observation notifications for the given path and observer.

Don't build and run yet – your app will crash if you do since you still haven't implemented the observer method. That comes next!

Translating direction vectors into movement

Next you'll translate the joypad's direction vector to a velocity vector that will move the car. You will need to define the maximum speed of the car and then multiply `relativePosition` vector by that speed – that will give you the car's momentous velocity. For example, a direction vector of (0.67,0.45) will set the car's velocity to (167.5,112.5) for a car with a maximum speed of 250:

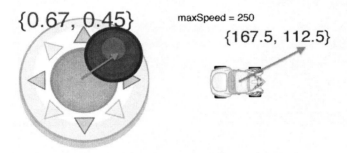

In **MyScene.m**, add the code that will determine the car's maximum speed based on the car type. First add a private instance variable to store the maximum speed:

```
int _maxSpeed;
```

And add this line at the end of `initializeGame`:

```
_maxSpeed = 125 * (1 + _carType);
```

This line at the end of `initializeGame` will set `_maxSpeed` to either 250, 375, or 500, depending on the car type. The value of `_carType` is 1, 2 or 3 – you can look it up in CircuitRacer-Prefix.pch.

Now that you can calculate the car's velocity based on the joypad's `relativePosition` and the car's maximum speed, add a method in `MyScene` to do that. First import `AnalogControl`:

```
#import "AnalogControl.h"
```

And add this method:

```
- (void)analogControlUpdated:(AnalogControl*)analogControl
{
  [_car.physicsBody setVelocity:
    CGVectorMake(analogControl.relativePosition.x * _maxSpeed,
                 -analogControl.relativePosition.y *_maxSpeed)];
}
```

This fancy new method takes in a reference to the analog control and sets the car's velocity to the `relativePosition` vector multiplied by `_maxSpeed`.

Note that you negate the y-axis. Can you guess why?

I hope you nailed it – the coordinate systems of UIKit and Sprite Kit differ. In UIKit, the y-coordinate increases towards the bottom of the screen, while in Sprite Kit it increases towards the top of the screen.

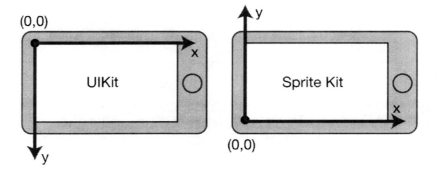

The last step is to add the method that gets called when the key-value observation notification fires. Add this method to the `MyScene` class:

```
-(void)observeValueForKeyPath:(NSString *)keyPath
                     ofObject:(id)object
                       change:(NSDictionary *)change
                      context:(void *)context
{
```

```
    if ([keyPath isEqualToString:@"relativePosition"]) {
        [self analogControlUpdated:object];
    }
}
```

This method receives several parameters that provide you with tons of useful information:

- keyPath tells you which key path (or class property) has changed on the observed object.

- object is a reference to the observed object.

- change is a dictionary with additional information about the change. For example, how exactly the value was changed, or for sets, whether an object was inserted or removed.

- context is an arbitrary object you can set when you first add the observation.

Since you have only one observer for only one property, your code is pretty straightforward – you just check if keyPath equals "relativePosition" (should always be true in this simple example) and if so, you call analogControlUpdated:.

Great, that connects all the dots on your game controls treasure map! Build, run and enjoy.

At this point you can control the car via the onscreen joypad and you can also test those track boundaries and crash into the obstacles.

Rotating sprites using a direction vector

One final touch – the car doesn't take those turns too well. By the time it gets to the other side of the track, it's running backwards! Luckily when you have the direction vector, it's quite easy to set the car sprite's zRotation so that it always faces the direction of movement.

Still in **MyScene.m**, import SKTUtils at the top of the file:

```
#import "SKTUtils.h"
```

Next scroll down and add at the end of analogControlUpdated:

```
if (!CGPointEqualToPoint(
        analogControl.relativePosition, CGPointZero)) {

  _car.zRotation =
    CGPointToAngle(
      CGPointMake(analogControl.relativePosition.x,
                  -analogControl.relativePosition.y));
}
```

First you check if the knob is in the neutral position. If so, you do not change the car's orientation. Otherwise you pass the relativePosition vector (with inverted y-axis) to CGPointToAngle from the SKTUtil library and simply set the result as the car's zRotation.

Build and run. Now the car turns around as you drive it towards the finish line! Sweet!

I hope that you're getting more and more accustomed to using the functions found in SKTUtils – as you've seen, they can greatly simplify your coding tasks.

In this section, you learned how to add UIKit controls to your game and how to communicate between UIKit and Sprite Kit classes. Your next big task is to monitor the car's progress on the track and decrease the number of laps remaining with each completed revolution. In other words: it's gameplay time!

Implementing the gameplay

In Circuit Racer, you need to know when the user successfully completes a lap. Unfortunately it's not as simple as just tracking when the car crosses the finish line – otherwise a clever player could make the car go back and forth across the finish line to win in no time!

So to determine when the user actually completes a lap, you will divide the track into four sections and decrease the laps remaining only if the car has passed through all four sections of the track. To do this, you're going to need to calculate the angle between the car sprite and the center of the track.

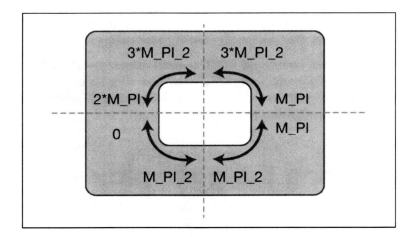

Your car starts at angle M_PI_2 (90 degrees) and when it passes M_PI (180 degrees), that means it's reached the next quadrant. Every time the car reaches the next target angle, you need to set a new target by adding M_PI_2. When the target angle is greater than 2*M_PI (on the left side of the scheme above) you need to set it back to M_PI_2, the starting car point.

Finally, each time the car passes through the M_PI_2 angle (the starting point) you need to decrease the laps remaining. That's the whole game logic right there!

Tracking the car

Let's put this into code. You will take care of the car tracking in the game loop. Add these changes to **MyScene.m**. Create a new private instance variable:

```
CGPoint _trackCenter;
```

Initialize it at the end of `initializeGame` to the track's position (i.e. the center of the screen):

```
_trackCenter = track.position;
```

Then implement `update:` as follows:

```
- (void)update:(NSTimeInterval)currentTime
{
  // 1
  static float nextProgressAngle = M_PI;
```

```
// 2
CGPoint vector = CGPointSubtract(_car.position, _trackCenter);

// 3
float progressAngle = CGPointToAngle(vector) + M_PI;
}
```

Let's go over each line in turn:

1. You set the initial value of nextProgressAngle to M_PI – that is, the track area on the right end of the screen.

2. You subtract _trackCenter and _car.position by using CGPointSubtract.

3. Finally, you use CGPointToAngle to get the angle for the subtraction result. Since CGPointToAngle returns values between –M_PI and M_PI, you add to the result another M_PI so you have only positive values for progressAngle. That makes calculations much easier.

Look at the last scheme on the previous page and you'll see how progressAngle is tied to the calculations you're going to make to track the car's progress through the four quadrants. Speaking of which, add this chunk of code at the end of update: to do your tracking:

```
// 1
if (progressAngle > nextProgressAngle &&
    (progressAngle - nextProgressAngle) < M_PI_4) {

  // 2 - advance on track
  nextProgressAngle += M_PI_2;

  // 3
  if (nextProgressAngle > 2*M_PI) {
    nextProgressAngle = 0;
  }

  // 4
  if (fabsf(nextProgressAngle-M_PI)<FLT_EPSILON) {
    //lap completed!
  }
}
```

Let's go over this bit-by-bit:

1. In the if condition, you check whether the current angle is greater than the next target, but you are only interested if the current angle is greater by just a bit: M_PI_4. This prevents the player from cheating by going backwards.

2. When the `if` condition is met, you increase the next target by `M_PI_2`, which is equal to one quadrant in the scheme above.

3. Then you check if the next target is greater than `2*M_PI` and if so, you reset the target to 0.

4. Finally, you check if the next target angle equals `M_PI` – that means the car just passed through the finish line and is heading to the right side of the screen.

Many programmers don't realize that they can't reliably compare two float variables by using `==`, so mind the equality condition to compare `nextProgressAngle` and `M_PI`.

You can read more about comparing float numbers here:
http://www.mikeash.com/pyblog/friday-qa-2011-01-04-practical-floating-point.html

Finally, replace the **//lap completed!** placeholder with:

```
_noOfLaps -= 1;
_laps.text = [NSString stringWithFormat:@"Laps: %i", _noOfLaps];
```

That'll take one lap off the lap count and update the UI accordingly.

Build, run and give the game a try – every time you pass through the finish line, you will see the number of laps decrease.

Gratuitous sound effects

Hey, completing a lap is fun! Let's spice it up a bit with some sound effects.

First, add these four instance variables to `MyScene` for all the sounds you'll eventually be using in Circuit Racer:

```
SKAction * _boxSoundAction;
SKAction * _hornSoundAction;
SKAction * _lapSoundAction;
SKAction * _nitroSoundAction;
```

Then initialize them at the end of `initializeGame`:

```
_boxSoundAction = [SKAction playSoundFileNamed:@"box.wav"
   waitForCompletion:NO];
_hornSoundAction = [SKAction playSoundFileNamed:@"horn.wav"
   waitForCompletion:NO];
_lapSoundAction = [SKAction playSoundFileNamed:@"lap.wav"
   waitForCompletion:NO];
_nitroSoundAction = [SKAction playSoundFileNamed:@"nitro.wav"
   waitForCompletion:NO];
```

Finally, add this line after setting the `_laps.text` in `update:`:

```
[self runAction:_lapSoundAction];
```

Build, run, and complete a lap – vroom, vroom!

Tracking time

To finish up this game, you need to keep track of time. In Circuit Racer, a player only has a certain number of seconds to complete the number of laps before they lose!

Make the following changes to **MyScene.m** to add the game timer. First, add a private instance variable:

```
NSTimeInterval _previousTimeInterval;
```

This new instance variable will keep the last time `update:` ran – this is important so you can calculate the delta time between runs of the game loop. If you don't keep track of how many times the game loop has run, you will certainly have uneven animations in your game, which is not nice at all.

Insert the following code **at the top** of `update:`:

```
if (_previousTimeInterval==0) {
  _previousTimeInterval = currentTime;
}

if (self.paused==YES) {
  _previousTimeInterval = currentTime;
  return;
```

```
  }

  if (currentTime - _previousTimeInterval > 1) {
    _timeInSeconds -= (currentTime - _previousTimeInterval);
    _previousTimeInterval = currentTime;
    _time.text =
      [NSString stringWithFormat:@"Time: %.lf", _timeInSeconds];
  }
```

Here you handle three cases via three if statements:

1. If _previousTimeInterval hasn't been initialized, simply save the current time. (I.e., update: runs for the first time)

2. If the scene is paused, do not decrease the player's remaining time. It may seem strange, but the app continues to call update: even while your scene is paused, as discussed in Chapter 16, "Saving and Loading Games".

3. Finally, if the delta time since the previous time check is more than a second, update _timeInSeconds and _previousTimeInterval to the current values and then update the UI with the new amount of time remaining.

That should get your timer ticking. Give it a try!

Implementing a UIKit callback

Since your ViewController is now taking care of the scene flow, whenever the game reaches either a win or lose state, you would like your MyScene class to pass the ball back to the view controller.

Open **MyScene.h** and declare a new property:

```
@property (nonatomic, copy) void (^gameOverBlock)(BOOL didWin);
```

`ViewController` will pass a block to be executed upon game finish to the scene class. The block takes in one Boolean parameter so that the code knows whether the player won or lost.

Go back to **MyScene.m** and at the end of `update:`, add:

```
if (_timeInSeconds < 0 || _noOfLaps == 0) {
  self.paused = YES;
  self.gameOverBlock( _noOfLaps == 0 );
}
```

The code easily detects a game-over state by checking whether the player is out of time or out of laps. You pause the scene in both cases and then simply invoke the game-over block, passing `YES` to the block if the player completed all laps, and `NO` in any other case. Easy-peasy!

Now open up **ViewController.m** to add the game over code. First add this method, which shows a game over message to the user:

```
- (void)gameOverWithWin:(BOOL)didWin
{
  UIAlertView *alert =
    [[UIAlertView alloc]
      initWithTitle:didWin ? @"You won!" : @"You lost"
      message:@"Game Over"
      delegate:nil
      cancelButtonTitle:nil
      otherButtonTitles:nil];
  [alert show];
}
```

Here you just add a simple alert view to display whether the player has won or lost. In your games, this might be a good opportunity to present a new view controller or run some kind of animation.

Now scroll up to `viewWillLayoutSubviews:` and add this right after this line `_scene = scene;`:

```
__weak ViewController *weakSelf = self;
_scene.gameOverBlock = ^(BOOL didWin){
  [weakSelf gameOverWithWin:didWin];
};
```

You create a weak copy of your view controller in order to use it inside the block you are going to pass to the scene. Then you set a simple block to `_scene.gameOverBlock` that calls `gameOverWithWin:`.

That's all there is to it —you now have the complete game logic implemented. Give the game a try and finish all the laps:

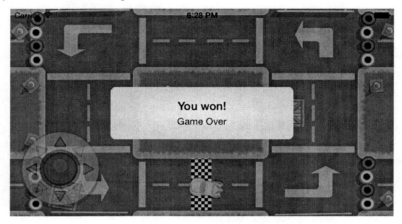

In this last chapter section you've learned how to pass the ball between SpriteKit and UIKit parts of your game. Next you will look into integrating UIKit in your game flow on an even bigger scale!

Navigating between screens

So far you don't have any navigation in your project. Well, it's time to add some. Like most classic racing games, Circuit Racer is designed to present the user with car and level selection screens when a game starts, and your next task is to implement them.

Adding a new view controller

Open **Main.storyboard**, grab a new view controller and drop it on the empty space in the storyboard:

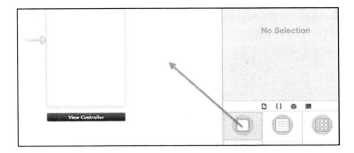

With the new view controller selected, open the Attributes Inspector, set the orientation to **Landscape** and tick the box that says **Is Initial View Controller**.

As the first order of business, drag an image view and hold it a bit before dropping it onto the view so it can resize itself to the view's frame:

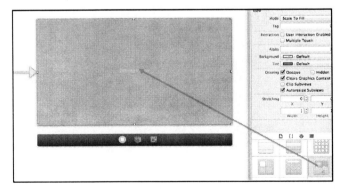

With the UIImageView selected, in the Attributes Inspector enter **bg-select-car.png** into the Image field. The screen background should show up.

Next add three buttons to the view controller, like so:

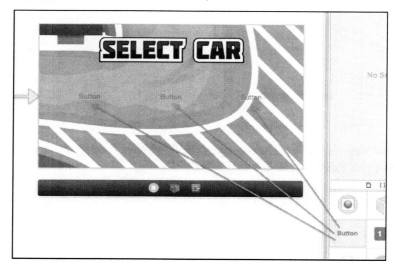

Select the button on the left and change the properties as follows: select **Custom** as the type, then delete the default button title and enter **btn-car1.png** for the image, and finally enter **1** for the tag:

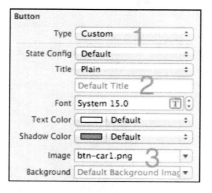

Select the button in the middle and make the same modifications, but for the image enter **btn-car2.png** and for the tag enter **2**.

For the button on the right, again make the same modifications, but for the image enter **btn-car3.png** and for the tag enter **3**.

You might need to realign the buttons so that they look nice on the screen (exact placement doesn't matter, just choose what looks good to you):

The provided assets make this screen looking great! And setting this screen up visually was a lot easier than if you had done it in plain Sprite Kit by manually setting positions for each button, eh?

In case you're curious, the dials below the cars indicate how fast each car is – remember how you made each car progressively faster based on the car number?

Adding additional view controllers

The first screen of the game is ready, but you need yet more screens. To get proper navigation you need to use a navigation controller.

To do this, first select the new view controller you just created by clicking on it in the dock:

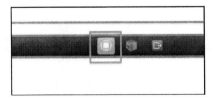

Then from Xcode's main menu, select **Editor/Embed In/Navigation Controller**. That should create a new navigation controller in the storyboard and also make it the initial controller that loads when the application starts.

With the new navigation controller still selected in the storyboard, open the Attributes Inspector and set **Landscape** for the orientation and select **None** for Top Bar. This last bit is important because otherwise you'll see a navigation bar item over your game scene.

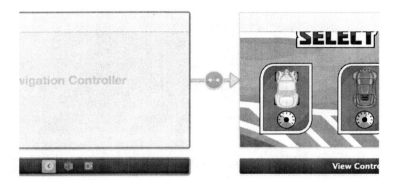

Now let's add the level selection screen, which from the user's point of view will be a difficulty selection screen. Start by dragging a new view controller onto an empty space in your storyboard. Once again, in the Attributes Inspector set the orientation to **Landscape**.

Just as before, drag in a UIImageView, let it grow until it resizes to take up all the space in the view and in the Attributes Inspector, set **bg-select-difficulty.png** as the image:

Now let's add buttons for the three difficulty levels. Just as for the previous screen, drag three UIButton instances one-by-one and this time, arrange them in a stack with equal spacing.

Select the top button and make the following adjustments in the Attributes Inspector: set **Custom** as the type, delete the prefilled title, enter **btn-easy.png** as the image and enter **1** as the tag.

For button in the middle, set the type to **Custom**, delete the prefilled title, enter **btn-medium.png** for the image and enter **2** as the tag.

Finally, for the button at the bottom, set the type to **Custom**, delete the prefilled title, enter **btn-hard.png** as the image and enter **3** as the tag.

Align the buttons again and you should end up with something like this:

Also add one more button in the bottom-left corner. Set its type to **Custom**, delete its title and enter **btn-back.png** for the image. This button will allow the player to go back and select a different type of car:

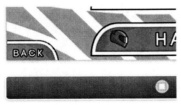

Great! Your storyboard is complete and it should look much like this, though don't worry if your controllers aren't aligned as beautifully as mine.

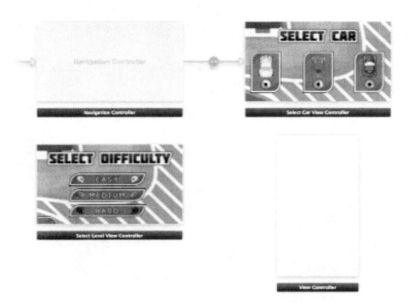

Implementing the navigation

Now let's add the code required for the navigation to work. As you've probably already guessed, the tags of the buttons correspond with the car and level types. You simply have to pass this info from screen to screen so that the user first selects a car, then a track and finally, the screen with the appropriate game shows up.

For this to work, you need two custom view controller classes. In Xcode's main menu, select **File\New\File…**, select the **Objective-C class** template and click **Next**. Enter **SelectCarViewController** for Class, enter **UIViewController** for Subclass of, uncheck any checked boxes and click **Next**. Finally, make sure the **CircuitRacer** target is checked and click **Create**.

Repeat these steps one more time but this time, call the new file **SelectLevelViewController**.

Now you need to connect your storyboard view controllers to your new custom classes. Open **Main.storyboard** again and zoom in on the car selection screen. Select the view controller object and switch to the **Identity Inspector** panel (third from left to right), then for both the Custom Class and the Storyboard ID, enter **SelectCarViewController**.

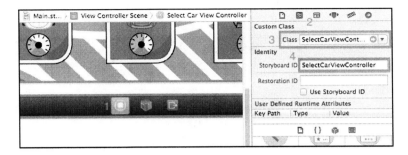

Now zoom in on the level selection view controller, select it, switch again to the Identity Inspection panel and for both the Custom Class and Storyboard ID, enter **SelectLevelViewController**.

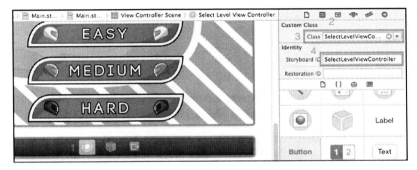

Select the original view controller that Xcode created for you and enter **ViewController** as the Storyboard ID:

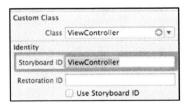

That takes care of configuring the controllers' identities. Next, open **SelectLevelViewController.h** and add a new property inside the class interface:

```
@property (assign, nonatomic) CRCarType carType;
```

This property will store the selected car type and will be set by the previous screen. Speaking of which, switch to **SelectCarViewController.m** and make the following changes.

Add these imports:

```
#import "SelectLevelViewController.h"
#import "SKTAudio.h"
```

Add this method:

```objc
- (IBAction)carButtonPressed:(UIButton*)sender
{
  [[SKTAudio sharedInstance]
    playSoundEffect:@"button_press.wav"];

  SelectLevelViewController *levelViewController =
    [self.storyboard instantiateViewControllerWithIdentifier:
      @"SelectLevelViewController"];
  levelViewController.carType = sender.tag;

  [self.navigationController
    pushViewController:levelViewController animated:YES];
}
```

At the top of the file, you import the next screen's controller and the audio library from SKTUtils, which you're going to need to play a sound when the user presses a button.

Next you define a new IBAction, carButtonPressed:, which plays an audio jingle and then fetches the next screen's view controller from the storyboard. You set SelectLevelViewController's carType property and then you push it to the screen.

Open **Main.storyboard** again and select the first button. Then, while pressing **ctrl** on your keyboard, drag with the mouse from the button to the view controller, like so:

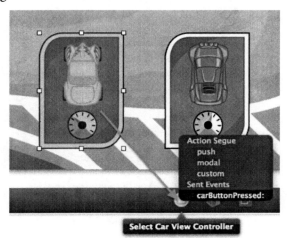

From the little popup menu, select **carButtonPressed:** to connect the button to the action. Repeat exactly the same procedure for the other buttons.

To add a touch of excitement to the game menu, let's play some wild racing tunes! Open up **SelectCarViewController.m** and add the following to `viewDidLoad`:

```
- (void)viewDidAppear:(BOOL)animated
{
  [[SKTAudio sharedInstance]
    playBackgroundMusic:@"circuitracer.mp3"];
}
```

This tune should get the players in the mood for a race.

Next open **ViewController.h** and add these two properties so that it can receive the player's game selections:

```
@property (assign, nonatomic) CRCarType carType;
@property (assign, nonatomic) CRLevelType levelType;
```

To finish up with `ViewController`, switch to **ViewController.m** and find the line where you create a `MyScene` instance:

```
MyScene *scene =
   [[MyScene alloc] initWithSize:_skView.bounds.size
                    carType:CRYellowCar
                    level:CRLevelEasy];
```

Replace it with the values you will be getting from the previous screen:

```
MyScene *scene =
   [[MyScene alloc] initWithSize:_skView.bounds.size
                    carType:self.carType
                    level:self.levelType];
```

Do you already see how everything's falling together to make this whole navigation thing work? I hope so. ☺

Open **SelectLevelViewController.m** again and add the following imports:

```
#import "ViewController.h"
#import "SKTAudio.h"
```

Then add these methods:

```
- (IBAction)backButtonPressed:(id)sender
{
```

```
    [[SKTAudio sharedInstance]
      playSoundEffect:@"button_press.wav"];
    [self.navigationController popViewControllerAnimated:YES];
}

- (IBAction)levelButtonPressed:(UIButton*)sender
{
    [[SKTAudio sharedInstance]
      playSoundEffect:@"button_press.wav"];

    ViewController *gameViewController = [self.storyboard
      instantiateViewControllerWithIdentifier:@"ViewController"];
    gameViewController.carType = _carType;
    gameViewController.levelType = sender.tag;

    [self.navigationController
      pushViewController:gameViewController animated:YES];
}
```

Here you define the action for the back button: it simply pops out the current view controller and plays a button sound effect.

For the level button pressed, you play the button jingle, fetch the next view controller from the storyboard, configure it and push it onto the screen.

Now to connect these actions, open **Main.storyboard** and select the **Select Level View Controller**. Just as you did before, hold down the **ctrl** key, **drag** with your mouse from the back button to the view controller and select **backButtonPressed:** from the popup menu. Then **ctrl-drag** from each of the difficulty buttons to the view controller and select **levelButtonPressed:** to connect them to this action.

Build and run the game and see how it all works together!

Everything works, except that the gameplay gets stuck at the point where you finish a game. Now that you have menus, you can just pop the gameplay view controller when the player finishes a game and bring them back to the game's GUI.

To quickly implement this, open **ViewController.m** and add the following new method:

```
- (void)goBack:(UIAlertView*)alert
{
  [alert dismissWithClickedButtonIndex:0 animated:YES];
  [self.navigationController popToRootViewControllerAnimated:NO];
}
```

And add this line at the end of `gameOverWithWin:`:

```
[self performSelector:@selector(goBack:) withObject:alert
  afterDelay:3.0];
```

The new `goBack` method hides the alert box and pops all view controllers back to the car selection screen. You simply call this method with a 3-second delay at the end of `gameOverWithWin:`.

Build and run the game once more, and you'll see that after you complete a level, win or lose, you're transported nicely back to the car selection, where you can try a different set of wheels.

Excellent! You've wrapped up the UIKit integration part of this book and can now extend your Sprite Kit games in many exciting ways with in-game HUDs and UIs, custom level selectors and anything else you can build with UIKit!

Challenges

You've achieved a lot in this chapter, but you can bring the project up one more notch! Solving this challenge requires you to apply what you've learned so far and make use of your UIKit skills in a new way.

As always, if you get stuck you can find the solutions in the resources for this chapter – but give it your best shot first!

Challenge 1: In-game menu

Like most games, Circuit Racer needs an in-game menu. In this challenge, you will add a pause button over the game scene and show a menu when a user taps the button.

Follow these simple instructions to implement this on your own:

1. Open **Main.storyboard** and switch the orientation of ViewController to landscape.

2. Add a button on top of your game scene in **ViewController** in your storyboard. Use the image **btn-pause.png** to fit it in the top-right corner.

3. Add an extra line to your **[ViewController viewDidAppear:]** method to send the SKView to the back, leaving the pause button visible at the front:

```
[self.view sendSubviewToBack:_skView];
```

4. Create a new IBAction method in ViewController called **showInGameMenu** and connect the pause button to it.

5. Make **showInGameMenu** show an alert with two buttons, one that says **Go to menu** and the other that says **Resume level**. Make your ViewController instance the delegate of the alert view.

6. To stop the level timer, set paused of the scene class to YES when you show the menu.

7. To get which button was pressed in the alert box you will need to add a – (void)alertView:(UIAlertView *)alertView didDismissWithButtonIndex:(NSInteger)buttonIndex method from the UIAlertViewDelegate protocol.

8. Don't forget to un-pause the scene, no matter which button the user pressed. If the user pressed **Go to menu**, simply call gameOverWithWin: and pass NO – this will end the game (with the you lose alert) and bring the player back to the menu.

If you implement all the steps, you should end up with a menu like this:

In addition to learning about UIKit in this chapter, you did a lot of review of Sprite Kit and should be feeling quite proficient.

This will give you the opportunity and the confidence to take on more advanced topics, starting with the next chapter – where you will control your Circuit Racer car via the built-in accelerometer!

Chapter 20: Accelerometer

By Marin Todorov

Apple's inclusion of the accelerometer was one of the big factors of the early success of the iPhone and iPod touch as gaming devices. Mobile gamers could play in a totally new and different way – by tilting the device. This allowed the players to change the point of view of the game, move the hero, or alter the game's gravity.

The accelerometer is a hardware component built into the iPhone that measures the acceleration over time caused either by gravity or by the movement of the device. It allows you, as a developer, to track the device's position in space and determine whether it is moving or still.

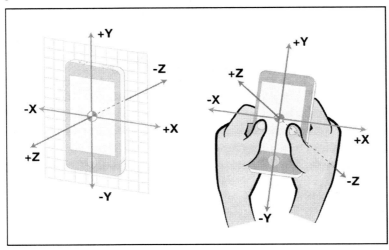

The accelerometer allows you to simplify a game's controls. It's more "natural" to tilt the device in the desired direction to move something within the game than it is to tap one button or another. This sort of feature is great for drawing casual gamers to your app – those who want to be able to play a game when they feel like it without thinking too much about the details.

Look at Doodle Jump, one of the early successes in the App Store. With it's accelerometer-driven game controls, it's so incredibly simple to play that almost anyone can pick it up and get started right away. That's what casual gaming is all about!

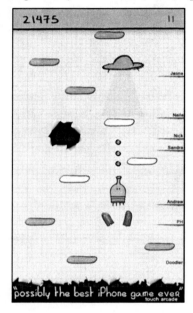

The topic of using the iPhone's accelerometer as game controller fits very well with the game you developed in the last chapter – Circuit Racer. The accelerometer is the perfect controller for a racing game, because steering with buttons is not much fun. Just look at some of the racing games in the App Store: Asphalt 7 and Need For Speed – Undercover, for example. They demonstrate that the accelerometer and driving are made for reach other:

In this chapter, you are going to learn how to read data from the accelerometer, turn this data into something useful, and allow the user to play Circuit Racer simply by tilting the iPhone.

> **Note:** This chapter begins where Challenge 1 left off in the last chapter. If you were unable to complete the challenges or skipped ahead from a previous chapter, don't worry – you can simply open **CircuitRacer-Starter** from the resources for this chapter to pick up where we left off.

Getting acceleration data

Run Circuit Racer and have a look at the way the game is set up so far. Players move through car type and level selection screens before reaching the main game scene, where they use an onscreen joypad to control the car:

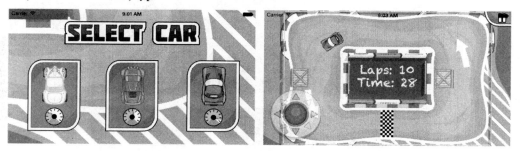

By the end of this chapter, the onscreen joypad will be history. You will be able to move the car solely by tilting the device.

> **Note**: To follow through this chapter, you will have to run the game **on the device** because there is no way to simulate the accelerometer while running the game in the iPhone Simulator on your computer.

In iOS, a framework called **Core Motion** takes care of connecting the hardware sensors like the accelerometer to your app. You normally "subscribe" one or more of your classes to updates from the sensors and can then read their measurements.

> **Note:** CoreMotion gives you access to the readings of three different sensors. The first is the accelerometer – you will learn tons about it while following through this chapter. The second is the gyroscope – it's a sensor measuring the device orientation in space, and the third is the magnetometer – it helps you out measuring magnetic fields. Accessing data from all those sensor works in a very similar fashion, so once you complete learning about the accelerometer, you can take on the gyro and magnetometer on your own.

Remember that when you switch on the accelerometer, it uses some extra energy to fetch the acceleration data, so you should only subscribe to it when you *need* the data – that is, when the game scene is actually displayed on the screen.

Turning the accelerometer on and off

It's time again to switch into coding mode! Open **ViewController.m** and make these few changes. First, add the following line just under the `#import` statements:

```
@import CoreMotion;
```

This imports the Core Motion framework, using the new syntax for importing frameworks introduced in Xcode 5. To learn more about this, check out Chapter 10 in *iOS 7 by Tutorials*, "What's New in Objective-C and Foundation."

Add this private instance variable:

```
CMMotionManager *_motionManager;
```

`CMMotionManager` is the class that gives you access to the accelerometer data. Here you declare a new instance variable `_motionManager` to get a hold of your manager instance.

Add this at the end of the `if` block in `viewWillLayoutSubviews:`, right after setting the `gameOverBlock`:

```
_motionManager = [[CMMotionManager alloc] init];
_motionManager.accelerometerUpdateInterval = 0.05;
[_motionManager startAccelerometerUpdates];
```

Here you create a new instance of the CoreMotion motion manager and instruct it to start reading acceleration data.

The code sets the `accelerometerUpdateInterval` to 0.05, meaning that the manager will read the accelerometer about 20 times per second.

That might seem like a lot at first sight, but since games are all about responsiveness, it could just as well be too few readings! The right frequency of accelerometer data varies per game type. For your own game, I encourage you to experiment with different intervals until you find the one that fits your gameplay. You also would not want to over-read the accelerometer – remember that doing this consumes a non-trivial amount of energy.

Now be a good iOS citizen and turn off the accelerometer as soon as the view is about to go off-screen. Add to `dealloc:`:

```
[_motionManager stopAccelerometerUpdates];
_motionManager = nil;
```

This way, as soon as the view controller is deallocated it will also stop the motion manager updates. How nice of you!

Getting the data

"But what are those updates and where can I find them?", you might be wondering. Never fear – `CMMotionManager` has a property called `accelerometerData` whose value gets updated constantly with the current accelerometer reading. It is up to you to repeatedly read this property and adjust your game accordingly.

The game loop update in `MyScene` feels like the right place to do this, so open **MyScene.h** and get cracking.

Import Core Motion to give `MyScene` access to `CCMotionManager`, like this:

```
@import CoreMotion;
```

And add this property:

```
@property (weak, nonatomic) CMMotionManager* motionManager;
```

You declare a weak property that will hold a reference to `ViewController`'s `motionManager`. Since `ViewController` owns both `MyScene` and a motion manager instance, you only need a weak reference to `motionManager`. This ensures that your scene does not hold onto your `CCMotionManager` when the `ViewController` tries to release it.

Go back to **ViewController.m** and at the end of `viewWillLayoutSubviews:`, where you create the motion manager instance, also add this:

```
_scene.motionManager = _motionManager;
```

Now your scene can get access to the accelerometer readings. I'm sure you're aching to see some output already, so let's take a peek at the accelerometer data.

Open **MyScene.m** and add this to the end of `update:`:

```
NSLog(@"accelerometer [%.2f, %.2f, %.2f]",
    _motionManager.accelerometerData.acceleration.x,
    _motionManager.accelerometerData.acceleration.y,
    _motionManager.accelerometerData.acceleration.z);
```

Now run the game again – don't forget that you have to keep running the game on your device throughout this chapter – and have a look at Xcode's output console:

```
2013-08-01 18:16:31.238 CircuitRacer[808:60b] accelerometer [0.57, 0.02, -0.59]
2013-08-01 18:16:31.257 CircuitRacer[808:60b] accelerometer [0.57, 0.02, -0.59]
2013-08-01 18:16:31.271 CircuitRacer[808:60b] accelerometer [0.62, -0.05, -0.85]
2013-08-01 18:16:31.287 CircuitRacer[808:60b] accelerometer [0.62, -0.05, -0.85]
2013-08-01 18:16:31.304 CircuitRacer[808:60b] accelerometer [0.62, -0.05, -0.85]
2013-08-01 18:16:31.321 CircuitRacer[808:60b] accelerometer [0.71, -0.02, -0.62]
2013-08-01 18:16:31.337 CircuitRacer[808:60b] accelerometer [0.71, -0.02, -0.62]
2013-08-01 18:16:31.354 CircuitRacer[808:60b] accelerometer [0.71, -0.02, -0.62]
2013-08-01 18:16:31.371 CircuitRacer[808:60b] accelerometer [0.73, -0.11, -0.50]
2013-08-01 18:16:31.392 CircuitRacer[808:60b] accelerometer [0.73, -0.11, -0.50]
2013-08-01 18:16:31.404 CircuitRacer[808:60b] accelerometer [0.73, -0.11, -0.50]
2013-08-01 18:16:31.421 CircuitRacer[808:60b] accelerometer [0.82, -0.08, -0.44]
2013-08-01 18:16:31.438 CircuitRacer[808:60b] accelerometer [0.82, -0.08, -0.44]
2013-08-01 18:16:31.454 CircuitRacer[808:60b] accelerometer [0.82, -0.08, -0.44]
```

Oh my! It definitely works, but what does it mean?

Interpreting the data

If you hold the device relatively still and just rotate it around its center, each of the x-, y- and z-components of the acceleration data will denote the rotation of the device towards its respective axis. The value of each axis ranges between -1 and 1.

Let's take a look at the x-axis acceleration only. Have a look at the diagram below to see how the x-axis is situated.

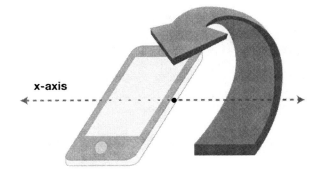

x-axis

The big arrow shows you how you rotate the device for the accelerometer to report acceleration around x.

And here's the how the three axes are situated together – note that unlike x- and y- axes which lay in the screen's surface, the z-axis just goes through the center of the screen upwards and downwards.

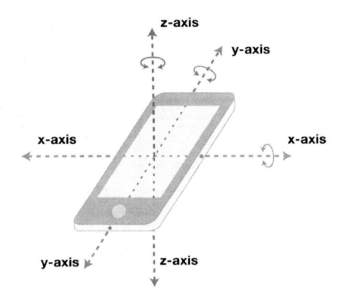

Now put your device on a table and then rotate it around one axis at a time while you watch the output console.

If you do this carefully, you should see only one data component change from 0 to 1, back to 0 and then to -1 as you rotate the device. This is a great way to understand how the accelerometer works.

All right, you now have the data – it's time to make some sense out of it.

Working with device orientation

The accelerometer code you are going to write in this chapter is based on a piece of code Alex Okafor wrote in a blog post of his called, "Lessons learned in Tilt Controls." The post summarized what Alex had learned while making *Tilt to Live*, a particularly great game released in the early days of the App Store that is heavily dependent on accelerometer controls. You can read the full post here:

http://www.paradeofrain.com/2010/07/lessons-learned-in-tilt-controls/

The biggest difficultly when working with the accelerometer is not fetching the current device position, but rather interpreting what the player *meant* by tilting the device to its current orientation. To do that, you first have to define a starting orientation.

Let's visualize the problem by considering again only the x-axis. Run the Circuit Racer game, navigate to the gameplay screen and then leave the device on a table. Look at the output console in Xcode. You should be seeing a lot of readings of about 0.00 for the x-axis, like so:

```
CircuitRacer[1898:60b] accelerometer [0.00, 0.01, -1.02]
CircuitRacer[1898:60b] accelerometer [0.00, 0.00, -1.03]
CircuitRacer[1898:60b] accelerometer [0.00, 0.00, -1.03]
CircuitRacer[1898:60b] accelerometer [0.00, 0.00, -1.03]
CircuitRacer[1898:60b] accelerometer [0.00, 0.01, -1.02]
CircuitRacer[1898:60b] accelerometer [0.00, 0.01, -1.02]
CircuitRacer[1898:60b] accelerometer [0.00, 0.01, -1.02]
CircuitRacer[1898:60b] accelerometer [-0.00 0.01, -1.05]
CircuitRacer[1898:60b] accelerometer [-0.00 0.01, -1.05]
CircuitRacer[1898:60b] accelerometer [-0.00 0.01, -1.05]
CircuitRacer[1898:60b] accelerometer [0.01, 0.01, -1.03]
CircuitRacer[1898:60b] accelerometer [0.01, 0.01, -1.03]
CircuitRacer[1898:60b] accelerometer [0.01, 0.01, -1.03]
CircuitRacer[1898:60b] accelerometer [0.01, 0.01, -1.04]
```

As you can see, the accelerometer's *neutral* position for the x- is when the device is horizontally flat, e.g. on a table.

Now rotate the device a bit around its x-axis (i.e. as pictured on the diagrams above) and monitor the output:

```
CircuitRacer[1898:60b] accelerometer [0.48, 0.02, -0.88]
CircuitRacer[1898:60b] accelerometer [0.48, 0.02, -0.88]
CircuitRacer[1898:60b] accelerometer [0.48, 0.02, -0.88]
CircuitRacer[1898:60b] accelerometer [0.53, 0.01, -0.86]
CircuitRacer[1898:60b] accelerometer [0.53, 0.01, -0.86]
CircuitRacer[1898:60b] accelerometer [0.53, 0.01, -0.86]
CircuitRacer[1898:60b] accelerometer [0.58, 0.01, -0.80]
```

The x-component increases and decreases in value, just as expected.

Now, think of all the times when you were playing an iPhone game while having your device lying flat on a table. That's right – it probably happened around zero times! Most of the time you hold your device at an angle – whatever feels comfortable to you.

This raises a difficult question for you: what position/orientation of the device would your typical player consider *neutral*? That is, from which device position will they most likely try to control your game? Probably not from a tabletop.

The answer is, the neutral position varies from person to person. You won't have a one-fits-all solution. Still, you can aim to satisfy most of the people, or even better, you can have several predefined positions for your player to choose from, like so:

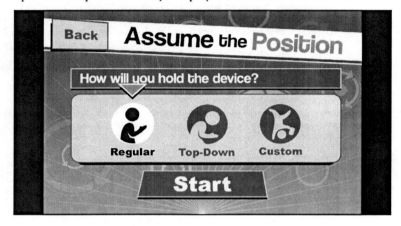

This is a screen from the original *Tilt to Live* game. The **Regular** position depictured on it is the position you will consider *neutral* in this chapter.

Tilt to Live's solution is actually quite smart – you should also consider it for your own games. Provide one or two default positions and let the player select how they intend to play the game. Alternatively if they select that they play the game in a Custom position – just save the readings from the accelerometer and make this position the *neutral*.

In any case implementing accelerometer based game controls is a non-trivial task. You better test your game with a number of people and consider their specific feedback in order to have the perfect game controls.

In this chapter you are going to implement one neutral position, similar to the one from *Tilt to Live*. Let's go!

Using accelerometer data

Now that you know more about how the accelerometer works and you understand the implications of device tilts, you can proceed to using the accelerometer data to move the car.

Getting the accelerometer vector

The game loop seems like a good place to move the car based on the accelerometer data, but it would be better to handle this in a separate method – it'll get messy inside update: if you do everything there.

In **MyScene.m**, add the following method:

```
- (void)moveCarFromAcceleration
{
  GLKVector3 raw = GLKVector3Make(
    _motionManager.accelerometerData.acceleration.x,
    _motionManager.accelerometerData.acceleration.y,
    _motionManager.accelerometerData.acceleration.z);

  if (GLKVector3AllEqualToScalar(raw, 0)) {
    return;
  }
}
```

And call this new method at the end of update::

```
[self moveCarFromAcceleration];
```

Okay, you are finally back to coding! You introduce a new method called moveCarFromAcceleration, which you call from the game loop. As the first order of business, you create a new three-dimensional vector called raw by calling GLKVector3Make(). In this new vector, you store the raw accelerometer data.

> **Note:** GLKVector3Make() and few other vector functions you'll use throughout this chapter are part of Apple's GLKit framework. One of the things GLKit provides is a bunch of extremely handy math functions like this that are heavily optimized for iOS hardware. In fact, much of SKTUtils is built on top of the GLKit math library!

> You can find the list of all GLKit functions dealing with three-dimensional vectors in GLKVector3.h. Fastest way to open that file is to ctrl-click on `GLKVector3Make()` and Xcode will take you to the header file where the function is defined.

At the end of the chunk of code above, you check if all the components of raw are equal to zero. That will be the case when there's no accelerometer data coming in yet. If there's no acceleration, there's no need to move the car around.

Defining the neutral orientation

Now comes the tricky part – defining the device's neutral position. Add it at the end of `moveCarFromAcceleration`:

```
static GLKVector3 ax, ay, az;

ay = GLKVector3Make(0.63f, 0.0f, -0.92f);
az = GLKVector3Make(0.0f, 1.0f,  0.0f);
ax = GLKVector3Normalize(GLKVector3CrossProduct(az, ay));
```

Let's discuss these vectors one-by-one.

Imagine that each of these three vectors defines the beginning origin and the direction of three axes – describing a whole three-dimensional coordinate system, in fact.

You define ay as (-0.63, 0, -0.92). This is a reading of the iPhone's accelerometer when you hold the device with two hands in front of you so that you are looking at the screen comfortably. This is, as you've seen, the most-used gaming position.

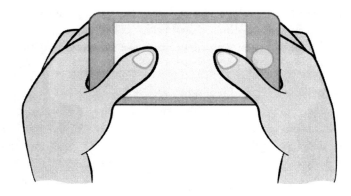

You define the az vector as (0, 1, 0). This is an auxiliary vector you need to build upon your ay vector and define a plane (you're going somewhere with this don't worry.)

Now your ay and az vectors define a rectangle and that looks approximately like so:

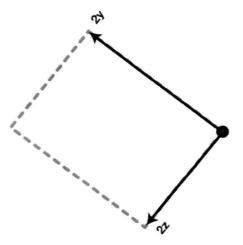

So when you add a third vector to those two above, that is both perpendicular to ay and az, you will get three perpendicular vectors which define for you a slightly tilted in 3D space coordinate system.

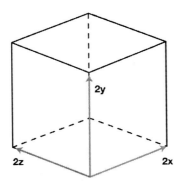

This will be your *neutral* coordinate system. I know it sounds quite complicated at this point, but all this you read just to understand better the why behind the what.

To make this a bit clearer, consider two coordinate systems. The first is aligned to the horizon and is the normal neutral position if the device is lying on a table. You could define it by using the three unit vectors (1,0,0), (0,0,1), and (0,1,0). The diagram below shows a cube that uses these three vectors as sides:

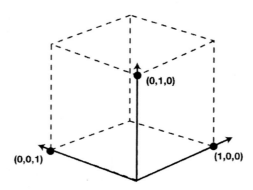

The second coordinate system is the one you just defined by ax, ay, and az, starting from ay, which is the vector reading of the accelerometer when people hold the device "normally." It looks like this:

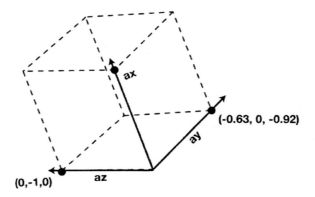

As you can see, this coordinate system is simply the first one rotated in space based on the new "neutral" ay. You need this rotated coordinate system so that you can use it as a starting point for reading the accelerometer.

Loosing a dimension – getting from 3D to 2D

So far, you have the current accelerometer vector (raw) and you have your new neutral coordinate system. So far you have your tilted 3D space coordinate system and your 3D accelerometer data. However your car moves only in 2D – the plane defined by the screen. In this section you will translate the 3D position of the accelerometer to a 2D vector, which you will use later on to set the car's velocity vector.

Let's see what the big idea is all about. Imagine you have a cube floating just above a small table. On top of the table there's a desk lamp. The shadow of the cube is the 2D projection on the table of the 3D cube – that wasn't so difficult eh?

To do that in code you will "project" (or "cast a shadow of" if you like that metaphor) the 3D acceleration vector over the plane define by (az, ax). Add this piece of code to moveCarFromAcceleration:

```
CGPoint accel2D = CGPointZero;
accel2D.x = GLKVector3DotProduct(raw, az);
accel2D.y = GLKVector3DotProduct(raw, ax);
accel2D = CGPointNormalize(accel2D);
```

You project the 3D `raw` vector over the `az` vector and get a scalar, which will be the x-component of your 2D vector. You do the same over the `ax` vector to get the y-component of your 2D vector.

At the end, you normalize the `accel2D` vector so that its values aren't too big or too small. Now the vector is perfect to use to determine direction, velocity, force, and so on – in fact, it's similar to the 2D vector you get from the joypad you developed in the last chapter.

Controlling for accelerometer "noise"

The accelerometer is a very "noisy" input device. It produces tons of data consisting of many small updates – sometimes it's more than you want!

It is very annoying for the player if the hero or the car in the game jumps around when the device is involuntarily tilted just a tiny bit. That's why you are going to implement an accelerometer *dead zone*.

Since your 2D acceleration vector is normalized, its components' values range from -1 to 1. Therefore, preventing the car from moving when the acceleration on the x or y-axis is less than 0.15 should give the player a nice comfort zone. The darker area in the image below represents the dead zone, in which you do not move the car:

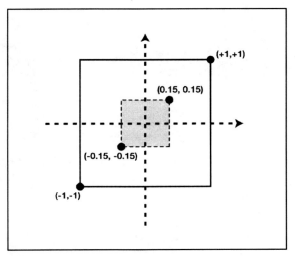

This simple piece of code should take care of the matter – add it to `moveCarFromAcceleration`:

```
static const float steerDeadZone = 0.15;
if (fabsf(accel2D.x) < steerDeadZone) accel2D.x = 0;
if (fabsf(accel2D.y) < steerDeadZone) accel2D.y = 0;
```

You define the dead zone as `steerDeadZone` and then you check if any of the x and y-coordinate values are less than the dead zone cap. In that case, you set the car's acceleration on that axis to zero.

You're almost there! Now you simply set the car body's velocity and let the physics simulation do the rest. Add this to `moveCarFromAcceleration`:

```
float maxAccelerationPerSecond = _maxSpeed;
_car.physicsBody.velocity =
    CGVectorMake(accel2D.x * maxAccelerationPerSecond,
                 accel2D.y * maxAccelerationPerSecond);
```

You multiply `accel2D` (the normalized direction vector) by the maximum speed per second and set the result as the body's velocity.

That's it! Give the game a try. You should be able to control the car by tilting the device:

In fact, you can now control the car both via the joypad and the accelerometer – it's your call!

Filtering out even more accelerometer noise

If you play a little longer with the car you will see it sometimes jittering and especially if you lean suddenly the device – the car jumps around hectically.

To prevent sudden changes of pace you will use another common trick in working with the accelerometer – a low pass filter.

The low pass filter will "smoothen" the changes of velocity in the car's movement by damping the change deltas on each coordinate.

Here's a visual representation of the effect of the low pass filter (taken from Apple's own accelerometer demo app).

https://developer.apple.com/library/ios/samplecode/AccelerometerGraph/Introduction/Intro.html

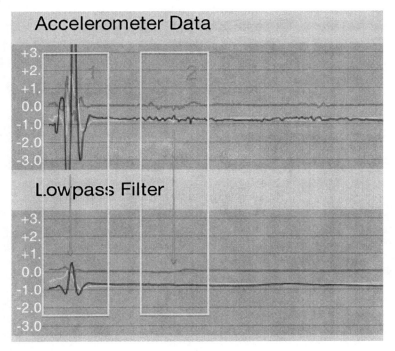

The graph represents the 3 coordinates of the acceleration vector. The above graph is the raw data and below you see the filtered values.

In region 1 you see the data from when I shook the device – in this case the filter smoothened the shock and prevented axis changes from -1.0 to 1.0 and back.

In region 2 you see the data from when I casually hold the device – the accelerometer picks up even the smallest shaking of my hand and therefore produces updates – that will make the car jitter. The low pass filter cuts out all these very small changes and the car will actually stands calmly ready to go.

Go ahead and add a new method that will take a raw 3D vector and will output the result of the low pass filter:

```
-(GLKVector3)lowPassWithVector:(GLKVector3)vector
{
    static GLKVector3 lastVector;
    static CGFloat blend = 0.2;

    vector.x = vector.x * blend + lastVector.x * (1.0 - blend);
    vector.y = vector.y * blend + lastVector.y * (1.0 - blend);
    vector.z = vector.z * blend + lastVector.z * (1.0 - blend);

    lastVector = vector;
    return vector;
}
```

This method always keeps the last accelerometer data vector in the static variable lastVector and uses it to dampen the changes on each coordinate from the new accelerometer data passed as vector parameter.

You can use this method as-is in your games. Try playing with the value of blend to see the effect it has on acceleration.

Now for the last bit – pass the accelerometer vector through your new low pass filter method. Back in moveCarFromAcceleration: find the line where you declare ax, ay, and az and insert the call above it:

```
raw = [self lowPassWithVector: raw];

static GLKVector3 ax, ay, az;
```

Run the game now and the car movement should look smoother. A side effect of the low pass filter is that it introduces inertia to the car movement and that's also real cool.

However, when you tilt the device the car does not rotate in the direction of the movement as it does when you press the joypad. Let's fix that before continuing.

Rotation dampening

As I said earlier, the accelerometer is quite a noisy input device. The acceleration can often jump around its neutral position, even with the dead zone you have in place, so you don't want to immediately rotate the car to any direction pointed to by the accelerometer.

You're going to dampen the car's orientation so that it doesn't jump straight to the new direction of acceleration, but instead responds with a bit of a delay. The car will rotate as the accelerometer instructs, but in several small steps rather than instantly.

Add this code to `moveCarFromAcceleration` to implement the rotation:

```
//1
if (accel2D.x!=0 || accel2D.y!=0) {

  //2
  float orientationFromVelocity =
    CGPointToAngle(CGPointMake(_car.physicsBody.velocity.dx,
                               _car.physicsBody.velocity.dy));

  float angleDelta = 0.0f;

  //3
  if (fabsf(orientationFromVelocity-_car.zRotation)>1) {
    //prevent wild rotation
    angleDelta = (orientationFromVelocity-_car.zRotation);
  } else {
    //blend rotation
    const float blendFactor = 0.25f;
    angleDelta =
      (orientationFromVelocity - _car.zRotation) * blendFactor;
    angleDelta =
      ScalarShortestAngleBetween(_car.zRotation,
                                 _car.zRotation + angleDelta);
  }

  //4
  _car.zRotation += angleDelta;
}
```

Here is what you are doing, step-by-step:

1. First you check if the accelerometer is in the dead zone. In that case, you don't rotate the car at all, as it's not moving on the track.

2. You get the angle from the acceleration vector and put it into `orientationFromVelocity`. You also declare the angle by which you will, at the end, rotate the car – `angleDelta`.

3. This next block is a tricky one – if the car needs to rotate from an angle of 175 degrees to 185 degrees that means the value of `zRotation` needs to change from 3.05 radians to -3.05 radians.

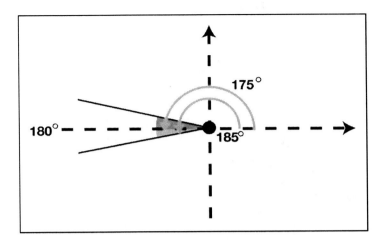

Therefore, if you apply damping to the rotation, it won't go over the 180-degree border, but will go all the way around the 0. It will actually rotate the long way around and that's not what you want

The quickest and best solution is to check whether the difference between the target and current angles is more than a whole radian and if so, simply set `angleDelta` straight to the new rotation value:

```
angleDelta = (orientationFromVelocity-_car.zRotation);
```

This introduces a miniature jump in the car rotation over the 180-degree margin, but it looks good and you don't have to worry about it.

On the other hand, if the new rotation is not going through the 180-degree margin, you want to apply damping to the rotation animation. First you fetch the difference between the target and current angles and take a small "step" in that direction:

```
angleDelta = (orientationFromVelocity - _car.zRotation) *
blendFactor;
```

For example, for a difference of 10 degrees, you get a resulting step of 2.5 degrees after multiplying by `blendFactor`, which you set to 0.25. This way the rotation will be smooth with no big and sudden jumps.

Finally, to make sure you are working with normalized angle values, you call `ScalarShortestAngleBetween` and overwrite what you had so far in `angleDelta` with the result.

4. The last line of your code adjusts the current car rotation by `angleDelta` (finally!). There you have it – smooth rotation in the flesh! Ahem, I mean in the code.

Build and run the game and see how the car now moves around with tilt control like it was absolutely real! Except, of course, that it doesn't turn into a smashed ruin when you hit the track walls.

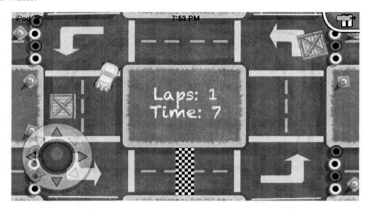

As a final touch, open **ViewController.m** and delete or comment out this entire section of `viewWillLayoutSubviews:` to remove the joypad:

```
const float padSide = 128;
const float padPadding = 10;
_analogControl =
  [[AnalogControl alloc] initWithFrame:
   CGRectMake(padPadding,
   skView.frame.size.height-padPadding-padSide,
   padSide, padSide)];
[self.view addSubview: _analogControl];

[_analogControl addObserver:scene forKeyPath:@"relativePosition"
                 options:NSKeyValueObservingOptionNew
                 context:nil];
```

What can I say? It was fun to learn how to create HUD controls with UIKit and you will definitely find yourself using those skills as a developer, but right now you are onto the next level of iOS sorcery – you are becoming a master of acceleration!

You now have a fully functional accelerometer-controlled mini-game! If you are interested in using more of the device's sensors with the Core Motion framework, have a look at Apple's documentation here:

https://developer.apple.com/library/ios/documentation/CoreMotion/Reference/CoreMotion_Reference/_index.html

You can fetch readings from the magnetometer and the gyroscope and create even more engaging games. The sky is the limit!

Challenges

Detect your neutral position

You still have the code that logs the current accelerometer reading to the output console. Monitor the output and figure what are the values for x, y, and z when you feel like holding the device "neutrally".

When you have the neutral values copy them over into the code and try the game again, does steering the car feel more natural? Remember that what is natural for you is not necessarily natural for everyone.

Now try playing the game in several different positions – e.g. while laying in bed, or sitting in a comfy chair. Check again the neutral x, y, and z values – they are pretty different compared to each other right?

Try different values for your neutral device orientation. See which one you would use in a game of yours.

Chapter 21: Game Center Achievements

By Kauserali Hafizji

So far in this book, all of the games you have created are single player only. However, players also want to be able to enjoy your game with their friends. Not only is it more fun to play games with others (whether on the same or opposite side), but it's also fun to boast about your achievements and high scores.

Luckily in iOS, adding social features like this is easy thanks to Apple's Game Center app and APIs. Over the next three chapters, you're going to learn all about Game Center and see how to put it to work in Circuit Racer. Specifically:

- In this chapter, you will learn about what Game Center is and take a quick tour of its features old and new, including those introduced in iOS 7. Along the way you will learn how to authenticate the local player, enable achievements and add support for them to your game.

- In the next two chapters, you will continue your investigations into Game Center by adding leaderboards and multiplayer support into Circuit Racer.

If you're ready to learn how to add a whole new level of interactivity to your game, put your racing gloves back on and get ready to rev your coding engine!

> **Note:** This chapter begins where Challenge 1 left off in the last chapter. If you were unable to complete the challenges or skipped ahead from a previous chapter, don't worry – you can simply open **CircuitRacer-Starter** from the resources for this chapter to pick up where we left off.

Introduction to Game Center

If you're an iOS gamer, you've probably come across Game Center already. Game Center consists of an app that acts as a central hub to browse your friends, leaderboards, achievements, and challenges:

Along with the app, Game Center provides a set of APIs that you can integrate into your game to support achievements, leaderboards, challenges, turn-based gaming, real-time multiplayer gaming, and more.

Not only is it a good idea to add Game Center support to your game to make it more fun, but adding Game Center support could potentially increase sales as well. If your game has Game Center support, you can benefit from a number of extra ways players can discover your app:

- **Listed on profile**. Your app will be listed on each player's game list, leaderboards, and achievements. If one of their friends checks out their profile, they might see your game!

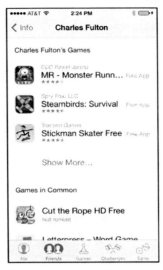

- **Friend challenges and requests**. Players can challenge their friends to beat the high scores in your game, or invite them to play a game if your game has multiplayer support. In either of these cases, they will have an option to download or buy your app, providing a viral growth mechanism.

- **More ratings**. If your app is in Game Center, when the user selects your app they have an easy way to rate your game or like it on Facebook. Anything that makes it easier for your players to rate your games is a good thing, as games with more and higher ratings are more likely to get downloads.

- **App Recommendations**. Games that have Game Center support can be auto-recommended to players based on what their friends play or other games they like. They are also more likely to be featured!

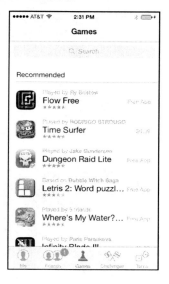

So adding Game Center support is a great idea, and Apple makes it nice and easy with the Game Center APIs. In this book, you will focus on achievements, leaderboards, and real-time multiplayer gaming and how to integrate it into a Sprite Kit game, since these are the most popular features of Game Center.

> **Note:** To learn more about turn-based gaming and challenges in Game Center, check out the Game Center chapters in *iOS 5 and iOS 6 by Tutorials*.

What's New in iOS 7

If you're a complete beginner to Game Center, you might want to skip this section since everything will be new to you anyway! ☺ But if you've used Game Center a bit and are curious what's new to iOS 7, read on.

Game Center has been out since iOS 4, and every new release of iOS has brought some new features to the APIs. Here's what's new with iOS 7:

- **A new user interface** for the Game Center app that fits in well with the iOS 7 style. As Apple said in the WWDC keynote, they ran out of green felt! ☺

- **Leaderboard sets.** This is an new feature that allows you to combine multiple leaderboards into a single group. This allows you to keep your leaderboards nicely organized into a hierarchy.

- **"Most recent" leaderboard type.** As the name suggests, this special kind of leaderboard will show the most recent score submitted by the player (rather than the highest score, which was the only option previously). This gives you more fine-grained control over what the ranking system is.

  For example, in a baseball game you might want to create a leaderboard to track the player's overall batting average. Since this batting average might increase or decrease over time, you want to always track the most recent submission rather than the highest or lowest.

- **Security changes to Game Center.** In iOS 7, Game Center includes some new features to prevent cheating in your apps, such as signed submissions, score management and score range.

- **Modal challenges.** Apple introduced challenges with iOS 6 and they are a neat way to keep players engaged. A modal challenge is one that is complete only when the challenged player has played the game in the same context as the challenging player.

  For example, consider a car racing game like Circuit Racer. If Player A challenges Player B to beat his/her time, Player B can only complete the challenge if s/he plays with the same car and on the same track as Player A.

You will learn about these new features in iOS 7 as you proceed through this chapter and the next. Let's get started!

Getting started

To do anything with Game Center, you first have to set up an app to use Game Center. This involves three steps:

1. Setting up your app for Game Center.

2. Register your app on iTunes Connect.

3. Enable Game Center features such as achievements and leaderboards.

Let's go through each of these steps one at a time. If you've used Game Center before, this may be routine for you by now. In that case, feel free to perform these steps yourself and skip to the "Authenticating local players" section.

Setting up your app for Game Center

Open CircuitRacer in Xcode if you haven't already, and switch to the CircuitRacer target settings. You will see the **Bundle Identifier** property in the **Identity** subsection under the **General** tab, as shown below.

Change the bundle identifier to a unique name. Each bundle identifier must be globally unique, and I've selected com.razeware.CircuitRacer already (and a few other variants for testing, like com.razeware.CircuitRacer3).

After you do, you might see a warning dialog like the following (if you don't see the warning just skip this step):

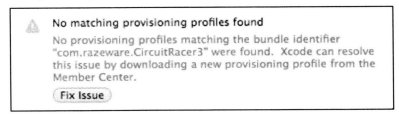

Click **Fix Issue**. This is a new feature in Xcode 5 that makes Xcode create an App ID and provisioning profile for you using your iOS developer account. If you're familiar with doing things the old way, this is a nice time saving!

Next, select the **Capabilities** tab and in the Game Center section click the **On** button. This also a new feature in Xcode 5 that makes it very easy to enable Game Center in your apps.

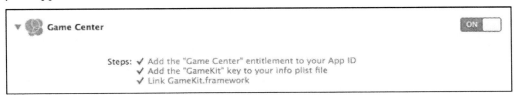

And that's it – with the click of two buttons, you're set up. Thanks, Xcode 5!

Registering your app on iTunes Connect

The next step is to create a new app on iTunes Connect. Log in to iTunes Connect, go to **Manage Your Apps** and click the **Add New App** button in the top-left corner. If you have both Mac and iOS developer accounts, you will be presented with a choice of app type – choose **iOS App**.

On the first screen, you need to provide a unique value in the **App Name** field, because it's the name that will appear in the App Store if you submit your app and it's accepted. I used "Circuit Racer," so you won't be able to use that name. Because this is only a test app, you could do something like **Your Name Circuit Racer**, using your actual name in place of the words "Your Name".

Enter **100** as the **SKU number** (this can be any number/word, so if you want you can set it to something else) and select the bundle identifier you created in the previous step.

> **Note:** SKU is short for stock-keeping unit, which is a unit that you personally make up to keep track of your applications.

Finally and most importantly, select the Bundle ID that you entered in your Xcode project.

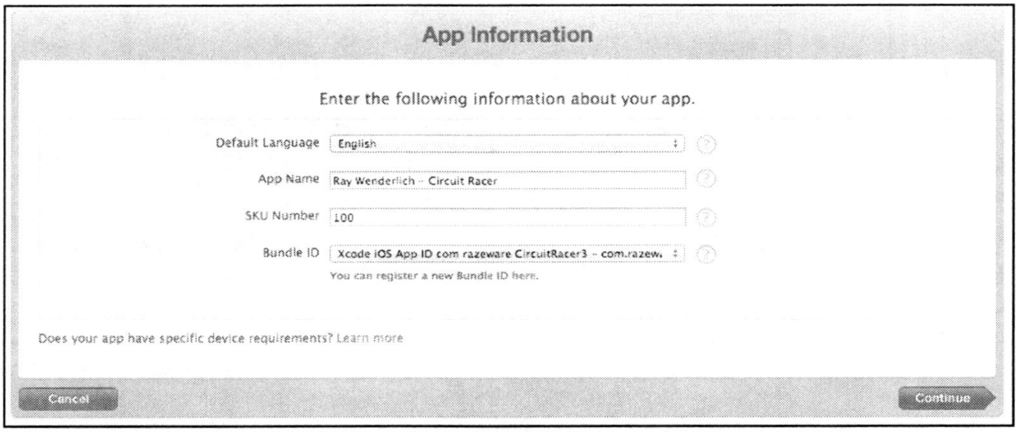

When you are done entering all the values, press **Continue**. Follow the prompts and enter all the required details. Since you just need to get through these steps for the purposes of this chapter, fill in only the necessary values and be as brief as you want to be.

You will need to upload a large app icon and a screenshot. To make the process easier, I have added an **iTunes** directory to the chapter's resources that includes the files you need.

> **Note:** Since Circuit Racer only works for the iPhone, you don't need to provide iPad-specific screenshots.

When you're done, click **Save**. If everything went well, you will be presented with the following screen:

Hurray! You have registered your app with iTunes Connect and completed the most perfunctory business. Now there are just a few more steps to activate Game Center.

Enabling Game Center achievements

You will only be dealing with Game Center achievements in this chapter, so select the blue **Manage Game Center** button on the right-side panel. You will be presented with the following screen to enable Game Center. Choose **Enable for Single Game**.

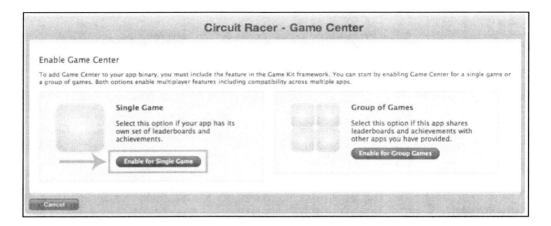

You will then see the following screen:

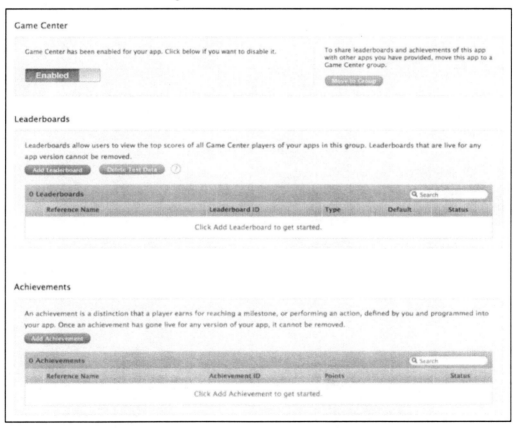

Now you've reached the exciting part. Circuit Racer will have four achievements for players to unlock:

1. **Destruction Hero:** Players will be able to earn this achievement multiple times and it will be hidden at first. You will award the achievement if the player hits the crates more than 20 times during a single race.

2. **Amateur Racer:** Players will earn this when they successfully complete the first level, that is, the easy difficulty level.

3. **Intermediate Racer:** Players will earn this when they complete the second level, that is, the medium difficulty level.

4. **Professional Racer:** Players will earn this when they complete the third level, that is, the hard difficulty level.

Let's create the first achievement. Click the **Add Achievement** button. You will be presented with a screen to enter some details about the achievement you want to create. In the **Achievement** subsection, enter the following:

- **DestructionHero** for the **Achievement Reference Name**. This is an internal name that you can use to search for the achievement on iTunes Connect.

- **[Your App ID].destructionhero** for the **Achievement ID**. This is a string that uniquely identifies each achievement. It is generally a good practice to use the App ID as a prefix while setting up the achievement ID. Be sure to use the App ID you set up above.

- **100** for the **Point Value**. This refers to the number of points the achievement is worth. Each achievement can have a maximum of 100 points and all achievements combined can have 1000 points maximum.

- Select **YES** for **Hidden**. This property will keep the achievement hidden until the player unknowingly achieves it.

- Select **YES** for **Achievable More Than Once**. As the name suggests, this property will ensure that the player can earn this achievement more than once. Moreover, when you set this property to YES, players will be able to receive achievement challenges from their friends even when they've already achieved them.

Achievement

Achievement Reference Name	DestructionHero
Achievement ID	com.razeware.circuitracer3.destructionhero
Point Value	100
	900 of 1000 Points Remaining
Hidden	Yes ⦿ No ◯
Achievable More Than Once	Yes ⦿ No ◯

Next select **Add Language** in the **Achievement Localization** section and enter the following details:

- **English** for the **Language**. Right now you're only adding a single localization (English) but if you are localizing your app you can repeat this process for other languages and select the appropriate language here.

- **Destruction Hero** for the **Title**. This is the title of the achievement that will appear in Game Center.

- **Bang into an obstacle more than 20 times** for the **Pre-earned Description**. This is the description you show before the player has earned the achievement. However in the case of this achievement it's hidden, so it doesn't actually matter what you put here.

- **Banged into an obstacle more than 20 times** for the **Earned Description**. This is the description you show after the player has earned the achievement.

- **achievement-destruction.png** for the **Image**. You need to add an image for each language, which in this case is just one. You can find this image file in the **iTunes** folder in the resources for this chapter.

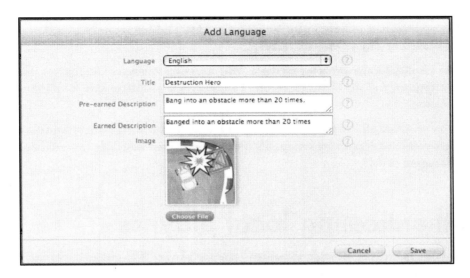

Click **Save** after you're done entering all the details. This should take you back to the main Game Center screen, only now you will see something in the Achievements section – Destruction Hero!

Now that you know what you're doing, create the other three achievements yourself by following the same process.

Here's a small table showing the values you should use, but be sure to replace **[Your App ID]** with your own App ID:

Achievement reference name	Achievement ID
Amateur Racer	[Your App ID].amateurracer
Intermediate Racer	[Your App ID].intermediateracer
Professional Racer	[Your App ID].professionalracer

Set each achievement to have **Point Value** set to **100**, **Hidden** set to **No**, and **Achievable More Than Once** set to **Yes**.

Also add English localizations for all three. You can enter whatever you like for the title and descriptions, and the iTunes directory contains an appropriate icon for all three achievements.

Once you've added all the achievements, click **Done** on the main Game Center screen. Now that you have everything set up, it's time to crack your knuckles and write some super-awesome code.

Authenticating local players

You're going to write some code to authenticate the player. Without an authenticated player, you can't use any features provided by Game Center.

Right-click on the **CircuitRacer** group in XCode and select **New Group**. Name the group **GameKit**. Next, right-click on the newly-created group and select **New File...**, choose the **Objective-C class** template and click **Next**. Name the class **GameKitHelper**, make it a subclass of **NSObject** and click **Next** again. Be sure the **CircuitRacer** target is checked and click **Create**.

This GameKitHelper class is where you're going to put all your Game Center code. An added benefit to you is that you'll be able to use this same class in of all your games without having to rewrite anything. I hope you agree that's pretty awesome!

Open **GameKitHelper.h** and replace the contents of the file with the following:

```
@import GameKit;

@interface GameKitHelper : NSObject

@property (nonatomic, readonly)
  UIViewController *authenticationViewController;
@property (nonatomic, readonly) NSError *lastError;

+ (instancetype)sharedGameKitHelper;

@end
```

All you've added here is a class method that will create and initialize a singleton GameKitHelper object, and two properties that provide access to a view controller and an NSError object. You'll see what those are for soon.

Next open **GameKitHelper.m** and add the `sharedGameKitHelper` method:

```
+ (instancetype)sharedGameKitHelper
{
  static GameKitHelper *sharedGameKitHelper;
  static dispatch_once_t onceToken;
  dispatch_once(&onceToken, ^{
    sharedGameKitHelper = [[GameKitHelper alloc] init];
  });
  return sharedGameKitHelper;
}
```

This method is straightforward; all you're doing is creating and returning a singleton.

Still in **GameKitHelper.m** add this private instance variable:

```
BOOL _enableGameCenter;
```

And add this initializer method that simply sets `_enableGameCenter` to true:

```
- (id)init
{
  self = [super init];
  if (self) {
    _enableGameCenter = YES;
  }
  return self;
}
```

By default, you're going to assume that Game Center is enabled on the user's device.

Add a new method named `authenticateLocalPlayer` that is responsible for authenticating the local player. Also add stubs for two methods called from `authenticateLocalPlayer`:

```
- (void)authenticateLocalPlayer
{
  //1
  GKLocalPlayer *localPlayer = [GKLocalPlayer localPlayer];

  //2
  localPlayer.authenticateHandler =
    ^(UIViewController *viewController, NSError *error) {
      //3
      [self setLastError:error];

      if(viewController != nil) {
        //4
```

```
            [self setAuthenticationViewController:viewController];
        } else if([GKLocalPlayer localPlayer].isAuthenticated) {
            //5
            _enableGameCenter = YES;
        } else {
            //6
            _enableGameCenter = NO;
        }
    };
}

- (void)setAuthenticationViewController:
  (UIViewController *)authenticationViewController
{
}

- (void)setLastError:(NSError *)error
{
}
```

I know it seems like a lot of code, so let's go through it step-by-step:

1. First you get an instance of the GKLocalPlayer class. This represents the player who is currently authenticated through Game Center on this device. Only one player may be authenticated on a device at a time.

2. Set the authenticateHandler of the GKLocalPlayer object. The Game Kit framework may call this handler multiple times.

3. Here you store any error the callback may have received using setLastError:, which is an empty method at the moment.

4. If the player has not logged into Game Center either using the Game Center app or while playing another game, the Game Kit framework will pass a view controller to the authenticateHandler. It is your duty as the game's developer to present this view controller to the user when you think it's feasible. Ideally, you should do this as soon as possible. You will store this view controller in an instance variable using setAuthenticationViewController:. This is an empty method for now, but you'll implement it in a moment.

5. If the player has already logged in to Game Center, then you set the authenticated property of the GKLocalPlayer object to true. When this occurs, you enable all Game Center features by setting the _enableGameCenter Boolean variable to YES.

6. If the user did not sign in – perhaps they pressed the Cancel button or login was unsuccessful – you need to turn off all Game Center features. As said previously, Game Center features are only available if the local player has logged in.

Since the authentication process happens in the background, the game might call the player's `authenticateHandler` while the user is navigating through the menu screens of the game or even while the player is racing.

In a situation like this, you're going to follow this strategy: whenever the game needs to present the GameKit authentication view controller, you will raise a notification, and whichever view controller is presently onscreen will be responsible for displaying it.

First you need to define the notification name. Add this line at the top of **GameKitHelper.m**:

```
NSString *const PresentAuthenticationViewController =
  @"present_authentication_view_controller";
```

Now add the following code inside `setAuthenticationViewController::`

```
if (authenticationViewController != nil) {
  _authenticationViewController = authenticationViewController;
  [[NSNotificationCenter defaultCenter]
    postNotificationName:PresentAuthenticationViewController
    object:self];
}
```

This simply stores the view controller and sends the notification.

The last method you need to fill out is `setLastError:`. This method will keep track of the last error that occurred while communicating with the GameKit service. Add the following code inside `setLastError::`

```
- (void)setLastError:(NSError *)error
{
  _lastError = [error copy];
  if (_lastError) {
    NSLog(@"GameKitHelper ERROR: %@",
        [[_lastError userInfo] description]);
  }
}
```

This simply logs the error to the console and stores the error for safekeeping.

Open **GameKitHelper.h** and add the following `extern` statement above the interface section:

```
extern NSString *const PresentAuthenticationViewController;
```

> **Note:** `extern` is a way of explicitly stating, for readability and compile-time enforcement, that you are just declaring this variable here and expect it to be defined elsewhere.
>
> The `extern` keyword itself, however, does not make the variable global. What makes a variable global is the position of its declaration in the file. If you declare a variable outside the interface in a class's header file, that variable is shared across and visible to all instances of your class, as well as to anyone who `#imports` the header.

Next add the following method declaration in **GameKitHelper.h**:

```
- (void)authenticateLocalPlayer;
```

You now have all the code in place to authenticate the local player. All you need to do is call this code in the relevant places in Circuit Racer.

Integrating with Circuit Racer

Pause for a moment to think about the architecture of the game. Each screen in the game is a separate view controller and is controlled by a navigation view controller. Therefore, you're going to implement authentication by creating a subclass of `UINavigationViewController`.

Go to **File\New\File...**, choose the **iOS\Cocoa Touch\Objective-C class** template and click **Next**. Name your class **CircuitRacerNavigationController**, make it a subclass of **UINavigationController** and click **Next** again. Be sure the **CircuitRacer** target is checked and click **Create**.

Next you need to set this class as the navigation controller for the game. Open **Main.storyboard** and select the navigation controller as shown:

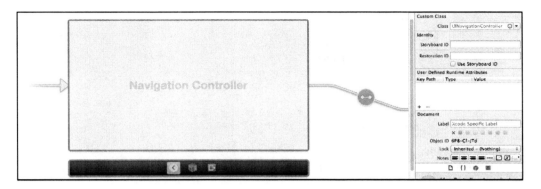

In the identity inspector, set the **Custom Class** property to
CircuitRacerNavigationController.

Great! Just a few more steps. Open **CircuitRacerNavigationController.m** and import
`GameKitHelper`:

```
#import "GameKitHelper.h"
```

Next implement `viewDidLoad` as follows by replacing the default stub with:

```
- (void)viewDidLoad {
  [super viewDidLoad];

  [[NSNotificationCenter defaultCenter]
      addObserver:self
      selector:@selector(showAuthenticationViewController)
      name:PresentAuthenticationViewController
      object:nil];

  [[GameKitHelper sharedGameKitHelper]
    authenticateLocalPlayer];
}
```

Here you are just registering for the `PresentAuthenticationViewController`
notification and making a call to the `authenticateLocalPlayer` method of the
`GameKitHelper` class.

> **Note:** As a general rule, you should always authenticate the local player as soon as the game starts.

Next add the following methods:

```
- (void)showAuthenticationViewController
{
  GameKitHelper *gameKitHelper =
    [GameKitHelper sharedGameKitHelper];

  [self.topViewController presentViewController:
    gameKitHelper.authenticationViewController
                                 animated:YES
                               completion:nil];
}

- (void)dealloc
{
  [[NSNotificationCenter defaultCenter] removeObserver:self];
}
```

The above methods are self-explanatory; you are simply presenting the authentication view controller over the top view in the navigation stack and deregistering for notifications when the object is deallocated.

It's time to build and run! If everything goes well, when the game launches you will be presented with the Game Center authentication view.

Enter your credentials and press Go. With Game Center, you only need to authenticate once. The next time you launch the game, Game Center will present a banner similar to the one shown below:

> **Note:** When you build a game in Debug mode the system automatically talks to Game Center's sandbox servers, which you can think of as a "test area" for your new achievements and leaderboards before the app goes live. You can see that you're in the sandbox by the *** Sandbox *** notification when you login. When you ship your app, it will automatically switch to production.

Adding achievements

In the previous section, you added four achievements to the game in iTunes Connect, so now you can go straight to writing code to award the achievements at the appropriate times within Circuit Racer.

Open **GameKitHelper.m** and add the following method:

```objc
- (void)reportAchievements:(NSArray *)achievements
{
  if (!_enableGameCenter) {
    NSLog(@"Local play is not authenticated");
  }
```

```
    [GKAchievement reportAchievements:achievements
             withCompletionHandler:^(NSError *error ){
                [self setLastError:error];
             }];
}
```

To report an achievement, you first need to create a GKAchievement object that stores the achievement's identifier and its percentage of completion. You'll create those later, but for now assume you have an array of these you wish to report to Game Center.

The good news is once you have this array, it's literally just one line to send: simply call GKAchievement's reportAchievements:withCompletionHandler:. This method automatically handles network errors for you, and resends the data to Game Center until it arrives successfully.

Declare the method in the **GameKitHelper.h** file, as shown below:

```
- (void)reportAchievements:(NSArray *)achievements;
```

Now let's integrate this into Circuit Racer for its specific achievements.

Integrating with Circuit Racer

Right-click on the **GameKit** group and select **New File…**, choose the **Objective-C class** template and click **Next**. Name the class **AchievementsHelper**, make it a subclass of **NSObject** and click **Next** again. Be sure the **CircuitRacer** target is checked and click **Create**.

Open **AchievementsHelper.h** and add the following import to access GameKit:

```
@import GameKit;
```

Next add the following constants above the implementation section in **AchievementsHelper.m**, but be sure to replace **.razeware** with **your own App ID**:

```
static NSString* const
  kDestructionHeroAchievementId =
@"com.razeware.circuitracer3.destructionhero";
static NSString* const
  kAmatuerAchievementId =
@"com.razeware.circuitracer3.amateurracer";
static NSString* const
  kIntermediateAchievementId =
@"com.razeware.circuitracer3.intermediateracer";
static NSString* const
```

```
    kProfessionalAchievementId =
@"com.razeware.circuitracer3.professionalracer";

static const NSInteger kMaxCollisions = 20;
```

> **Note:** Make sure the achievement IDs map exactly to the ones you've created in iTunes Connect. Remember – capitalization matters!

Next add the following method:

```
+ (GKAchievement *)collisionAchievement:
  (NSUInteger)noOfCollisions
{
  //1
  CGFloat percent = (noOfCollisions/kMaxCollisions) * 100;

  //2
  GKAchievement *collisionAchievement =
    [[GKAchievement alloc] initWithIdentifier:
     kDestructionHeroAchievementId];

  //3
  collisionAchievement.percentComplete = percent;
  collisionAchievement.showsCompletionBanner = YES;
  return collisionAchievement;
}
```

This is a helper method that makes it easy for you to report progress for the "Destruction Hero" achievement. Remember, this achievement is granted once a user has collided with 20 crates in a single race.

collisionAchievement: takes a parameter specifying the number of collisions that have occurred so far. It returns a GKAchievement that you can send to the reportAchievements method in GameKitHelper that you just wrote.

Here is brief stepwise breakdown of the method:

1. You can report achievement progress even if it is only partially complete. This calculates the percent complete based on the number of boxes hit so far compared to the maximum boxes (20).

2. You create a GKAchievement object using the Destruction Hero achievement identifier.

3. You set the `percentComplete` property of the `GKAchievement` object to the one calculated in the first step.

Now that you have a helper method to create the Destruction Hero achievement, let's do the same for the achievements corresponding to each difficulty level. Remember you will unlock these achievements only when the player has completed each level.

Add the following method:

```
+ (GKAchievement *)achievementForLevel:(CRLevelType)levelType
{
  NSString *achievementId = kAmatuerAchievementId;
  if (levelType == CRLevelMedium) {
    achievementId = kIntermediateAchievementId;
  } else if(levelType == CRLevelHard) {
    achievementId = kProfessionalAchievementId;
  }

  GKAchievement *levelAchievement =
    [[GKAchievement alloc] initWithIdentifier:achievementId];

  levelAchievement.percentComplete = 100;
  levelAchievement.showsCompletionBanner = YES;
  return levelAchievement;
}
```

This method is similar to `collisionAchievement:`. It creates an achievement depending upon the game level.

Before moving on, add declarations for these methods in **AchievementsHelper.h**:

```
+ (GKAchievement *)collisionAchievement:
  (NSUInteger)noOfCollisions;
+ (GKAchievement *)achievementForLevel:(CRLevelType)levelType;
```

Now that you have these helper methods in place, you need to make use of them in the actual game. Open **MyScene.m** and import both your helper classes:

```
#import "AchievementsHelper.h"
#import "GameKitHelper.h"
```

Add a private instance variable to track the number of collisions between the car and the boxes:

```
NSUInteger _noOfCollisionsWithBoxes;
```

Initialize this variable in `initWithSize:carType:level:`, just after you set `_levelType`:

```
_noOfCollisionsWithBoxes = 0;
```

Next you need to tell the scene about physics collisions. The cars and boxes are already set up to collide and generate contact messages, but right now, no one is listening. Add the following above the implementation section:

```
@interface MyScene()<SKPhysicsContactDelegate>
@end
```

Now add this line at the end of `initializeGame`:

```
self.physicsWorld.contactDelegate = self;
```

Finally, you need to implement `didBeginContact:`. Add this method:

```
- (void)didBeginContact:(SKPhysicsContact *)contact
{
  if (contact.bodyA.categoryBitMask +
      contact.bodyB.categoryBitMask == CRBodyCar + CRBodyBox){

    _noOfCollisionsWithBoxes += 1;

    [self runAction:_boxSoundAction];
  }
}
```

You call this method every time the car and box collide. You need to increment the counter you declared earlier by 1, and just for fun, play a collision sound, too.

Okay! All that's left to do now is to actually report achievements. Add the following new method:

```
-(void)reportAchievementsForGameState:(BOOL)hasWon
{

  NSMutableArray *achievements = [NSMutableArray array];

  [achievements addObject:
    [AchievementsHelper collisionAchievement:
     _noOfCollisionsWithBoxes]];

  if (hasWon) {
    [achievements addObject:
      [AchievementsHelper achievementForLevel:_levelType]];
```

```
    }

    [[GameKitHelper sharedGameKitHelper]
        reportAchievements:achievements];
}
```

This method is easy to understand. You pass in a Boolean variable that describes if the player has won or lost a game. If the player has won, you create an achievement for that level and report it to Game Center. Either way, you always report the collision achievement.

Inside `update:`, add the following line just before the call to `self.gameOverBlock`:

```
[self reportAchievementsForGameState:( _noOfLaps == 0 )];
```

It's time to build and run again, and run some tests. I know it might be difficult to finish all three levels but if you want those achievements, you better complete those laps before the time's up! Every time you earn an achievement, Game Center will show a banner like this:

Achievement unlocked: You have successfully added achievements into your game!

Initializing the built-in user interface

You now have achievements in your game, but what if your player wants to see what achievements he or she has unlocked so far?

At this point, their only option is to check their achievements in the built-in Game Center app. But of course, this requires the player to leave your app, which is never a good thing. It would be much better if there were a way for a player to see their progress right from within your app – and luckily, there is!

The GameKit framework provides a class called GKGameCenterViewController that allows your players to view their achievements, leaderboards, and challenges right from within your app. Let's try this out and add this into Circuit Racer.

Open **GameKitHelper.m** and add the following method:

```
- (void)showGKGameCenterViewController:
  (UIViewController *)viewController
{
  if (!_enableGameCenter) {
    NSLog(@"Local play is not authenticated");
  }
  //1
  GKGameCenterViewController *gameCenterViewController =
    [[GKGameCenterViewController alloc] init];

  //2
  gameCenterViewController.gameCenterDelegate = self;

  //3
  gameCenterViewController.viewState =
    GKGameCenterViewControllerStateAchievements;

  //4
  [viewController presentViewController:gameCenterViewController
                              animated:YES
                            completion:nil];
}
```

The above method is responsible for creating and displaying the GKGameCenterViewController. The steps involved in doing so are:

1. First initialize an object of GKGameCenterViewController.

2. Set the delegate of the `GKGameCenterViewController`. Game Center informs the delegate when the user finishes interacting with the `GKGameCenterViewController`. You'll look into that in just a moment.

3. Set the default view state to `GKGameCenterViewControllerStateAchievements`. This means that when you display the Game Center view controller, the first view you show is the achievements view.

4. Finally, present the view controller.

Next you need to implement the `GKGameCenterControllerDelegate` protocol. In **GameKitHelper.m**, add the following above the implementation section:

```
@interface GameKitHelper()<GKGameCenterControllerDelegate>
@end
```

Next implement the required delegate method:

```
- (void)gameCenterViewControllerDidFinish:
  (GKGameCenterViewController *)gameCenterViewController
{
  [gameCenterViewController dismissViewControllerAnimated:YES
                                               completion:nil];
}
```

And now the last step: declare `showGKGameCenterViewController:` in **GameKitHelper.h**, as shown below:

```
- (void)showGKGameCenterViewController:
  (UIViewController *)viewController;
```

That's all it takes to present the `GKGameCenterViewController` – all you need to do now is integrate it into Circuit Racer.

Integrating with Circuit Racer

First things first, you need a new view controller to act as the "home screen" for Circuit Racer. To do this, open **Main.storyboard** and drag a new View Controller into the storyboard. In the **Attributes Inspector**, set the **Orientation** to **Landscape**:

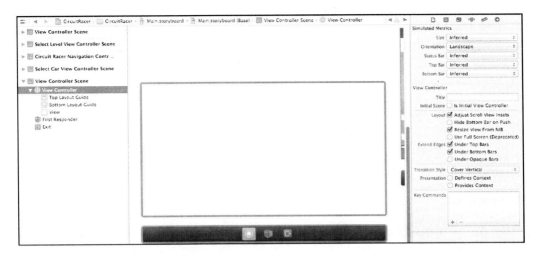

Drag an image view into the view controller and make it fill the entire view controller. Set the image to **bg-main-menu.png**. Then drag two buttons to the view controller, set them to **Custom**, delete their titles, and set the images to **btn-play.png** and **btn-gamecenter.png**.

At this point your view controller should look like this:

Next create a new file with the **iOS\Cocoa Touch\Objective-C** class template, enter **HomeScreenViewController** for the class and **UIViewController** for Subclass of. Click **Next** and then **Create**.

Back in **Main.storyboard**, select your new view controller and in the Identity Inspector, set the Class and Storyboard ID to **HomeScreenViewController**:

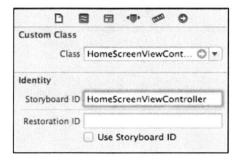

Next, control-drag from the Circuit Racer Navigation Controller to the Home Screen View Controller. In the popup that appears, select **root view controller**:

This makes the Home Screen View Controller appear before the Select Car View controller.

Finally, you need to add action methods for both buttons. Select **HomeScreenViewController** and make sure the Assistant Editor is open with **HomeScreenViewController.m** visible. Control-drag from the play button to **HomeScreenViewController.m**, enter **playGame** for the name, and click **Connect**. Repeat for **gameCenter**, but enter **gameCenter** for the name.

Now open **HomeScreenViewController.m** and add the following import statements:

```
#import "GameKitHelper.h"
#import "SelectCarViewController.h"
#import "SKTAudio.h"
```

Next implement `playGame:` and `gameCenter:` methods as follows:

```
- (IBAction)playGame:(id)sender {

    [[SKTAudio sharedInstance]
      playSoundEffect:@"button_press.wav"];

    SelectCarViewController *carViewController =
      [self.storyboard instantiateViewControllerWithIdentifier:
       @"SelectCarViewController"];

    [self.navigationController
      pushViewController:carViewController animated:YES];
}

- (IBAction)gameCenter:(id)sender {
    [[SKTAudio sharedInstance]
      playSoundEffect:@"button_press.wav"];
    [[GameKitHelper sharedGameKitHelper]
      showGKGameCenterViewController:self];

}
```

Build and run. Once you've authenticated the player, pressing the Game Center button will open up the `GKGameCenterViewController`, which looks like the image on the following page:

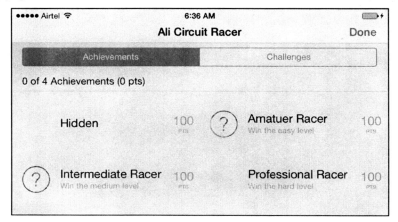

I hope you're as pleased as I am with the new Game Center UI in iOS 7.

And that's it – you have now added Game Center, achievements, and a game center view controller into Circuit Racer! In the coming two chapters, you will learn about the changes in Game Center leaderboards and about multiplayer APIs. But first – a quick challenge for you!

Challenges

Before you proceed to the next chapter, here is a challenge that will ensure you've understood majority of the chapter.

If you get stuck, you can find the solutions in the resources for this chapter, but give it your best shot first!

Challenge 1: Racing addict achievement

Create a new achievement in iTunes Connect called **Racing addict**. Hide it initially and award it if the player plays the game at least 10 times in a row.

Here are a few hints to do this:

• Create a static variable to track the number of times the local player has played the game.

• Every time the game completes, check to see if that variable has crossed 10.

• You can use one of the images for the other achievements to create this achievement.

Chapter 22: Game Center Leaderboards

By Kauserali Hafizji

In the last chapter, you learned the steps required to set up your game to use Game Center, authenticate the local player and enhance the player's experience with achievements. You also implemented Game Center's built-in user interface.

In this chapter, you are going to focus on another awesome Game Center feature: leaderboards. Think of a leaderboard as a database of the scores of all the players playing your game. The biggest advantage of adding leaderboards to your game is that it allows players to see how they are doing in comparison to other players.

Traditionally, building a leaderboard required a lot of server-side infrastructure, not to mention considerable time spent working on the server-side component. Game Center makes it easy to add this feature to your game – just add a few lines of code and you're all set.

Let's try this out and add some leaderboards to Circuit Racer!

Note: This chapter begins where Challenge 1 left off in the last chapter. If you were unable to complete the challenges or skipped ahead from a previous chapter, don't worry – you can simply open **CircuitRacer-Starter** from the resources for this chapter to pick up where we left off.

However, to follow along with this chapter you will have to set up an entry in iTunes Connect for Circuit Racer and a number of achievements. For instructions on how to perform these steps, see the previous chapter.

Supporting leaderboards

To add leaderboards to your game, you need to perform five steps. Here's a quick overview, then we'll go through each step with Circuit Racer.

1. **Authenticate the local player.** Remember that to use any Game Center feature, you first need to authenticate the local player.

2. **Create a strategy for using leaderboards in the game.** Decide how many leaderboards the game is going to have and how each leaderboard will interpret scores.

3. **Configure leaderboards in iTunes Connect.** Add each leaderboard and set its name and formatting, such as the score range. Optionally, add an image for each leaderboard.

4. **Add code to report scores to Game Center.** Similar to how you added code to send an array of `GKAchievements` to Game Center in the previous chapter, you need to add similar code to send an array of `GKScores`.

5. **Add code to display the leaderboards to the player.** You'll use the `GKGameCenterViewController` as you did for achievements. Optionally, you can also retrieve the score data and display the leaderboard in a custom user interface.

The rest of this section will go through these steps one-by-one.

Step 1: Authenticating the local player

You added support for player authentication to Circuit Racer in the previous chapter, so you can skip this step. If you'd like to go over the process one more time, have a look at `authenticateLocalPlayer` in the `GameKitHelper` class.

Step 2: Creating a leaderboard strategy

To support leaderboards, your game needs to have a scoring mechanism that allows the game to calculate a fixed score every time the player finishes a race. The only restriction Game Center puts on this score is that it needs to be a 64-bit integer.

Since Circuit Racer is a race against time, let's keep the scoring mechanism as the time required to complete a track. This means the game will report the amount of time it took for the local player to complete each track. Those players who finished the track in the shortest amount of time will be at the top of the leaderboard.

Sounds like a plan!

Before you move onto the next step, you also need to decide on the number of leaderboards your game will support. It's not mandatory to have multiple leaderboards, but it's usually a good idea, as it gives the player a fine-grained look at the position they hold among all the game's players.

In Circuit Racer, the player chooses a car and then selects a difficulty level. To account for all the possible car/difficulty combinations, you're going to create a total of nine leaderboards. For example, the first leaderboard will be **Car_1_level_easy_fastest_time**. Your other leaderboards will similarly cover all the other car and difficulty level combinations. Later, in the chapter you will use these nine leaderboards to create leaderboard sets. Keep reading to know more.

Step 3: Configuring leaderboards in iTunes Connect

Login to iTunes Connect using your credentials and select the **Manage Your Apps** option, then choose your Circuit Racer app – its exact name is unique and will be whatever you called it when going through the last chapter. Select the **Manage Game Center** option on the right.

Select the **Add Leaderboard** button under the Leaderboards section.

Leaderboards

Leaderboards

Leaderboards allow users to view the top scores of all Game Center players of your app. Leaderboards that are live for any app version cannot be removed.

Add Leaderboard   Delete Test Data ⓘ

0 Leaderboards				🔍 Search
Reference Name	Leaderboard ID	Type	Default	Status
Click Add Leaderboard to get started.				

Then select the **Single Leaderboard** option to create a new leaderboard.

> **Note**: The other option (Combined Leaderboard) allows you to create a new "virtual leaderboard" that combines the results of several leaderboards.
>
> For example, if you wanted you could create a leaderboard for Circuit Racer called "Any car level easy fastest time" that combines the results of "Car 1 level easy fastest time", "Car 2 level easy fastest time", and "Car 3 level easy fastest time".
>
> You would still report your scores to each individual leaderboard – this just provides an easy way to aggregate the results for players across several leaderboards that share the same score format type and sort order.

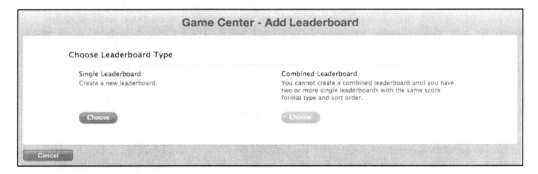

If you're wondering what each of those fields on the next page are, don't fret! Enter the following values:

- **Car 1 level easy fastest time** for the **Leaderboard Reference Name**. This is a string that represents the internal name for the leaderboard. You can use this string to search for leaderboards within iTunes Connect.

- **[Your App ID].car1_level_easy_fastest_time** for the **Leaderboard ID**. This string uniquely identifies the leaderboard. You will use this identifier to report scores to Game Center. It's usually best practice to use the App ID as a prefix.

- **Elapsed Time – To the Second** as the **Score Format Type**. This field specifies the format of the scores you'll send for this particular leaderboard. It also tells Game Center how to interpret the scores. Your game's scoring mechanism is based on time, so you choose the appropriate format.

- **Best Score** as the **Score Submission Type**. This field specifies which score the leaderboard will display first, the best or the most recent one.

- **Low to High** as the **Sort Order**. This field dictates how the scores are arranged in the leaderboard. In our case since the lowest time refers to the highest score, select here.

- **1 to 60** for the **Score Range**. Even though this field is optional, I recommend you add a value here. You will learn more about this field in the sections to come, so stay tuned. For now, you enter **1** and **60**, which are the lowest and highest values from the game's **LevelDetails.plist** file.

Single Leaderboard	
Leaderboard Reference Name	Car 1 level easy fastest time
Leaderboard ID	com.razeware.circuitracer3.car1_level_easy_fastest_time
Score Format Type	Elapsed Time – To the Second
Score Submission Type	⦿ Best Score ◯ Most Recent Score
Sort Order	⦿ Low to High ◯ High to Low
Score Range (Optional)	1 To 60
	0:00:01 0:01:00

The next step is to add a language. Select the **Add Language** button in the **Leaderboard Localization** section. The important thing to keep in mind is that these are the settings that affect what your users will see, so choose wisely.

Fill in the following details:

- **English** for the **Language**.

- **Yellow Car Easy Level Fastest Time** for the **Name**. This is the name of the leaderboard that players will see.

- **Elapsed Time (hours, minutes, seconds, ex. 5:01:18)** for the **Score Format**. This is the format Game Center will use to display the scores in the leaderboard.

- **seconds** for the **Score Format Suffix**. This is the suffix that Game Center adds to the score submitted by the device. Circuit Racer measures a player's score in seconds.

You can optionally upload an image for each language. In this chapter, you won't be adding any images to leaderboards, though I highly recommended that you do so in your own games as this shows up in Game Center.

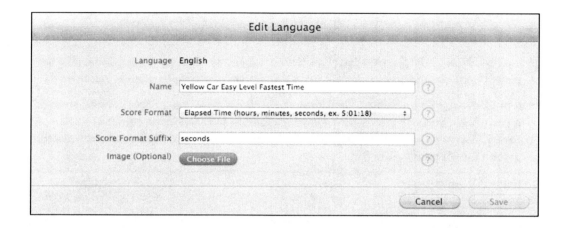

> **Note:** You can add multiple languages to each leaderboard and Game Center will display the correct language according to the locale set on the phone.

Select the **Save** button when you are done entering all the details. This will create a new leaderboard, as shown below.

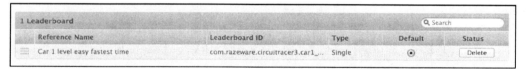

Now you need to create the other eight leaderboards for the game. Since you already know how to create a single leaderboard, doing the rest should be easy. Make sure you follow the table below while entering the data required for each leaderboard.

Yes this is a bit tedious, but think of it this way - by the time you're done you'll be an expert at setting up leaderboards in iTunes Connect! ☺

Reference Name	Leaderboard ID	Score range
Car 1 level medium fastest time	[Your App ID].car1_level_medium_fastest_time	1 – 50
Car 1 level hard fastest time	[Your App ID].car1_level_hard_fastest_time	1 – 35
Car 2 level easy fastest time	[Your App ID].car2_level_easy_fastest_time	1 – 60
Car 2 level medium fastest time	[Your App ID].car2_level_medium_fastest_time	1 – 50
Car 2 level hard fastest time	[Your App ID].car2_level_hard_fastest_time	1 – 35
Car 3 level easy fastest time	[Your App ID].car3_level_easy_fastest_time	1 – 60
Car 3 level medium fastest time	[Your App ID].car3_level_medium_fastest_time	1 – 50
Car 3 level hard fastest time	[Your App ID].car3_level_hard_fastest_time	1 – 35

Enter whatever you like for the English localization for each, based on the previous examples.

After you're done entering all the details, your leaderboards table in iTunes Connect should look like the one below:

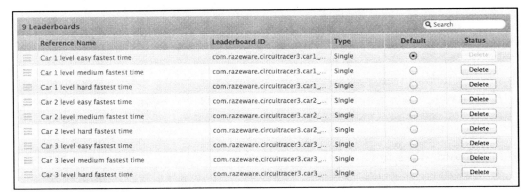

When you've added your leaderboards, click **Done** to go back to your app's information page, and then click **Done** to get back to the Manage Your Apps page.

Step 4: Reporting scores to Game Center

Now that you've got the leaderboards set up in iTunes Connect, it's time to write some code. To keep things simple, you're going to add a method to the `GameKitHelper` class that will report a score to a leaderboard identified by its leaderboard ID.

Make sure Circuit Racer is open in Xcode, then open **GameKitHelper.m** and add the following method:

```
- (void)reportScore:(int64_t)score
    forLeaderboardID:(NSString *)leaderboardID
{
  if (!_enableGameCenter) {
    NSLog(@"Local play is not authenticated");
  }
  //1
  GKScore *scoreReporter =
    [[GKScore alloc]
      initWithLeaderboardIdentifier:leaderboardID];
  scoreReporter.value = score;
  scoreReporter.context = 0;

  NSArray *scores = @[scoreReporter];

  //2
  [GKScore reportScores:scores
   withCompletionHandler:^(NSError *error) {
     [self setLastError:error];
   }];
}
```

The above code is responsible for creating and sending a score to Game Center. Here is a step-wise explanation:

1. First the method creates an object of type `GKScore` that holds information about the player's score. Game Center expects you to send out scores using this object. It also returns objects of type `GKScore` when you retrieve scores.

   As you can see, a `GKScore` simply stores a value – the number to send to the leaderboard, which in this case is the number of seconds. You can also set a `context` for each score, which is an arbitrary 64-bit unsigned integer that you can associate with a score value, for use when you retrieve scores later. You don't need this for Circuit Racer, so you set it to 0.

2. Next the method reports the score using `GKScore`'s `reportScores:withCompletionHandler:` class method. The code calls the completion handler when Game Center is done processing the scores, and again this method takes care of auto-resending scores on network failures. Here you just log any error that Game Center may have returned.

Open **GameKitHelper.h** and declare the above method as shown below:

```
- (void)reportScore:(int64_t)score
   forLeaderboardID:(NSString*)leaderboardID;
```

Awesome! You now have all the code in place to send scores to Game Center. To do this, open **MyScene.m** and add the following two private variables:

```
int _maxtime;
NSDictionary *_leaderboardIDMap;
```

You'll use the first variable, _maxtime, to store the total amount of time the player has to complete the current level. You'll use this to find out the amount of time it took the player to complete the current track.

The second variable, `_leaderboardIDMap`, is a dictionary where the key is a string with format CarType_LevelType and the value is its corresponding leaderboard ID. For example, the key **1_1** would have a leaderboard ID of **com.razeware.CircuitRacer.car1_level_easy_fastest_time**.

Next you need to initialize the above dictionary. Inside `initWithSize:carType:level:`, add the following code snippet before the call to `initializeGame`:

```
_leaderboardIDMap =
@{[NSString stringWithFormat:@"%d_%d",CRYellowCar,CRLevelEasy] :
 @"com.razeware.circuitracer3.car1_level_easy_fastest_time",
 [NSString stringWithFormat:@"%d_%d",CRYellowCar,CRLevelMedium] :
 @"com.razeware.circuitracer3.car1_level_medium_fastest_time",
 [NSString stringWithFormat:@"%d_%d",CRYellowCar,CRLevelHard] :
 @"com.razeware.circuitracer3.car1_level_hard_fastest_time",
 [NSString stringWithFormat:@"%d_%d",CRBlueCar,CRLevelEasy] :
 @"com.razeware.circuitracer3.car2_level_easy_fastest_time",
 [NSString stringWithFormat:@"%d_%d",CRBlueCar,CRLevelMedium]:
 @"com.razeware.circuitracer3.car2_level_medium_fastest_time",
 [NSString stringWithFormat:@"%d_%d",CRBlueCar,CRLevelHard] :
```

```
@"com.razeware.circuitracer3.car2_level_hard_fastest_time",
[NSString stringWithFormat:@"%d_%d",CRRedCar,CRLevelEasy] :
@"com.razeware.circuitracer3.car3_level_easy_fastest_time",
[NSString stringWithFormat:@"%d_%d",CRRedCar,CRLevelMedium]:
@"com.razeware.circuitracer3.car3_level_medium_fastest_time",
[NSString stringWithFormat:@"%d_%d",CRRedCar,CRLevelHard] :
@"com.razeware.circuitracer3.car3_level_hard_fastest_time"
};
```

This initializes the dictionary with the necessary leaderboard IDs. Make sure you use the exact leaderboard IDs that you gave to iTunes Connect, and remember that capitalization matters.

Next add the following line to `loadLevel`:

```
_maxtime = _timeInSeconds;
```

This just stores the maximum time for the current level.

Next add this new method:

```
- (void)reportScoreToGameCenter
{
  int64_t timeToComplete = _maxtime - _timeInSeconds;
  [[GameKitHelper sharedGameKitHelper]
   reportScore:timeToComplete
   forLeaderboardID:
     _leaderboardIDMap[[NSString stringWithFormat:@"%d_%d",
       _carType, _levelType]]];
}
```

This simply calls the method you added to `GameKitHelper` to report a new score.

Now inside `update:`, add a call to `reportScoreToGameCenter` just before calling the `gameOverBlock`:

```
[self reportScoreToGameCenter];
```

Finally, it's time to test everything. Build and run the project.

After you successfully complete a track, the game will automatically report your score to Game Center. Check the debug console to see if anything went wrong. If you don't see any error logs, then you can trust that Game Center got your score.

YAY!!!!

Step 5: Displaying leaderboards to the player

The last thing to do is to display those leaderboards. Game Center does provide helper methods that retrieve the scores in each leaderboard using the `GKLeaderboard` object. Once you have the scores, you can present the leaderboards to the player in any view.

However, there's a much easier way to display leaderboards if you don't want to create your own custom user interface, using the the `GKGameCenterViewController`. You added support for this view controller in the last chapter, so all you need to do now is make a few changes to display leaderboards in it.

Open **GameKitHelper.m** and navigate to the method named `showGKGameCenterViewController:`. In it, change `viewState` from `GKGameCenterViewControllerStateAchievements` to `GKGameCenterViewControllerStateDefault`, as shown below:

```
gameCenterViewController.viewState =
    GKGameCenterViewControllerStateDefault;
```

This sets up the view controller to display both leaderboards and achievements, rather than just achievements.

Build and run. Tap on the **Game Center** button on the home screen and you should see the leaderboards you set up in iTunes Connect with any scores you've earned since you began sending scores to Game Center.

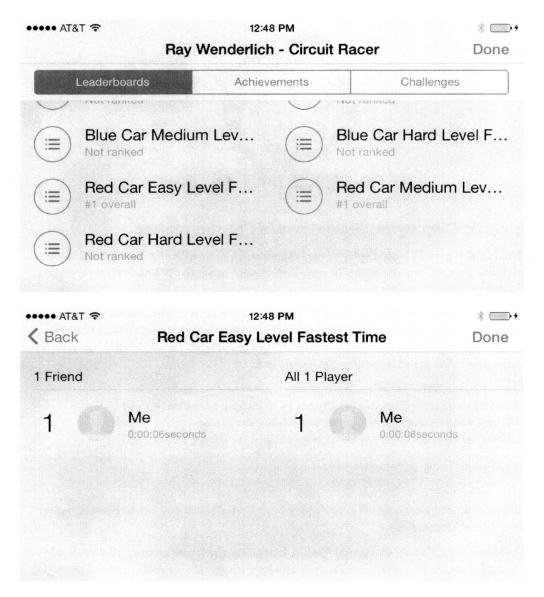

Congratulations, you have added leaderboards to your app!

If you just wanted to learn how to add basic leaderboards to your app, feel free to stop reading now and skip ahead to the next chapter. But if you want to learn about some more advanced things you can do with leaderboards, read on!

Leaderboard sets

Now that you are familiar with leaderboards, I'd like to tell you about an amazing new feature introduced in iOS 7 called leaderboard sets.

Leaderboard sets give developers the ability to combine several leaderboards into a single group. Think of a leaderboard set as a tagging framework. Each leaderboard can belong to one or several groups/sets. This allows you to organize your leaderboards into a structured hierarchy, rather than the "9-long list of leaderboards" mismatch you currently have, which can be overwhelming to players.

To add support for leaderboard sets in Circuit Racer, you need an organizing strategy. You are going to group your leaderboards according to car type. Thus, all the

Yellow car	*Blue car*	*Red car*
car1_level_easy_fastest_time	car2_level_easy_fastest_time	car3_level_easy_fastest_time
car1_level_medium_fastest_time	car2_level_medium_fastest_time	car3_level_medium_fastest_time
car1_level_hard_fastest_time	car2_level_hard_fastest_time	car3_level_hard_fastest_time

leaderboards for the yellow car will belong to the "Yellow car" group, and so forth.

To visualize this, take a look at the table below:

> **Note:** You could also organize the leaderboards according to difficulty level. Since leaderboard sets provide the capability to tag leaderboards multiple times, it would be easy to do it both ways.

Login to iTunes connect and open the **Manage Game Center** page for Circuit Racer, as you've done before.

Under the leaderboards section you will find a button titled **Move All Leaderboards to Leaderboard Sets**. Click that button to create the first leaderboard set.

On the next screen, enter **Yellow Car** for the **Leaderboard Set Reference Name** and **[Your App ID].yellowcar** for the **Leaderboard Set ID**.

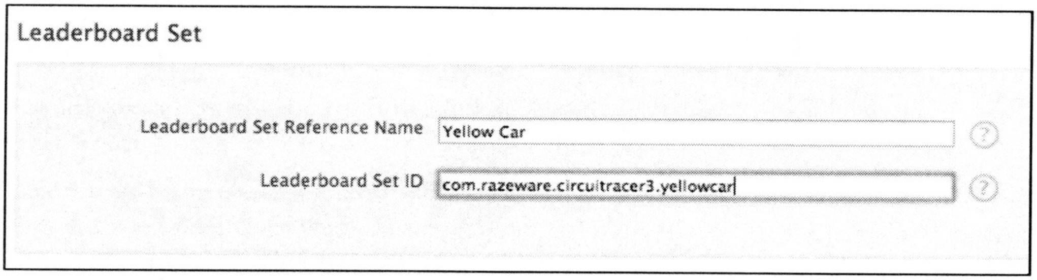

Leaderboard Set

Leaderboard Set Reference Name   `Yellow Car`   ⑦

Leaderboard Set ID   `com.razeware.circuitracer3.yellowcar`   ⑦

Select the **Continue** button when you are done entering the data.

Next you need to add leaderboards to this set. On the next screen, under the section **Leaderboards in This Set**, select the **Add to Leaderboard Set** button. Since this is the Yellow Car group, all the leaderboards pertaining to the first car should be a part of this group.

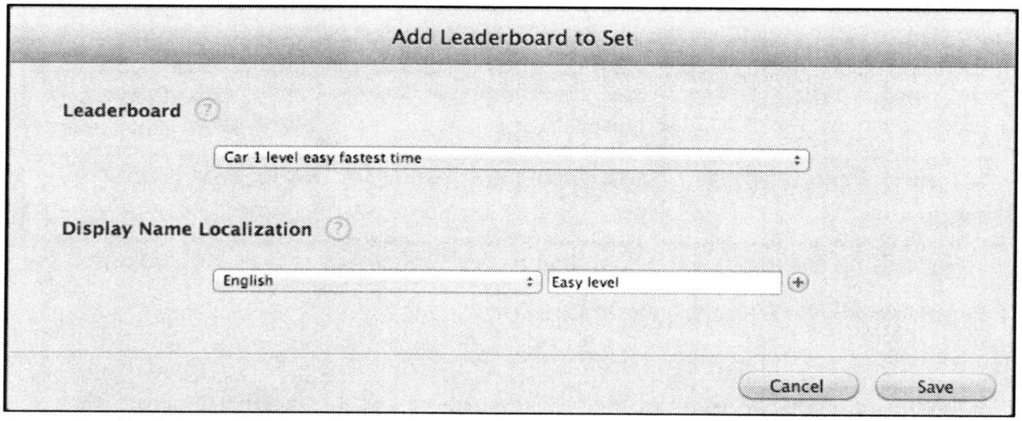

Add Leaderboard to Set

Leaderboard ⑦

`Car 1 level easy fastest time` ⬍

Display Name Localization ⑦

`English` ⬍   `Easy level` ⊕

Cancel   Save

As shown in the image above, you first select the leaderboard you want to add to the set. Next you enter a display name for the leaderboard within the set. Since the set is named "Yellow Car", it makes sense to name the **car1_level_easy_fastest_time** leaderboard **Easy level**. After you've done that, click **Save**.

In the same fashion, add the other two leaderboards pertaining to the yellow car to this set, naming them **Medium level** and **Hard level**.

Now you need to name the leaderboard set. Under the **Leaderboard Set Localization** section, select the **Add language** button. Select **English** as the language and enter **Yellow car** for the display name, then click **Save**.

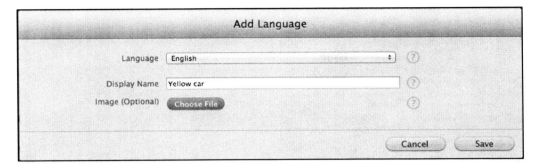

Although you are not going to add a locale-specific image now, it is always a good idea because it shows up in Game Center.

Using the **Add Leaderboard set** option on the first section of the page, repeat the above procedure for the blue and red cars. Make sure you give them ID values of **[Your App ID].bluecar** and **[Your App ID].redcar** to remain consistent with the yellow car leaderboard set, replacing **.razeware** with **your own App ID**, of course.

> **Note:** If you decide to support leaderboard sets, you need to ensure that every leaderboard is part of at least one group.

Finally, when you've organized all the leaderboards into there respective sets, select the **Save** button at the bottom-right. You should now see three display sets under the **Leaderboard Sets** section, as shown below:

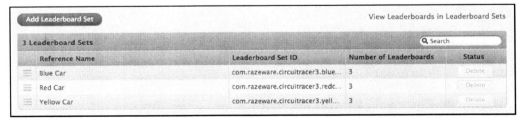

Note that there is a link called **View Leaderboards in Leaderboard Sets**. This can be quite useful to visualize your leaderboard sets – click it and you'll see the image on the following page:

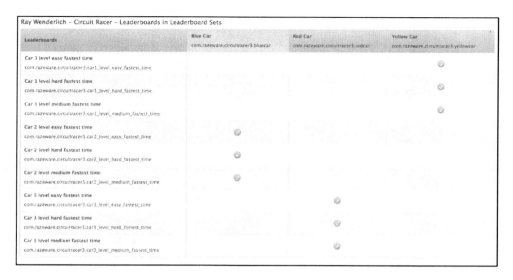

That's it! You now have everything ready in iTunes Connect. The next step is to show the leaderboard sets to the user/local player. Once again, the easiest way to do that is to use the `GKGameCenterViewController`.

But you don't need to add any code! Simply build and run. When you tap on the Game Center button on the home screen, the `GKGameCenterViewController` opens up and shows the leaderboard sets you created in iTunes Connect. Note that it might take a few minutes for your leaderboards to show up in your app – if it doesn't appear right away wait a few minutes.

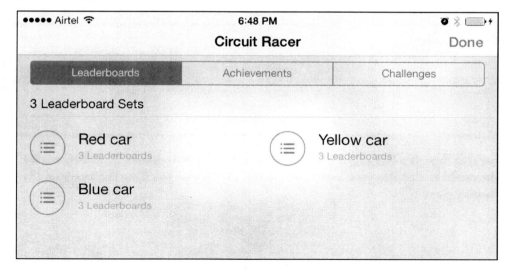

Ah, sweet simplicity! You now see just three leaderboards where before there were nine, and it is a lot easier to navigate between them thanks to the hierarchical organization.

Security in Game Center

You should be quite familiar with Game Center's features, so let's take a quick look at the different ways in which Game Center provides security.

How does submission work?

Before discussing Game Center's security features, let's first consider how the system handles submissions.

When your game sends a score to Game Center, it doesn't send it directly to the Game Center servers. Instead it sends the score to the *gamed* daemon, which in turn sends it to the servers.

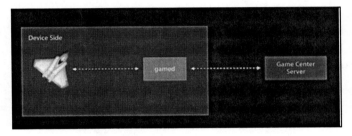

Why does the system manage communication that way? To answer that question, imagine that the device sending out the score has an Internet connectivity problem. In such a situation, the *gamed* daemon stores the scores and will send them to the Game Center servers when the Internet connection is back.

This means you don't have to do anything in case the Internet connection is wonky. Game Center takes care of all the heavy lifting for you.

Limit cheating

Believe it or not, there are people out there who are going to cheat and submit unearned scores, even some that are not humanly possible to achieve! iOS 7 gives you three ways to combat cheating within your game:

1. **Signed submissions:** This feature is totally free and you don't need to make any changes to your game to use it. In iOS 7, when your game submits scores/achievements to the *gamed* daemon, it automatically attaches a cryptographic signature to the submission. Game Center rejects any submission that does not have this signature.

2. **Score range:** Another way to limit cheating is to use the score range property on a leaderboard. The score range specifies minimum and maximum values that you think a player can achieve for a particular leaderboard. Any score that is higher or lower than the specified range is accepted by Game Center, however it is never shown to another player. Since Game Center holds onto the score, if you later find out that it is possible to get such a score, changing the set range will make that score visible. You already set up score ranges when creating your leaderboards earlier.

3. **Score/player management:** New in iTunes Connect is the player/score management console (To view this console login to iTunes connect and just select any leaderboard. iTunes will show you a list of the top 100 players in that leaderboard). This helps you, the developer, to view scores that were submitted in a leaderboard. You can chose to remove a score from a leaderboard and you can even chose to remove a player, thereby preventing him or her from posting scores to that leaderboard again. This is an extremely powerful tool and as the saying goes, "With great power comes great responsibility." Make sure that you use this power appropriately and only when needed.

And that's it for leaderboards – except for one final challenge for you!

Challenges

This chapter just has one challenge for you – to give you a bit more practice with leaderboard sets.

Note that you don't actually need to make any changes to your project to complete this challenge, so there is no solution project for this chapter.

Challenge 1: Leaderboard sets

Make three new leaderboard sets that organize the nine leaderboards you created in this chapter by difficulty level. Remember that you only have to make the changes in iTunes Connect and the GKGameCenterViewController will automatically show them in the leaderboards section.

Chapter 23: Game Center Multiplayer

By Kauserali Hafizji

Out of all of the potential features you could add to your game, adding multiplayer support is one of the best. Being able to play with or against other players can make your game a whole lot more fun, and a more memorable and unpredictable experience. It also can help to increase the word of mouth visibility of your game – after all, if players like your game they will want to recommend it to their friends so they can play together!

In the old days, creating a multiplayer game on iOS was a lot of work, involving a lot of complicated networking and back-end code to find players and create matches. These days, Game Center solves most of this for you, and lets you focus just on your game.

Using Game Center APIs, your game can host matches in real time, either between the player's friends or by "auto-matching" random players from around the world. You can also send data between players and broadcast events to keep the game state in synch.

In this chapter, you are going to add multiplayer support to Circuit Racer, so multiple players can race each other in real time.

Even though the game in this chapter is only one simple example of what a multiplayer game could be, we've ensured that the GameKitHelper class you'll develop is reusable. That means you can use it in your own games, and it is a great starting point for more sophisticated implementations.

> **Note:** This chapter begins where the project left off in the last chapter. If you were unable to complete the challenges or skipped ahead from a previous chapter, don't worry – you can simply open **CircuitRacer-Starter** from the resources for this chapter to pick up where we left off.

> However, to follow along with this chapter you will have to set up an entry in iTunes Connect for Circuit Racer and a number of achievements and leaderboards. For instructions on how to perform these steps, see the previous chapters.

Choosing a multiplayer strategy

The first decision you have to make is whether you want to make a turn-based game or a real-time game — both are supported with Game Center, but they use different APIs.

Turn-based games are those in which only one user can play at a time. Chess is a classic example. Real-time games are those in which all the players can make their moves simultaneously, such as in a racing game.

Circuit Racer being a racing game, you're going to implement a real-time multiplayer strategy in which two players compete against each other to finish a set number of laps around a track. The one who finishes first wins. Simple enough?

> **Note:** This chapter focuses on real-time multiplayer games. To learn more about turn-based multiplayer games, check out the Game Center chapters in *iOS 5 and iOS 6 by Tutorials*.

The second decision you have to make is how many players the game will support. Game Center supports up to a maximum of 4 simultaneous players (unless you use a hosted server, as discussed in a minute). To keep things simple, for Circuit Racer you will only support 2 simultaneous players.

To implement this strategy, you need to use the Game Center matchmaking API to find 2 players who want to play the game. Once you've got a match, you need to send data back and forth between the devices, the most important of which representing the positions of each car as they round the track.

Game Center provides two ways to send data between players in a match:

1. **Peer-to-peer:** If you use this method, you don't need to worry about much of the complicated networking code such as setting up connections or writing back-end code. Instead, you can use Game Center APIs to easily send data between devices. In

the background, Game Center will automatically create the appropriate connections and will route data through Game Center's servers and ensure that it reaches the other devices.

2. **Hosted game:** This method is best for developers who want to host the networking layer on their own servers rather than use Game Center's. This might be useful if you already have the networking layer in place and just want to use Game Center's matchmaking API to create a match, or if you want to support more than 4 simultaneous players.

For this tutorial, you are going to stick with the first method and route all the data through Game Center's servers.

Player matchmaking

Before you can begin a game, you first need to find a set of players who want to play together. This is called **matchmaking** in Game Center terms.

Lucky for you, Game Center includes some APIs that make this easy. Let's learn how to use them!

Open **GameKitHelper.h** and add the following protocol at the top of the file:

```
@protocol GameKitHelperDelegate <NSObject>
- (void)matchStarted;
- (void)matchEnded;
- (void)match:(GKMatch *)match didReceiveData:(NSData *)data
    fromPlayer:(NSString *)playerId;
@end
```

This protocol defines how the `GameKitHelper` object will communicate with the outside world when using multiplayer APIs. There are three events of which the implementing object will be notified:

1. **Match started:** This notifies the implementing object that a suitable match has been found and the game can be started.

2. **Match ended:** This notifies the implementing object that a match has ended. There are a number of reasons this might happen, such as player disconnection or networking errors.

3. **Match data received:** This tells the implementing object that data has been received from the other end, such as updates to game state.

Next add the following properties to the `GameKitHelper` interface:

```
@property (nonatomic,assign) id<GameKitHelperDelegate> delegate;
@property (nonatomic,strong) GKMatch *multiplayerMatch;
```

The first property is the `delegate`, which represents the object that will receive all the multiplayer events you created in the protocol above. The `GKMatch` object represents the network between the devices involved in the multiplayer game being set up and played.

Add the following method declaration:

```
- (void)findMatchWithMinPlayers:(int)minPlayers
                     maxPlayers:(int)maxPlayers
       presentingViewController:(UIViewController *)viewController
                       delegate:(id<GameKitHelperDelegate>)delegate;
```

Open **GameKitHelper.m** and add the following private instance variables:

```
BOOL _multiplayerMatchStarted;
UIViewController *_presentingViewController;
```

Define this new method as shown below:

```
- (void)findMatchWithMinPlayers:(int)minPlayers
                     maxPlayers:(int)maxPlayers
       presentingViewController:(UIViewController*)viewController
                       delegate:(id<GameKitHelperDelegate>)delegate
{
  //1
  if (!_enableGameCenter) {
    NSLog(@"Local player is not authenticated");
    return;
  }
```

```
    //2
    _multiplayerMatchStarted = NO;
    _multiplayerMatch = nil;
    _delegate = delegate;
    _presentingViewController = viewController;

    //3
    GKMatchRequest *matchRequest = [[GKMatchRequest alloc] init];
    matchRequest.minPlayers = minPlayers;
    matchRequest.maxPlayers = maxPlayers;

    //4
    GKMatchmakerViewController *matchMakerViewController =
      [[GKMatchmakerViewController alloc]
        initWithMatchRequest:matchRequest];
    matchMakerViewController.matchmakerDelegate = self;
  [_presentingViewController
    presentViewController:matchMakerViewController
    animated:NO completion:nil];
  }
```

This may seem like a lot to digest, so let's go through it step-by-step to understand what this method does.

1. The method first checks if the local player is authenticated. If not, the method exits without attempting to do anything else.

2. If the player is authenticated, the method then sets the properties and instance variables to an appropriate value.

3. Next the method creates an object of GKMatchRequest. What does the GKMatchRequest object do? Well, it does exactly what the name implies: it creates a match request with the appropriate criteria. In this case, you've used the min and max players. Later, you will set these to 2 because you want only 2 player matches in Circuit Racer.

4. The method then uses the GKMatchRequest object to initialize the GKMatchMakerViewController.

Just like there is a built in view controller to display leaderboards and achievements (GKGameCenterViewController), Apple provides a built in view controller to help players with the matchmaking process (GKMatchMakerViewController). This allows players either to create a match with one of the their Game Center friends or with a random player it finds.

Game Center does provide APIs that you can use to programmatically create a match (check out `GKMatchmaker` if you're curious), however using `GKMatchMakerViewController` is much simpler and gives you a clean iOS 7-style layout for free.

At this point, build the game. Xcode will generate a warning like the one shown below:

When you drill down, you'll notice that you've set the delegate of the `GKMatchMakerViewController` to `self`, however you haven't marked your class as implementing the delegate protocol nor implemented any of the required methods. To fix this add the protocol to the interface section in **GameKitHelper.m** (new code highlighted):

```
@interface GameKitHelper()<GKGameCenterControllerDelegate,
GKMatchmakerViewControllerDelegate>
```

Also add the following methods of the `GKMatchMakerViewControllerDelegate` protocol:

```
- (void)matchmakerViewControllerWasCancelled:
  (GKMatchmakerViewController *)viewController
{
    [_presentingViewController dismissViewControllerAnimated:YES
                                             completion:nil];
    [_delegate matchEnded];
}

- (void)matchmakerViewController:
  (GKMatchmakerViewController *)viewController
    didFailWithError:(NSError *)error
{
    [_presentingViewController dismissViewControllerAnimated:YES
                                             completion:nil];
  NSLog(@"Error creating a match: %@",
        error.localizedDescription);
    [_delegate matchEnded];
}

- (void)matchmakerViewController:
  (GKMatchmakerViewController *)viewController
                didFindMatch:(GKMatch *)match
```

```
    {
        [_presentingViewController dismissViewControllerAnimated:YES
                                                    completion:nil];
        _multiplayerMatch = match;
        _multiplayerMatch.delegate = self;
        if (!_multiplayerMatchStarted &&
                _multiplayerMatch.expectedPlayerCount == 0) {
            NSLog(@"Ready to start the match");
        }
    }
}
```

You have added three of the protocol's methods. Here is a brief description of each:

- `matchMakerViewControllerWasCancelled::` This method is called when the user cancels the `GKMatchMakerViewController`. All you have to do here is dismiss it, as the user does not want to play a multiplayer game. You also call `matchEnded` on the delegate object to notify that you could not create the match.

- `matchMakerViewController:didFailWithError::` This method is called when the match making API fails to create a match. The only things to do here are to dismiss the view controller, log an error to the console and call `matchEnded` on the delegate.

- `matchMakerViewController:didFindMatch::` This is where things get interesting. This method is called when Game Center successfully finds a match. You store the `GKMatch` object in an instance variable and set the delegate of the `GKMatch` object to `self`.

In `matchMakerViewController:didFindMatch:`, notice that you are checking the `expectedPlayerCount` property of the `GKMatch` object. This property represents the number of players that have yet to join the game before it can begin. If this property is 0, then all the required players have joined and the game can start.

The last piece of the puzzle is the GKMatchDelegate. When you create a match, you set the delegate property of the GKMatch object to self. GKMatch informs this delegate of important events related to the match.

In **GameKitHelper.m**, add the protocol to the interface section as shown below (new code highlighted):

```
@interface GameKitHelper()<GKGameCenterControllerDelegate,
GKMatchmakerViewControllerDelegate,GKMatchDelegate>
```

You will now add the GKMatchDelegate protocol methods one by one so that they are easy to understand. At the bottom of the implementation section, add the following method:

```
- (void)match:(GKMatch *)match didReceiveData:(NSData *)data
   fromPlayer:(NSString *)playerID
{
  if (_multiplayerMatch != match)
    return;

  [_delegate match:match didReceiveData:data
       fromPlayer:playerID];
}
```

This method is called when you receive data from the other player's device. All you're doing is passing data to the delegate, which in your case is the scene object – more on that later.

Add the following method below the match:didReceiveData: method:

```
- (void)match:(GKMatch *)match didFailWithError:(NSError *)error
{
  if (_multiplayerMatch != match)
    return;

  _multiplayerMatchStarted = NO;
  [_delegate matchEnded];
}
```

The above method is called when there is an error while playing the match. In this case, you send a matchEnded message back to the delegate.

Now add the last and final delegate method:

```
- (void)match:(GKMatch *)match player:(NSString *)playerID
  didChangeState:(GKPlayerConnectionState)state
```

```
{
  if (_multiplayerMatch != match)
    return;

  switch (state) {
    case GKPlayerStateConnected:
      NSLog(@"Player connected");
      if (!_multiplayerMatchStarted &&
          _multiplayerMatch.expectedPlayerCount == 0) {
        NSLog(@"Ready to start the match");
      }
      break;
    case GKPlayerStateDisconnected:
      NSLog(@"Player disconnected");
      _multiplayerMatchStarted = NO;
      [_delegate matchEnded];
      break;
  }
}
```

The above method is invoked every time a player's status changes. There are two possible states: either the player is connected to a match or the player is disconnected from the match. In the first case, you check to see if all the players have joined in and then take some action, about which you will learn more in the next section. In the second case, you simply end the match.

That's it! You now have the entire arsenal in place to create a multiplayer game.

Testing your matchmaking code

In this section, you are going to test if all the matchmaking code you wrote in the GameKitHelper class works as expected.

To do this, open **Main.storyboard** and add a new button to the HomeScreenViewController, below the Game Center button. As you did for the other buttons, set its type to **Custom** and delete its title. Set the image for the button to **btn-multiplayer.png** – you can find this image inside the **Update files** folder in the resources for this chapter.

Then with the assistant editor open and displaying **HomeScreenViewController.m**, control-drag from the multiplayer button to **HomeScreenViewController.m** to create a method that will be called when the button is tapped. In the popup that appears, enter showMatchMakerViewController for the name, and click connect.

Next open **HomeScreenViewController.m** and implement the method as follows:

```
- (IBAction)showMatchMakerViewController:(id)sender
{
  [[GameKitHelper sharedGameKitHelper]
    findMatchWithMinPlayers:2 maxPlayers:2
    presentingViewController:self delegate:self];
}
```

You now need to implement the GameKitHelperDelegate protocol. Modify the interface of **HomeScreenViewController.m** as shown below (new code highlighted):

```
@interface HomeScreenViewController () <GameKitHelperDelegate>
```

Next implement the methods of the protocol as follows:

```
#pragma mark GameKitHelperDelegate methods
- (void)matchStarted
{
  NSLog(@"Match has started successfully");
}
```

```
- (void)matchEnded
{
  NSLog(@"Match has ended");
}

- (void)match:(GKMatch*)match didReceiveData:(NSData*)data
    fromPlayer:(NSString*)playerId
{

}
```

Notice that in these methods you only have logs that print the current state, since you're just testing the GameKitHelper API.

Make sure you have at least one physical device, two devices are best, but if necessary you can use the Simulator as the second device. You also need two Game Center accounts.

Build and run to install the app on your device. Then build and run on a second device, or in the Simulator. Finally, open the app on the first device so that you now have your new code running in both places, with one of them connected to Xcode so you'll be able to see its log messages in the console.

Select the **Multiplayer** button on both the devices after you see the game center login banner. This will launch the GKMatchMakerViewController, as shown below.

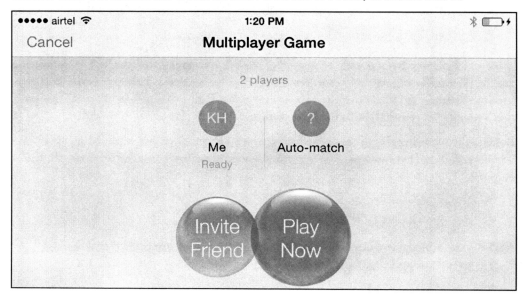

Select the **Play Now** button to create a match between two players. This may take sometime. Since you are using Game Center in sandbox mode, only your devices will be available for a match. You can't go cruising for n00bs yet! ☺

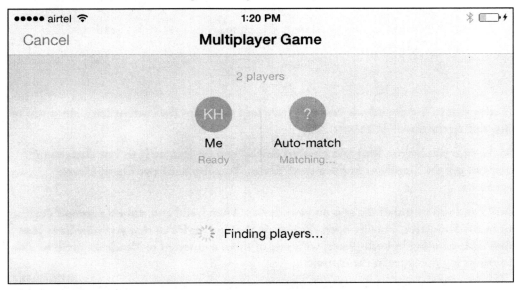

After Game Center creates the match, your game dismisses the GKMatchMakerViewController and you should see the following log on the console:

```
CircuitRacer[5985:70b] Ready to start the match
```

w00t – this shows that a match between the two players has automatically been made for you by Game Center. At this point the connection between the devices is active and you can start sending data between the two devices using Game Center's built-in APIs – and that's exactly what you'll do in the next section.

But first, try sending the game to the background on one of your devices to see what happens. After a few minutes, on your other device you should see the following in the console:

```
CircuitRacer[5985:70b] Player disconnected
CircuitRacer[5985:70b] Match has ended
```

This shows that when your game is in the background, the connection between the devices goes away and the match ends.

Network coding strategy

Now that you have all the code in place to create a multiplayer match, let's briefly return to talking strategy.

Assigning Player 1

The problem is, how do you decide which player gets which car? Another way to think about this is that you need to find a way to decide which player is Player 1. You're going to use the following strategy:

As soon as the match is started, each side will generate a random number. You will consider the one who generates the bigger number to be Player 1. In the rare case that both players generate the same number, you will simply generate another number and try again.

Being Player 1 has certain unavoidable advantages: it is this player's device that decides when the game starts and when it ends.

> **Note:** The same strategy can be extrapolated to support 3 or more players. In such a case the players will be ordered in a descending fashion depending upon the random number they generate.

Player aliases

Since the game has two cars that will be on the screen at the same time, it could sometimes be difficult for the players to know which car belongs to which player. You can solve this problem by using player aliases, the nicknames chosen by every Game Center user. To get these, you simply query Game Center using the GKPlayer API, which you will learn more about in the sections to come.

You're going to place a player alias above each car, thus telling anyone watching the screen which player is in control of that car.

Game states

One tricky thing about developing multiplayer real-time games is that you have no control over the order in which things happen. For example, one side could have finished initializing the game as well as sent the random number for player assignment, all before the other player has even started.

To keep track of things, you're going to keep track of the current state the game is in, and only perform certain actions in certain states. On each player's side, the game will move logically from one state to the next, allowing you to keep the devices synchronized.

The following diagram illustrates the states that Circuit Racer will have:

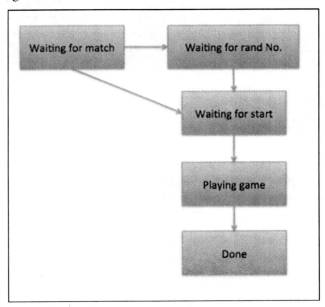

Let's go through each state in detail:

- **Waiting for match:** The game is waiting for Game Center to return a match and look up the player aliases.

- **Waiting for random number:** Once the game has the match and the player aliases, it generates a random number and sends it to the other side(s). Then it moves into this state and waits for a random number from the other device(s) in turn.

- **Waiting for start:** Once the game receives a random number, it knows if it is Player 1 or Player 2. If the game is Player 2, it moves into this state and waits for Player 1 to send a "start" message.

- **Playing game:** Once Player 1 has sent a start message (or Player 2 receives it), the game moves to this state – the one representing the game is active. In this state, the game sends data such as the car positions back and forth between the two players.

- **Done:** In this final state, the game ends and decides on a winner.

That's it for the high level plan – let's see what it looks like in code!

Multiplayer Game Scene

Currently `MyScene` only supports a single car at a time. To support multiple players, you need a modified version of this scene that supports multiple players.

To keep this chapter's focus purely on Game Center, I have created a starter point that includes refactored code and serves as a starting point for multiple players. You can find this in the **CircuitRacer-After Multiplayer Game Scene** folder – open this in Xcode now.

Let's go through all the changes:

1. *Main.storyboard*: The multiplayer button on the home screen now sends a message to the `playMultiplayerGame:` method of the `HomeScreenViewController`.

2. *HomeScreenViewController.m*: This view controller no longer implements the `GameKitHelperDelegate` protocol. Instead, this will be implemented by the `MultiplayerNetworking` class (more on this later).

3. *ViewController.h:* A new property, `noOfCars` is added.

4. *ViewController.m*:

    a. In `viewWillLayoutSubviews` if the `noOfCars` property is set the game scene is initialized with a new initialization method, `initWithSize:numberOfCars:levels:`.

    b. In case the number of cars is greater than 1, an object of `MultiplyerNetworking` is created.

    c. The scene is set as the delegate of the `MultiplayerNetworking` object.

    d. Finally the `GKMatchMakerViewController` is shown and the `MultiplayerNetworking` object is set as the delegate of the `GameKitHelper` object.

5. *MyScene.h*: A new initialization method is added that takes as a parameter the number of cars that will race.

6. *MultiplayerNetworking*: This is a new class and will contain all the networking code for a multiplayer race. Think of it as separate module that will handle all the heavy lifting and will communicate with the scene through a protocol.

7. *GameKitHelper.m:* The `matchStarted` delegate method is invoked when all the players have joined the multiplayer match.

Take a moment to go through all the changes mentioned above. You will notice that now the game scene has an array of cars. In case the game is initialized in single player mode the array will only have one car, whereas in multiplayer mode it will have two cars.

With the segregation of the networking code the game scene will just be responsible for game play and the networking engine (`MultiplayerNetworking`) will inform the scene about the positions of the other cars. This way the code is separated out and a clean interface is maintained.

Moving forward, you will make changes to the `MultiplayerNetworking` class and add real-time multiplayer support.

Before you proceed, let's try the new project out. But before you do, switch to your target settings and change the Bundle Identifier to whatever you chose for your App ID earlier:

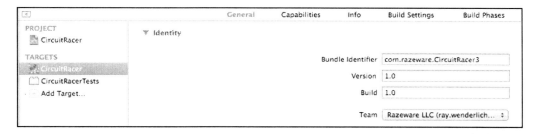

Also, do a clean build (Project\Clean) and delete your existing project from your devices before continuing to make sure you are starting from a clean slate.

Now build and run and select the **Multiplayer** button on the home screen. You will see that the game takes you to a view controller that will present the `GKMatchMakerViewController`:

This basically bypasses the screens that appear for a single player game that allow you to choose the track and car type (to keep things simpler).

Adding networking code

Your scene is set up and you have the ability to create a match. Now you need to add the networking code that will structure communication between each device. This is it – the heart of your multiplayer implementation!

Setting up the game states

Remember the game states I mentioned? Add the following structure at the top of **MultiplayerNetworking.m**:

```
typedef NS_ENUM(NSInteger, GameState) {
  kGameStateWaitingForMatch = 0,
  kGameStateWaitingForRandomNumber,
  kGameStateWaitingForStart,
  kGameStatePlaying,
  kGameStateDone
};
```

Define the message types and structures for each of the messages you will be sending back and forth by adding the following new `typedef`s at the top of **MultiplayerNetorking.m**:

```
typedef NS_ENUM(NSInteger, MessageType) {
  kMessageTypeRandomNumber,
  kMessageTypeGameBegin,
  kMessageTypeMove,
  kMessageTypeLapComplete,
  kMessageTypeGameOver
};

typedef struct {
  MessageType messageType;
} Message;

typedef struct {
  Message message;
  uint32_t randomNumber;
} MessageRandomNumber;

typedef struct {
  Message message;
} MessageGameBegin;

typedef struct {
```

```
  Message message;
  float dx, dy, rotate;
} MessageMove;

typedef struct {
  Message message;
}MessageLapComplete;

typedef struct {
  Message message;
} MessageGameOver;
```

Each structure represents a type of message you will send to the other device. Notice that each message structure has a message type. This is so that when you receive data, you can safely cast the data into a `Message struct` since that is the first part of every `struct`. Then, using the `messageType` value, you can determine the type of message sent.

Add the following instance variables to the implementation section of **MultiplayerNetworking.m**:

```
  uint32_t _ourRandomNumber;
  GameState _gameState;
  BOOL _isPlayer1, _receivedAllRandomNumbers;
  NSMutableArray *_orderOfPlayers;
```

These variables keep track of the random number for the local device and the ones received from the other player(s). These numbers will be used to sort all the players in the game and this will help in determining player order, more on this in the next section.

Sending data and starting the game

Begin implementing the networking code by first modifying `matchStarted` and adding two stub methods:

```
  - (void)matchStarted
  {
    NSLog(@"Match has started successfully");
    if (_receivedAllRandomNumbers) {
      _gameState = kGameStateWaitingForStart;
    } else {
      _gameState = kGameStateWaitingForRandomNumber;
    }
    [self sendRandomNumber];
    [self tryStartGame];
  }
```

```
- (void)sendRandomNumber
{

}

- (void)tryStartGame
{

}
```

matchStarted first checks if the game has received random numbers from all players of the match. If it has, then it moves the game state to the "waiting for start" state.

Before you fill out the stub methods, you need to initialize the game state variable and generate a random number. Add the following two statements to the top of init: method:

```
_ourRandomNumber = arc4random();
_gameState = kGameStateWaitingForMatch;
```

Next add a method to send data to other players in the match:

```
- (void)sendData:(NSData*)data
{
  NSError *error;
  GameKitHelper *gameKitHelper =
    [GameKitHelper sharedGameKitHelper];
  BOOL success =
    [gameKitHelper.multiplayerMatch
     sendDataToAllPlayers:data
            withDataMode:GKMatchSendDataReliable
                   error:&error];
  if (!success) {
    NSLog(@"Error sending data:%@", error.localizedDescription);
    [self matchEnded];
  }
}
```

To send data across the network with Game Center, all you have to do is call sendDataToAllPlayer:withDataMode:error: on the match object, like you see here. GKMatchSendDataReliable ensures that the data you send is guaranteed to get there (as long as the network connection stays alive), at the cost of slower delivery times compared to GKMatchSendDataUnreliable.

Now that you have the power to send data, add the following code to sendRandomNumber:

```
MessageRandomNumber message;
message.message.messageType = kMessageTypeRandomNumber;
message.randomNumber = _ourRandomNumber;
NSData *data =
  [NSData dataWithBytes:&message
                 length:sizeof(MessageRandomNumber)];
[self sendData:data];
```

The above code creates a structure of type **MessageRandomNumber** and assigns the random number created on initialization to the message. It then sends the message to the other player(s) in the match.

Next add the following new method:

```
- (void)sendBeginGame
{
  MessageGameBegin message;
  message.message.messageType = kMessageTypeGameBegin;
  NSData *data =
    [NSData dataWithBytes:&message
                   length:sizeof(MessageGameBegin)];
  [self sendData:data];
}
```

And add the following code to **tryStartGame**:

```
if (_isPlayer1 && _gameState == kGameStateWaitingForStart) {
  _gameState = kGameStatePlaying;
  [self sendBeginGame];
}
```

This method checks if the local player is Player 1. If so, it moves the game state further to "playing game" and sends a **MessageGameBegin** message. Remember, only Player 1 can send this message.

Build and run on two devices, and create a match as usual. When you're done, check the console for any errors. If everything goes well, you should see the following message on the console:

```
CircuitRacer[3337:60b] Match has started successfully
```

Receiving data

Until now, you've been adding code to send data to other players in the match. Lets handle the other part of the equation: receiving data. Add the following define statements at the top of the **MultiplayerNetworking.m** file.

```
#define playerIdKey @"PlayerId"
#define randomNumberKey @"randomNumber"
```

Next add the following stub methods, you will fill these out in just a minute.

```
-(void)processReceivedRandomNumber:
  (NSDictionary*)randomNumberDetails {

}

- (BOOL)isLocalPlayerPlayer1
{
  return NO;
}
```

Modify `match:didRecieveData:fromPlayer:` to handle the random number message:

```
//1
Message *message = (Message*)[data bytes];
if (message->messageType == kMessageTypeRandomNumber) {
  MessageRandomNumber *messageRandomNumber =
    (MessageRandomNumber*)[data bytes];

  NSLog(@"Received random number:%d",
    messageRandomNumber->randomNumber);

  BOOL tie = NO;
  if (messageRandomNumber->randomNumber == _ourRandomNumber) {
    //2
    NSLog(@"Tie");
    tie = YES;
    _ourRandomNumber = arc4random();
    [self sendRandomNumber];
  } else {
    //3
    NSDictionary *dictionary =
      @{playerIdKey : playerId,
        randomNumberKey : @(messageRandomNumber->randomNumber)};
    [self processReceivedRandomNumber:dictionary];
  }
```

```
//4
if (_receivedAllRandomNumbers) {
    _isPlayer1 = [self isLocalPlayerPlayer1];
}

if (!tie && _receivedAllRandomNumbers) {
    //5
    if (_gameState == kGameStateWaitingForRandomNumber) {
        _gameState = kGameStateWaitingForStart;
    }
    [self tryStartGame];
}
}
```

That's a long method (and there's much more to come), so let's take it one step at a time:

1. The received data is cast into a **Message struct**. Using the **messageType** field, you check for the type of **Message** received. For now, the method only handles random number messages.

2. You compare the number with the locally generated number and if it is a tie – meaning the numbers are identical – you send another random number. (And immediately go play the lottery! ☺)

3. If the received number is not equal to the one generated locally the method creates a dictionary which stores the random number and the player Id of the player who sent it.

4. When all random numbers are received and the order of the players is determined the **_receivedAllRandomNumber** variables will be true. In this case you check if the local player is Player 1.

5. Finally, if it wasn't a tie, and all random numbers have been received you advance the game state and call **tryStartGame**, which makes Player 1 initiate the game by sending the **kMessageTypeGameBegin** message.

You now have all the code in place to handle incoming random number messages. However, you still need to add code to process the received numbers and arrange all the players in order. Let's do that now. Add the following to the **init:** method of **MultiplayerNetworking.m**

```
_orderOfPlayers = [NSMutableArray array];
[_orderOfPlayers addObject:
    @{playerIdKey : [GKLocalPlayer localPlayer].playerID,
```

```
    randomNumberKey : @(_ourRandomNumber)}];
```

The _orderOfPlayers array will store details of each player along with their random number. This array will later be sorted on the basis of the stored random number and that will be the order of players in the game. Add the following code to the processReceivedRandomNumber: method.

```
//1
if([_orderOfPlayers containsObject:randomNumberDetails]) {
  [_orderOfPlayers removeObjectAtIndex:
    [_orderOfPlayers indexOfObject:randomNumberDetails]];
}
//2
[_orderOfPlayers addObject:randomNumberDetails];

//3
NSSortDescriptor *sortByRandomNumber =
  [NSSortDescriptor sortDescriptorWithKey:randomNumberKey
    ascending:NO];
NSArray *sortDescriptors = @[sortByRandomNumber];
[_orderOfPlayers sortUsingDescriptors:sortDescriptors];

//4
if ([self allRandomNumbersAreReceived]) {
  _receivedAllRandomNumbers = YES;
}
```

Here is a brief explanation:

1. The method first checks if the dictionary is already present in the _orderOfPlayers array. In case of a tie when the random number is re-sent this condition will be true. In such as situation the object is removed from the array.

2. The method then adds the received data to the _orderOfPlayers array.

3. The _orderOfPlayers array is then sorted on the bases of the random number generated by each player.

4. Lastly in case all the random number messages have been received the method sets the _receivedAllRandomNumbers Boolean variable to true.

At this point Xcode will show an error saying that the allRandomNumbersAreReceived method is not declared. Let's fix that now. Add the following method to the implementation section.

```
- (BOOL)allRandomNumbersAreReceived
```

```
{
  NSMutableArray *receivedRandomNumbers =
    [NSMutableArray array];

  for (NSDictionary *dict in _orderOfPlayers) {
   [receivedRandomNumbers addObject:dict[randomNumberKey]];
  }

  NSArray *arrayOfUniqueRandomNumbers =
    [[NSSet setWithArray:receivedRandomNumbers] allObjects];

  if (arrayOfUniqueRandomNumbers.count ==
      [GameKitHelper sharedGameKitHelper].
        multiplayerMatch.playerIDs.count + 1) {
    return YES;
  }
  return NO;
}
```

The above method is a helper method and will return a Boolean value, this value will be true in case all the received random numbers are unique and when random number from all players are received.

Remember the `isLocalPlayerPlayer1` method you added above. Lets add some code to it.

```
- (BOOL)isLocalPlayerPlayer1
{
  NSDictionary *dictionary = _orderOfPlayers[0];
  if ([dictionary[playerIdKey]
        isEqualToString:[GKLocalPlayer localPlayer].playerID]) {
    NSLog(@"I'm player 1");
    return YES;
  }
  return NO;
}
```

The above method is also a helper method that will return a Boolean value. This value is true if the local player is Player 1.

Build and run, and now when the game initiates a match, each device will send out a random number and use that data to name one of the devices as Player 1.

The console output for Player 1 will show the following logs (note that the ordering may be different for you due to network timing):

```
CircuitRacer[3348:60b] Receive random number:637481014
CircuitRacer[3348:60b] I'm player 1
CircuitRacer[3348:60b] Match has started successfully
```

The next message type to handle is the game begin message. Append the following code snippet to the `match:didReceiveData:fromPlayer:` method.

```
else if (message->messageType == kMessageTypeGameBegin) {
  _gameState = kGameStatePlaying;
}
```

Remember that only Player 1 can send out the begin game message, so when Player 2's device receives this message, its game state moves to `kGameStatePlaying`.

When the device receives a move message from another player, you need to change the position of the car that that player is driving. Now, since the `MyScene` class is responsible for game play, the `MultiplayerNetworking` class needs to tell the scene to move that car, more on this in the next section.

Add the following to the same method to handle "move messages":

```
else if (message->messageType == kMessageTypeMove) {
  MessageMove *messageMove = (MessageMove*)[data bytes];

  NSLog(@"dX:%f dY:%f Rotation:%f", messageMove->dx,
    messageMove->dy, messageMove->rotate);
}
```

Next you're going to handle the lap complete message. This message is used to tell other players the number of laps the local player has completed around the track. Later, this information will be used to determine a winner.

Add the following private variable to **MultiplayerNetworking.m**:

```
NSMutableDictionary *_lapCompleteInformation;
```

Initialize the above private variable in the `init` method as shown below.

```
_lapCompleteInformation = [NSMutableDictionary dictionary];
```

Next add the following helper method to the implementation section.

```
- (void)setupLapCompleteInformation
```

```
{
  NSArray *array = [GameKitHelper
    sharedGameKitHelper].multiplayerMatch.playerIDs;

  for (NSString *playerId in array) {
    [_lapCompleteInformation setObject:@(_noOfLaps)
      forKey:playerId];
  }
  _lapCompleteInformation[[GKLocalPlayer localPlayer].playerID]
    = @(_noOfLaps);
}
```

The above method initializes the `_lapCompletedInformation` dictionary. When the match starts all players will need to complete the max number of laps hence the method stores the player Id and total laps (5 in our case) in it.

Add a call to the above method at the end of the `matchStarted` method.

```
[self setupLapCompleteInformation];
```

When you receive a lap complete message you need to reduce the number of laps left for that player by 1. Let's add a helper method that does just this.

```
- (void)reduceNoOfLapsForPlayer:(NSString*)playerId
{
  NSNumber *laps = _lapCompleteInformation[playerId];
  laps = [NSNumber
           numberWithUnsignedInteger:laps.integerValue - 1];
  _lapCompleteInformation[playerId] = laps;
}
```

You now have everything in place to handle the lap complete message. Add the following to the `match:didReceiveData:fromPlayer:` method.

```
else if (message->messageType == kMessageTypeLapComplete) {
  [self reduceNoOfLapsForPlayer:playerId];
}
```

Just one more type to handle, append the following to the same method

```
else if(message->messageType == kMessageTypeGameOver) {

}
```

You will add code to the previous condition in the next section. For now the `MultiplayerNetworking` class can send and receive all types of messages. You're getting close to a full-fledged multiplayer game. Hurray!

Handling movement data

You still need to add code to move the cars. Don't worry – you're getting there. ☺

Since, the `MultiplayerNetworking` class is responsible for deciding which car belongs to which player you need to add a method to the `MultiplayerProtocol` that will inform the implementing object (which in our case is `MyScene`) the car that belongs to the local player.

Add the following method declaration to the `MultiplayerProtocol` in **MultiplayerNetworking.h**:

```
- (void)setCurrentPlayerIndex:(NSUInteger)index;
```

Next open **MultiplayerNetworking.m** and add modify the `tryStartGameMethod` as shown below (new code highlighted):

```
- (void)tryStartGame
{
  if (_isPlayer1 && _gameState == kGameStateWaitingForStart) {
    _gameState = kGameStatePlaying;
    [self sendBeginGame];

    //first player
    [self.delegate setCurrentPlayerIndex:0];
  }
}
```

The above code will inform the scene that the local player is player 1. But what if the local player is not Player 1. Well, in that case you need to find out the index of the local player and send that to the scene. Add the following helper methods to **MultiplayerNetworking.m**:

```
- (NSUInteger)indexForLocalPlayer
{
  NSString *playerId = [GKLocalPlayer localPlayer].playerID;

  return [self indexForPlayerWithId:playerId];
}

- (NSUInteger)indexForPlayerWithId:(NSString*)playerId
```

```
{
    __block NSUInteger index = -1;
    [_orderOfPlayers enumerateObjectsUsingBlock:^(NSDictionary
      *obj, NSUInteger idx, BOOL *stop){
        NSString *pId = obj[playerIdKey];
        if ([pId isEqualToString:playerId]) {
          index = idx;
          *stop = YES;
        }
    }];
    return index;
}
```

The above methods are self-explanatory; all that these methods do is that they find out the index of a player based on the player's Id.

Next append the following code to section in which a message of type game begin is handled in the `match:didReceiveData:fromPlayer:` method.

```
[self.delegate setCurrentPlayerIndex:[self
  indexForLocalPlayer]];
```

With all that done open **MyScene.m** and implement the `setCurrentPlayerIndex:` method as shown below.

```
- (void)setCurrentPlayerIndex:(NSUInteger)index
{
    _currentIndex = index;
}
```

Build and run, select the Multiplayer button on the home screen. Once a match has been created you will see that each player is assigned a car depending on the random number they generate. However, when a car moves its position is not updated on the other device.

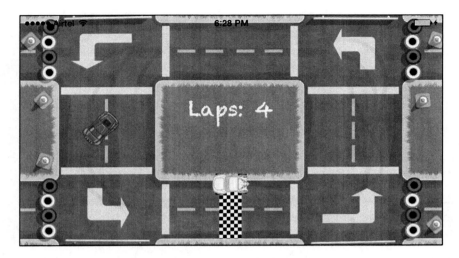

Let's add code to send each player's move to the other device. Add the following method to **MultiplayerNetworking.m**:

```
- (void)sendMove:(float)dx yPosition:(float)dy
         rotation:(float)rotation
{
  MessageMove messageMove;
  messageMove.dx = dx;
  messageMove.dy = dy;
  messageMove.rotate = rotation;
  messageMove.message.messageType = kMessageTypeMove;
  NSData *data = [NSData dataWithBytes:&messageMove
                              length:sizeof(MessageMove)];
  [self sendData:data];
}
```

Define the above method in `MultiplayerNetworking` interface in **MultiplayerNetworking.h** as shown below:

```
- (void)sendMove:(float)dx yPosition:(float)dy
         rotation:(float)rotation;
```

Now that you can send the position of the local player's car as he drives around the track, let's add a call to the above method in **MyScene.m**. Append the following at the end of the `moveCarFromAcceleration`:

```
[_networkingEngine sendMove:(car.physicsBody.velocity.dx)
                 yPosition:(car.physicsBody.velocity.dy)
                  rotation:car.zRotation];
```

This will send the velocity and rotation of the local player's car to the other players in the match.

> **Note:** Since the `update:` method is called every frame the code above will also be sending out position details every frame. This is quite inefficient and can be improved. For now, don't worry about it and read ahead.

Earlier, while writing `match:didReceiveData:fromPlayer:`, you added a log statement to print the values received if the message is of type `kMessageTypeMove`. Build and run the game on two devices to test out if the data gets through so far.

> **Note:** If you are running one of your apps on the Simulator, make sure that's the app sending output to the console, so that you can use your device to drive a car.

The console should show you statements like the one below:

```
CircuitRacer[6813:70b] dX:192.398346 dY:-54.615707 Rotation:-
0.272531
```

At this point, you are sending and receiving position and rotation values for each player. You now need to use the received data to change the position of the opponent's car.

To do that, define the following method declaration in `MultiplayerProtocol` in `MultiplayerNetworking.h`:

```
- (void)setPositionOfCarAtIndex:(NSUInteger)index
    dx:(CGFloat)dx dy:(CGFloat)dy rotation:(CGFloat)rotation;
```

Next, add the following line of code at the end of the section that handles "move messages" in the `match:didReceiveData:fromPlayer:` method in **MultiplayerNetworking.m**.

```
[self.delegate
  setPositionOfCarAtIndex:
    [self indexForPlayerWithId:playerId]
  dx:messageMove->dx
  dy:messageMove->dy
  rotation:messageMove->rotate];
```

Add the implementation of the above method in **MyScene.m** as shown below:

```
- (void) setPositionOfCarAtIndex:(NSUInteger)index
                              dx:(CGFloat)dx dy:(CGFloat)dy
                        rotation:(CGFloat)rotation
{
  SKSpriteNode *car = _cars[index];
  [car.physicsBody setVelocity:CGVectorMake(dx, dy)];
  if (rotation != 0) {
    [car setZRotation:rotation];
  }
}
```

Build and run. As you drive around the track you will see the position of your car update on the other device.

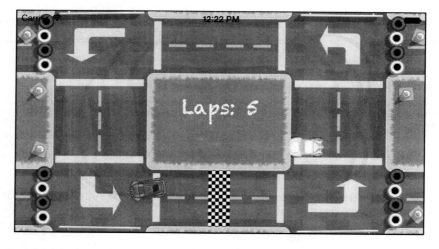

Take a break and play with the game. Race against yourself if you have to – one hand on each device! No cheating. ☺

Ending the match

Okay! It's time to add a game over condition and determine the game's winner. For this you first need to send a lap complete message when the player completes a lap. Add the following method to **MultiplayerNetworking.m**.

```
- (void)sendLapComplete
{
  MessageLapComplete lapCompleteMessage;
  lapCompleteMessage.message.messageType =
    kMessageTypeLapComplete;

  NSData *data =
    [NSData dataWithBytes:&lapCompleteMessage
                   length:sizeof(MessageLapComplete)];
  [self sendData:data];
  [self reduceNoOfLapsForPlayer:
    [GKLocalPlayer localPlayer].playerID];
}
```

Next, declare the above method in the interface section as shown below:

```
- (void)sendLapComplete;
```

Open **MyScene.m** and add the following code in section where the lap over condition is checked in the `update:` method. This should be placed below the code that plays the `_lapSoundAction`:

```
[_networkingEngine sendLapComplete];
```

With that in place switch to **MultiplayerNetworking.m** and add the following method.

```
- (BOOL)isGameOver
{
  NSArray *playerIds = [_lapCompleteInformation allKeys];

  for (NSString *key in playerIds) {
    NSNumber *laps = _lapCompleteInformation[key];
    if (laps.unsignedIntegerValue == 0) {
      return YES;
    }
  }
  return NO;
}
```

The above method checks the `_lapCompleteInformation` dictionary to see if any player in the match has completed all levels.

According to our strategy only Player 1 can send out the game over message. Let's first add a method to send this message. Add the following method below the `isGameOver` method.

```
- (void)sendGameOverMessage
{
  MessageGameOver gameOverMessage;
  gameOverMessage.message.messageType = kMessageTypeGameOver;
  NSData *data = [NSData dataWithBytes:&gameOverMessage
                    length:sizeof(MessageGameOver)];
  [self sendData:data];
}
```

Along with the above method you also need a way to determine if the local player has won. Since, you store the number of laps each player has completed you can use that information and find out. Add the following helper methods below the `sendGameOverMessage` method.

```
- (BOOL)hasLocalPlayerWon
{
  NSUInteger winningIndex = [self indexForWinningPlayer];
  NSDictionary *dict = _orderOfPlayers[winningIndex];

  if ([dict[playerIdKey]
      isEqualToString:[GKLocalPlayer localPlayer].playerID]) {
    return YES;
  }
  return NO;
}

- (NSUInteger)indexForWinningPlayer
{
  NSArray *playerIds = [_lapCompleteInformation allKeys];

  NSString *winningPlayerId;
  for (NSString *key in playerIds) {
    NSNumber *laps = _lapCompleteInformation[key];
    if (laps.unsignedIntegerValue == 0) {
      winningPlayerId = key;
      break;
    }
  }

  return [self indexForPlayerWithId:winningPlayerId];
```

```
    }
```

Using the above methods you can easily determine who has won the game. However, you need a way to tell the game scene about the results. For this add the following method declaration to the `MultiplayerProtocol` in **MultiplayerNetworking.h**:

```
- (void)gameOver:(BOOL)didLocalPlayerWin;
```

There are two places where you need to check the game over condition:

1. When a lap complete message is sent.

2. When a lap complete message is received.

Append the following code to the `sendLapComplete` method in the **MultiplayerNetworking.m** file.

```
if ([self isGameOver] && _isPlayer1) {
  [self sendGameOverMessage];
  [self.delegate gameOver:[self hasLocalPlayerWon]];
}
```

The above piece of code first checks if the game is over and only if the local player is Player 1 it sends out the game over message. Also, using the new `gameOver:` method the delegate is notified that the game is over.

Also add the above code to the end of the section that handles the lap complete message in the `match:didReceiveData:fromPlayer:` method.

In case the local player receives a game over message the networking engine should inform the scene that the game has been completed. For this add the following code to the section that handles the game over message in `match:didReceiveData:fromPlayer:`

```
[self.delegate gameOver:[self hasLocalPlayerWon]];
```

Phew! This is a coding marathon. There's just one more piece left. Open **MyScene.m** define the `gameOver:` method of the `MultiplayerProtocol` as shown below.

```
- (void) gameOver:(BOOL)didLocalPlayerWin
{
  self.paused = YES;
  self.gameOverBlock(didLocalPlayerWin);
}
```

To add some finishing touches modify the `matchEnded` method in
MultiplayerNetworking.m (new code highlighted).

```
- (void)matchEnded
{
  NSLog(@"Match has ended");
  [[GameKitHelper sharedGameKitHelper].multiplayerMatch
    disconnect];
  [_delegate matchEnded];
}
```

In case of any network errors the above code will disconnect the local player from the
multiplayer game.

Build and run the game on two devices. You should now be able to play a full-fledged,
two-player, real-time racing game! ☺

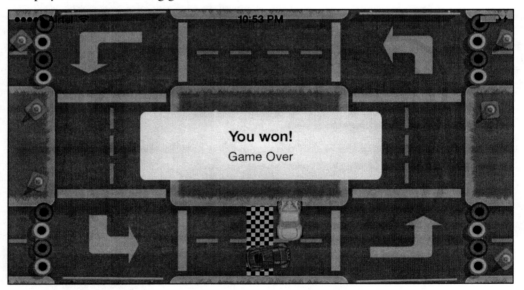

Congratulations, you have made a multiplayer game with Game Center and Sprite Kit!

If all you wanted to learn was the basics, feel free to stop reading here and skip to the
next chapter. But if you want to add a little polish and get some extra practice, keep
reading!

Displaying player aliases

You've been tooling around with your fully-functional multiplayer game, maybe trying to rope a friend or family member into a match. During your testing, you may have come across one problem: it is sometimes difficult to understand which car belongs to which player, since the players are selected randomly. Although, if you take a look at the code Player 1 will always be the yellow car and Player 2 will be the blue one.

Your strategy calls for displaying a player alias above each car, so get to it!

The first step is to retrieve details about all the players in the match. So let's start there.

Retrieving player data

The strategy you are going to adopt here is when the match starts you will first lookup details of all the players in the match. Only then will the `matchStarted` delegate method be called. Using this strategy you have player details before the match starts.

Open **GameKitHelper.h** and add the following property to the `GameKitHelper` interface:

```
@property (nonatomic, strong)
  NSMutableDictionary *playersDictionary;
```

You're going to use this property to store the details of the players in the match.

Next open **GameKitHelper.m** and add the following method to it:

```
- (void)lookupPlayersOfAMatch:(GKMatch*)match
{
  NSLog(@"Looking up %d players", match.playerIDs.count);

  [GKPlayer loadPlayersForIdentifiers:match.playerIDs
            withCompletionHandler:
   ^(NSArray *players, NSError *error){
     if (error) {
       NSLog(
         @"Error looking up players of multiplayer match:%@",
         error.localizedDescription);
       _multiplayerMatchStarted = NO;
       [_delegate matchEnded];
     } else {
       _playersDictionary =
         [NSMutableDictionary
          dictionaryWithCapacity:players.count];
```

```
        for (GKPlayer *player in players) {
          NSLog(@"Found player: %@", player.alias);
          [_playersDictionary setObject:player
                                  forKey:player.playerID];
        }
        [_playersDictionary setObject:[GKLocalPlayer localPlayer]
            forKey:[GKLocalPlayer localPlayer].playerID];
        _multiplayerMatchStarted = YES;
        [_delegate matchStarted];
      }
    }];
  }
```

This method looks up the details of all the players in the match. It calls
loadPlayersForIdentifiers:withCompletionHandler: of GKPlayer, which
returns player details in an array. You log any error that occurs and send a matchEnded
message through the delegate. If there is no error, the method stores all the players in the
_playerDictionary instance variable and sends a matchStarted message.

Inside match:player:didChangeState:, change the GKPlayerStateConnected
switch case to the following:

```
NSLog(@"Player connected");
if (!_multiplayerMatchStarted &&
  _multiplayerMatch.expectedPlayerCount == 0) {
    NSLog(@"Ready to start the match");
  [self lookupPlayersOfAMatch:_multiplayerMatch];
}
```

Be sure not to delete the break.

Likewise, replace the code inside the matchmakerViewController:didFindMatch:
method with the following:

```
[_presentingViewController dismissViewControllerAnimated:YES
  completion:nil];
_multiplayerMatch = match;
_multiplayerMatch.delegate = self;
if (!_multiplayerMatchStarted &&
  _multiplayerMatch.expectedPlayerCount == 0) {
  NSLog(@"Ready to start the match");
  [self lookupPlayersOfAMatch:_multiplayerMatch];
}
```

Build and run the game on two different devices or one device plus the Simulator. Just as you did before, select the **Multiplayer** button on the home screen in both apps. You should now see logs in the console similar to the following:

```
CircuitRacer[6074:70b] Ready to start the match
CircuitRacer[6074:70b] Looking up 1 players
CircuitRacer[6074:70b] Found player: Olieh
CircuitRacer[6074:70b] Match has started successfully
CircuitRacer[6074:70b] Received random number:-1447889139
CircuitRacer[6074:70b] I'm player 1
```

Now that you have all the information about the players you need a way to map each player alias with a specific car. The strategy you used in `MultiplayerNetworking` was that all the players are sorted in an order that matches the car they are driving. Using the same approach you will add code to create an array that has all player aliases in the same order.

Add the following method to **MultiplayerNetworking.m**:

```objc
- (void)retrieveAllPlayerAliases
{
  NSMutableArray *playerAliases =
    [NSMutableArray arrayWithCapacity:_orderOfPlayers.count];

  for (NSDictionary *playerDetails in _orderOfPlayers) {
    NSString *playerId = playerDetails[playerIdKey];
    GKPlayer *player = [GameKitHelper
      sharedGameKitHelper].playersDictionary[playerId];
    [playerAliases addObject:player.alias];
  }
}
```

The above method uses the player Id of all the players in the match to retrieve their aliases from `GameKitHelper`. This method should be invoked when the order of players has been determined, which mean when the game starts.

Add the following code at the end of `sendBeginGame` and at the end of the section that handles the game begin message in `match:didReceiveData:fromPlayer:` method.

```objc
[self retrieveAllPlayerAliases];
```

Now that all player aliases are in order all you have to do is notify the game scene about these aliases and the game scene will be responsible for drawing them above each car.

For this add the following method declaration to `MultiplayerProtocol` in
MultiplayerNetworking.h:

```
- (void)setPlayerLabelsInOrder:(NSArray*)playerAliases;
```

Let's add code to invoke the above method on the delegate object. Add the following to
the end of the `retreiveAllPlayerAliases` method in **MultiplayerNetworking.m**.

```
[self.delegate setPlayerLabelsInOrder:[NSArray
  arrayWithArray:playerAliases]];
```

You're all set with the networking engine. Let's switch to the game scene now. Open
MyScene.m and add the following helper method.

```
- (SKLabelNode*)addPlayerLabelWithText:(NSString*)text
    atPosition:(CGPoint)position
{
  NSLog(@"Adding player with label: %@", text);
  SKLabelNode *label =
    [SKLabelNode labelNodeWithFontNamed:@"Marker Felt"];
  label.position = position;
  label.fontSize = 18;
  label.fontColor = [SKColor whiteColor];
  label.text = text;
  [self addChild:label];
  return label;
}
```

The above method creates an object of `SKLabelNode` and adds it to the game scene. The
text and position for the label are parameters to the method.

Next add the following private variable to `MyScene`.

```
NSMutableArray *_playerLabels;
```

This variable will hold references to all the `SKLabelNode`s in the scene.

Since the player aliases will only be shown when the player chooses to play a multiplayer
match initialize the above variable in the `initWithSize:numberOfCars:level:`
method.

```
_playerLabels = [NSMutableArray arrayWithCapacity:_noOfCars];
```

Finally, you have to implement the `setPlayerLabelsInOrder:` method of the
`MultiplayerProtocol`. Add the following method at the end of **MyScene.m**

```
- (void)setPlayerLabelsInOrder:(NSArray*)playerAliases
{
   [playerAliases enumerateObjectsUsingBlock:
     ^(NSString *string, NSUInteger idx, BOOL *stop) {
     SKSpriteNode *car = _cars[idx];
     SKLabelNode *label =
       [self addPlayerLabelWithText:string
          atPosition:CGPointMake(car.position.x, car.position.y +
       30)];
     [_playerLabels addObject:label];
   }];
}
```

Build and run the game, when the game starts you will see player aliases above the cars they are driving. Here is an image that shows this in action:

The labels take some time to show up, this is because it takes some time for the game to decide who is Player 1. Once that is done the aliases are displayed on screen.

You will notice that the labels don't follow the cars. Let's fix this now.

Add the following code to the end of the
setPositionOfCarAtIndex:dx:dy:rotation: method in **MyScene.m**.

```
SKLabelNode *playerLabel = _playerLabels[index];
playerLabel.position = CGPointMake(car.position.x,
  car.position.y + 30);
```

All this does is change the position of the label to match the position of the car. Next,
you need to change the position of the local player's label. For this add the following to
the end of the moveCarFromAcceleration: method.

```
SKLabelNode *playerLabel = _playerLabels[_currentIndex];
  playerLabel.position = CGPointMake(car.position.x,
car.position.y + 30);
```

Build and run the game. You will now see the labels move along with the cars – and you
are done with the multiplayer version of Circuit Racer!

Challenges

There are three challenges this time, to give you some extra practice using the Game
Center multiplayer APIs.

As always, you can find the solutions in the resources for this chapter, but give it your
best shot first!

Challenge 1: Display player photos

In the last section of this chapter, you added player aliases to each car. You can retrieve a
player's game center photo using similar APIs. Your challenge is to do just that, then add
code to display each photo above their respective car.

Follow these simple instructions to implement this on your own:

1. Similar to how you implemented the retrieval of player aliases; write a method in
   MultiplayerNetworking.m that will retrieve player photos. Call this method
   retrieveAllPlayerPhotos. This method will loop over all the player ids' in
   _orderOfPlayers and using the loadPhotoForSize:withCompletionHandler:
   method the photo will be retrieved. Since the method to download the photo is
   asynchronous every time the success handler is invoked check to see it you have all the
   photos.

2. Invoke this new method when the game begin message is sent or is received. This way you're making sure that all the photos will match the order of the cars.

3. Add a method declaration in `MultiplayerProtocol` to notify the scene about the downloaded photos.

```
-(void)setPlayerPhotosInOrder:(NSArray*)playerPhotos;
```

4. Once all photos have been downloaded invoke the above method on the delegate.

5. Open **MyScene.m** and implement the `setPlayerPhotosInOrder:` method.

6. Add a private variable to store all player photos in **MyScene.m**:

```
NSMutableArray *_playerPhotos;
```

7. Initialize the `_playerPhotos` variable in the `initWithSize:numberOfCars:level:` method.

```
_playerPhotos = [NSMutableArray arrayWithCapacity:_noOfCars];
```

8. Similar to the `addPlayerLabelWithText:atPosition:` method create another helper method that will add the player photo to the scene. This method should ideally have a signature as shown below:

```
-(SKSpriteNode*)addPlayerPhotoWithTexture:(SKTexture*)texture
    atPosition:(CGPoint)position
```

9. Fill out the `setPlayerPhotosInOrder:` method of the `MultiplayerProtocol`. This method will go through all the images, add them to the scene using the helper method you added above and then add the photo nodes to the `_playerPhotos` array. This is very similar to the `setPlayerLabelsInOrder:` method.

10. At this point when you build and run the game you should see photos of each player above their respective car. However the photos don't move with the cars and are really big in size. To fix this set a size to the photo node in the `addPLayerPhotoWithTexture:atPosition:` method and the below code to the end of the `moveCarFromAcceleration:` method.

```
if (_playerPhotos.count > 0) {
  SKSpriteNode *photo = _playerPhotos[_currentIndex];
  photo.position =
    CGPointMake(car.position.x, car.position.y + 70);
}
```

Similarly, you need to move the opponent's photo as they move around the track. To do this add the following to the end of `setPositionOfCarAtIndex:dx:dy:rotation:` method

```
if (_playerPhotos.count > 0) {
  SKSpriteNode *photo = _playerPhotos[index];
  photo.position =
    CGPointMake(car.position.x, car.position.y + 70);
}
```

Build and run the game. Your game scene should now show you photos of all the players in the match.

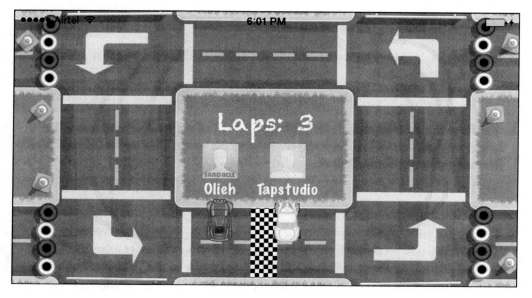

Challenge 2: Honk at other players

This should be a fun challenge. When a player taps on the screen a horn is sounded on all the other players' devices.

Follow these simple instructions to implement this on you own:

1. First you need a way to detect a tap on the scene. For this open **ViewController.m** and add a private `UITapGestureRecognizer` variable.

```
UITapGestureRecognizer *_tapRecognizer;
```

2. Initialize the above variable in the `viewWillLayoutSubviews` method, above the part where the `MultiplayerNetworking` class is initialized.

```
_tapRecognizer = [[UITapGestureRecognizer alloc]
    initWithTarget:self action:@selector(tapDetected)];

[self.view addGestureRecognizer:_tapRecognizer];
```

3. Add an empty selector that will be called when a tap is detected.

```
- (void)tapDetected
{

}
```

4. Open **MyScene.h** and define a public method as shown below.

```
-(void)tap;
```

5. Switch to **ViewController.m** and modify the `tapDetected` method as shown below.

```
- (void)tapDetected
{
    [_scene tap];
}
```

6. Open **MultiplayerNetworking.m** and define a new type of message.

```
typedef struct {
    Message message;
} MessageHonk;
```

7. Also define this new message type in the `MessageType` enum. Name it `kMessageTypeHonk`.

8. Add a method to the implementation section to send a message of type `MessageHonk`. This should be quite easy to do since you have already written similar methods (take a look at the `sendGameOver` method), make sure you name the method `sendHonkMessage`.

9. Declare the `sendHonkMessage` as public by adding it to the interface section of the header file.

10. Open **MyScene.m** and add the `tap` method.

```
- (void)tap
{
```

```
    [_networkingEngine sendHonkMessage];
}
```

11. Until now your game has the ability to send a honk message. Let's take care of the receiving part now. Add the following method to `MultiplayerProtocol`.

```
-(void)playHorn;
```

12. Open **MultiplayerNetworking.m** and add an else condition to handle the honk message to `match:didReceiveData:fromPlayer:`

```
else if(message->messageType == kMessageTypeHonk) {
    [self.delegate playHorn];
}
```

13. Open **MyScene.m** add implement the `playHorn` method of `MultiplayerProtocol`.

```
- (void)playHorn
{
    [self runAction:_hornSoundAction];
}
```

Build and run. When you tap the screen on any device a horn will be sounded on all other devices playing the match. Cool ehh!

Challenge 3: Reduce network traffic

In this challenge you're going to reduce the number of messages being sent to Game Center. Currently the game is sending 60 messages per second, this is not efficient.

There are several ways in which this can be optimized one such approach is: To monitor the velocity and direction of the local player's car. We will send out a message to game center only when there is a change in these values. The way the game scene is written as of now when it receives a move message it sets the velocity and rotation of a car. This is good, as the car will keep moving with that velocity until another message is received.

However, the problem with the above approach is that since the game is currently using the accelerometer the frequency of change of direction is very high. Hence to solve this problem you're going to limit the number of messages sent to 10 per second. Since the game already interpolates between the previous and new value you don't need to worry about that.

Follow these simple steps to get this working:

1. Modify the moveCarFromAcceleration method signature to the following

```
-(void)moveCarFromAcceleration:(SKSpriteNode*)car
  currentTime:(NSTimeInterval)currentTime
```

2. At the end of the update: method replace the call to moveCarFromAcceleration: with the following.

```
[self moveCarFromAcceleration:car currentTime:currentTime];
```

3. In the update: method, modify the condition that checks if a second has passed to the following.

```
if (currentTime - _previousTimeInterval > 1 &&
  !_isMultiplayerMode)
```

Since there is no time label in multiplayer mode the above will ensure that the condition is never true.

4. In the moveCarFromAcceleration:currentTime: method replace the call to sendMove:yPosition:rotation method of MultiplayerNetworking with the following.

```
if (currentTime - _previousTimeInterval >= 0.1
   && _isMultiplayerMode) {
   _previousTimeInterval = currentTime;
   [_networkingEngine sendMove:(car.physicsBody.velocity.dx)
                     yPosition:(car.physicsBody.velocity.dy)
                      rotation:car.zRotation];
}
```

The above code will ensure that only 10 messages are sent per second. This reduces the amount of networking traffic drastically.

At this point you should have a very good idea as to how you should go about creating a multiplayer game. The GameKitHelper class as well as parts of the MultiplayerNetworking class can be reused in your own games to support multiple players.

So go ahead and add multiplayer support to your game to make your games more fun!

Chapter 24: AirPlay

By Marin Todorov

You have already added a ton of great features into Circuit Racer, from a custom UI to accelerometer-driven controls to multiplayer capability. In this chapter you are going to add one final feature that will take Circuit Racer over the top – AirPlay.

AirPlay is Apple's protocol for wirelessly streaming content (like photos, music, videos, or the screen itself) from one device (like your iPhone or iPad) to another (like an Apple TV). The ability to project your iPhone's display on the big screen is great for games, since it allows you to provide a much more exciting and immersive experience.

Since AirPlay has built in screen mirroring, you can actually start Circuit Racer and mirror it straight to your Apple TV without adding a single line of code:

However, with built-in screen mirroring, both your device and the Apple TV shows the same content. It would be a lot cooler if you could show something different on the iPhone than what you display on the Apple TV – like a steering wheel, for example!

That's exactly what you're going to learn how to do in this chapter. By the time you're done, you'll have the controls on your device and the game on your external display, like so:

> **Note:** This chapter begins where Challenge 3 left off in the last chapter. If you were unable to complete the challenges or skipped ahead from a previous chapter, don't worry – you can simply open **CircuitRacer-Starter** from the resources for this chapter to pick up where we left off.
>
> However, to follow along with this chapter you will have to set up an entry in iTunes Connect for Circuit Racer and a number of achievements. For instructions on how to perform these steps, see the previous chapters.

Mirroring your screen

To follow along with this chapter, it is helpful to have an Apple TV for testing, but it not required.

If you don't have an Apple TV, there are some tools you can use to convert your Mac into an Airplay receiver that you can use instead, such as AirServer (http://www.airserver.com/) or Reflector (http://www.airsquirrels.com/reflector/). Both of these apps have a free trial, so choose one and download, install, and run it.

Next, perform the following steps whether you are using an Apple TV or AirServer/Reflector:

1. Slide up on the home screen of your iPhone to see the home screen menu.

2. If you have an Apple TV nearby or AirServer/Reflector running, you will see an **AirPlay** button appear. Tap that to see the list of those devices.

3. Tap a device to connect to it.

4. Turn the **Mirroring** switch to on.

5. Finally, when you see an AirPlay icon in your status bar, that means you are streaming your screen to the external device.

The next image shows how my iPod's mirrored screen looks on my MacBook (I am using Reflector to do that while developing and testing).

Feel free to try out Circuit Racer – you'll see that the exact same content is displayed on both devices. In the rest of this chapter, you'll work to make it diferent!

> **Note:** Please mind that AirPlay needs excellent WiFi connection to stream Retina quality video to your Apple TV or Macbook. My experience shows that even a single wall between you and your WiFi router can cause AirPlay streamed video to lag considerably.

UIKit and AirPlay

You might think you need to import and use an additional framework to enable AirPlay for your game, as well as go through a lengthy setup. And you would be completely right to expect that. It's a tricky problem to stream video wirelessly.

The folks at Apple, however, are a smart bunch and have endeavored to make your life easier. They have built support for displaying content wirelessly right into UIKit!

The UIScreen class provides you with a list of the available screens via a method named screens. Usually you have only one screen available, the device screen, but not sometimes you have more.

Whenever you activate AirPlay in the way described above, you will get another UIScreen object in the NSArray returned from screens. It's then up to you to create some content on this second screen for UIKit to stream over the air to your second screen:

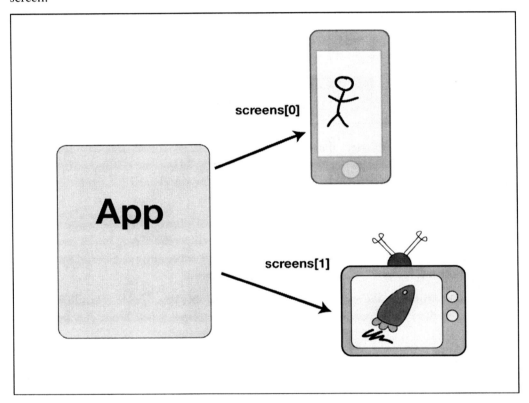

Because an iOS device only has a limited amount of processing power and Sprite Kit games are heavyweight, it's typical to only use display a Sprite Kit scene on one of the screens. The other screen typically uses UIKit controls, which require much less overhead.

In Circuit Racer, you will display the Sprite Kit game on one screen, and a UIKit view controller on another screen that displays a steering wheel. Let's get started!

Getting started

Let's start by adding a new view controller that will display a steering wheel on the device's screen during the gameplay.

Inside Circuit Racer, open **Main.storyboard** and drag a new view controller into the canvas:

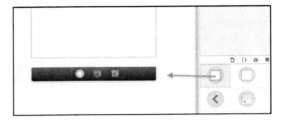

Click on the black bar to select the view controller and in the **Attributes Inspector**, select the **Landscape** orientation. Switch to the **Identity Inspector** tab and enter **SteeringWheelViewController** as both the class and the storyboard ID. So far, so good — now let's add some content.

Drag and drop an image view onto the new view controller and, with the image view selected, go to the **Attributes Inspector** and enter **steering-wheel.png** in the image field and **Center** as the mode. Also, make the image view the exact same size as the image by selecting **Editor\Size to Fit Content** from the main menu.

Before you continue, make sure **Auto Layout** is **off** for this app. To do this, click the canvas and in the File Inspector make sure the **Use Autolayout** box is not checked:

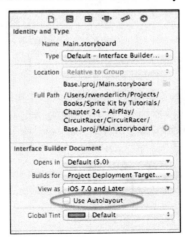

Now select the steering wheel again – you might need to click aside and click the image view again. Then from Xcode's menu, select **Editor/Align/Horizontal Center in Container**. That will center the image horizontally on the screen. Now click aside, select the steering wheel again and click **Editor/Align/Vertical Center in Container**.

You should now have something like this for your view controller:

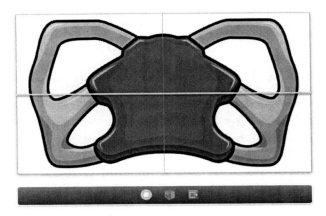

Add a button on top of the steering wheel. Set **steering-wheel-horn.png** as the image, set **Custom** as the type and an empty string as the title. Resize the button to the image's size with **Editor\Size to Fit Content**. Then drag the button around and align it in the center of the screen. Two blue guides will appear – when they do, drop the button on that spot.

Cool! Your steering wheel controller is looking good:

Now you need to add a basic class for this view controller. Go to **File\New\File...**, choose the **iOS\Cocoa Touch\Objective-C class** template and click **Next**. Name your class **SteeringWheelViewController**, make it a subclass of **UIViewController** and click **Next** again. Be sure the **CircuitRacer** target is checked and click **Create**.

For the moment, you are all done with the steering wheel. You'll come back to this class when it's time to display it on the device, but for now, what about that second screen?

Connecting to an external screen

I mentioned earlier that you detect external screens via [UIScreen screens]. You're going to add the code for that in this section, as well as learn how to split different parts of the game between two screens.

Moving the main view to the external screen

Open **ViewController.m** and scroll to **viewWillLayoutSubviews:**. At the top of this method, you create an SKView and an SKScene and add them to the current view. Your present task is to simply move the SKView instance to the external screen.

You want to preserve the current functionality if the player is not connected to an AirPlay device, so you're going to adjust the existing code to handle both AirPlay and non-AirPlay cases. Find this line:

```
[self.view addSubview: _skView];
```

And wrap it inside the following if statement (new lines are highlighted):

```
if ([UIScreen screens].count == 1) {
  [self.view addSubview: _skView];
}
```

This is exactly the same functionality as before, but now it is comfortably wrapped in a condition that checks if there is only one screen available to the application.

Now you can add the code for a second screen. Inside the @interface block in the same file, add a new instance variable (just under _motionManager):

```
UIWindow *_secondWindow;
```

Go back to viewWillLayoutSubviews: and, just after the code you added a moment ago, add an else branch:

```
else {
  //1
  UIScreen *gameScreen = [UIScreen screens][1];
  CGRect screenBounds = gameScreen.bounds;

  //2
  _secondWindow = [[UIWindow alloc] initWithFrame:screenBounds];

  //3
  _secondWindow.screen = gameScreen;
  _secondWindow.hidden = NO;
}
```

This code might look unfamiliar even if you are experienced with UIKit. In a typical iPhone app, you don't need to create new **UIWindow** objects – one is always created for you automatically. So what's going on here?

Let's explore what the code above does step by step:

1. First you store a reference to the second screen in **gameScreen** for quick access. You also grab the bounds of that screen. Note that the extra screen can have arbitrary dimensions, depending on your TV size and form. Forget good old 320x568 form factor – now you are in for a resolution based on the TV you're connected to. For example, a 1080p TV might have 1920x1080 resolution, and a 1990's TV might have 704x480 resolution.

2. You create a new window with the size of the external screen.

3. Now you come to the most important step in the process – you assign the new window to the external screen by setting its **screen** property. This instructs UIKit to take the content of this window and stream it over AirPlay. Finally, you set the **hidden** property of the window to **NO** because newly created windows are hidden by default.

Believe it or not, that's all the setup you need to do. When you create some content and put it in **secondWindow.view**, it'll show up on your extra screen. Off you go!

Note: There is a gotcha about the last piece of code. _secondWindow *needs* to be an instance variable because otherwise, it does not get retained by any other objects and gets released at the end of viewWillLayoutSubviews:.

If you do not have any non-ARC experience, consider this: in viewWillLayoutSubviews: you create a new object instance _secondWindow, but afterward you do not actually use it anywhere in the code. Therefore Cocoa Touch decides you don't need it and deletes it from memory. To show Cocoa Touch that you will be using _secondWindow for something, you make it an instance variable. This way nobody can get rid of it but you. ☺

You are moments away from giving the game a try, but first add this at the end of the else block you just added:

```
_skView.transform =
  CGAffineTransformMakeScale(screenBounds.size.width/568,
                             screenBounds.size.width/568);

_skView.center = CGPointMake(screenBounds.size.width/2,
                             screenBounds.size.height/2);

[_secondWindow addSubview:_skView];
```

Since the screen can be of any arbitrary resolution, you make a scaling transformation based on the original width of 568 points and scale your skView so that it takes up the entire TV screen.

Next you position the skView in the center of the screen and finally, you add it to your _secondWindow.

This should be enough to display the game scene on your external screen. Build and run, choose your car and track, and see what happens. The image below shows the device streaming to the Reflector app on my MacBook:

Assets for different screen resolutions

In this chapter you are taking the easiest path to handling different screen resolutions – having one set of image assets fit to a 568x320 screen size and scaling the whole scene to fit the external screen.

There are also more advanced approaches to doing that. Since the TV resolution can vary quite a bit if you always scale up your assets they sometimes might be a bit blurred.

Therefore to provide best experience in your AirPlay game you would like to have several sets of assets – fit for different screens. You will scale them to fit the exact TV resolution, but there will be definitely less blur.

However just to present all sides to this topic – I have to mention that providing big image assets might cause stream lags for the players that don't have such a great WiFi connectivity. The larger assets also will require more CPU time and memory, so you would have to carefully keep performance in mind.

As always in life you will have to compromise between quality and performance. The best way to address this will be to test with different asset sizes and different network conditions and see what kind of quality vs. performance ratio suits your game.

Splitting content between two screens

When you first run the game, you will see the game menus mirrored on both your device and AirPlay screens. When you start one of the levels, however, your device's screen becomes empty, even while you continue to see the game on the external screen.

This proves the concept already! Your two screens are displaying different content. You have the steering wheel screen ready, so why not show it?

At the top of **ViewController.m**, import the wheel controller:

```
#import "SteeringWheelViewController.h"
```

Once again, at the end of the else branch in viewWillLayoutSubviews:, just after the line where you add skView as a subview of _secondWindow, add these lines:

```
//1
SteeringWheelViewController* steeringController =
  [self.storyboard instantiateViewControllerWithIdentifier:
  @"SteeringWheelViewController"];

//2
UIScreen* controllerScreen = [UIScreen screens].firstObject;
CGSize controllerScreenSize = controllerScreen.bounds.size;

//3
steeringController.view.frame = CGRectMake(0, 0,
  controllerScreenSize.height, controllerScreenSize.width);

//4
[self addChildViewController:steeringController];
[self.view addSubview:steeringController.view];
```

Let's take these sections in turn:

1. First you grab a copy of SteeringWheelViewController from your storyboard.

2. Then you get a hold of the UIScreen object for your device – the main screen is always at index zero, or [UIScreen screens].firstObject – and fetch its size in controllerScreenSize.

3. At the end, you set the frame of the wheel controller's view to match the dimensions of the screen. You need this extra step because when you push a view controller on top of the navigation stack or present it modally, UIKit takes care to properly resize your view. You're going to add the wheel view onscreen yourself, so you need to resize it in advance.

4. Finally, with the wheel properly positioned and sized, you simply add the view to the current view controller's hierarchy. You also have to add the view controller to the view controller hierarchy.

Build and run and choose your car and track again, and you will see your steering wheel appear on your device's screen:

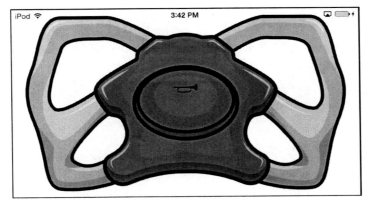

Well done! Before you go on further, run the project while you are *not* connected to an AirPlay device to reassure yourself that you can still play the game exactly as before.

> **Note:** When your device locks, you will be disconnected from the AirPlay device, so remember to check whether the AirPlay connection is still active if you don't see your game on the big screen.

Adapting the accelerometer controls

When you enable AirPlay for a game, you're going to want to make a number of adjustments to your gameplay and interface so that your players continue to have a great experience.

For one thing, your controller – the iOS device – now has the appearance of a steering wheel, so you should let your users steer with the device as if it were actually a wheel. This requires quite a change in the accelerometer logic.

Basically, you will change the controls so you tilt left to turn the wheels of the car to the left, and tilt right to turn the wheels to the right. The car will always move at a set velocity in the direction it's facing.

Let's put this into code!

New steering behavior

Open **MyScene.m** and add the empty placeholder for the method that will move the car based on the steering tilt:

```
- (void)moveCar:(SKSpriteNode*)car
  fromSteering:(CGPoint)steering
{

}
```

Now in order to reuse as much of your existing `moveCarFromAcceleration:currentTime` method as possible, find the line where you set the car's velocity. Scroll to `moveCarFromAcceleration` and find this line towards the middle of the method body:

```
car.physicsBody.velocity =
    CGVectorMake(accel2D.x * maxAccelerationPerSecond,
                 accel2D.y * maxAccelerationPerSecond);
```

At this point of the code, you have a 2D vector that gives you the tilt of the device on the axes in which you are interested. Let's intercept the method before setting the car's velocity and use `accel2D` for steering purposes.

Do that by replacing the line above with the following:

```
if ([UIScreen screens].count>1) {
  [self moveCar:car fromSteering:accel2D];
} else {
  car.physicsBody.velocity =
    CGVectorMake(accel2D.x * maxAccelerationPerSecond,
                 accel2D.y * maxAccelerationPerSecond);
}
```

Just before you set the velocity of the car, you check if there's an external screen connected and if so, you pass the control over to `moveCarFromSteering:`. In this way, you elegantly allow the player to have a full game experience both on the device and when connected to an external screen.

Note: The tracks in Circuit Racer are very small and have tight corners, and the cars move very quickly. So when players are using their iPhone as a steering wheel controller you will need to adjust a bit the maximum speed the cars do on the track to fit the gameplay for the new controls.

Inside `moveCarFromSteering:`, add the initial code to calculate the car's current rotation:

```
static float _maxSteeringAngle = 0.025f;
float angleDelta = -steering.x * _maxSteeringAngle;

car.zRotation += angleDelta;
```

`_maxSteeringAngle` is the maximum angle delta by which the car would rotate at full tilt of the steering wheel. Since `steering.x` spans between -1 and 1, you safely multiply it by the max angle to get the delta angle based on the current device tilt.

Once you have the delta angle, you simply add it to the current `zRotation` of the car. Unlike previously, you first calculate the car's orientation and will now use that to build the car's velocity.

You can quite easily make a direction vector out of the car's rotation angle with SKTUtils on your side – just call `CGPointForAngle()` and you'll be done. Append this to the method:

```
CGPoint directionVector = CGPointForAngle(car.zRotation);
car.physicsBody.velocity = CGVectorMake(
  directionVector.x * _maxSpeed * 0.67,
  directionVector.y * _maxSpeed * 0.67);
```

You turn `car.zRotation` into the normalized vector `directionVector`. In the next line, you create a velocity vector by multiplying the normalized vector by the car's max speed. And that's all!

Note: Remember when I said the blue and red cars were too fast to steer this way? By multiplying by 0.67, you are decreasing the car's maximum speed. This is the quick way to adjust the game mechanics to the steering input mode without too many complications.

OK, run the game and choose the yellow car and any track you want. Hold the device in front of you with two hands and try to steer the car by tilting left and right. Whohoo!

Adjusting the steering sensitivity to the car speed

If you try playing the game with all cars right now you will notice that playing with the yellow car feels okay, but the two faster cars are somewhat difficult to handle.

Well if you think about it – this should not come as a surprise! The cars are reaching different maximum speed, but they do turn around with the same maximum angle delta - `_maxSteeringAngle`.

To mimic better how the cars would behave in real world you should allow the more powerful cars to also turn quicker – they're moving with greater speed after all!

Go to `moveCarFromSteering:` and remove the line where you set a static maximum turning angle delta:

```
static float _maxSteeringAngle = 0.025f;
```

Then declare a new instance variable of `MyScene` class with the same name:

```
float _maxSteeringAngle;
```

What's left is to set a different value depending on how powerful the car engine is. Move on to `initializeGame` and add this line:

```
_maxSteeringAngle = 0.018f + _carType*0.0075f;
```

This code will set the maximum angle delta to 0.0255 for the yellow car, 0.033 for the blue car, and 0.0405 for the red car. This will allow the red car to turn almost two times faster than the yellow car. That's more like it!

Give the game another try! The red is still really powerful and sometimes it can feel like you're driving a bumping car, but practice will make you better driver ☺

The controls will take a little bit to get used to. Tip: don't get too excited – rotating in a circle won't help you cross the finish line on time!

Preventing screen dimming

At this point, you need to resolve one problem with using the device as a controller. Usually iOS dims the screen if the user does not tap for a given period of time, so you need to add a small piece of code to prevent that.

Open **SteeringWheelViewController.m** and add these two methods:

```
- (void)viewDidAppear:(BOOL)animated
{
  [UIApplication sharedApplication].idleTimerDisabled = YES;
}

-(void)viewWillDisappear:(BOOL)animated
{
  [UIApplication sharedApplication].idleTimerDisabled = NO;
}
```

When the steering wheel shows up onscreen, you disable the idle timer, and when it's pushed out you enable it again. That was easy!

Adding interactivity to your controller

For an even more engaging experience, it helps give your game controller some extra controls. But as you'll see, when increasing the interactivity of your AirPlay controller, it's important to take a measured approach.

In this last section of the chapter, you'll connect the horn button on the steering wheel so that it plays a sound when the user taps it. Then as the chapter's challenge, you'll add a nitro boost effect to the game, allowing your players to temporarily increase the car's speed over the maximum value.

Adding a central button

Open **SteeringWheelViewController.h** and add at the top:

```
#import "MyScene.h"
```

Next, inside the @interface body, add a new property:

```
@property (strong, nonatomic) MyScene *scene;
```

Now that your controller has a scene property, you can react to user interactions and invoke the corresponding actions on the scene instance.

Speaking of the scene, switch to **ViewController.m** and at the end of the long else branch in viewWillLayoutSubviews:, just after the line that adds steeringController.view as a subview of self.view, set the steeringController's scene property:

```
steeringController.scene = scene;
```

Let's do something very easy. On your steering wheel you have a horn button just waiting for you to connect it. That's a perfect task for demonstrating how to connect your controller class with the scene displayed on the external screen.

Open **MyScene.h** and add a new method declaration:

```
- (void)playHorn;
```

This makes the method that you implemented to play the horn sound in the previous chapter public.

Now you need to connect the button from `SteeringWheelViewController` to this method inside `MyScene`.

Open **SteeringWheelViewController.m** and add the method you're going to call when the player taps the horn button on the device screen:

```
- (IBAction)actionHonk:(id)sender
{
    [self.scene playHorn];
}
```

To connect the button, open **Main.storyboard** and while holding the ctrl key, drag from the horn button to the view controller object. From the little popup that appears, select **actionHonk**:

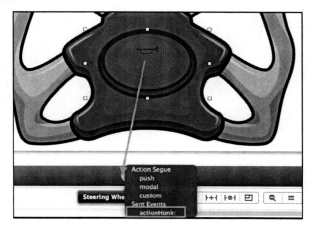

Build and run the game and give your new horn a try – *honk! honk!*

Keeping the player's attention on the main screen

But... wait! The more attentive of you are certainly already protesting.

In the beginning of this chapter, I told you that encouraging the player to tap on the screen isn't ideal when using AirPlay because it distracts the player from looking at the external screen. Well, what I said is still valid, but...

The key to using the device as a controller is *simplicity*. If you have one button in the middle of the screen, like your horn button above, the player does not necessarily need to look at the device to press it.

Another successful use case would be if you had two buttons on the controller's screen, one taking up the entire left half and another taking up the entire right half. Players won't likely find it distracting to press those buttons, since they are so large and easy to find.

Further use of the device in an AirPlay setup would be to move parts of the HUD to the device screen. Just have a look at the game *MetalStorm: Online* – it shows all of the airplane's indicators and the game's HUD on the device screen so the external display can be beautiful and uncluttered:

Congratulations – you've made it through the final Circuit Racer chapter. Just think – only six chapters ago, you had nothing but an empty track! I hope you feel inspired by the various technologies that you've seen during the long journey here.

Challenges

Are you up for one more Circuit Racer challenge? Don't stop when you're so close to the end!

There's just one challenge for this chapter, and it's to add an extra feature to your steering wheel view controller to implement a nitro boost feature.

As always, you'll find the solution to this challenge in the resources for this chapter, but give it your best shot first!

Challenge 1: Nitro boost

Every racing game needs a nitro boost for those long stretches before the finish line. To review what you've learned in this chapter and build upon it, your challenge is to add a nitro boost feature to Circuit Racer.

If you've played some racing games on your iPhone, then you probably know that the nitro boost is usually activated by a swipe up gesture – a motion that the user can perform without having to look at the device screen.

Below is an outline of the steps you'll need to take to get the nitro boost working. I'll leave it up to you to flesh them out in code:

1. Add a `nitro` method to your scene class (make it public) that does the following:

    a. Store `_maxSpeed` into a helper variable and double its value. This will give your car a boost in speed.

    b. Run a block action after 0.5 seconds that sets the `_maxSpeed` back to its original value – the nitro party is over.

    c. Play the `_nitroSoundAction`.

2. In `SteeringWheelViewController`, have a Boolean value called `_allowedToNitro`, which you set to YES in `viewDidLoad` so that the player can initially use a nitro boost.

3. Then add a `UISwipeGestureRecognizer` to the controller's view and set its direction property to `UISwipeGestureRecognizerDirectionUp`. You can read up on gesture recognizers here:
   https://developer.apple.com/library/ios/documentation/uikit/reference/UIGestureRecognizer_Class/Reference/Reference.html

4. Have your gesture recognizer invoke a method that in turn calls `[MyScene nitro]`. Then set `_allowedToNitro` to NO and run a block action in 5 seconds that sets it back to YES. Make sure that you call the `scene`'s `nitro` method only when `_allowedToNitro` equals YES.

Build and run, and swipe to give your car a neat speed boost!

And that ends the development of Circuit Racer. But don't mourn the end – you can always take the game's development even further by yourself by adding new tracks, difficulty levels, cars or anything you like. If you do add something cool, don't forget to share it with other readers in the book forums!

Section VI: Bonus Chapters

To thank you for purchasing this book, we have some bonus chapters for you!

The first two chapters are about getting the most performance out of your game, and the third is about learning how to get great art for your game – whether you hire someone or take the do-it-yourself approach.

These bonus chapters come as an optional PDF download, which you can download for free here:

- http://www.raywenderlich.com/store/ios-games-by-tutorials/bonus-chapters

We hope you enjoy the bonus chapters!

Chapter 25: Performance: Texture Atlases

Chapter 26: Performance: Tips and Tricks

Chapter 27: Making Art for Programmers

Conclusion

We hope that you have enjoyed your adventure through this book. If you followed along the entire way, you have made five complete iOS games with Sprite Kit from scratch – spanning everything from zombies to cats to badasses named Arnold. You now have all the knowledge it takes to make a hit game, so why not go for it?

Come up with a great idea, prototype a game, get people to play it, watch them for feedback and keep iterating and polishing your game based on all you have learned. Be sure to set aside time in your schedule to add juice to your game, and make sure you have killer art and sound effects, following the advice in the book.

We can't wait to see what you come up with! Be sure to stop by our forums and share your progress at http://www.raywenderlich.com/forums.

You might also be interested to know that we have a monthly blog post where we review games written by fellow readers like you. If you'd like to be considered for this column, please visit this page after you release your game: http://www.raywenderlich.com/reviews

We have one final question for you: Did we succeed in our goal to write the best book on game programming you've ever read? Please email us anytime at ray@raywenderlich.com to let us know either way.

Thank you again for purchasing this book. Your continued support is what makes the tutorials, books and other things we do at raywenderlich.com possible. We truly appreciate it.

Best of luck in all your iOS adventures,

— Tom, Mike, Jake, Ali, Matthijs, Chris, B.C., Vinnie, Rod, Marin, Ray and Vicki

(the raywenderlich.com Tutorial Team and friends!)

CPSIA information can be obtained at www.ICGtesting.com
Printed in the USA
LVOW09s0253170414

381977LV00023B/557/P